Language of

Language of the Gods

By

B R Taylor

2016

©Copyright 2016 by B R Taylor

All rights reserved

Pictures sourced from Creative Commons or edited by B R Taylor

Source: Creative Commons. Copyright permission expressly granted.

Pictures available for commercial purposes; pictures which can be modified, adapted or built upon.

@ www.creativecommons.org

Cover designed

By

B R Taylor

ISBN-13: 978-1533157683 (CreateSpace-Assigned)
ISBN-10: 1533157685

Publishers: CreateSpace, an Amazon company

Dedication

This book is dedicated to all those souls who have suffered at the hands of manipulative rapacious imperialism, in all its colours and forms. Souls caught up in oceans of distorted truths, false beliefs, propaganda and accidental circumstances. Brothers and sisters of humanity used as pawns to advance hidden agendas disguised as servicing the greater good and progress. I also dedicate this book to those who seek the truth no matter what the cost, a truth lost and neglected under a mountain of falsehoods and divided opinions.

The greatest gift one generation can give to the next is a solid foundation of truth, the right coordinates with real answers to what, where, who and why; along with the confidence and freedoms to seek wisdom and understanding to all of nature's gifts and mysteries. I also dedicate this book to both my parents Jean and Richard, a sun and moon union who conceived a flickering star after their Christmas party in 1967, without which I would not have had the body and mind to walk this unconventional path.

Preface

This book was the result of years of research into the relationship between human consciousness and the universe, the microcosm and the macrocosm, and how the controlling powers have utilised this relationship along with ancient knowledge for themselves, while suppressing our ability to become truly enlightened. I have set out to expose how various controlling systems have, for thousands of years, undermined the common man's connection to higher mind consciousness; using methods such as deceit, fear, debt and division, the elite have kept themselves firmly at the top. With an array of sophisticated techniques, they not only divide us physically but also spiritually by offering us perverted versions of spirituality disguised as monotheistic planet worshipping cults. I also set out to discover a correlation between true spirituality, the energetic cycles of the planets and what the ancient Egyptians were trying to tell us. From a deep understanding of natural cosmic cycles, I also wanted to know if it was possible to gain an insight into what forces will be prominent in our near future and how they will influence the geopolitical landscape.

Contents

- Page 1 **Introduction**
- Page 2 **Chapter 1) Consciousness and the collective**
- Page 3   Five sense reality
  - The collective
- Page 4   Extra sense
  - Sixth sense and premonitions
- Page 5   Mediums, clairvoyance, channels and the intuitive
- Page 6   Astral projection
- Page 9   Science of consciousness
  - The double slit experiment
- Page 11 Mind over matter
- Page 12 The placebo effect
- Page 12 Hypnotist
- Page 14 Epi-genetics
- Page 14 Eureka moments
  - Free will
- Page 16 Notes for chapter 1
- Page 17 **Chapter 2) Astrotheology**
- Page 19 Astrotheology
  - Natal charts
- Page 20 Luke 22:10 the Last Supper
- Page 22 Fish, feet and belief
- Page 23 Judas betrays Jesus
  - The Spear of Destiny
- Page 24 Noah's ark
- Page 24 Ark of the Covenant
- Page 25 The Holy Grail
- Page 26 Matthew, Mark, Luke and John
- Page 27 Adam and Eve
- Page 28 The Age of Aquarius
- Page 30 The Uranus connection
- Page 31 Paganism
- Page 33 Notes for chapter 2
- Page 34 **Chapter 3) The control system**
- Page 35 The banking cartel
- Page 37 Most wars are banking wars
- Page 40 World War One
- Page 43 The Armistice
- Page 43 Treaty of Versailles

- Page 45 World War Two
- Page 47 The final political testament of Adolf Hitler
- Page 49 Iraq and the petrodollar
- Page 51 Libya 2011
- Page 53 War on terror
- Page 56 Notes for chapter 3
- Page 58 **Chapter 4) War on consciousness**
- Page 59 The attack on food
- Page 61 Processed foods
- Page 62 Breakfast cereals
    - Microwaves
    - PH of the body
- Page 64 War on drugs
- Page 65 Vaccinations
- Page 68 Polio vaccine
    - Reactions to vaccines
- Page 70 Scientific studies and cases
- Page 73 The flu vaccine
- Page 75 Reducing the population
- Page 77 Notes for chapter 4
- Page 81 **Chapter 5) Corporations**
- Page 82 Legal fiction
- Page 84 The Vatican's trust
- Page 85 The UNITED STATES CORPORATION
- Page 86 Commercial courts
- Page 87 The TV license
    - The police
- Page 90 Psychopathic disconnect
- Page 91 Democide
- Page 92 Different forms of government
- Page 95 Obsolescence
- Page 97 The perfect consumer
- Page 98 The corporate persona
- Page 101 Notes for chapter 5
- Page 102 **Chapter 6) The British Empire**
- Page 103 Napoleon
- Page 115 The Nazi Party
- Page 120 Post war globalization
- Page 124 Sir Edward Heath and the Magna Carta
- Page 125 The dark side of empire
- Page 127 Notes for chapter 6

- Page 129 **Chapter 7) Secret societies**
- Page 131 Tax exempt foundations
- Page 133 Bilderberg
- Page 134 Skull and bones
- Page 136 Bohemian grove
- Page 137 CFR
- Page 138 Freemasons
- Page 143 Masonic oaths
- Page 145 Masonic symbols
- Page 152 Origins of Freemasons and the Roman Catholic Church
- Page 159 Notes for chapter 7
- Page 161 **Chapter 8) Perverting the course of history**
  - Basic orthodox view of history
- Page 162 Charles Darwin
- Page 163 Sirius
- Page 167 Egypt
- Page 171 The Great Pyramid
- Page 176 The clock of Giza
- Page 182 Pyramids everywhere
- Page 183 Dogons
- Page 184 Elongated skulls
- Page 185 Paracas
- Page 187 The Serapeum
- Page 188 Bulls and rams
- Page 191 Looting and the destruction of ancient cultural heritage
- Page 193 Iraq
  - World map
- Page 194 Political correctness and social taboos
- Page 196 Climate change
- Page 199 Notes for chapter 8
- Page 201 **Chapter 9) Perverting spirituality**
- Page 202 Getting connected
- Page 203 Seven days of creation
- Page 203 Judaism and Saturn
- Page 206 Orthodox history of Judaism
- Page 211 Virtues and vices
  - Christianity and Jupiter
- Page 214 Islam and Venus
- Page 218 Buddhism and Mercury
- Page 221 Hinduism
- Page 220 Pantheism

v

- Page 223 Nazism
- Page 225 Resignation of the Pope
- Page 226 Religious and spiritual trinity
- Page 227 The sacred secret
- Page 233 Notes for chapter 9
- Page 235 **Chapter 10) Zionism**
- Page 237 Isis cults
- Page 251 House of Rothschild
- Page 254 The Isis connection
- Page 257 Notes for chapter 10
- Page 259 **Chapter 11) Controlling information**
- Page 260 Mainstream media
- Page 261 TV
- Page 264 Propaganda and WW1
- Page 265 Books
- Page 267 Internet technology
- Page 268 Mobile phones
- Page 270 Hollywood
- Page 272 Corporate music industry
- Page 273 Notes for chapter 11
- Page 275 **Chapter 12) The attack on education**
- Page 278 The modern school
    - Home schooling
- Page 279 Repetition
- Page 280 Debt
    - International curriculum
- Page 282 Programming
- Page 284 Why English
- Page 285 Changing your belief system
- Page 286 Saturn connection
- Page 287 Notes for chapter 12
- Page 288 **Chapter 13) Astrological natal charts of famous people**
- Page 304 Notes for chapter 13
- Page 305 **Chapter 14) Astro-geopolitics**
- Page 308 Wheels within wheels
- Page 321 The future
- Page 322 It's already happening
- Page 324 Notes for chapter 14
- Page 325 **Chapter 15) Non-human entities**
- Page 328 The war in heaven
- Page 329 Spirit and soul

- Page 332 Tutankhamun's mask
- Page 337 Interdimensional entities
- Page 338 Extra terrestrials
- Page 339 Who is in control?
- Page 346 The Pharaoh/Masonic connection
- Page 347 Satanic rituals
- Page 348 Intrusive thoughts and mind parasites
- Page 349 Cloning and synthetic humanoids
- Page 349 Underground bases
- Page 351 Stargates and portals
- Page 353 Notes for chapter 15
- Page 354 **Chapter 16) Globalisation**
    - The advantages of globalisation
- Page 355 An optimistic view of globalization
- Page 357 A pessimistic view of a future under globalization
- Page 365 Notes for chapter 16
- Page 366 **Conclusion**
- Page 370 Notes for the conclusion
- Page 371 **Author's bio**
- Page 372 Other books by this author

Language of the Gods

Introduction

This book is a journey of discovery into the nature of reality, and our conscious connection to universal energy. We are not simply biological vessels with a life expectancy of 70 years; we are and always have been a spirit and soul reflection of the universe, the creators of our own destiny and the world we inhabit. Along with a detailed analysis of cosmic forces, the book will attempt to shed light on how various systems of control have manipulated our sense of perception, distorting who we are and what our true potential is. It will attempt to show how, over the past 2000 years, we have been subjected to various forms of control, from an array of monotheistic religions, each adopting a different planet/God as its ideological representative; to corporate and global institutions, all designed with the intention of dividing humanity on both a physical and spiritual level. Much of what passes as the word of God, in many religious text books, are accounts of planetary and solar cycles, disguised as personified parables. We will examine how the control system under the British Empire evolved from its overt peak during the 19th century into a web of secret societies, international corporations and financial institutions, steering humanity towards a new imperialism known as globalisation, and how they use universal cycles as guidance for their own geopolitical policies, while at the same time undermining and ridiculing its potential publicly. The book will try to expose some of the greatest deceptions found in society, inversions of truth and perversions within all kinds of modern institutions, shackling humanity under cycles of perpetual debt and economic slavery.

As we move into the Age of Aquarius, a new Age of "knowing", revolution, technology and independence, we shall look at the overall geopolitical situation and how the control system has adapted to keep humanity within the confines of their globalisation project, handicapping us with their view of world events and their perverted view of history. We will examine how the elite are using the ancient Egyptian cult of ISIS as a catalyst to promote the "GEN-ISIS" of this New Age.

We are truly entering a time of turbulence, but with a basic understanding of universal energetic cycles and how human consciousness manifests reality, one will be in a better position to appreciate the changes taking place and the forces behind those changes without fear. The book will not only try to open your eyes to new esoteric information and new concepts, but will attempt to shed light on some of the important questions of life, giving us a better perspection of the past, present and future, allowing us more control over our own lives and to harmonise with new energetic changes emanating from the universe.

This book is written based on my personal interpretation of information and events gathered, readers might develop their own view and understanding from it. Some subjects tackled in this book are of a sensitive nature and it is not my intention to disrespect or offend anyone with alternative beliefs.

Chapter 1. Consciousness and the collective

First, we must understand the various forms of human consciousness, from the individual focal to the higher mind or timeless sea of universal consciousness; it is as vast and eternal as the untamed imagination, contained within the physical body for a human lifetime. A biological framework of genetics, holding the consciousness within the constraints of our five senses. We all resonate a spectrum of frequencies, emanating from the heart/mind partnership, like an orchestra playing a unique symphony vibrating outwards influencing all those in its wake. Groups Interact with one another creating what is known as a collective frequency, group think or collective consciousness.

The subconscious is the internal emotional part of our mind, the background store deep within us. Our conscious minds are limited to what we focus on at any given moment. The subconscious is all the other possibilities, the underside of the iceberg, the 70 - 90% in reserve, remembering everything like a digital hard drive. If we were to make a comparison with an orchestra, the focal consciousness is the melody whereas the subconscious is all the other instruments combined. In ancient astrology, the Sun represents the will, the external projection or focal consciousness, whereas the Moon represents our internal emotions and the subconscious. Water is often used to represent internal emotion, the spirit, Moon energy and the subconscious. The ratio between our conscious and subconscious mind is replicated outwards towards the macrocosm in similar proportions. The bodies water content, the Earth's land to sea relationship and the amount of dark matter in the universe are all found to have these similar relative properties, leaving one appreciative as to synchronicity and connection between all these areas, "as above so below".

Above all this is a higher mind, an ocean of universal consciousness, a place outside our physical reality where earthly constraints have no bounds. The place we came from and the place we return. The connection to this higher mind sea of infinite possibility is a natural part of the human experience, but most modern societies have lost sight of this, restricting man's interaction with this vast endless source of timeless wisdom.

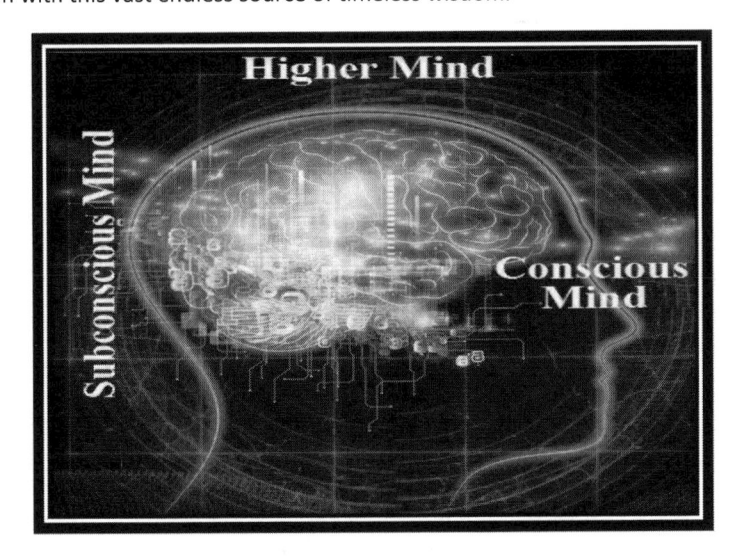

Five sense reality

When you close your eyes, and relax, your consciousness lies deep within you. Where is it exactly? Is it just behind the eyes, is it in the centre of the brain or is it outside the physical but somehow connected to it? I suggest it is in all these areas with the consciousness acting as the benchmark to all creation. Each of our five senses are decoding the energy that surrounds us, energy within an electrical magnetic universe, frequencies stimulating each sense as they communicate back to the consciousness. Sound is probably the easiest to understand but they all work on the same principle. The brain decodes this energy flowing into your version of perceived reality; therefore, the world you think and believe to be outside yourself is being constructed in your head deep within your consciousness.

If you take away all your senses apart from the one of touch, your reality will be limited. The more senses you add the greater your perception within time and space. What would your reality be if you had six or seven senses and what would these extra senses do? The individual like the pebble thrown in the pond resonate a personal set of unique frequencies, energy vibrations which flow out from the biological centre. This symphony of frequencies is limited only by the imagination. A happy person will give off a happy blend of frequencies, whereas an angry person will transmit angry energy. Just as the cosmos influences the new born baby with its own unique array of planetary energies, individuals influence their surroundings with their multi layered interactions within the collective.

The collective

We can now see how the individual is a transmitter/receiver of energetic frequencies, while the five sense/mind receives; the heart/mind connection transmits. When you have a group of people all resonating their unique rainbow of energies, the collective frequency within a proximity is produced. This collective frequency is picked up and decoded back by each individual's senses and projected into their reality. This collective consciousness is a force in itself, with each individual playing a role in its creation, both transmitting and receiving. This is why you invariably become who you associate with. The collective has power in numbers, a single raindrop on a tin roof makes very little sound, but millions of droplets all resonating at the same frequency can deafen the occupants below.

You will notice when an angry person walks into a room full of happy people, the frequency given off by that person will start to influence the collective, diluting the happy frequency that once dominated the room. There are many ways to influence the collective, either consciously or subconsciously. Anyone in authority over a group who understands these basic principles is in a powerful position to manipulate their reality.

The collective consciousness is multi-faceted, like cogs in a machine these collectives interact and have varying levels of influence, from the group, community and national level to the global consciousness, all influencing and shaping our reality. The lower levels are influenced through proximity and five sense stimuli whereas the national and global collectives are manipulated through the perception of various forms of media outlets.

Collective Consciousness

Extra senses

The universe is a giant soup of interacting electrical frequencies,[1] radiating in all directions. Our senses respond to constant stimulation from these energy fields. Our physical brains together with our consciousness decode and project back what we understand to be reality, the final stage in a perpetual updating process. The more senses we have tapping into this information field the greater our conscious awareness will be. Many people have the ability to enhance their basic five sense reality. Some have an active sixth sense or GUT feeling, (the Swedish for GOD is GUD, similar pronunciation to the English word GUT). This connection to the higher mind or source is giving them stimuli of one form or another. The greater our attachment to the five-sense earthly material realm of the corporate control system, the more dormant our other senses may become. Ancient cultures without modern distractions focused on the expansion of their other senses, even opening up their seventh sense, the third eye, allowing them to astral project, giving their consciousness the ability to break free from the physical body and move within the realms of the higher mind, a place free from the constraints of time and space.

Sixth sense and premonitions

There are various ways to improve your sixth sense, gut intuition. Keeping in good physical health is paramount, balancing oneself chemically and biologically, providing the backdrop for ample energy to maximize natural inner potential and inner strength not to look outside oneself towards the control system for all the answers. Meditate, relax and take time to build a healthy balance between mind and body, Keep a good temperament and an open mind.[2]

Below are some practical ways to improve your sixth sense intuition:

- Take time to focus and listen to your intuition. Learn to meditate.
- Don't look outside yourself for all the answers; you would be giving your power away.
- Pay attention to your dreams.
- Spend more time being creative, time stimulating right brain activities.
- Eat a natural and healthy diet and spend more time with nature.
- Avoid toxic things, e.g. smoking, alcohol and junk food. Treat yourself with care and respect.

Occasionally we receive information from source or higher mind consciousness, energetic vibrations in the form of premonitions, pre-empting things to come, feelings that are so strong and out of the ordinary that special attention is paid to the information received. Abraham Lincoln had one such premonition, in the form of a dream, during the end of March 1865, he retired to bed exhausted and began to dream. In his dream, he found himself wandering around the Whitehouse hearing people sobbing. He pursued the sounds of crying to find out what the commotion was. He eventually went downstairs and entered the East Room where he saw a casket; a body lay in it with its head covered. Soldiers guarded the casket with many people mournfully gazing upon the corpse. In his dream Lincoln demanded to know who had died, "The President" replied one of the soldiers "he was killed by an assassin", at that moment the mourners gave a loud burst of grief which woke Lincoln from his dream. Disturbed at the vividness of what he had just witnessed, he made a mental note. Two weeks later on April 14th 1865, Abraham Lincoln was shot and killed by John Wilkes Booth. His body was laid in a casket and placed in the East Room of the Whitehouse guarded by soldiers.[3]

One must ask, where does this information come from? When you understand the various levels of consciousness, it is all very simple. Lincoln's conscious mind was connecting to source during his sleep, a place outside the constraints of the physical body and time; therefore, he was able to observe the past, the present and the future simultaneously. Meditation is another common way to stimulate your sixth sense awareness.

Mediums, clairvoyance, channels and the intuitive

These various forms of psychics all have the ability to connect to the higher consciousness, giving them a view of things outside normal affairs. Through various forms of connecting they all possess unique gifts, some see visions or colours some have feelings and emotions, others hear voices. These gifts come in all shapes and sizes just like the people themselves, it's as natural as the variations in eye colour, however modern man-made religions would like us to believe, anything extra sensory is the work of the Devil, and if you participate you will burn in hell for eternity. What they really mean is they don't want you expanding your awareness and looking within yourself for answers; they want you to look towards them for answers keeping a firm grip on the reins of control.

- Clairvoyance: The ability to see things without the physical eye

- Clairaudience: The ability to hear without the physical ear
- Clairsentience: The ability to feel without the physical body

Behind the physical five senses there are spiritual senses. A psychic is just someone who has finely tuned themselves to the art of perceiving extra information that most people will overlook. The psychic deciphers this information and turns it into something tangible. The intuitive on the other hand tends to get flashes of insight that need little or no translating, these flashes of inspiration, ideas or apprehensive feelings can appear at any time and are unpredictable. A channel is a person who can turn down their own conscious focused mind and allow psychic/spiritual/intuitive messages to flow through them as a host. The medium will focus on specific spirits or energies in order to draw the information they need. They commonly use what they call a spirit guide to help them contact deceased love ones. What they all have in common is they are all connecting to various levels of consciousness outside the normal five senses. In their various ways, they tune into the higher mind collective, the ocean of consciousness. We all exist in this timeless energy; it's just a matter of tuning yourself into that frequency.

You should now have a basic understanding of the way in which consciousness works, its various layers within the restrictions of the physical body. There are endless frequencies outside what our normal senses can decode. Throughout history cultures and civilizations have developed their extra senses, but today's world is mainly dormant under the framework of modern society, a system unwilling to relinquish power back to the individual.

Astral-projection

A further expansion of the senses beyond the sixth and into higher levels of awareness, an individual can train themselves to free the conscious mind from the constraints of the physical body, enabling the person to enter the astral planes of unlimited possibility. The subject literally leaves the physical and travels through time and space, with an energetic copy of the flesh body, to wherever the mind's focus wishes to go. Advanced forms of meditation can lead you into astral-projection.[4] The use of binaural beats is an effective tool when starting out. The sounds will stimulate your extra senses with the hypnotic sounds and frequencies produced. According to Robert Bruce of Astrodynamics,[5] many people naturally astral-project during sleep and meditation but they have difficulty remembering the event. Just like dreaming, we know we had a good dream but just can't quite remember the details.

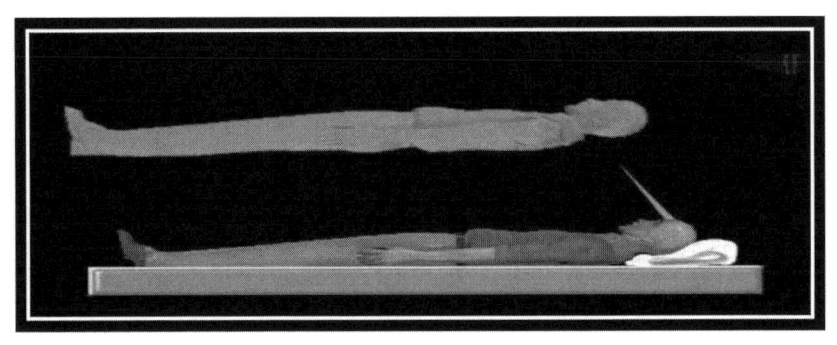

Remote viewing is the projection of the mind as opposed to astral-projecting the energetic copy of the flesh body. The remote viewer is like an eye in the sky, performed usually with specific objectives. The mind's eye will go where the consciousness takes it, asking for guidance from the higher mind. In 1975 the United States Government sponsored a $20 million program called the "STARGATE PROJECT", to determine any potential military value to psychic phenomena, including remote viewing. The program was terminated after 20 years, deemed unusable. One must ask if it was unusable, why did it take 20 years to come to this conclusion considering the amount of resources thrown at the project?[6] Police have also used remote viewers to aid some difficult cases; one such case took place in California in 2006. A photographer from Las Vegas named Robert Knight had become worried about his long-time friend and radio DJ, Stephen Williams. Knight had not heard from Williams for an unusually long time, knowing a psychic and remote viewer, Knight approached Angela Smith for assistance, she was more than happy to help. She gathered a team of six trainees together to see what they could come up with. After many sessions of remote viewing the team concluded, there was a body in water; a fishing net, and all this was to be found off the southern coast of California near Catalina Island. Soon after this an unidentified body was found off Catalina Island and broadcast to the media. When Knight heard the news, suspecting it was his friend Stephen Williams, he called the county morgue and told them he may know the identity of the body. He told them Stephen had three fingers missing on his left hand, from an accident fifty years earlier. They put him on hold and went to check, and were astonished to find the fingers missing just like knight had said. After the body had been identified as Mr Stephen Williams, Knight told the police of a possible suspect. An investment adviser named Harvey Morrow, who had befriended Stephen prior to his disappearance, with the aim of investing his fortune. The police were unable to find Morrow and asked if the remote viewers could shed some light on his whereabouts. Once again, the remote viewers got together to look outside their five senses for answers. After many sessions, they concluded that Morrow had fled to the British Virgin Islands. On this tip off the police finally found Harvey Morrows, arrested and later convicted him. He is now serving life for the murder of Stephen Williams.[7]

Near death experience

Another form of OOB (out of body) is the near-death experience NDE. People involved in accidents or operation complications have found themselves looking at their bodies from an outside perspective, observing events unfold in fine detail. They somehow create an energetic copy of their flesh body, just like in astral projection, where the consciousness has shifted to a new vantage point. In 1987, Barbara Bartolome a 31-year-old mother of two from Santa Barbara, California was booked to go into hospital for her final discectomy and laminectomy, as part of her back treatment. The day before the operation the doctors wanted to perform a myelogram, a procedure to inject iodine dye into the spine to look for problems on X-Rays. The nurse injected the die into Barbara's neck while she was lying on the X-Ray table. The table was then supposed to lift Barbara steadily upright to allow gravity to aid the die descend down her spine. This didn't happen. She lay flat and began to hyperventilate; she eventually blacked out and immediately went from her physical body to a place on the ceiling, looking down on herself and the heads of the doctors. From her new vantage point she heard one of the doctors call out "Code Blue". This call is used to indicate a patient requiring resuscitation or otherwise in need of immediate medical attention. From her new position on the ceiling she felt very calm, relaxed and content. Presuming she had died she noticed a presence next to her, a familiarity as though she had known this presence always. While the resuscitation was going on below she began to communicate with this presence, she made it clear she wanted to go back into her body and be with her children again, telling the presence that she had not yet fulfilled her life's purpose and needed to go back. The commotion below intensified, she saw an oxygen mask being placed over her face and a man position a small box on the ledge next to the X-Ray table. She made a comment to the presence about the box, asking what it was. At that moment, she found herself positioned in front of the box looking straight at it. She realized after a while it was a heart monitor. When the box was turned on the line on the screen was flat from left to right, with a continuous beep. Barbara went back to the ceiling to be with the presence. Below her the Neurosurgeon and Orthopaedic surgeon were talking about the delayed arrival of the defibrillator to the X-Ray room. It was taking too long. The Orthopaedic surgeon told everyone to stand clear. He stepped forward towards Barbara's lifeless body and struck her in the chest with the full force of his fists. This procedure is regarded as a last-ditch attempt at shocking the heart into beating again. The second time he struck Barbara's chest, in an instant, she went straight back into her body and opened her eyes. She was so amazed and excited to be back in her body that she was trying to talk under the oxygen mask. The nurse told her to keep quiet because they needed to stabilize her. After a small bout of silence Barbara started talking again, to the astonishment and disbelief of the doctors and nurses surrounding her, she spoke of being on the ceiling looking at everything unfold below. It was only when she mentioned the conversation between the Neurosurgeon and the Orthopedic surgeon about the defibrillator and how she was struck in the chest twice that the staff stopped what they were doing and stood in amazement at what she was telling them.[8] How can this woman see and hear all that was going on around her when her heart had stopped and she was unconscious. Barbara's account of her near-death experience is common amongst NDE's; there are thousands of recorded cases all over the world. It's as though the physical body and the Light body exist simultaneously but your focal consciousness can only occupy one or the other at any given time.

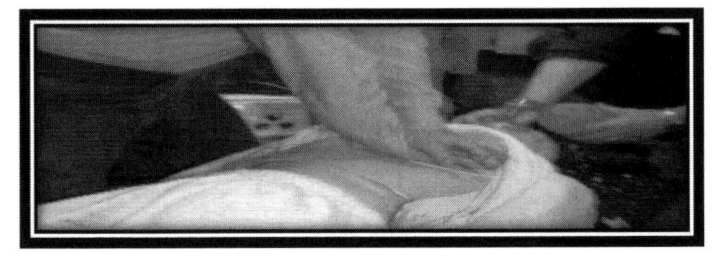

Science of consciousness

"The day science begins to study non-physical phenomena; it will make more progress in one decade than in all the previous centuries of its existence." - Nikola Tesla

To understand the nature of the universe one must think in terms of energy, frequency and vibrations. Science works best when in harmony with nature. The universe is a vast endless source of energy, we just need to open our consciousness and understand what we are being shown. Throughout history there has been many experiments designed to measure the relationship between our physical reality and our consciousness.

The double slit experiment

Unexpected results were obtained when performing Thomas Young's double slit experiment at the quantum level. The results turned the world of science on its head, with many scientists today, still unable to comprehend what they are witnessing.

Experiment 1) Matter is fired at a screen with one slit; behind the slit is a second screen which collects the matter coming through the first slit. For this example, small ball bearings are used. The pattern which appears on the second screen is what would be expected, a slit pattern.

Experiment 2) a wave is fired through a single slit, creating a pattern on the back screen with the highest intensity right behind the slit and a gradual reduction to either side.

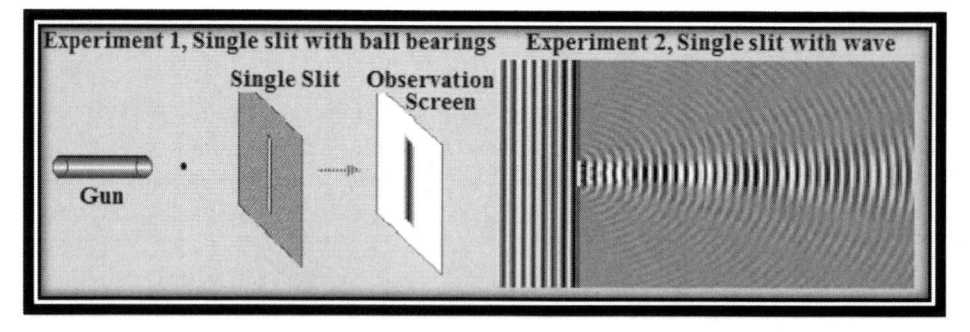

Experiment 3) Waves are passed through two slits. We see that the waves going through the slits produce two separate waves which interfere with each other diffracting the wave pattern. On the back screen, we see an interference pattern of light and dark bands.

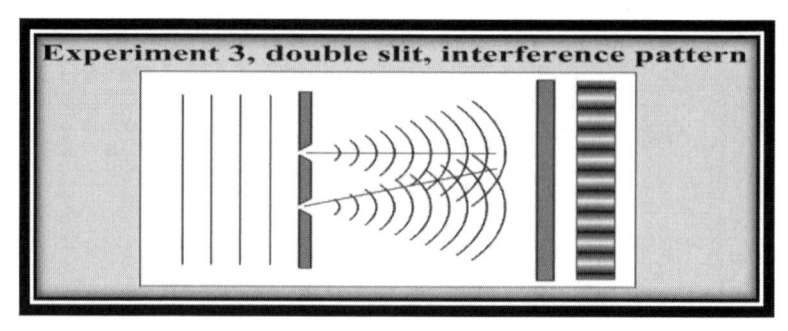

When firing ball bearings at two slits you get a double slit pattern on the back screen, which is to be expected. When we go quantum and fire small particles of matter like electrons at the screen something unexpected happens. First, they fired a steady stream of electrons, lo and behold; a single slit shaped pattern appeared on the back screen just like in experiment 1 with the larger ball bearings. The next thing they did was to fire a stream of electrons through two slits. With astonishment, the electron particles behaved like waves and created an interference pattern on the screen.

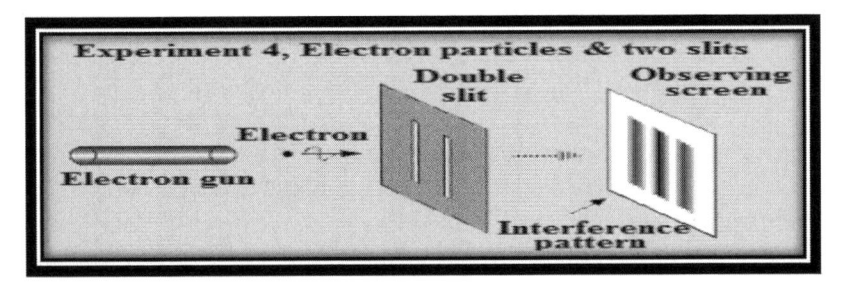

Experiment 4, Electron particles & two slits

How can matter create an interference pattern like a wave? They should act like the ball bearings and pass through both slits leaving a double slit pattern on the back screen. This baffled scientists so they performed the experiment again, this time firing one electron at a time. The results were the same, a slit pattern with one slit, and an interference pattern with two. It suggests that the single electron leaves the gun and becomes a wave, goes through both slits, interferes with itself to hit the screen like a particle. They needed to pay more attention to the electron, was it going through slit A or slit B. They set up a sensor to monitor one of the slits. When they ran the experiment, they found 50% of the electrons went through slit A and 50% went through slit B, which was to be expected, but to their surprise the interference pattern on the screen had gone, replaced by the double slit pattern. They turned the sensor off and fired the electrons. The interference pattern came back again. Sensor on, double slit, sensor off, interference pattern.

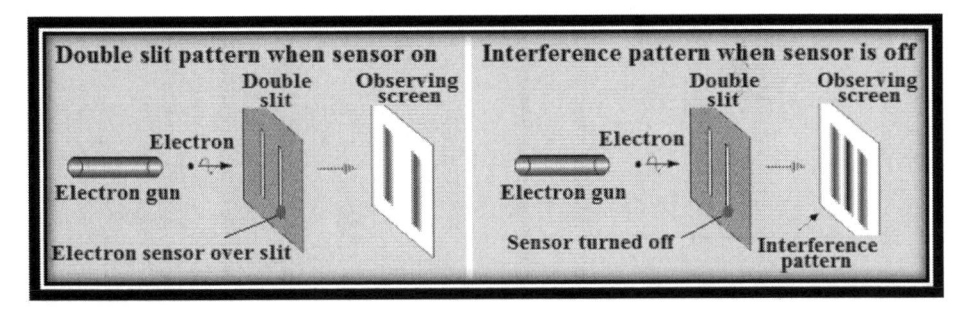

How can this be, just the act of observing the single electron will cause it to behave like a particle, but when no one is observing, the electron reverts back to a waveform.[9] The double slit experiment is a prime example of how matter on the quantum level is both physical and a wave. We find this with the physical and astral body, both existing simultaneously. The focal consciousness can only occupy one position at any given moment, as demonstrated by the near-death experience. If the consciousness is not in the physical it will occupy the wave or light body and vice versa. It appears that many things in the universe are multi-dimensional. When consciousness is observing matter, the waveform collapses and we see only physical. When the consciousness is not observing, it will continue to behave as such. This must be the natural state otherwise we would find ourselves in the company of spirits and light beings.

Mind over matter

At the Institute of Heartmath, various studies have been carried out to see if a positive heart/mind relationship can influence or even alter human DNA. According to the institute, positive feelings fortify our energy system and nourish the body at the cellular level; adversely a negative mind-set will deplete energy in the system brought about by focusing on those negative emotions. In the Modulation of DNA Conformation article 2003, the Institute concluded that aspects of DNA strands could be influenced by human intention, especially when the heart/mind was positively strong. The founder Doc Childre postulates that an energetic connection occurs between the DNA in the cells and the higher mind consciousness and that the heart serves as a key access point through which information connects to the physical system. He also says that a strong positive heart/mind state increases this coupling. His theory proposes that people who maintain this strong heart coherence with increased coupling to the higher mind will be more capable of altering their DNA.[10] With the body being a biological transmitter/receiver of energetic frequencies, the heart/mind relationship is the prime focal point in beating out and transmitting your unique spectrum of electromagnetic frequencies into your surroundings. The Institute of Heartmath's results have shown how important a positive mindset is when influencing an individual's reality. It will be equally as important influencing the collective. The control system on the other hand seems to bend over backwards with submerging humanity in a constant stream of negativity.

At Princeton University's Engineering Anomalies Research Lab (PEAR), a number of trials have been conducted over many years to see if individuals can influence the output of a computer known as (REG) random events generator, which randomly creates one's or zero's. The initial experiment tested two groups of individuals, one psychically gifted and the other not so. After many trials, they both produced similar positive results. Statistically more significant than what could be expected by chance. Next, they performed studies with pairs of individuals who knew each other. Together they would try to influence the outcome of (REG). With many pairs and trials, they found the results exceeded that of the individual trials. Couples in a relationship created what the research lab called a coherence effect and performed six times better than the initial individuals. Robert John and Brenda Dunne at (PEAR) suggested that emotional closeness might create resonance between individuals and result in a stronger influence.[11] The next stage was to perform the trials on groups of people. The groups that had a more focused and coherent collective mind set produced the best results. They were three times better than individuals and six times better when all meditating together.[12] This shows in a limited way the power of the collective mind or consciousness on reality. If we all focus on the same objective, we may have the ability to create whatever world we want. From the point of view of the control system, in order to keep itself in command, it must disguise our true potential and thrust us into a social structure of fragmented and competing individuals.

The placebo effect

The placebo effect is an artificially simulated phantom treatment for a medical condition designed to deceive the individual. The effect suggests that the mind of the patient is responsible for healing the ailment. Many studies have shown this effect to be real and effective. There is also a common belief among doctors that there is no placebo effect when it comes to surgery. During the late 90s a study was carried out on patients with debilitating knee pain. The patients were divided up into three separate groups.

- Group 1) They would have surgery to shave the damaged cartilage in the knee.
- Group 2) They would also have surgery with the joint being flushed out and cleaned.
- Group 3) The placebo group were tricked into believing they had surgery. After sedation, an incision was made to the knee then stitched back up.

All three groups went through rehabilitation programs as normal. The results concluded that the placebo group improved just as much as the other two groups who had been through real surgery. They also stated in the conclusion that healthcare researchers should not underestimate the placebo effect regardless of its mechanism.[13] The opposite of the placebo effect can be just as real, being told you have a terminal illness by someone in a position of authority, whether genuine or not, is sometimes enough to shock the system into ill health. Could even lead to terminal illness or bring on a heart attack through stress.

Hypnotism

Modern hypnosis has its roots in the work of Franz Mesmer, a German physician, 1734 - 1815. He came up with the theory that a natural energetic frequency is being transferred between animated and inanimate objects. He called this animal magnetism or mesmerism. Contrary to what most people believe a hypnotized subject is not asleep during hypnosis, the reality is far from that. Under hypnosis the individual's subconscious senses are one hundred times better than normal, being far more alert than in your conscious state. Like the iceberg the conscious part just above the water represents only a fraction, the will, the analytical, rational part of the mind. The subconscious is the permanent memory, your habits, self-preservation and emotions. If one was to make a comparison with a computer the conscious mind would be the processor and the subconscious the hard drive. The subconscious is so powerful like a digital camera; it records everything and forgets nothing. 2.3 million pieces of data per second. We only forget things at the conscious level. To become hypnotized, accessing the subconscious directly, the subject must fulfil three basic criteria.

1) Relaxed: Both physically and mentally, aiming for deeper relaxation.

2) Concentration: The consciousness must focus on something, sound or visual. This along with relaxation creates a shift in the alpha state of consciousness allowing communication with the subconscious directly.

3) Cooperation: Through suggestion the hypnotherapist can alter the belief system and programming of the subconscious mind. The subject must want the change and cooperate

willingly; otherwise the conscious mind via what is known as the critical faculty, the bouncer on the door between the conscious and unconscious will reject the suggestion.

Self-preservation is one of the most important jobs of the subconscious; it protects the mind and guards the individual from threats. Under this self-preservation negative suggestions go into the subconscious far more easily than positive ones. You could say the conscious mind is an employee of the subconscious, filtering any suggestion of change given from outside. Once in the hypnotic state suggestions can be placed directly into the subconscious. Only if the conscious and critical faculty are willing, can alternative programming begin. In the event of a person wanting help to give up smoking, a new belief system concerning smoking can begin when the suggestion has passed into the subconscious. The hypnotist is able to access all parts of our subconscious memory even as far back as early childhood. Throughout our lives we are being surreptitiously hypnotized, any form of conditioning to teach or lead us through thinking is a form of hypnosis. Institutions like schools, churches, governments and family environments all play a role somewhere. Watching television is a perfect way to become hypnotized, fulfilling all the criteria for hypnotism, you're relaxed; you're concentrating and very much open to suggestion. Watching TV turns off the conscious analytical brain so we uncritically process the information. It induces a passive state of communication straight to the subconscious; due to its self-preservation, negative suggestions go into the subconscious far easier than positive ones. This may be why so much negative news and violence is broadcast. You are being hypnotized.[14] [15] There seems to be a conscious effort by the control system to target directly into the subconscious by all means available. The range of frequency's each individual contributes to the collective is made up from his or her conscious, subconscious and higher mind connection. If the control system can go directly to the subconscious, the most powerful aspect of the mind then it becomes clear how much of an influence they can have.

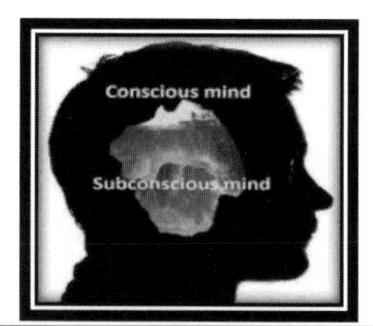

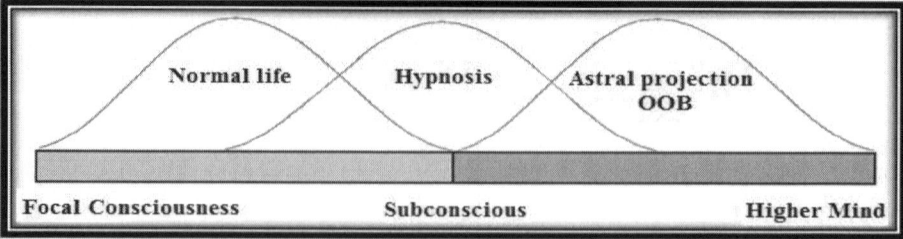

Epi-genetics

To make each individual the way they are, requires a complicated variety of factors and influences. Scientists have debated the nature or nurture hypothesis for decades. Recently a new concept has crept into the mainstream scientific community, the study of epigenetics. Human DNA is the body's biological instruction manual, the basic building blueprint for the body's cellular construction and function, bear in mind that nearly 98% of human DNA is non-coding or junk DNA. Attached to that is another layer of coding information, which activates, deactivates, accentuates or suppresses certain aspects of your DNA's base code, this is known as epigenetics, it's what tells the proteins in the cells to process those parts of the DNA sequence in certain ways, creating a unique individual. This is why each cell, beginning with the same DNA sequence can grow into either skin cells, muscle cells or whatever is required, it's all down to epigenetic tagging. The important thing to note about epigenetic tagging is that it is not fixed like the DNA sequence; these tags can change during a person's lifetime in response to outside influences and/or energetic alterations emanating from the individual's attitude and belief systems. So, with your mind you really can alter your body's expression of its core DNA. The environmental and emotional stimuli which you place yourself in will affect you at the cellular level; this allows the human to adapt to almost any situation he finds himself in, given enough time and the right attitude. The growing cells of a new baby will be epigenetically influenced by all outside factors of an electromagnetic and energetic nature that includes the universe and the position of planetary bodies.

Eureka moments

Inspiration seemingly from nowhere, enlightening the conscious mind with solutions to all kinds of problems. As previously mentioned the individual's extra senses promote this inspiration.

Some great eureka moments:

1) Albert Einstein's Theory of Relativity. While riding home in a car he was struck by the sight of Bern's clock tower, Switzerland. Realizing at once, he interpreted it as time beating at different rates throughout the universe depending upon the speed one is moving.

2) Nikola Tesla's alternating current. While Tesla was out walking mulling over the problems inherent with direct current, inspiration struck him and he came up with the idea of alternating current. On his way home, he continued to make pictures in the dirt with his walking stick. A prolific inventor, Tesla often sat meditating, visualizing his ideas.

3) George de Mestral's Velcro. While out walking his dog, he noticed many burrs stuck to his trousers. On his return home, he viewed the tiny hooks of the burrs under his microscope, at that point the eureka moment struck him. Velcro was born.

Free will

The will is your external projection of focal consciousness. Free will is the sole individual's ability to choose from a path of choices unhindered. The subconscious is instinctual or reactionary. To have will power is to have dominion over your basic instincts, and to exercise free will is to choose the most suitable option available as opposed to allowing basic reactions to manifest. It is the conscious taking precedent over the subconscious. The social objectives of the control system are to encourage fast paced, reactionary living, an environment leaving little room for rational free will to be employed. It is not in the interest of the control system for the majority to be well informed critical thinkers able to form fact based independent opinions and to say "NO" occasionally. They want obedient consumers whose base carnal desires react in all the right pre-empted ways.

Conventional science insists that the brain is made from the same particles as everything else in the universe, from mountains to sand, oceans to rain drops. They insist that these particles are not conscious. So where does the consciousness reside? I suggest they are looking at it the wrong way around. Consciousness is the benchmark, this is where we are, and all the physical constructs we perceive around us are projections from our eternal conscious imagination. Bill Hicks explained it best when he said:

"All matter is merely energy condensed to a slow vibration, that we are all one consciousness experiencing itself subjectively, there is no such thing as death, life is only a dream, and we are the imagination of ourselves". - Bill Hicks

Notes for chapter 1

(1) Wallace Thornhill, David Talbott, Electric Universe, Mikamar, 2007, http://www.amazon.com/Electric-Universe-Wallace-Thornhill-Talbott/dp/0977285138

(2) Belleruth Naparstek, Your Sixth Sense, Harper Collins, 2009, https://www.harpercollins.com/9780061723780/your-sixth-sense

(3) Ward Hill, lamon, Reflections of Abraham Lincoln (1847-1885), A.C McClurg & Co, 1895, https://archive.org/details/recollectionsab00lamogoog

(4) Sylvan J Muldoon, Projections of the astral body, Muller Press, 2011, http://www.amazon.com/Projection-Astral-Body-Sylvan-Muldoon/dp/1447402251

(5) Robert Bruce, Astrodynamics.com, https://www.astraldynamics.com/

(6) Stargate Project, Wikipedia.org, https://en.wikipedia.org/wiki/Stargate_Project

(7) Joe Schoenmann, Seeing dead people, Las Vegas Sun, May 5 2012, http://lasvegassun.com/news/2012/may/05/seeing-dead-people-remote-viewers-nevada-help-solv/

(8) Barbara Bartolome, NDE Radio, Lee Witting, March 26 2014, http://www.youtube.com/watch?v=LVPsqECaUWY

(9) Double Slit Experiment, Wikipedia.org, https://en.wikipedia.org/wiki/Double-slit_experiment

(10) McCarty Atkinson, Tomasind, Modulation of DNA Conformation, Institute of heartmath, 2003, https://www.heartmath.org/

(11) R Jahn, B Dunne, Margins of reality, The role of consciousness in the physical world, Harcourt Brace, Jovanovich, 1987 p257

(12) http://www.collectivewisdominitiative.org/papers/kenny_science.htm#end233

(13) A controlled trial of arthroscopic surgery for osteoarthritis of the knee, The New England journal of medicine, July 11 2002

(14) Aric Sigman, Remotely controlled, Vermilion, 2007, http://www.goodreads.com/book/show/1086351.Remotely_Controlled

(15) Alan Marriott, The Academy of hypnosis, http://www.theacademyofhypnosis.com/

Chapter 2. Astrology/Astrotheology

Astrology or applied astronomy is the discipline of using the position of the planets with their individual unique energetic frequencies to unlock the forces behind our physical reality, and to understand how these various energy fields play off against one another as they influence what we perceive with our five senses. The surrounding soup of cosmic electrical energy changes with endless cyclical movements of huge planetary bodies, gracefully moving and interacting across the heavens. Reality is a subjective construct in the minds of each individual, whose proximity varies within this electrical energy field, together with their programmed internal beliefs, a personal version of reality is experienced. Each planet radiates a signature frequency, a tapestry of energies making it unique. Like a room with an angry person, the energy given off will influence individuals and the collective depending upon where the individual positions himself.

Planet	Attributes	Action	Symbol
Sun	Self, Will, Focal Consciousness	I Will Act	☉
Moon	Emotion, Needs, Feelings, Subconscious	I React	☽
Mercury	Communication, Mind	I Communicate	☿
Venus	Love, Liking, Pleasure	I Harmonise	♀
Mars	Physical energy, Action	I Assert	♂
Jupiter	Expansion, Abundance	I Expand	♃
Saturn	Time, Seriousness, Discipline, Restriction	I Control	♄
Uranus	Revolution, Change	I Deviate	⛢
Neptune	Dreams, Illusions	I Refine	♆
Pluto	Transformation	I Transform	♇

Understanding the basics of astrology is necessary when trying to comprehend the forces behind our reality; the universe has a profound relationship with human consciousness. Astrology helps to expose the true origins of man-made religions, rooted within the zodiac and the journey of the Sun (God's Sun) as it moves through endless cycles within the twelve astrological houses (12 disciples) of the zodiac. The zodiac wheel represents many aspects of life and many time frames, all working together like a majestic time piece of synchronized universal consciousness.

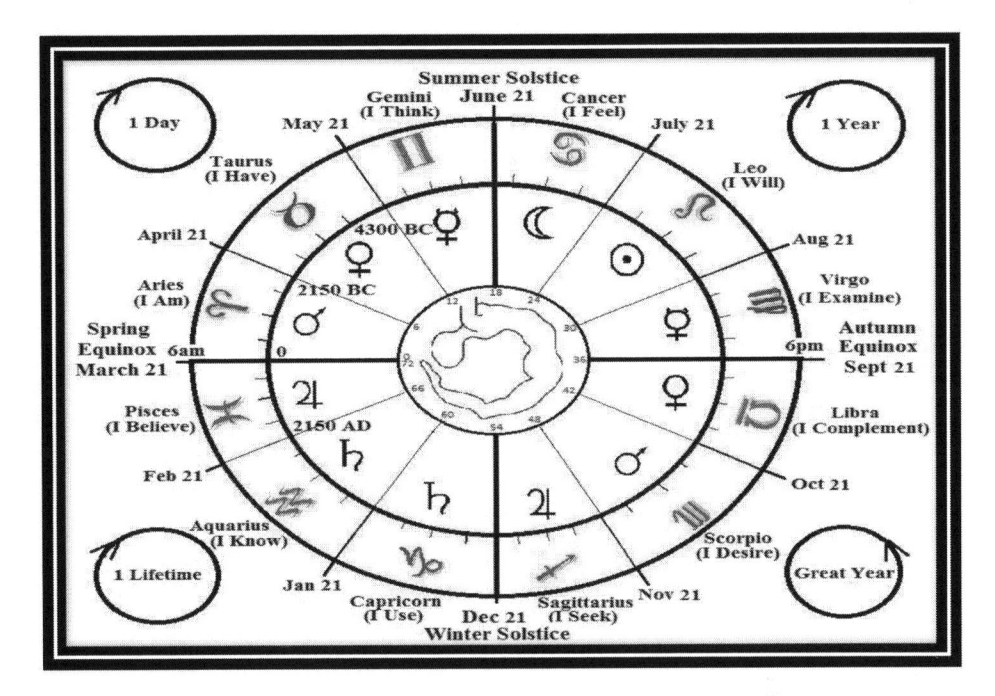

One cycle of the zodiac can represent 1 day, 1 year, 1 lifetime or even the Great Year (25,800 years), always beginning at Aries and ending in Pisces. The human body is also represented within the various houses, the head at Aries the heart at Leo and the feet at Pisces.

Day cycle: At the equator, the Sun will appear on the horizon at 6am, the beginning of a new day. God's Sun has risen to light the world, beginning in Aries and setting in Libra, the balancing scales, day and night. The Sun then loses its power and disappears into the underworld for 12 hours, only to be reborn again as man's risen saviour the very next day.

Year cycle: Always beginning in March, the start of the ancient astrological year. Remnants of which are still apparent today, September comes from Sept meaning 7, Oct (octopus) for 8 and Dec (decimal) for 10, which makes more sense when viewing the ancient astrological calendar. In the year cycle, we see the summer/winter solstices and the spring/autumn equinoxes together making up the cross of the zodiac in which God's Sun finds himself moving around. The Sun reaches its highest and strongest point at the summer solstice; it then begins its descent one degree per day into the southern hemisphere, reaching its lowest and weakest point at the winter solstice on December 22. A strange thing occurs at this point, the Sun appears to stop moving south for three days, rising in the same position on the horizon each morning, as though it had died for three days. Eventually on December 25 the Sun moves 1 degree north, the start of a six-month journey back towards the northern hemisphere. This is the birth of the new Sun.

The Great Year: This is a full cycle of 25,800 years, the precession of the constellations moving slowly backwards in the night sky. For the past 2,000 years the constellation of Pisces has been behind the Sun each spring equinox morning as it appears on the horizon, steadily moving towards the Age of Aquarius, continually emitting energy vibrations towards the Earth. Before Pisces it was the Age of Aries and before Aries we had Taurus, and so on.

One lifetime: A full cycle can represent an average human life, approximately 72 years. 6 years in each sign, starting at Aries and ending with Pisces.

Astrotheology

Astrotheology is the merging of man's religious beliefs with the ancient wisdom of astrology/astronomy. Many people scoff when you mention the zodiac and star signs, yet most religions in modern society have deep roots within it. When looking at the 2,150-year precession of the zodiac signs we notice that we are now on the cusp of a transition from Pisces into Aquarius. Pisces has a unique energy, simplified as the motto (I believe), creating an epoch of 2,150 years of believing. Aquarius is the Age of "insight and knowing" with its motto (I know), which just happens to coincide with the expansion of the Information Age we are experiencing today. The Age of Pisces is represented by two fish and ruled by the planet Jupiter. The Pope sits on the throne of Peter (Jupiter), while God's Sun with its Piscean backdrop is known as Jesus. In ancient Greek Zeus was the God of the sky, lightning and thunder, known by the Romans as Jupiter, together they give us Jupiter-Zeus (Ju-zeus or Jesus). Christians still use the fish as a symbol for their beliefs, many unaware that it represents the zodiac sign of Pisces. Before Pisces it was the Age of Aries the ram, ruled by the planet Mars. Here we see Moses or Marses coming down from Mt Sinai blowing the ram's horn, telling his followers to forget the sacred bull (Taurus), now they must follow the ram (Aries). During this latest transition into Aquarius, man's religions must find a way to throw off the old throne of Peter and replace it with the water bearer (Aquarius), ruled by Saturn in ancient astrology and Uranus and Saturn in modern astrology.

Natal charts

Also known as a birth chart, this is a way of mapping the universe at your particular time and place of birth, creating a visual representation of planetary energies which influence and interact various areas of a person's life. At your moment of birth, you are said to be a biological reflection of the cosmos surrounding you, (as above so below). Your physical make-up is constructed from the orientation of electrical energies and frequencies flowing towards you, essentially capturing that specific moment of combined universal energy, which cements itself at your cellular level, making you unique. The natal chart can help us understand core influences. After your birth, the planets continue to move across time and space, once again having an effect on your development, the new position of planetary energies will play off against the fixed biological energy of the original natal planetary positions, fixed at your time of birth. These new positional interactions are known as transits.

The zodiac wheel represents many areas of life, it is divided up into manageable parts, expressing all aspects of our physical experience, with 12 signs, 12 houses and the planets, an experienced astrologer can gain great insight into a person's personality, strengths and weaknesses. By using this knowledge an individual can choose a more suitable path in life, harmonizing with his biological and spiritual nature.

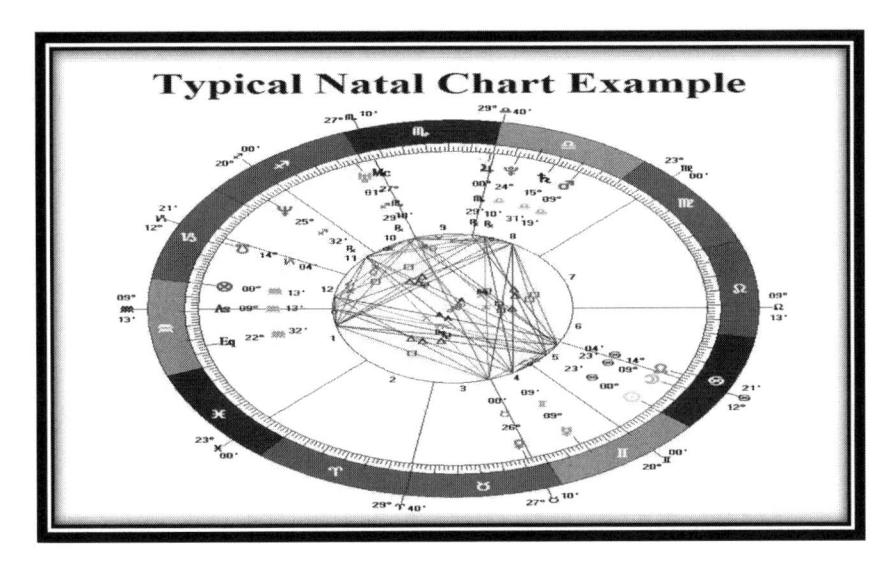

Luke 22:10, the Last Supper

They said to him "where do you want us to prepare it?" And he said to them, "when you have entered the city, a man will meet you carrying a pitcher of water, follow him into the house that he enters. And you shall say to the owner of the house, the teacher says to you. Where is the guest room in which I may eat the Passover with my disciples?"

Understanding this verse is crucial to understanding man's religions and the cycles of the zodiac. The Last Supper on the throne of Peter (Jupiter) is the last in the Age of Pisces before the natural transition into Aquarius. **When you have entered the city a man will meet you carrying a pitcher of water, Follow him into the house that he enters.** This is the house of the zodiac called Aquarius. **And you shall say to the owner of the house, the teacher says to you.** In the traditional version of the zodiac, before Uranus was discovered, Saturn ruled the house of Aquarius. Saturn represents many things, seriousness, organization, order, authority, also known as Old Father Time or the Teacher.

Where is the guest room where I may eat the Passover with my disciples? During the transition from Pisces into Aquarius, on the cusp, both Jupiter and Saturn will have equal dominance over the shared house position in the zodiac. Here Jupiter becomes the guest in the new house ruled by Saturn, Old Father Time, and the teacher. The Passover is the movement from one house boundary into the other. There are 12 disciples with Jesus; representing the 12 houses of the zodiac. Jesus the Sun of God, the Sun in the sky, our risen saviour, he is coming in the clouds, he wears a crown of thorns and walks on water.

God's Sun with his crown of thorns walking on water

The Sun of God also turns water into wine and heals the sick. The Sun evaporates water from the ocean, which condenses over the land and turns into rain. The rain will water the grapes which are used to make wine. Vitamin D is produce by the body when exposed to sunlight. Vitamin D is one of the best ways to boost the immune system when fighting illness, hence God's Sun heals the sick.

In the late 15th century, Leonardo da Vinci painted "The Last Supper", a magnificent work depicting the last meal with Jesus and his disciples. If you look at the picture from an astrological perspective, it takes on a whole new dimension.

Jesus represents the Sun, the central focus of the zodiac and his disciples represent the 12 houses. Da Vinci paints the disciples into four groups, these depict the four seasons, three in each, the first three on the far left represent Aries, Taurus and Gemini; with the colours of fire, earth and air to suit. The other interesting point about the third disciple is the way he holds his hands out, as though he is trying to simulate the two twins of Gemini, the sign associated with the arms and hands. As we go along we see three more disciples Cancer, Leo and Virgo; water, fire and earth with colours to match the seasons. On the right side of Jesus is a man with his arms stretched out acting like a pair of scales, which of course is Libra. The colours of their clothes begin to fade and become drab reflecting the autumn and winter months of fading light and misery. The man second to last is Aquarius, an air sign of mind and intellect. He holds one hand upside down on the table simulating the double wave symbol of Aquarius. Finally, we see Jesus in the centre dressed in mostly blue and orange, signifying the masculine and feminine. I suspect da Vinci was trying to represent the Sun in Pisces a water sign, or the spirit and soul aspect of the Sun's energy.

Feeding The 5,000 with 2 fish and 5 loaves seems a daunting task, certainly in need of a miracle. When viewing it through the eyes of the astrologer, it becomes child's play. The 2 fish represent Pisces and the house of bread is Virgo, between these two-opposing spring and summer months there are 5 signs in which the Sun shines its brightest, allowing all the plants and crops to grow. In Biblical terms 5 symbolizes God's grace. So, between the two fish of Pisces and God's grace in Virgo, we should have no problem feeding everyone. But don't forget to say grace before settling down for dinner. Also, Jesus represents the Sun during the Age of Pisces, ruled by the planet Jupiter, a planet of expansion and abundance.

Feet, fish and belief

The Bible has many references to feet, fish and belief, all aspects of Pisces; fish the symbol; feet the body parts, and belief the motto or energetic frequency coming from the Piscean constellation. According to the website (**knowing Jesus**) there are 103 Bible verses about feet.[1] After the Last Supper Jesus washes his disciple's feet. The Pope is also partial to washing and kissing feet.

"Your Lord and teacher have washed your feet, so you also should wash one another's feet. I have given you an example, you should do as I have done for you" - John 13:14-15

There are 17 Bible verses about fish and fisherman and 29 verses about belief. Not surprising when you know what fish and belief represent here. The world has had 2,150 years of this energetic backdrop influencing humanity, no wonder humanity experienced thousands of belief systems throughout the world during the Piscean Age.

"And he said to them, follow me and I will make you fishers of men". Matthew 4:19

Judas betrays Jesus

The story of Judas betraying Jesus for thirty pieces of silver is well known throughout the Christian world. After the Last Supper Judas identifies Jesus with a kiss in the garden of Gethsemane. He betrays Jesus for 30 pieces of silver which leads to his death on the cross. In astrological terms, Judas represents the sign of Scorpio. A scorpion will bite you leaving a mark which looks like two lips; this is known as the kiss of death. On the zodiac wheel Scorpio is 30 days away from the winter solstice on December 22nd. The point at which the Sun appears dead on the zodiac cross for three days. The 30 pieces of silver represent the Moon 30 nights after Scorpio.

The Spear of Destiny

The Spear of Destiny or the Holy Lance, the name given to the weapon supposedly used by a Roman soldier to pierce the side of Jesus as he hung on the cross during the final stages of his crucifixion. Good Friday is a Christian holiday celebrating the crucifixion of Christ; it normally takes place on the Friday preceding Easter Sunday, this year, 2015, it fell on April 3rd. If we analyse this from an astrological perspective, we see that April 3rd is in the middle of Aries, a sign ruled by the planet Mars. The symbol for Mars is a shield and a spear. If we place a human body over the three decans of Aries we see that the spear of Mars pierces the body in the same place as all the depictions of the piercing of Jesus throughout history, at the transitional point from cardinal Aries to fixed Aries. It's just another Astrological story about planets journeying around the zodiac wheel. The Spear of Destiny is believed by many to be a real artifact, containing special powers, and he who possesses the spear shall rule the world.

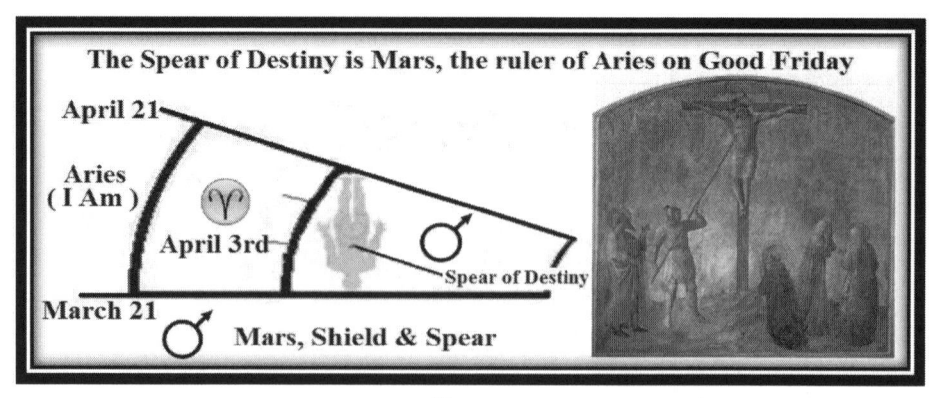

Noah's ark

Throughout the centuries explorers and archaeologists have been searching for the remains of Noah's Ark, believing it to be a physical construct, misguided they overlook the astrological explanation choosing instead to spend vast sums of money searching the globe for evidence. An arc is a section of a circle, in this case a section of the zodiac circle, beginning in Aquarius through Pisces finally ending in Aries. This is the real Noah's Arc.

Noah is the personification of Aquarius the water man. Pisces is the two fish or animals two by two. During these months in the depths of winter the weather can be extreme, too cold to leave your livestock outside in the elements, it would be considered a wise move to bring them in, two by two to shelter from the harsh weather. Finally, the Arc ends in Aries the ram, representing dry land, new beginnings and prosperity once more.

According to the early church Noah's Arc landed on Mt Ararat. Could this be the Sun in Aries, the final stages of Noah's Arc? (AR-Aries) (RA-Sun). We also need to consider the constellation Argo Navis; such a large collection of stars, the ancients divided it into 3 sections. Carina-(Keel), Puppis-(Stern) and Vela-(Sail).

Aquarius and Pisces have so many watery constellations the ancients referred to it as the Sea. To the side of Argo Navis is the constellation of Columba represented by the dove.[2]

"Then he sent forth a dove from him to see if the water had subsided from the face of the ground "Genesis 8:8

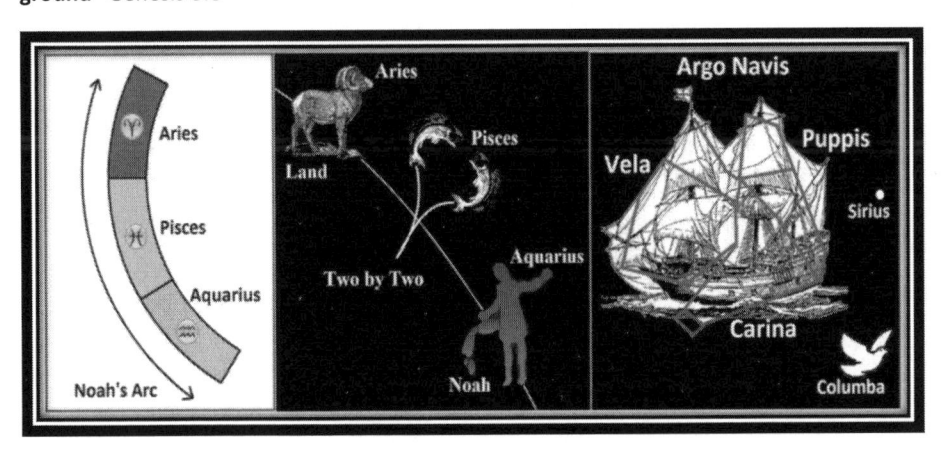

Ark of the Covenant

The Ark of the Covenant is a chest supposedly containing the ten commandments of Moses. A covenant is a formal alliance or agreement made by God with humanity, a communicative contract. All communication falls within the domain of the planet Mercury. While Noah's Arc is found in the winter of the zodiac wheel, the Arc of the Covenant can be found on the opposite side, in the height of summer, God's contract with humanity in the form of communication within the Holy Trinity, the father, Sun/son and Holy Spirit or the higher, focal and subconscious mind. When we look at this arc in the zodiac from Cancer through to Virgo we find the ruling planets of the Moon-Cancer, Sun-Leo and Mercury-Virgo, making up the Arc of the Covenant, Mercury represents communication within all realms of consciousness. This is the Holy Trinity and the Arc of the Covenant all in one.

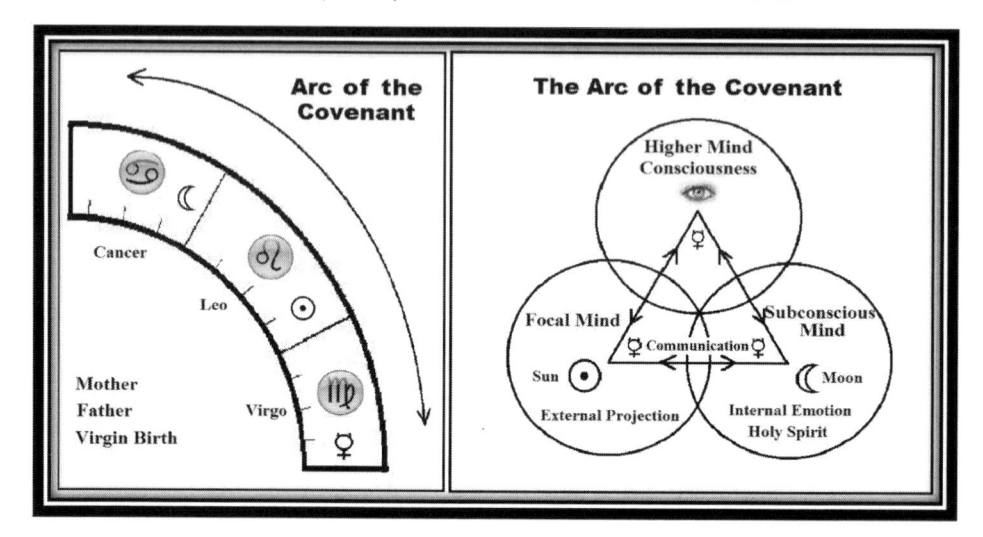

The secret to the Arc of the Covenant is strong communication between all the realms of consciousness. This is how we create our reality. They were right when they said the Ten Commandments were held in a chest. The body part associated with Cancer and Leo is the chest. All of humanity is believed to possess instinctive common sense and universal laws written on their hearts.

"They show that the requirements of the law are written on their hearts, their consciences also bearing witness, and their thoughts sometimes accusing them and at other times even defending them." - Romans 2:15 (NIV)

The Holy Grail

The Holy Grail is generally considered to be the cup from which Christ drank at the Last Supper, it is also the same cup used by Joseph of Arimathea to catch the blood of Jesus as he hung on the cross. To understand this in its true sense, a grasp of the three areas of consciousness must be understood, the Father, Son and Holy Spirit. The cup is symbolic and represents the element of water, the emotional level of consciousness; love, feelings, relationship and connections. Just like in Tarot the cup is the symbol for water and our internal emotions. Communication between all three levels of consciousness within the Arc of the Covenant takes place on an emotional and spiritual level. The grail represents the filling of the cup with emotional communicative energy, flowing between higher mind, focal and the subconscious, in essence an energetic emotional lubricant, the blood or life's energy from God's Sun suspended on the cross of the zodiac at the centre of the astrological wheel.

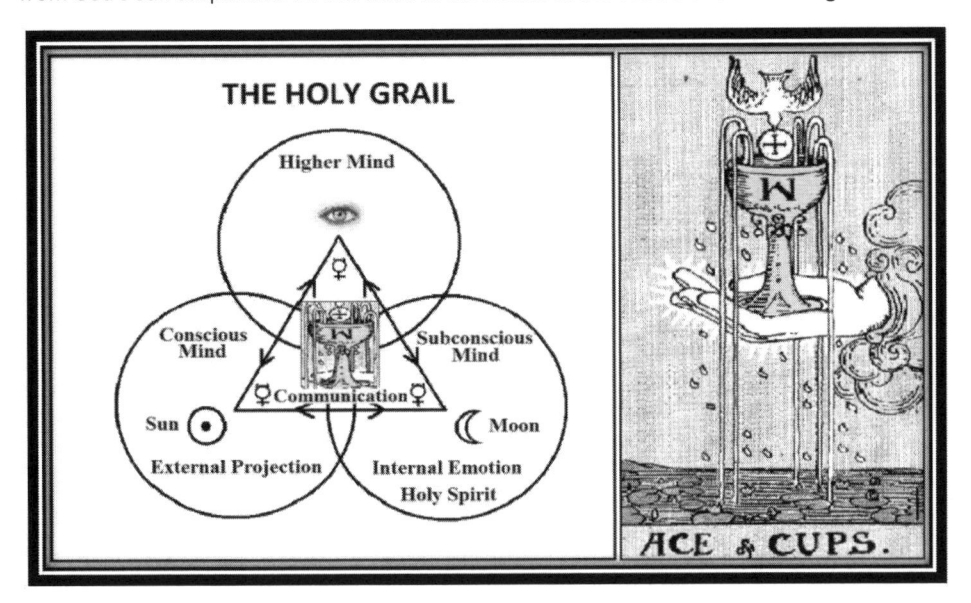

THE HOLY GRAIL

Higher Mind / Conscious Mind / Subconscious Mind / Sun - External Projection / Moon - Internal Emotion / Holy Spirit / Communication

ACE of CUPS.

Matthew, Mark, Luke & John

The four Evangelists, writers of the gospels or are they the four seasons of the zodiac, the equinoxes and the solstices?

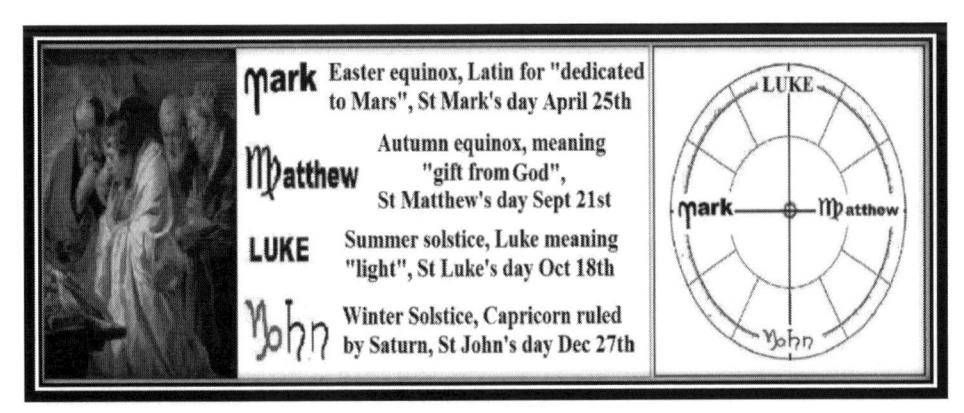

mark — Easter equinox, Latin for "dedicated to Mars", St Mark's day April 25th

matthew — Autumn equinox, meaning "gift from God", St Matthew's day Sept 21st

LUKE — Summer solstice, Luke meaning "light", St Luke's day Oct 18th

John — Winter Solstice, Capricorn ruled by Saturn, St John's day Dec 27th

Mark is a boy's name meaning "dedicated to Mars". The first cardinal sign of Aries, ruled by the planet Mars. Mark represents Aries the spring equinox. St Mark's day is celebrated on April 25th in the middle of spring. Matthew in Latin means "Gift of God", representing the autumn equinox, a name beginning with "M", which is also the symbol for Virgo. St Matthew's day is celebrated on 21st September. Luke is Latin for light representing the summer solstice, the time of year when the Sun is at its brightest. The only anomaly here is that St Luke's day falls on October 18th. John is a composite of the symbols or glyphs for

Capricorn and Saturn, Saturn is the ruler of Capricorn the cardinal sign following the winter solstice and St John's day is on December 27th.

In a universe full of electromagnetic energetic, the change in these fields can be instantaneous with the movement of celestial bodies. The angles of the planets relative to you and each other are important. Some angles produce a beneficial influence and some not so. Over the centuries the control system through religion has twisted this ancient wisdom and transposed the word angle into angel. The most recognized angels are Michael, Gabriel and Satan. Michael is the angle of the Sun in the sky; Gabriel represents the angle of the Moon[3] and Satan, the Devil or the fallen angel, is simply the personification of the planet Saturn, a planet of materialism, power and worldliness. All planetary bodies can have both positive or negative effects depending on their angle and our relative position. Giving one's life over to the pursuit of money and power alone is to neglect many other important aspects of life such as emotions, relationships, higher ideals and spiritual development. An excess of materialism, ignoring human values can be considered as evil, dark, or the work of the Devil. Ruling the sign of Capricorn, Satan is often portrayed as half goat and half human, the ruler of the underworld, during the darkest days of winter, at the lowest and weakest point for the Sun on its journey around the zodiac.

Adam and Eve

On a 24-hour zodiac cycle, Adam and Eve simply represent the day and the night, light and dark, good and evil. Adam is to be found in the garden during spring and summer when the Sun is strong enough to stimulate growth. Eve (Evening) gets the better of Adam in Libra, the scales of right and wrong, good and evil, decision making, where we descend further away from the protection of the Sun, in full power, at midday and during the summer solstice. Here we move into the houses of desire, seeking, using and knowing, the houses of late autumn and winter. Coincidently, In the northern hemisphere the majority of apples and other fruits are ripe for picking during September, the month of harvesting, the same month Virgo changes into Libra, where we start our journey towards the underworld.

"When the woman saw that the fruit of the tree was good for food and pleasing to the eye, and also desirable for gaining wisdom, she took some and ate it. She also gave some to her husband, who was with her, and he ate it." Genesis 3:6[4]

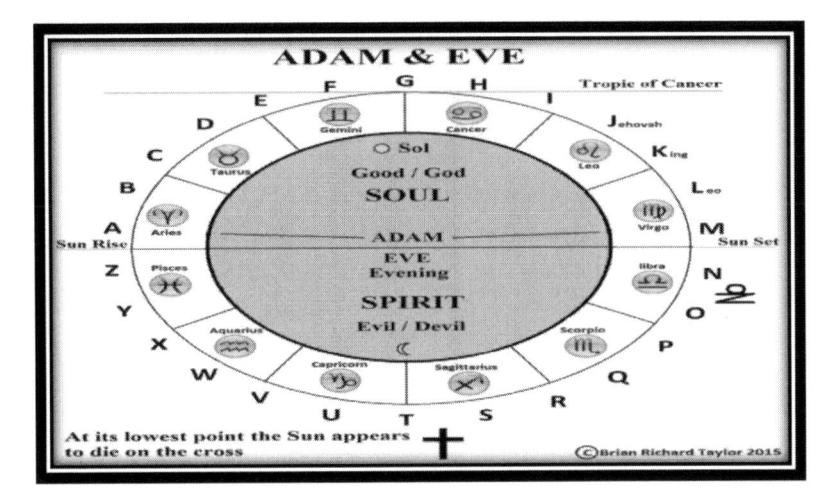

The control system throughout the ages has disguised the true nature of universal wisdom and adopted many of the meanings and symbols for its own purposes. They draw you away from understanding the bigger picture, away from your natural connection to source (higher mind Logos). The media portrays astrology as a laughable pseudo-science, publishing horoscopes based on only the Sun sign, a fraction of what you are, only the external projection of the consciousness, a prediction so general and lacking, it is no more helpful than a doctor diagnosing a patient from a 10 second telephone conversation.

I have tried to demonstrate how man's religions have used astrology for its own purposes, disguising truth with deception, inventing stories and explanations which seem plausible to the naive because they are stimulating man's spiritual nature. The only difference being, they make you look outside yourself for answers, depowering your true potential and enslaving you in their dogma. The participants within religions self-police one another into rigid formalities condemning astrology as the work of the Devil. The truth is there is nothing to fear, the Devil does not exist, only in the minds of those believers. Fear has always been used by the control system to weaken its subjects into submission and slavery. As mentioned in chapter 1 fear and negative suggestions go straight into the subconscious due to its defence mechanism.

At present, there is a steady transformation of universal energy influencing humanity. The Age of Aquarius, the Age of knowing, wisdom and awareness is expanding human consciousness as we speak. This unstoppable process will alter the way in which the control system operates. People need order but not exploitation. Within this new frequency range humanity will evolve for the better, throwing off the ageing shackles of Piscean beliefs together with its abundance of blind faith.

The Age of Aquarius

When you are born you are biological reflections of universal energy which surrounding you. You come out of this world not into it. During this 2150-year Age of Aquarius humanity will be under the influence of the water bearer, with Uranus and Saturn ruling the heavens. This will alter the backdrop of energetic frequencies affecting all biological organisms. Saturn's energy is serious, organizing and restrictive, along with hard work, frustrations and constraints. It will propel certain sections of humanity to organize better and take responsibility for the world in a more serious manner. This too will influence the evolvement of the control system, throwing everything they can to prop up their antiquated methods, moving forward with new techniques of greater control and restrictions. Uranus on the other hand is a planet resonating unpredictability, out of the blue events and a rebellious nature, something which will work contrary to the efforts of relative control. This will initially propel humanity to struggle against saturnine systems of order. As this transition approaches humanity will be better equipped to sense deceptions and lies. The wizard behind the curtain pulling at the levers will struggle to maintain dominance within this new energetic backdrop. During this Age of (I know), the wizard's curtain should fall, and all those who have eyes will see it for what it really is.

"There is no top or bottom, no absolute positioning in space. There are only positions that are relative to the others. There is an incessant change in the relative positions throughout the universe and the observer is always at the centre" — Giordano Bruno[5]

The Saturn connection

Saturn is an energetic body in the universe, Old Father Time and the Teacher. Its unique energetic identity can be expressed as seriousness, control, restriction, limitation, authority, discipline, patience etc. Just like a parent Saturn's energy will teach us mastery over our lives, with hard work, dedication and patience helping us to mature within our life's purpose. Saturn takes 30 years to fulfil a cycle and return to one's natal position. At 45 Saturn sits opposite to the natal Saturn, influencing many people to experience a midlife assessment or crisis. Saturn commands us to get to work on time, disciplined and responsible we must learn to manage time constraints and work hard. The rigid cultural systems which we live under influencing our behaviour are also Saturnian in nature. The worship of Saturn is commonplace, but most people don't realize it, they go about their lives oblivious to its influence. The education system is a prime example of saturnian energy, with the discipline of teaching within time constraints, mastering each given subject, until the individual students achieves graduate status, a single degree of academic knowledge within 360 geometric degrees of the potential universal wisdom. In many cultures and belief systems Saturn is represented by the colour black and the shape of a cube. Unaware of this the graduates, on completion, celebrate by wearing Saturnian black robes with square satanic mortar boards on their heads. Announcing, to all, that their minds have been squared off and their new focal consciousness resonates with Saturn's seriousness. Wedding ceremonies also engage in Saturn's symbolism. The serious nature of marriage with its vows and restrictions are cemented with an exchange of rings, Saturnian rings designed to influence the couple as they live within the serious constraints of a saturnian energetic union.

The Kaaba in Mecca is a black cube, and to some is a symbolic representation of the planet Saturn. The ceremony of walking around the Kaaba in an anti-clockwise direction is a physical symbolic gesture re-enacting the rings of Saturn, which also go in an anti-clockwise direction. This act is a physical one, installing all the characteristics of Saturn into one's faith, limitation, restriction, authority, seriousness and control. The North Pole of Saturn has a strange hexagon in its atmospheric weather system which may explain why a cube is used to represent Saturn, the hexagon is simply a cube viewed from a specific angle.

The Uranus connection

Uranus is the 7th planet from the Sun; it has the 3rd largest radius of all the planets with the 4th largest mass. A cold planet composed of ice and rocks, discovered by William Herschel, observing the heavens from his home in Somerset, England in 1781. From an astrological point of view Uranus gives off an energetic frequency associated with unpredictability and out of the blue events; it is revolutionary, rebellious, with individual free will. It influences erratic and bizarre behaviour, with freedom and creativity being important aspects to this planet, along with breaking the status quo. Many people consider the timing of its rediscovery to be no coincidence, when taking into account its energetic construct and the year it was recorded, which happened to be right between the American and French Revolutions.

Uranus takes 84 years to complete a full cycle around the Sun, whereas Saturn only takes 29. This means Uranus will occupy a single house within the zodiac for approximately 7 years. At the halfway point when the planet has transited opposite your natal Uranus surprises are more likely to occur. This is usually around the age of 42, around the time of a midlife crisis. The electromagnetic opposition creates stressful torque within the biological individual, pulling many people away from their normal routine, breaking the status quo. Another transit aspect within the Uranus cycle is the square, the 90-degree position from the natal Uranus which occurs around the age of 21 and 63, influencing changes of an unpredictable and out of the blue nature.

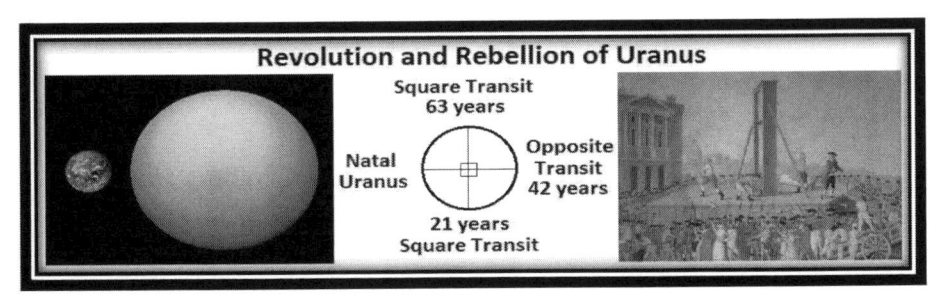

For one thousand years, in the first half of the Aquarian Age, Uranus will rule, overshadowed in the latter half by Saturn. In the Bible Jesus says **"The kingdom of heaven is at hand"**. What does he mean by this? When one takes the Greek word for heaven (Ouranos), and substitutes it for the word heaven, Jesus's prophecy takes on a whole new dimension.

"The kingdom of Ouranos (Uranus) is at hand"

He suggests we all need to repent for the kingdom of Uranus is at hand, suggesting we must change our attitude or mind-set, be remorseful for the kingdom of Jupiter will come to an end, and a new one will begin. A global paradigm shift will naturally occur due to the outpouring of watery spirit from the cardinal beginnings of the Aquarian Age, the energy of awakening, revolution and independence will rain down upon the Earth.

Paganism

Paganism is a term for a belief system which identifies nature as the body of the divine, a wide group of indigenous, polytheistic religious traditions, stretching far into the ancient world, generally referring to country people, living off the land as opposed to living in the cities. Before Christianity it had no religious structure, which you would associate with religions today. As Christianity grew so did the semi structural development of Paganism. Early Christians referred to these diverse cults, who did not believe in their version of God, as Pagans. For example, Taoism is the paganism of China; Hinduism is the paganism of India and Shinto the Paganism of Japan. Pagans believed the stars were divinity, Apollo was the God of the Sun, his sister Diana was the Goddess of the Moon, this was also the case with all the known planets. Paganism was once dominated by the belief in astrology and star worship, the ancient wisdom, blending one's own unique path with that of the collective cycles of the planets and the universe, each life being an individual manifestation of mother Earth, an individual experience connected to each other and the surrounding world, our lives being both personal and part of a collective.

Astrology played a major role in early societies, one of the earliest known zodiac wheels was found in Egypt during the Napoleonic campaign, in 1821 what is known as the Dendrah zodiac was removed and now lies in the Louvre, Paris, estimated to be 6,000 years old. Ancient wisdom of bygone civilizations, those advanced societies capable of building the great pyramids took astrology seriously. The Catholic Church in its attempts to dominate and spread its sphere of influence throughout the known world rejected all forms of divination including astrology. They wanted people subservient to the Church, giving over their individual power to its belief system. As part of the early control system they intended to eradicate individual forms of spirituality and replace it with an external manmade collective indoctrination.

When the flag of the UK is placed on the zodiac wheel along with the dates of the eight major pagan festivals, you will discover that all the red lines point to these festivals. The flag is asymmetrical; it has a right and wrong way up. The red diagonal cross of St Patrick is not central; its position only corresponds perfectly with four pagan festivals when it is off centre and the correct way up. The official explanation for this is far from convincing. In my view the Union Jack is a pagan flag.

The Union Jack's official explanation: **"In 1801, an Act of Union which made Ireland a co-equal member of the United Kingdom made it necessary to add a symbol for Ireland to the flag, but without obliterating any of the existing symbols. If the St. Patrick's cross had been centred on the diagonal stripes, then St. Andrew's cross would have been relegated to an inferior position, basically serving only as a border for St. Patrick's. But Scotland was the senior of the two kingdoms, so this was unsatisfactory. The solution was to divide the diagonal stripes diagonally, so that the red St. Patrick's cross would take up only half of each stripe, and so that half devoted to St. Andrew would take the place of honour. Thus, in the two hoist quarters, the white St. Andrew's cross occupies the upper position, and in the two fly quarters, the red St. Patrick's cross occupies the upper position."**[6]- Design of the Union Jack

Pagan Festivals

Summer Solstice,	June 21st	Beltane	May 1st
Winter Solstice,	December 22nd	Lughnasadh	August 1st
Spring Equinox,	March 20th	Samhain	October 31st
Autumn Equinox,	September 23rd	Imbolk	February 1st

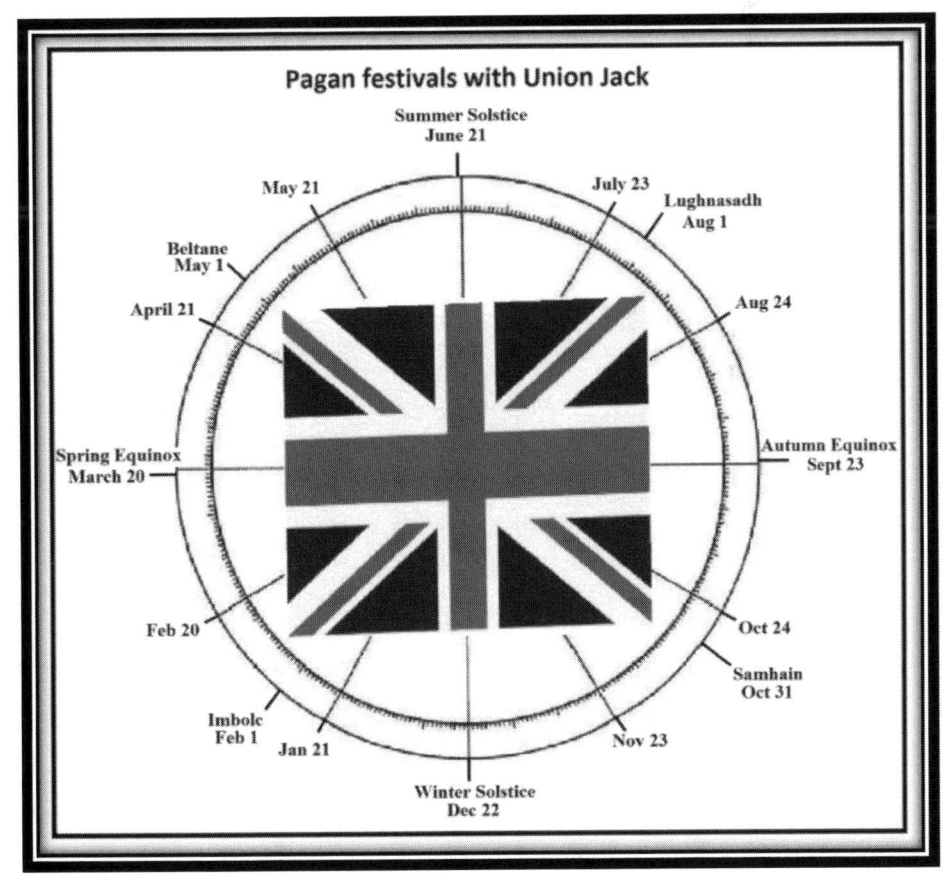

Pagan festivals with Union Jack

- Summer Solstice — June 21
- May 21
- July 23
- Lughnasadh — Aug 1
- Beltane — May 1
- April 21
- Aug 24
- Spring Equinox — March 20
- Autumn Equinox — Sept 23
- Feb 20
- Oct 24
- Samhain — Oct 31
- Imbolc — Feb 1
- Jan 21
- Nov 23
- Winter Solstice — Dec 22

Beltane is a pagan/Gaelic May Day festival, half way between the spring equinox and the summer solstice. It marks the beginning of summer when cattle were taken out to summer pastures, in the middle of Taurus the bull.

Lughnasadh another pagan/gaelic festival marking the beginning of the harvest season, halfway between the summer solstice and the autumn equinox.

Samhain is from sunset on 31st October till sunset on 1st November, the end of the harvest season, halfway between the autumn equinox and the winter solstice, the time when cattle were brought down from summer pastures. Offerings of food and drink were left out to pagan Gods and spirits to bring good fortune and help survive the winter. Feasts were had in which the souls of dead kin were beckoned to attend meal times with a place set for them. People would go door to door reciting verses in exchange for food.

Imbolk is a pagan festival marking the beginning of spring, halfway between the winter solstice and the spring equinox. A festival associated with the goddess Brighid. Feasts were had and holy wells were visited, the water bearer of Aquarius.

Notes for chapter 2

(1) Knowing Jesus, www.bible.knowing-jesus.com/topics/Feet

(2) The Unspoken Bible, www.usbible.com/astrology/noahs_flood.htm

(3) Gabriel · Astrological definition of Gabriel · Astrology Encyclopaedia · November 12, 2014, www.astrologyweekly.com/dictionary/gabriel.php

(4) Genesis 3:6, New International Version, Biblica, 2011

(5) Giordano Bruno, Philosopher, www.wsws.org/en/articles/2000/02/brun-f16.html, 16th century

(6) Design of the flag, http://www.flagpole86.com/article-flag.asp?prono=15

Chapter 3.

The control system

Before we explore how humanity is being manipulated, on various levels, we must first gain an insight as to what the control system is and who the players are, a multi layered system of influential cogs, grinding together, pulling humanity along a road of twists and turns, which most of us would prefer not to go down. Cogs of various sizes and strengths, lubricated with the flow of personnel and resources from various secret societies, organisations and think tanks. No one person or entity sits on the throne with total control, levels of power shuffles backwards and forwards along a sliding scale of time and influence, occasionally battling it out in brutal bloodletting orgies with the children of those unfortunate generations butchered in its wake. There has always been some form of control over humanity, a necessary influence, encouraging productivity and stimulating potential. Without this external sense of motivation, the majority will aimlessly drift through life accomplishing very little. But there is a point at which the control system interferes and becomes counterproductive to the natural evolution of man.

"The very word "secrecy" is repugnant in a free and open society; and we are as a people inherently and historically opposed to secret societies, to secret oaths and secret proceedings. We decided long ago that the dangers of excessive and unwarranted concealment of pertinent facts far outweighed the dangers which are cited to justify it. Even today, there is little value in opposing the threat of a closed society by imitating its arbitrary restrictions. Even today, there is little value in insuring the survival of our nation if our traditions do not survive with it. And there is very grave danger that an announced need for increased security will be seized upon those anxious to expand its meaning to the very limits of official censorship and concealment. That I do not intend to permit to the extent that it is in my control. And no official of my Administration, whether his rank is high or low, civilian or military, should interpret my words here tonight as an excuse to censor the news, to stifle dissent, to cover up our mistakes or to withhold from the press and the public the facts they deserve to know. For we are opposed around the world by a monolithic and ruthless conspiracy that relies on covert means for expanding its sphere of influence--on infiltration instead of invasion, on subversion instead of elections, on intimidation instead of free choice, on guerrillas by night instead of armies by day. It is a system which has conscripted vast human and material resources into the building of a tightly knit, highly efficient machine that combines military, diplomatic, intelligence, economic, scientific and political operations. Its preparations are concealed, not published. Its mistakes are buried not headlined. Its dissenters are silenced, not praised. No expenditure is questioned, no rumour is printed, no secret is revealed. No President should fear public scrutiny of his program. For from that scrutiny comes understanding; and from that understanding comes support or opposition. And both are necessary. I am not asking your newspapers to support the Administration, but I am asking your help in the tremendous task of informing and alerting the American people. For I have complete confidence in the response and dedication of our citizens whenever they are fully informed." - President John F Kennedy, The president and the press speech 1961.[1]

The cogs of the control system

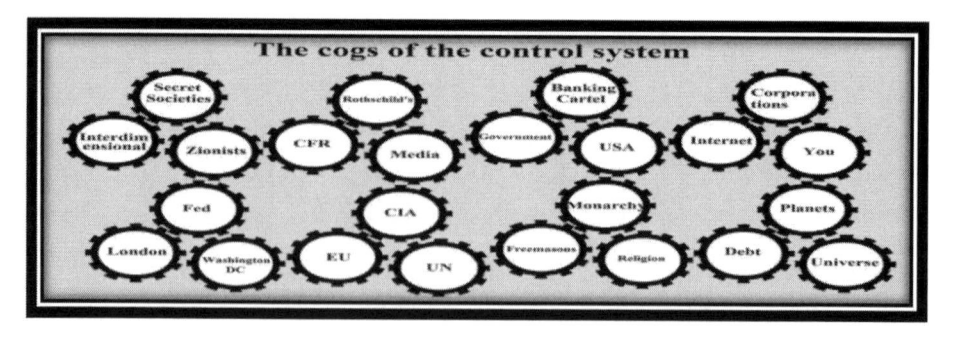

Secret Societies · Rothschild's · Banking Cartel · Corporations · Interdimensional · Zionists · CFR · Media · Government · USA · Internet · You · Fed · CIA · Monarchy · Planets · London · Washington DC · EU · UN · Freemasons · Religion · Debt · Universe

The banking cartel

"**Let me issue and control a nation's money and I care not who writes the laws.**" Mayer Amschel Rothschild (1744-1812), founder of the House of Rothschild.

Most people are now aware of the international banking cartels influence as a major player in the control system. The issuance of a nation's currency determines who is master and who is slave. The sovereign governments of this world have always had the legal option to issue their own currency, without debt attached. Created in the treasury it would trickle down through the system like blood in the veins of the nation, ensuring enough liquidity to lubricate the engines of industry, without the burden of compounding interest. Unfortunately, most modern nations borrow money from private central banks with interest attached. This money is offered into circulation forcing tax to be collected to pay off the nation's huge debt obligation. In the past freeing the nation from debt slavery was a major campaign issue when seeking votes from the electorate, something has changed, now this topic rarely gets mentioned. Considering it was the main cause of the majority of wars throughout the past 200 years, it should be at the top of the list.

"**He who controls the money supply of a nation controls the nation**" - James Garfield 20th president of the United States.[2]

Other quotes taken from: Famous quotations on banking.[3]

"**If the American people ever allow private banks to control the issue of their currency, first by inflation, then by deflation, the banks...will deprive the people of all property until their children wake-up homeless on the continent their fathers conquered…. The issuing power should be taken from the banks and restored to the people, to whom it properly belongs.**" – Thomas Jefferson in the debate over the Re-charter of the Bank Bill (1809)

"**I believe that banking institutions are more dangerous to our liberties than standing armies.**" – Thomas Jefferson

"**History records that the money changers have used every form of abuse, intrigue, deceit, and violent means possible to maintain their control over governments by controlling money and its issuance.**" James Madison

"**If congress has the right under the Constitution to issue paper money, it was given them to use themselves, not to be delegated to individuals or corporations**". -Andrew Jackson

"The Government should create, issue, and circulate all the currency and credits needed to satisfy the spending power of the Government and the buying power of consumers. By the adoption of these principles, the taxpayers will be saved immense sums of interest. Money will cease to be master and become the servant of humanity". - Abraham Lincoln

"When a government is dependent upon bankers for money, they and not the leaders of the government control the situation, since the hand that gives is above the hand that takes... Money has no motherland; financiers are without patriotism and without decency; their sole object is gain." – Napoleon Bonaparte, Emperor of France, 1815

"That this House considers that the continued issue of all the means of exchange – be they coin, bank-notes or credit, largely passed on by cheques – by private firms as an interest-bearing debt against the public should cease forthwith; that the Sovereign power and duty of issuing money in all forms should be returned to the Crown, then to be put into circulation free of all debt and interest obligations..." Captain Henry Kerby MP, in an Early Day Motion tabled in 1964.

"Banks lend by creating credit. They create the means of payment out of nothing." Ralph M Hawtry, former Secretary to the Treasury.

"Our whole monetary system is dishonest, as it is debt-based... We did not vote for it. It grew upon us gradually but markedly since 1971 when the commodity-based system was abandoned." The Earl of Caithness, in a speech to the House of Lords, 1997.

"The bank hath benefit of interest on all moneys which it creates out of nothing." William Paterson, founder of the Bank of England in 1694, then a privately-owned bank

"The few who understand the system will either be so interested in its profits or be so dependent upon its favours that there will be no opposition from that class, while on the other hand, the great body of people, mentally incapable of comprehending the tremendous advantage that capital derives from the system, will bear its burdens without complaint, and perhaps without even suspecting that the system is inimical to their interests." The Rothschild brothers of London writing to associates in New York, 1863.

"Money is a new form of slavery, and distinguishable from the old simply by the fact that it is impersonal – that there is no human relation between master and slave." Leo Tolstoy

"It is well enough that people of the nation do not understand our banking and money system, for if they did, I believe there would be a revolution before tomorrow morning." Henry Ford, founder of the Ford Motor Company.

Most people believe the evolution of the control system has their best interests at heart. They consider the monetary system to be a carefully oiled machine, which is designed to benefit the majority. When a nation borrows itself into debt, no matter how hard its citizen's work, it can only sink further into debt, enslaving its citizens. Each generation finds itself paying more tax for fewer services because of its inherited obligation to pay off the compounding interest on huge government borrowing. Disguised through inflation the debt can never be repaid as only the principle is sent into circulation. Eventually when there is not enough money, due to deflation, bankruptcies ensue, transferring tangible assets into the hands of the international financiers connected to the Ponzi scheme. History is full of examples of the dangers inherent in usury, money changers and goldsmiths were regularly thrown out for exploiting their host nations. The Romans eventually allowed usury with careful restrictions, while Christianity was opposed to it for quite some time, this all changed in England under Henry VIII, with his 1545 Act, allowing usury of up to 10%, meanwhile Muslims have always been against usury. The modern banking system can be linked to the creation of the Bank of England in 1694, a private central bank which was set up to stabilise pricing and lend money to the government. With a panel of shareholders, the BOE would lend money on interest for empire building, while making the shareholders richer, the citizens were not only asked to fight in numerous conquests but also required to pay the tax burden for the privilege. The partnership between the City of London financiers and the government, allowed the British Empire to eventually influence 1/3 of the globe, becoming the benchmark for other competing empires, all financed by the same banking cartel. This process turned the empires into tools for the objectives of the global financiers. Wars and invasions encouraged to line the pockets of the shareholders and to export influence. Like all loans, conditions would be attached making the financiers masters over the governments of each nation. Incidentally, the City of London is a private corporation owned primarily by large financiers, outside the normal controls of the host nation. The Rothschild's the most influential banking family in history began in a modest building in Frankfurt during the mid-17th century, eventually controlling most, if not all private central banks. In 1946, after the Second World War, the Bank of England was nationalised, with all stock brought into public ownership. This only took place after the Bretton Woods agreement of 1944 which transferred the baton of world currency and financial global dominance over to the United States Dollar and the private Federal Reserve.

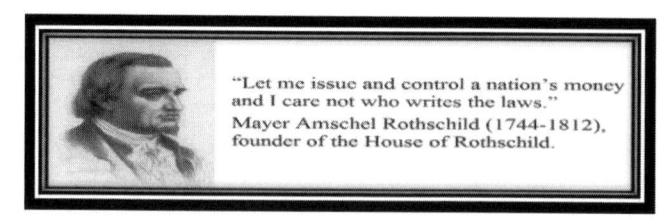

> "Let me issue and control a nation's money and I care not who writes the laws."
> Mayer Amschel Rothschild (1744-1812), founder of the House of Rothschild.

Most wars are banker's wars

Since the creation of the Bank of England, the European banking cartel has used the private central bank as a mechanism to control a nation through debt slavery. After the defeat of Napoleon, the Rothschild's controlled most private central banks in Europe, and had the means and desire to expand their monetary system throughout the world. The American Colonies initially used government issued currencies with no external debt attached, freeing the settlers from the exploits of the old world. The American Revolution according to Benjamin Franklin was primarily due to King George III Currency Act, forcing the colonies to abandon their government issued currencies in favour of notes from the Bank of England, which were issued on interest.

"The refusal of King George 3rd to allow the colonies to operate an honest money system, which freed the ordinary man from the clutches of the money manipulators, was probably the prime cause of the revolution" - Benjamin Franklin (founding father of the US)

The Americans won their revolution in 1776 and continued to issue their own currency. However, the tenacious European banksters paid off congressmen, bribed statesmen and worked tirelessly behind the scenes. In 1791 their efforts paid off, the First Bank of America was created and given a 20-year charter. This European controlled private central bank set to work bringing America under the shackles of the debt trading system. After 20 years it became apparent what their real motives were. Congress refused to renew the charter, for it was enriching the bank while ruining the nation's economy. When the government stated its intentions to go back to issuing its own currency, Nathan Rothschild in England was purported to have said.

"Either the application for the renewal of the charter is granted, or the United States will find itself involved in a most disastrous war." - Nathan Rothschild. Congress refused to renew the charter. **"Teach these impudent Americans a lesson. Bring them back to Colonial status."**- Nathan Rothschild[5]

The war of 1812 began, financed by the Bank of England, designed to bring the United States back under colonial rule or to submerge them under so much debt they would need a new private central bank to pay it off. The latter happened; the Second Bank of America was created and given a 20-year charter. In 1832 Andrew Jackson campaigning for his 2nd term as President promising to remove the bank's charter. Even though congress granted a renewal the new President vetoed against it. Congress was unable to overturn the veto and the bank ceased to exist.[6]

"Gentlemen! I too have been a close observer of the doings of the Bank of the United States. I have had men watching you for a long time, and am convinced that you have used the funds of the bank to speculate in the breadstuffs of the country. When you won, you divided the profits amongst you, and when you lost, you charged it to the bank. You tell me that if I take the deposits from the bank and annul its charter I shall ruin ten thousand families. That may be true, gentlemen, but that is your sin! Should I let you go on, you will ruin fifty thousand families, and that would be my sin! You are a den of vipers and thieves. I have determined to rout you out, and by the Eternal, (bringing his fist down on the table) I will rout you out!"- Andrew Jackson before ending the banks charter.[7]

Shortly after this, an assassination attempt was made on Andrew Jackson's life; fortunately, it failed when the assassin's guns misfired. During the commotion, the attacker received multiple injuries from the angry Jackson who beat him violently with his walking cane. After which, the attacker spent the rest of his life in a mental asylum.

The United States became prosperous, even though the European banksters were determined to control their money system, as they connived behind the scenes. During the 1860's the Confederates seceded from the Union. Abraham Lincoln, the new president, was determined to bring them back under Union control. The private banks were playing off both sides; offering to finance Lincoln at 30% interest while financing Britain and France's alliance with the Confederates. Lincoln was rumoured to have said, **"He would not free the black man by enslaving the white man to the bankers"**. He issued his own currency, state owned and interest free, called the Greenback which threatened European monetary dominance, in response, an editorial was purported to have appeared in the London Times in 1865, which captured the essence of the difficulty faced by Lincoln.

"If that mischievous financial policy, which had its origin in the North American Republic, should become indurated down to a fixture, then that government will furnish its own money without cost. It will pay off debts and be without a debt. It will have all the money necessary to carry on its commerce. It will become prosperous beyond precedent in the history of civilized governments of the world. The brains and the wealth of all countries will go to North America. That government must be destroyed or it will destroy every monarchy on the globe."-- Purported to be from the London Times 1865

France and Britain, on the side of the Confederates considered sending troops to aid the demise of Lincoln's efforts to unify the country. The British had landed troops on the Mexican border ready to aid the south. Russia had an alliance with Lincoln and a naval presence in New York harbour under Admiral Popoff, and San Francisco's harbour under admiral S Lesowsky, both were placed under the command of Lincoln.[8] Russia too had control over its state owned bank and was fully aware of the dangers of private central banks and the intentions of the European bankers. Czar Alexander II told the British that if they sent their troops into America they could consider themselves at war with Russia.[9] After 4 years of fighting, on 9th April 1865, with 750,000 dead, Lincoln finally secured his victory. Promising to continue with the Greenback he was later assassinated on 15th April. After Lincoln's death the Greenbacks were steadily recalled with the funding Act of April 12 1866.[10] After numerous attempts the Russian Czar was also assassinated in 1881.

Determined to have total control over the United States money supply, the international financiers set about planning for a new private central bank. After the panic of 1907, which many believed to have been orchestrated by the banking cartel, in order to create an atmosphere favourable for their interests, a private meeting was arranged with influential bankers together with Senator Nelson Aldrich on Jekyll Island, Georgia, in 1910. They would thrash out a plan for a new bank which they initially called the Aldrich Plan. After many attempts congress refused to pass the proposal with President Taft and the public still opposed the idea of a private central bank. Disguising its true nature, the plan was amended and renamed the Federal Reserve Act. On December 22nd 1913 during the Christmas recess, with most congressmen at home, the bill was rushed through the house. The new president Woodrow Wilson, who had defeated Taft that March, fulfilled his obligation to his financial sponsors by signing the bill into law on December 23rd 1913. At the same time, after the ratification of the 16th amendment, the IRS was authorised to collect income tax. Now the international banking cartel had just what they wanted, control of one of the most powerful nation's money supply. It was now a perfect time for a great war to get as many nations as possible under the heavy burden of debt. Furthermore, this would allow the banking cartel to impose new conditions on those in debt, create the new world in their own image.

Woodrow Wilson published a book called "The New Freedom" 1913. In it he expresses his concern about what he called the money trust or credit trust.

"There has come about an extraordinary and very sinister concentration in the control of business in the country. However it has come about it is more important still that the control of credit also has become dangerously centralised.

The great monopoly in this country is the monopoly of big credit, so long as that exists, our old variety of freedoms and individual energy of development are out of the question. A great industrial nation is controlled by its system of credit; our system of credit is privately concentrated. The growth of the nation and all our activities are in the hands of a few men. The money trust or as it should be called this credit trust of which congress has begun an investigation is not a myth, it is no imaginary thing.

We have come to be one of the worst ruled, one of the most completely controlled and dominated governments in the civilised world. No longer a government by free opinion, no longer a government by conviction and the vote of the majority but a government by the opinion and duress of a small group of dominant men". - Woodrow Wilson 1913.[11]

World War One

"The death of Lincoln was a disaster for Christendom. There was no man in the United States great enough to wear his boots and the bankers went anew to grab the riches. I fear that foreign bankers with their craftiness and tortuous tricks will entirely control the exuberant riches of America and use it to systematically corrupt civilization." Otto von Bismarck (1815-1898), German Chancellor, after the Lincoln assassination

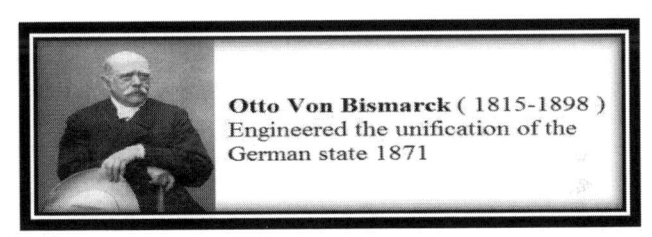

Otto Von Bismarck (1815-1898)
Engineered the unification of the German state 1871

Otto Von Bismarck the first chancellor of Germany and a major player in the unification of the nation was well aware of the ambitions of the international financiers. As chancellor, Germany quickly morphed into the leading powerhouse of Europe. Even though it had a private central bank, the German government placed strict controls on its operations. Prior to 1914, Germany had positioned itself at the forefront of modern manufacturing; by 1908 it was depriving Britain of its European and American markets. 20 years after Bismarck had unified the country, a study was put together by London bankers, they were alarmed to find that 2/3 of the English and European markets had gone into the hands of Germany. Worst of all was that Germany's trade with the world was, on the whole, conducted without the need of international banking finance. They were free from debt slavery. Britain, burdened by its long-established debt based monetary system could not hope to match the efficiency and honest prosperity of the new Germany. Their ship building, both military and domestic was surpassing that of the British. In 1911 H G Wells wrote his thoughts about the new Germany.

"We in Great Britain are now intensely jealous of Germany. We are intensely jealous of Germany not only because the Germans outnumber us, and have a much larger and more diversified country than ours, and lie in the very heart and body of Europe, but because in the last hundred years, while we have fed on platitudes and vanity, they have had the energy and humility to develop a splendid system of national education, to toil at science and art and literature, to develop social organization, to master and better our methods of business and industry, and to clamber above us in the scale of civilization. This has humiliated and irritated rather than chastened us." H G Wells (An Englishman looks at the world).[12]

Britain was under pressure to survive, keeping its empire intact, they were convinced they had no other option but to destroy their competitors. The international financier's globalisation plan was also in jeopardy. Unable to compete on a level footing, Britain and the financiers set about using diplomacy and secret treaties designed to completely encircle Germany with a wall of steel. The only reason World War 1 didn't break out earlier was because the Federal Reserve System was not in place, it had to be set up prior to the big war, to control the vast amount of borrowing which would be needed for the conflict. Finally, with everything ready, only 6 months after the creation of the Federal Reserve, the match was lit, on June 28th 1914, the assassination of Archduke Franz Ferdinand of Austria triggered the mobilisation and eventual slaughter of millions of young men, innocent men who had no idea in the world what they were really fighting for. Even though the conflict began in Sarajevo, the focus soon shifted to the real target, it wasn't long before the gates of hell were opened and all guns pointed at Germany.

At the start, in 1914, the main participants were Great Britain, France and Russia against Germany, Austria-Hungary and Turkey. By 1916 according to Benjamin Freedman,[13] the Germans had almost won the war.

"The German submarines, which were a surprise to the world, had swept all the convoys from the Atlantic Ocean, and Great Britain stood there without ammunition for her soldiers, stood there with one week's food supply facing her -- and after that, starvation. At that time, the French army had mutinied. They lost 600,000 of the flower of French youth in the defence of Verdun on the Somme. The Russian army was defecting. They were picking up their toys and going home, they didn't want to play war anymore, they didn't like the Czar. And the Italian army had collapsed. Now Germany -- not a shot had been fired on the German soil. Not an enemy soldier had crossed the border into Germany. And yet, here was Germany offering England peace terms. They offered England a negotiated peace on what the lawyers call a status quo ante basis. That means: "Let's call the war off, and let everything be as it was before the war started." Well, England, in the summer of 1916 was considering that. Seriously! They had no choice. It was either accepting this negotiated peace that Germany was magnanimously offering them, or going on with the war and being totally defeated."- Benjamin Freedman 1961 speech at the Willard Hotel

Another player in the control system steps into the picture. The Zionists, a political ideology hiding behind Judaism, influenced heavily by the international financiers of Europe and now America, controlling many banks and much of the media, they offered a deal to the British. If they could persuade the pro German Americans to enter the war on the side of the British, they would want in return, control of Palestine for their own use. The British agreed to the proposal after considering all the options available. Motivated with the promise of a Jewish state, the Zionists set about altering public opinion in America against the Germans. At that time the American Republic and Bismarck's Germany, were singing from the same hymn sheet, both mistrustful of private central banks and the ambitions of the British Empire. Furthermore, most Americans were unaware that their new Federal Reserve was a private owned central bank. At that time, the Americans had great affinity with the Germans, many were descendants of the German people. The international financiers with the British had been pressurising Woodrow Wilson and the Americans to join in the efforts since the start of hostilities. The sentiment for neutrality was strong even with the sinking of the Lusitania in 1915 and the loss of 1198 lives. In 1917 Germany offered a military alliance with Mexico and stepped up their U-boat activities in the North Atlantic, this was enough for the media to villainize Germany, using propaganda they were able to alter the public's perception, the Germans became Huns, shooting Red Cross nurses and cutting babies hands off. Wilson asked congress for a war to end all wars; congress voted and declared war on Germany on April 6th 1917. Fulfilling their part of the bargain, the Zionists approached the British and asked for something in writing, to show that the British would keep their word; the receipt they received in writing was known as the Balfour Declaration.[14]

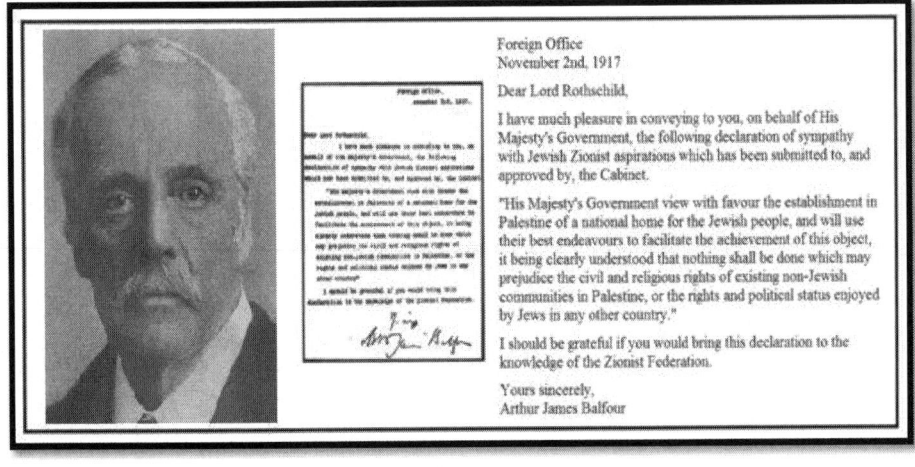

The Armistice

After 4 years of fighting with 16 million dead, the worst conflict the world had ever seen, the war finally came to an end, with the signing of the Armistice, a ceasefire on the 11th November 1918. A peace treaty was organised in Paris, to carve up Europe and slap penalties on Germany. According to Benjamin Freedman, an attendee of the conference, there were 117 Zionist Jewish delegates representing Zionism and International finance. Eustace Mullins writes:

"After the Armistice, Woodrow Wilson assembled the American Delegation to the Peace Conference, and embarked for Paris. It was, on the whole, a most congenial group, consisting of the bankers who had always guided Wilson's policies. He was accompanied by Bernard Baruch, Thomas W. Lamont of J.P. Morgan Co., Albert Strauss of J & W Seligman bankers, who had been chosen by Wilson to replace Paul Warburg on the Federal Reserve Board of Governors, J.P. Morgan, and Morgan lawyers Frank Polk and John W. Davis. Accompanying them were Walter Lippmann, Felix Frankfurter, Justice Brandeis, and other interested parties. Mason's biography of Brandeis states that "In Paris in June of 1919, Brandeis met with such friends as Paul Warburg, Col. House, Lord Balfour, Louis Marshall, and Baron Edmond de Rothschild."

"Indeed, Baron Edmond de Rothschild served as the genial host to the leading members of the American Delegation, and even turned over his Paris mansion to them, although the lesser members had to rough it at the elegant Hotel Crillon with Col. House and his personal staff of 201 servants."

"The bankers at the conference convinced Wilson that they needed an international government to facilitate their international monetary operations."[15]

While Europe was being carved up to the victors, the Zionists produced the Balfour Declaration, saying Palestine was to be allocated to them. The German delegates, astonished and surprised, realising for the first time why America had entered the war, and what the hidden agenda had been, they felt betrayed. Woodrow Wilson on his return remarked.

"This war, in its inception was a commercial and industrial war. It was not a political war."
- Woodrow Wilson[16]

Treaty of Versailles

Determined to fulfil their objectives and disable Germany as an economic threat, the international financiers along with the Allies put together the Treaty of Versailles. Considering Germany didn't start the war, it was blamed and made to pay for all participants, amounting to three times the value Germany itself. The treaty fulfilled its purpose, by carving up Europe making it easier for the international financiers and the empire to divide and rule each territory, creating new frictions which could be used to promote future conflicts. The reparations on Germany were so severe that it crippled the nation for the next 15 years. The new German Rothschild influenced private central bank proceeded to target private wealth, ruining the middle classes through the promotion of hyperinflation. The banksters wielding so much power and influence that they left no stone unturned as they looted Germany from within.

The Bolshevik Revolution

The international financiers had two major objectives at the start of the war, firstly to destroy German economical capabilities and secondly to remove the Russian Tsar from power, and once eliminated would finance a socialist style government. The Tsars were not looked at favourably by the financiers or the British Empire. Tsar Alexander 2's role in supporting Lincoln during the American civil war of 1881-1885 reflected this position. The Tsars similar to Bismarck understood the ambitions of this small group of dominant men. Even though Russia was on the side of France and Britain, the banksters plan was to get Russia and Germany fighting against one another, weakening them to such an extent that a takeover would be easy. The plan went well, Russia started the war with the world's largest army, approximately 5 million soldiers, but through bad management, infiltration and subversion the army soon became stagnant. A previous attempt at a revolution was thwarted in 1905, with concessions made by Tsar Nicholas 2, to civil rights and parliamentary power sharing. By the end of 1916, 1,700,000 Russian soldiers had died. Riots and strikes were a daily occurrence and many soldiers were abandoning their posts to go home, the country was falling apart. Under this backdrop, in February 1917, Tsar Nicholas 2nd was forced to abdicate. Power was transferred to a socialist government led by Alexander Kerensky. Around this time the international financiers had maneuvered America to take the place of Russia by declaring war on Germany, eliminating their temporary advantage. The international financiers through Max Walberg financed Trotsky and Lenin's 1917 October revolution,[17] which actually took place on the 7th November.[18] The Bolsheviks took over power and declared a ceasefire in December.

To keep the full extent of their involvement out of the public domain, the international financiers ordered the execution of the Tsar and all his family. They were executed on 17th July 1918.

"The Bolshevik revolution actually was financed by wealthy financiers in London and New York. Lenin and Trotsky were on the closest of terms with these moneyed interests both before and after the Revolution". The Creature from Jekyll Island[19]

World War Two (round 2)

The years after WW1 saw Germany desperately trying to hold itself together under the heavy burden of reparations placed upon it by Versailles. The German private central bank had broken away from government control and was fermenting hyperinflation. At its height, in November 1923, a loaf of bread cost a staggering 200,000,000,000 marks. The citizens demoralised and depressed looked towards the National Socialists for solutions, led by Adolf Hitler they promised to reform the nation and shake off the shackles of Versailles. When Hitler was voted into office and became Chancellor in January 1933, one of the first things he did was to take back control of Germany's central bank, outraged at this the international financiers, many of them Jewish Zionists, called for a global boycott of German goods and services. They used their influence to begin an economical war with Germany and its National Socialist government. On March 24th 1933 the Daily Express, a UK tabloid, published its Friday edition with the headlines "JUDEA DECLARES WAR ON GERMANY."[20]

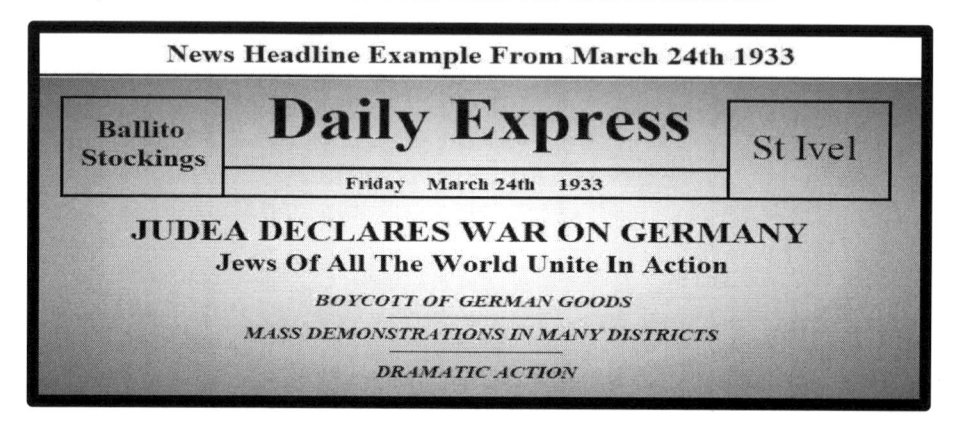

News Headline Example From March 24th 1933

Daily Express

Ballito Stockings | St Ivel

Friday March 24th 1933

JUDEA DECLARES WAR ON GERMANY
Jews Of All The World Unite In Action
BOYCOTT OF GERMAN GOODS
MASS DEMONSTRATIONS IN MANY DISTRICTS
DRAMATIC ACTION

The German cabinet was assembled to figure out what their reaction should be to this war declaration. They decided that a national boycott of all Jewish goods and services would be an appropriate response. The following week on April 1st, storm troopers were dispatched across the country, marking all Jewish businesses with notices, asking the German public to avoid conducting business with Jewish people.

Nazi boycott of Jewish businesses April 1st 1933

Over the next five years the National Socialists managed to transform Germany from a defeated, bankrupt, husk, into one of the most powerful military nations on the planet. Within two years the 5.6 million German unemployed had been reduced by 50%. Furthermore, by 1938 there were only 0.4 million unemployed. This transformation was felt all around the world, known as the German miracle, Time Magazine even nominated Adolf Hitler as man of the year for 1938.

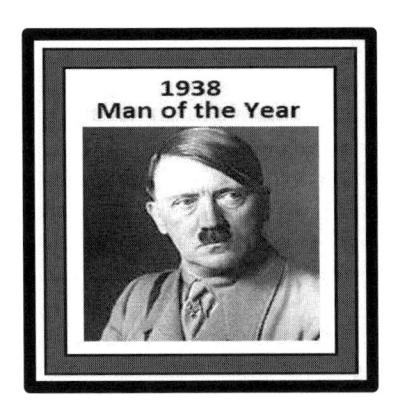

1938 Man of the Year

Decoupled from the world's monetary system, if left unhindered would allow Germany to advance into a position of unstoppable strength. The international financiers along with Great Britain had to act soon, or it would be too late.

"**We will force this war upon Hitler, if he wants it or not.**" -- Winston Churchill (1936 broadcast)

"**Germany becomes too powerful. We have to crush it**." -- Winston Churchill (November 1936 speaking to US - General Robert E. Wood)

"**This war is an English war and its goal is the destruction of Germany.**" -- Winston Churchill (- autumn 1939 broadcast)

Germany tore up the Treaty of Versailles and started to reunify all the areas it had lost after WW1, indirectly liberating them from the banking cartels debt slavery system. 400,000 Germans left Poland between 1919 and 1921, across the new boarder into Germany. Many Germans were persecuted and murdered in various pogroms across the Polish divide. Germany felt obliged to find a solution; with 35,000 estimated deaths, they sent troops across the border on 1st September 1939. Two days later both France and Britain, under an alliance pact with Poland, declared war on Germany. Russia also invaded Poland from the east on 17th September 1939. If the invasion of Poland was the prime reason for declaring war on Germany, why did Russia become an Ally when it was also guilty of participated in the same invasion? The mind-set of the people who lived then was divided, depending on whose version of propaganda you were exposed to. The Brits unaware of the level of control the international financiers had on their own monetary system and government were convinced they were fighting the just war and the Germans were sub-human, Jew hating murderers. The Germans too believed they were fighting the good war, liberating Germany from the oppression of the International banksters and the Bolshevik threat from the east. The majority of Austrian's were overwhelmingly in favour of unification with Germany, they lined the streets with flowers as they welcomed the Germans in. France also politically divided fell in under six weeks. Again, Russia was primed, financed by the international banksters, led by Stalin, their role was to smash and weaken Germany into another humiliating defeat. The propaganda ministries on both sides would vilify one another in an attempt to motivate their citizens into fighting the just war.

In 1940 Winston Churchill became Britain's wartime Prime Minister, determined to see the destruction of Germany to the bitter end while ignored Hitler's many peace offerings. Churchill was a single-minded attack dog and a close ally to the international financier's aspirations. Rudolf Hess 2nd in command under Hitler flew to Scotland to negotiate a peace deal with the Scottish aristocracy, only to be arrested and gagged in prison till his death in 1987. Once the Americans entered the war, the Germans, with their troops bogged down on the eastern front, suspected defeat was just a matter of time. Again, the international financiers managed to persuade a huge global alliance to join the demise of Germany. The country was flattened, bombed back to the Stone Age. Berlin became a wasteland with thousands of dead. In the end over 60 million people perished, the worst war ever witnessed by humanity. The only winners were the international financiers; they picked up the pieces and continued their plan of global dominance. If one reads Adolf Hitler's last will and testament, written on April 29th 1945, when he blames International Jewry for the defeat of Germany, could he be referring to the international financiers, most of who happen to be Zionist Jews.

The final political testament of Adolf Hitler

"More than thirty years have now passed since I in 1914 made my modest contribution as a volunteer in the First World War that was forced upon the Reich.

In these three decades, I have been actuated solely by love and loyalty to my people in all my thoughts, acts, and life. They gave me the strength to make the most difficult decisions, which have ever confronted mortal man. I have spent my time, my working strength, and my health in these three decades.

It is untrue that I or anyone else in Germany wanted the war in 1939. It was desired and instigated exclusively by those international statesmen who were either of Jewish descent or worked for Jewish interests. I have made too many offers for the control and limitation of armaments, which posterity will not for all time be able to disregard for the responsibility for the outbreak of this war to be laid on me. I have further never wished that after the first fatal world war a second against England, or even against America, should break out. Centuries will pass away, but out of the ruins of our towns and monuments the hatred against those finally responsible whom we have to thank for everything, international Jewry and its helpers, will grow.

Three days before the outbreak of the German-Polish war I again proposed to the British ambassador in Berlin a solution to the German-Polish problem—similar to that in the case of the Saar district, under international control. This offer also cannot be denied. It was only rejected because the leading circles in English politics wanted the war, partly on account of the business hoped for and partly under influence of propaganda organized by international Jewry.

I have also made it quite plain that, if the nations of Europe are again to be regarded as mere shares to be bought and sold by these international conspirators in money and finance, then that race, Jewry, which is the real criminal of this murderous struggle, will be saddled with the responsibility. I further left no one in doubt that this time not only would millions of children of Europe's Aryan peoples die of hunger, not only would millions of grown men suffer death, and not only hundreds of thousands of women and children be burnt and bombed to death in the towns, without the real criminal having to atone for this guilt, even if by more humane means.

After six years of war, which in spite of all setbacks will go down one day in history as the most glorious and valiant demonstration of a nation's life purpose, I cannot forsake the city which is the capital of this Reich. As the forces are too small to make any further stand against the enemy attack at this place, and our resistance is gradually being weakened by men who are as deluded as they are lacking in initiative, I should like, by remaining in this town, to share my fate with those, the millions of others, who have also taken upon themselves to do so. Moreover I do not wish to fall into the hands of an enemy who requires a new spectacle organized by the Jews for the amusement of their hysterical masses.

I have decided therefore to remain in Berlin and there of my own free will to choose death at the moment when I believe the position of the Fuehrer and Chancellor itself can no longer be held.

I die with a happy heart, aware of the immeasurable deeds and achievements of our soldiers at the front, our women at home, the achievements of our farmers and workers and the work, unique in history, of our youth who bear my name.

That from the bottom of my heart I express my thanks to you all, is just as self-evident as my wish that you should, because of that, on no account give up the struggle but rather continue it against the enemies of the Fatherland, no matter where, true to the creed of a great Clausewitz. From the sacrifice of our soldiers and from my own unity with them unto death, will in any case spring up in the history of Germany, the seed of a radiant renaissance of the National-Socialist movement and thus of the realization of a true community of nations.

Many of the most courageous men and women have decided to unite their lives with mine until the very last I have begged and finally ordered them not to do this, but to take part in the further battle of the Nation. I beg the heads of the Armies, the Navy, and the Air Force to strengthen by all possible means the spirit of resistance of our soldiers in the National-Socialist sense, with special reference to the fact that also I myself, as founder and creator of this movement, have preferred death to cowardly abdication or even capitulation.

May it, at some future time, become part of the code of honour of the German officer—as is already the case in our Navy—that the surrender of a district or of a town is impossible, and that above all the leaders here must march ahead as shining examples, faithfully fulfilling their duty unto death.

Above all I charge the leaders of the nation and those under them to scrupulous observance of the laws of race and to merciless opposition to the universal poisoner of all peoples, international Jewry."

Given in Berlin, this 29th day of April 1945. 4:00 A.M.   ADOLF HITLER

Various quotes

"After visiting these places, you can easily understand how that within a few years Hitler will emerge from the hatred that surrounds him now as one of the most significant figures who ever lived." - John F Kennedy Personal diary (1 August 1945)[21]

"I believe now that Hitler and the German people did not want war. But we declared war on Germany, intent on destroying it, in accordance with our principle of balance of power, and we were encouraged by the 'Americans' around Roosevelt. We ignored Hitler's pleadings not to enter into war. Now we are forced to realize that Hitler was right." - Attorney General, Sir. Hartley Shawcross, March, 16th, 1984[22]

"I see no reason why this war must go on. I am grieved to think of the sacrifices which it will claim. I would like to avert them." - Adolf Hitler, July, 1940.

Winston Churchill agrees: "**We entered the war of our own free will, without ourselves being directly assaulted**." - Guild Hall Speech, July 1943.

"**The last thing Hitler wanted was to produce another great war**." - Sir. Basil Liddell Hart (The History of The Second World War)[23]

"We made a monster, a devil out of Hitler. Therefore we couldn't disavow it after the war. After all, we mobilized the masses against the devil himself. So we were forced to play our part in this diabolic scenario after the war. In no way we could have pointed out to our people that the war was only an economic preventive measure."- US foreign minister James Baker (1992)

"**What thrust us into war were not Hitler's political teachings: the cause, this time, was his successful attempt to establish a new economy. The causes of the war were: envy, greed, and fear.**" - Major General J.F.C. Fuller, historian, England[24]

"**During the entire period of the telegram war, in 1939-1940, lengthy negotiations took place between the German and British foreign ministries, in which the British suggested to cancel the war if Germany would reinstate the gold standard and reintroduce interest rates.**" - Lieutenant-Colonel J. Creagh Scott, 11th August 1947, Chelsea Town Hall, London[25]

Iraq and the petrodollar

After Bretton Woods, with the US Dollar becoming the world's reserve currency, the United States was in a unique position, forcing the world to trade using paper which their central bank, the Fed, created out of nothing. Sellers would exchange their goods and services for dollars, initially redeemable with gold, at $35 per oz. Many oil producing nations would deposit USD's back into US banks perpetuating what is known as the Petro Dollar Cycle. Any nation buying real goods would first have to purchase dollars from the exchange of their tangible goods and services. The fed would pump out all this money with interest attached, trapping the whole commercial world within its web of compounding interest.

During the Vietnam war America's spending escalated, it spent so much money fighting that it had to print its way out, devaluing its currency. The French, the old colonial rulers of Vietnam were suspicious of Anglo-American ambitions, concerned about its obligation under Bretton Woods, asked for its Gold in exchange for its USDs. Nixon under pressure refused to pay the French, putting an end to the Bretton Woods gold standard in 1971. The dollar, the world's currency was now free to inflate itself into oblivion.

In 1973 the major oil producing nations were intending to sell oil using their own currencies. Threatened by this, the Anglo/American alliance, through OPEC, persuaded these nations to trade on the dollar in exchange for power, stability, military support and arms deals, causing the petro dollar cycle to flourish. Having no gold to fulfil its new obligations the United States had to back its promises with its military industrial complex, bigger than all the other countries combined.

Kuwait a independent emirate under the protection of the British from 1914, with a largely impoverished population, discovered oil with the Kuwait Oil Company in 1934, a creation of the Anglo-Persian oil company known as BP (British Petroliam). Exploration was delayed until after WW2. The use of Kuwait oil began in 1951, and by 1952 had become the largest oil producer in the Persian Gulf. In 1961 after Kuwait became independent from British protection, Iraq claimed the country under the rationale that it had once been part of Iraq's suzerainty. Kuwait's Emir asked for assistance from the British Government who sent troops and military aid. Later during a coup in 1963 Iraq's Prime Minister was killed, after which Iraq reaffirmed its acceptance of Kuwait's sovereignty and its 1913 and 1932 boundaries.

In August 1990, after allegations of slant drilling into Iraq's oil supplies, Saddam Hussain sent his troops into Kuwait claiming it to be an Iraqi province. The United States along with 34 coalition nations led a counter attack on 23rd Feb, 1991, within 4 days Saddam's forces had been pushed back or destroyed. The coalition allowed Saddam Hussain to stay in power, choosing to tame the puppet dictator, who they manoeuvred into power years earlier.

First Iraq Conflict 1991

Determined to get revenge on the Americans, Saddam Hussain, in the autumn of 2000, chose to trade his 3.3 billion barrels of oil on the euro instead of the dollar. America who purchased 2/3 of Iraq's oil was furious. Instead of just printing dollars for the oil, they had to produce goods and services in exchange for euros to pay for Saddam's oil. The Petrodollar cycle had been broken. The US had no choice but to act, their global reserve currency scam was in jeopardy. They needed a good excuse to justify an invasion. They couldn't give the real reason otherwise the financial scams fragility would be exposed, and all other previous conflicts could come into question. They came up with the idea of WMD's, Saddam Hussain was accused of possessing weapons of mass destruction, which he could deploy within 45 minutes, they also stated that he had something to do with 9/11, but the bush administration couldn't give the specifics. The media were relentless, happy to pump it out day and night, influencing the collective consciousness of the west. A few honourable men and women tried to expose the extent of the lies but paid heavily. Dr David Kelly a United Nations weapons inspector with doubts about the validity of the WMD claims, was found dead in July 2003, by an apparent suicide. The second Iraq war began on 1st May 2003, and has been ongoing in various forms ever since. By 10th June 2003 Iraq's oil was switched from euro's back to dollars. Saddam Hussain was eventually captured and executed.

Second Gulf War 2003

Libya 2011

Libya is a country on the Mediterranean coast of North Africa with over 150 tribes in 2 main groups, the Meghabra in the west and the Wagfalla in the east. Before Gaddafi the country was divided into two administrative parts, attempts to unite these groups previously failed. Oil was discovered in 1959 under King Idris, who allowed most of the profits to be siphoned off by the international oil companies. On September 1st 1969, with countrywide support, a coup d'état took place putting Colonel Muammar Gaddafi in power, unifying the nation. Over the next few decades Libya became one of the richest countries in Africa. With its 100% state owned bank, retaining its oil wealth for the benefit of its people, the country had freed itself from the burden of debt and obligations to the international financiers. It had fewer people living below the poverty line than most European countries and life expectancy was around

75. Unlike America, the incarceration capital of the world, Libya had very little crime and few incarcerations. Most Libyans had a house and a car with negligible energy costs, free health care and education. Anyone wishing to start a farm was given free land with a house and free seeds for planting. A newly married couple received $50,000 housing money to start their new family. Loans were Interest free and the government paid half toward your new car. With similar independent economics to the German economic miracle of the 1930s, Libya had positioned itself outside the global debt slavery financial system, the Libyans therefore had an unfair advantage over the rest of the debt burdened world. This was frowned upon by the international community but tolerated up to a point. When Gaddafi began influencing and exporting his success into other neighbouring countries, his fate was sealed in the eyes of the control system.

Libya was Africa's largest exporter of oil, before the US-NATO bombing campaign, with 1.7 million tons per day. With all this oil trading on US dollars, the status quo was accepted, but in 2000 Gaddafi organised **the World Mathaba Conference**. Most African nations and other like minded countries, such as Malaysia, Indonesia and Iran attended. They set out to create a new African oil trading currency, freeing themselves from the exploits of the international monetary system. The currency was called the Gold Dinar. Just months before the invasion, Libya had 144 tons of gold ready and prepared to trade oil for dinars instead of US Dollars, this would have **haemorrhaged** the American economy and changed the balance of power throughout the world. At the Mathaba conference, well attended by most African leaders, many views were aired against the **oligarch's** controlling international trade, finance and governance. Gaddafi deplored the control of 80% of the world's wealth by 400 families of Geo-oligarchs, but wouldn't go into detail as to who they were. Other speakers at the Mathaba conference contributed their views.[26]

"**The Conference represented our victory against colonialism and imperialism, apartheid and racism. We have a political struggle because economic control is in the hands of the forces we politically destroyed. We face hurdles in our quest to improve the standard of living of our people. We must reinvigorate the Mathaba to face new challenges. The forces of yesterday that defeated imperialism must reconstitute the Mathaba. There must be regional solutions for regional problems and international solutions for international problems. We must create a political union of African States. For unity, it is necessary that peace prevail. We must have a mechanism for conflict management.**"- President Robert Mugabe of Zimbabwe

"**We are not free, as we do not have economic freedom. The younger generation says that we cannot entirely blame outside forces. We are revolutionaries to liberate people from bondage. We fail because some of us are agents of the same people we are supposed to fight against. Some of us were approached not to sign the declaration that will herald unity and freedom of Africa. We produce the bulk of the world's raw materials so why are we still poor. We produce what is enriching the first world today. Some of us are fighting proxy wars in Africa for the benefit of others. Africa has never colonised any one. Some people who prolonged apartheid are now waving the banner of democracy and freedom. The African debt burden is not globalised. It is still Africanised.**"-President Yaya Jameh of Gambia

"We must restructure the World Mathaba and impose ourselves in the world. We must impose ourselves on world communities. We must confront the concept of globalisation. There is a conflict between imperialism and us. The United States wants globalisation to be American globalisation. We shall fight to create international globalisation to serve us. What we have is a clash of wills. The imperialist project will fail. We have Daniel Ortega and Hugo Chavez as members of the Mathaba."-Muammar AL Gaddafi of Libya

The first casualty of war is the truth, so the propaganda began. The excuse they came up with to invade and change the regime, was that Gaddafi was killing his own people, and they had to go in and free them in the name of democracy. Considering in early July 2011, 1.7 million Libyans turned up in Tripoli to support Gaddafi, 95% of the city and 1/3 of the whole country's population, probably the largest demonstration the world had ever seen, for a man who was supposedly killing his own people. The truth of it is that western intelligence services and private mercenaries had been fermenting dissent in the Middle East for almost 30 years. They just sent more trouble makers into Libya and blamed Gaddafi. The media and the UN followed orders, the rest is history. Gaddafi was later found and murdered by his captors in a shameful display of cowardice and abuse of power. Before the western backed rebels even formed a new government, they created a new private central bank in the east, controlled by the international financiers, who took over from Libya's state owned bank, which was up and running before the war ended. Libya has now been smashed and the lives of most of its population returned to a future of debt slavery and imposed scarcity.

Liberation and Democracy in Libya

War on terror

When trying to understand the objectives and aspirations of the international financiers, their global plan of world economic unity, under their control becomes a little clearer, and why specific targets are chosen in conflicts advancing this agenda. It really is like a grand chess game, predicting the next move on the geopolitical level when understanding the mind-set of those moving the pieces is made easier. History tells us the dangers associated with usury, how host nations become swallowed up by the money manipulators. The Roman Empire eventually succumbed to it; Europe weary of the mistakes of the past banned it for centuries. Host nations seduced by the initial flow of easy money become servants to the wishes of the money masters, no longer sovereign states carving out their own futures. They invariably become pawns in an international game of debt expansion, bullying other nations into submission. The majority of traditional religions would not allow usury, but as the years progressed most of them became victims. Interest of any kind is forbidden in Islam, to obey Muslim law specific codes of banking have been developed, they front weight the loans to avoid interest. The Quran forbids usury:

"Those who charge usury are in the same position as those controlled by the devil's influence. This is because they claim that usury is the same as commerce. However, God permits commerce, and prohibits usury. Thus, whoever heeds this commandment from his Lord, and refrains from usury, he may keep his past earnings, and his judgment rests with God. As for those who persist in usury, they incur Hell, wherein they abide forever" (Al-Baqarah 2:275)

"O you who believe, you shall not take usury, compounded over and over. Observe God, that you may succeed." (Al-'Imran 3:130)

"And for practicing usury, which was forbidden, and for consuming the people's money illicitly. We have prepared for the disbelievers among them painful retribution." (Al-Nisa 4:161)

"The usury that is practiced to increase some people's wealth, does not gain anything at God. But if people give to charity, seeking God's pleasure, these are the ones who receive their reward many fold." (Ar-Rum 30:39)

Any country adopting anti-usury principles will eventually be targeted by the international financiers. To complete their plan of a single global financial system, with them as masters and the rest of us as debt slaves, they must eliminate all forms of competition. The war on terror is an excuse to infiltrate and undermine any country that will not play ball with this agenda. Iran is a major participant and foot hold in the Islamic world. All efforts will be focused on destabilising them. Iran's allies are being picked off, one by one. Syria a long-time ally is being dismantled as I write this book. The war on terror has no end, they can create a new villain any time they want, a pretext to a new invasion. Iran has not attacked another country for 200 years, yet it is constantly vilified in western media as a threat to the stability of the Middle East. They fulfil all their obligations under the IAEA, unlike Israel who ignore demands to legitimise their secret stash of nuclear weapons. Under this dangerous backdrop of expansive ambitions for a greater Israel, Iran is accused of trying to acquire a nuclear weapon, considering those countries who didn't have nuclear weapons have already fallen, I think I would try to acquire one too, as a necessary form of defence. With 1.6 billion Muslims in the world, 1/4 of the world's population, the control system has to be very careful, if they back them into a corner, united, the Muslim world could unleash a backlash so massive it would send everyone back to the Stone Age. There seems to be many cogs of the control system involved in this war on terror, each furthering their own ambitions. In some way, they have a common objective, the push for globalisation.

Who is threatening who, US military bases surrounding IRAN

Map showing US Military Bases (marked with stars) in countries surrounding Iran: Turkey, Syria, Iraq, Israel, Saudi Arabia, Oman, Yemen, Pakistan, Afghanistan, and near Kazakhstan. Other labeled regions: Russia, Egypt, Arabian Sea.

Countries attacked by bombing, sabotage or attempted government overthrows since 1945

IRAN	US	
	Korea and China 50-53	Panama 1989
	Guatemala 1954	Iraq 1991
	Indonesia 1958	Kuwait 1991
	Cuba 1959-1961	Somalia 1993
	Guatemala 1960	Bosnia 1994, 1995
	Congo 1964	Sudan 1998
	Laos 1964-73	Afghanistan 1998
	Vietnam 1961-73	Yugoslavia 1999
	Cambodia 1969-70	Yemen 2002
	Guatemala 1967-69	Iraq 1991-2003
	Grenada 1983	Iraq 2003-2015
	Lebanon 1983, 1984	Afghanistan 2001-15
	Libya 1986	Pakistan 2007-2015
	El Salvador 1980s	Somalia 2007-8, 2011
	Nicaragua 1980s	Yemen 2009, 2011
	Iran 1987	Libya 2011, 2015
		Syria 2014-

Notes for chapter 3

(1) John F. Kennedy, Speech, The President and the Press: Addressed before the American Newspaper Publishers Association, April 27, 1961,
http://www.jfklibrary.org/Research/Research-Aids/JFK-Speeches/American-Newspaper-Publishers-Association_19610427.aspx

(2) James A Garfield, United States President, Quote.
http://www.brainyquote.com/quotes/quotes/j/jamesagar383440.html

(3) The money masters, famous quotations on banking,
http://www.themoneymasters.com/the-money-masters/famous-quotations-on-banking/

(5) Chapter 49 — The History of Banking. Control in the United States (An article of Alain Pilote, first published in the Sept.-Oct., 1985 issue of the Vers Demain Journal.)
http://michaeljournal.org/plenty49.htm

(6) Veto of the Bank of the United States, (1832), Andrew Jackson
http://college.cengage.com/history/us/resources/students/primary/veto.htm

(7) From the original minutes of the Philadelphia committee of citizens sent to meet with President Jackson (February 1834), according to Andrew Jackson and the Bank of the United States (1928) by Stan V. Henkels. http://en.wikiquote.org/wiki/Andrew_Jackson

(8) Modern History/American Civil War/Wartime Diplomacy/US-Russian Relations
http://en.wikibooks.org/wiki/Modern_History/American_Civil_War/Wartime_Diplomacy/US-Russian_Relations

(9) Cornelius Carl Veith, Citadels of Chaos, 1949, Meador publishing co, Chapter 4

(10) United States Notes, Wikipedia, http://en.wikipedia.org/wiki/United_States_Note

(11) Woodrow Wilson, The New Freedom, A call for the emancipation of the generous energies of a people, Doubleday Page & Co, Chapters 8-9, 1913

(12) H G Wells, An Englishman looks at the world,1914, chapter 4 (of the new reign 1911), Biblio Bazaar

(13) Benjamin Freedman's 1961 Speech at the Willard Hotel,
https://www.youtube.com/watch?v=HhFRGDyX48c

(14) Balfour decliration, November 2nd 1917,
http://en.wikipedia.org/wiki/Balfour_Declaration

(15) CHAPTER EIGHT World War One [SECRETS OF THE FEDERAL RESERVE By Eustace Mullins]

(16) Woodrow Wilson, Quote, http://en.wikiquote.org/wiki/Woodrow_Wilson

(17) How Jewish International Finance Functions ,THE DEARBORN INDEPENDENT, issue of 9 July 1921, http://www.jrbooksonline.com/intl_jew_full_version/ij60.htm

(18) October Revolution, http://en.wikipedia.org/wiki/October_Revolution

(19) G Edward Griffin, the creature from jekell island, page 123, American Media,U.S.; 3rd edition (17 Aug 1999)

(20) Daily Express, March 24, 1933: JUDEA DECLARES WAR ON GERMANY, https://www.google.co.uk/search?q=daily+express+judea+declares+war+on+germany&biw=1898&bih=958&source=lnms&tbm=isch&sa=X&ved=0ahUKEwjHl_X1kt_MAhXCAcAKHbLSCCwQ_AUIBigB#imgrc=boSBh09yBm6nHM%3A

(21) John F Kennedy, after visiting such Nazi strongholds as were found in Berchtesgaden and Kehlsteinhaus; Personal diary (1 August 1945); published in Prelude to Leadership (1995), http://en.wikiquote.org/wiki/John_F._Kennedy

(22) Attorney General, Sir. Hartley Shawcross, March,16th, 1984, Wikiquotes. http://en.wikiquote.org/wiki/Talk:Hartley_Shawcross,_Baron_Shawcross

(23) B.H. Liddell Hart (Military Historian), History of the second world war, Konecky & Konecky; English Language edition (May 18, 2007)

(24) Major-General John Frederick Charles Fuller ,The Second World War, 1939-1945: a strategical and tactical history, Duell, Sloan and Pearce (1948).

(25) Juri Lina ,Archetects of deception, 2004, http://www.slideshare.net/UnitB166ER/the-architects-of-deception-by-juri-lina

(26) The world Mathaba conference 2000, http://mathaba.net/wm/wm.html

Chapter 4.

The war on consciousness

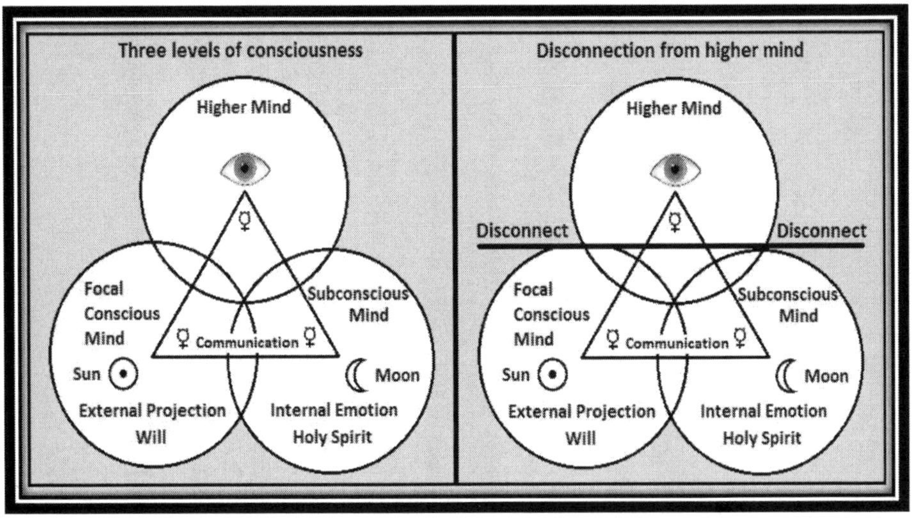

Three levels of consciousness
Higher Mind
Focal Conscious Mind
Subconscious Mind
Communication
Sun
Moon
External Projection Will
Internal Emotion Holy Spirit
Disconnection from higher mind
Higher Mind
Disconnect
Disconnect
Focal Conscious Mind
Subconscious Mind
Communication
Sun
Moon
External Projection Will
Internal Emotion Holy Spirit

For any system of control wishing to keep itself in power, must have mastery over the consciousness of the majority of its subjects. This is done using an endless array of subtle yet sophisticated techniques. From cradle to grave our minds are targeted with new inventive ways to neutralise our capacity to connect to Logos consciousness, frustrating the balance of communication between ourselves and higher levels of awareness. All part of an attempt to render us vulnerable to manipulative influences from various mechanisms under the overriding control of our ruling masters, who steadily conditioned us to look towards them for guidance and support. This latest generation of socially engineered individuals are primed and positioned to become yet another useful asset unwittingly lubricating the gears of their own suppression. The vast majority believe their participation and support for this latest version of control, is in the name of progress, and for the greater good of humanity, advancing living standards and freedoms for future generations.

A boy in school was once asked by his teacher.

Teacher - "**What do you want to be when you grow up?**"
Boy -" **I want to be happy.**" replied the boy
Teacher - "**You don't understand the question.**"
Boy - "**You don't understand life** "said the boy.

There really is a war on, it is a war for your mind, its tentacles are far reaching, penetrating nearly every aspect of our lives, It has been long in the making yet still has a fair way to go.

"**Just look at us. Everything is backwards. Everything is upside down. Doctors destroy health, lawyers destroy justice, universities destroy knowledge, governments destroy freedom, the major media destroy information, and religion destroys spirituality**." - Michael Ellner[1]

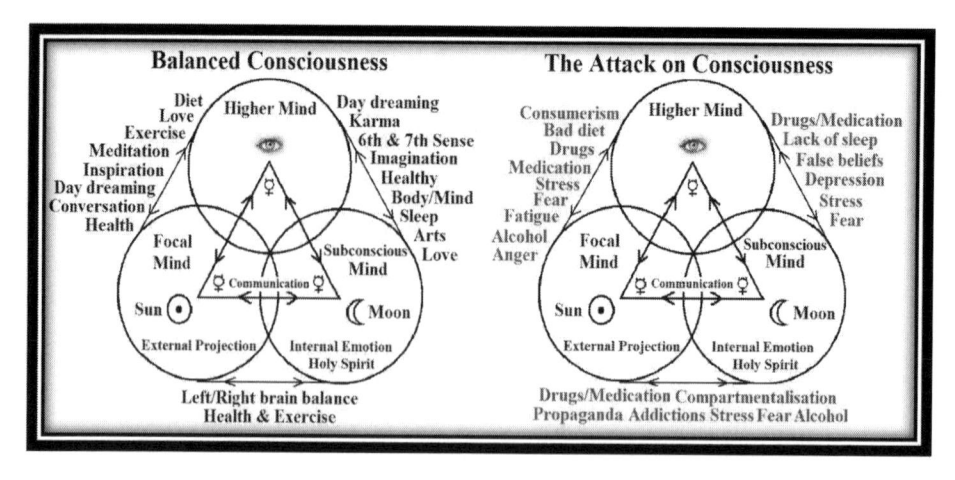

The attack on food

Our reality is the projection of our combined consciousness within the energy fields which surround us. Food is just another form of energy, vibrating at a given frequency. Nature's bounty is full of fresh, nutritious, quality foods grown within the Sun's life-giving properties, transferred to the body on consumption. In contrast corporate foods, highly processed, lacking in life, light and nutrition give us little of real value. For the mind and body to be in harmony, in good health, and functioning within a balanced consciousness, it needs a moderate supply of fresh vitamins and minerals. A modest supply in modest proportions, enough to satisfy the minds desire for more nutrients. Highly processed corporate foods with cheap ingredients, preservatives and additives, on the whole, contain quantity without quality. This lack of vital nutrients convinces the mind and body, after eating, that it is still hungry. An unfulfilled diet turns an individual into an enlarged unfulfilled person, an unhappy and ineffective addition to the human collective. With corporate foods, one will develop a corporate body, a corporate appetite and finally become a corpse.

Genetically Modified Organisms (GMO), are the result of a laboratory process, genes from the DNA of one species are extracted and artificially merged with the genes of a different plant or animal. The foreign genes may have originated from bacteria, viruses, insects, animals or even humans. Some of the world's largest global agricultural companies, specialising in GMO seeds, have produced what are called suicide seeds. GURT (Genetic use restriction technology), is a genetic modification which causes the second generation of seeds to be sterile, forcing the grower to turn to the seed producer for his annual supply. India, one of the world's largest producers of cotton was targeted by one of these companies as part of their conquest for seed control around the globe. From the mid-1980s, a company, I shall not name beginning with M, modified their cotton seeds with a toxic gene which turned them into suicide seeds, allowing them to benefit financially from royalties, claiming they had created something new, where in fact they had just perverted an existing seed found in nature. The intellectual rights relating to seeds, something nature produces for free is widely considered as a fraudulent scam. The globalisation project of the past 20 years has allowed these companies to infiltrate domestic markets all over the world, replacing diversity and destroying localised varieties found throughout nature, varieties which have taken thousands of years to evolved, adapt and thrive in specific locations. This one size fits all policy regarding GMO seeds, competing against natures abundant varieties and natural selection is staggeringly naive. With their vast wealth, these companies have managed to lock local markets into licensing arrangements, influence local and regional governments, coheres huge swathes of the farming community, and expand their global monopoly. With glossy literature and slick promotional videos, thousands of Indian farmers, of modest means have been lured into the world of these GMO seeds. They were offered attractive loans only if they would use the new seeds and pesticides, which promised better yields while costing many times more than the local variety. These GMO seeds didn't always perform as expected, throwing many farmers into financial debt, even ruin. Some unable to pay their loans were forced to turn their land and what little assets they had over to these unscrupulous corporations, in the end many farmers took their own lives. Ironically the suicide seeds brought about suicide farmers. Over the past 20 years, with 95% of India's cotton seeds controlled by M, over 291,000 Indian farmers have committed suicide under the pressure of crippling debt. M has been heavily criticised and accused of contributing to these appalling statistics. In 2009 alone 17,638 Indian farmers committed suicide, 1 every 30 minutes. The other problem associated with GMO crops is cross contamination, gene pollution, or genetic drift. Over time it is inevitable that the GMO crops will encroach and pollute organic farms, turning their natural crops into the intellectual property of the large agricultural corporations who own the GMO technical patents. The Corporations claim they are trying to help feed the world and fight famine in under developed countries. In reality they are expanding their monopolies, gaining more control of the food supply and manipulating the situation to make the world's farmers dependent on their seeds and pesticides.[2][3] The debate over the safety of GMO will go on for decades, the long term effects on human biology is still in its infancy. The introduction of new genes into fruit or vegetables may result in new toxins, new bacteria, new allergens, and even new diseases.[4] What is clear is the increase in global control and dependency of our food supply, once free, now in the hands of the international corporations. Science is a tool and can be used for good or bad, it is certainly clever but not always wise. In the hands of a psychopathic corporation with a profit centred agenda, the results can be devastating, with a negative benefit to the overall good of humanity. The control of the cotton seeds is only the beginning. The objectives of these giant corporations are to do away with natural seed diversity, of which they cannot profit from, substituting all seeds with their artificial patented versions, eventually controlling everything we grow and eat. Genetically modified seeds produce genetically modified foods; genetically modified foods genetically modify those who wish to eat them. The natural balance of frequencies within nature's bounty are being carelessly tampered with, something humanity may never recover from.

Processed foods

The main reason for processing food is to eliminate micro-organisms and extend shelf life. The closer your diet is to nature the better the food is for your body. Each process destroys valuable nutrients and alters some properties. Simply cooking, chopping or combining one food with another is considered a process, and exposing food to high levels of heat, light and/or oxygen will also reduce its nutrient value. Vitamins B and C can be washed out especially during the boiling process. It is preferable to eat vegetables raw keeping intact the delicate vitamins, minerals, photochemical, antioxidants and enzymes. The greater the heat and longer the cooking time the greater the nutrient destruction. When the body craves nutrients, chemicals are produced giving the feeling of hunger, when nutrient rich foods are consumed the body and mind become satisfied, a balanced chemistry will hold off the hunger feeling for a healthy amount of time, keeping the body trim. If the individual consumes dead food, lacking in essential nutrients but full of calories, the body will over eat and still feel hungry, unable to satisfy a craving for nutrients, the body soon expands, blossoming towards obesity. In this modern age of plenty the United States has developed a problem with an overweight population. Submerged in fast corporate living, two out of every three adults are overweight. One third is considered obese. (5) This problem only gets worse each year, spreading around the west like a virus, influenced by each other's behavioural patterns. Overweight people are contributing to the human collective with their gluttonous appetite for none nutritious corporate processed foods.

In 2008 a study was conducted and published in the (Journal of Agriculture and Food Chemistry). The study concluded that raw broccoli appears to deliver anti-cancer compounds 10 times more efficiently than cooked broccoli.(6) Another study conducted at the Roswell Park Cancer Institute in Buffalo, found that eating small amounts of raw broccoli and cabbage over a period of time, reduced the risk of bladder cancer by as much as 40%.(7) There is little doubt that eating plenty of fresh minimally processed high quality vegetables is one of the best ways to stay healthy.

Typical nutrient losses for vitamins and minerals during the cooking process

Nutrient	Freeze	Dry	Cook	Cook+Drain		Nutrient	Freeze	Dry	Cook	Cook+Drain
Vitamin A	5%	50%	25%	35% 10%		Folate	5%	50%	70%	75% 30%
Retinol Activity Equivalent		5%	50%	25%		Food Folate	5%	50%	70%	75% 30%
Alpha Carotene		5%	50%	25% 35%		Folic Acid	5%	50%	70%	75% 30%
Beta Carotene	5%	50%	25%	35% 10%		Vitamin B12	0%	0%	45%	50% 45%
Beta Cryptoxanthin		5%	50%	25% 35%		Calcium	5%	0%	20%	25% 0%
Lycopene	5%	50%	25%	35% 10%		Iron	0%	0%	35%	40% 0%
Lutein+Zeaxanthin		5%	50%	25% 35%		Magnesium	0%	0%	25%	40% 0%
Vitamin C	30%	80%	50%	75% 50%		Phosphorus	0%	0%	25%	35% 0%
Thiamin	5%	30%	55%	70% 40%		Potassium	10%	0%	30%	70% 0%
Riboflavin	0%	10%	25%	45% 5%		Sodium	0%	0%	25%	55% 0%
Niacin	0%	10%	40%	55% 5%		Zinc	0%	0%	25%	25% 0%
Vitamin B6	0%	10%	50%	65% 45%		Copper	10%	0%	40%	45% 0%

Breakfast cereals

The breakfast cereal found in many family homes has been promoted by big corporations as the natural way to start the day. Many cereals are produced from a process called extrusion where grains are mixed with water to form slurry. This mixture is then forced through an extruder, a tiny hole shaping each cereal at high temperature and pressure. After expanding they are sprayed with a mixture of sugar and oil, an overall process which destroys most of the initial nutrients that the grain once offered. Many studies have been conducted to see what the effects are from living on these cereals for prolonged periods. One such study, in 1960, at the University of Michigan, a tongue in cheek study, experimented on three groups of rats. The first group were fed on cornflakes and water. Group two were fed on the cardboard box which the cereal came in and water. The third group were fed on rat chow with water. As expected the third group stayed relatively healthy, the second group, fed on the box, became lethargic, eventually dying of malnutrition. What astounded the research team was the death of the first group eating the cornflakes, they died before the rats that where fed on the box, furthermore before death they threw fits, bit each other and finally died of convulsions. The experiment was not meant to be a serious study but the results were far from funny. It has been suggested that the extrusion process breaks down the organelles and disperse the proteins which then become toxic.[8]

Microwaves

Contrary to popular belief, microwaves are one of the worst ways to cook food. They excite water molecules within the food, vibrating violently at extremely high frequencies creating heat from molecular friction. This results in a molecular decomposition of the essential vitamins leaving the food nutritionally sparse. Additionally, microwaving creates new compounds not naturally found in humans or in nature, called radiolytic compounds. Time will tell what these compounds are doing to your body in the long run. With a huge global market for microwaves, they serve the corporations well, contributing to many people's feeling of hunger, due to eating dead foods within a vicious cycle of corporate food consumption.

PH of the body

The bodies PH balance is important for maintaining good health. It has been known for decades how detrimental an acidic diet can be to the human body. None processed foods found throughout nature generally lean towards the alkaline side of the PH scale; occasionally we find some natural foods being mildly acidic. Foods full of naturally occurring nutrients promote health and keep the bodies PH in good order. Processed foods on the other hand tend to be more acidic, contributing to an increase in health problems for people throughout developed countries, who find themselves being seduced by advertising and other social pressures, into consuming highly processed acidic foods. Excess acid in the body can lead to many problems such as indigestion, nausea, bloating, gout, cataracts, constipation, strokes, allergies, heart disease, diabetes, osteoporosis and cancer. Research has shown a link between acid PH and cancer. Cancer thrives in an acidic environment, producing lactic acid as it grows. Some research scientists suspect a link between PH, Candida and cancer. The yeast fungus called Candida is present in all of us, when the fungus overwhelms the gut's probiotic presence the Candida becomes an overall health threat. Cancer tumours have been found to reside amongst Candida colonies. It seems the best way to keep the gut healthy and the Candida under control is to consume fresh alkaline foods within nature's bounty.[9] Before the expansion of modern super markets, most foods were bought and produced locally, keeping them fresh and close to nature's source. The average family also grew a limited selection of fruit and vegetables in their own gardens, contributing to a healthier lifestyle. Processed packaged foods are convenient for the modern time poor corporate worker, but generally not as good for their health. Pre-made boxed meals, microwaved, ready to eat in 10 minutes is a recipe for disaster. No wonder developed countries are seeing an explosion in the rates of cancer, diabetes and other life threatening illnesses.

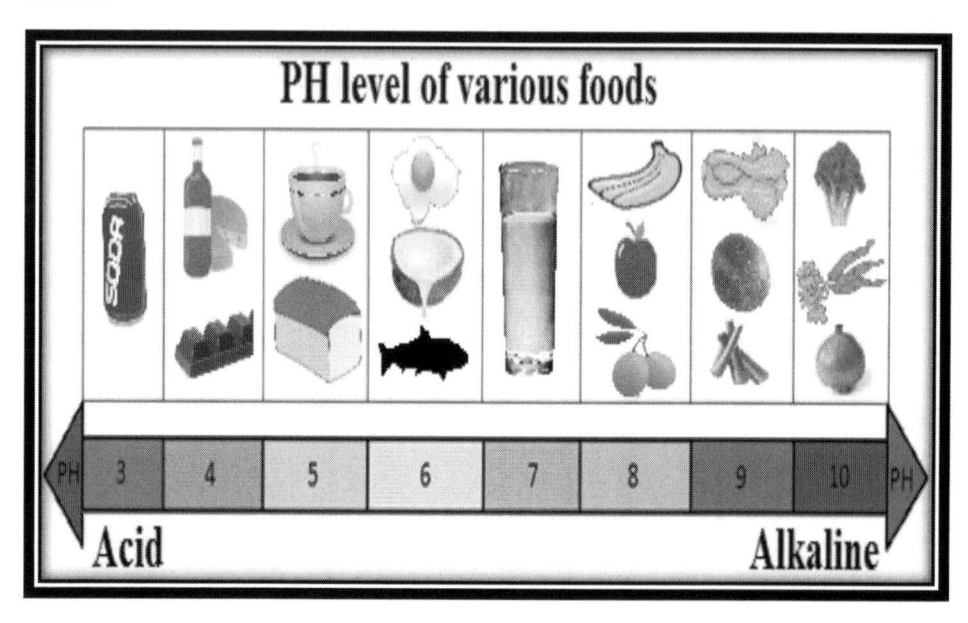

PH level of various foods

Acid — 3, 4, 5, 6, 7, 8, 9, 10 — Alkaline

They say, you are what you eat, to a certain extent this is true. The human body on one hand is delicate and fragile but on the other hand robust and resilient. What we put into our bodies is far more important than what most people realise. Outside our five senses, within the electrical universe everything is giving off a frequency, food is no exception. Nature provides us with an abundance of perfect foods found throughout the world, helping to sustain a healthy balance of mind and body, keeping communication flowing between all levels of consciousness. These natural foods have harnessed life giving energies emanating from the Sun which pass onto us. Highly processed foods lose that energy. In their arrogance the corporations try to compete with this balance, they pervert nature at the DNA level with profit motivated science, trying to control all aspects of our food production, supply and consumption, even how we cook the food. The main objective of these corporations is to entice you away from healthy self-sufficiency, into a life of unhealthy dependency on their inferior products. Linked at the higher levels within the control system, it becomes clear that processed food dependency will also favour the large pharmaceutical corporations, offering medications and temporary relief for symptoms brought about by poor nutrition.

War on drugs

War of drugs or Pharmageddon would be a better title to this section. As Michael Ellner put it, "**Doctors destroy health**". In the United States, in one year alone, out of approximately 400,000 annual deaths from conventional medical mistakes, 106,000 were the result of prescription drugs.[10][11] Looking more like a war against humanity for profit. It may have been better in some cases to have put more faith in the body's own immune system, feeding it well and letting nature take its course, instead many people choose to be doctored to death. The big pharmaceutical corporations, driven by profit and drug sales, are disrupting many people's biological balance, neutralising their capacity to influence the collective consciousness. Through long term dependency on drugs and medical procedures, the companies profit from drawn out treatments to which many people would have been better off using natural remedies, better diet and/or life style changes. New illnesses are being invented, like ADD and ADHD, along with factory made prescriptions ensuring years of sales. According to a CDC report "Health, United States 2013,"[12] between 2007 and 2010, 48% of all Americans were taking some form of prescription drug, that's an increase from 39% during the years of 1988 to 1994, a huge market with immense resources and lobbying capacity. Depression a natural human emotion caused by a combination of factors, once regarded as a signal that the sufferer should make some form of adjustment to their lives, is now an opportunity for big pharma to make profit. Their front line sales team known as doctors and psychiatrists are eager to prescribe anti-depressants as the solution, happy pills that mask over the problem by artificially stimulating the bodies chemical balance, allowing the individual to continue with their problematic lives is now common. 10% of all Americans are currently on anti-depressants, the largest group being women in their 30's and 40's, at a staggering 23%.[13] Some of these anti-depressants are so strong it can take several months to wean yourself off them. Some of the side effects, (side effects are really effects of the drug, unwanted) are so severe, even worse than the initial depression itself. With side effects like suicide why would anyone contemplate using them in the first place?

Side effects of Anti-depressants
Insomnia, Irritability, Nervousness, Anxiety, Violent thoughts and actions, Suicidal thoughts or suicide, Agitation, Tremors, Hostility, Sweating, Irregular heartbeat, Aggression, Criminal behavior, Confusion and incoherent thoughts, Paranoia, Hallucinations, Psychosis, Akathisia (a painful inner agitation; inibility to sit still)

Treating oneself is not good for business; the pharmaceutical corporations don't want competition, especially if it eats into potential profits. Food supplements have always been a good way to boost the body's natural immune system, avoiding the need for patented treatments, but many supplements are under attack from a barrage of strict regulations imposed on them by government agencies, acting on behalf of a few large corporate monopolies. Marijuana, one of nature's miracle plants has been under attack for decades, lobbied against and demonised by the under belly of main stream consensus and the corporate media, labelled as an illegal substance in many parts of the western world, its natural medicinal properties, with very few side effects, are seen as a threat to the profits of big pharmaceutical cartels. There are hundreds of documented cases of miraculous cures for a variety of illnesses even cancer, all from the use of marijuana or marijuana extracts, the big boys don't want people growing their own medicine and becoming self-sufficient. It is interesting to note that before the U.S Federal Government outlawed cannabis in the 1930's it was listed in the 1851(3rd edition) of the U.S Pharmacopoeia (list of drugs and drug ingredients) and was the primary treatment for over 100 separate illnesses and diseases.[14]

Vaccinations

"Was the government to prescribe to us our medicine and diet, our bodies would be in such keeping as our souls are now." - Thomas Jefferson[15]

A vaccine is the introduction of an antigenic material into the body stimulating the immune systems adaptive immunity to future infections of more virulent strains. In 1796 Edward Jenner observed that milkmaids had developed immunity to smallpox. Jenner theorised that the less dangerous cowpox had given them immunity. He noted that the puss in their cowpox blisters could be used as protection from the smallpox virus. He tested his theory on an 8 year old boy named James Philips, Injecting the milkmaid's puss into both arms producing a light fever and some discomfort but no full blown infection. Immunisation was born, but it wasn't all plain sailing, many people died during these early attempts at immunisation through adverse reactions and a multitude of other infections. Many sceptics voiced their opinions against the risks associated with vaccination, concluding that there are better ways to fight the disease, for example improvements in living standards, better sanitation, clean water and better nutrition. Unfortunately, no accurate records exist as to how many people were inoculated and how many developed smallpox as a result. The problem was that inoculated people were contagious during the mild illness which occasionally triggered epidemics. Dr Lettsom wrote in 1806 that there were 72 deaths from smallpox per thousand people in the 42 years prior to inoculation and 89 per thousand in the 42 years following.

Councillor Asbury, Chairman of Sheffield's Health Committee, wrote in 1927,

"It has been calculated that from 1721 to 1758 smallpox inoculation was responsible for the deaths of no less than 22,700 persons from smallpox in London alone."[16]

In 1840 an Act of Parliament was passed making the act of Variolation/Inoculation Illegal

Writing in the British Medical Journal (21/1/1928 p116) Dr L Parry questions the vaccination statistics which showed a greater death rate amongst the vaccinated than the unvaccinated, he asks:

"How is it that smallpox is five times as likely to be fatal in the vaccinated as in the unvaccinated?

"How is it that in some of our best vaccinated towns - for example, Bombay and Calcutta - smallpox is rife, whilst in some of our worst vaccinated towns, such as Leicester, it is almost unknown?

"How is it that something like 80 percent of the cases admitted Into the Metropolitan Asylums Board smallpox hospitals have been vaccinated, whilst only 20 percent have not been vaccinated?

"How is it that in Germany, the best vaccinated country in the world, there are more deaths in proportion to the population than In England - for example, in 1919, 28 deaths in England, 707 In Germany; In 1920, 30 deaths In England, 354 In Germany. In 1919 There were 5,012 cases of smallpox with 707 deaths; in England In 1925 There were 5,363 cases of smallpox with 6 deaths. What is the explanation?"[17]

Dr. Charles Nichols of Boston quoted in the BMJ 2002

"In India, according to an official return presented to the British House of Commons by Viscount Morley, there have been, during 30 years, 1877 to 1906, 3,344,325 deaths from smallpox of persons presumably vaccinated, for vaccination is universally enforced in India....In each and every community where vaccination ceases and strict sanitation is substituted, smallpox disappears. There are no exceptions to this."[18]

During 1871-1873 when Europe adopted a vaccination program it was swept with the worst smallpox epidemic in recorded history. In 1872 when Japan started its compulsory vaccination program the disease steadily increase for each consecutive year. In 1892 throughout Southeast Asia there were more than 165,000 cases with 30,000 deaths in a wholly vaccinated population. Around the same time Australia had no compulsory vaccination program to which only 3 deaths were recorded over a fifteen year period.

"There is no question but that perfect sanitation has almost obliterated this disease, smallpox, and sooner or later, will dispose of it entirely. Of course when that time comes, in all probability, the credit will be given to vaccination." Dr John Tilden MD (1851-1940)

Throughout the 19th and 20th century, prior to the introduction of mandatory vaccination programs, the number of deaths from childhood diseases like measles, whooping cough and diphtheria was falling to a small manageable rate, due to other factors such as better sanitation, housing, nutrition and water supply. The 1968 measles vaccination program statistically reduced the death rate by little more than half from previous decades, averaging around 70 people per year, in a population of 51 million. Over the next 20 years the average recorded yearly death rate from measles dropped to approximately 10, for the 5 years leading up to the 1988 introduction of the combination vaccine MMR (measles, mumps, rubella). With these diseases almost already eradicated the MMR was surprisingly made mandatory. For the next 6 years, statistics recorded an average of 2 deaths per year from measles. Still determined to completely eradicate the disease, in 1994 a second round of MMR vaccine was introduced, making little significant difference to the overall number of deaths. The following graphs taken from The UK Office of National Statistics 20th century mortality files 1901-2000[19] show clearly a huge decline in the death rate from measles prior to the introduction of the mandatory vaccination programs.

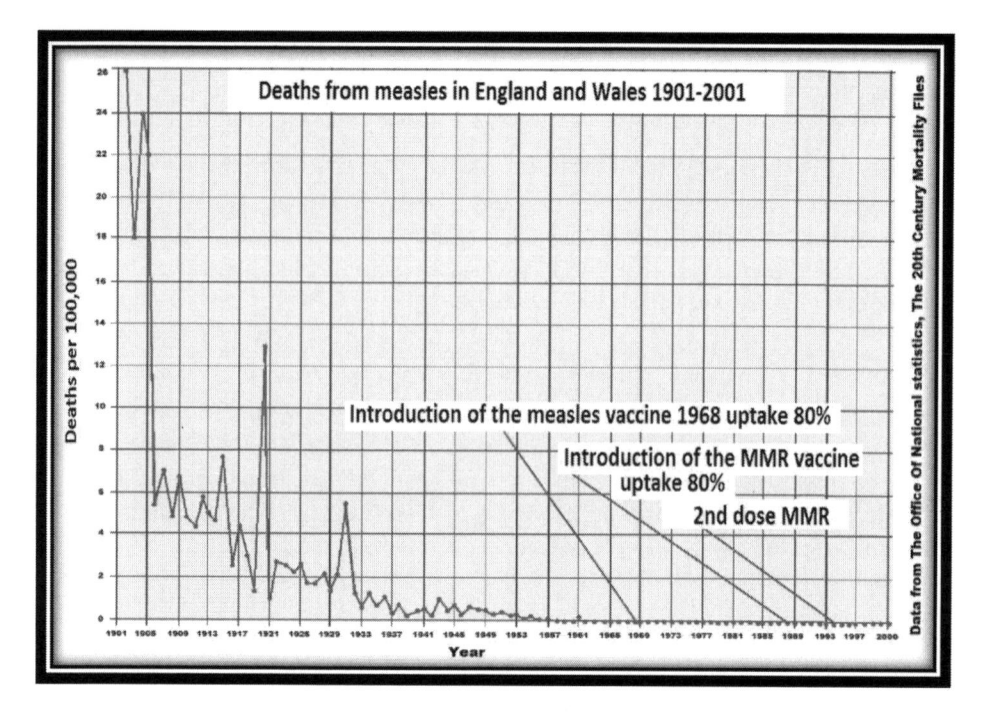

Deaths from measles in England and Wales 1901-2001

Introduction of the measles vaccine 1968 uptake 80%
Introduction of the MMR vaccine uptake 80%
2nd dose MMR

Data from The Office Of National statistics, The 20th Century Mortality Files

"I would consider the risks associated with measles vaccine unacceptable even if there were convincing evidence that the vaccine works, there isn't. While there has been a decline in the incidents of the disease it began long before the vaccine was introduced". Dr Robert Mendelsohn MD

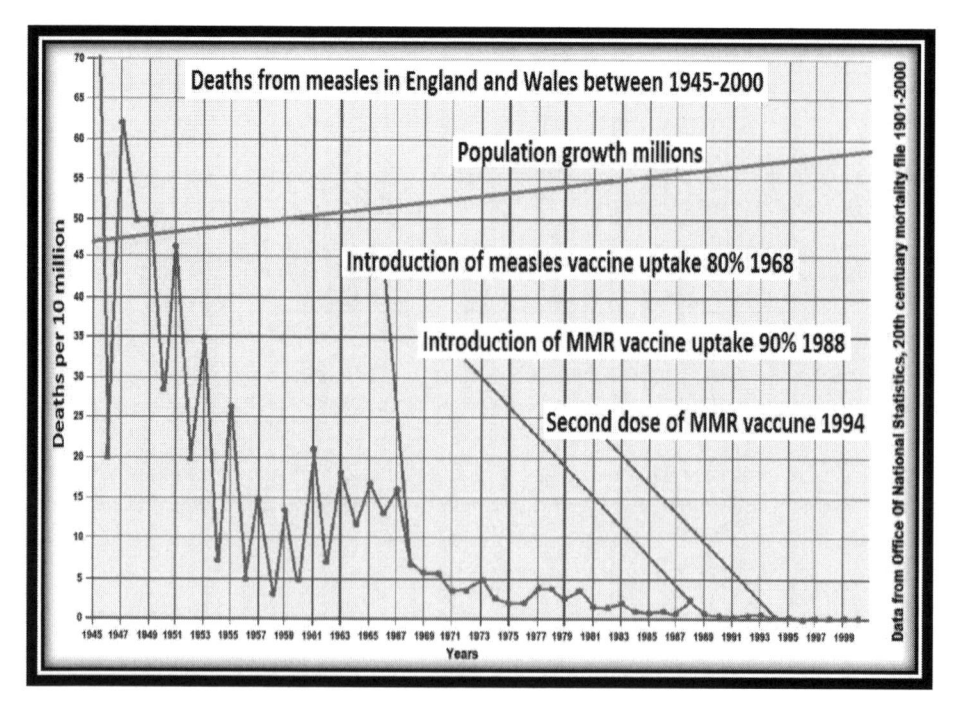

Deaths from measles in England and Wales between 1945-2000

Population growth millions
Introduction of measles vaccine uptake 80% 1968
Introduction of MMR vaccine uptake 90% 1988
Second dose of MMR vaccune 1994

Data from Office Of National Statistics, 20th centuary mortality file 1901-2000

Polio vaccine

Up to 95% of all polio infections cause no symptoms. The vast majority of the remaining 5% develop minor symptoms such as, fever, headache, diarrhoea, stiffness and pains. Those people are usually back to normal within 2 weeks. In approximately 0.5% of cases, muscle weakness is experienced leading to an inability to move. The majority of these patients fully recover. From the small number who don't fully recover, some will have permanent disability, 5% of children and up to 30% of adults within this group will die from the disease.[20] Considered by many one of medicines major breakthroughs the SV40 polio vaccine was widely distributed. But by 1963 numerous studies had established the carcinogenicity of the SV40 vaccine and its capacity to cause tumours and a variety of cancers in hamsters; by this time over 100 million American children and adults had been injected with the vaccine.[21] From the WHO's own literature they estimate that from every 1 million doses of the oral polio vaccine it would cause at least 2 cases of paralysis.

Even being vaccinated is not a guarantee that you will avoid a disease. Your body can be loaded with antibodies but still get the illness, even die from it. You can also have no antibodies and not catch the disease. In 1988 there was a measles outbreak at a college in Colorado, 84 students caught the illness even though over 98 percent of students had documentation of adequate measles immunity.[22] This is not a rare occurrence, the measles-rubella (MR) or MMR vaccination rate is greater than 99% in the Chinese province of Zhejiang; however the incidence of all three of these diseases still remain high,[23] the question of vaccination effectiveness must be raised with this evidence in mind.

How effective are vaccines? There was an influenza outbreak in a 99% vaccinated population among the crew of the USS Ardent, February 2014. Quote from a CDC report.

"On February 10, 2014, the USS Ardent, a U.S. Navy minesweeper, was moored in San Diego, California, while conducting training. Over the course of 3 days, 25 of 102 crew members sought medical care because of influenza-like illness."[24]

Reactions to vaccination

Modern immunisation is a multibillion dollar industry with doctors and patients alike demanding the full spectrum of vaccinations, with the underlining assumption that modern vaccines are 100% safe, mainly ignorant to the shots ingredients and unaware of the possibility of unwanted side effects. The majority of people are under the impression that the science on the matter has been settled. Most research is financed by big pharmaceutical corporations, with their interests paramount. The scientific research into the opposing view on vaccine safety has remained largely underfunded. The financial implications of undermining big pharma's adopted approach are huge. Their resources allow them to influence legislation designed to favour more sales through mandatory vaccination programs. The whole industry has become a belief system driven by fear and propaganda, with many parents unable to have rational discussions around the subject without becoming emotionally charged, even resorting to alienating some parents who wish to opt out of the vaccination programs all together. We are even seeing authorities in some areas taking children away from parents and forcibly injecting them with vaccines, in the process labelling the parents as the abusers. Some schools have begun refusing unvaccinated children from attending classes, citing the health risk they pose to the vaccinated children, fuelling another avenue of division within established communities, the pressure at both ends of the arena steadily grows. In the pro vaccine camp there is an attitude that only vaccines and prescription drugs from the large pharmaceutical companies can save you, giving little credence to natural remedies, nutritional supplements or the body's own immune system, a system which has developed over millions of years, with all our unvaccinated ancestors leading us to where we are today, responsible for the survival of the human species since time began. Now with a global population of 7 billion, these factors seem to go unnoticed. The establishment and pro vaccine lobby groups seem to shy away from the existence of many credible scientific studies showing adverse reactions or permanent harm being caused by vaccines, promoting instead their total safety record and effectiveness. A young child developing and growing needs time to mature naturally, its fragile body and immune system is just beginning, but modern vaccine programs bombard the infant with artificial stimuli injected straight into the blood stream, bypassing the body's natural defence mechanisms. By the age of two, a child in the United States receives up to twenty four vaccination injections. Is it any wonder a percentage of children develop allergies and adverse behavioural problems. During the 1970's the disorder known as autism was virtually unheard of, with only 1 in 10,000 diagnosed with the illness. Since the increase in vaccines, especially multiple vaccination products, there has been an explosion in the number of autism cases. This could be due to a variety of environmental factors but many scientists and doctors are pointing the finger towards a link between the two.

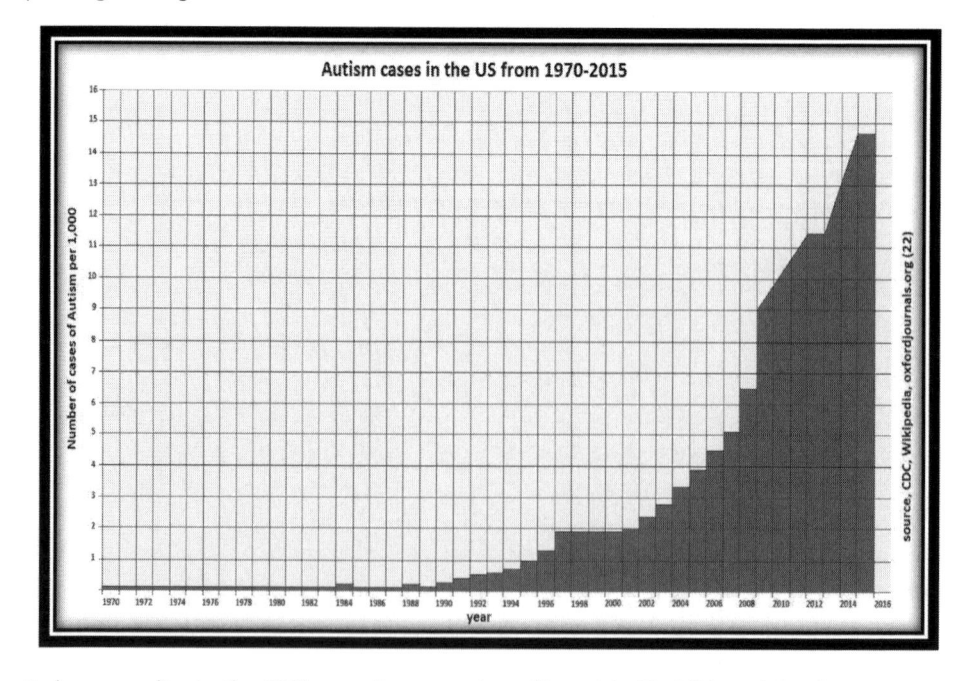

Autism cases in the US from 1970-2015

Today, according to the CDC's own figures autism affects 1 in 68 children. It has been suggested that if this increase continues, by 2025 we could see 1 in 20 children suffering from the illness.

Scientific studies and cases

There are many documented scientific reports showing a relationship between vaccines and adverse reactions, even autism, from credible sources and medical journals. I will list a selected few here.

A study published in the 2010 journal, Annals Of Epidemiology, conducted by Stony Brook University Medical Centre New York, has shown that giving the Hepatitis B vaccine to baby boys triples their risk of developing Autism.[25]

A study published in the 2002, Laboratory Medical Journal determined that vaccination may be one of the triggers for autism.

"We are far from certain that vaccines help trigger autism, but we are farther still from certain they do not. Published science and clinical experience are converging rapidly to form a more accurate image of autism. We are learning that autism implies a physically ill child with associated immune, gut, and nutritional problems. Besides helping target biological interventions for autism, understanding the underlying physical problems enhances our grasp of the possible role of vaccines."[26]

A pilot study was carried out at the University of Pittsburgh School of Medicine during 2010. Infant monkeys were given vaccines officially recommended for human infants by the CDC and the American Academy of Paediatrics (AAP). The study found that some of the monkeys exhibited autism-like symptoms.[27]

Sunday Times publication, 29th August 2010.

"A mother whose son was severely brain damaged by the MMR vaccine in an extremely rare reaction has won her battle for justice after 18 years. Jackie Fletcher secured a legal ruling that has forced the government to accept that its vaccination programme left her son Robert, now 18, severely disabled and to pay him compensation."[28]

The Mail Online reported the following, January 2013.

"Parents who claim their 10-year-old boy developed autism as a result of being injected with an MMR vaccine when he was a baby have been awarded more than £600,000 in a landmark court decision in America. Saeid and Parivash Mojabi claimed that son Ryan suffered a 'severe and debilitating injury to his brain' after being administered with two measles-mumps-rubella vaccinations in December, 2003 and in May the following year."[29]

CBS News, September 10th 2010. Hannah Poling's parents receive $1.5 million compensation for damages to their child. Hannah's father Dr Jon Poling is a Neurologist.

"Hannah was described as normal, happy and precocious in her first 18 months. Then, in July 2000, she was vaccinated against nine diseases in one doctor's visit: measles, mumps, rubella, polio, varicella, diphtheria, pertussis, tetanus, and Haemophilus influenza. Afterward, her health declined rapidly. She developed high fevers, stopped eating, didn't respond when spoken to, began showing signs of autism, and began having screaming fits. In 2002, Hannah's parents filed an autism claim in federal vaccine court. Five years later, the government settled the case before trial and had it sealed. It's taken more than two years for both sides to agree on how much Hannah will be compensated for her injuries."[30]

Italian court awarded Valentino Bocca's family Euros 174,000 after the Italian Health Ministry conceded the MMR vaccine caused autism

"On September 23, 2014, an Italian court in Milan award compensation to a boy for vaccine-induced autism. A childhood vaccine against six childhood diseases caused the boy's permanent autism and brain damage. Based on expert medical testimony, the court concluded that the child more likely than not suffered autism and brain damage because of the neurotoxic mercury, aluminium and his particular susceptibility from a genetic mutation. The Court also noted that Infanrix Hexa contained thimerosal, now banned in Italy because of its neurotoxicity, "in concentrations greatly exceeding the maximum recommended levels for infants weighing only a few kilograms." Presiding Judge Nicola Di Leo considered another piece of damning evidence: a 1271-page confidential GlaxoSmithKline report (now available on the Internet). This industry document provided ample evidence of adverse events from the vaccine, including five known cases of autism resulting from the vaccine's administration during its clinical trials."[31]

The United States has a National Vaccination Injury Compensation Program. If a claim is made for damages to a child from suspected adverse reactions to vaccines, the parents must go through what is known as the vaccine injuries court, a secret tribunal with no reporters or public allowed, even the pharmaceutical companies don't have to attend. There is no required disclosure process, so potential incriminating documents can end up hidden in the hands of vaccine manufacturers. The irony here is that if an award is made for damages, inflicted on a child through vaccinations, the payment comes from a trust fund set up out of tax payer's money. Since 1989 there has been 13,804 cases brought to the vaccine court in the United States, 2,700 cases in 2012 alone. Overall 3,941 were successful, awarded compensation totalling 2.88 billion dollars.[32]

If modern vaccinations are so safe and effective then why the need for a Vaccination Injury Compensation Program at all.

"This forced me to look into the question of vaccination further, and the further I looked into it the more shocked I became. I found that the whole vaccine business was indeed a gigantic hoax. Most doctors are convinced that they are useful, but if you look at the proper statistics and study the instance of these diseases you will realise that this is not so." - Dr Archie Kalokarinos MD[33]

By two years of age some US children receive as many as twenty four vaccination injections, in the UK children under two years old receive ten injections incorporating combination vaccines instead of twenty four separate injections. The following chart is a NHS recommended routine immunisation schedule for the UK along with ingredients and side effects.

The complete routine immunisation schedule 2013/14 UK

Vaccination schedule		Ingredients	Side Effects
Two months old	Diphtheria, tetanus, pertussis (whooping cough), polio and Haemophilus influenzae type b (Hib)	DTaP/IPV/Hib (Pediacel)	What the medicinal ingredient is: Each 0.5 mL dose of PEDIACEL® contains: diphtheria toxoid, tetanus toxoid, acellular pertussis vaccine (pertussis toxoid, filamentous haemagglutinin, fimbriae types 2 and 3, pertactin), inactivated polio vaccine, Hib conjugate vaccine. What the non-medicinal ingredients are: Aluminium phosphate, 2-phenoxyethanol, polysorbate 80, bovine serum albumin, trace amounts of formaldehyde, glutaraldehyde, neomycin, streptomycin and polymyxin B.	Common side effects your child may have are: fever, crankiness; some swelling and soreness in the area where they get their needle; (i.e. nurse, doctor) are a high fever, convulsions, an inconsolable high pitch cry that lasts for several hours, shock (pale, limp and non responsive); or an allergic reaction (hives, wheezing, difficulty breathing, swelling of the face or mouth). More common: Fever, Rare: Chest pain chills coughing, wheezing, or shortness of breath difficult or labored breathing difficulty with swallowing fast heartbeat noisy breathing seizures skin itching, rash, or redness sneezing sore throat swelling of the face, throat, or tongue tightness in the chest
	Pneumococcal disease	PCV (Prevenar 13)	Each 0.5 mL dose of Prevenar 13 contains the following active ingredients: • 30.8 micrograms of pneumococcal purified capsular polysaccharides • 32 micrograms of CRM197 protein plus the following inactive ingredients: • aluminium phosphate • sodium chloride • succinic acid • polysorbate 80 • water for injections	
	Rotavirus	Rotarix (Rotarix)	The lyophilised vaccine contains: amino acids, dextran, Dulbecco's Modified Eagle Medium (DMEM), sorbitol, and sucrose. OMEM contains the following ingredients: sodium chloride, potassium chloride, magnesium sulfate, ferric (III) nitrate, sodium phosphate, sodium pyruvate, D-glucose, concentrated vitamin solution, L-cystine, L-tyrosine, amino acids solution, L-glutamine, calcium chloride, sodium hydrogencarbonate, and phenol red.	Very rare (affect less than 1 in 10,000 people in all age groups) Swollen glands. Dizziness. Fainting or seizures. Pins and needles or numb sensations. Nausea, vomiting or abdominal pain. Aching joints. Skin reactions such as rash, hives or itching. Allergic reactions such as anaphylaxis, narrowing of the airways (bronchospasm) or swelling of the lips, throat and tongue (angioedema).
Three months old	Diphtheria, tetanus, pertussis, polio and Hib	DTaP/IPV/Hib (Pediacel)		
	Meningococcal group C disease (MenC)	MenC (NeisVac-C or Menjugate)	Active ingredient: each 0.5mL dose contains 10 micrograms of meningococcal polysaccharide group C conjugated with 10 to 20 micrograms of tetanus toxoid protein, adsorbed to aluminium hydroxide (adjuvant). Inactive ingredient: aluminium hydroxide (1.4mg, equivalent to 0.5mg aluminium), sodium chloride (4.1mg) and water for injection to 0.5mL. No preservative is added to the formulation.	
	Rotavirus	Rotarix (Rotarix)		
Four months old	Diphtheria, tetanus, pertussis, polio and Hib	DTaP/IPV/Hib (Pediacel)		Uncommon (affect between 1 in 100 and 1 in 1000 children) Crying. Diarrhoea. Vomiting. Feeling generally unwell. Allergic eczema. Very rare (affect less than 1 in 10,000 children) Swollen glands. Dizziness. Headache. Sleepiness. Allergic reactions.
	Pneumococcal disease	PCV (Prevenar 13)		
Between 12 and 13 months old – within a month of the first birthday	Hib/MenC	Hib/MenC (Menitorix)	What Menitorix contains: The active substances are: Haemophilus type b polysaccharide (polyribosylribitol phosphate) 5 micrograms conjugated to tetanus toxoid as carrier protein 12.5 micrograms Neisseria meningitidis group C (strain C11) polysaccharide 5 micrograms conjugated to tetanus toxoid as carrier protein 5 micrograms The other ingredients are: Powder: trometamol, sucrose Solvent: sodium chloride, water for injections	(affect between 1 in 100 and 1 in 1000 people) Cold-like symptoms, eg runny nose, cough. Diarrhoea. Vomiting. Loss of appetite. Swollen glands. Swollen salivary glands may occur about three weeks after having the vaccine. Unknown frequency Feeling generally unwell. Fitting (convulsions). Allergic reactions. Pain in the joints (more common in adult women). Decrease in the normal number of blood cells called platelets in the blood (idiopathic thrombocytopenic purpura). Children who experience this side effect (which involves easy bruising or bleeding for longer than normal) within six weeks of receiving their first dose of MMR vaccine should have a test to measure the levels of antibodies in their blood before they are given a second dose of the vaccine. If the tests show that the child is not fully immune to measles, mumps and rubella it is recommended that the second MMR dose is still given. Redness, irritation and watering of the eyes (conjunctivitis). Swelling of the testicles. Nerve problems such as Guillain-Barré syndrome.
	Pneumococcal disease	PCV (Prevenar 13)		
	Measles, mumps and rubella (German measles)	MMR (Priorix or MMR VaxPRO)	The active ingredients of PRIORIX are live weakened measles, mumps and rubella viruses in a dry powder. Each 0.5mL dose contains not less than : • 10³·⁰ CCID50 (cell culture infectious dose 50%) of the Schwarz measles • 10³·⁷ CCID50 of the RIT 4385 mumps; and • 10³·⁰ CCID50 of the Wistar RA 27/3 rubella virus strains. The inactive ingredients in the vaccine are: lactose, neomycin sulphate, amino acids, sorbitol and mannitol. The vaccine is mixed with sterile Water for injection before use.	
Two and three years old	Influenza (from September)	Flu nasal spray (Fluenz) (annual) (if Fluenz unsuitable use inactivated flu vaccine)		Very common or common (affect more than 1 in 100 people) Pain, redness and swelling at the injection site. Irritability in children. Feeling weak or tired. Headache. Pain or swelling in the joints. Fever. (This can be reduced with paracetamol or ibuprofen – ask your doctor, nurse or pharmacist for advice.) Shivering. Nausea and vomiting. Diarrhoea. Rash, bruising or itching at the injection site. Unknown frequency Swollen glands. Swelling of the injected arm. Allergic reactions such as hives, facial swelling or shortness of breath. Convulsions. Fainting. Temporary pins and needles or numbness in the injected arm. Nerve problems such as Guillain-Barré syndrome, brachial neuritis or facial palsy.
Three years four months old or soon after	Diphtheria, tetanus, pertussis and polio	dTaP/IPV (Repevax) or DTaP/IPV (Infanrix-IPV)	What the medicinal ingredient is: INFANRIX-IPV contains the following medicinal ingredients: diphtheria and tetanus toxoids, three purified pertussis antigens (pertussis toxoid, filamentous haemagglutinin and pertactin (69 kiloDalton outer membrane protein)) and inactivated polio virus types 1, 2 and 3. What the important nonmedicinal ingredients are: INFANRIX-IPV contains the following nonmedicinal ingredients: sodium chloride, aluminium salts, Medium 199 (as stabilizer including amino acids, mineral salts and vitamins), water for injections and may contain trace amounts of neomycin and polymixin.	
	Measles, mumps and rubella	MMR (Priorix or MMR VaxPRO) (check first dose has been given)		Common side effects More than one in 10 girls who have the Gardasil HPV vaccine experience: fever nausea (feeling sick) pain(ed arms, hands, legs or feet. Fewer than one in 10,000 restriction of the airways and difficult breathing (bronchospasm) The frequency of these side effects is unknown: blood problems, leading to unexplained bruising or bleeding chills fainting or brief loss of consciousness feeling dizzy general feeling of being unwell Guillain Barre syndrome joint pain lymphadenopathy/muscle pain or tenderness seizures (fits) tiredness vomiting weakness
Girls aged 12 to 13 years old	Cervical cancer caused by human papillomavirus types 16 and 18 (and genital warts caused by types 6 and 11)	HPV (Gardasil)	The ingredients are proteins of HPV Types 6, 11, 16, and 18, amorphous aluminium hydroxyphosphate sulfate, yeast protein, sodium chloride, L-histidine, polysorbate 80, sodium borate, and water for injections.	
Around 14 years old	Tetanus, diphtheria and polio	Td/IPV (Revaxis), and check MMR status	Aluminum hydroxide, Formaldehyde, Neomycin, 2-Phenoxyethanol, Polymyxin B, Polysorbate 80, Streptomycin, Diphtheria toxoid, Tetanus toxoid, Virus: polio	
	MenC	MenC (Meningitec, Menjugate or NeisVac-C)++		
65 years old	Pneumococcal disease	PPV Pneumococcal polysaccharide vaccine (Pneumovax II)	Active ingredient: The active ingredient of PNEUMOVAX 23 is a mixture of inactive parts from 23 of the most common types of pneumococcal bacteria. Each 0.5 mL of vaccine contains: 25 micrograms of each polysaccharide type. Inactive ingredients: phenol • sodium chloride solution	Very common (affect more than 1 in 100 people) Pain, tenderness, swelling, redness or hardening of the skin at the injection site. Fever (high temperature). Unknown frequency Nausea and vomiting. Headache. Weakness or loss of strength (asthenia). A general feeling of being unwell (malaise). Pain in the muscles or joints. Inflammation of joints (arthritis). Swollen glands (lymph nodes) Rash or hives. Allergic reactions such as anaphylaxis or swelling of the lips, throat and tongue (angioedema).
65 years of age and older	Influenza	Flu injection (annual)		
70 years old	Shingles (from September)	Shingles (Zostavax)	Active ingredient: a weakened form of the varicella-zoster virus. Inactive ingredients: sucrose, hydrolyzed porcine gelatin, sodium chloride, monosodium L-glutamate, sodium phosphate dibasic, potassium phosphate monobasic, potassium chloride	Call your doctor at once if you have a serious side effect such as: fever, swollen glands, sore throat, flu symptoms, breathing problems, or severe or painful skin rash. Less serious side effects include: pain, warmth, redness, bruising, itching, or swelling where the shot was given; diarrhea; joint or muscle pain, headache, or mild skin rash.

It's very easy to manipulate figures. To lower the statistical risks of adverse reactions to vaccines, all that needs to happen is an overall failure to report the incidents adequately.

"Former FDA Commissioner David Kessler estimated in a 1993 article in the Journal of the American Medical Association that fewer than 1 percent of all doctors report injuries and deaths following the administration of prescription drugs. This estimate may be even lower for vaccines. In one survey that our organization conducted in New York in 1994, only 1 doctor in 40 reported to the Vaccine Adverse Events Reporting System (VAERS)."[34]

It appears that the majority of reactions are not reported, although these statistics are used by the government and the medical community to convince themselves and the public as to the safety of the whole vaccine industry. Is it possible that the risks from the initial childhood diseases are fewer than the risks associated with modern vaccination programs. Could it be that the benefits from improvements in living standards have been compromised by the dangers inherent in multi toxic vaccines? Would it have been better to opt out, leave things alone and let nature guide humanity into taking the easier option and a more natural one? The estimated global revenue for the vaccine industry for 2016 is approximately $52 billion; more than double that of 2009.[35] With the help of the WHO, government legislation and main stream media, this figure should grow year on year. In 2004 a report was published in the Journal Paediatrics by the CDC, the report was received by the medical community as a green flag for the MMR vaccine, suggesting there was no significant correlation with autism. However, in the summer of 2014, one of the co-authors of the paper came out and admitted the CDC had omitted vital damning statistics, suggesting that the risk to African American male babies developing autism from the MMR vaccine was twice that of the rest of the population. He stressed how regretful he was for the cover up. His conscience eventually took precedence over the pressure placed upon him from his superiors and their alternative agenda.

STATEMENT OF WILLIAM W. THOMPSON, Ph.D., REGARDING THE 2004 ARTICLE EXAMINING THE POSSIBILITY OF A RELATIONSHIP BETWEEN MMR VACCINE AND AUTISM

My name is William Thompson. I am a Senior Scientist with the Centres for Disease Control and Prevention, where I have worked since 1998.

I regret that my co-authors and I omitted statistically significant information in our 2004 article published in the journal *Paediatrics*. The omitted data suggested that African American males who received the MMR vaccine before age 36 months were at increased risk for autism. Decisions were made regarding which findings to report after the data were collected, and I believe that the final study protocol was not followed.[36]

The flu vaccine

Every winter people are encouraged to get a flu shot, especially the over 65's, pregnant women and people with serious medical conditions, each year influenza is estimated to impact up to 10% of the world's population. The various manufacturers of flu vaccines produce well over 300 million doses which are distributed to over 100 countries, each manufacturer having its own brand with its own unique mix of ingredients. It is important to know what is in these vaccines and what is being injected directly into the blood stream. Some vaccine manufacturers add Thimerosal to the mix, an organic compound containing 49.5% mercury, used as a preservative to help prevent contamination from harmful microbes. Formaldehyde is another favourite with some manufacturers.

> # Ingredients of Vaccines - Fact Sheet. CDC Website
> Common substances found in vaccines include:
> - Aluminum gels or salts of aluminum which are added as adjuvants to help the vaccine stimulate a better response. Adjuvants help promote an earlier, more potent response, and more persistent immune response to the vaccine.
> - Antibiotics which are added to some vaccines to prevent the growth of germs (bacteria) during production and storage of the vaccine. No vaccine produced in the United States contains penicillin.
> - Egg protein is found in influenza and yellow fever vaccines, which are prepared using chicken eggs. Ordinarily, persons who are able to eat eggs or egg products safely can receive these vaccines.
> - Formaldehyde is used to inactivate bacterial products for toxoid vaccines, (these are vaccines that use an inactive bacterial toxin to produce immunity.) It is also used to kill unwanted viruses and bacteria that might contaminate the vaccine during production. Most formaldehyde is removed from the vaccine before it is packaged.
> - Monosodium glutamate (MSG) and 2-phenoxy-ethanol which are used as stabilizers in a few vaccines to help the vaccine remain unchanged when the vaccine is exposed to heat, light, acidity, or humidity.
> - Thimerosal is a mercury-containing preservative that is added to vials of vaccine that contain more than one dose to prevent contamination and growth of potentially harmful bacteria.
>
> http://www.cdc.gov/vaccines/vac-gen/additives.htm

Formaldehyde has been shown to cause cancer in animals and according to the Department of Health and Human Services (DHHS), formaldehyde may **"reasonably be anticipated to be a carcinogen"**. A recent mass spectrometry test found that levels of mercury in one vaccine product was as high as 50 ppm.[37] The EPA (Environmental Protection Agency) has set the maximum contamination level of drinking water at 2 ppb, making the mercury in the vaccine 25,000 times higher. All the government health agencies and the medical establishment insist these levels are safe and recommend that the vulnerable in society take the flu shot each year. In 1976 during the presidency of Gerald Ford, a United States Army Private came down with a particular strain of swine flu, a few days later he died. Fearing the worst, health officials convinced the president that a nationwide epidemic was on its way and the only sensible solution would be a national vaccination program. With the help of the media and the medical profession, at a cost of $135 million, 46 million Americans lined up for the flu shot. As time went by it became evident that the suspected epidemic had not occurred, the private was the only known death along with 13 cases of hospitalisation. However, in the aftermath of the vaccination program over 4,000 people had made claims due to adverse reactions to the flu shot. There were approximately 500 cases of Gillain Barre Syndrome, a paralysing neuromuscular disorder, leaving sufferers with varying degrees of permanent disability which resulted in 25 deaths.[38] This whole episode in the history of the flu vaccine industry is a clear example where the act of doing nothing would have been the better option. During the campaign two doctors from Australia, in a TV interview, were voicing their concerns about the vaccines potential to kill a person who had heart problems; the program was seen by another American rival mafia boss to the Gambino family. With this new information the rival mafia boss using inside contacts within the Gambino family convinced Carlos Gambino, head mafia boss, to take the flu shot.

"Gambino died of a heart attack on October 15, 1976 at his home. Unverified Mob rumours at the time went so far as to suggest that a rival ordered his spies within the Gambino family to persuade Gambino to take a swine-flu shot, knowing that a frail individual with a heart ailment and hardening of the arteries might succumb. According to federal sources, Gambino did get his flu shot shortly before his death."[39]

The normal testing standard for a new vaccine is to perform at least two double blind field trials, showing efficacy and trials showing proof of long term safety. This normally takes years of research. With the seasonal flu vaccine a group of professionals meet to predict the strain most likely to occur during the following season. This varies from one year to the next. It's almost impossible to test against a strain that has not come yet, and long term safety tests just don't happen. All the flu vaccines are experimental vaccines with the public used as guinea pigs. The initial idea behind a vaccine was to give the subject lifetime immunity. Profit seems to be the main motive when making a product that is only guessing at the seasonal strain and offering no lifetime immunity.

According to physician, Dr Mark Geier, a realistic estimation of deaths in the US from influenza, is approximately 600 annually,[40] most of whom are elderly with additional complications. If the vaccine only has a low efficacy rate the question must be asked, is it worth risking the possibility of a potential adverse reaction each time one takes the shot. Efficacy rates vary depending upon the source, anywhere between 9% and 70%, so if we take an average of 40% that would mean 240 deaths possibly prevented out of the annual 600. According to the CDC's own figures there are now only 0.8 per million cases of GBS caused by the influenza vaccine as opposed to 10 per million back in 1976.[41] If all 300 million Americans took the Flu shot that would produce 240 cases of Guillain Barre Syndrome, varying in severity. Not only would you see GBS but many other types of adverse reactions. The manufacturers would, of course, make a great deal of money for themselves and their shareholders, shouldering no liability for the vaccines ill effects, due to government legislation put in place after the 1976 swine flu disaster.

Reducing the population

Is it possible that behind the mask of the vaccination program, there is another agenda; an agenda derived from the control systems secret think tanks? With a desire to tackle global population expansion, even reducing it by some degree. Bill Gates head of the Bill and

Melinda Gates Foundation, a foundation promoting global vaccination programs across the planet is pushing to vaccinate as many children as possible.

"There remains an urgent need to reach all children with life-saving vaccines. One in five children worldwide are not fully protected with even the most basic vaccines" - Bill & Melinda Gates Foundation, vaccines strategy overview.

During the TED (Technical Entertainment Design) conference, in 2012, Bill Gates gave a presentation talk on "Saving the planet" from Global Warming due to CO_2 emissions. During the talk he advocates the use of vaccines for global population reduction.

"The world today has 6.8 billion people, that's heading up to about 9 billion. Now if we do a really great job on new vaccines, health care, reproductive health services, we could lower that by perhaps 10 or 15%"- Bill Gates TED conference 2012

Bill Gate's father, William H Gates Sr, was the former head of Planned Parenthood, a eugenics organisation founded by Margaret Sanger, who wrote the book "*The Pivot of Civilisation*" which promotes the eradication of "human weeds", the end of charity, for the segregation of misfits, cretins, morons and the maladjusted, and also the sterilization of genetically inferior races. With a background like that it's understandable why Bill Gates is in such a powerful position, he could be useful for the control systems future ambitions.

"Diet, injections, and injunctions will combine, from a very early age, to produce the sort of character and the sort of beliefs that the authorities consider desirable, and any serious criticism of the powers that be will become psychologically impossible. Even if all are miserable, all will believe themselves happy, because the government will tell them that they are so." Bertrand Russell. The Impact of Science on Society. 1951.

While there is an ongoing attack on the natural balance of communication between all levels of consciousness, reducing us to just intellectual awareness, through the administration of pharmaceutical products, food processing and environmental suggestions. Over hundreds of years our mental and physical powers which only mystics, mediums and seers now possess have slowly been filtered out of most people's daily lives, now assuming that our modern limited consciousness is the norm. The control system imposes bans on some natural products which alter or enhance a person's state of focal consciousness, through strict laws and legislation, unless of course one of their corporations are profiting out of a patented version. The Amanita Muscaria (a psilocybin mushroom), the Ergot fungus, the fermented grape, Ayahuasca and Cannabis are all found within nature's bounty and used by our ancestors to stimulate communication between levels of consciousness, to achieve higher states of focal awareness. This is deemed unacceptable within the rigid boundaries of a control system that need a perpetually subservient population looking toward them for guidance and solutions.

Notes for chapter 4

(1) Michael Ellnor, Qoute, http://www.whale.to/b/ellner_h.html

(2) The Seeds Of Suicide: How Monsanto Destroys Farming, Globalresearch.org, http://www.globalresearch.ca/the-seeds-of-suicide-how-monsanto-destroys-farming/5329947

(3) Rising suicide rate for Indian farmers blamed on GMO seeds, RT, November 22, 2014, http://rt.com/news/206787-monsanto-india-farmers-suicides/

(4) BAD SEED: Danger of Genetically Modified Food, https://www.youtube.com/watch?v=go_29vbOdlI

(5) Weight-control Information Network, statistics, web site, http://win.niddk.nih.gov/index.htm

(6) Raw broccoli appears to deliver anti-cancer compound 10 times as efficiently as cooked, Journal of Agricultural and Food Chemistry, Oct 25, 2008, http://www.prohealth.com/library/showarticle.cfm?libid=14055

(7) Mike Adams, Natural news, Raw Broccoli, Cabbage Slash Bladder Cancer Risk, http://www.naturalnews.com/023655_Isothiocyanates_raw_foods.html

(8) Dirty Secrets of the Food Processing Industry, The Western A price Foundation, http://www.westonaprice.org/health-topics/dirty-secrets-of-the-food-processing-industry/

(9) PF louis, Four things you need to know about cancer and candida, Natural News, December 8th 2012, http://www.naturalnews.com/038266_cancer_Candida_correlations.html

http://www.canceractive.com/cancer-active-page-link.aspx?n=1089

(10) Gary Null (Phd), Death by medicine, Report, Pdf, http://www.webdc.com/pdfs/deathbymedicine.pdf

(11) James John T, Phd, A New, Evidence-based Estimate of Patient Harms Associated with Hospital Care, Journal of patient safety, September 2013 - Volume 9 - Issue 3, http://journals.lww.com/journalpatientsafety/Fulltext/2013/09000/A_New,_Evidence_based_Estimate_of_Patient_Harms.2.aspx

(12) CDC Report, Health, United States 2013, http://www.cdc.gov/nchs/hus/chartbook.htm#chartbook_special_feature

(13) Peter Wehrwein, Astounding increase in anti depressant use by americans, Harvard health publications, Harvard medical school. http://www.health.harvard.edu/blog/astounding-increase-in-antidepressant-use-by-americans-201110203624

(14) Canibis for cancer and medical marijuana, http://www.cannabiscure.info/

(15) Thomas Jefferson, quote, Notes on the state of Verginia (1781–1783), publiser JW Randolph. Issue 1 page 266, http://en.wikiquote.org/wiki/Notes_on_the_State_of_Virginia

(16) Jennifer Craig, BSN, MA, Ph.D, February 26, 2010, Smallpox Vaccine: Origins of Vaccine Madness, International medical council on vaccination, http://www.vaccinationcouncil.org/2010/02/26/smallpox-vaccine-origins-of-vaccine-madness/

(17) FATALITY RATES OF SMALL-POX IN THE VACCINATED AND UNVACCINATED, British Medical Journal, 116 (Published 21 January 1928),Cite this as: BMJ 1928;1:116, http://www.bmj.com/content/1/3498/116.1

(18) History of vaccination and anti-vaccination programmes in India, British Medical Journal, (Published 24 August 2002) Cite this as: BMJ 2002;325:430. http://www.bmj.com/rapid-response/2011/10/29/re-history-vaccination-and-anti-vaccination-programmes-india

(19) Graph Data from Office of national statisticks, uk, 20th centuary mortality files 1901-2000. http://www.ons.gov.uk/ons/publications/re-reference-tables.html?edition=tcm%3A77-215593

(20) Polio infection, Wikipedia, http://en.wikipedia.org/wiki/Poliomyelitis

(21) SV40, Simian Virus 40 (SV40): A Cancer Causing Monkey Virus from FDA-Approved Vaccines http://www.sv40foundation.org/cpv-link.html

(22) Hersh BS, Markowitz LE, Hoffman RE, Hoff DR, Doran MJ, Fleishman JC, Preblud SR, Orenstein WA. A measles outbreak at a college with a prematriculation immunization requirement. Am J Public Health. 1991 Mar;81(3):360-4. http://www.ncbi.nlm.nih.gov/pubmed/1994745

(23) Wang Z, Yan R, He H, Li Q, Chen G, Yang S, Chen E, Difficulties in eliminating measles and controlling rubella and mumps: a cross-sectional study of a first measles and rubella vaccination and a second measles, mumps, and rubella vaccination. PLoS One. 2014 Feb 20;9(2):e89361, http://www.ncbi.nlm.nih.gov/pubmed/24586717

(24) Theodore L Aquino DO, Gary T Brice, CDC Report, Influenza Outbreak in a Vaccinated Population — USS Ardent, February 2014, October 24, 2014 / 63(42);947-949, http://www.cdc.gov/mmwr/preview/mmwrhtml/mm6342a3.htm

(25) Epimology of Autism, Wikipedia, http://en.wikipedia.org/wiki/Epidemiology_of_autism

Ausism spectrum disorder, Centers for disease control statistics, http://www.cdc.gov/ncbddd/autism/data.html

Autism spectrun disorder in young children, http://ije.oxfordjournals.org/content/38/5/1245.full.pdf

(25) Gallagher CM, Goodman MS, Hepatitis B vaccination of male neonates and autism diagnosis, NHIS 1997-2002. J Toxicol Environ Health A. 2010;73(24):1665-77. http://www.ncbi.nlm.nih.gov/pubmed/21058170

(26) Bernard Rimland, PhD, Woody McGinnis, MD, Vaccines and Autism, Autism Research Institute, San Diego, CA, laboratorymedicine> september 2002> number 9> volume 33. http://labmed.ascpjournals.org/content/33/9/708.full.pdf

(27) Laura Hewitson, Brian J. Lopresti, Carol Stott, N. Scott Mason and Jaime Tomko ,Acta Neurobiol Exp 2010, 70: 147–164, Influence of pediatric vaccines on amygdala growth and opioid ligand binding in rhesus macaque infants: A pilot study, Department of Obstetrics and Gynecology, University of Pittsburgh School of Medicine, Pittsburgh, PA, USA; http://www.ane.pl/pdf/7020.pdf

(28) Sarah-Kate Templeton, Mother wins MMR payout after 18 years, Sunday Times, Published: 29 August 2010, http://www.thesundaytimes.co.uk/sto/news/uk_news/Health/article381972.ece

(29) David Gardner, Mail Online, Published: 01:32 GMT, 15 January 2013, American parents awarded £600,000 in compensation after their son developed autism as a result of MMR vaccine, http://www.dailymail.co.uk/news/article-2262534/American-parents-awarded-600-000-compensation-son-developed-autism-result-MMR-vaccine.html

(30) Sharyl Attkisson, CBS News, September 10, 2010, 10:44 AM, Family to Receive $1.5M+ in First-Ever Vaccine-Autism Court Award, http://www.cbsnews.com/news/family-to-receive-15m-plus-in-first-ever-vaccine-autism-court-award/

(31) Mary Holland JD, Recent Italian Court Decisions on Vaccines and Autism, Feb 27th 2015, Health impact News, http://healthimpactnews.com/2015/u-s-media-blackout-italian-courts-rule-vaccines-cause-autism/

Paul Bignell, The Independent, Italian court reignites MMR vaccine debate after award over child with autism, Sunday 17 June 2012, http://www.independent.co.uk/life-style/health-and-families/health-news/italian-court-reignites-mmr-vaccine-debate-after-award-over-child-with-autism-7858596.html

(32) HRSA, Compensation program statistics report for february 2015, United States, http://www.hrsa.gov/vaccinecompensation/statisticsreport.pdf

(33) Dr Archie Kalokarinos MD, Interview, International Vaccine Newsletter, June 1995, http://www.whale.to/v/kalokerinos.html

(34) Testimony of Barbara Loe Fisher, Co-Founder & President National Vaccine Information Center, U.S. House Government Reform Committee - August 3, 1999 "Vaccines: Finding a Balance Between Public Safety and Personal Choice". http://www.whale.to/vaccines/fisher.html

(35) Nick Taylor, Vaccine market worth $52 billion in 2016, In-Pharma technologist.com, 18th Jan 2010, http://www.in-pharmatechnologist.com/Regulatory-Safety/Vaccine-market-worth-52bn-in-2016

(36) William Thompson Phd, Statement, http://www.morganverkamp.com/august-27-2014-press-release-statement-of-william-w-thompson-ph-d-regarding-the-2004-article-examining-the-possibility-of-a-relationship-between-mmr-vaccine-and-autism/

(37) Mike adams, Natural News, Why flu shots are the greatest medical fraud in history, dec 10, 2014,
http://www.naturalnews.com/047942_flu_shots_medical_fraud_vaccine_quackery.html

(38) 1976 swine flu outbreak, Wikipedia,
http://en.wikipedia.org/wiki/1976_swine_flu_outbreak

(39) Carlos Gambino, Wikia,
http://organizedcrimeencyclopedia.wikia.com/wiki/Carlo_Gambino

(40) Mark Geier, Phisician http://en.wikipedia.org/wiki/Mark_Geier

(41) CDC, Preliminary Results: Surveillance for Guillain-Barré Syndrome After Receipt of Influenza A (H1N1) 2009 Monovalent Vaccine --- United States, 2009--2010
http://www.cdc.gov/mmwr/preview/mmwrhtml/mm59e0602a1.htm

Chapter 5. Corporations

The word corporation comes from the Latin corpus, the word for "body" or "body of people". The early forms of corporations appeared in the 17th century; a body of investors would get together for a specific purpose, usually for the good of the community, they would create a corporation to fulfil certain objectives. In those days, the corporations were granted a charter and brought into legal existence by a monarch or parliament, the charter had time restrictions and purpose limitations. Once the objectives were reached the corporate charter would cease on completion. If any corporation went outside its legal perimeters other than its original purpose the charter could be revoked. Limitations were strict in order to control the power of corporations over the rights of the citizens. As the British Empire expanded so did the corporations. The British East India Company was one of the best-known examples, acting on the government's behalf; it would bring in massive revenue from its exploits, becoming increasingly integrated with the British military and colonial policies. The great advantage for the corporation was its limited liability. Those who made the initial investment could protect their personal wealth from future liabilities, whereas an individual trading under his own name was personally liable and risked losing everything. The corporation therefore could take far more risks. The American Revolution was not only about freeing the colonies from the British usurious banking system and King George III Stamp Act; it was also fermented by the monopolistic exploits of some British corporations. The Boston Tea Party, in 1773, was a demonstration against the East India Company's monopoly over trading routes. After the revolution, the United States imposed tough restrictions on the corporations, forbidding them from influencing elections, public policy and other areas of civic society, wisely limiting corporations from exploiting the American people, only granting charters for projects that benefited the public. The pecking order under the new constitution was the people, the government, the banks then the corporation. Back in Europe the corporations had fewer restrictions shielding investors by limiting liabilities over their personal wealth. Over time, these corporations grew larger and more influential making those benefiting from its profits very wealthy.

The money masters realised that through the corporate structure they could influence and control labour, resources, community rights and political sovereignty. During the Industrial Age the European common man found himself working 12 hours a day, 7 days a week for some of these corporations, lubricating the engines of industry and setting the sails of influence in the direction of the wealthy elite. As the 20th century unfolded the corporations set about influencing everything in their wake. Since then there has been a constant battle between the rights of the common man and the expansive nature of the corporation. Corporations see humans as a resource commodity with no other value than economic. The whole nature of the corporation is psychopathic with no empathy for humanity, expanding and consuming as it grows regardless of consequence. The corporations have now grown into international monsters, some having greater profits than the GDP of small nations. They swallow up local business, land, communities and assets, morphing into beasts that our ancestors fought vigorously to restrain. They now finance most political parties, crushing the labour movements which were set up as a counter measure to ensure fairness and equality. They attack and subvert regulation allowing them greater scope for expansion and exploitation. Their tentacles have spread into nearly every area of modern life, influencing education, health, justice, entertainment and even spirituality. The new pecking order is the banks, the corporations, the government then the people. The corporations have the best lawyers and enough wealth to disregard local laws which attempt to restrict their rapacious activities. They pay private police and armies to put down dissent amongst workers and to bully communities, essentially becoming a new form of oligarch. We are now living in a corporatocracy, where consumerism has become the new religion, with the Television and the main stream media acting as an altar to which victims are preyed upon and sacrificed into debt. Political candidates are elected by the citizens but ruled by armies of corporate lobbyists, passing whatever legislation is needed to keep the money rolling in. Franklin D Roosevelt made a speech on April 29th 1938, a message to congress.

"The first truth is that the liberty of a democracy is not safe if the people tolerate the growth of private power to a point where it becomes stronger than their democratic state itself. That, in its essence, is Fascism—ownership of Government by an individual, by a group, or by any other controlling private power.

The second truth is that the liberty of a democracy is not safe if its business system does not provide employment and produce and distribute goods in such a way as to sustain an acceptable standard of living." - Franklin D Roosevelt[1]

Legal fiction

There are two main types of laws in this world, the law of the land (Common Law) and the law of the sea (Universal Commercial Code (UCC), Maritime Admiralty Law). In order to conduct business on an international basis, one country trading with another, a strict business code was adopted based on Roman Vatican Cannon Law. Ships would traverse the globe exchanging goods under this system, backed up by naval pursuits if the law wasn't adhered to and contracts weren't fulfilled. In order to do business fluently under UCC law a legal fiction had to be created so the flesh and blood human could conduct business with corporations under the Jurisdiction of its statutes. This allowed things to be done in law, which, without the legal fiction, would not be possible. Throughout the 19th Century corporations expanded their influence, dominating commerce, it was therefore necessary to incorporate the common man into this system, turning him into a commodity. An ingenious but deceptive method was adopted by those countries participating in this trading strategy, this was the main reason why the birth certificate was created. When you are born, your parents unwittingly register your birth and with this registration the government creates a company under the same name e.g. "PETER PAN". From that moment on all official documents denoting the legal fictitious company baring your name will use capital letters. As the company was a creation of the government it is also they that own and control it. The great deception here is that they did not tell you this; they also didn't want you to know, so they could use this company as a tool to attach liabilities to the real you and secure future government borrowing with your legal fiction as security. Most people are unaware that nearly everything has a legal fiction attached to it; the system can only survive if this is the case. You the flesh and blood person are not required under common law to acquiesce to the demands of a corporation, unless you have a legal binding contract with them, a contract of full disclosure where both parties are aware of all aspects of the contract and both parties have provided a valid signature. Bearing in mind the majority of people are unknowingly acting for their namesake corporation which throws into question the legality over full disclosure. The corporations can only do business with the legal fiction and has no control over the real person. PETER PAN the company was created alongside the flesh and blood boy, created and named by his parents. But in the absence of the knowledge of the existence of the company, people are led to believe that everything applies to the boy. When officials acting for the control system ask the question "Are you Peter Pan?" What they really mean is "Do you accept the liabilities for PETER PAN the corporation". When you agree by saying "YES", you are unknowingly accepting the liabilities for the corporation (person), which the control system own and use to establish their authority over you. The government and its institutions all of which are corporations, have authority over you only by your consent. Statutes (Acts of Parliament) only apply to the legal fiction whereas common law applies to the flesh and blood human. Common law is simple and has evolved over hundreds of years.

- You must not injure or kill anyone.
- You must not steal or damage things owned by someone else.
- You must be honest in your dealings and not swindle anyone.

Parliamentary laws are vast, an endless stream of legislative statutes designed to find new ways of extracting wealth from the common flesh and blood person through the legal fiction he is unwittingly representing, designed to keep him in perpetual debt slavery, working his entire life for a pension that vanishes on the date he goes to collect it.

This transition into what is essentially a corporatocracy has been a long process. British corporations, as we understand them today, came into being in 1844 with a UK Parliamentary Act allowing the corporation to define their own purpose. The power to control them passed from the government to the courts. In 1855 shareholders were awarded limited liability protecting individual wealth from the consequences of their corporate behaviour.

In 1963 the D-U-N-S numbering system was introduced allocating a unique number to each business entity. With minimal effort, you can discover that political parties, government institutions and even your local police force have a D-U-N-S number, signifying a corporation. When you do a search, you will discover that the House of Commons is a commercial company (number UC2279443), The Labour Party is a commercial company, the House of Lords, the United Kingdom Corporation Ltd, the Ministry of Justice, the Bank of England and every Court and Police Force up and down the country; even the Secretary of State for Trade and Industry is a company. Consequently, in order to interact with all these corporations, the legal fiction attached to the individual must be created, and to survive it must also be hidden from public scrutiny.[2]

The Vatican's trusts

We must go back a long way in history to appreciate where this all began and why it is the way it is. The Canaanite Phoenicians (1500 – 539 BC) were the pioneers of this trading system, with their vast maritime superiority; they managed to dominate commerce throughout the Mediterranean from Tyre, where Lebanon/Israel is now. With all their ships, they managed to impose tariffs and tax on commercial activity making themselves rich and feared. The Phoenician alphabet is believed to have been behind all modern western alphabets, spreading into Greece and Rome through its trading activities. Alexander the Great took Tyre in 332 BC putting an end to its 1000-year maritime monopoly. It is believed by some scholars that the wealth from Phoenicia eventually moved into Venice creating another maritime trading culture, the Venetians.

After the decline of Rome and the transfer of power over to the Vatican the Papacy had learnt a lot about commerce and set about enslaving all of humanity by setting up a system of ownership targeting all property and souls. After the Knights Templar had been defeated at Acre, 24 miles south of Tyre in 1291, the Roman Catholic Church began to put in motion their plan to own the world. In 1302 Pope Boniface VIII, through Papal bulls, created the first express trust in history, the "**Unam Sanctum**", Attached to that trust were three "**Cestui Que Vie**" trusts, or crowns, each one targeting specific areas of ownership.

- Nicolas V, 1455: Romanus Pontiflex – 1st Testamentary Deed and Will and 1st Crown of People as Permanent Slaves.
- Sixtus IV, 1481: Aeterni Regis – 2nd Testamentary Deed and Will and 2nd Crown over land.
- Paul III, 1531: Convocation – 3rd Testamentary Deed and Will and 3rd Crown over Souls.

With these three **Cestui Que Vie** trusts or Papal bull crowns, the Roman Catholic Church, unchallenged, believe they have ownership, the keys to all land, bodies and souls. This is why the Pope's crown has three tiers. All courts now operate on trust law, based on Vatican ecclesiastical cannon law; they manipulate people into representing their corporate legal fiction or trust, which are essentially underpinning these three papal trusts.[3]

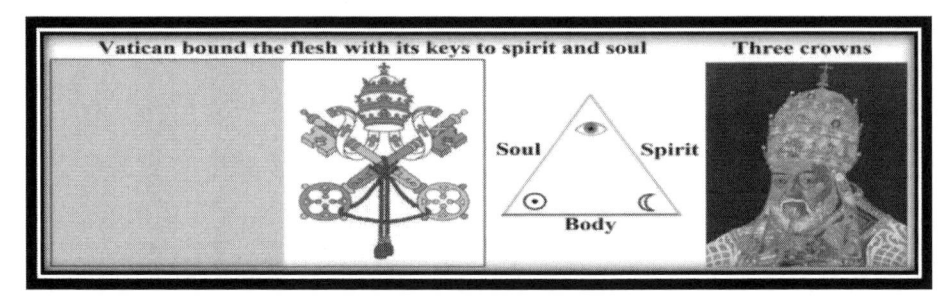

The UNITED STATES CORPORATION

After the American Civil War, the United States was in a terrible financial mess. The international financiers had achieved one of their objectives. They either wanted the Union bankrupt or divided and controlled by themselves. The Union survived but 4 years of war had taken its toll in lives and the economy. With Lincoln, out the way the international financiers offered financial help to the Union with conditions attached, they wanted to create an independent government for the ten-square mile District of Columbia, a separate entity in the host nation, like the City of London and the Vatican. This new independent government was to be a corporation under the name, THE UNITED STATES. The name is all capitals signifying a corporate legal fiction. On February 21st 1871 the 41st congress passed the Act of 1871, Act titled: "An Act to provide a government for the District of Columbia." This new corporation was owned by international bankers and the aristocracy of Europe. The constitution of 1787 was rewritten with one word changed. The original constitution reads "Constitution for the United States of America". The new one reads "CONSTITUTION OF THE UNITED STATES OF AMERICA", all capitals signifying a corporation with the word "for" changed to "OF". This is a constitution of a corporation dictating policy as opposed to a constitution of the people. Many may still believe the President of the United States is the president of the republic, he is, in fact, the president of a corporation owned by foreign interests. This may explain why the British and the Israeli Zionists have a special relationship with the United States, they may well be its owners.

When the United States and Britain, under their special relationship decide to expand the influence of democracy throughout the world, in reality they are using democracy as an excuse to make the world safer for banking usury and corporate ecclesiastic commerce, helping them to gain a greater monopolistic foot hold in whatever country is next on the list, this is essentially globalisation. The American war machine is nothing more than a group of companies lobbying the corporate government for a greater involvement in world affairs, they profit from mass slaughter and human misery on a global scale. Major General Smedley Butler of the United States Marine Corps, said it best in his book "War is a Racket".

"Like all the members of the military profession, I never had a thought of my own until I left the service. My mental faculties remained in suspended animation while I obeyed the orders of higher-ups. This is typical with everyone in the military service."

"War is a racket. It always has been. It is possibly the oldest, easily the most profitable, surely the most vicious. It is the only one international in scope. It is the only one in which the profits are reckoned in dollars and the losses in lives."

"A racket is best described, I believe, as something that is not what it seems to the majority of the people. Only a small "inside" group knows what it is about. It is conducted for the benefit of the very few, at the expense of the very many. Out of war a few people make huge fortunes."

"I spent 33 years and four months in active military service and during that period I spent most of my time as a high class muscle man for Big Business, for Wall Street and the bankers. In short, I was a racketeer, a gangster for capitalism. I helped make Mexico and especially Tampico safe for American oil interests in 1914. I helped make Haiti and Cuba a decent place for the National City Bank boys to collect revenues in. I helped in the raping of half a dozen Central American republics for the benefit of Wall Street. I helped purify Nicaragua for the International Banking House of Brown Brothers in 1902-1912. I brought light to the Dominican Republic for the American sugar interests in 1916. I helped make Honduras right for the American fruit companies in 1903. In China in 1927 I helped see to it that Standard Oil went on its way unmolested. Looking back on it, I might have given Al Capone a few hints. The best he could do was to operate his racket in three districts. I operated on three continents." — Smedley D. Butler, War is a Racket.[4]

The Evolution of The American Flag

Commercial courts

The commercial court system has evolved from the law of the sea, Maritime Admiralty Law. A universal commercial code (UCC), designed to allow the flow of business to take place between corporations and the flesh and blood person through the deceptively created Legal fiction. Going to court for any civil action, is not a good idea, as the only function of a court is to judge between the two disagreeing parties, and then penalise the loser. The court is not interested who wins or loses because the objective of the court is to make a profit as a commercial enterprise for its owners; its purpose is to acquire money from anybody who is foolish enough to attend. A civil commercial court summons (which is really an invitation) to go to court, is not in your name, but in the name of the legal fiction which they are hoping to fool you into representing. Any financial institution is also a legal fiction and doesn't really exist. The modern commercial court is effectively a representation of a ship, exercising its authority under the Law of the sea.

Commercial Courts, UCC, Maritime Admiralty Law

The Judge will try to entice you into representing the legal fiction by asking "is PETER PAN in court" or "are you PETER PAN"? By answering yes to this you are unwittingly accepting responsibility to represent the fictitious corporation known as PETER PAN, where liabilities will be placed upon you. A recent case took place in the UK where the local council took Roger Hayes to court for failure to pay his council tax. On the 11/JAN/2011 the County Court of Birkenhead conceded to the right of Roger Hayes to act as 'third party representative' for the legal fiction of MR ROGER HAYES. In essence, the court agreed that they were two separate entities. This is the court transcript from Roger Hayes.[5]

Judge: Can we first find out who is in the court... is MR ROGER HAYES in the court?
Me: Sir, I am third party representative for MR ROGER HAYES.
Judge: Are you MR ROGER HAYES?
Me: No sir, I am the third party representative for MR ROGER HAYES... you may address me as Roger.
Judge: I will not address you as Roger, I will call you MR HAYES
Me: Sir, I am not MR HAYES, the court is required to address me as I request and I request that you address me as Roger. (NOTE – court protocol dictates that a defendant or respondent can be addressed the way they choose – the Judge then referred to me as 'the gentleman' but avoided referring to me as MR HAYES).
Judge: If you are not MR ROGER HAYES then I will take note that MR ROGER HAYES is not represented in court.
Me: In that case sir, you will have to also note that the council is not represented in court. (NOTE. This would mean that the case would have to be dismissed, finding for the defendant, because the plaintiff had not appeared)
Judge: I can see that that the council has representation in the court.
Me: Then you will have to acknowledge that MR ROGER HAYES has representation in the court. We are all equal in the eyes of the law... if council has third party representation then so does MR ROGER HAYES. The council is a corporation and so is MR ROGER HAYES.
Judge: MR ROGER HAYES is not a corporation.
Me: Yes it is.
Judge: No it isn't, it is a PERSON.
Me: A PERSON is a corporation.
Judge No it isn't.
Me: Define person.
Judge: I don't have to.

Me: Then let me do it for you sir. A PERSON is a corporation (NOTE: This is defined in a law dictionary) Sir, are you familiar with the Cestui Que Vie Act of 1666?
Judge: I am familiar with many laws.
Me: Sir, I asked if you were familiar with the Cestui Que Vie Act of 1666, if you are not Sir, then with respect you are not competent to judge in this matter and that gives rise to a claim of denial of due process.
Judge: Let's hear from the council.
Me: Sir we can only move on to the council's presentation when the court has confirmed that MR ROGER HAYES is represented in court.
Judge: Fine.

And the case continued.... with me (Roger Hayes) acting as third-party representative for the legal fiction MR ROGER HAYES and with the judge eventually telling the council to go away and prove its case. The Judge was obviously very keen to avoid a charge of denial of due process i.e. a challenge to his competence. It was much easier for him to side with me and pass the buck back to the council. Smart judge.

It is interesting to see how the deception of the legal fiction, a corporation is vigorously upheld by court room employees, eager to impose the will of the control system, either through ignorance or a subconscious consumption of expectations of the corporate persona.

The TV licence

In Britain, the citizens receive a demand to pay a TV licence. The demand is addressed to the legal fiction, in capital letters not the human. This demand is optional because it is not the real you who is being billed but it is you who decide whether to pay or not. As a physical being you are bound under common law but not legal statutes, common law does not demand you pay tax or a TV licence. The interesting thing here is that the legal fiction who is only a piece of paper can be considered deaf, dumb and blind and does not even own a TV set, therefore is not required to have a licence. The company employed to send out demands put fear in the minds of the public by sending out vans with peculiar devices attached to the roofs, in an attempt to frighten people into paying. All you need to do is write on their envelope "NO CONTRACT - RETURN TO SENDER ". There is no contract. A contract is when there is full disclosure, where both parties are aware of all aspects of the contract and both parties have provided a valid signature.

The police

The Police or Policy enforcement officers have deviated from their initial role as constables, defenders and upholders of constitutional/common law, to a new dominant role as statutory tax collectors for corporate government legislation. Police forces are now commercial enterprises dedicated to creating profit; they extract our money using various forms of penalty notices and fines. Police officers take an oath of office which gives them authority to uphold common law. Many police do not appreciate the difference between optional 'Legal' statutes and 'Lawful' common law requirements which are not optional and apply to us all. In order for the Police officer to extract money from the public, it is essential that the officer persuades the person into representing and taking responsibility for the legal fiction of the same name. His first attempt at establishing authority over you is to ask for your name. This is not an innocent question. There are many legalese questions designed to trap you into contractually representing the legal fiction, the officer may ask "Do you understand", in legalese terms he is trying to establish authority by getting you to stand under his official capacity. There are many web sites dedicated to this and go into specific details on how to avoid the many pitfalls, I will only give a brief outline here. An offence under common law has only been committed if there is a victim; someone killed or injured; someone who has had possessions damaged, or stolen; or someone who has been defrauded. If the police officer continues pushing you to agree to pay his corporate fine, then a good question to ask might be "who is the victim?", or "what is the charge, am I free to go?". The police officer now has a problem because you have not agreed to represent your legal fiction, binding yourself to his legal statutes. By not being aggressive or offensive, you have to be very careful not to fall under his legalese traps otherwise you become subject to his legal not lawful authority. It is all a big game carefully crafted in order to extract your wealth in a perfectly "legal" way.

Modern Police Force

Most governments are now corporations; we essentially live within a huge corporation. Behind the scenes the global corporate control system is co-owned either at board level or at shareholder level. It could be argued that through co-ownership of all the key corporations, that the entire global structure is one giant corporation. The owners of which are likely to be the same group who own and control the major private central banks. It has become virtually impossible to live a life on this planet without having some form of corporation imposing its will upon you. The course and direction of human evolvement is now more or less in the hands of these giant interlocking entities. Through the implementation of new legislation and corporate procedures, insurance requirements and media manipulation humanity is programmed to compete against one another for the best deck chair with the best view on the Titanic, wilfully ignorant and oblivious to the direction the ship is heading. Working hard to stoke the engines and maintain a well-oiled machine, this ship will go in one direction, the direction of greater corporate control and power consolidation into fewer hands. The personality of the corporation is that of a psychopath, having no emotion or empathy. The corporate machine is a cold calculating one, it makes decisions that solely pay homage to the bottom dollar, the wellbeing and needs of the human race coming up a distant second - if at all.

PSYCHOPATHS	CORPORATIONS
Callous disregard for the feelings of others	✓
Incapacity to maintain enduring relationships	✓
Reckless disregard for the safety of others	✓
Deceitfulness, repeated lying and conniving others for profit	✓
Incapacity to experience guilt	✓
Failure to conform to social norms with respect to lawful behaviors	✓

The government corporation is most definitely psychopathic in nature, attracting power hungry psychopathic personalities into its midst. Power corrupts and absolute power corrupts absolutely. The ambition of the government corporation is to advance the globalisation agenda at the expense of sovereign nation states and the wishes of its people. **"They will have globalisation whether they like it or not"**. The government corporation will use all force necessary to achieve its corporate objectives, sometimes deceiving its population and its young men into fighting a righteous and noble fight. Most people in the west go to work daily for some form of corporation, devoting their minds, bodies and souls to what they believe to be progress. Small business, sole traders and family businesses are straining under the effects of the monopolistic corporate monsters growing up around them. Corporate colleges and universities prepare and encourage each new generation to participate in this perpetual New Age corporate collective.

Psychopathic disconnect

There are, in simplistic terms, two main types of psychopathy, the natural psychopath and the environmental psychopathic persona. As mentioned in chapter 2, a balanced individual is one who possesses good communication within all three realms of consciousness, the focal, sub and higher mind/Logos. The psychopath on the other hand has a flaw in the connection to higher mind, it is often said that they have no soul. All they have is the untethered focal and subconscious, with an inability to self-regulate through universal law which comes from the higher mind connection to the Logos, a regulating mechanism which governs the majority of those who are considered as decent people. Furthermore, like the psychopath the corporation's externally projected image becomes paramount, its sub-conscious workings of staff menders and policy, are expected to leave their connection to universal higher consciousness at home along with their coordinates relating to common decency.

Having the status of a person, the corporation falls within the parameters of a natural psychopath. The other aspect here, also mentioned in chapter 2, is that within a collective environment you generally take on the persona of the people and environment you associate with. This creates the type 2 psychopath, the environmental psychopathic persona. People who are not generally considered to be natural psychopaths but become heavily influenced by their peers and their environment to behave in a psychopathic manner, a good example of this would be the armed forces or the police force.

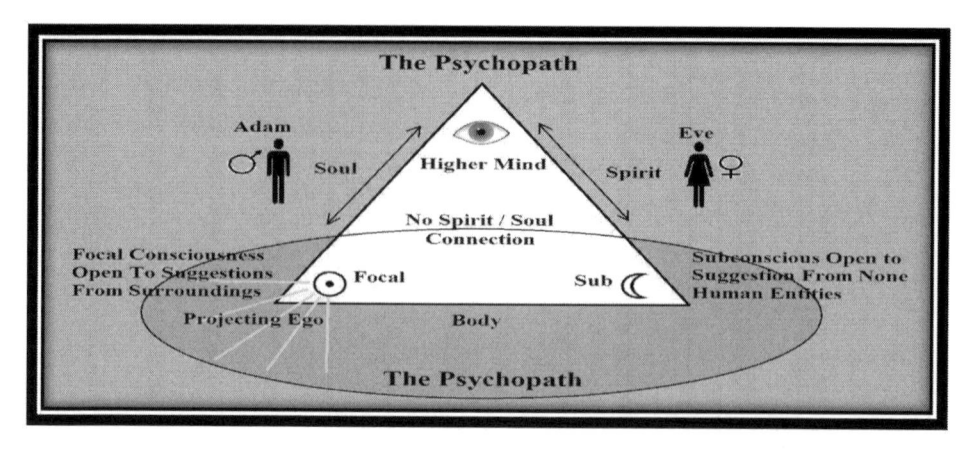

The Psychopath

Adam — Soul — Higher Mind — Spirit — Eve

No Spirit / Soul Connection

Focal Consciousness Open To Suggestions From Surroundings — Focal — Sub — Subconscious Open to Suggestion From Non Human Entities

Projecting Ego — Body

The Psychopath

It has been suggested in some ancient writings that this void, or lack of connection to the higher mind allows the parasitic mind to be influenced by outside energies, not always of a human nature and not always with our best interests at heart. Our ancestors understood the dangers associated with psychopaths, shamans were given the task of identifying them at an early age, to prevent these individuals gaining positions of power within the community. They would either make everyone aware or remove them permanently through some lethal endeavour. In our modern Plutocratic Corporatocracy, we have created the perfect environment for the natural psychopath to thrive, gaining power, as they ascend, up the ranks of the corporations. They sit comfortably and feel at home in the psychopathic environment of these large corporations, influencing all those around them into behaving in a similar fashion. People with a balanced connection to source may feel a conflict of interest in such an environment, their healthy connection to the higher mind should trigger their conscience to move away from this unhealthy situation. If they decide to stay they will be swimming against the tide emotionally, running the risk of a mental breakdown.

Large corporations seek out functioning psychopaths to work within the higher levels of its structure. These people are able to detach themselves from humanity and push the interests of the psychopathic corporation to the next level. They can order the deaths of thousands without feeling any adverse emotions while continuing in their quest for narcissistic perfection. Our history is full of these types of people, once they reach the top in government, gaining total power, people die, they die in the millions, this is known, in academia, as democide (the murder of any person or people by their government).

Democide

The number one cause of unnatural deaths on the planet over the past 120 years is known as democide, when your government kills you. It is estimated that over 260,000,000 unarmed civilians have died at the hands of psychopathic, untamed, out of control governments from the beginning of the 20th century, to the present. If you add military deaths to this calculation the number is a staggering 350,000,000 people murdered in this way.[6]

DEATHS BY DEMOCIDE FROM 1900 TO TODAY		
CHINA	1949-87	76,702,000
USSR	1917-87	61,911,000
COMBINED WESTERN COLONIALSIM	-	50,000,000
GERMANY	1933-45	20,946,000
JAPAN	1936-45	5,946,000
CHINA	1923-48	3,468,000
CAMBODIA	1975-79	2,035,000
TURKEY	1909-18	1,883,000
VIETNAM	1945-87	1,670,000
POLAND	1945-48	1,585,000
PAKISTAN	1958-87	1,503,000
YOGOSLAVIA	1944-87	1,072,000
NORTH KOREA	1948-87	1,663,000
MEXICO	1900-20	1,417,000
RUSSIA	1900-17	1,072,000
TOTAL CIVILIAN DEATHS		**260,000,000**
TOTAL DEATHS WITH MILITARY		**350,000,000**

The next level of global control and dominance is likely to have low tolerance for dissent, as before, any new form of global government, unchecked could find new ways to implement democide on its unarmed and unsuspecting populations. This time it can be subtle, with the desire to take full control over all aspects of life and society, working towards a future of sustainable development (Agenda 21),[7] they want global governance, a unified global economic system, a global army to quash dissent and a reduction in population to a sustainable level by phasing out, what some describe as, "**useless eaters**". In June 1979, a monument was erected in Elbert County, Georgia, in the United States by unknown persons, it supports this idea of sustainable development and depopulation, known as the Georgia Guidestones, a granite monument conveying a message, a set of 10 guidelines in 8 modern languages and 4 ancient languages. Today's global population is approximately 7.125 billion people; the proposal is to reduce this down to a mere 500 million, a staggering 93% reduction.

The Georgia Guidestones

Different forms of government

There are many different types of governance, many different names for various levels of subordination under a command and control structure, simplified, it is the amount of power the control system has over the individual that differs. Only two forms of governance exist in a practical sense, they are oligarchy, ruled by a few; or a republic, ruled by law. Dictatorship or monarch, ruled by one, is not a genuine reality, as the ruler always has either their councils or bureaucrats to dispense power, making them essentially an oligarchy. Democracy the rule of the majority or mob rule is also a flawed conception. The problem with it is that the minds of the majority can be manipulated to overrule the freedoms of the few, it is essentially two wolves and one sheep voting on what is for dinner. The founding fathers of America knew history, and the pitfalls associated with a democracy, that is why they chose to be a republic.

"I do not say that democracy has been more pernicious on the whole, and in the long run, than monarchy or aristocracy. Democracy has never been and never can be so durable as aristocracy or monarchy; but while it lasts, it is more bloody than either. ... Remember, democracy never lasts long. It soon wastes, exhausts, and murders itself. There never was a democracy yet that did not commit suicide. It is in vain to say that democracy is less vain, less proud, less selfish, less ambitious, or less avaricious than aristocracy or monarchy. It is not true, in fact, and nowhere appears in history. Those passions are the same in all men, under all forms of simple government, and when unchecked, produce the same effects of fraud, violence, and cruelty. When clear prospects are opened before vanity, pride, avarice, or ambition, for their easy gratification, it is hard for the most considerate philosophers and the most conscientious moralists to resist the temptation. Individuals have conquered themselves. Nations and large bodies of men, never." - John Adams[8]

"It has been observed that a pure democracy if it were practicable would be the most perfect government. Experience has proved that no position is more false than this. The ancient democracies in which the people themselves deliberated never possessed one good feature of government. Their very character was tyranny; their figure deformity." - Alexander Hamilton[9]

Throughout history honest forms of democracy don't last long, they are soon swallowed up by powerful interests and turn quickly into an oligarchy. For this reason, it can never be a sustainable option for a stable government. It should also be noted here that the Romans began as a republic with twelve tablets of Roman law which limited government power, leaving the people alone to be productive. As time went by the Romans moved towards a democracy, forgetting its essence of freedom and its proper limitation of government. They quickly went from a democracy to an oligarchy, ruled by a succession of Caesars, eventually collapsing under the weight of corruption and debt.

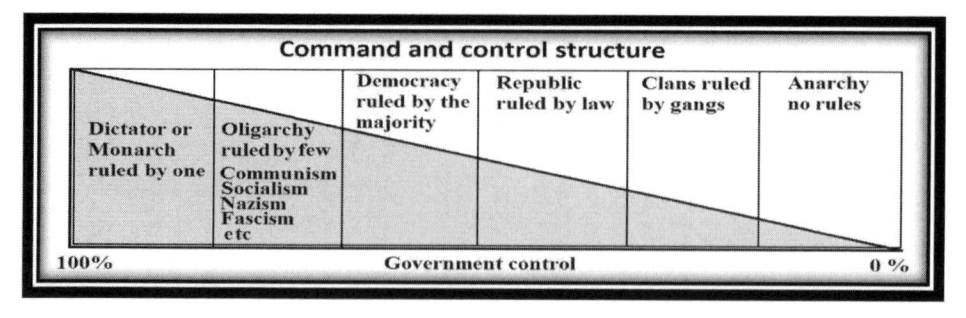

Command and control structure					
Dictator or Monarch ruled by one	Oligarchy ruled by few Communism Socialism Nazism Fascism etc	Democracy ruled by the majority	Republic ruled by law	Clans ruled by gangs	Anarchy no rules
100%		Government control			0 %

A republic is a system based on law, a law which limits the power of government to leave the people alone to pursue life, liberty and happiness. The superior aspect of a republic is its ability to protect the rights of minorities who wish to live outside the social norms of the majority, creating a tolerant harmonious social variety of peoples. The United States was set up as a republic not as a democracy, to protect the rights of all its citizens. The word democracy does not appear in the bill of rights or the constitution. The founders studied history and did all they could to keep America from becoming a democracy. It is ironic, now that the corporations have taken over, that they wave the banner of democracy, their version of democracy. It is really another form of oligarchy, corporate oligarchy with a psychopathic nature spreading its tentacles all over the globe. Anarchy cannot be counted for it is also another temporary measure, with everyone having to arm themselves to protect what they have from each other, without law there can be no freedom. The vacuum of power is soon replaced by another form of control. In practical terms that leaves only two main systems of government, a republic or an oligarchy; it is up to us which one we choose. How free do you want to be?

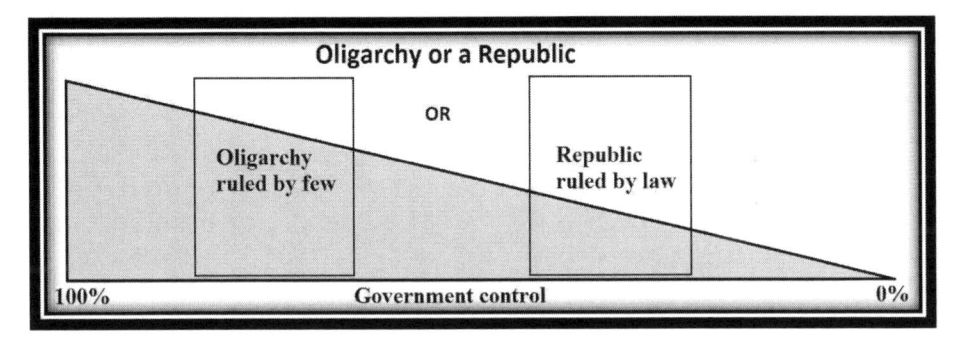

Oligarchy or a Republic

OR

Oligarchy ruled by few

Republic ruled by law

100%   Government control   0%

Some famous quotes about democracy:[10]

"**The best argument against democracy is a five-minute conversation with the average voter.**"- Winston Churchill

"**The difference between a democracy and a dictatorship is that in a democracy you vote first and take orders later; in a dictatorship, you don't have to waste your time voting.**"- Charles Bukowski

"**Dictatorship naturally arises out of democracy, and the most aggravated form of tyranny and slavery out of the most extreme liberty.**" -Plato

"**Democracy is the road to socialism.**" -Karl Marx

"**The tyranny of a prince in an oligarchy is not so dangerous to the public welfare as the apathy of a citizen in a democracy.**" -Charles de Montesquieu

"**Democracy is a pathetic belief in the collective wisdom of individual ignorance.**" -H. L. Mencken

"**Propaganda is to a democracy what the bludgeon is to a totalitarian state**". -Noam Chomsky

The corporations cannot expand to the extent that we see today under a republic, the strict limitations on adverse power over the people is not advantageous to them. The corporations can thrive within a democracy and more so under an oligarchic democracy. This according to Franklin D Roosevelt is corporate fascism. The control system works for and perpetuates its system of control, fiercely gaining more power and more resources, ultimately enslaving and diminishing the freedoms of the individuals within its grasp. We now operate under a tiered system, at the top there is a small group of wealthy families, who own all the major banks and corporations, controlling humanity through mechanisms of managed scarcity, with economic models requiring permanent growth and endless consumption. They employ vast armies of people to harvest the earth's natural resources, who slave in factories to produce inferior products which break once out of guarantee. This built in life obsolescence, designed to keep demand up, will eventually turn the whole planet into one giant rubbish dump. Participants of this system are so busy running on the tread mill, devoting their time and energy, unknowingly keeping the rest of their fellow humanity in servitude. On the whole, they are wilfully unaware that they are feeding a beast which will eventually devour them.

Obsolescence

There are three main ways corporations stimulate the demand for their products, which ensure sustainable factory commitments and growth into the future. Design, pricing and built in obsolescence, all used to gain market share and seduce consumers into buying things they don't need, to impress people they don't know, with money they don't have, to prop up an artificially created debt based monetary system that creates money out of thin air, pushing more debt onto the shoulders of each new generation. Planned obsolescence is a subtle, secret mechanism at the heart of the modern consumer society. In the early part of the 20th century manufacturers took greater pride in their products, offering goods which would last, even outliving the consumers who purchased them. The only drawback was once most customers had made the first purchase, they had no reason to purchase again. After the initial brand release the factories became idle as demand dropped, at this time light bulbs where being produced which could last 5,000 hrs or more. Every year a fire station in Livermore, California celebrates the birthday of one of its light bulbs. Invented by Adolphe Chaillet, the bulb has been burning continuously since 1901, a design certainly made to last. Edison's first commercial bulb went on sale lasting on average 1500 hrs. By the mid 1920s, light bulbs were being made to last a good 2500 hrs. In the winter of 1924, the world's bulb manufacturers came together to form a cartel. Each member had strict guidelines to produce inferior bulbs, lasting no more than 1000 hrs. Any member found producing better bulbs would incur a fine. By the 1940s the new standard became 1000 hrs, effectively conning the consumer and artificially stimulating demand for light bulbs. Planned obsolescence was born. Many inventors have filed patents for bulbs which purport to last a staggering 100,000 hrs, but the power of the corporate cartels made sure these products would not reach the general market. Today most products are designed with obsolescence in mind, targeting a price range, where the consumers expect only a limited life's usage. This keeps the factories full, full of people devoting their precious lives on churning out garbage products that devour natural resources, which eventually end up in the back yard of some third world country, designated to become the world's global rubbish dump.

1901 Lightbulb, Rubbish Dump, Sweatshops

During the middle of the last century, the USSR was governed differently, centrally planned by the state, the government stipulated that all white goods (fridges and washing machines) should last a minimum of 25 years. It doesn't take much effort to produce good products. The modern western corporate manufacturing system has become psychopathic, yet people participate en masse, underpinning its existence and devoting their life's purpose to promoting this expansion. Other mechanisms at the corporation's disposal, are designed to seduce the minds of the consumer, stimulating their desire to want more and to want the latest, this is achieved through new fashions and escalating specifications. Even though planned obsolescence may be attached to a product, it is in the interest of the manufacturing corporation to tempt the consumer into parting with their existing functional goods and money in exchange for the latest brand or design. All the large corporations interlock to form a powerful array of control and influence, tweaking policy throughout the system, enhancing their agenda and maximising profits. With subtle techniques of hypnotic suggestion, aided by the mainstream media, advertising and through perverted social expectations, they stimulate the consumers inferiority complex, installed into them by their corporate upbringing. This is a never-ending cycle; there is always a new model or a new brand to pursue. The illusion of freedom and happiness through unlimited consumption has been set in the focal and subconscious minds of the citizens of the developed west over three generations, creating nations of shallow, materialistic, unsatisfied debt slaves, obsessed with out purchasing their friends and neighbours with the latest tat.

From September 1st 2012 a push was made by many governments to ban the sale of the old style incandescent light bulbs, in favour of what they call energy efficient lighting or eco friendly. The definition of eco-friendly is "not harmful to the environment". These governments argue that the new light bulbs will dramatically reduce your energy bills and greenhouse gas emissions, which they say is linked to manmade global warming. The bulbs are purported to last up to 10 times longer than its traditional counterpart. This, of course, is because all incandescent bulbs where made to break by the bulb cartels back in the 1920s, so we can't use that as a reason for the change. The amount of energy required to produce these new bulbs during the manufacturing process is vastly greater than the traditional incandescent bulb, with over 30 separate electronic components and a glass tube that contains a cocktail of toxic carcinogenic chemicals including mercury. Some of these toxins are emitted even during normal use. How they can say this is eco-friendly is beyond me. It must be corporate governmental double speak for an agenda they are keeping to themselves. Although there is a saving on the running costs, with less than half the required power consumption, many people have reported serious health problems which they believe to be caused by these CFL (compact fluorescent lights). If one of these toxic bulbs breaks in your home, the official recommendation by the Federal Environment Agency is to evacuate your home for at least 15 minutes, leaving all the windows open and turning off the heating. It is estimated that only 10% of these CFL bulbs are disposed of in the proper recommended fashion, leaving the other 90% to pollute and toxify waste dumps and other areas of the environment in which they end up, certainly not eco-friendly in my mind. The CFL light bulb fiasco is another example of corporations infiltrating policy makers to legislate in favour of corporate interests. It's no surprise that the light bulb cartel, 80 years later positioned themselves amongst the gears of the European Union, gaining a tactical advantage and promoting their monopoly. In a rush to push forward this new legislation, the European commission failed to carry out proper trials and tests prior to the new rules becoming law. The lack of tests, ensuring the safety of these new bulbs, exposes the real balance of power throughout this new European community, putting the interests of the corporations before that of the citizens.[11]

The perfect consumer

In a global corporatocracy, the will and ambitions of the corporation become the driving force behind future global policy. The flesh and blood human becomes subordinate to the corporate legal fiction, which he is expected to devote his life representing. With a rapacious desire of the corporations to expand, they have a need to be free from hindrance of laws and cohesive human collectives. The perfect environment for the untamed, monopolistic control of the corporation is one full of fragmented individual consumers, resonating the psychopathic frequency of the corporation, influencing a new form of collective consciousness. One reason for the rapid push for global integration is to destabilise cultures and eliminate national identity. A single individual is much easier to control and influence, especially if they are not and don't feel part of a collective. An individual through hypnotic suggestion and subliminal messaging can be made to do and want just about anything. A strong collective consciousness has the power to resist this influence. The modern forced integration policy, which has been going on for a few decades, is gaining momentum. They say they want multiculturalism, but that already existed, the world was full of a multitude of independent cultures. The term multiculturalism is a misnomer; it is another disguise for the real agenda. They are trying to produce a global monoculture.

A culture is a people with a certain way of thinking, behaving, working, dressing etc. they have their own traditions, language and unique identity. To take them away from their culture is to dilute and break their tie to that collective. If you shake the planet up like a jar of multi coloured marbles you end up with a mass of individuals which produces a monoculture. Those traditional collective communities who shared the same unique values and identities would no longer exist. This whole monoculture project is for the benefit of the corporations, it is not designed to benefit the community or the individual.

The nature of the new corporate educational system is to churn out effective participants in this global corporate game of consumption. They graduate with all the right degrees of corporate compatibility, unaware of the mechanisms in place controlling them. Given false coordinates, to mislead and confuse, wrapped up in debt, they eagerly position themselves as willing servants to their new corporate masters.

The corporate persona

To resonate and fit in line with the perceived expectation of a corporate employee, the individuals will slowly develop a corporate personality or persona. Similar to an actor when playing a role, their focal conscious expression takes on a serious saturnian energetic overtone, aligning themselves with the corporate identity. Along with the persona comes an array of attached mannerisms, such as corporate speech, corporate movements, corporate twitches, laughs, coughs and other bizarre idiosyncratic expressions. The corporate persona can become a stressful act running averse to one's natural behaviour. With the evolution of technology, the corporate persona has many new accessories to lean on and hide behind, while pursuing the corporate agenda. To become an accepted member of the corporate club an individual finds it necessary to wear the appropriate attire. Suits and uniforms have always been used as a motivating tool, enabling the individual to perform as expected within the frequency range of corporate activities. Once inside the suit or uniform, with the business card and identity tag, an air of pseudo confidence will transform a person, the face and mannerisms will change, activating pre-programmed beliefs of seriousness, expressing their idea of how a person should behave when working as part of the corporate control system. The female species have their own brand of corporate persona, along with hair style, make up, noisy shoes, power suits and matching hand bags, locking them into saturnine frequencies which help them produce the required corporate results. Most of these people would find it virtually impossible to fulfil the corporate requirements dressed in just their underpants or an orange robe worn by Buddhist monks. The police use the uniform to great effect, dark hats, helmets and accessories, resonating a serious and authoritarian manner, keeping the line of division firmly on the side of the policy enforces. To prove your obedience to the corporate control system, it is generally expected that a collar and tie is worn. A collar is used to shackle a slave and also during perverted sexual S&M role play. The collar is worn by the slave or gimp to show his submissive rank. The tie is also expected to be worn when taking on the corporate persona, symbolising your physical tie to your collar and shackled subordination. If these obedient corporate slaves ever feel the need to express themselves and be creative, they are free to choose more than one type of knot that expresses their devotion to their chosen servitude.

Collar & Tie

Many people with rebellious natures will struggle to fit into and accept this type of role, instead they adopt an anti-corporate persona which can be just as artificial and comes with its own mixed bag of colourful expressions. Referred to by the corporatists as bums, losers, hippies, New Age, etc. some of them will go to extraordinary lengths when disassociating and identifying themselves as corporate opposites.

As the control system develops, gaining more power and influence, members of the community will take on some form of corporate persona, depending upon their own unique set of circumstances. People will identify themselves with a pre-programmed belief of how specific groups behave, the doctor, the builder, the lawyer and the policeman, each one distinguishable from years of media insinuation and categorisation. A suggestive belief of how each form of corporate persona is to conduct themselves within society. If all forms of organisation and control are removed, the individual loses the artificial benchmark of the corporate role model, and when left, with only themselves to rely on, without external distractions; they should develop their own uniqueness, finding equilibrium and clarity within all realms of consciousness.

Professional arrogance is a symptom of narrowing one's self to the corporate persona. Advancing so far up the corporate sphincter, the individual can develop blind arrogance within their chosen field or profession. Unwilling and sometimes unable to see outside the professional prison they build for themselves, they defend the corporate position in a somewhat deluded and arrogant manner. An example of this would be the doctor who refuses to acknowledge any alternatives which do not run in line with his adopted version of medicine, handed down to him by big pharma and the established medical corporations. No matter how tyrannical the control system becomes, there will always be a percentage of people willing to represent the corporate power structure at any cost, power junkies. This is one reason why psychopaths are attracted to corporations, not only does the environment resonate with the soulless personality of the psychopath; it also gives them an identity and structure to hide behind. Once in the corporate persona, a normal and balanced individual can be persuaded to carry out some of the most extreme acts of psychopathy. In a military role, murder and violence become common place. Abuse, brutality and prejudice can be seen within many police forces. In high finance and commerce throughout the city, economic exploitation is generally expected. All physical expressions of psychopathic, corporate and saturnine energy, distorting the natural equilibrium and balance within the collective consciousness. Corporations have convinced many people that the only way to be attractive to others is through branded labels, cosmetics and surgical procedures, they fail to mention the traditional method of smiling, even the most unattractive people become pleasing to the eye when they smile.

The United States Constitution

We the People of the United States, in order to form a more perfect union, establish justice, insure domestic tranquility, provide for the common defence, promote the general welfare, and secure the Blessings of Liberty to ourselves and our Posterity, do ordain and establish this Constitution for the United States of America.

Article 1.

Section 1. All legislative Powers herein granted shall be vested in a Congress of the United States, which shall consist of a Senate and House of Representatives.

New Global Constitution

We the corporations of the planet, in order to form a more perfect union, establish jurisdiction, insure domestic obedience, provide for the common defence, promote the general enslavement of humanity and secure the blessings of corporate expansion and their prosperity, do ordain and establish this constitution for the planetary global union.

Bound sticks with axe head, fasces symbol for fascism

Notes for chapter 5

(1) Franklin D Roosevelt, speech on April 29th 1938, Message to Congress.
http://en.wikiquote.org/wiki/Franklin_D._Roosevelt

(2) Your Strawman, Website, http://www.yourstrawman.com/

(3) Courts, Names and the Cestui Que Vie Trust, Dec 8th 2013,
http://truthseeker1313.com/2013/12/08/courts-names-and-the-cestui-que-vie-trust/

(4) Major General Smedly Butler, War Is A Racket, 1935,
http://en.wikipedia.org/wiki/War_Is_a_Racket

(5) Roger Hayes, Court testimony, David Icke's forum, 15,2,2011
http://www.davidicke.com/forum/showthread.php?t=158003

(6) Alex Jones, Democide, blueprint of mad men, 2012,
https://www.youtube.com/watch?v=xCTlPqA9-wQ

(7) Agenda 21, United Nations earth summit conference, 1992,
http://en.wikipedia.org/wiki/Agenda_21

(8) John Adams, Founding father of America, The Letters of John and Abigail Adams Quotes,
http://www.goodreads.com/work/quotes/17049308-the-letters-of-john-and-abigail-adams

(9) Alexander Hamilton, 1787-06-26, Quote, http://en.wikiquote.org/wiki/Democracy

(10) Democracy quotes, http://www.brainyquote.com/quotes/keywords/democracy.html

(11) Toxic Light, The dark side of energy saving bulbs. 2012
https://www.youtube.com/watch?v=x0x3rbHFwQU

Chapter 6. The British Empire

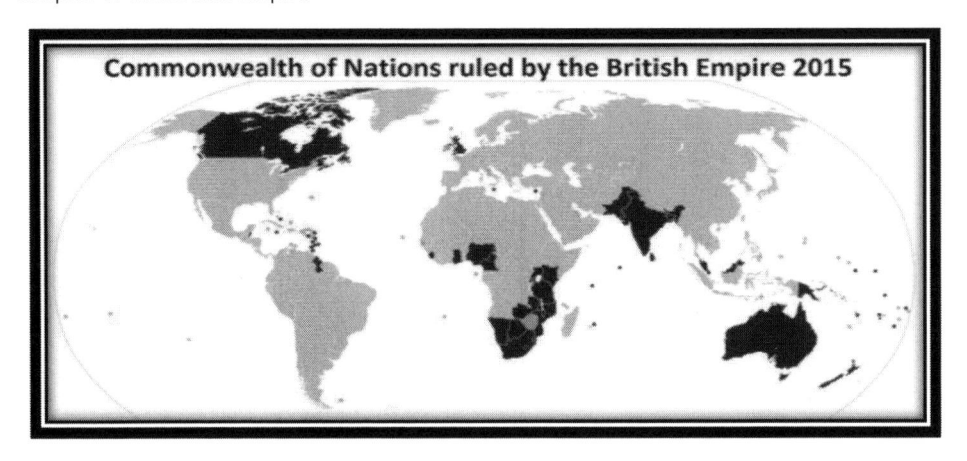

Commonwealth of Nations ruled by the British Empire 2015

The British Empire, as most people traditionally view it, evolved out of the ancient empires of Greece, Egypt and Rome, systems of command and control imposed from hierarchies of influential elitists. The controlling powers and organisations behind these systems don't always disappear; they change with the times, evolve and relocate, sometimes going underground. Empires rise and fall, drawn through time on an ocean of changing human consciousness, this one is no different, it eventually found itself a safe haven, an Island protected on all sides by water.

The British Empire was the largest empire the modern world had ever seen. From the British Isles in Northern Europe, the United Kingdom ruled over its dominions, colonies, protectorates and mandates, at its peak, covering 1/4 of the Earth's land mass, 458 million people, 1/3 of the human population. From the early days of Henry VIII, his ambitions and advancements in ship design, allowed for a vast armada of floating gun decks and war ships to be produced, propelling England forward as the world's dominant marine power, eventually ruling the waves. His ambitions became an enormous strain on the financial resources of the monarch, which persuaded him to bring usury back with the Act of 1545; this allowed him to borrow what he needed for empire building. Before seeing the full benefits of his imperialistic dream, Henry's appetites got the better of him, dying bloated and overweight in 1547. By the mid-18th century the empire had grown, controlling parts of India, Africa, the West Indies and North America. This first phase of empire was forged from military exploits and expeditions, the control of trade routes and merchants drove it forward, developing vast networks of commercial activity which helped finance even greater expansion all over the known world. This phase was challenged during George III rule (1760-1820), when the American colonies revolted against the strict exploits and controls of British corporations. The Colonies temporarily freed themselves in 1776 with their revolutionary war for independence, where a new constitution and bill of rights emerged. George was also challenged in Europe after the French revolution by Napoleon, who by 1812 had most of Europe under his control. All this pressure against the empire took its toll on the King, by 1815, George III had become gripped by insanity, unable to tie his own shoe laces, he became just an acting figure head, aimlessly wandering the corridors of Windsor Castle, the head of what had now become a world super power. To the policy makers, business expansion and the control of trade became priority. The funding and arming of antagonists and revolutionaries did not worry the empire, with their alliances and resources they only saw opportunity in provoking division. No single country could match up to the empires ability to restrain new tyrants. They could lose the odd battle, but in the end, would win the war. Always thinking ahead, they didn't care how many were killed, what was destroyed and how long it took. They always had a contingency plan for a new order out of chaos, and their version of corporate order came from the entangled mess and chaos they helped to ferment. After the American Revolutionary War, an atmosphere of independent republicanism began to spread unsettling many aristocrats in England, but the elite had a plan, a plan to use any difficulty to their advantage.

Napoleon

The British Empire's recipe for ruling was to divide and conquer, to create false issues, arouse petty passions and stimulate base instincts, steering people in the direction required for imperialism. The British were masters in the art of diplomacy and secret warfare, their favourite tactic was to get everyone fighting amongst themselves through rival factions, revolts, provocateurs, psyops, coups and manufactured enemies, they would light multiple touch papers and stand back, watching from the shores of their well-defended island. They would wait until all sides had exhausted themselves, physically and financially, then send in their armies, representatives and diplomats to negotiate solutions that favoured the advancement of their own control and power. They will finance tyrants, dictators, emperors and kings, as long as the tyrant poses no threat to the British Isles, the empire will continue to do business, supporting useful idiots who do the fighting for them, The British will pick their moment, and when the time is right, send in their troops to slay the dragon. The power of the empire rests in the hands of a relatively small but powerful group, wealthy influential families setting the direction for future conquests. Its subjects, servants, merchants and mercenaries are the blood circulating in the veins of a beast, feeding it as they go about their daily lives, a beast born from the will of a privileged few who control the many. During the American revolution of independence, Britain persisted in asking Catherine the Great of Russia for assistance. She was not impressed by the British conduct during the Seven Years War (1754- 1763), during which she witnessed Britain discreetly exit the conflict leaving Russia's Prussian allies vulnerable to defeat. Catherine considered these efforts disloyal; she became concerned and saw Britain as an untrustworthy ally. She was determined to stay officially neutral in this new conflict, but continued to trade with the colonies believing that an independent America would be ideal for future Russian business interests. With America free from Britain the empire would have to turn to other countries like Russia for necessary supplies and resources. Britain, at its greatest time of need, saw Russia's position as a humiliating stab in the back. Now the empire was storing up enemies all across the known world. Louis XVI of France (1774 - 1792) had also allied with the independent United States against the British, partially motivated by revenge for losses during the Seven Years' War; the French had been secretly supplying the United States from 1775. The financial and military aid made by France was a major contributing factor for America's victory against the British. George III was not too happy with either Louis XVI or Catherine the Great and by 1778 found himself in a global war with very few allies. Britain had to figure out a way of getting the upper hand, manipulating events which would see their rivals fighting amongst themselves, weakening each other before a final British victory. After the American Revolution of 1776, the defeated British were keen to quash further ambitions of rebellion towards freedom, independence and republicanism, revolution was in the air and also in the minds of the collective consciousness. The British elite were not enamoured by the spread of independence, fearing a loss to their positions and prestige, especially if it came to the shores of their island. The British establishment considered a revolution in Europe beneficial in destabilising enemy powers and getting even with Louis XVI and the Russians. The French revolution of 1789 went on for approximately ten years, abolishing feudalism and dismantling the old rule from the privileged classes' along with the Catholic Church. The young French republic was plagued with various difficulties, the new administration known as the Directory found itself swamped by financial instability, suspended elections and corruption accusations. It eventually collapsed in a coup led by Napoleon Bonaparte, who became a useful tool in some ways for the British. If Napoleon had ambitions to march across Europe, exposing this fragile republic to new enemies and debt, weakening Russia, Prussia and Austria in the process, then the British, from their well-defended island, would sit back and watch the spectacle. Financed by British owned banks and money from the Louisiana Purchase, Napoleon went on the rampage.[5] By 1812 he had control of most of Europe. The British had many contingencies in place, options available when restraining their new tyrant, as long as they controlled the seas they could control the game, they would make new allies, drawing other nations into fighting when and where necessary, weakening Napoleon and everyone else, eventually creating an opportunity for the British to play their final hand in his defeat.

By placing a tarantula in your enemy's bed, does not mean you have a love for tarantulas.

Napoleon was born on August 15th 1769 on the island of Corsica, six months after the French invasion which toppled the independent republic run by Pasquale Paoli. Corsica was now a province of the French Empire, ruled by Louis XV, and the richest country in Europe. The small island of Corsica had been heavily influenced by Britain, although there was no formal alliance, Britain historically supported the Corsican government. During the invasion, the Corsican resistance put up a brave fight but with few men and the lack of credible help from the British, they eventually fell.

"I was born when Corsica was perishing. Thirty thousand Frenchmen spewed on to our shores, drowning the throne of liberty in waves of blood... The cries of the dying, the groans of the oppressed and tears of despair surrounded my cradle from the hour of my birth." -Purported to be from Napoleon

Napoleon's father Letizia worked as a representative of the Corsican government, he moved to France and in 1778 secured a place for Napoleon at the Royal Military College, where he enrolled at the age of 9. He moved over to the Royal Military Academy in Paris when he was 15, a finishing school which turned officers into gentlemen, only to begin his training as a soldier at 16. On July 14th 1789 Paris erupted into riots, the start of a ten-year period of unrest, the revolution had begun. After his training at the age of 23, he went back to Corsica and threw himself into politics, hoping to join forces with his childhood hero Pasquale Paoli, who was still in control of the Corsican government. Paoli didn't trust this young upstart and they were soon at war with each other. After a brief skirmish in which Napoleon was defeated, Paoli chose to banish him from his home Island forever. On 10th June 1793, he sailed to France with his widowed mother, brothers and sisters. They were now a refugee family. Paris was still in turmoil, the revolutionaries had executed King Louis XVI back in January, beheading him with a guillotine. Still eager to purge France of elitist parasites the revolutionaries continued to look for more heads to roll. Napoleon, back in France was reinstated in the army as an artillery captain; he was sent on his first active mission, at the seaport town of Toulon, south of France. It was here Napoleon's abilities were noticed; his input in throwing out the British fleet secured him a promotion to Brigadier General.

Back in Paris on October 5th 1795 crowds of Parisians stormed onto the streets along with national guardsmen determined to restore the monarchy. The government called on Napoleon to repel the attackers, with his unit he turned his cannons on the approaching crowd opened fire and blew them to pieces. Three weeks later, at the age of 26, he was promoted to General and Commander for the Army of the Interior. After a quick marriage to his wife Josephine, Napoleon was sent to the Italian Alps where he was given the job of supreme commander of all French forces throughout Italy; his brief was to challenge the Austrian Empire and their Italian allies. Even though he was a general, he had never commanded an army before. As soon as he arrived his subordinates knew from his demeanour exactly who was in control, one of his generals was reported to have said, "**I don't know why but the little bastard scares me**".

By 1797 he had taken Italy and finished off Austria, he showed no mercy. After a brief rest back in France, Napoleon was sent to Egypt where he was to create problems for the British by disrupting their trade routes. The British were quite happy to see this new general's exploits as long as he didn't cause them any problems. Napoleon sailed to Egypt, taking Malta along the way, eventually anchoring his ships 20 miles north of Alexandria and on July 1st 1798 he took the city with minimal effort. Organising his troops, he then marched onto Cairo to face 21,000 Mamluks in the Battle of the Pyramids. At the battle Napoleon grouped his men into giant impregnable military squares, protecting themselves from the Mamluks and their Cavalry, which came at the French from all directions. Over 6,000 Egyptians died to only 300 French, the battle was a huge success for Napoleon. While the French were enjoying their new conquest in Cairo, the British decided to act against this new upstart to protect trading interests. The empire sent the British fleet to Egypt under the command of Lord Horatio Nelson. On August 1st Nelson spotted the French fleet anchored in Aboukir Bay and ordered an immediate attack. Splitting his ships into two divisions, Nelson annihilated Napoleons fleet. From the 17 ships engaged only 4 escaped, the rest became a mixture of splinters and drift wood, putting a temporary end to Napoleons ambitions by trapping him and 35,000 French soldiers in Egypt.

On August 23, 1799, after more than a year in Egypt, exploring and conquering, Napoleon secretly set off for France, leaving 30,000 of his men behind. By October 9th he was back in Paris and within a month had seized power by controlling the French government. By the age of 33 he had become a King in all but name. Realising they had a loose cannon who had to be reined in, the British declared war on France on May 18th 1803. The plan of the British was to use diplomacy, creating allies against Napoleon, getting everyone else attacking and weakening him, making sure he didn't get a foothold on the British mainland, and when he is vulnerable they would go in for the kill.

On 2nd December 1804, in a ceremony at Notre Dame, attended by the Pope, Bonaparte was made Emperor of the French Empire. Britain's defence policy was to control the seas and dominate the oceans with the world's most powerful navy, destroying competition before it had the chance to challenge British supremacy. From the start of hostilities, Napoleon had wanted to invade the British Isles; he knew he needed a formidable fleet to smash the British Navy, which would open the conflict up for a future land invasion. For two years he had tried to assemble a combined Franco-Spanish fleet at the port of Cadiz, under a blockade imposed on him by the British. Napoleon had amassed 33 fighting vessels with a plan to break the blockade and sail them to the Caribbean where they would meet up with another fleet, on their return they would release ships at Brest, north west France, emerging from the blockade with superior numbers to smash the British fleet in the English Channel. Anticipating a move, a fleet of 27 British ships under the command of Admiral Nelson, sailed toward the 33 vessels trying to leave the blockade at Cadiz. They engaged at the Cape of Trafalgar, south of Cadiz. Nelson, the superior tactician went straight for the kill, destroying 2/3 of the enemy's fleet, losing his own life in the process by catching a bullet fired from the upper rigging of an enemy's ship. Even though he was killed he managed to keep his whole fleet intact. Britain was safe for the immediate future. Austria and Russia had now allied with Britain, who would watch from afar letting them do most of the land fighting. In 1907, after many battles, Napoleon met up with Alexander I of Russia at Tilsit where they struck up an alliance. The British Empire was becoming isolated, Napoleon had implemented an embargo on all British goods, known as the Continental System, the Berlin decree of 1806 forbid the import of British goods into all European countries allied with France. This was in response to the British naval blockade forbidding ships leaving French ports. The British would try to contain Napoleon by cutting off supplies reaching his troops. In 1808 Napoleon became suspicious of the Spanish for secretly trading with the British, he decided to invade. To Napoleon's surprise the Spanish fought the French vigorously in a protracted brutal rebellion lasting 5 years. Unable to break the Spanish, the war ate away at Napoleon's patience and resources. Britain still able to trade around the world was sustaining itself, but the blockade finally took its toll and decimated the Russian economy. Unable to survive, Russia started to trade once again with the British, turning its back on the Continental System. This Infuriated

Napoleon who drew up plans to take control of Russia. The British had passed new legislation requiring all neutral American ships wishing to trade with Napoleons Europe, first to stop off at England to pay a trade duty; this allowed the British to check all goods destined for Europe. During this period, the powerful British Navy had seized over 100 "enemy" ships, not only taking the goods but also the sailors, during the first years of the 19th century the British had Impressed over 6,000 men into its 120,000 ranks. Not only were the British impressing sailors and interfering with trade, they were also stirring up trouble with the native Indians, arming them against the Americans. This was too much for James Madison who took his grievances to congress. On June 18th 1812 America declared war on the British; this had now become a world war.

Back in Europe with over 600,000 men, the biggest army ever assembled, Napoleon crossed the Neman River and marched into Russia. Anticipating the war would be over in 3 weeks, he headed for Moscow, after 2 months of marching Napoleon had lost 150,000 men from exhaustion, sickness and desertion. The Russians had not yet engaged the approaching army, they sat back waiting, letting the elements do the fighting for them. By the end of the summer, at Borodino, the Russian troops finally faced the enemy. After fierce fighting, which lasted 9 hours, the Russians dispersed, leaving Napoleon proclaiming victory, he believed Moscow was his. A few days later he entered the capital; it was deserted. The Russians had set fire to the city and refused to surrender or negotiate. Napoleon wrote to the Tsar offering peace terms, but Alexander I ignored him. Bitterly disappointed Napoleon sat it out for 5 weeks, waiting for negotiations to commence. Unable to sustain his position, on October 19th Napoleon led his army out of Moscow, heading back to France. Three weeks later it began to snow, the Russian winter had come early. Over the next few weeks the temperature fell to a staggering -22. Their food ran low and his men were cold and exhausted, his army froze to death in the open fields, attacked on all sides by Cossacks as they retreated, the situation became hopeless. From the initial 600,000, only 93,000 men returned to France, all the rest were lost. This was to be the beginning of the end for the Emperor of France. Smelling blood, the British went in for the kill, allied themselves with his neighbours, they began the slow death of his grip on Europe. By the fall of 1813 Napoleon's armies were hopelessly outnumbered and in retreat all across Europe. In March of 1814 the French sat back and watched as Tsar Alexander I of Russia marched into Paris and forced Napoleon to renounce his throne. Pleased with the result, the British along with their allies, did not choose to kill Napoleon, instead they sent him into exile on the Mediterranean Island of Elba. Frustrated and still full of ambition, eleven months later, Napoleon recruited a small army for one last attempt at restoring his throne. He was finally defeated in June 1815 at the Battle of Waterloo by British and Prussian forces. In the decades of fighting an estimated 5 million had perished throughout the Napoleonic Wars. Once again Britain, partly responsible for financing navy and military support for much of the resistance Napoleon encountered, emerged as the world's most dominant power. Although the British loss of life was significant, considering it was at war with so many factions, it was mild compared to other participants. Britain had succeeded in either ruining its competitor's economies, or getting their neighbours to fight them. Finally, to ensure the end of Napoleon's thirst for conquest, the victorious controlling powers of Europe sent him to an island far out in the South Atlantic, the Island of St Helena, where he spent his final years under constant surveillance. He died in 1821 aged 51.

Longwood House, St Helena, Napoleon's retirement home

After having been reduced to bankruptcy, inflation and despair, from a war which lasted 25 years, the new French government, subsidised by international financiers within the city of London, became the junior partner in an alliance with the British, lasting for over 100 years. The next phase of the British Empire was to integrate, control and utilise the industrial revolution, creating not only a military empire but an industrial one. Over the next century under the reign of Queen Victoria, the British Empire was at the forefront of new technology and innovations, with this superiority came and even greater expansion to its dominance. With a network of modern communication and transportation links the empire grew exponentially, by 1850 Britain had become the largest manufacturing centre on Earth, about 50% of all global manufacturing was produced in the UK. By this time the city of London's financial district was at the core of the British economy and the empire. At the beginning of the 20th century, most of Europe's ruling Monarch's descended from either Queen Victoria of England or Christian IX of Denmark, they were nearly all related to one another, a simple way to keep power within the family. From 1871 onwards, the new unified Germany began to surpass the British economically with its technical achievements, social reforms and global exports. While the British elite were still using divide and rule tactics to keep themselves on top, Germany under Chancellor Otto von Bismarck created revolutionary new social welfare programs uniting the nation. Germany was the first to introduce a variety of social welfare programs; they created national insurance for sickness, accidents and disabilities; universal healthcare for all it citizens along with compulsory education and even a state pension. The National Socialist education policy became the envy of the west with the highest literacy rate in the world at 99%. This level of education provided the nation with more numeracy and literature skills, creating a society with more engineers, chemists, opticians, skilled managers, knowledgeable farmers and skilled military and factory personnel. In just 63 years from 1850 to 1913 the German population had nearly doubled from 35 to 67 million. Its steel production had surpassed both Britain and the United States. By 1914 Germany was producing half of all global electrical equipment and had now become one of the biggest exporters in the world. The British Empire could not compete on equal terms, its policy of divide and rule, keeping the majority of its subjects in perpetual scarcity, had allowed them to rule for the past 250 years. The only option they could see available, in order to survive, was to destroy its competitors, and Germany had become its main rival. The empire realised it had to intensify its alliance with the international financiers, to create a powerful partnership which would have the tools necessary to propel itself through the 20th century and beyond together creating a financial, industrial, and military powerhouse. The empire had to survive, nothing was off the table, all means necessary; through concealment, distraction and manipulation, it will survive no matter what the cost. If the Kaiser couldn't bring his country into line with Britain's version of globalisation, it would find itself at war economically and if necessary militarily. Once the American banking system was under the control of the international financiers in December 1913, the green light was given for the disembowelment of Germany.

The British Empire is ruthless and expansive. It controls all its subjects through commercial monopolies, corporate contracts, financial dominance, military persuasion and diplomatic arm twisting. The real heart of the empire lies within the City of London, an independent corporation in the heart of the capital, controlling all finance from an entity known as the "CROWN". The City/Crown Corporation is outside the normal jurisdiction of British laws; it has its own courts, laws, flag, police force and mayor. Just like the Vatican City State and Washington DC, all separate entities within their host nations. This triad, an alliance of control, now work together to form a global force expanding the globalisation project; they are also exempted from a variety of taxes. The Vatican controls world religion, the City within London controls world finance and Washington DC controls the world's military muscle. These three cities all possess common attributes aligning themselves with particular universal energetic frequencies, along with Saturnine ceremonies, symbols and other similarities they all possess an ancient Egyptian obelisk, which is situated within each city state. There is a zodiacal Union Jack pattern beneath the obelisk in St Peters square, the throne of Peter (Jupiter), a definite astrological depiction of the path of the Sun as it moves around the zodiac. The presence of these ancient obelisks is not yet fully understood by the general public, maybe the people behind the positioning of these structures know the full extent of their importance, there potential impact on the surrounding area's energetic fields and frequencies.

The Vatican State and Church is the largest financial power, wealth accumulator and property owner in existence. Not only does the Catholic Church hoard its wealth, it also hoards its knowledge, ancient books and manuscripts, some of which came from the ruins of the great library at Alexandria, knowledge and wealth kept from the rest of humanity, while at the same time controlling them through scarcity and ignorance.

Egyptian obelisks in the three city states

Washington DC St Peter's Sq, Vatican City The City, London

The characters behind the Crown Corporation are kept secret, ensuring anonymity, disguising the true masters behind globalisation. Within the City, this Crown entity is controller of the Bank of England, the US Fed, the IMF, Lloyds of London, the stock exchange, branch offices to most British banks, over 200 foreign banks, at least 50 US banks. It houses most of the main stream media monopolies and Fleet Streets newspapers, it is also home to various major cartels and corporations whose tentacles stretch across the globe. The Queen of England is only a figurehead for the Crown, the directorate of the corporation. The empire is essentially ruled by the Crown Corporation. The City became a sovereign state of its own in 1694 at the time William of Orange privatised the Bank of England. The Crown Empire uses commercial law, maritime admiralty law, and ecclesiastic Vatican cannon law to enforce its will and conduct business as a means of commercial control throughout the world.

Some of the richest families on the planet control the Crown Corporation, families such as the Rothschild's, Warburg's, Oppenheim's and the Schiff's. These families and their descendants direct the Crown Corporation's activities which own the titles to worldwide Crown land and colonies. The City carries on its day to day business of local government with medieval ceremonies and ancient customs, its voting power vested in secret guilds with names of traditional crafts such as, Grocers, Fishermen, Mercers and Skinners. All this tradition and ceremony is a mask blinding the eyes of the public to the real deal going on behind the scenes. The British parliament serves as a public relations front, preoccupied with the day to day trivia of legislation and population control, taking the eye off the hidden power which these ruling elitist families possess.

The banking cartel within the city maintains a tight fiscal control of global monetary policy. Through various mechanisms and relationships with central banks of each nation they determine the value of all currencies and therefore the financial status of each country. The United States is just another Crown colony, the president acts for the interests of the Crown Corporation, through his role as president of the Virginia Corporation, (Act of 1871). Using their vast wealth and influence the Crown Corporation finances agents to promote their cause in positions of influence, offering huge material wealth to all who are willing to manipulate the outcome favouring the expansion and aspirations of this global entity. Through secret societies they recruit useful members of each community, grooming them to carry out their objectives.

The City/Crown Corporation operates as a super government, a secret government, creating continuity behind the charade of party politics. No important incident occurs in any part of the world without their participation in some form, neutralising competition and ensuring overall survival, dominance and expansion. British foreign policy has always been a constant succession of cycles, shifting alliances, isolation, financial control, diplomacy and war. China, Russia, the United States, Germany and France are in order the most populous and have been the most independent nations in the world and therefore, represent the most dangerous threat as competitors toward the British Empire. All these nations have been victims in one way or another to British repression. The empire through its control of education and media has the ability to alter the belief systems of the majority of its subjects; they will persuade the public's perception on who their new enemy is. Over the centuries nearly every country has been in its crosshairs, not because their people are bad, it's just because the empire has decided they are to be brought in line with the policies of the Crown Corporation. If they choose to set brother against brother or mother against son, to advance their agenda, I'm sure they will find a way to do so.

In his book "A Study of War" professor Quincy Wright shows the statistical breakdown of the most warring countries of Europe from 1480 - 1940, the percentage of time each country is at war.

> **Percentage of time each country is at war**
> England 28%   France 26%   Spain 23%   Russia 22%   Austria 19%
> Turkey 15%   Poland 11%   Sweden 9%   Italy 9%   Netherlands 8%
> Germany (including Prussia) 8%   Denmark 7%

It's no surprise to see Britain at the top with a whopping 28%, that's nearly 1/3 of its entire existence over the past 500 years, warring with Tom, Dick or Harry in the name of expanding the British Empire, presumably in a defensive capacity.

"**The principle victims of British policies are unpeople—those whose lives are deemed worthless, expendable in the pursuit of power and commercial gain. They are the modern equivalent of the 'savages' of colonial days, who could be mown down by British guns in virtual secrecy, or else in circumstances where the perpetrators were hailed as the upholders of civilisation.**" - Mark Curtis[1]

"**To plunder, to slaughter, to steal, these things they misname empire; and where they make a wilderness, they call it peace.**"- Publius Cornelius Tacitus (Roman Historian 55-117)

"**Why should we not form a secret society with but one object the furtherance of the British Empire and the bringing of the whole uncivilised world under British rule for the recovery of the United States for the making the Anglo-Saxon race but one Empire. What a dream, but yet it is probable, it is possible.**" -Cecil Rhodes[2]

Cecil Rhodes 1853-1902, was a British businessman, South African politician, and a great believer in British colonialism. Rhodes used his diplomatic skills to negotiate with the elite ruling classes of the British Empire. Aware of his qualities and aspirations, which ran in line with the empires objectives, they worked together and formed a useful alliance; Rhodes would act as a well-paid agent for the Crown, while the empire would protect his interests through force and diplomacy. Rhodes left a fortune in his will to secret societies and Rhodes scholarships, all with the intention of advancing his dream.

"**I contend that we are the finest race in the world and that the more of the world we inhabit the better it is for the human race. Just fancy those parts that are at present inhabited by the most despicable specimens of human beings what an alteration there** would be if they were brought under Anglo-Saxon influence, look again at the extra employment a new country added to our dominions gives." - Cecil Rhodes[3]

His vision for an imperial federation which would unify Britain and the United States in to a controlled globalised system throughout the whole world would begin to materialise after his death. At the turn of the 20th century the British Empire was vulnerable under its old format, the sheer weight of US, Russian and German industrial and commercial growth was in competitive terms, too great for the empire to compete against alone, a new approach had to be devised. In 1909, with the Rhode's legacy, Lord Alfred Milner and others created a secret society known as the Round Table, a group of influential individuals all with a common purpose, the survival of the empire. With its wealth and influence, it financed agents to infiltrate all major spheres of power, steering policy towards a favourable outcome. From this successful group other organisations, offshoots where born, interconnecting in a huge web creating a shadow government of continuity, irrespective of who was in power within the old frameworks of democracy. A network of secret societies, government agencies and institutes, just as Cecil Rhodes had envisaged. The objective was to consolidate power in to the hands of global governance, a one world financial system with a one world army, all controlled by the same forces behind the British Empire. In his book Tragedy and Hope, Carroll Quigley identifies the Round Table as "The hub of the international Anglophile network".[4] It has been speculated that offshoots of this Round Table group work together to consolidate power into the hands of the three city states, these organisations include:

- League of Nations - 1920
- Royal Institute of International Affairs/Chatham House - 1920
- Council on Foreign Relations - 1921
- United Nations - 1945
- Bilderberg Group - 1954
- Club of Rome - 1968
- Trilateral Commission - 1973

After WW1 the British Empire, weakened and financially indebted, had taken control of some of Germany's colonies and removed most of Europe's colonial competing figure heads. Now at its peak, the new balance of power was firmly in their hands. In 1917 before the end of the war the British monarch, the directorate of the Crown Corporation, decided to change its German name from "Saxe-Coburg & Gotha" to the more English sounding name of "Windsor", as a public relations exercise, disguising their family ties to the country it had just smashed. With global dominance as the prime motivation for their actions, they realised that all variations of nation states, whether a democratic republic, a liberal democracy or a right-wing utopia, was giving too much power to the common man, stifling the advancement of the elite's globalist totalitarian agenda. Now inseparable from the international financiers of Wall St and London, frustrated with the slow progress of democracy, the diplomatic and secret intelligence apparatus of the Empire allowed them to push for global dominance through networks of communists, fascists and socialist movements, sponsoring numerous dictatorial figure-heads after the Great War. During the 1920's and 30's a wave of fascist movements spread throughout the world. Contrary to popular belief, they were not independent movements springing up spontaneously, but part of a larger plan. The push for control was on. They will set man against man, beast against beast, until they get what they want, more for themselves and less for everyone else.

List of fascist movements throughout the world from 1922 onwards

1 The Axis
- 1.1 Italy (1922–1943)
- 1.2 Germany (1933–1945)
- 1.3 Japan (1931–1945)

2 Other countries
- 2.1 Austria (1933–45)
- 2.2 Brazil (1937–1945)
- 2.3 Chile (1932-1938)
- 2.4 China, Republic of (1932–1945)
- 2.5 Croatia (1941–1945)
- 2.6 Finland (1929–1932)
- 2.7 France (1940–1944)
- 2.8 Greece (1936–1941)
- 2.9 Hungary (1932–1945)
- 2.10 Norway (1943–1945)
- 2.11 Portugal (1932–1974)
- 2.12 Poland (1930s)
- 2.13 Romania (1940–1944)
- 2.14 Serbia
- 2.15 Slovakia (1939–1944)
- 2.16 Spain (1936–1975)
- 2.17 South Africa

3 Fascism in democratic nations
- 3.1 Australia (1931 – late 1930s)
- 3.2 Canada (1930s–1940)
- 3.3 Belgium (1930s–1945)
- 3.4 Ireland (1932–1933)
- 3.5 Mexico (1930–1942)
- 3.6 The Netherlands (1923–1945)
- 3.7 Lebanon
- 3.8 United Kingdom (1932–1940)

https://en.wikipedia.org/wiki/List_of_fascist_movements

Benito Mussolini, the founder and leader of Italy's National Fascist Party, became Prime Minister in 1922, when he led his black-shirts to seize power by marching on Rome. He rapidly turned Italy into a corporate police state, taming its population into submissive participants. He had many backers and supporters, from international financiers to the Vatican. In 1926 Thomas Lamont, a partner of Morgan, later to become JP Morgan, arranged a loan of $100 million for Mussolini's government.[6] Using its influence within the media, they promoted Mussolini in the minds of the general public, publications in Time, Fortune and Life magazine, referred to him as a "Triumphant Reformer" and the "Wonderful Benito". Time magazine alone featured him on its cover eight times over 20 years.

Throughout the 1920's Mussolini's corporate fascist movement was promoted by the agents of the empire and the Catholic Church as a role model for other fascists to follow. Italy's treatment by the allies during ww1 had left a very bitter taste in the mouths of the Italians. In the years that led up to the war, Italy had naturally sided with Germany and Austria, in theory they should have joined them at the beginning. Italy sat out waiting to see how the war would progress. In the early months of 1915, British agents made a deal with the Italian leadership, an agreement called the Secret Treaty of London. The treaty was too tempting for the Italians to refuse; it offered them large sections of territory around the Adriatic Sea. The Allies wanted a new front in the south, splitting and weakening the Central Powers. On April 26th 1915 Italy came in on the side of Britain and France. By 1917 the Italians had only got 10 miles into Austrian territory, then came the disaster of Caporetto, where the Italians had to fight the whole of the Austrian army, along with 7 divisions of German troops, the Italians lost 300,000 men in the offensive. By the end of the war the Italians had 2,197,000 casualties, with 600,000 dead. The country was bankrupt with inflation running rampant. Being on the side of the victors, the Italians expected their fair share of the spoils. At the Treaty of Versailles, they got very little, bringing deep humiliation and resentment from the Italian people, they felt betrayed by Britain, who seized nearly all the captured territory for itself, 1.4 million square miles, giving only 360,000 to France for their 6 million war casualties. The failure of the Italian government at Versailles, made them look weak in the eyes of the Italians, this helped pave the way for the rise of Mussolini and his fascists in Italian politics.

In 1923 a Captain General in the Spanish military, Miguel Primo de Rivera, overthrew the government and declared himself as dictator. Touted in the media, at the time, as the Spanish Mussolini, he was later overshadowed by Francisco Franco, another fascist dictator. Similar events were unfolding in Germany with the Nazi Party, Inspired by both Mussolini's march on Rome and Miguel Primo's overthrow of the Spanish government, the German Nazi Party leader Adolf Hitler attempted a coup in late September 1923, The famous Beer Hall Putsch, unfortunately for the Nazi's, the putsch failed, landing Hitler and his conspirators in Jail for over a year, the Nazi's finally gained power in 1933 with the help of London and the international financiers, both channelling funds through the Reich-bank's chairman Hjalmar Schacht, into the coffers of the Nazi Party. By the late 30's any country in the crosshairs of the empire had some form of fascist party either in government, challenging government or marching up and down the streets pretending to be the government.

The British Empire had wanted total control of the United States ever since those turbulent days of George III and the American Revolution. Even though the Crown Corporation had control of the Federal Reserve and the Virginia Corporation of the United States, it saw Roosevelt as a traditionalist and part of the old democratic process and upholder of the constitution. A plan was hatched in 1933; a coup to overthrow Roosevelt's elected government, it was a plot by a group of wealthy industrialists, to create a fascist veteran's organisation. Unfortunately, the plot was uncovered by General Major Smedley Butler, and brought to light in the United States House of Representatives. In 1934, Butler testified before a Special Committee on Un-American Activities, in his testimony, Butler stated that:

"A group of several men, representing mainly Wall-Street banking interests had approached him to help lead a plot to overthrow Roosevelt in a fascist military coup" - General Smedley Butler

In their final report, the committee supported General Smedley Butler's claims on the existence of the plot, but the matter was mostly forgotten, with no more investigations or prosecutions. The press also went silent showing very little interest.[7]

Joseph Stalin took over from the Wall Street backed Lenin following his death in 1924, to lead the next phase of control within the Soviet Union, another form of ism, Bolshevik communism, similar to fascism when looking at its top down command and control structure, just another dictatorship, leaving the people exposed to the mercy of their narcissistic, psychopathic leaders. The Idea of allowing all these dictators to exist next to each other, was to keep them in line and impose the will of the elite on the common citizen, vulnerable citizens who looked towards their leaders for solutions to many of the manufactured problems of the day, vulnerable citizens living in fear surrounded by potential enemies which made it easier to steer public policy in the direction required for globalisation. This global game of chess, played by the elite, meant keeping the dictators in check, they could only do this by surrounding them with other dictators, just as ruthless and just as well armed, capable of invasion at a moment's notice. Arming them was big business especially for the arms manufacturers, the corporations and the big banks. The only problem was keeping it all together, keeping them in line with global policy. What would happen if one or more of your dictators had ambitions and ideas of their own?

The Nazi Party

Already planning ahead, the international financiers allied themselves by financially helping the German National Socialist Party. The Zionist faction within world Jewry had plans to create a homeland for the Jews in Palestine, to be run by a Zionist government. The National Socialists (NA) and the Zionists (ZI) both had common goals concerning the Jews in Europe; the German National Socialists would help the Zionists round up all European Jews and send them to Palestine. The Zionists had difficulty in the past persuading Jewish families to resettle in the new homeland, which Britain gave to the Rothschild/Zionists, through the Balfour Declaration, at the end of WW1. Many were reluctant to leave because they had established successful businesses, and were comfortable in Germany and other parts of Europe. Certain objectives needed to be realised from the next war, a war that seemed inevitable, especially if the British Empire and the Crown Corporation had something to do with it.

1) The expulsion of Jews from Europe to Palestine:

The Transfer Agreement 25th August 1933, an agreement made between the Zionist Federation of Germany, the Anglo Palestinian Bank and the economic authorities of Nazi Germany, designed to facilitate the emigration of German Jews to Palestine. For the Rothschild/Zionists to fulfil their desire of populating Palestine with European Jews, a situation would have to be created in Europe to make them move, a situation which would make staying intolerable.[8]

2) The destruction of German companies and the seizure of assets, companies who were not controlled by international finance or the Crown Corporation:

Any large German company which had become a successful contributor to the German economy, with no ties of debt to international finance, free to produce and compete against factories and corporations under the control of the empire, would find themselves in the cross hairs. This strong competitive position was seen as unfair, incompatible with the status quo and balance of power in Europe, a balance which tilted on the side of the empire and the Crown Corporation. The objective was to smash the whole country back to the Stone Age, forcing them to rebuild everything, using borrowed money from Rothschild/Zionist international financiers and City of London Banks, placing them under the control of the empires financial debt based monetary system permanently. Between 1940 - 1945, 61 German cities, with 25 million people, were destroyed, devastated beyond recognition, in a bombing campaign initiated by the British government working for the Crown.[9]

3) Get the Bolsheviks and the Germens to annihilate one another:

One would expect the Red Army, an ally of Britain and the United States to receive help and supplies for their war effort. One would not expect allied companies to be supplying Germany at the same time. But surprisingly this was the case. A swift victory over Nazi Germany didn't seem to be the prime objective for the elite; a prolonged war fulfilling multiple objectives appeared to be the game plan. A number of large US corporations, financial institutions and industrial figures where conducting business for both sides during the whole conflict. Standard Oil shipped enemy fuel through Switzerland, Ford trucks supported German troops throughout occupied Europe, and IG Farben adopted a business as usual policy. The same old British Empire tactics where being employed, get your rivals to fight amongst themselves, weakening each other to a point which allows you to go in and pick up the pieces, then create the new world in your own image, in the meantime arm and finance them until they are crippled with extreme debt . A long protracted war would produce more devastation and a greater opportunity for restructuring in the aftermath, consolidating old power structures, transferring control into fewer hands, favouring international finance, the Empire and the Crown Corporation.[10]

4) Create an atmosphere, from the aftermath, suitable for the establishment of global governance, through institutions such as the United Nations, the IMF and other global projects, the next stepping stone for world dominance:

After WW1, the League of Nations was set up as an attempt to prevent future wars, and cement the participating nations into following the diplomatic aspirations of the empire. Unfortunately, the league was regarded as weak, unable to prevent future wars from happening, and many countries withdrew once they became suspicious of ulterior motives. A bigger and better version would be necessary after WW2. In 1945 the United Nations was created, under the same pretext of preventing wars. The old Bank of England needed a new face, greater scope and more persuasive power to propel the empire into the future. During the final stages of WW2, the Bretton Woods conference, formally known as the United Nations Monetary and Financial Conference was set up. By the end of July 1944, the IMF was established, coming into formal existence in 1945. For the next phase of global monetary control, the shelves of the old private central Bank of England were moved over into the IMF. The empty husk of the BOE was then sold off in 1946, to the British people in a public relations exercise called nationalisation. Many institutions sprang up after WW2, for more global control and influence, part of the new evolvement of the British Empire and the Crown Corporation. The World Health Organisation (WHO), a specialised agency of the UN was created in 1948, to manage international public health. The UN really has become the foundation for global governance.

> **Specialised Agencies of the United Nations**
> 1 Food and Agriculture Organization (FAO)
> 2 International Civil Aviation Organization (ICAO)
> 3 International Fund for Agricultural Development (IFAD)
> 4 International Labour Organization (ILO)
> 5 International Maritime Organization (IMO)
> 6 International Monetary Fund (IMF)
> 7 International Telecommunication Union (ITU)
> 8 UN Educational, Scientific and Cultural Organization (UNESCO)
> 9 United Nations Industrial Development Organization (UNIDO)
> 10 Universal Postal Union (UPU)
> 11 World Bank Group (WBG)
> 11.1 International Bank for Reconstruction and Development (IBRD)
> 11.2 International Finance Corporation (IFC)
> 11.3 International Development Association (IDA)
> 12 World Health Organization (WHO)
> 13 World Intellectual Property Organization (WIPO)
> 14 World Meteorological Organization (WMO)
> 15 World Tourism Organization (UNWTO)
> 16 Former specialized agencies
> 17 Related Organizations
> 17.1 Comprehensive Nuclear-Test-Ban Treaty
> 17.2 International Atomic Energy Agency (IAEA)
> 17.3 Organisation for the Prohibition of Chemical Weapons
> 17.4 World Trade Organization (WTO)

5) Create enormous debt, another controlling lever for the international financiers, and to take control over all European banking institutions.

After 1945 all participants of the war had become burdened by excessive government debt, the price they had to pay for their involvement. No matter which side they were on, the government debt was owed to the international financiers. The Treaty of Versailles, after WW1, was designed to cripple Germany economically, the Potsdam Conference in July 1945 was equally damaging, and it made sure Germany would pay dearly, blamed for the cause of the war; they would have to pay reparations. The country was finished they had been smashed six ways to Sunday, but the country was still ransacked, under the deindustrialisation policy. Machinery and manufacturing plants were dismantled and transported to France and the UK, anything left was destroyed. The country had to start from scratch, with money borrowed from the newly formed IMF, on terms and criteria imposed by the IMF and the international financiers. German reparations also came in the form of forced labour, over 4 million POW and civilians were used in this way throughout Europe and the Soviet Union. Germany paid Israel 3 billion DM in Holocaust reparations and 450 million DM to the world Jewish congress to compensate survivors in other countries, no reparations were paid to Romani gypsies, homosexuals, Christians, Catholics, Muslims or any other identifiable group caught up in the turmoil.

The lender is always master over the borrower, the international financiers knew that in the aftermath of the war, with all governments in debt, they would be calling the shots and have immense leverage when the new Europe and its new geopolitical scene was being established. The Romans used the leather whip as a mechanism of control, the international financiers use debt. The pen is mightier than the sword and the balance sheet is mightier than the whip.

6) Change global public opinion towards the Jews, by giving them victim status; this will help to shield future Zionist policies from criticism as they hide behind the Jewish religion.

It is in the Interests of the Rothschild/Zionist international financiers to shield themselves from public scrutiny. What better way than to hide behind a barrage of smoke and mirrors, creating an atmosphere of the perpetual victim, changing the belief system in the minds of the masses. Using all techniques available, pumped out daily, watering those seeds within the subconscious, from education to media, from politics to official history, forbidding the inquisitive from asking sensitive questions. Masked through mechanisms of legislation and intimidation, the public cannot be allowed to know the game, the players or the truth. The perpetual victim status is set like stone in the collective consciousness of each generation, targeting raw emotions, allowing the Zionist control grid to bomb, butcher and burn all who stand in the way of their aspirations of a greater Israel and greater financial control, becoming a rogue state within the boundaries of human decency and tolerance. The hypocrisy is monumental all because they hide behind victim status; no one wants to be labelled as an anti-Semite.

7) Cause as much chaos as possible, for a new order to be implemented afterwards.

During the early stages of the war, which many believe was forced on Germany, Hitler offered numerous peace proposals. Churchill was having none of it, allied with the international financiers; the annihilation of this competitor was part of the overall strategy for their globalisation project. There was no way they wanted to share power with Hitler. One such peace offering came to the attention of Joseph P Kennedy, the US Ambassador to the United Kingdom, and father of JF Kennedy. He revealed the terms of this offer to the former President of the US, Herbert Hoover who couldn't understand why Britain would not accept.

"With the onset of mass air raids Churchill's political difficulties shrank. He could turn the blandest gaze on fresh peace emissaries like the one behind which the British legation correctly detected Hitler's hand that now arrived in Sweden. A Berlin lawyer, Ludwig Weissauer, had travelled to Stockholm to contact Sir Victor Mallet through a senior judge and friend of the Swedish monarch, Professor Lars Ekeberg. But now Churchill was running Britain's foreign policy. Through Halifax, he forbade Mallet to meet Weissauer. The British

envoy, who sincerely desired a negotiated peace, ascertained Berlin's terms nonetheless. They were as before: for Germany, the continent; for Britain, her overseas empire. Ekeberg asked for an answer by the eleventh. Halifax and Cadogan brought the resulting Stockholm telegram over to No.10 on the tenth and left Churchill to think it over. If you want any more questions asked, Mallet had promised in it, I can easily get them put by Ekeberg, again without committing anyone and as though coming from me alone. Churchill tossed the telegram aside. When the F.O. mandarins returned at 7:30pm, he had drafted a rejection and was sprawled in bed in his flowered Chinese dressing gown, drawing on a Havana cigar. Kennedy learned of this episode and revealed it to former President Herbert Hoover. Told Hitler's terms, the former president gasped: Why didn't the British accept? Nothing but Churchill's bullheadedness, replied Kennedy". -David Irving (Churchill's War)[11]

On 10th May 1941, The German Deputy Fuhrer Rudolf Hess, in a last ditched attempt to negotiate a peace deal flew to meet the peace movement in Britain, unknown to him, with all angles covered; this fake peace movement was controlled by Churchill. Hess was captured and spent the rest of his life in prison, silenced forever.

Baron von Weizaecker, about Hitler **"He had set his heart on peace. Herr von Ribbentrop seemed less predisposed toward it. He sent the Führer his own word picture of a future Europe like the empire of Charlemagne.' To the Swedish explorer Sven Hedin Hitler voiced his puzzlement at Britain's intransigence. He felt he had repeatedly extended the hand of peace and friendship to the British and each time they had blacked his eye in reply. 'The survival of the British Empire is in Germany's interests too**,"- David Irving (Hitler's War)[12]

All the new fascist dictators were happy to receive funding from Wall Street and London's financiers, happy to play their expected roles at dictatorship, unaware that they were being set up in a global game of chess for a massive conflict, a new world war which would see the deaths of nearly 80 million people, and the total destruction of Germany. Hitler and the Germans were backed into a corner.

Ironically in 1939 when the Germans seized about 100,000 square miles of Poland, the British in the same year seized 218,259 square miles in other parts of the world, expanding their own empire. Britain declared war on Germany for invading Poland on 1st Sept 1939, but became allies with Russia who invaded Poland on 17th September 1939. An example of double standards which certainly poses many questions as to what the real agenda was behind the scenes. Once the war was under way, it became a giant exercise in logistics and negotiations. The objectives set out initially by the Anglo/Zionist alliance were to be fulfilled at all costs, no matter how many deaths or peace offerings the Germans made, annihilation was the plan and annihilation was delivered. A point came early on when Hitler and the leading National Socialists realised they had been manoeuvred into an impossible position, their dreams of an independent Germania were not, and never were going to be part of the British Empires future plans, they had no choice but to throw everything they could at what they saw as a fight for survival, it became an all-out war to the bitter end.

The real power of the British Empire and the Crown Corporation lay in the hands of a few individuals, the British Parliament and its citizens have little or no say in the important foreign affairs of the empire, but those citizens within that empire must fight when international finance and the City feel it necessary to call upon them. In Andrew Carnegie's book "Triumphant Democracy" he writes:

"My American readers may not be aware of the fact that, while in Britain an act of Parliament is necessary before works for a supply of water or a mile of railway can be constructed, six or seven men can plunge the nation into war, or, what is perhaps equally disastrous, commit it to entangling alliances without consulting Parliament at all. This is the most pernicious, palpable effect flowing from the monarchical theory, for these men do this in "the king's Name," who is in theory still a real monarch, although in reality only a convenient puppet, to be used by the cabinet at pleasure to suit their own ends."-(13)

Post war globalisation

After WW2, the control systems power lay in fewer hands, an alliance between the International financiers, the Crown Corporation, the Vatican and the American Military Industrial Complex, all major players in the creation of the post war era. Their objective was to put in place the foundations for globalisation, the next stepping stone to global governance. Through the United Nations and the IMF, individual sovereign nation states would be brought in line to operate as interdependent, reliant, servants of the new post war global system, any country stepping out of line would find itself under economic pressure from the international financial community. With its network of secret societies and government institutions, globalist ideology was rewarded and encouraged, anyone with contrary beliefs were squeezed out of the frame. Over the next 70 years Europe was brought closer together under the guise of trade agreements, deregulation and an end to future wars within its borders. This all looked good on the surface, a step in the right direction for progress. While on one hand the union offered positive practicalities, but on the other hand it was taking independent control away from sovereign nations, cultures which had taken centuries of blood and sweat to develop. The ability to self-govern, or at least have some influence over one's own life, has always been a strong factor in the formation of free societies, most wars stem from this, without peaceful resolution you have violent revolution. The EU had to tread carefully, concealing its game plan from the majority, slowly moving its agenda, using disguise, deception and force; it would seek to take control of all aspects of our lives.

1951 - The European coal and steel community was formed: A trade agreement to bring the major coal and steel producing countries of Europe under a single system.

1957 - The Treaty of Rome: This treaty was the foundations for the EEC, signed in March.

1958 - EEC, the European Economic Community was created: The predecessor to the EU, an economic trading union, designed to deregulate and unify trading procedures with all members.

1973 - The UK joins the EEC after being turned down twice in the past. A UK referendum was held in 1975 to stay in the EEC, the British public voted to stay, believing it to be just a trading union and would benefit them economically.

1986 - Single European Act is signed: This was a further reduction in trade barriers.

1989 - Fall of the Berlin wall: Many people perceived the fall of the Berlin wall to be the start of western influence over the east. It never occurred to them that an eastern Soviet style system could spread westwards. The formation of the EU is now seen as such.

1993 - The Maastricht Treaty: The formal treaty on the European Union.

2002 - The Euro was introduced: A single currency introduced to all but a few of the member countries, another step closer to political and monetary union.

2004 - The EU constitution was established: A new constitution was created in which all members were to adopt. This was rejected in a referendum by the French and the Dutch which brought the ratification to an end in 2005.

2007 - The Lisbon Treaty: The Treaty was created as an alternative to the failed constitution; it effectively is the constitution under another name. The Irish rejected the Lisbon Treaty with a referendum, but the control system would not take no for an answer, a second referendum was organised along with a huge propaganda campaign. The Irish eventually voted yes.

At this moment in time, 2015, there are currently 28 members.

The name Europe comes from Europa, a Greek mythological figure, a Phoenician woman abducted by Zeus in the form of a white bull. Europa is the 6th closest moon to the planet Jupiter, it's the 6th largest moon in our solar system, and if you count our moon as one of the influential bodies Jupiter becomes the 6th body from the Sun. The flag for the European Union is an astrological expression of the Sun in the 12 houses of the zodiac.

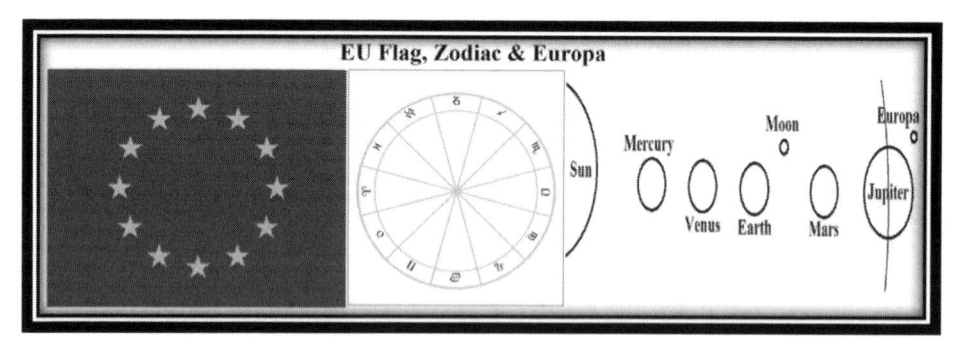

EU Flag, Zodiac & Europa

Although the main stream has associated astrology and hermeticism with crackpots and pseudo scientists, the establishment consistently align themselves with its influence and synchronicity. Many of their symbols, ceremonies and flags have some form of astronomical/astrological taint to them, and the timing of specific events are suspiciously astrological in nature. It's as though the elite are aware of the natural power within this ancient science, maybe using it for their own ends while ridiculing it in the eyes of the masses. The European Parliament building has been designed to look like the Tower of Babylon (baby-London). This is no accident. The whole creation of the European Union is as though they are trying to recreate Babylon or a modern version of the Roman Empire, both societies heavily influenced by ancient universal wisdom.

Tower of Babylon & EU Parliament

The latest phase of globalisation is to create economical parity, more of a level playing field throughout the globe. This is being done by suppressing the economies of western countries whilst stimulating the east. The jack boot of debt is being stamped across Europe, forcing stagnation and austerity on European participants, while stimulating growth in the underdeveloped countries, all this is taking place now, a huge project, with the vast majority of global finance and commerce under the control of the international financiers and globalists. The wars, conflicts and confrontations we see are both public relations exercises and regime change operations. Any country or region frustrating global control and expansion are being dealt with; it's just a matter of time until all resistance has gone. ASEAN union is being formed in South East Asia, the Africa Union is under way and so is a new American Union, a new partnership between North and South America, these new unions will be brought together through trade agreements, just like in the European Union model. The only potential obstacle to globalisation are the minds of the people, it is vital to the success of this great project, that the beliefs of the citizens are brought in line with the positive aspects of global union, avoiding the negative aspects, the main one being, where does an individual escape to if he does not like the system imposed upon him by an all-encompassing one world union. The whole idea of individual states and sovereignty was to have more diversity of cultures and a variety of ways to live one's life. If any individual was unhappy with one country's social mechanisms, they were free to go somewhere they felt more comfortable. Nations would have to compete on merit, setting a good example in order to attract investment keeping the citizens happy. A one world government, especially if it is unelected and unrepresentative, will ensure the individual has nowhere to escape to, he has to do what he is told, lump it and be quiet. Judging by the ferocity and speed of the globalisation project, the deception, imposition of its will, its corruption and pseudo transparency. The concealing of real objectives, the forcing through of legislation sometimes without being read or fully understood, leads many feeling a little uneasy at what is being created and the effects it will have on the average citizen.

After the signing of the treaty of Rome in 1957, two of the founders of the treaty were reflecting on their achievement. Baron Robert Rothschild (House of Rothschild) reflected on his conversation with Paul Henri Spaak (Belgian Foreign Minister), where Spaak's said:

"I think we have re-established the Roman Empire without a single shot being fired."[14]

The modern political process has become a scientific operation in mass mind manipulation, the altering of public opinion through various aspects of media, education and political theatre, essentially ensuring that all turkeys will vote for Christmas, that's if you still have faith in today's voting system. An interesting aspect to this is the hidden influence the Vatican has within the globalisation project, another major power player in the game. The Treaty of Rome laid the foundations of the EU project, and was lodged in Rome on the 12 Oct 2009, a fascinating twist when considering the partnership between the three city states.

Using levers of government debt, the international financiers through the IMF and World Bank impose conditions, social reforms and criteria favouring globalisation and interdependency between member states. The sensible days of sovereignty, self-determination and self-sufficiency have nearly come to an end.

"Europe's nations should be guided towards the super state without their people understanding what is happening. This can be accomplished by successive steps, each disguised as having an economic purpose, but which will eventually and irreversibly lead to federation." Jean Monnet, April 30th 1952.

"What is at stake is more than one small country. It is a big idea, a new world order where diverse nations are drawn together in common cause to achieve the universal aspirations of mankind; peace and security, freedom and the rule of law. Such is a world worthy of our struggle and worthy of our children's future." George HW Bush Sr. President of US, congress speech, September 11th 1991.

"We have before us the opportunity to forge for ourselves and for future generations a new world order, a world where the rule of law, not the law of the jungle, governs the conduct of nations. When we are successful, and we will be, we have a real chance at this new world order, an order in which a credible United Nations can use its peacekeeping role to fulfil the promise and vision of the U.N.'s founders." Transcript of George HW Bush speech from the Oval office January 16, 1991.

"2009 is the first year of global governance with the establishment of the G20 in the middle of the financial crisis." He continued, **"The climate conference in Copenhagen is another step toward the global management of our planet."** Herman Van Rompuy (new EU President speech 19 Nov 2009).

"I think a new world order is emerging and with it the foundations of a new and progressive era of international cooperation. We have resolved that from today we will together manage the process of globalisation to secure responsibility from all and fairness to all, and we've agreed that in doing so we will build a more sustainable and more open and a fairer global society." Gordon Brown speech to the G20 Press Conference, London, 2 April 2009.

"There is no salvation for civilization, or even the human race, other than the creation of a world government." Albert Einstein as quoted by Charles Kegley, World Politics: Trend and Transformation (2008) p. 537.

Globalists are given positions of influence within the mechanisms of power centralisation. Agents manipulated or self-propelled, believing the project will lead to a brighter future, with its immense bureaucracy restrained and shielded from corruption. Most dissenting opposition is quietly pushed out of favour, dropped from lists of influential agents ensuring common coherence and success. There is an irony, a perverted twist, globalised governance set up under the pretext of preventing future wars and saving the planet from our over consumption, is itself propagating war and promoting environmental exploitation, caused by their parasitical financial systems and global corporations thirst for profit and expansion. The common man does not want war or an over complicated life, most people do not need to surround themselves with unnecessary symbols of success. These are belief systems employed to entice man into participating in a rat race of competition, a divide and rule policy, another mechanism of control, mastered by the British Empire and its evolving successors. Power corrupts and absolute power corrupts absolutely.

"The greatest weapon of mass destruction is corporate economic globalization." -- Kenny Ausubel

Sir Edward Heath and the Magna Carta

In 1973 Edward Heath, acting British Prime Minister, signed our political sovereignty away with his entry into the European Common Market. When Heath's government enacted the European Community Act 1972, providing for the incorporation of European Union Law, he did this without a referendum, the British electorate were not consulted, he therefore breached the spirit of the UK constitution.

The Magna Carta 1215, the Petition of Rights 1628, the Bill of Rights 1689 and the Act of Settlement 1701.

In 1974, following Ted Heath's Premiership and defeat, Harold Wilson became Prime Minister, aware of Heath's treasonous error, Wilson set about rectifying this problem, in 1975 he arranged a retrospective referendum, hoping to obtain permission from the British people, for something they had been made to join. The referendum was worded in such a way as to legitimise the error. The question asked:

"Do you think the UK should stay in the European Community (Common Market)"?

The problem was, Heath had already signed the entrance documents illegally, without consulting the electorate on this constitutional matter, the wording of the referendum was specifically designed and the phrase "Stay in" was deceptive. The UK could not stay in something which legally they could not have entered. Parliament did not have the right to sign away British sovereignty without first consulting the electorate. The reality behind most memberships of the European Union have been similar acts of deception, a grand scale of smoke and mirrors, all players and agents aware of the deception, as political globalists they happily go along with the deceit, believing they are working for the overall good of humanity. I'm sure some of Saddam's henchmen or Hitler's SS were equally as passionate about their cause, but this is no excuse for lies and deception. If it is genuinely in humanities best interest then there is no reason to disguise the truth.

In 2013 the annual budget for this extra layer of command and control bureaucracy, cost the European community 150 billion Euros. The UK contribution alone was approximately £11 billion, which equates to over £400 for the average UK household.[15] To put that in perspective, the British Government's budget for its own general government was only £13.5 billion and the budget for the whole countries secondary education during 2013 was £21 billion.[16]

Sir Edward Heath's body was laid to rest in Salisbury Cathedral, ironically in the same place as the Magna Carta, entombed and laid to rest within a glass display case.

The dark side of empire

Divide and rule has been used for millennia by controlling systems to weaken their competitors, breaking them into manageable chunks, playing one off against another. The British Empire, masters at divide and rule, wrote the manual on the subject, from centuries of exploitation. When people become aware of this they can see division in nearly every area of life from cradle to grave. Division of religion, race, age, nationality, sex, income bracket, educational bracket, political persuasion, sexual perversion, philosophical ideology, neighbourhood, manhood, fashion, musical taste, car you drive, watch you wear, phone you use, restaurant you frequent and possessions you hoard, naming just a few. All used as a mechanism to keep us apart and under control while the elite's large financial institutions and corporations expand exponentially. Using government agencies, NGO's and secret operations the British plough huge funds into competing factions, suppressing any cohesion or potential competitor to their interests. They sponsor and initiate rival factions, guerrilla warfare and overthrow elected representatives, especially in resource rich, third world countries, ensuring weak and unstable economies, allowing them to run off with the raw materials, furnishing their own exploits at a fraction of the cost. Africa is a great example; the perpetual problems and reoccurring divisions allow the rest of the world to pillage its raw materials for next to nothing. The British Empire along with other colonial powers used similar tactics to fulfil their objectives. The methods they adopted came in three variations and combinations, depending upon each situation, known as settlement, indirect rule or divide and rule.

Settlement: Settlers from host colonies would be encouraged to relocate to new countries or areas, occupying the land and building settlements. They would impose their colonial style of government over as much of the region as they could by taking control of everything around them. During the settlement process the indigenous people would either be displaced or exterminated. When the British arrived in Zimbabwe they renamed it Southern Rhodesia after Cecil Rhodes. The new colonial settlers awarded themselves exclusive ownership of

3,000 acres of land each. The original black Africans living on that land were declared to be tenant farmers, lacking rights of ownership. When Zimbabwe became independent in 1980 there were 300,000 white settlers, less than 10% of the population controlling 40% of Zimbabwe's prime agricultural land. President Mugabe introduced land reform policies designed to distribute the land equally amongst the indigenous people of the area. This settlement tactic is being used today in Palestine by the Israelis, a country for years lived on by one type of people (Palestinians), signed over by another group of people (British Empire), to a third party (Zionists). The indigenous Palestinians are going the same way as the North American Indians and the Australian Aborigines; they either leave or face progressive extermination.

Indirect rule: The controlling colonial powers would co-opt local elites, bribing kings, councils and mafia to work as agents for the colonies, making them wealthy from this new money. The co-opted elites also benefited from protection as long as they acquiesce to the wishes and demands of the empire. This created tensions between indigenous communities, suspecting corruption and allegiances to colonial powers, failing in their duty to serve the indigenous people who they were supposed to represent, a technique used throughout India, Africa and the British West Indies, and becoming the preferred tactic used in the modern era. Governments and officials are indirectly ruled by debt, the international financiers and global corporations have immense power when it comes to bribing or as they like to call it, conditions of loan requirements.

Divide and rule: This is a conscious effort by outside powers to pit one group against another, driving wedges between differences within a community, artificially stimulating rivalry and fragmentation. The British have used this to bring about the changes they want, all over the world, from Northern Ireland to Africa, North America to India, Muslims v Hindu, Catholics v Protestants. All human beings, expressions of universal energy and beauty, fighting one another over a belief system offered to them by their controlling masters. Instead of uniting with their brothers and sisters, in a collective consciousness, together towards real freedom and liberty, they compete, butcher and burn one another, forcing their version of control, accepting the mandates, madness and rituals of empire. Today we see the whole of the Middle East divided, more divisions than a football league, Sunny v Shia, Arab v Jew, Christian v Muslim all useful divisions for the globalists to prey on. They will arm them all and contain the madness. The latest in a long line of covert conquests, just like Europe in the 1940's, the new empire will roll in when the end is near, initially as a UN peace keeping force, offering up terms and solutions, favouring the aspirations of empire and the expansion of globalisation.

The British Empire has progressed and evolved, allied with international finance (Zionism), the Vatican (Roman Catholic Church) and the American Military Industrial Complex, this new force, a western elitist ideology is determined to bring the whole world totally under its system and influence. A deceptive force designed to enslave every human within its web of debt and servitude. Disguising its intentions as humanitarian, peaceful and democratic, stopping at nothing until its totalitarian governance, a single system of surveillance and control is in place.

Notes for chapter 6

(1) Mark Curtis, Unpeople, Victims of British policy, dec 28th, 2004, published by Vintage books.

(2) Cecil Rhodes, Confession of Faith, 1877, https://mikemcclaughry.wordpress.com/the-reading-library/the-basement-just-dox/just-dox-british-intelligence/cecil-john-rhodes-confession-of-faith-1877/

(3) Cecil Rhodes, last will and Testament, 1902, University California Library, https://archive.org/stream/lastwilltestamen00rhodiala/lastwilltestamen00rhodiala_djvu.txt

(4) Carroll Quigley, Tragedy and Hope, 1966, Collier-Macmillan company, https://books.google.co.th/books?id=q3XVBAAAQBAJ&printsec=frontcover&dq=tragedy+and+hope+carroll+quigley&hl=en&sa=X&ved=0CB0Q6AEwAGoVChMInMirtrmTxgIVCqq8Ch2puABV#v=onepage&q=tragedy%20and%20hope%20carroll%20quigley&f=false

(5) Patrick Scrivener, The war of 1812, reformation.org 2015, http://www.reformation.org/war-of-1812.html

(6) John Hoefle, The British Empire's Fascism Stalks America, EIR Strategy, March 20, 2009, Laurouchepub.com , http://www.larouchepub.com/eiw/public/2009/2009_10-19/2009-11/pdf/12-18_3611.pdf

(7) The Plot Against FDR, McCormack Dikstein Committee, Wikisource, http://en.wikisource.org/wiki/McCormack-Dickstein_Committee#Origin_of_the_files

(8) Edwin Black, The transfer agreement, 1984, Dialog Press, http://www.transferagreement.com/

(9) The bombing of Germany during ww2, Metapedia.org http://en.metapedia.org/wiki/Bombing_of_Germany_during_World_War_II

(10) Charles Higham, Trading with the enemy, Hale London, 1983, https://libcom.org/library/allied-multinationals-supply-nazi-germany-world-war-2

(11) David Irving, Churchill's War, The Struggle for power, 2003, Volume 2, page 445, Focal Point Publications, http://www.fpp.co.uk/books/Churchill/1/WSCv1pt2.pdf

(12) David Irving, Hitler's War, page 244, 2002, Focal Point Publications, http://www.fpp.co.uk/books/Hitler/2001/HW_Web_dl.pdf

(13) Andre Carnegie, Triumphant Democracy, 1912, C Scribner's Sons. https://books.google.co.th/books?id=Z_hCAQAAMAAJ&q=andrew+carnegie+triumphant+democracy+1886&dq=andrew+carnegie+triumphant+democracy+1886&hl=en&sa=X&ved=0CBsQ6AEwAGoVChMItc_6pfCTxgIVlTS8Ch2jeQB1

(14) Paul Belien, Eurocrat Empire Building, The Brussles journel, on Wed, 2007-03-28 07:47, http://www.brusselsjournal.com/node/2018

(15) Szu Ping Chan, EU budget, what you need to know, The Telegraph, 11:44AM GMT 14 Nov 2014, http://www.telegraph.co.uk/finance/financialcrisis/11221427/EU-budget-what-you-need-to-know.html

(16) UK budget analyst, http://www.ukpublicspending.co.uk/education_budget_2013_2.html

Chapter 7. Secret societies

"Why should we not form a secret society with but one object the furtherance of the British Empire and the bringing of the whole uncivilised world under British rule for the recovery of the United States for the making the Anglo-Saxon race but one Empire. What a dream, but yet it is probable, it is possible." -Cecil Rhodes (1853-1902)

"The very word "secrecy" is repugnant in a free and open society; and we are as a people inherently and historically opposed to secret societies, to secret oaths and to secret proceedings. We decided long ago that the dangers of excessive and unwarranted concealment of pertinent facts far outweighed the dangers which are cited to justify it." Part of John F Kennedys speech, press association 1961 (full speech in chapter 3)

The empire has and will use all options available to it, nothing is off the table. If necessary they will assassinate leaders, presidents and monarchs, as long as the replacement runs favourable to their imperialistic aspirations. There is no greater mechanism for social change other than war, if the empire requires a war to bring about change, they will have a war, manipulating people and events to initiate it. Their eyes and ears are everywhere, all dissenters are filed and observed, and through secret societies individuals are manoeuvred and coerced into performing sometimes illegal acts, designed to help the empire while the individual believes naively they are advancing their own personal cause. During the latter half of the 19th century, collectivist movements and groups of socialists began to appear, forming organisations and societies, believing that human civilisation can only survive and advance under a global collectivist system, a system which would be organised top down by people like themselves. In this future world, the majority of the citizens have no rights, they are given privileges by their superiors, and they are only born to serve the greater good of the collective. There were two basic camps of collectivists, both with the same goals but with different approaches. The Marxists, a group of collectivist socialists, who saw a fast-revolutionary approach as the solution, this method was only suitable in countries where democracy was weak, where the people were already acclimatised to mild forms of dictatorships. The other camp preferred a slower approach, using propaganda, legislation, education and media to bring a nation around to their way of thinking. They realised that in societies with strong participatory democracies, that they would have to infiltrate slowly, going unnoticed by the majority. This group are known as Fabians, a semi secret society who use two symbols within their movement, a turtle and a wolf in sheep's clothing, named after the Roman general Quintus Fabius Maximus Verrucosus, who became famous for avoiding direct military engagements, instead preferring wars of slow attrition. Fabianism or Fabian strategy has come to mean a gradual slow cautious policy.

Both these groups work together to control world populations, aiming to bring about a unified global collectivist society. The Marxists/Leninist camp made great gains throughout the east, sponsored by the international financiers, using communism as an expression of their socialist collectivism, predominantly in the Soviet Union and China. The Fabians' on the other hand had to be patient, they had to develop strong influences at all levels of government and society, based in London they nurtured many offshoots and socialist organisations, which sprang up across the globe promoting collectivism. The Fabians are wolves in sheep's clothing whereas Marxist/Leninists are wolves in wolves' clothes. Many prominent labour party politicians have been members of the Fabian Society including, Ramsey McDonald, Clement Attlee, Tony Benn, Harold Wilson, Tony Blair and Gordon Brown. Other famous Fabians include George Bernard Shaw, HG Wells and Bertrand Russell.[1]

Collectivists see the state as the new God, the new emperor, the new religion. Your individuality must be moulded to fit within the parameters set out by the state, you must serve the state to justify your existence otherwise you're an unworthy misfit or a home-grown terrorist, a threat to the legitimacy of statism and collectivism. Their new definition of extremist is anyone who challenges their established order no matter how extreme it becomes. All subjects within the new social order must be restricted within a narrow band of conscious expression, revoking the natural biological reflection of endless universal possibilities, limiting freedom, liberty and self-expression. To achieve their objectives the collectivists, have their members actively perverting media, politics, education, history and science, with the aim of advancing their ideological cause, firmly believing that the final end game justifies their deceptive moves and infiltrations. We are told that man is responsible for climate change, we are told who our new enemies are, those who we should fear and fight, we are told that we must give up our freedoms for security, give up our sovereignty for harmony, we are told that austerity is necessary, that there is no more money for our communities but on the other hand we see plenty of money for war. We are told to be vaccinated and that GMO's are safe, we are conditioned to accept the official versions of events and not to question anything, just keep on shopping, watching TV and eating, and eventually everything will be just fine. The problem associated with all variations of collectivism, whether it is communism, socialism, fascism, Nazism or globalism, is that they all eventually resort to brute force to maintain power and to perpetuate themselves. David Rockefeller an agent for the international financiers expressed his admiration for the collectivist experiment in China under Chairman Mao, fully aware that at least 45 million people had been worked, starved or beaten to death in the process, Mao is possibly the greatest mass murderer in history.

"**Whatever the price of the Chinese Revolution, it has obviously succeeded, not only in producing more efficient and dedicated administration, but also in fostering a high morale and community purpose. The social experiment in China under Chairman Mao's leadership is one of the most important and successful in human history.**"(David Rockefeller, New York Times, 1973.)

To the globalist, the human cost involved in this collective experiment is not an issue. This is why George Bush and Tony Blair can take their countries to war on lies; they are not interested in the truth or conflicting evidence. Their overall mission is to force through the next phase of globalisation, it is their job to make the next phase of the agenda plausible to the general public, they are just PR men for the controlling corporations. They would not have been allowed in office if their views or wishes ran contrary to globalisation. Since the fall of the Berlin wall, the west has become more like the east and the east has become more like the west, merging the two variations of collectivism towards unification. Once practical parity has been achieved, sometime in the near future, a new level of global administration will emerge from some manufactured crisis, a new tier of bureaucracy, out of reach of most people whom it will control and supposedly represent. In 1948 another Fabian George Bernard Shaw wrote:

"I am a communist, but not a member of the Communist Party. Stalin is a first-rate Fabian. I am one of the founders of Fabianism and as such very friendly to Russia" - George Bernard Shaw 1948[2]

From Fabianism to Cecil Rhodes, most secret and semi-secret societies operate from a central core outward. The inner ring or circle contains the big wigs, the influential elite and trusted associates, who hold most of the cards and are setting the direction of policy. From this inner circle, a slightly larger ring or organisation is formed around them, attracting members who have no knowledge of the inner ring, its members or its influence. These outer ring members are carefully selected, who either have genuine aspirations parallel to the objectives of the inner core, or are compromised through various techniques. This outer ring creates another outer ring and so on until it interacts and influences mainstream society. At the outside level, they pay for the services of innocent naive people who perform various tasks advancing the desires of the inner circle and controlling elite. Using this method, the wizard can remain anonymous behind the curtain, invisible to the casual observer, as he propels the old form of empire into a new form of collectivist global governance. The opposing camps of collectivism can use their differences within the theatre of geopolitics to play one off against the other, distracting and confusing the vast majority within the public realm, creating an excuse to mould each political and social system towards the final stage of globalisation.

Tax exempt foundations

There are many tax exempt foundations in the United States and the world who masquerade as charitable organisations, created from the private wealth of a few rich individuals. These philanthropic organisations are perceived by many as beneficial to society's progress. But what are their true intentions? And what are the trustees and policy makers really up to? In the early 50's the US Congress set up a special committee to investigate some of the most well-known tax-exempt foundations, including the Ford Foundation, the Carnegie Endowment, the Rockefeller and Guggenheim Foundations. The Reece Committee asked Norman Dodd to form a team of investigators to look into the workings of these foundations. At that time, there was a suspicion of anti-American activities underlining their operations. During the early stages of the investigation Mr Dodd met with the then president of the Ford Foundation, Mr H Rowan Gaither, on their first meeting Gaither admitted that the foundations policy makers were under the influence of directives which came all the way from the Whitehouse. They were instructed to use their grant making powers to aid a comfortable merger of everyday life in the United States with the lives of the people in the Soviet Union. This was an underlining objective which was to be secretly done behind the scrutiny of the general public. Following this Mr Dodd met with the relatively new president of the Carnegie Endowment Foundation, Mr Joseph E Johnson and his young staff. Due to the work involved answering all the questions posed by the investigation team, the president of the Endowment offered all the minute books going back to the foundations conception, Dodd's team had two weeks to plough through the material looking for all the answers they needed. He appointed Katherine Casey a bright lawyer with a balanced temperament. However, with limited time, they had to focus on specific time periods in order to uncover what they were ultimately looking for.

In 1908 the topic of discussion within the minute books of the Carnegie Endowment, was in the form of a recurring question.

Question "Is there any means known more effective than war, assuming you wish to alter the lives of an entire people? ". They concluded

Answer "No, there is no more effective means other than war known to alter the lives of an entire people."

1909 Question "How do we involve the United States in a war?"

Answer "We must control the State Department"

Question "how do we do that?"

Answer "We must take over and control the diplomatic machinery of this country."

During World War 1, the Carnegie Endowment recorded in their minute books a shocking transcript of a telegram dispatched to President Wilson, **cautioning him to see that the war doesn't end too quickly**.

After the war was over the Endowment recorded their new objectives, **to ensure the American way of life does not revert back to how it was before the war**, in order to do that they concluded that they must control the American educational system. They also concluded that the task was too big for them alone, so they asked for help from the Rockefeller Foundation, who accepted the challenge. Domestic education was to be handled by the Rockefeller Foundation while international education was to be handled by the Carnegie Endowment. They concluded that the key to success lay in the teaching of American history, or at least their version of it.

"He who controls the past controls the future. He who controls the present controls the past." George Orwell- 1984

The foundation approached four of the most prominent history teachers of the day, asking for assistance in their new plan of altering the manner in which American history was taught. Realising the implications, the teachers turned them down flat. It left the foundation with no other choice but to build their own stable of historians and history teachers. Eventually they had twenty new recruits who went on to become the nucleus of the American Historical

Association. By the end of the 1920s the Carnegie Endowment spent an enormous sum putting together a comprehensive study, they concluded that the future of America belongs to, (**collectivism, administered with characteristic American efficiency**).

In the final report Dodd's investigation concluded that tax exempt foundations were working in harmony towards the control of education within the United States. Their overriding objective was to orientate the educational system away from supporting the principles embodied in the Declaration of Independence and the Constitution.[3][4]

On August 19th 1954 Carroll Reece (member of the House of Representatives) summed up his investigation headed by Norman Dodd.

"It has been said that the foundations are a power second only to that of the Federal Government itself ... Perhaps the Congress should now admit that the foundations have become more powerful, in some areas, at least, than the legislative branch of the Government."[5]

This is a perfect example of how the controlling elite have been secretly manipulating the beliefs of the American population for nearly a century, a defined intent to bring the majority of the citizens within a constitutional republic closer towards a socialist collectivist globalisation project. On one hand, the citizens still believe they are free sovereigns in the greatest democratic republic in the world, while on the other hand working feverishly to impose the will of a tiny group of influential men, hell bent on creating a new world in their image, in line with their own personal arrogant beliefs, convinced that their vision of the future is better in the long run for everyone else. With new foundations springing up and working together towards a common goal, some of which appear, on the surface, as humanitarian. The Bill and Malinda Gates Foundation have a new motto "**A Call for Global Citizens**". This motto aims to influence the global educational system into manufacturing favourability towards their corporate monopolistic sales and aspirations, socially engineering the fragile minds of this new generation, targeting them as early as possible. Manmade global warming/climate change has infested every nook and cranny within the students learning experience, persuasive suggestions have targeted their fragile minds from all directions within a new common core educational program, another belief system designed to manoeuvre humanity into the web of socialistic collectivism, ruled by international financiers and international corporations. The days of well-informed critical thinkers, a population of wise, logical and balanced reasoned men and women are fast becoming extinct. The controllers do not want this in the ranks of the masses, they want obedience and compliance, a population progressively dumbed down enough to blindly accept all the latest government issued concepts and smart enough to implement and force them on the rest of humanity. With full control over the educational system, the 21st century human commodity will slot nicely within the advancing global collectivist project, functioning in line with policy. Through education, vaccination and persuasion our new citizens are being groomed like stable horses, to participate in the next phase of the death stars construction.

Bilderberg

The Bilderberg group, conference, meeting or club has recently become a semi-secret /private society, arranging annual conferences for approximately 150 influential political leaders, industrialists, financiers, academics, media moguls and elitists, with connections to the Council on Foreign Relations (CFR), the Trilateral Commission, the IMF and many of the world's global and international organisations. They interact at the highest level to gather and share ideas and objectives, ensuring the globalisation project is focused and on track. During the conference and its many seminars, fresh plans can be put into motion, attention will be highlighted by members and think-tanks who feel it necessary to tweak and adjust policy to maintain their projected schedule. All necessary participants within these areas will be brought in line with new expectations. The group evolved its name from the hotel in Oosterbeek, Netherlands, where it held its first meeting back in 1954.[6] The list of attending participants to these meetings is quite staggering, no doubt a reflection of how important the event has become amongst the influential elite. A comprehensive list can be found on the internet; here I will list a few significant ones.[7]

List of Bilderberg participants

King Philippe of Belgium (2007–2009, 2012)	Tony Blair (1993), Prime Minister 1997–2007 UK
Prince Charles, Prince of Wales (1986)	Gordon Brown (1991), Prime Minister 2007– 2010
Prince Phillip, Duke of Edinburgh (1965, 1967)	Edward Heath, Prime Minister 1970–1974 (deceased)
Queen Beatrix of the Netherlands	Alec Douglas-Home (1977–1980),
Prince Bernhard of the Netherlands (1954–1975)	Margaret Thatcher (1975, 1977, 1986) Prime Minister
Willem-Alexander of the Netherlands (2008)	David Cameron (2013) Currently Prime Minister
King Harald V of Norway (1984)	Timothy Geithner (2008, 2009), Treasury Secretary US
Haakon, Crown Prince of Norway (2011)	Henry Kissinger (1957–2013) 56th
Juan Carlos I of Spain, King of Spain (2004)	United States Secretary of State
Queen Sofía of Spain (2008–2011)	Richard Perle (2011) Secretary of Defense 1981–1987
Stephen Harper, (2003), Prime Minister of Canada	Colin Powell (1997)
Christine Lagarde (2013), Minister of Finance	Condoleezza Rice (2008), 66th US Secretary of State
Helmut Schmidt, West German Chancellor	George P. Shultz (2008), 60th US Secretary of State
Angela Merkel (2005), German Chancellor	Bill Clinton (1991), President 1993–2001
George Osborne Shadow Chancellor	Gerald Ford (1964, 1966), President 1974–1977
Peter Mandelson Business Secretary (2008–2010)	John Kerry (2012)
Denis Healey former Chancellor of the Exchequer	Rick Perry (2007), Governor of Texas 2000–2015
Kenneth Clarke Chancellor of the Exchequer	David Petraeus (2013), former Director of the CIA
Ben Bernanke (2008, 2009),Chairman of the Fed	David Rockefeller, Sr. Chase Manhattan Bank

List of Bilderberg participants : https://en.wikipedia.org/wiki/List_of_Bilderberg_participants

The Bilderberg group has now become a major cog of the global shadow government, interacting with many different established organisations, working together to create a new world socialist collective, a new feudalist system ensuring greater control and compliance, towards a society aligning itself with the serious controlling and restrictive energies of Saturn.

Skull and Bones

Skull and Bones is a secret society located within the grounds of Yale University, established in 1832 by William Huntington Russel. The university was founded by Eli Yale a wealthy opium trader within the East India Company. Russel was also involved in the drug business; his successful shipping firm dominated the United States side of the Chinese opium trade. The Skull and Bones secret order became a recruiting ground to preserve power and commercial interests of prominent families in the area, connected and profiting primarily from the opium business. Drugs in those days were not illegal, they acted as a mechanism of control and influence, addicting people from all walks of life, generating profit and political leverage for the seller, traders who cared not for the wellbeing of their victims, saw the world through the eyes of a psychopath, interested only in their own economic and political power. The opium trade eventually led to the Opium Wars which brought about the British Empire's control over Hong Kong. Each year the Skull and Bones secret society would select a mere 15 new recruits from their first-year students. In their final year, at Yale, they would become members of the order through an initiation ceremony. Each generation of elitist families would ensure their sons were chosen, keeping the power tight within the same circles. George W Bush was a member along with his father and grandfather, a family name synonymous with bonesmen. Being nominated a bonesman would certainly guarantee you a prominent position in the outside world, financial success in areas of politics, banking, law and commerce, it was bonesmen taking care of bonesmen. Considering only 15 new recruits are initiated each year, the number of bonesmen in top jobs is vastly disproportionate to the rest of the population. During the 2004 presidential campaign, the electorate were given two choices, George W Bush or John Kerry, both members of skull and bones, swearing an oath of secrecy, opposing each other in public but uniting together in secret. Just like many other secret societies, being initiated takes one through an array of macabre occult rituals. The S&B is no different, it has been reported that while the initiate lays helpless in a coffin, he is flanked by one member dressed as the devil and another dressed as a hooded skeleton, chanting, (the hangman = death, the Devil = death and death =death). In the temple itself, there is a room they call the tomb, which houses numerous human skulls and bones presented in display cabinets, where an unhealthy fixation of death seems to be the overriding theme. There is a rumour that Prescott Bush with fellow bonesmen, robbed the grave of the Apache Chief Geronimo back in the early part of the 20th century, furthermore, they took his skull and displayed it in a glass case within the tomb of their temple at Yale.

The symbolism behind the 322 and the Skull and Bones is still secret, but one can speculate as to its origins. A theory is that it represents the second chapter of a German fraternity created at Yale University in 1832. Another explanation comes from Genesis 3:22

Then the LORD God said, "Behold, the man has become like one of Us, knowing good and evil; and now, he might stretch out his hand, and take also from the tree of life, and eat, and live forever " Genesis 3:22 The American standard Bible

Yale University and the Skull & Bones secret society has had some interesting involvements in Chinese politics, partially due to their participation within the countries active opium trade.

With the exception of the Carter administration 1976-1980, all United States Ambassadors to Beijing since Henry Kissinger's deal with Mao, in the early 70's, have been members of the Skull and Bones secret society. This is quite a feat when you consider that only 15 are initiated each year. At the start of the 20th century Yale Divinity School established a number of schools and hospitals throughout China, known as "Yale in China". Perceived by many as another none profit philanthropic charitable organisation, it was designed to develop educational programs in China which would further relations and understanding between the Chinese and American people. It could also be seen as a front for altering their collective perception, influencing political change in the beliefs of the Chinese people. Writing in the Yale daily news, Jonathan Spence a professor of Chinese history at Yale University reveals that "Yale in China" supported Mao Zedong's rise to power. In 1919 when Mao was 26, the student's union invited him to take over editorship of the Yale journal. Mao accepted the position where he quickly changed its format, promoting his own social criticisms and Marxist ideology.[8][9] China was in the throes of great change after the fall of the old imperialistic system, a new republic under Sun Yat-Sen could see China competing against the west, economically and militarily. The western elitists preferred a tough approach, one which would keep China in a perpetual state of backwardness, a command and control structure which was simple and authoritarian, keeping a boot firmly stamping on China's progress for decades. Mao's communist party could do just that. Once Mao was in full control he turned China into the world's largest opium producer.

Bohemian grove

Is a large forested area in northern California, where a 140-year-old private San-Francisco men's art club holds a two-week encampment for its members and their guests, which include some of the world's most powerful men. Senior members of the grove, with over 40 years' service, are elevated to the prestigious position and status of "Old Guard", which gives them priority treatment and VIP seating at seminars and ceremonies. The Bohemian Grove's mascot is an owl, a 30-foot concrete statue standing centre stage at the head of the lake in the grove. This owl is said to be a symbol of wisdom. At the start of the event a ceremony called "Cremation of Care" is performed in front of the 30-foot owl, a mock human sacrifice along with its burning takes place in front of a large audience by a selection of robed members purporting to be exorcising demons, with the intention of ensuring the success of the ensuing two weeks. This whole ceremony has a definite ancient occultist overtone. The Bohemian club has a patron saint, John of Newpomuk, similar to Freemasonry and the story of Hiram Abiff, their saint suffered death rather than disclose closely guarded secrets, reminding members of their expected cooperation.

Bohemian Grove
Cremation of care ceremony

> **Famous attendees of the Grove**
>
> | | | |
> |---|---|---|
> | George H W Bush | Dick Chaney | Al Gore |
> | George W Bush | Bill Clinton | Robert Kennedy |
> | Herbert Hoover | Dwight D Eisenhower | Richard Nixon |
> | Henry Kissinger | Gerald Ford | Colin Powel |
> | Ronald Reagan | Henry Ford | Donald Rumsfeld |
> | Theodore Roosevelt | Newt Gingrich | William Taft |
> | Jimmy Carter | | |
>
> http://americansagainstnwo.tripod.com/id14.html

"Democracy must be built through open societies that share information. When there is information, there is enlightenment. When there is debate, there are solutions. When there is no sharing of power, no rule of law, no accountability, there is abuse, corruption, subjugation and indignation." Atifete Jahjaga (President of Kosovo)

"There is nothing so despicable as a secret society that is based upon religious prejudice and that will attempt to defeat a man because of his religious beliefs. Such a society is like a cockroach — it thrives in the dark. So do those who combine for such an end." William H Taft 27th President of the US (Speech to the Young Men's Hebrew Association in New York 20 December 1914).

Council on Foreign Relations

Founded after the Great War in 1921, the CFR purports itself to be an independent, nonpartisan membership organisation, think tank and publisher. It currently has 4900 members from the highest levels of government, business, finance and media, its main goal is to influence politics, foreign policy and international economics towards the consolidation of power, promoting globalisation, free trade agreements and reducing financial regulation for the transnational corporations. It is not a secret society but it has an agenda which is contrary to national sovereignty and nationhood. Its president Richard Haass was carefully selected back in 2003 to carry forward the CFR's tradition. Before becoming president of the CFR Haass was director of policy planning for the US Department of State, he has also been vice president and director of foreign policy at the Brookings Institute and senior associate at the Carnegie Endowment for International Peace. A Rhodes Scholar Haass holds both masters and doctor of philosophy degrees from Oxford University. Many of the members within the CFR are involved in many other organisations and influential positions within government, a revolving door of likeminded globalists, infiltrating all levels of society. Within the organisation a number of think tanks shape today's international policy, one think tank is known as the David Rockefeller Studies Program, contributing to the CFR's publication called the Foreign Affairs Journal, which helps shape public opinion towards their future aspirations. In the late 1930's both the Ford Foundation and the Rockefeller Foundation promoted the CFR with large monetary contributions. Britain has its own version, known as the Royal Institute of International Affairs, running in step with both the CFR and the Trilateral Commission, diverting foreign policy away from the citizens ability to control their sovereign destiny towards a secret socialistic collective global agenda.[10][11]

Influential CFR Members		
Henry Kissinger	Jim Geithner	Condoleezza Rice
Madeline Albright	Mikhail Gorbachev	David Rockefeller IV
James Baker	Newt Gingrich	George Shultz
George H W Bush	John Kerry	George Soros
Zbigniew Brezinski	John McCain	Paul Wolfowitz
Jimmy Carter	Rupert Murdock	Allan Dulles
Dick Cheney	Janet Napolitano	Gerald Ford
Bill Clinton	Henry Paulson	Herbert Hoover
Hillary Clinton	David Petraeus	Richard Nixon
Alan Greenspan	Colin Powell	Paul Warburg

"We cannot leap into world government through one quick step.... The precondition for eventual and genuine globalization is progressive regionalization because by that we move toward larger, more stable, more cooperative units." -Zbigniew Brezinski, (Centre for strategic and international studies CSIS), State of the world forum 1995

Freemasons

The Masons are not a secret society but a society with secrets, a large international organisation with an estimated 5 million members in nearly every country in the world. It is based on medieval stone mason's guilds, Old Testament symbolism, ancient Egyptian mystery religions and the construction of Solomon's Temple. They publicly refer to themselves as "morality veiled in allegory". There are many levels within Freemasonry, known as degrees, with the majority falling into the Blue Lodge Order. From here they progress up 3 degrees before splintering off to either the Scottish Right or York Lodge's. The highest known degree is the 33rd degree, which is the Grand Sovereign Inspector General. A significant number of the influential elite within western society are Freemasons, including politicians, lawyers, barristers and policemen, all looking out for one another as fellow Masons, swearing an oath to secrecy and allegiance. It could be considered as a religious order, because no one can be a fellow Mason unless they believe in the Masonic God, the God of light and universal wisdom. Oblivious to its true purpose, many Freemasons think they are just part of an old boys' network, hoping to further their own personal careers and social status, they lack the understanding of what Freemasonry is built upon. Like all religions its core belief system is based around astronomy and astrology, which is easily identified by analysing Masonic rituals and symbolism.

Nimrod: The Freemasons regard Nimrod as one of the founders of Masonry, he is generally considered as the one who proposed building the Tower of Babel, and directed its construction. Nimrod is often associated with the constellation of Orion. He was also renowned for his rebelliousness against God.

Sirius: A star twenty times brighter and bigger than our own Sun, was worshipped in ancient Egyptian mythology. The legend of Isis, Osiris and Horus originated from our ancestors who studied the heavens focusing on the Sirius constellation, which became the ancient Egyptian trinity similar to the Father, Sun and Holy Spirit. Sirius is the sister to our Sun, moving within a binary which completes a full cycle every 25,800 years. Freemasonry use Sirius symbolism and its components throughout all levels of their fraternity, suggesting that they worship the planets, the luminaries and just like the ancient Egyptians, pay homage to Sirius, the Sun behind our Sun. In Masonic Lodges Sirius is known as the "Blazing Star".

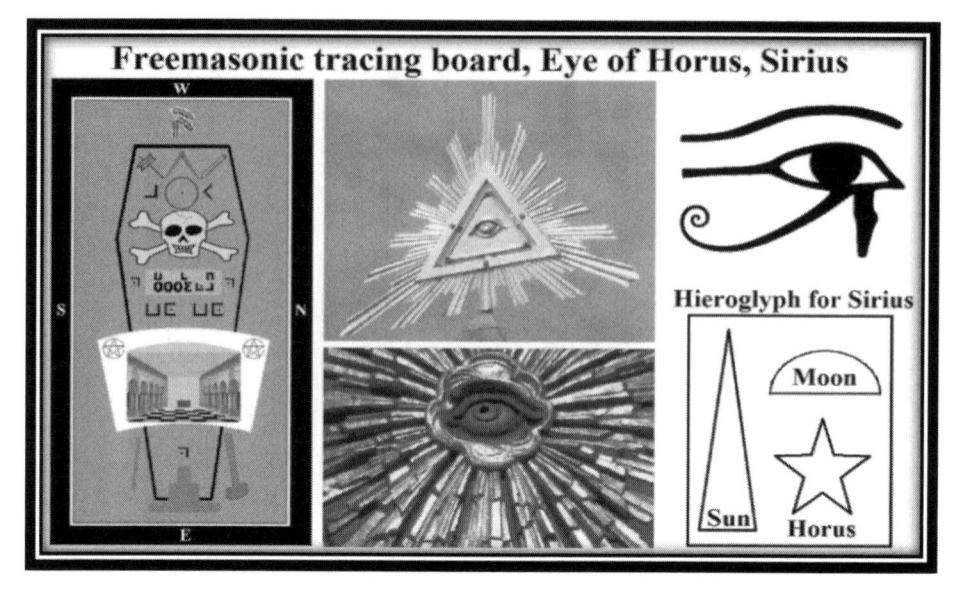

Egyptian symbolism plays a large role in Freemasonry. The legend of Osiris is fairly simple. Isis and Osiris were married. Seth, Osiris's brother murdered him and took over his throne, after which, Isis restored Osiris back to life to conceive a son Horus. Seth killed Osiris again by chopping up his body into many pieces, scattering them in the river. Isis searched for the pieces, finding all but his penis; she raps the body parts together and once again revives Osiris. After Horus's birth Isis sends Osiris to rule the underworld. The interesting thing here is the triad relationship, just like in Christianity, and the three areas of consciousness. Here the resurrection of Osiris is the re-erection of his missing penis, enabling him to create new life. The obelisk is a stone representation of Osiris's missing member.

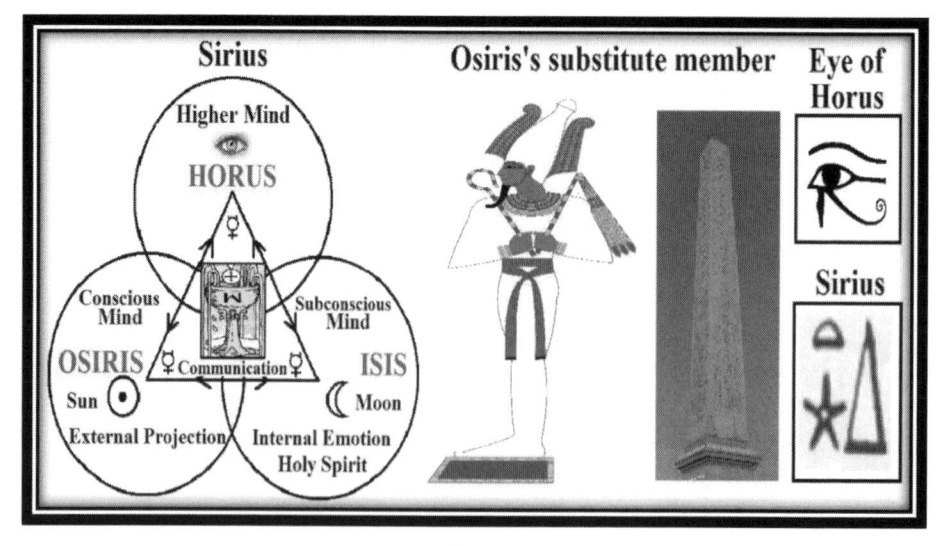

The position of Sirius in the sky is important from an astronomical or astrological point of view. It reveals a great deal when trying to understand the mysteries behind Masonic symbolism and ancient knowledge. Most Freemasons have no idea in the world what they are part of and what it all means. Many great scholars have pointed out that our Sun like the majority of stars in the universe; exist in a binary, in this case with Sirius, orbiting elliptically around one another. Its only now, with modern equipment that we are in a position to acknowledge how informed and advanced our ancestors were. We have been placed under the illusion that these primitive cultures were wattle and daub dummies, unable to even make a wheel. They say truth is sometimes stranger than fiction; we will unravel more on this part of the mystery later in the book.

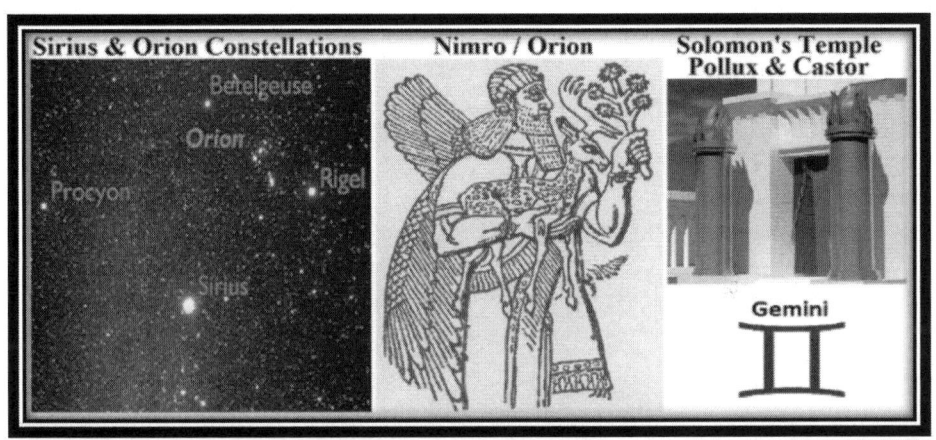

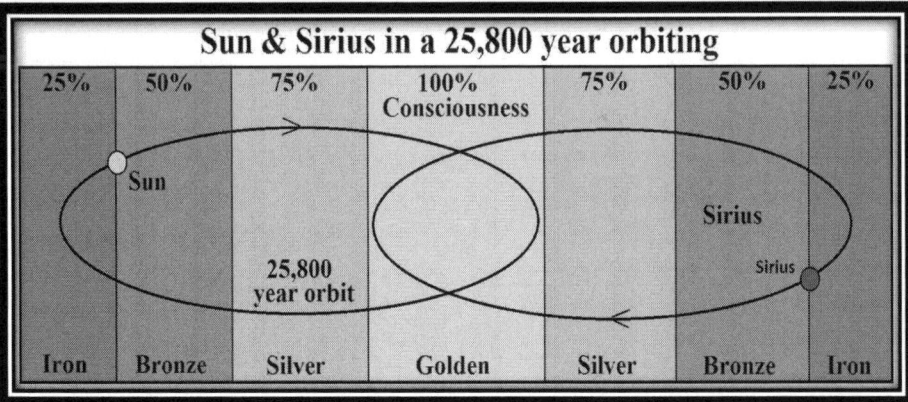

Sirius & Orion Constellations	Nimro / Orion	Solomon's Temple Pollux & Castor
Betelgeuse, Orion, Procyon, Rigel, Sirius		Gemini ♊

Sun & Sirius in a 25,800 year orbiting

25%	50%	75%	100% Consciousness	75%	50%	25%
	Sun		25,800 year orbit		Sirius	Sirius
Iron	Bronze	Silver	Golden	Silver	Bronze	Iron

Within this binary there is another triad, our Sun, the focal consciousness, the God of the physical realm; Sirius, the God of the subconscious, the emotional realm; and the higher mind or universal consciousness. The ancients understood how the universe was an expression of the three areas of our minds, "as above so below". Our Sun influences the physical world while Sirius keeps the spiritual realm alive. Sirius belongs to a constellation known as Canis Major, Canis means dog in Latin, also known as the Dog Star. The ancient Egyptians had a deity known as Anubis. During the first dynasty, he was God of the afterlife, depicted with the head of a dog. Anubis was replaced during the middle kingdom by Osiris who became lord of the underworld.

Canis Major	Dog Star	Anubis	Triad: Sun, Sirius, Universe

As the new initiate Freemason progresses up the ladder of degrees within the Masonic fraternity, they are enlightened with ancient knowledge and wisdom, enabling the penny to eventually drop and their level of understanding concerning occult mysteries and holy science becomes clearer. An emphasis is made in the holy sciences, holy meaning holistic or whole. Once you see the whole picture, within the science of light, you become illuminated. Man's religions in general do not enlighten the believer, instead the truth is twisted clouding and distorting their view of reality, neutralising their capacity to have a meaningful influence on human progress. Solomon's Temple plays an important role in Freemasonry. An ancient temple, supposedly constructed by King Solomon and his Master Masons, headed by a man named Hiram Abiff. The temple was to hold the Arc of the Covenant. There is no archaeological evidence to support the physical existence of this temple, only the account mentioned in the Bible.[12] When we examine the whole concept of Solomon's Temple from an astrological perspective, it all begins to add up. Solomon is a constructed name which refers to the Sun in three ancient languages.

- SOL: Latin for the Sun
- OM: Aum pronounced (Om) means the Sun in Hindu Sanskrit
- ON: In biblical Hebrew Heliopolis (city of the Sun) was referred to as "ON"
- SOL-OM-ON is just the Sun in three ancient languages. The temple is often depicted as two pillars, the entrance to the First Holy Temple.

The story told by Freemasons, is that Hiram Abiff, the Master Mason, during the final stages of constructing Solomon's Temple, was approached by three lesser stone workers, they threatened him with death unless he revealed the Master Mason's secret password, which would grant them wisdom and power. Hiram Abiff refused to divulge the password and was subsequently murdered by the three ruffians. King Solomon later found the body and reburied the remains in an ornate temple. The murderers were eventually executed. The Masons hold Hiram Abiff in great esteem, as an example of honour amongst Master Masons, keeping their oaths and secrets even to the point of death. Hiram Abiff is mentioned in the Bible but there is no account of his murder. His name is interesting from an astrological point of view. Hi-ram refers to Aries, the ram, the hi-ram is the top of the head, Aries represents that part of the body, above the head is the crown chakra or Hiram. Abiff starts with A and B the first two letters of the alphabet, letters associated with Aries, the first days of the ancient calendar. The (iff) falls in line with the tropic of Cancer.

English Alphabet in the Zodiac Wheel

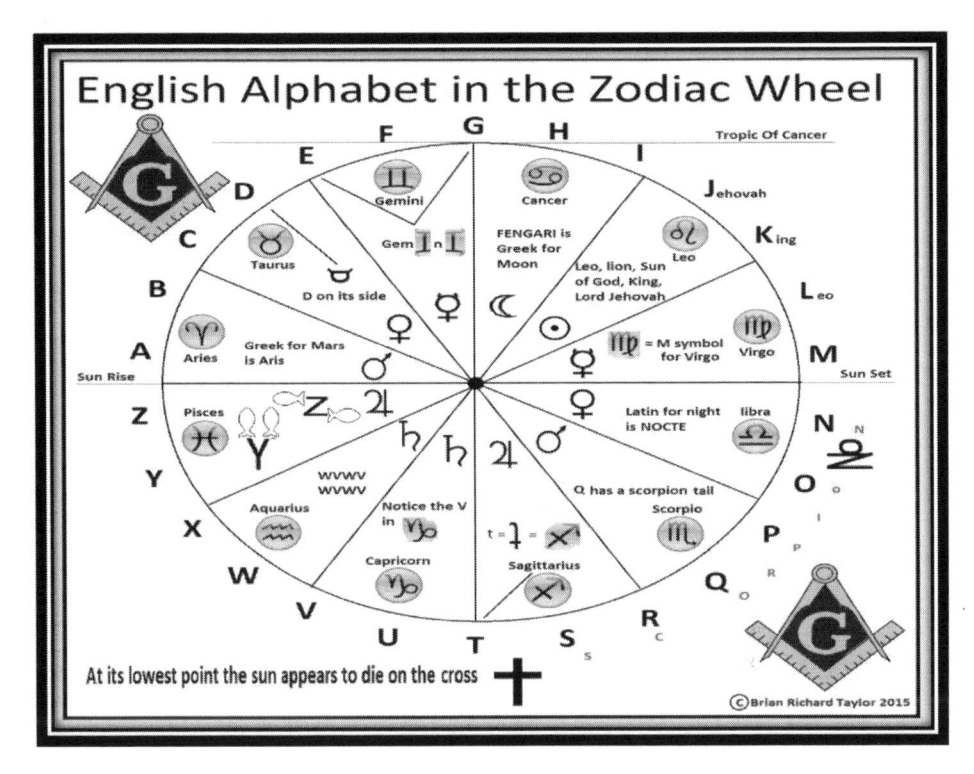

At its lowest point the sun appears to die on the cross

©Brian Richard Taylor 2015

The G in the centre of the famous Freemasons emblem is the highest letter in the zodiac alphabet; it could also be associated with the G in Gemini, its twin pillars, Castor and Pollux, the pillars to Solomon's Temple.

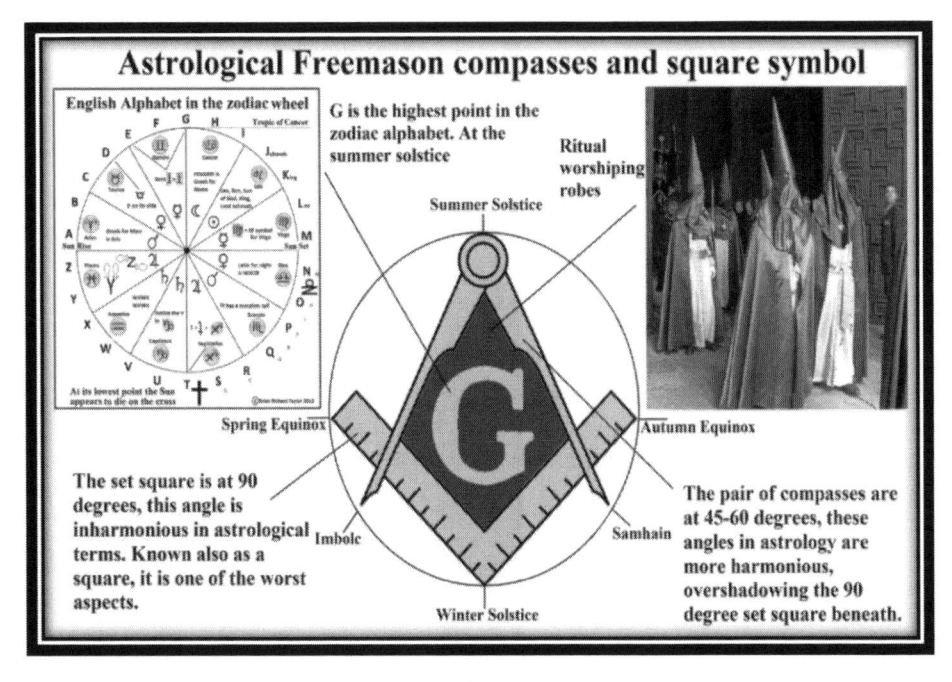

Astrological Freemason compasses and square symbol

G is the highest point in the zodiac alphabet. At the summer solstice

Ritual worshiping robes

Summer Solstice
Spring Equinox
Autumn Equinox
Imbolc
Samhain
Winter Solstice

The set square is at 90 degrees, this angle is inharmonious in astrological terms. Known also as a square, it is one of the worst aspects.

The pair of compasses are at 45-60 degrees, these angles in astrology are more harmonious, overshadowing the 90 degree set square beneath.

Symbolism is very important in the process of reprogramming a belief system into the subconscious mind, aligning oneself with the energetic frequencies associated with the symbols or ceremonies used. All new recruits must take part in rituals and ceremonies attaching emotional stimulus to suggestions, transforming the individual into a pliable and useful member for future Masonic aspirations, the outer circle of fresh initiates rarely come into contact with the inner circle of established Hiram Masons, who still have a modicum of influence towards the direction and course of progress within modern society.

Masonic oaths

At each level of Freemasonry, from the 1st degree to the 33rd, the Mason must perform a ritual ceremony and take an oath to keep secret passwords and knowledge within the brotherhood. The penalty for divulging these secrets can be horrific.

- 1st degree penalty: Throat cut, tongue buried in the sands of the sea.
- 2nd degree penalty: Heart plucked out, placed on highest pinnacle of temple.
- 3rd degree penalty: Disembowelled, bowels burnt to ashes.
- 7th degree York right: Top of skull taken off, brain exposed to noon day Sun.

At the 33rd degree level, it has been reported that the initiate is asked to drink wine from a human skull, symbolising Holy Communion with a Masonic twist. The oaths within the brotherhood of international Freemasonry transcend national and political allegiances, creating a powerful unaccountable and influential organisation throughout the world. As a Mason progresses up the ranks of the fraternal order, his fellow Masons will do all they can to protect him from outside harm. It's a big club and their oaths are taken (Siriusly), even to the point of protecting fellow members who are involved in criminal activities. In 1826 a Mason by the name of William Morgan aired his intentions to publish a book exposing the Freemason's secrets, still under his Masonic oath, he found himself arrested, under spurious accusations, later to disappear and was never seen again, the Freemasons where blamed for his death causing a huge anti-Masonic backlash which gave them a bad image over the next few decades, many members left and lodges had to closed. Eventually by the end of the 19th century their numbers had recovered. Around the time of Albert Pike any person of renown who was respected in the circles of high society would join the Freemasons.

Some researchers have concluded that Jack the Ripper was a Freemason, performing Masonic ritual killings throughout London's Whitechapel during the 1880s. When reviewing their thesis, it does carry some weight. They propose that the 2nd air to the English throne, the Duke of Clarence, a Freemason, had fallen in love with a common Catholic prostitute, Annie Crooks. He married her and they had a daughter. Annie was set up with a place to live and a nanny to help take care of the baby. The nanny they hired eventually turned to prostitution to increase her income, and began spreading news of the royal secret amongst other Whitechapel prostitutes. Eventually some of the prostitutes threatened to expose the story to the press unless they were paid off. At that time, the Prime Minister Robert Cecil was a Freemason, the police commissioner, Sir Charles Warren was a Freemason and so was Sir William Gull, the royal physician. It is suggested that either the Queen or the Prime Minister gave the go ahead to eliminate this threat to the royal establishment's reputation. It is claimed that the royal physician was called upon to neutralise the problem, Gull went on a killing rampage to protect his fellow Masons who also protected him. The interesting part of this case is the way the victims were murdered; it was as though they were in accordance with Masonic oath penalties, throat cut from ear to ear, and bowels ripped out of the body etc. Prior to being called Jack the Ripper, the killer referred to himself as "Leather Apron". Just like the item which is given to Master Masons, a lamb skin or leather apron. It has been suggested that the reason why Leather Apron was never caught, was because he was surrounded and protected by other fellow Masons in high positions.

Many influential figures throughout history have been Freemasons, with an allegiance which takes precedence over many other aspects of their lives. Cecil Rhodes was a member of the Bulawayo Lodge in Rhodesia, in 1895 he donated some land over to the order for the construction of a temple. During the 2nd World War, two of the leaders of the Allied coalition, Churchill and Roosevelt, were Freemasons, brothers united in war and united within international Freemasonry. Germany on the other hand, in 1934 ordered the disbandment of Freemasonry, the confiscation of its property and the closure of all its Lodges. Masons were seen as a threat to the German National Socialist revolution, they were prohibited from participating in public service work or having any connections within the National Socialist Party. Freemasons in German concentration camps were regarded as political prisoners and were made to wear a red inverted triangle.

On August 8th 1935, the Fuhrer, Adolf Hitler, announced a final end to all Masonic Lodges throughout Germany, he published an article in a National Socialist Party newspaper accusing the Masonic order of conspiring with international Jewry to create and control a world republic. As the war progressed, the German ban on Freemasonry applied to all occupied countries as well as nations allied with Germany.

Famous Freemasons

Benjamin Franklin	Douglas Macarthur	Joseph Bonaparte
George Washington	Harry S Truman	George VI
Franklin D Roosevelt	Cecil Rhodes	Albert Einstein
Winston Churchill	Thomas Edison	Sigmund Freud
J Edgar Hoover	Edward VII	Karl Marx
Silvio Berlusconi	Prince Albert Victor	Alexander I (Russia)
Andrew Jackson	Nathan Mayer Rothschild	George W Bush
Theodore Roosevelt	Buzz Aldrin	George H W Bush
Gerald Ford	Allister Crowley	Joseph Stalin
William McKinley	Henry Ford	Lindon B Johnson
William Taft	James Garfield	Manly P Hall

Tehran Conference 1943

A meeting of Masons, Stalin, Roosevelt & Chirchill

Masonic symbolism

There are many examples of Masonic artwork, in paintings, aprons and tracing boards, rich with astrological symbolism.

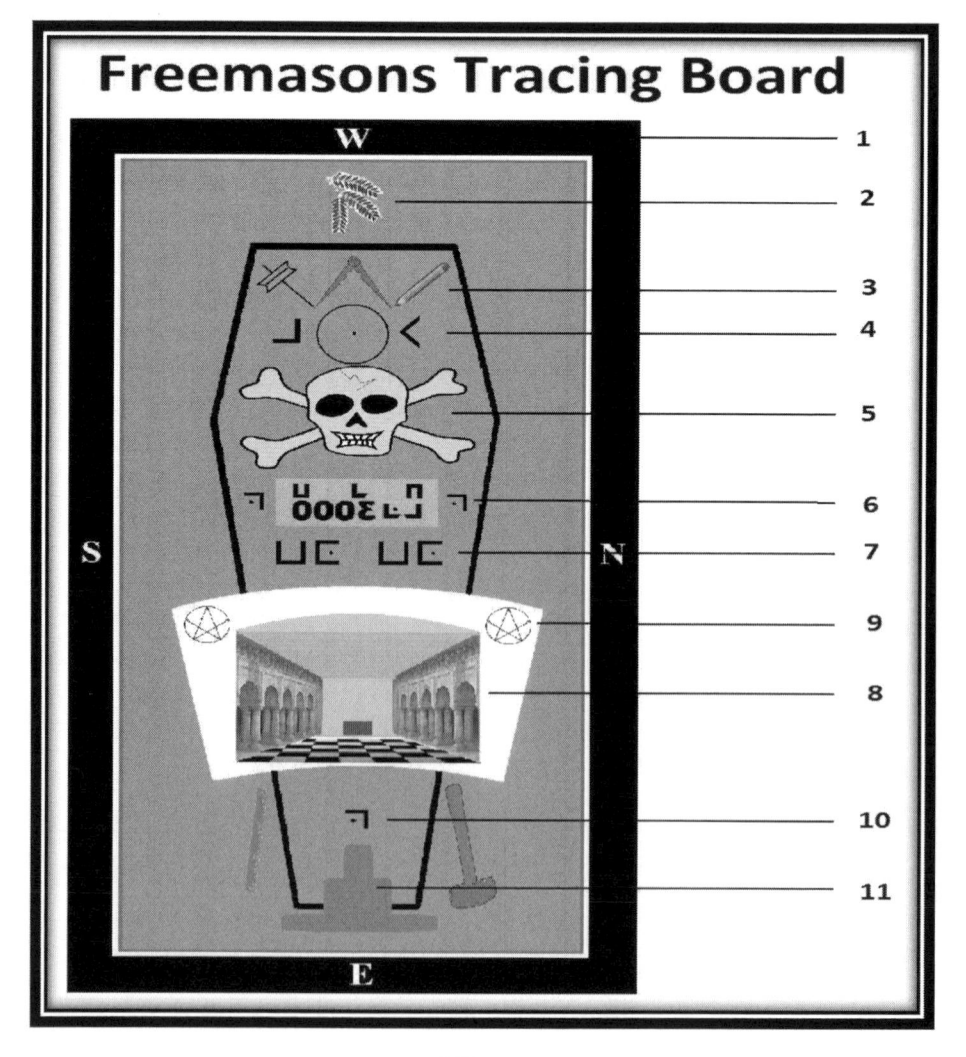

Freemasons Tracing Board

1) N S E W   The four cardinal points of the compass.

2) 3 sprigs of Acacia, spices are used to make incense for rituals. Smoke from the bark is thought to keep demons away. Moses's burning bush was thought to be an acacia tree and the Christian crown of thorns is also thought to have been made from acacia.

3) Tools used by a master mason. Plumb line, compass and a pencil, Forming a W for worship The plumb is similar to the Ancient South Korean trigram symbol for heaven. ☰ Kun Heaven
The pencil is focal consciousness, the half circle made by the compass represents the sub conscious and the plumb line is higher mind consciousness.

4) Freemasonry has its own secret alphabet, disguised as shapes and symbols.

A	B	C	J	K	L			
D	E	F	M	N	O		S	W
G	H	I	P	Q	R		T U X Y Or	
							V Z	

A	B	C					
D	E	F	J		N O P	S	W
G	H	I	K L	Q R	X Y		
			M	T U V	Z		

⌐ = A   ⟨ = L   A and L refers to Anno Lucis, a freemasonic dating system which began 4004 BC

(·) = Astrological symbol for the Sun

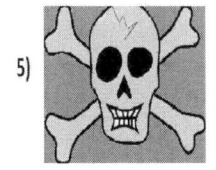

5) Skull and Crossbones, represents Saturn / Cronos in Capricorn, the sign of the Zodiac associated with the skeletal structure of the human body. The traditional bones used to make the cross are taken from human thighs, from the knees upwards, this is also associated with Capricorn (Cap for Knee caps).

6) To decipher this part of the puzzle, we need to look at its inverted reflection.

⌐ Π ⌐ ⌐ ⌐ = H A B (Hiram Abiff)

⌐⌐3000 = A L 3000 (Annos Lucis 3000)

7) ⊔∊ ⊔∊ Flip ∃⊔ ∃⊔ = MB MB   Either referring to Masonic Blue lodge, or
Mason Brother revered.

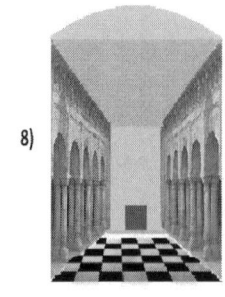

8) There are 5 arch ways either side, an illuminated arch at the end, and the arch which one enters through. 12 in total, representing the 12 houses of the Zodiac, with the 2 luminaries, the Sun and the Moon ruling one each.

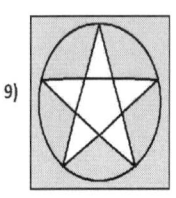

9) The pentagram, 5 pointed star is associated with Venus, the planet of love and liking. If this is inverted it represents the opposite of what Venus stands for. Venus is a planet which produces a pentagram pattern as it orbits around the earth.

Five inferior conjunctions of Venus repeat in a processing pentagram

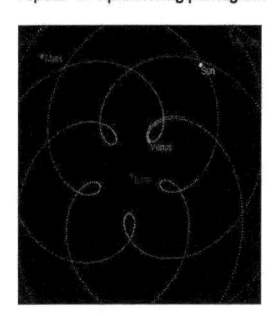

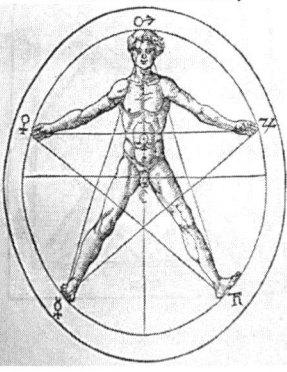

Balanced human harmony

Inverted energy of Venus, Associated with negative demonic energy

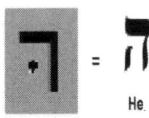

10) ה = ה   "He" is the fifth letter of the Hebrew alphabet, "He" also represents Helium which has a relative atomic mass of 4,003. Masonic year of creation is 4004 BCE.
He

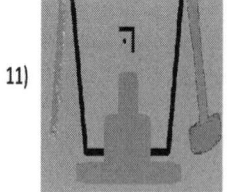

11) Tools used by Master Masons, also the tools used to murder Hiram Abiff. Just like in Christianity where they use the cross to symbolise the death of Christ, the Masons use these tools to evoke similar emotions.

When a person decides that they want to join a Freemason's Lodge, they must first ask to join. If you are a suitable candidate, you may be asked to fill out a petition form. Your request for membership is then voted on by existing members using a secret ballot system. The traditional method they use is also based on astrological symbolism. A white ball is chosen for yes, a black ball or cube is chosen for no. The white ball represents Venus energy of love and liking, whereas the black ball or cube represents Saturn's serious and restrictive energy. Most members will be unaware of this, blindly accepting it as a glorified game of marbles. The planet Venus is shrouded by a layer of reflective clouds made from sulphuric acid; this gives the planet a light yellowish white appearance.

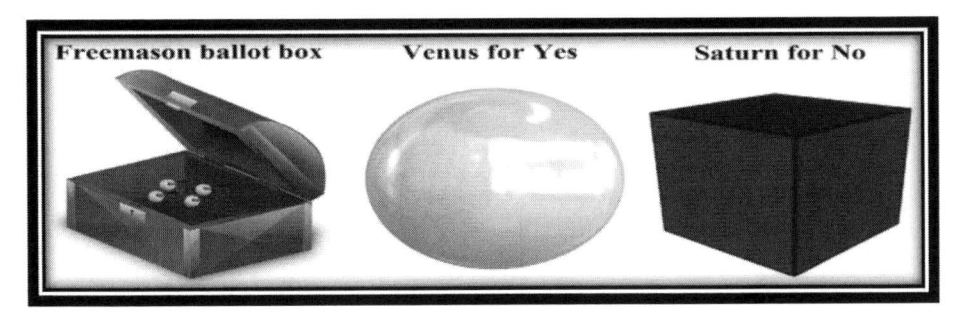

Freemason ballot box — **Venus for Yes** — **Saturn for No**

The Masons believe that human history began 4004 BC, a date confirmed by Bishop James Ussher, Archbishop of Armagh and Primate of Ireland from 1625-1656. He calculated that creation began on the nightfall preceding 23rd Oct 4004 BCE.[13] To find today's date we just add 4004 to the equation, so 2015 would be 6019. The significance of the 3000AL (Anno Lucis), refers to the time of Solomon, and their chronological time for the construction of Solomon's Temple.

The holistic ancient science of astrology, "as above so below", can be represented as wheels within wheels. The science works from the Great Year down to a 12 hour clock. If we take the Great Year to be 25,800 years, which is one full revolution of the binary system between our Sun and Sirius, and we divide each epoch of approximately 2150 years into its own complete zodiac cycle, each sign becomes 180 years. When we add the dates of biblical events, some interesting astrological correlations occur.

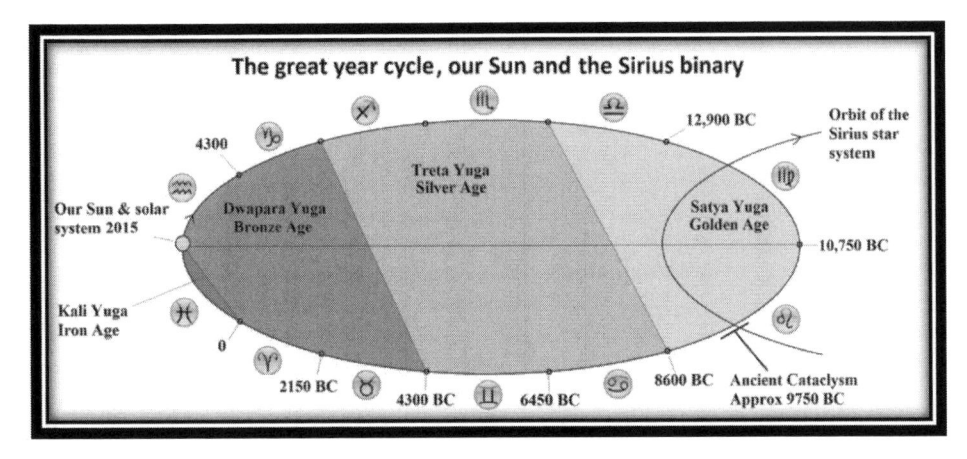

The great year cycle, our Sun and the Sirius binary

- Our Sun & solar system 2015
- Kali Yuga Iron Age
- Dwapara Yuga Bronze Age — 4300 BC, 2150 BC
- Treta Yuga Silver Age — 4300 BC, 6450 BC, 12,900 BC
- Satya Yuga Golden Age — 8600 BC, 10,750 BC
- Orbit of the Sirius star system
- Ancient Cataclysm Approx 9750 BC

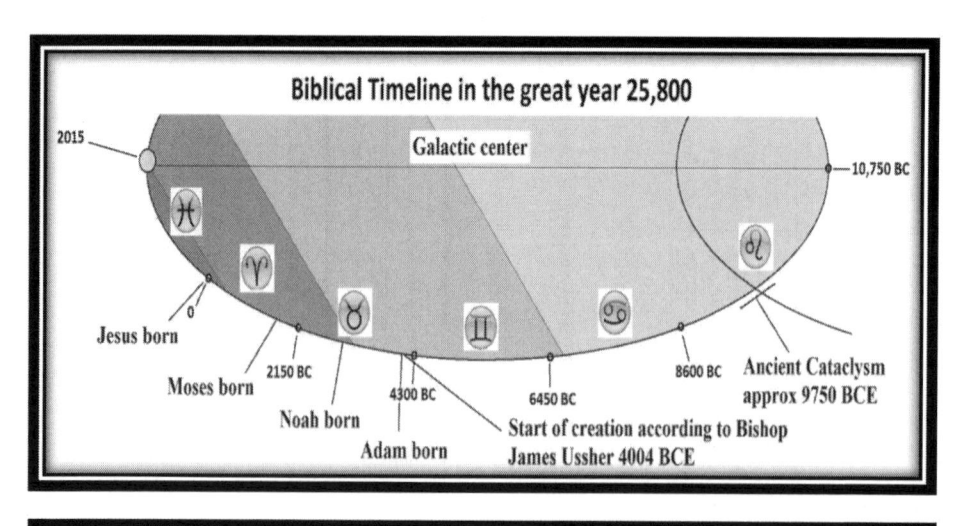

Biblical Timeline in the great year 25,800

- 2015
- Galactic center
- 10,750 BC
- Jesus born — 0
- Moses born — 2150 BC
- Noah born — 4300 BC
- Adam born — 6450 BC
- Start of creation according to Bishop James Ussher 4004 BCE
- 8600 BC
- Ancient Cataclysm approx 9750 BCE

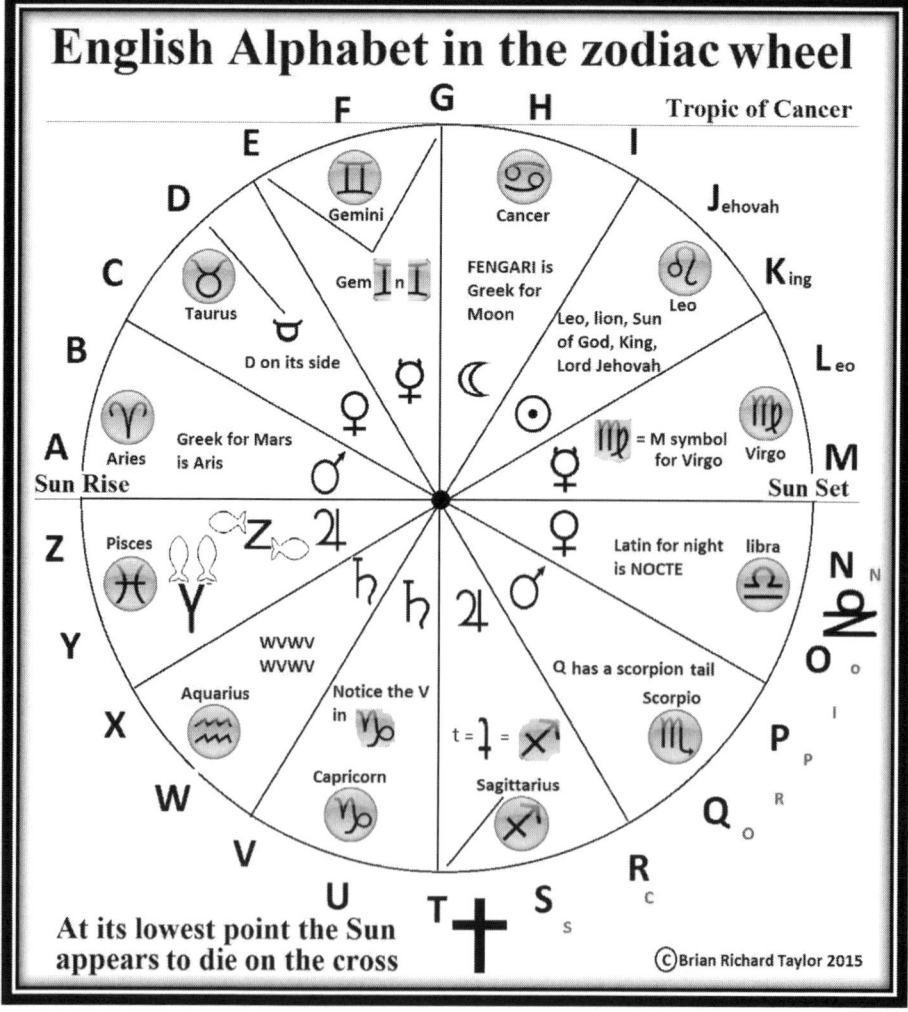

English Alphabet in the zodiac wheel

Tropic of Cancer

- A — Aries, Sun Rise
- B
- C
- D — D on its side
- E
- F
- G
- H
- I
- J — Jehovah
- K — King
- L — Leo
- M — Virgo = M symbol for Virgo, Sun Set
- N — libra, Latin for night is NOCTE
- O
- P
- Q — Q has a scorpion tail, Scorpio
- R
- S
- T — At its lowest point the Sun appears to die on the cross
- U
- V — Notice the V in Capricorn
- W
- X — Aquarius
- Y — WVWV WVWV
- Z — Pisces

Greek for Mars is Aris

Gem I n I

FENGARI is Greek for Moon

Leo, lion, Sun of God, King, Lord Jehovah

t = ↑ = ✗

©Brian Richard Taylor 2015

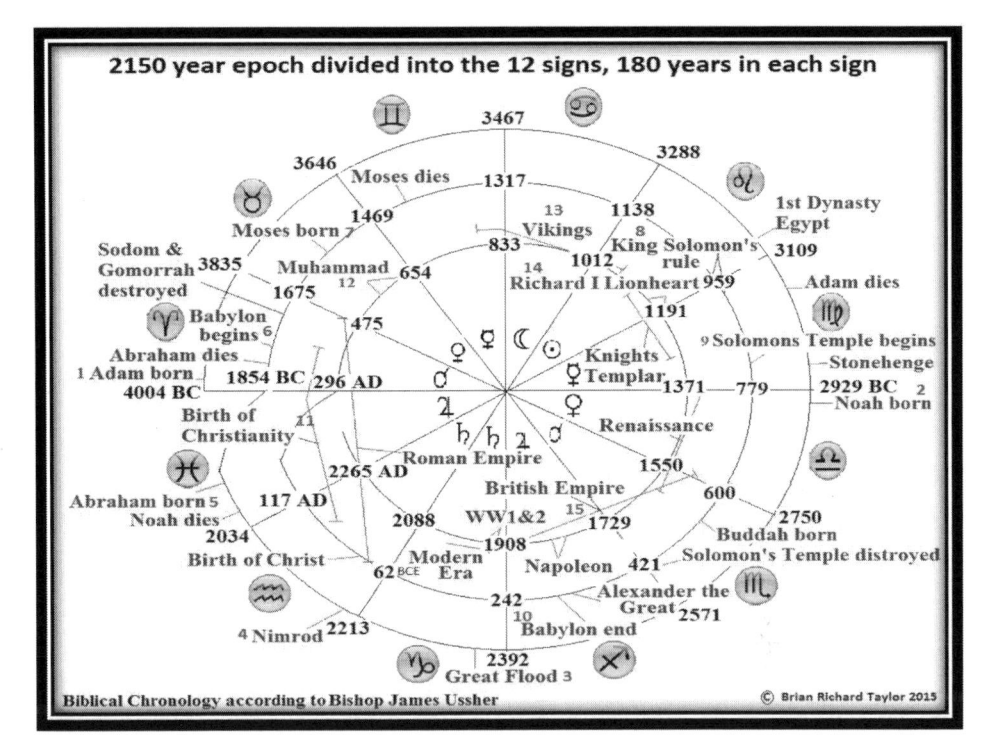

2150 year epoch divided into the 12 signs, 180 years in each sign

[Circular chart showing Biblical Chronology according to Bishop James Ussher, © Brian Richard Taylor 2015, with the following labels around the zodiac wheel:]

- Gemini: 3467, Moses dies 1317, 3646
- Cancer: 3288
- Taurus: Moses born 1469, 13 Vikings 833, 3646
- Leo: 1138, 1st Dynasty Egypt, King Solomon's rule 1012, 3109
- Aries: Babylon begins 6, Abraham dies, 1 Adam born 4004 BC, Muhammad 1675, 14 Richard I Lionheart 959, Adam dies, 1854 BC / 296 AD, 654, 12, 475
- Virgo: 9 Solomons Temple begins – Stonehenge 2929 BC, 2 Noah born, 1191
- Pisces: Abraham born 5, Noah dies 2034, Birth of Christianity, 117 AD, 2265 AD
- Libra: Knights Templar 1371, 779, Renaissance 1550
- Aquarius: Birth of Christ 62 BCE, Modern Era, 2088, WW1 & 2 1908, Roman Empire, British Empire 1729, 600, 2750 Buddah born, Solomon's Temple destroyed 421
- Scorpio: Alexander the Great 2571
- Capricorn: 4 Nimrod 2213, 242, Napoleon, Babylon end
- Sagittarius: Great Flood 3, 2392, 10

Center symbols: ♀ ☿ ☾ ☉ ♂ ♃ ♄ ♆

Biblical Chronology according to Bishop James Ussher   © Brian Richard Taylor 2015

1) Adam is born in Aries, the first astrological month of a new year, Adam dies in the opposite sign of Virgo, Represented by the letter M, A to M, Adam.

2) Noah is born in Libra; the two letters associated with this sign are N and O, Noah.

3) The Great Flood begins at the start of the astrological position of Noah's Arc, Capricorn through to Pisces.

4) Nimrod and Christ are born within 1 epoch of each other.

5) Abraham emerges as we move from Pisces into Aries, the ram, ABram, Abraham. Traditionally Abraham was born at the time of Nissan, the first month in the Jewish calendar, March-April the Passover. According to the Talmud, Abraham, Isaac and Jacob were all born and died during the month of Nissan.

6) Babylon begins in Aries, associated with the astrological letter B, BABylon.

7) Moses was born on the 7th Adar, in Taurus, the sign of the bull. Moses brought his people out from the Age of Taurus into the new Age of Aries.

8) King Solomon, SOL-OM-ON is the Sun in three different languages, which falls in the sign of Leo, a sign ruled by the Sun.

9) According to Seder Olam Rabbah, a 2nd century Hebrew language chronologist, Solomon's Temple was constructed in 832 BCE and destroyed in 422 BCE.[14] This places the temple many years after King Solomon, the temple also begins 1 epoch after Stonehenge.

10) At the bottom of the zodiac, we see a great deal of destruction, Babylon ends, Solomon's Temple ends, there is a Great Flood, WW1 & 2 along with Napoleon.

11) The birth of Christianity, along with its developments takes place within the sign of Pisces.

12) Muhammad and Islam began in the sign of Taurus, ruled by Venus, a whole epoch after Moses. The traditional symbol for Islam is the five-pointed star, the crescent Moon and the colour green. The five-pointed star represents Venus, love and liking, the crescent Moon is our Moon and our internal emotional subconscious. Taurus is a fixed earth sign, hence the colour green.

13) The Vikings began their exploits in Gemini, a sign ruled by Mercury, expanding their empire throughout the sign of Cancer, ruled by the Moon. The Vikings worshiped a God called Oden or Woden. Woden's day is where the English get there Wednesday from. Oden and Wednesday both represent the planet Mercury.

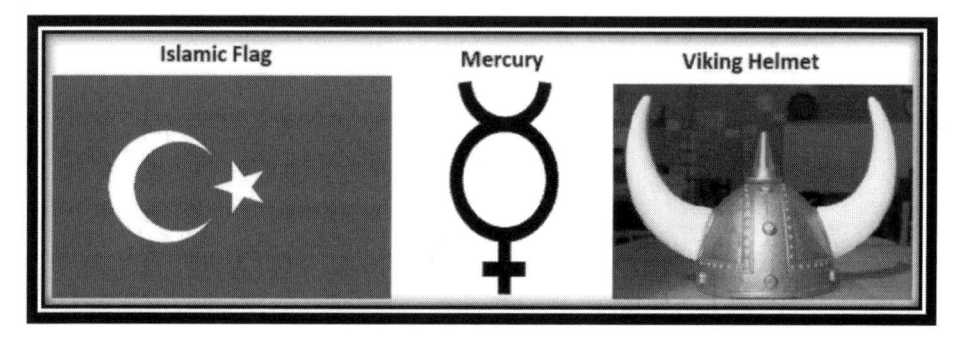

| Islamic Flag | Mercury | Viking Helmet |

14) Richard the Lionheart becomes King of England; this takes place in the sign of Leo the lion, one epoch after King Solomon and 2 epochs after the first Egyptian, Sun worshipping dynasty.

15) The British Empire begins throughout the Scorpio years ruled by Mars, the planet of proactive physical energy and war. The empire expands throughout the Sagittarian sign ruled by Jupiter the planet of expansion. It consolidates and transforms itself during the new era ruled by Saturn.

Freemasonry incorporates much of ancient Greeks religious and philosophical ideas. Another God from that period was Dionysus, the Greek God of the grape harvest, wine making and drinking, later becoming patron of the arts, he was also associated with rebirth and death and mystery religions. Alcohol was an important addition to the Dionysian's lifestyle, performing drunken fertility rituals and alcohol fuelled gatherings. Anything to do with harvesting falls under the sign of Virgo; Dionysus is another deity, this time representing Virgo in the house of bread.

It should be clear by now why Freemasons have, throughout history been accused of being a secret order empowered by occult knowledge. The top levels of Freemasonry are party to esoteric knowledge and secrets closely guarded from one generation to the next. The vast majority of low level Masons, are given mostly exoteric meanings, an invented, modified explanation of the truth, twisting ancient knowledge to conceal the light from shining on anyone unworthy or unprepared to receive it. Only the high-level Masons know the full extent of this knowledge and their influence throughout geopolitics and world events.

Origins of Freemasonry and the Roman Catholic Church

To understand Freemasonry, one must go back to the Knights Templar (The order of Solomon's Temple), a military order officially endorsed by the Roman Catholic Church. Their purpose was to make the Holy Land, from Antioch to Jerusalem, safe for Christian pilgrims. That was their perceived purpose but beneath it all was an enterprising business aspect, the Catholic Church wanted to control trade routes in this important junction between east and west. The Templar's spent 200 years attacking Muslims to secure bases and ports in the Holy Land. To fund these operations, they amassed an immense network of proceptories (communities) throughout Europe, involved in all sorts of business ventures to raise revenue for their front-line operations, essentially becoming the first multinational corporation. With regular donations and tax exemptions they became extremely wealthy, allowing them to conduct many crusades. In 1291 they were finally defeated, killed or chased out of the Holy Land by Muslim forces. While they were organising for another crusade, King Philip IV of France and Pope Clement V arranged for the arrest and disbandment of the Order of the Knights Templars. Philip was heavily in debt to the Templars and saw them as a state within a state, a threat to his authority. The Pope also saw no reason for their existence after their final defeat at the Siege of Acre; he also saw them as a potential threat to his business interests and authority. The Templar's, after years of service, were rounded up, tried for heresy and burnt alive at the stake, their land and assets were transferred over, by the Pope, to the Knights Hospitaller, a similar order whose main role was the health and welfare of pilgrims, a form of medieval Red Cross. The Knights Hospitaller, with all the land and wealth they inherited from the Templars, created a new headquarters in Rhodes and became known as the Knights of Rhodes, they then moved to Malta to become the Knights of Malta. After their defeat to Napoleon and later the British they eventually moved back to Rome where they still exist today. Many organisations mirroring the Knights of Malta have sprung up over the years, even adopting the same name, but only one has the endorsement of the Pope. The structure of these orders is very important, similar to that of the Freemasons; they are a secret order with secret oaths and various levels of hierarchy, with a Grand Master at the helm. They also have ancient pharaonic symbolism along with pharaonic knowledge and Egyptian deity worship.

| Flattened Pyramid | Knights Templar | Knights of Malta |

The Roman Catholic Church was the most dominant business/religious enterprise on the planet, spreading its influence all over the world. This all came to an end in the 16th century with the reformation and the birth of the Protestant movement (Christians Protesting against Catholicism). England broke away beginning the process under Henry VIII, later much of Europe descended into chaos sparking the Thirty Years War 1618-1648. The war was initially between Protestants and Catholics but later evolved into basic raw power and control. Many anti Catholics fled to the New World and the colonies of North America. The Protestant movement, aware of history and how much of a threat the knights Templar organisation became to the Roman Catholic Church, decided to create their own version, a secret order, an army of influential men able to infiltrate society promoting their beliefs, free from Papal rule, using a similar structure as the Templars, they called themselves Freemasons. During this time, much of Europe prohibited Jews from certain occupations, however they were welcome within Freemasonry due to their opposition towards Catholicism, this new intellectual army was uniting Christians and Jews against Rome. There is a great deal of Jewish symbolism within Freemasonry and generally a greater ratio of Jews inside lodges as opposed to outside. The Masons and the Catholic church both drew their underlining principle influences from ancient Egypt, this is why you find Obelisks, planets, stars and astrology in both Catholic and Masonic circles. They keep much of the important knowledge at the high levels. Only 1.9% of the founding fathers of America were Catholic, the majority were Protestant.[15] Although these versions of Protestantism had splinted off into different variations, they were still on the other side of Catholicism. Many were also Freemasons. Although they fought the British who were also Protestant, America was not freeing itself from the Catholic Church just to be enslaved by the Church of England (Anglican Church) and the corporations of King George III. The republic was created on similar lines to the old Roman Republic, before it was taken over by Julius Caesar using the pharaonic model of supreme figure head. This revised republic model became a symbol of new freedom all over the western world, many countries were envious.

Prior to the French Revolution Catholicism was the official religion of France, almost all its 28 million citizens were Roman Catholics. Many scholars believe that the Freemason movement had a role to play in the revolution,[16] with the intention of destroying the Catholic Church's hold over the country and the Pope's overall influence. King Louis XVI and his wife Mary-Antoinette, both Roman Catholics were executed, all churches were closed, public worship was forbidden and church bells were removed and melted down.[17] By the time Napoleon came to power, in 1799, the people were begging for a return of their spiritual institutions. Ready to accommodate religious beliefs Napoleon restored relations with the church, under his terms, mainly to prevent counter revolutions and to help promote his rule. On 16th July 1801 he created the **Concordat**,[18] Catholicism was to be recognised only as the religion of the majority of the French citizens, denying it any privileges within the state. The church was also required to give up all claims to property lost during the revolution, and all clergy were to swear an oath of loyalty to the government. In this new relationship, the Pope had very little authority. Eager to show who was boss, Napoleon insisted the Pope attend his crowning ceremony at Notre Dame Cathedral which made him Emperor Napoleon I. He was not a religious man but could see the use religion had in controlling the people; he also introduced a feast day for the new St Napoleon. Although he restored some of the Catholic Church's prestige, he had disdain for Rome; the concordat was introduced in all conquered territories, bringing the Catholic Church, throughout Europe, firmly under his heel. Napoleon's older brother, Joseph, became the Grand Master of the Grand Orient of France (1804 – 1815), managing its growth and reputation throughout France.[19] It has never been firmly established whether Napoleon himself was a Freemason, but many believe he was, or at least sympathetic to their cause. The relationship between Napoleon and the Pope was not good; it was a continuous conflict with the breaking point culminating in 1808 when Napoleon occupied Rome, this immediately led to the Pope's decision to excommunicate him. In retaliation Napoleon had the Pope arrested and eventually taken to France, where he became Napoleon's prisoner until 1814. The French Revolution was a watershed for Catholicism throughout the whole of Europe giving the Masons just what they wanted. This could be one reason why Napoleon was not executed after Waterloo, the British and the Masons could not have done a better job on the Catholic Church if they had tried themselves. The Concordat remained in effect until 1905.

The Statue of Liberty which stands in New York harbour, proudly symbolising liberty and freedom, donated by French Grand Orient Temple Masons to Masons of New York, in 1884, celebrating 100 years of the first Masonic Republic. The statue is the Roman Goddess Libertas which is the equivalent to the Egyptian Goddess ISIS.

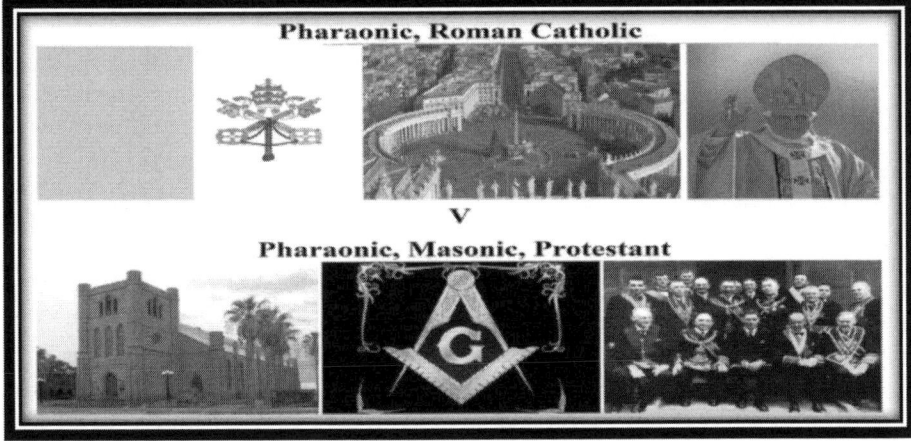

The Catholic Church had to find some way of getting their power and assets back, business is business, and both sides had a lot to lose. They chose to favour fascist dictatorships over democracies, because dictators could get the job done quickly, they worked closely with some of the most ruthless tyrants in history, as they moved slowly into position, all over Christendom, beginning with Rome.

"In 1922, Achille Ratti, freshly appointed cardinal, had been the surprising choice to succeed Pope Benedict XV. He took the name Pius XI. Later that same year, amid widespread violence, Benito Mussolini, the thirty-nine-year-old Fascist leader, became Italy's prime minister. Since then the two men had come to depend on each other. The dictator relied on the Pope to ensure Catholic support for his regime, providing much-needed moral legitimacy. The Pope counted on Mussolini to help him restore the Church's power in Italy " - Excerpt: The Pope and Mussolini, David I Kertzer[20]

The Roman Catholic Church has been opposed to Freemasonry since it became a noticeable threat back in 1738, and has made numerous pronouncements forbidding Catholics from becoming Freemasons. In 1983, Joseph Ratzinger issued a "**Declaration on Masonic Association**" which states:

"**The faithful who enrol in Masonic associations are in a state of grave sin and may not receive Holy Communion, the Church's negative judgement in regard to Masonic association(s) remains unchanged since their principles have always been considered irreconcilable with the doctrine of the Church and therefore membership in them remains forbidden**" - Declaration on Masonic association

In 1931 an anti-Catholic republican government came to power in Spain, they secularised education and prohibited religious education in schools, they also turned over all church's property to the state. This among other things helped trigger the Spanish Civil War, a brutal war between the legitimately elected republican government and nationalist dictator Francisco Franco. The Nationalists had a powerful ally, the Catholic Church, and the war was seen by many as a new crusade.

"**We are faced with a war that is taking on each day the character of a crusade**"- Francisco Franco, unification of the fighting forces, 18th April 1937

After the war, the close association between Franco's Nationalists and the Catholic Church legitimised the dictatorship, which in turn restored the church's former privileges. South America, predominantly Roman Catholic was awash with dictators of all kinds of persuasions, all batting for the Catholic Church. Central Europe was also very much Catholic, trying to keep itself together under the growing threat of Masonic/Zionist backed Bolshevism. The Russian Tsar and his family were Eastern Orthodox, which is the closest you will get to Catholicism without the Pope's overriding control. After his downfall and later execution, the Bolsheviks took over, with a policy to eradicate all religion which they intended to implement across Europe. Along with the rise of dictators throughout Europe, came a ban on Freemasonry which was outlawed in Fascist Italy, Spain and Germany.

The relationship between Catholics and Jews has always been a difficult one, traditionally the Catholic Church has been anti anyone who is not Catholic, and so anti-Semitism is a natural progression. It has also had a long history of killing people in the most vile and grotesque ways. The support for Hitler's National Socialist government in Germany was seen as beneficial for the church's future. Germany could stop the spread of Bolshevism and relocate all the Jews out of Europe by placing them in the heart of the Muslim world, forcing the Jews and Muslims together, driving a divisive wedge in the old crusader states. Hitler was brought up in a Catholic environment; his mother was a devout Roman Catholic. What effect this had on him is not clear, but Hitler himself was not in favour of any organised religion. A concordat was signed between the Pope and Germany in 1933, securing the rights of the church within the Reich; Hitler saw this as the Catholic Church's approval of his regime which gave him international respectability. He would later renege on this contract, by imprisoning both Catholics and Jews in his labour camps. Hitler was fully aware that Germany was surrounded, Freemasons in the west, Bolsheviks in the east and Roman Catholics in the south, he trusted no one, believing they all wanted to destroy his Reich. From the church's perspective, they could be seen as just looking after their own business interests regardless as to what Hitler's intentions were.

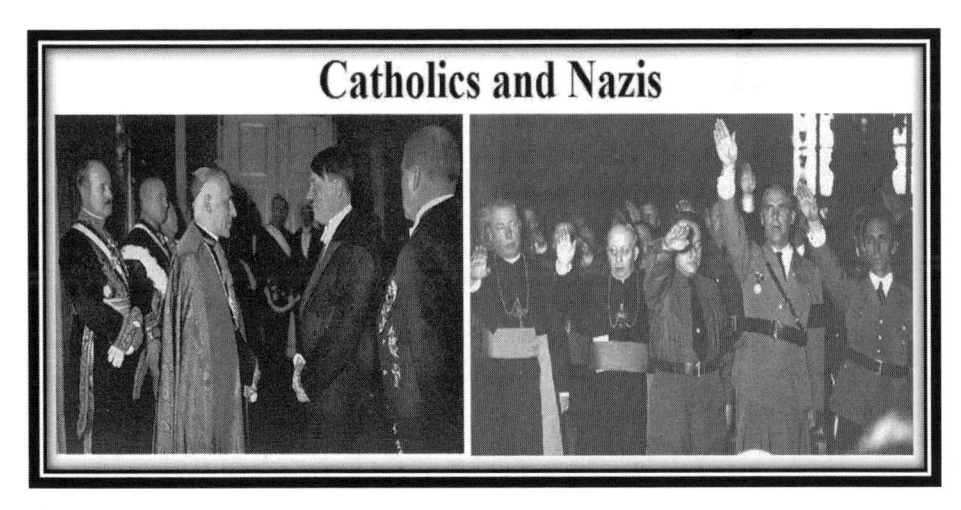

Catholics and Nazis

It is interesting to note that during the last days of World War Two, Hitler was rumoured to have escaped into Spain then Argentina, both Catholic countries. In August 1945 two atomic bombs were dropped over Japan, one on Hiroshima and one on Nagasaki, both with a significant Catholic population. The city of Nagasaki was evangelised by Jesuits in 1549 and became an important Catholic centre in the Far East. The Nagasaki bomb fell on the Urakami district right in the heart of the Catholic area, killing over 35,000 people including 70% of the 12,000 Catholics who lived there.[21] This was a true Holocaust by definition.

Holocaust - "destruction or slaughter on a mass scale, especially caused by fire or nuclear war".

Incidentally the new president of the United States, who sanctioned the bomb's use, was a high ranking Freemason, Harry S Truman. The official reason for dropping the bomb was questionable because Japan was already in the negotiating stages of surrendering. Truman's allegiance to Freemasonry appears to have superseded his role as President.

"Although I hold the highest civil honour in the world, I have always regarded my rank and title as a Past Grand Master of Masons the greatest honour that had ever come to me". - Harry S Truman.[22]

Freemason Truman Drops Atomic Bomb On Nagasaki

After the war, the Masonic alliance came away with more power than they went in with, they now had control over most of Europe and still held onto the world's reserve currency. The Americans were looking forward to putting the war behind them and moving forward. In 1961 the first and only Roman Catholic president sat in the Whitehouse, his name was John Fitzgerald Kennedy. Many people at the time voiced their concerns over this conflict of interest. By the 60's many people considered the Catholic Church and other religious organisations as ageing institutions with limited power, and in this new post war modern world religious divisions could be overlooked. Kennedy was regarded by many as one of the greatest presidents the US had ever seen, respected by the people as a progressive forward-thinking leader, he energised and motivated the nation during his short time in office. Whether his Catholic background had anything other than coincidence to do with his assassination is something most of us will never know, only those hiding behind national security and official secrets are partial to that information. Bobby Kennedy and JFK junior were also Roman Catholics. One thing we can be sure of was Kennedy's opposition to secret oaths and secret societies.

"The very word "secrecy" is repugnant in a free and open society; and we are as a people inherently and historically opposed to secret societies, to secret oaths and to secret proceedings" - Part of John F Kennedy's speech, press association 1961 (full quote in Chapter 3)

Vice President Lyndon Johnson, who immediately took over the presidency from Kennedy after his death, was a Freemason, so was J. Edgar Hoover and at least three members of the Warren Commission, Chief Justice Earl Warren, Richard Russel and Gerald Ford. It is also important to point out the number of former US presidents who were also Freemasons,

George Washington, Andrew Jackson, James Polk, James Buchanan, Andrew Johnson, James Garfield, William McKinley, Theodore Roosevelt, William Taft, Warren Harding, Franklin Roosevelt, Harry Truman, Lyndon Johnson and Gerald Ford.[23] The Roman Catholic Kennedys were in the heart of Freemason territory condemning secret societies, not a good mix if you want to reach retirement age.

The economical aspect is also important because the Masons have on their side the world's reserve currency, and most of the international banking institutions. It is easy for them to apply financial pressure on adversaries and none conformers, I personally don't regard the level of poverty in many Catholic countries as a coincidence.

The Infiltration of both the Masons and the Vatican, by one another, has been going on for centuries, each side trying to gain the advantage and undermine their opponent's institutions from within. The Vatican being one of the biggest financial powers, wealth accumulators and property owners in existence, sets itself up as a favourable target for takeover. If any organisation could add this to its portfolio it could easily control the whole planet.

"Today evil doers all seem allied in a tremendous effort inspired by and with the help of a society powerfully organized and widely spread over the world; it is the Society of Freemasons. In fact, those people no longer even try to dissimulate their intentions, but they actually challenge each other's audacity in order to assail God's August Majesty. It is now publicly and overtly that they undertake to ruin the Holy Church, so as to succeed, if it is possible, in the complete dispossession of Christian nations of all the gifts they owe to Our Saviour Jesus Christ. As a result, in the space of a century and a half, the sect of the Freemasons has made incredible progress. Making use at the same time of audacity and cunning, Masonry has invaded all the ranks of social hierarchy, and in the modern States it has begun to seize a power which is almost equivalent to Sovereignty" - Pope Leo XIII April 20 1884

"Let us remember that CHRISTIANITY and Freemasonry are essentially incompatible, to such an extent, that to become united with one means being divorced from the other. Let us, therefore, expose Freemasonry as the enemy of God, of the Church and of our Motherland "- Pope Leo XIII Dec 8th 1892

It has been suspected that Freemasons have infested the Catholic Church especially during the Post WW2 era. There have been many articles and accounts written about Masonic infiltration, even suspecting them of being involved in the death of Pope John Paul I, in 1978. The new Pope was only 33 days into his new role when he was found dead in his bed, suspected of having a heart attack. In David Yallop's book, "In God's Name",[24] he identifies a link between Freemasons within the Vatican, and the death or murder of the new Pope. These Freemasons in the Vatican are known as P2 (propaganda due), the Grand Orient Masonic Lodge of Italy, founded in 1805 during the Napoleonic kingdom of Italy. Interestingly, one of the P2 Masons suspected of being involved, Gian Roberto Calvini, was also the Vatican's banker, later found hanging from scaffolding under Blackfriars Bridge in London's banking district, in June 1982.

If Masons have infested the Vatican to the point at which it is no longer independent, their ability to oppose the spread of Masonic power and its version of globalisation has finally been neutralised. As a result, the Roman Catholic Church has opened its doors to paedophiles, homosexuals and women priests, internal division which most likely would have been resisted before. The Masonic takeover could explain Tony Blair's recent conversion to Catholicism, he is now on safe territory, and it's also beneficial to his public relations campaign, when seeking the job of Master of the Universe. His new Catholic status could bring him 2 billion new supporters.

"Ever since I began preparations to become a Catholic, I felt I was coming home ... this is now where my heart is, where I know I belong." - Tony Blair

Note for chapter 7

(1) Fabian society, New World Encyclopaedia,
http://www.newworldencyclopedia.org/entry/Fabian_Society

(2) Evening Herald (Dublin, Ireland), February 3, 1948, reprinted in Economic Council Letter (National Economic Council), Issue 278, Part 397 (1952), p. 290.

(3) G Edward Griffin, interview with Norman Dodd, 1982. Special committee to investigate tax exempt foundations, 1953-4, https://www.youtube.com/watch?v=YUYCBfmIcHM

(4) Norman Dodd, the Dodd report to the Reece committee on foundations, 1954, PDF,
http://brynmawrcollections.org/traces/archive/files/552952f585af5ef916a246c55fcb7a76.pdf

(5) Carroll Reece, August 19, 1954, Reece summed up his investigation,
http://modernhistoryproject.org/mhp?Article=FinalWarning&C=2.5

(6) Daniel Estulin, The True Story of the Bilderberg Group, TrineDay publishers, 2009

(7) List of Bilderberg participants, https://en.wikipedia.org/wiki/List_of_Bilderberg_participants

(8) Jonathan Spence, Yale Daily News no. 96 February 29 1972, http://digital.library.yale.edu/cdm/compoundobject/collection/yale-ydn/id/135148/rec/14

(9) Yale China Association, wikipedia, https://en.wikipedia.org/wiki/Yale-China_Association#cite_note-1

(10) Science and Nature, Horizon, BBC, 17/9/14, http://www.bbc.co.uk/sn/tvradio/programmes/horizon/solomon_qa.shtml

(11) Craig, G. Y. and E. J. Jones. A Geological Miscellany. Princeton University Press, 1982, Bishop James Ussher dates creation. Page 2, http://www.lhup.edu/~dsimanek/ussher.htm

(12) Seder Olam Rabba, 2nd century Hebrew language chronologist, https://en.wikipedia.org/wiki/Seder_Olam_Rabbah

(13) James Perloff, The Shadows of Power: The Council on Foreign Relations and the American Decline, 1988, Western Island Publishers.

(14) Members Of the CFR, Wikipedia, https://en.wikipedia.org/wiki/Members_of_the_Council_on_Foreign_Relations

(15) Religious Affiliation of the Founding Fathers of the United States of America, http://www.adherents.com/gov/Founding_Fathers_Religion.html

(16) Freemasons in the French Revolution, http://freemasonry.bcy.ca/texts/revolution.html

(17) Gemma Betros,The French revolution and the Catholic church, History today, Published in History Review Issue 68 December 2010, http://www.historytoday.com/gemma-betros/french-revolution-and-catholic-church

(18) Concordat 1801, wikipedia, https://en.wikipedia.org/wiki/Concordat_of_1801

(19) Joseph Bonaparte, https://en.wikipedia.org/wiki/Joseph_Bonaparte

(20) David I Kertzer, The Pope and Mussolini, the secret history of Pius xi and the rise of fascism in Europe. http://www.npr.org/books/titles/265793344/the-pope-and-mussolini-the-secret-history-of-pius-xi-and-the-rise-of-fascism-in-#excerpt

(21) BR Anthony Josemaria, The Catholic Holocaust of Nagasaki, Homiletic and pastoral review, 2010, http://www.hprweb.com/2010/08/the-catholic-holocaust-of-nagasaki-why-lord/

(22) Honolulu lodge F&A.M, Official Website, Masonic Quotes. http://honolulufreemasons.org/masonic-quotes/

(23) Presidents of the US who were Freemasons, Wikipedia, https://en.wikipedia.org/wiki/List_of_Presidents_of_the_United_States_who_were_Freemasons

(24) David Yallop, In Gods Name, Basic Books 2007, http://www.goodreads.com/book/show/733940.In_God_s_Name

Chapter 8. Perverting the course of history

"**He who controls the past controls the future. He who controls the present controls the past.**" -George Orwell 1984

"**History is a set of lies that people have agreed upon.**" -Napoleon Bonaparte

"**Our past is only a little less uncertain than our future, and like the future, it is always changing, always revealing and concealing.**" -Daniel Boorstein, Hidden History

"**The historian must serve two masters, the past and the present.**" -Fritz Stern, the Varieties of History

"**History will be kind to me for I intend to write it.**" -Winston Churchill

"**Study the historian before you begin to study the facts.**" -Edward H. Carr

Which has the greater influence, the past on the present or the present on the past? As the victors write the history books, they also massage previous known versions, selecting what suits them and deselecting what doesn't. The aim is to control the collective minds of its citizens who passively accept what is referred to as official history (his - story). You could argue that the only certain thing about history is that it happened in the past, the rest is an official exercise in social engineering of the public consciousness. The greater the power and influence of the control system, the greater the potential for perverting and manipulating the truth. Every empire, kingdom or dictator has, in some way, secured its power base on a glorified version of the past, aligning themselves with destiny and divinity, as they promote an impressive version of history designed to subordinate their citizens, who are taught to fear and respect their new all-powerful masters.

Basic orthodox view of history

Once upon a time there was nothing, around 13 billion years ago energy and matter spontaneously exploded into existence, from this void of nothingness sprang the universe, this is known as the Big Bang Theory. Around 1 billion years later stars magically appeared which lit up that universe. Our solar system, its planets and the Earth all evolved around 4.6 billion years ago. The gravitational collapse of a giant molecular cloud, collected in the centre to form our Sun, along with various concentrated pockets of dense clouds which formed moons and planets. Our Moon formed relatively recently, between 30 and 50 million years after the Earth. A hypothesis known as the Giant Impact theory, concluded that a body the size of Mars struck the Earth ejecting a huge amount of matter into orbit; this matter later became spherical and formed what we know today as the Moon. At some point in the Earth's early beginnings conditions arose creating the perfect environment for life to emerge. Single cellular organisms appeared around 3.8 billion years ago, 3 billion years later the first multi cellular plants appeared, probably green algae. Over time these cells became more specialised, unique and interdependent.

This current Phanerozoic phase started approximately 540 million years ago, it is divided into three sub eras, the Palaeozoic, the Mesozoic and the Cenozoic. With the Palaeozoic era being 540 million to 250 million years ago. It was a period where many modern groups of life began to evolve. The land was inhabited initially by plants, then by animals, on an enormous continent known as Pangaea. This was followed by the Mesozoic era, from 250 to 66 million years ago, also divided into sub sections with the Triassic, Jurassic and the Cretaceous era. Each era became disrupted by some form of global extinction event. The Cenozoic era, which we are in now, began after such an event around 66 million years ago, a global cataclysm which saw the end of the dinosaurs. The Cenozoic era also has three sub divisions, the Paleogene, Neogene and Quaternary periods. Any life which survived up to this point diversified into the species we see today. The mega continent of Pangaea began to break apart around 180 million years ago, separating to form new smaller continents. There have been many global extinction events which have taken place over the Earth's evolvement; some so catastrophic they put an end to upwards of 95% of all life on Earth.

Around 6 million years ago two branches split from small apes living in the Saharan regions of Africa. The offspring of which evolved into chimpanzees and the Homo sapiens we see today. Modern Homo sapiens are thought to have originated around 200,000 years ago, spreading all over the planet. By 9,000 BC they had reached the tip of South America where they existed in small groups of hunter gatherers. Only when language evolved to a point where communication between generations preserved knowledge did social cultures and communities develop. At this point, agricultural communities began to emerge around the fertile crescent within the Middle East, developing into small villages and towns. Around 8,000 BC surplus food allowed Priests and governing classes to emerge leading to the growth of culture and civilised societies, Sumer around 4,000 – 3,000 BC is thought to be one of the first civilised cultures, followed by Egypt, the Indus Valley and China.

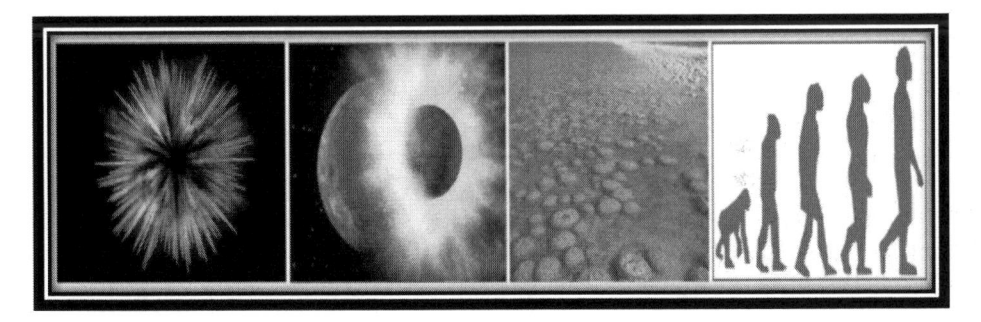

Charles Darwin

Charles Darwin was born into a wealthy upper-class family in 1809, in the town of Shrewsbury, Shropshire, England. His father Robert Darwin was a successful society doctor and financier. Charles is best known for his contribution toward the theory of evolution and natural selection, but there is more behind the Darwin story than we are commonly told. The theory of evolution had been established by a French naturalist by the name of Jean-Baptiste Lamarck, fifty years prior to Darwin's time. Lamarck was the first valid understanding of the evolution process that was scientifically published. A more advanced understanding of the natural processes surrounding evolution was later put forward in a manuscript written by Alfred Russell Wallace, who wrote a paper entitled *"Natural Selection"*. Wallace sent his manuscript to Charles Darwin asking for his opinion, to see if it was worthy of further publication, and if so, would Darwin forward it to Sir Charles Lyell at the Royal Society. Darwin profoundly impressed by Wallace's paper did indeed take it to Sir Charles Lyell, but wanted to be the provider of the theory of evolution to the world himself. They pondered over Wallace's complete understanding of natural selection and evolution, wondering what course of action they should take. Both Darwin and Lyell were part of the upper class Victorian elite, they decided to change the priority of the paper, claiming that Darwin had also written a manuscript offering his theory on the same subject, he therefore, quickly wrote an abstract purporting to this. This agreement between Darwin and Lyell was known as "The Delicate Arrangement".[1] A meeting was arranged at the Linnean Society of London to present "**A theory of evolution, presented by Charles Darwin & Alfred Russel Wallace** ". As Wallace was an educated man from the subordinate classes, it was more favourable within the establishment to have Darwin leading the charge. The problem was that Darwin and Wallace each had a different approach when presenting their theories on natural selection. The theories were similar but the perspective made all the difference.

Darwin's perspective on the theory of natural selection: Survival of the fittest. Every day is a constant struggle, you must compete and strive to get to the top, otherwise you will be taken over by someone fitter than yourself and you will die. Only the select few at the top will survive, the rest are worthless inferior specimens who deserve to become extinct.

Wallace's perspective on the theory of natural selection: The world of evolution is based on the elimination of the weakest. All you need to do to survive is make sure you're not the ones at the bottom, strive not to be the weakest. With this perspective, you do not have to unnecessarily compete with everyone else to get to the top, just make sure you're not last, the one left behind, at the bottom.

Two similar theories but two different approaches both can alter a person's belief system and both can offer up and play out as a perception within reality. Wallace had a more relaxed, realistic understanding of the natural selection process, not as severe as Darwin's approach depicting a constant battle for survival. It was necessary for the establishment at that time to promote a perverse version of the natural selection process, the Wallace approach did not favour a belief system fit for empire building and the aspirations of the elite classes running the British Empire. If a nation was to adopt the Darwinist approach as the foundation for their nation's policy, they could artificially promote competition within society stimulating its citizens into competing with one another, which in turn would fuel the growth of their debt based monetary system together with a multitude of social divisions.

Sirius

Why Sirius? what is so important about this star system over all the others. In 1844 the German astronomer Friedrich Wilhelm Bassel noticed the bright star Sirius had a slight oscillation to its course compared to its neighbours, he concluded that Sirius A had a companion star Sirius B, which orbited in a binary every 50 years. Sirius A is the brightest star in our night sky, easily identifiable to the naked eye; it is twice the mass of our own Sun but twenty-five times brighter. Sirius B, a collapsed red giant, which collapsed around 120 million years ago became a white dwarf, a star with the same mass as our Sun but a radius 0.0008th the size, such a large mass in a small volume creates a dense structure thousands of times denser than anything seen in our own solar system, its gravitational influence is enormous. Many modern scholars have come to the conclusion that not only is Sirius A in a binary with Sirius B but the whole Sirius star system is also in a binary with our own solar system, an elliptical binary which takes approximately 25,800 years to complete a full cycle. This cyclical binary was very important to our ancient ancestors; they went out of their way to build enormous, complicated structures hoping to pass on knowledge which would be valuable to future generations. Bearing in mind Sirius is the most important star within the order of Freemasonry, and the most important star to the ancient Egyptians, who had advanced knowledge of astrology and astronomy. One may ask what is so important about Sirius.

This is a hypothesis which I feel fits all pieces of the puzzle together, making sense of the importance of Sirius and what our ancestors were trying to tell us. Every 25,800 years our solar system and the Sirius star system move closer together, the gravitational and electromagnetic influence of the Sirius system on our comparatively small solar system is so profound it has the potential to cause cataclysms of biblical proportions. The planets, asteroids, meteors and space debris trailing behind the gravitational pull of the Sirius star system is something which our solar system encounters as it passes through on its elliptical orbit with its sister star Sirius. During this period anything can happen, the possibility of planets being struck by giant asteroids, meteors or whatever else lurks 8.6 light years away is increased. It all depends upon how close our solar system mergers with the Sirius system, they could pass too close for comfort before beginning the long 12,900-year descent back out again. The familiar line up of planets within our solar system could change dramatically, throwing the planets into different orbits by the combined forces of these two gigantic systems passing one another, a potential which could have devastating effects upon life on Earth, increasing the chance of cataclysms and chaos, throwing all types of species into extinction along with sea rises and Ice Ages. Pockets of humanity have managed to survive previous cataclysms, holding onto remnants of the once advanced civilisations they belonged to, leaving behind some form of knowledge for us to decipher.

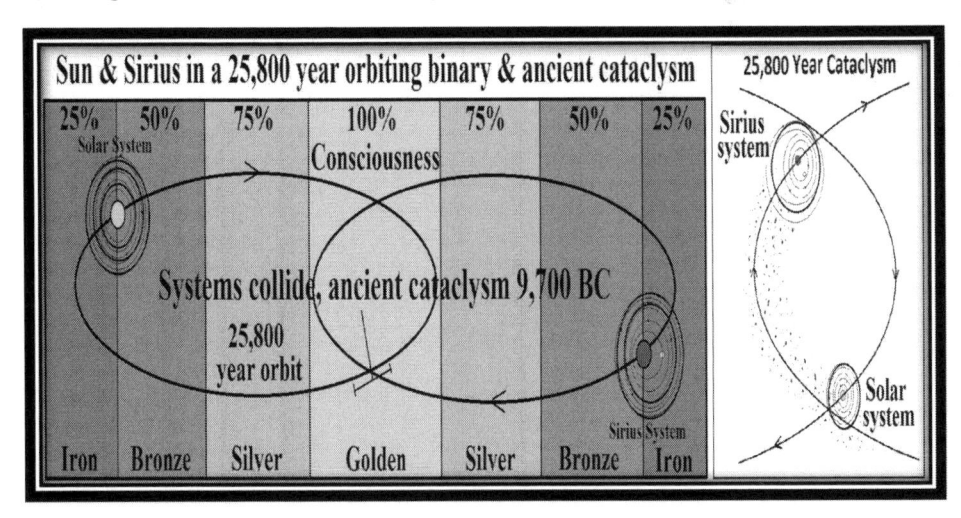

Our solar system has just moved out of the Kali Yuga or Iron Age within the Great Year cycle, a turning point where we begin the 12,900-year ascension towards Sirius. The last time these systems passed each other was approximately 12,000 years ago, a point in which archaeological evidence points to a global catastrophe. In a recent article by Graham Hancock titled "Fingerprints of a global cataclysm 12,800 years ago", he writes.

"Vast swathe of our planet that geologists call the Younger Dryas Boundary Field. Across this huge "fingerprint" spanning North America, Central America, parts of South America, most of Europe and parts of the Middle East as well, the tell-tale traces of multiple impacts by the fragments of a giant comet have been found. Some of these fragments were TWO KILOMETRES or more in diameter and they hit the earth like a blast from a cosmic scatter-gun around 12,800 years ago." - Graham Hancock[2]

An article titled "**Did a Comet Hit Earth 12,000 Years Ago?**", published in the Scientific American, also points to the same time period.

"Roughly 12,900 years ago, massive global cooling kicked in abruptly, along with the end of the line for some 35 different mammal species, including the mammoth."[3]

The book "**Cataclysm, Compelling Evidence of a Cosmic Catastrophe in 9500 B.C.** ".

"Follow this multi-disciplinary, scientific study as it examines the evidence of a great global catastrophe that occurred only 11,500 years ago. Crustal shifting, the tilting of Earth's axis, mass extinctions, up thrusted mountain ranges, rising and shrinking land masses, and gigantic volcanic eruptions and earthquakes--all indicate that a fateful confrontation with a destructive cosmic visitor must have occurred. The abundant geological, biological, and climatological evidence from this dire event calls into question many geological theories and will awaken our memories to our true--and not-so-distant--past." - Cataclysm 1997[4]

How do we know our Solar system is in a binary with Sirius? Today's astronomers agree that Sirius is a whitish blue star, but it hasn't always been described this way. Over 2000 years ago the star system was noted as being red like Mars. Ptolemy an ancient writer of Alexandria during the 2nd century AD, a mathematician, astronomer, geographer and astrologer, referred to Sirius as reddish.

"**The star in the mouth, the brightest, which is called ' The Dog ', and reddish** ". Claudius Ptolemy, Almagest, book viii, 150AD

Many references in our ancient past referred to Sirius as being red, how can this be? were they colour blind, or playing a joke on us, we all know Sirius is blue, its unmistakably blue. When you consider that our solar system and the Sirius star system are in a perpetual binary, 12,900 years moving away from one another and 12,900 moving together, it all makes sense. There is a scientific reason for the colour change; it's called the '**Doppler shift"**, light and sound appear at different frequencies depending on whether they are moving towards us or moving away. A car with its horn activated will appear high pitched as it moves towards us, then low pitched as it moves away. The same is true for light; an object moving towards us will be seen in the higher frequencies i.e. blue, whereas an object moving away will be seen at the lower frequencies of red. The ultra violet light range is of a higher frequency than the infra-red spectrum. This is also true with considering ourselves as human biological entities, transmitter receivers of electromagnetic energy. When you're attracted to someone, both parties will resonate at a high frequency, within an excitable energy range, its natural, it's just two people moving together. When you're repulsed or moving away from someone, whom you dislike, your energies are both vibrating at lower ends of this electromagnetic spectrum, a frequency of hatred instead of love, you see red.

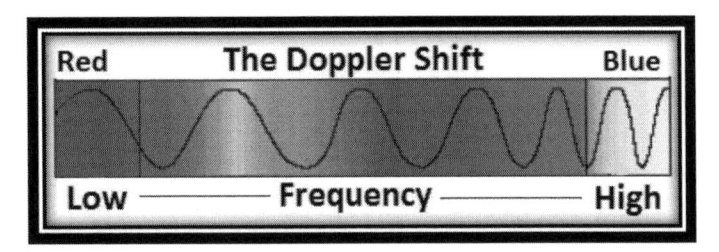

Red   **The Doppler Shift**   **Blue**

Low ———— **Frequency** ———— **High**

When Sirius is moving towards us it will appear blue, and when it moves away it will appear red. It all makes perfect sense because we have only recently turned from the furthest point in the binary to our long journey back towards the Golden Age of enlightenment, connecting with Sirius, the start of 12,900 years of ascension.

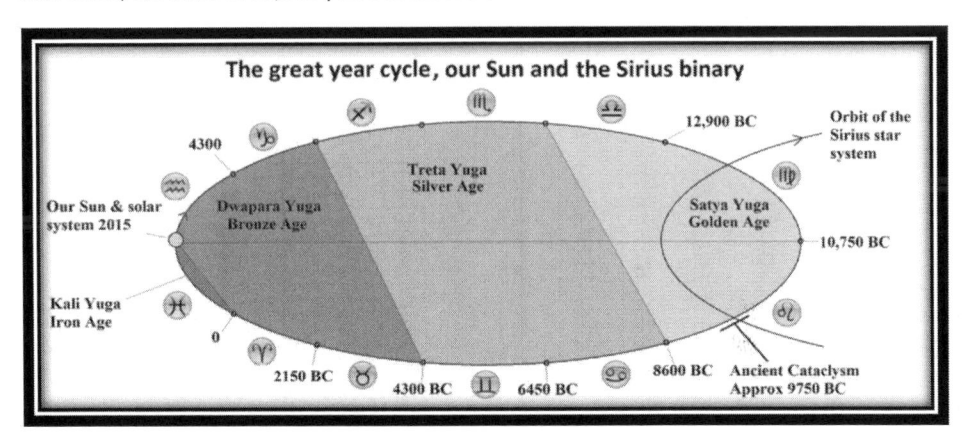

The great year cycle, our Sun and the Sirius binary

- 12,900 BC — Orbit of the Sirius star system
- 4300
- Treta Yuga Silver Age
- Our Sun & solar system 2015
- Dwapara Yuga Bronze Age
- Satya Yuga Golden Age
- 10,750 BC
- Kali Yuga Iron Age
- 0
- 2150 BC
- 4300 BC
- 6450 BC
- 8600 BC
- Ancient Cataclysm Approx 9750 BC

Our Sun is the energy source for our physical consciousness, our projected reality, and focal consciousness. Sirius is the source of our subconscious, ISIS, our inner emotions, the closer we get to Sirius the greater our connection with the universal subconscious, we essentially become enlightened, spiritual beings, connecting to source and wisdom within a natural elevating cycle. At this moment, we are still a long way out, our base characteristics as collective humanity is still grounded to the physical realm, battling constantly with our animal instincts, wilfully ignorant of higher mind potential within cosmic energy, this will gradually change as we move through the Bronze Age, Dwapara Yuga, towards the silver and finally back into the Golden Age of enlightenment, a 25,800 year cycle. Everything in the universe resonates a symphony of unique frequencies, influencing the mind, body and soul. The closer we get to any one of these sources the greater the impact. During the day our Sun energises our focal consciousness, we awake from a sleep in which we appear to be unconscious or deep inside the subconscious mind, the Sun's energy helps to pull us back into focal consciousness. this will be true with Sirius, our subconscious minds are generally habitual and inaccessible to the majority concerned with focal matters and materialism, but the closer we get to the source of our subconscious, Sirius, the greater the awakening. Our ancestors left us clues to this knowledge, if only we were smart enough to understand. The highest levels of Freemasonry and various other secret societies understand the significance of Sirius, but keep it under lock and key, only for the initiated that have proven themselves worthy of sacred knowledge. Our ancient ancestors also knew the value of astronomy and astrology, the foundation to a system of spirituality and wisdom, only to be perverted throughout the ages by a variety of controlling elitists, pulling humanity away from enlightenment and the science of light.

Our history is cyclical, not lineal, as main stream Darwinism suggests. They want us to believe that we are at the pinnacle of evolving human species, adapting to our new environment from the primeval slime which we came from, over thousands of years, each generation more intelligent and advanced than anything that went before. This cannot be true for two reasons, first we are in a cyclical binary with Sirius, a binary which transforms humanity in a perpetual cycle of high and low consciousness. Secondly, we have the evidence of ancient advanced civilisations going back at least 12,000 years or even longer. The pyramids of Giza in Egypt, the ancient ruins of Puma Punka, at Tiwanaku in Bolivia; ancient megalithic stone blocks at Baalbek, in Lebanon, weighing over 1000 tons each, foundations to old temples which modern technology couldn't produce today, although, according to Darwin, we are at the cutting edge of civilisation, surpassing anything that ever existed before. For over 100 years the Darwinist camp have not been able to produce a missing link, no matter how hard they try they cannot find it, this is simply because there isn't one to be found. Our real history is being kept under lock and key by our controlling classes, who not only have access to ancient records, they only allow the masses to see a version of history (his – story) which they see fit to dispense, a version keeping us ignorant of who we are, where we came from and what our true potential is.

Ancient Technology & Megalith blocks

Egypt

Egyptian history has been officially whitewashed, perverted by a network of Caucasian colonialists, who have for many years controlled the flow of information and evidence, with an agenda to distance ancient Egypt away from its original African ancestry. Many Pharaohs were predominantly black men, black Africans. Modern history books on Egypt subtly divert the reader away from ancient black African culture, even placing Egypt away from the African continent and into the Middle East. The western spheres of power have influenced the world's view of Egyptian history detaching the black man as far as possible from being part of an advanced civilisation, possibly more advanced than the one we see in many parts of the world today, a civilisation which may have had a hand in building the great temples and pyramids in Egypt, an achievement which would not be possible now, even with our level of technology. Most of modern society has a tainted and arrogant belief that they are at the forefront of the most advanced civilisation in all of human history, choosing to ignore some of the awesome megalithic and stone structures strategically placed all over the world by our distant ancestors. From the early days of Napoleon there has been a subtle attempt to manipulate the facts, evidence and findings, to support a lineal Darwinist view of history, myths and lies have been created, pulling humanity away from its true origins, a history if understood clearly would empower and liberate individuals as opposed to a select few who conceal the truth and all its benefits for themselves.

Over the past few decades the official mainstream historical view concerning the Great Pyramid and the Giza plateau has increasingly come under fire, as more and more questions are making the old view and methods of its construction seem naive and ill conceived. With a lineal Darwinist approach to history, no matter how much evidence is stacked up and presented, the old school Egyptologists and lineal historians are trapped by the growing mountain of anomalies, all they can do is ignore them, brush them into a corner, labelling them as farfetched conspiracies. They turn their attention and concentrate instead on emphasising anything which fits into their official narrative. With a lineal historical belief, any idea of a civilisation prior to the ancient dynastic Egyptians capable of advanced technological achievements cannot be entertained, it pulls the rug from under the feet of the establishment, and discredits the whole lineal approach. If you detach yourself from this cemented version of history, viewing it instead as a perpetual cycle of rising and falling civilisations, moving through time and space, cycles of high and low consciousness, forever changing as our solar system moves through an elliptical binary with the Sirius star constellation, then true history and material evidence concerning the Giza makes more sense and gracefully falls into place when viewed through cyclical history.

The official view of the Great Pyramid of Giza.

- The Pyramid was built during the reign of Khufu between 2580 - 2560 BC.
- It was built as a tomb.
- It only took between 10 and 20 years to construct.
- 146.5 meters high, the tallest man-made structure in the world for over 3,800 years.
- 2.3 million blocks of stone, weighing between 2 and 30 tons, transported from nearby quarries, 5.9 million tons.
- The largest granite stones found in the Kings chamber weigh between 25 – 80 tons, transported from Aswan 500 miles away.
- 5.5 million tons of limestone and 8,000 tons of granite.
- Stones were cut with a mean joint gap of only 0.5 mm wide, cut with basic copper chisels, drills and saws.
- Blocks moved into place with ropes, pulleys ramps and thousands of slaves.

- To place all these blocks within a 20-year time period, they would have had to position 800 tons of stones every day, that's 12 blocks perfectly place each hour.
- The 4 sides of the base have an accuracy error of only 58mm.
- The base is horizontal and flat to +- 15mm.
- The 4 sides are closely aligned to the 4 cardinal points, only 4 minutes off true North.
- The ratio of the parameter to height is equal to 2 Pi. (although Pi was considered to have been first calculated by Archimedes of Syracuse 287-212 BC).
- The outer mantle consisted of 144,000 casing stones, highly polished to an accuracy of 1/100th of an inch.
- The pyramid had 8 sides which only became apparent from the air during the dawn and sunset of the spring and autumn equinox, when the Sun casts a shadow along the side.

Tools supposedly used to build ancient Egypt

The Great pyramid of Giza, advanced technology

Inside the Great Pyramid, shafts and chambers

Anybody with a clear head can see that producing an enormously complex and precise structure of this magnitude using primitive tools of copper chisels and stone hammers is impossible, not feasible, and all within a 20-year period. The established mainstream club of historians ask us to believe in this official fairy tale to keep the lineal historical theory alive, no matter how impractical and absurd it becomes. If it comes from the mouth of authority figures i.e. established Egyptologists, most people will unquestioningly believe it. The vast majority of people no longer possess minds capable of critical thinking; it has been weaned out of them, minds socially engineered and gullible enough to accept what they are told by anyone touting as an authority figure.

A group of scholars and scientists have recently made a concerted effort to uncover an array of evidence showing ancient machine tooling, marks left behind which could have only been created using some form of high technology. This is still dismissed by the main stream.

Evidence of ancient machine tooling of hard stone

Basic orthodox view of Egyptian history

For over 3000 years Egypt had one of the most successful civilisations ever to exist in this modern cycle, from 3200 to 30 BC, a culture based around polytheism, the worship of many Gods. Situated at the north-east corner of Africa, along the great river Nile, the initial settlers began to farm around the fertile banks of the river, wove linen and made pottery, they later developed the skill to produce and use bronze. King Menes aka Narmer was the first king to unite both upper and lower Egypt, unifying both kingdoms. This period was known as the Old Kingdom, it lasted till 2181 BC. Many pyramids and temples were built; the first stepped pyramid by Pharaoh Djoser was assembled in 2648 BC along with pyramids by Sneferu and Khufu. Towards the end of the Old Kingdom, Egypt became weak and fragmented; it split due to internal disputes and civil wars, this is referred to as the first intermediate period, ending in 2055 BC when Mentuhotep II managed to once more reunite Egypt, this period is known as the Middle Kingdom, a 400-year period lasting until 1650 BC. During this time people from the area known as Israel/Palestine began to settle in Egypt. Around 1650 BC people from the north east known as the Hyksos, a mix of Asiatic and Semitic components invaded Egypt; they seized power in the north splitting the country once again by leaving the south under the rule of native Egyptians. In 1550 BC the Hyksos were driven out allowing Egypt to be united once more, bringing in the period known as the New Kingdom, this lasted for approximately 500 years, a prosperous, strong and united time, even expanding their territory into Palestine and Syria. They built magnificent temples, and even had a female Pharaoh named Hatshepsut, who ruled Egypt from 1479 – 1458 BC. In 1352 BC Amenhotep

IV became Pharaoh upon his father's (the magnificent King Amenhotep III) death. Amenhotep IV outlawed the traditional polytheistic ancient religions in favour of a monotheistic culture, the worship of a single deity, the Sun disk God Aten. To reflect his devotion to his new God, Amenhotep IV changed his name to Akhenaten. When he died his son Tutankhamun reverted Egypt back to its ancient polytheistic roots. Finally, in 1077 BC the New Kingdom declined, never to recover to its former glory, the north and south split once more bringing in the third intermediate period. In 747 BC kings from the south managed to reunite Egypt before the Persians took control in 525 BC, this was followed by Alexander the Great, ruler of the ancient Greek Kingdom of Macedon, he dominated Asia and North-East Africa up until his death in 323 BC. The Greeks continued to rule Egypt under a General named Ptolemy along with his descendants for 300 years. Finally, Egypt was swallowed up as another province of the Roman Empire, Cleopatra being the last active Pharaoh of Ptolemaic Egypt from 51 BC to 30 BC

The Great Pyramid

According to Christopher Dunn an Engineer from Manchester, England, who wrote the book "*The Giza Power Plant*", the Great Pyramid of Giza, far from being a tomb was a large acoustic device which used the technology of harmonic resonance. Its granite and lime stone structure harmonised with the Earth's natural frequencies, converting Earth's vibrational energies into electrical energy. He shows how the chambers and passage ways within the pyramid maximise and amplified its acoustic qualities. Could this be the same technology discovered by Nikola Tesla when solving the clean energy problem?[5]

The interesting aspect here is the positioning of the shafts within the Great Pyramid, shafts 8.6 x 8 inches wide coming off both the King and Queen's chambers, according to Robert

Bauval's Orion Correlation Theory,[6] they point outward towards star constellations, The southern shaft coming from the Kings chamber pierces the outer shell of the pyramid and points to Alnitak, one of the stars in Orion's belt. The north shaft points to Thuban in the constellation Draco. The Queen's chamber also has shafts which terminate 20 feet short of the surface, pointing to Sirius in the south and Ursa Minor in the north. Some main stream scientists have dismissed this theory for not being close enough to support an accurate correlation. From the perspective of this book, energy frequencies and the law of attraction, one can theorise what the Pyramids could have been used for. During a previous Golden Age, when human civilisation was at a high point in conscious cohesion, both the focal and the subconscious were equally represented within our external reality, harmonising effortlessly with one another and higher mind consciousness. An ancient civilisation aware of the complexities of the universe, how it all works and their place within it, could have anticipated the transition out of the Golden Age into the silver and bronze. To combat the loss of balancing energetic frequencies coming from our binary sister Sirius, along with possible other influential constellations, an ancient civilisation possibly had the foresight and advanced technology to set about creating an artificial frequency generator, which was so huge, it would withstand any future cataclysm or environmental change, safeguarding a high level of conscious cohesion for future generations.

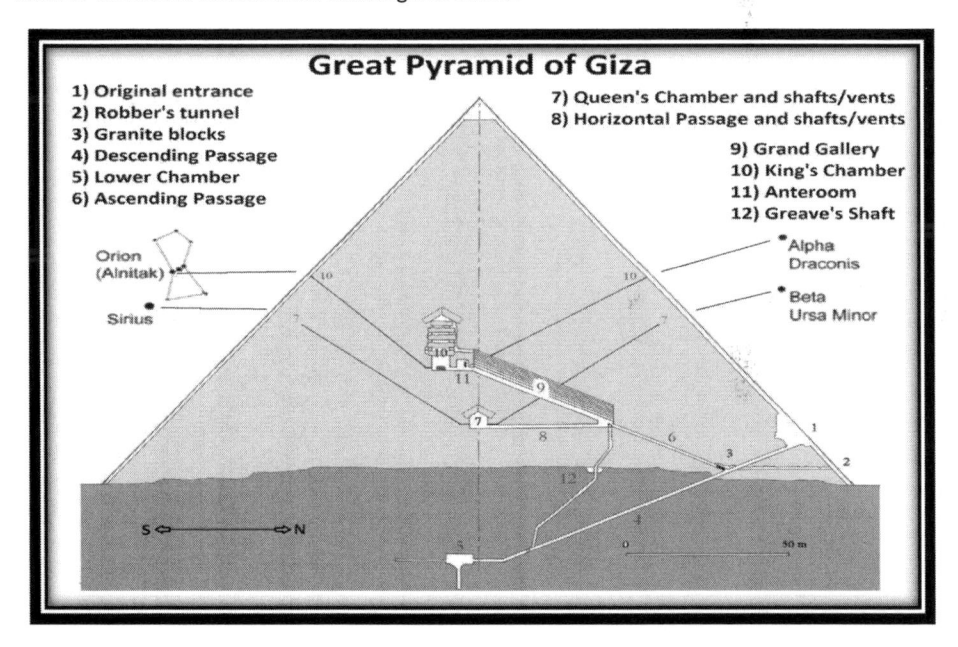

Great Pyramid of Giza

1) Original entrance
2) Robber's tunnel
3) Granite blocks
4) Descending Passage
5) Lower Chamber
6) Ascending Passage
7) Queen's Chamber and shafts/vents
8) Horizontal Passage and shafts/vents
9) Grand Gallery
10) King's Chamber
11) Anteroom
12) Greave's Shaft

The Earth's natural energy frequency is harnessed in the lower chambers of the Pyramid, water from the Nile flows into its subterranean passageways, energy is directed upwards to be enhanced as a neutral base frequency within the Queen's chamber, this energy becomes amplified as it progresses up the Grand Gallery, reaching a maximum potential at the top, here the neutral energised frequency is influenced by an input signal coming from shafts attached to the King's chamber, specific signals coming from celestial constellations would merge with the enhanced base energy to form the required amplified frequency. Once inside the King's chamber this highly energised energetic frequency can oscillate upwards influencing the rest of the pyramids colossal infrastructure, and out to the surrounding areas, similar to today's electromagnetic fog emanating from phone masts and modern technology, a fog influencing our biological cellular makeup and collective consciousness.

If we assume the ancients built the Great Pyramid to reflect the interrelationship between the universe and the human consciousness some remarkable coincidences reveal themselves, "as above so below". If the King and Queen's chambers represent the focal and subconscious, the shafts and tunnels should fit neatly into this thesis for it to be a plausible explanation. The shafts from the King's chamber do indeed support this, as they extend to the surface, the physical realm exposed to the Sun which represents the focal consciousness, the male and Osiris. The Queen's chamber on the other hand should represent the subconscious, the spirit world and the feminine Isis. The shafts from the Queens chamber do not extend to the surface, they terminate short, in my view this is an attempt to express the hidden none physical spiritual realm, the subconscious and the Sirius star system, to which the shaft aligns itself to. You would also expect the feminine Queen's chamber to have some form of connection to water (internal emotion), another connection with the subconscious, indeed this is what we see, a network of lower watery chambers attached to the Queen's chamber.

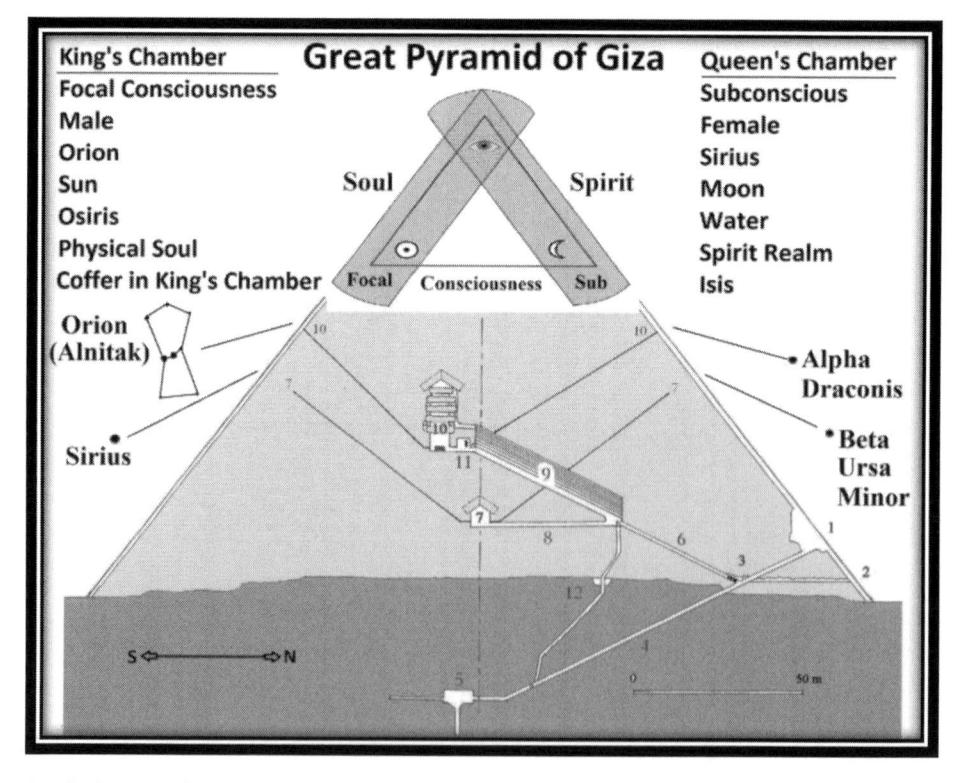

King's Chamber	Great Pyramid of Giza	Queen's Chamber
Focal Consciousness		Subconscious
Male		Female
Orion		Sirius
Sun	Soul Spirit	Moon
Osiris		Water
Physical Soul		Spirit Realm
Coffer in King's Chamber	Focal Consciousness Sub	Isis
Orion (Alnitak)		Alpha Draconis
Sirius		Beta Ursa Minor

The shafts may also play an important role during the day. As the Sun moves from east to west in its seasonal cycle, the north side of the pyramid is in shadow for approximately 100 days of the year. Once the Sun is elevated to 51.84 degrees, the north face becomes illuminated. From its lowest point at the winter solstice to the highest point in summer, the Sun's angle moves in proximity to the southern face of the pyramid. At a certain point, around midday, it casts light into the exposed shaft, energising it and creating a potential between itself and the opposing shaft in shadow on the north side. The energetic frequency coming from the Sun is not alone; it too has cosmic energy which emanates from behind it. This maybe one of many important signals needed to stimulate the pyramids designed function. The word Pyramid can be broken down as **Pyra**, Greek for fire, and **mid** for middle or centre, "**fire in the middle**", although the ancient Khemitians used the term Per-Neter for pyramid Per meaning "**House**" and Neter meaning "**God or Goddess**". Whoever chose the word pyramid all those years ago to describe these ancient structures were onto something, this also fits in with the hypothesis of a powerful frequency generator as opposed to a tomb. I would also suggest that another purpose for the Great Pyramid is that of an astronomical calendar, keeping accurate time and identifying certain cyclical events.

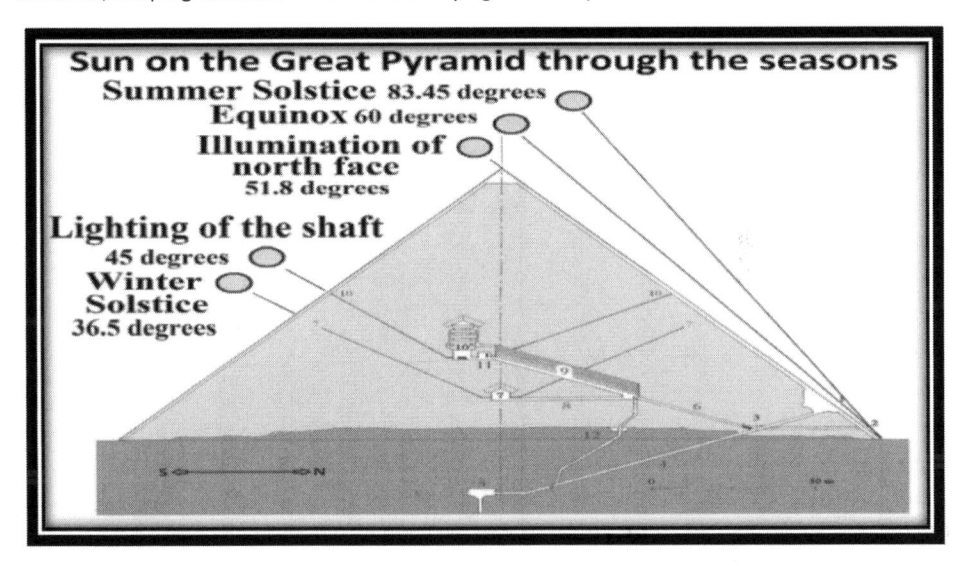

Sun on the Great Pyramid through the seasons
- Summer Solstice 83.45 degrees
- Equinox 60 degrees
- Illumination of north face 51.8 degrees
- Lighting of the shaft 45 degrees
- Winter Solstice 36.5 degrees

When we transpose the angular positions of the Sun as it seasonally moves up the southern face into Gregorian calendar dates, we see some interesting correlations.

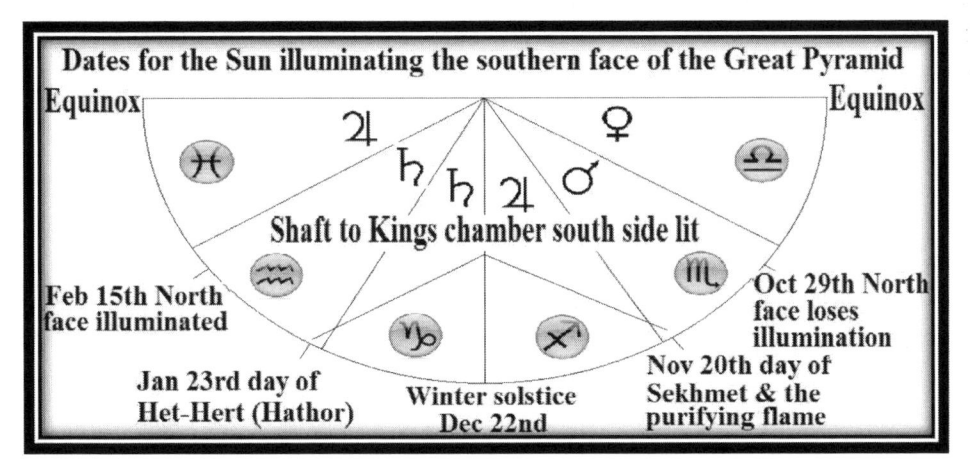

Dates for the Sun illuminating the southern face of the Great Pyramid

- Equinox
- Shaft to Kings chamber south side lit
- Feb 15th North face illuminated
- Jan 23rd day of Het-Hert (Hathor)
- Winter solstice Dec 22nd
- Nov 20th day of Sekhmet & the purifying flame
- Oct 29th North face loses illumination
- Equinox

October 29th: The Sun has progressed southwards to a point at which it no longer illuminates the north face of the Great Pyramid. This date is the ancient Egyptian religious festival of **'Going forth Het-Hert (Hathor) and the Ennead'**. The Ennead refers to a group of nine deities in Egyptian mythology, worshipped at Heliopolis, the **City of the Sun** an ancient city on the northern edge of Cairo. The nine deities consisted of Atum, his children Shu and Tefnit, their children Geb and Nut and finally their children Osiris, Isis, Set and Nephthys. They all go forth with Hathor, the daughter of Ra, who was the goddess of Love, beauty, dance, music and fertility, similar attributes to Venus.

The Sun lights up the southern shaft to the Kings chamber around midday on the 20th November; this is another ancient Egyptian festival, the **'Day of Sekhmet and the purifying flame'**. Sekhmet was the destructive daughter of Ra; her body spread a fiery glow, depicted as a woman with a lion's head. She symbolises vengeance and retribution, Ra ordered Sekhmet to go out and eat people. After many days she wouldn't stop, she liked it; Ra tricked her by turning beer red and scattering it over the land. Thinking it was the blood of the people Sekhmet drank all she could, falling asleep after three days. When she awoke she no longer craved the blood of the people and was transformed into the good Goddess Hathor. This makes perfect sense as the day of Sekhmet precedes the winter solstice, where the Sun is at its weakest, it is then followed on January 23rd by the **'day of Het-Hert (Hathor)'**, the transformed Sekhmet and good daughter of Ra. From here the Sun begins its journey back north towards the majestic and optimistic days of summer. The shaft on the south side of the Kings chamber is perfectly angled to signify this time of the year.

The 15th February also holds an ancient Egyptian festival, the time at which the north face of the Great Pyramid is illuminated once again. This festival is known as, **'the majesty of Geb proceeds to the throne of Busiris to see Anubis, who commands the council on the requirements of the day'**. Geb was the Egyptian God of the Earth, a member of the Ennead and husband to Nut. He was also father to Osiris, Seth, Isis and Nephthys. Anubis was one of the best-known Gods in all Egypt, depicted as a seated dog or a man with a dog's head; he was a guide to the deceased pharaoh as he journeyed to the next world.

The ability to keep an accurate track of time was important to our ancient ancestors, especially seasonal time and yearly cycles. It was the job of the Priesthood to safeguard this valuable information and keep on top of astronomical and celestial cycles. They created mythological stories and personified the stars and constellations in order to remember, record and pass on this important knowledge. Modern man's religions have perverted the original purpose of the priesthood and spirituality, a spirituality which once ran parallel and in harmony with nature's cosmic cycles. When terms are analysed which reference modern priesthood cults, you see similarities to astrological expressions of time keeping.

Priests: Ancient astrological time keepers, aligning their knowledge of the stars to deity worshiping festivals. In the time of David, the priests were divided into 24 courses or classes. (1 Chronicles 24:7-18). 24 hours of the day. Pri in Latin means the first, which is the premier position of a sequence. Pri (first) est or east, the place of the Sun's rising, first in the east.

Cardinals: Are senior ecclesiastical leaders within the Catholic Church. There are four cardinal points on the zodiac wheel; these cardinal points are the spring and autumn equinoxes and the winter and summer solstices.

Deacons: A ministry within the Christian Church associated with some kind of service. Deacons are also portions of a zodiac sign; each sign has three ten-degree deacon divisions.

Arch Bishop: Bi-shop, two positions, day/night, good/evil. The zodiac arc or arch representing time polarities like day and night.

Pastor in Latin is Sheppard; A Sheppard takes care of sheep, Aries the ram, the first or Pri house within the zodiac, the wheel of universal time.

Father: Father Time, Saturn, Chronos.

Monk: One of the roles of the monk (moonk) was to observe and calculate Moon cycles, in the monastery (moonastery). Each month (moonth) the Moon would complete one full cycle. Meditation and connecting with internal emotional consciousness is also a reflection of Moon energy. The practice of head shaving among some monks could be an attempt to make the head look more like the Moon.

"**Participation in collective observances like the recitation of the disciplinary code on new Moon and full Moon days**" - Life and education in a Buddhist monastery, Buddhist studies, Buddahnet.net

Modern priesthoods within today's religious cults promote a distorted historical belief system in the minds of the masses; by perverting the course of history they help the control system steer mankind along a narrow path of dogmatic subordinate compliance.

The clock of Giza

If time was one of the most important aspects in the lives of our ancestors, it's safe to presume that most of their great engineering achievements and monuments were specifically designed with this in mind. We know the ancients based their time keeping on astronomy and the position of the Earth in comparison to the stars. If we consider the pyramids on the Giza Plateau as a giant astronomical calendar or clock, built as a permanent reminder, not only of the yearly seasonal cycles but primarily to reflect the cycle of the Great Year, the 25,800-year binary cycle with Sirius, the most important of all the cycles, projecting and predicting future levels of human consciousness and cosmic events.

If we look at the array of structures on the Giza plateau we see many pyramids, all different sizes and in various positions. Many Egyptologists presume the positioning is a random reflection of human spontaneity, but when you consider the depth of knowledge the ancient builders had towards the movements of the stars and constellations, it makes sense that they would reflect this knowledge in their architecture. If we take a plan of the pyramids and plot a circle from the corner of the Great Pyramid, the back of the sphinx and the corner of the pyramid of Queens, we essentially contain all the relevant pyramids within a giant circle. We can also place a square within that circle which touches all four sides; this square runs along two sides of the Great Pyramid and one side of Menkaure, the smallest of the three pyramids. A diagonal within that square will pass straight through the centre of the two large pyramids and the edge of the small one. This is our 25,800-year clock face.

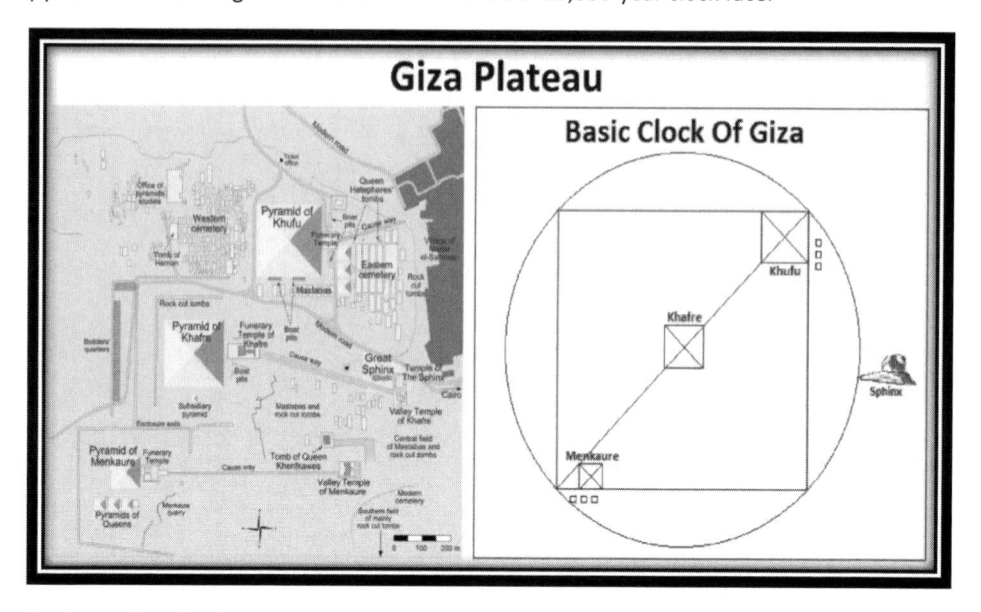

We know that the three main pyramids correspond to the stars in Orion's belt; we also know how close the shaft in the King's southern chamber was to the constellation of Orion. We have Osiris, Isis, and Horus, all Gods of ancient Egypt associated with Sirius and Orion. With this we can make an assumption that the three small pyramids south of Menkaure and east of the Great Pyramid could also represent the three stars in Orion's belt at different time periods. Today when Orion appears on the horizon the three stars in Orion's belt are vertical to one another, just like the three small pyramids east of Khufu's pyramid. The last time Orion's belt appeared horizontal on the horizon was approximately 11,000 BC. From this we can deduce the time zones and proximity in the Great Year clock of Giza.

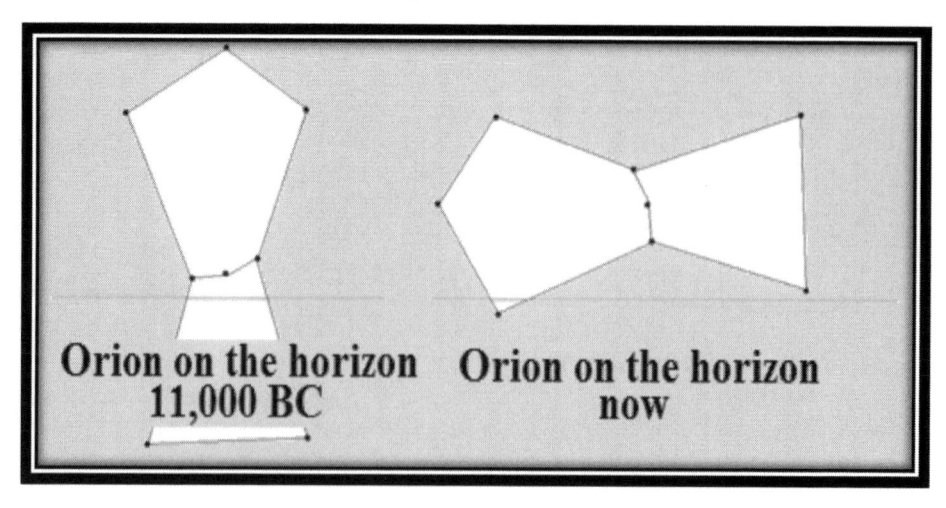

If we now place our clock with dates according to the zodiac constellations, we reveal an interesting reflection of the Great Year, fixed into the bedrock on the Giza Plateau.

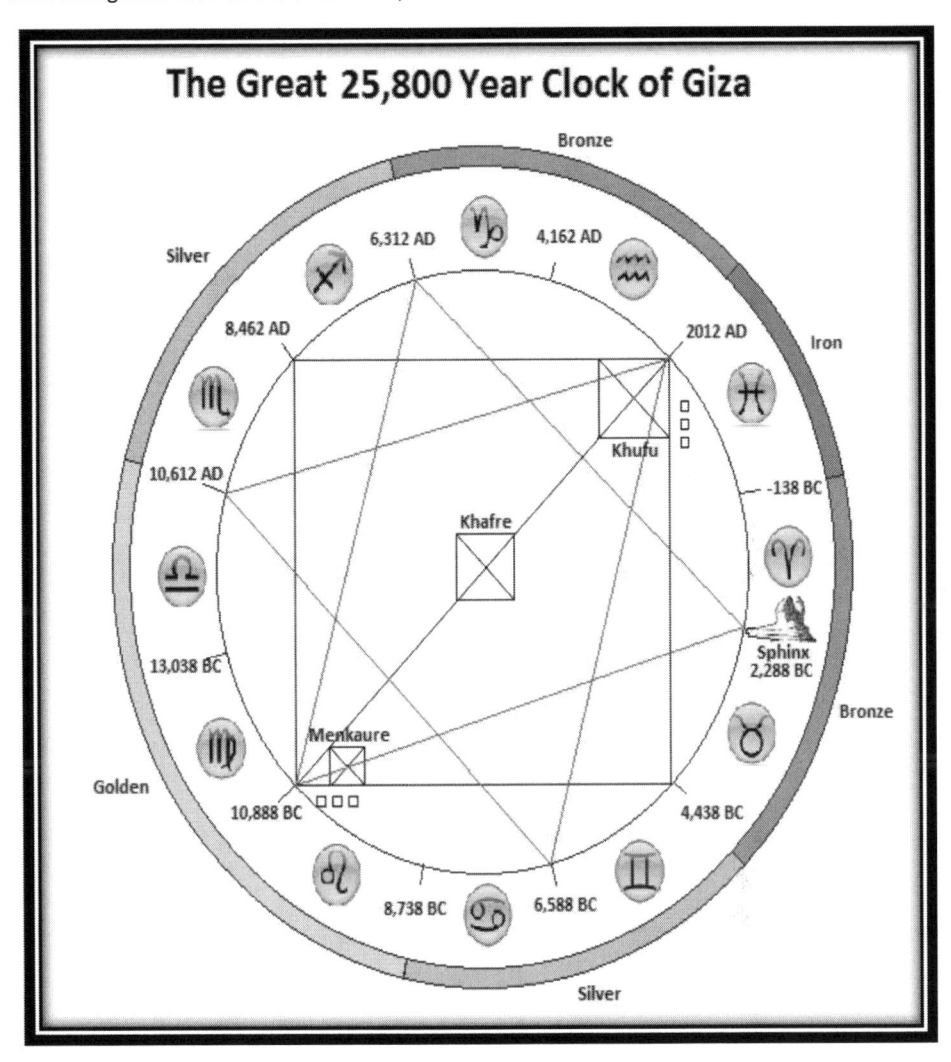

The Great 25,800 Year Clock of Giza

- Bronze
- Silver
- 6,312 AD
- 4,162 AD
- 8,462 AD
- 2012 AD
- Iron
- Khufu
- 10,612 AD
- -138 BC
- Khafre
- 13,038 BC
- Sphinx 2,288 BC
- Bronze
- Menkaure
- Golden
- 10,888 BC
- 4,438 BC
- 8,738 BC
- 6,588 BC
- Silver

A few interesting points can be made from analysing this particular clock, which all add to its credence. The Sphinx at some time in its past had its head re-carved; the body is much older than main stream Egyptologists like us to believe. It could have been there for anything up to 50,000 years. We also find many ram headed Sphinxes at the temple in Karnak, our Sphinx on the Great Year clock is positioned at the beginning of the Aries epoch, the Age of the ram, with the head being the part of the body associated with Aries. Pisces and Aquarius, the fish and symbolic water signs are both found where the Nile flowed during the dynastic days of the Pharaohs. Libra, the balancing scales of day and night, where the Sun descends over the horizon, happens to be, of all places, on the west side where the Sun sets. A Star of David can be drawn over the points dividing each epoch. More details about the Giza clock can be found in the work of Johan Oldenkamp PhD.[(7)]

Ram headed Sphinxes & Nile

Nile River

Lineal Darwinian historians set a scene in which our ancestors were all primitive, supposedly the further back we go in history the more primitive they were, oblivious to certain aspects of the real world, in which the evidence does not always support this concept of history. There must have been an ancient culture with a high level of knowledge about the universe, star systems and planets, and how they interacted. How can this be? where and whom did they get the information from? The complexity of astronomy and the pure synchronicity and symmetry of astrology does not come from primitive people; it comes from intelligent enlightened beings, and to understand this maybe a clue to finding who our real ancestors really were. The answers we are looking for may still be hidden under tons of earth and sand. In a recent interview, Zahi Hawass, Egypt's First Minister of Antiquities, said:

"I believe that we've only found about 30 percent of Egyptian monuments, that 70 percent of them still lie buried underneath the ground. You never know what the sand will hide in the way of secrets" - Zahi Hawass[8]

Enoch & Thoth

If the dynastic Egyptians didn't build the Great Pyramid, then who did? An interesting perspective has been proposed by Ken Klein, in his work,"***The Great Pyramid, Lost Legend of Enoch***".[9] He makes a good argument that the pyramids where constructed hundreds of years prior to Khufu's birth. Radio carbon dating has been conducted on organic matter found within the mortar joints on some blocks within Khufu's pyramid. The results gave a wide range of years, from 2858 BC to 3809 BC.[10] Another Egyptian artifact known as the "Inventory Stela", states that the Great Sphinx existed prior to the time of Khufu.

"In 1857, Auguste Mariette, founder of the Egyptian Museum in Cairo, unearthed the much later Inventory Stela (estimated Dynasty XXVI, c. 678–525 BC), which tells how Khufu came upon the Sphinx, already buried in sand"[11]

During his time as Pharaoh, Khufu did indeed build a number of pyramids; he built small pyramids to the east of the Great Pyramid, one in particular was dedicated to his mother Queen Hetepheres. The puzzling thing here is the standard of workmanship. If Khufu did build the Great Pyramid, then what when wrong, what happened to his attention to detail, and his master craftsmen, did they all go on strike, leaving the one-armed apprentice alone to build his mother's pyramid, it doesn't add up. The difference is huge, the precision, skill and care of construction used on the Great Pyramid is just not present on the small ones built by Khufu. This suggests that they were not done at the same time by the same people.

Queen Hetepheres Pyramid

Ken Klein also makes a strong case that the origins of the Egyptian religion stem from the time of Enoch, Noah's grandfather, born 622 years and seven generations after Adam. There are striking similarities between Enoch and the Egyptian deity known as Thoth.

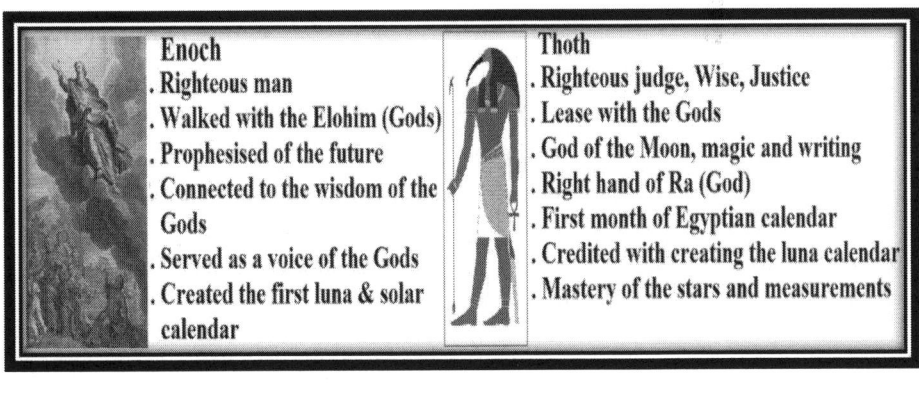

Enoch	Thoth
. Righteous man	. Righteous judge, Wise, Justice
. Walked with the Elohim (Gods)	. Lease with the Gods
. Prophesised of the future	. God of the Moon, magic and writing
. Connected to the wisdom of the Gods	. Right hand of Ra (God)
. Served as a voice of the Gods	. First month of Egyptian calendar
. Created the first luna & solar calendar	. Credited with creating the luna calendar
	. Mastery of the stars and measurements

When we plot Enoch's birth on the epoch zodiac calendar, we see that he was born in the sign of Cancer, the only sign in the zodiac ruled by the Moon. Enoch was the only living being to leave the Earth without dying. At the age of 365 he was **taken by the Gods**. The father of the lunar and solar calendar is taken by the Gods after 365 years, which just happens to be the number of days in the year, another coincidence.

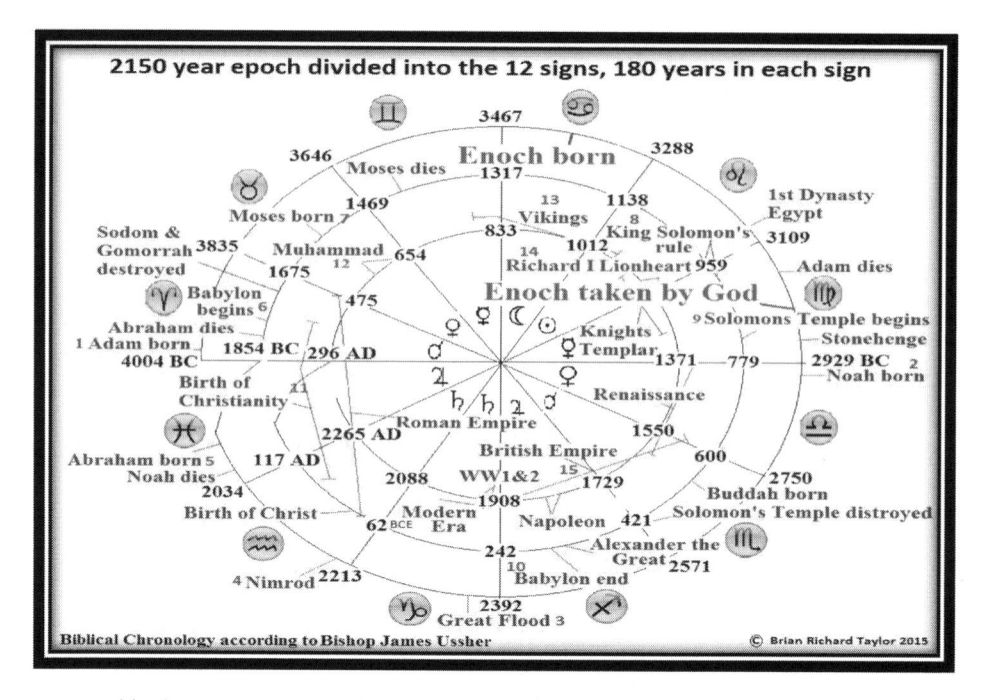

2150 year epoch divided into the 12 signs, 180 years in each sign

Biblical Chronology according to Bishop James Ussher   © Brian Richard Taylor 2015

Is it possible that such an important event in human history was to be reflected in a stone monument, giving future generation's clues as to where the Gods took Enoch? They do say that the Gods ruled the Earth in those days. It would make sense that such a high level of sophistication and technological brilliance found in the Great Pyramid could be the creation of those Gods who once lived amongst men. Gods so knowledgeable about the cosmos and universal energies, they left us with a guide to their wisdom, in the form of the astrological zodiac, a synchronised poetical calendar, reflecting time, space and consciousness, wheels within wheels, the language of the Gods. The Great Pyramid, not only an astrological calendar but possibly a permanent reminder of Enoch's ascension into the heavens with the Gods. An event so profound in its day, a record was necessary. An empty coffer, precisely cut from some of the hardest granite known to man, placed in the Kings chamber, an empty coffer for the only man who escaped an Earthly death, leaving this world in the company of the Gods. Thoth essentially became the Egyptian's version of Enoch, by using animal characteristics the Egyptians made statements about their deities. Thoth was commonly depicted as a nocturnal Ibis bird with a curved beak, representing the Moon.

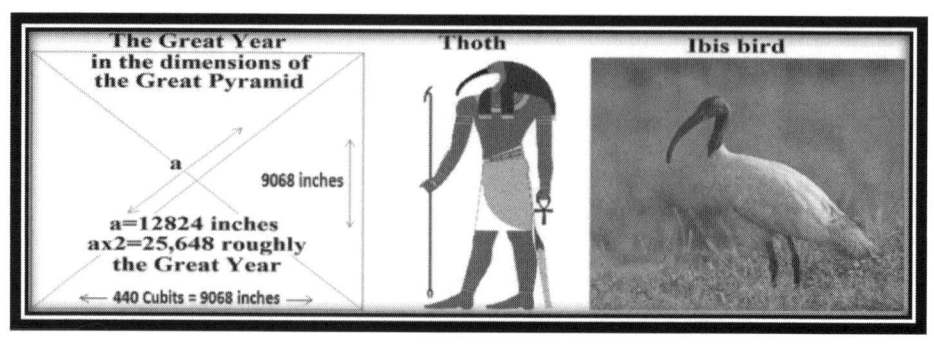

The Great Year in the dimensions of the Great Pyramid

a = 12824 inches
a×2 = 25,648 roughly the Great Year
← 440 Cubits = 9068 inches →

Pyramids everywhere

Most people are unaware of the scale and quantity of pyramid building which our ancestors undertook, most consider the Egyptian pyramid legacy as unique. The truth is, if you delve deep enough into the subject you will find hundreds of these structures, different shapes and sizes all over the planet, Egypt is not isolated in this matter. There are many variations, different types of pyramids to be found, there are the traditional triangular pyramids, like the ones found on the Giza Plateau, flat topped pyramids like in Mexico and China, there are also cylindrical types like Silbury Hill in England. No one knows the true number and full extent of pyramids scattered over the globe and under the oceans, there could be thousands depending upon how strict your criteria is.

Orthodox archaeologists and bureaucrats have shied away from discussing the pyramids in China, even with pictorial evidence and various testimonies referencing their existence. The closed nature of the Chinese control system makes it difficult to access some ancient monuments for any serious scientific analysis. Near the ancient capital of Xian, lies dozens of ancient pyramids which the authorities acknowledge do exist, labelling them as trapezoidal burial tombs dating from the Han Dynasty 206 BC – 220 AD. Recently the Chinese authorities have begun to plant fast growing trees over many of these structures, hoping to dress them up as natural hills.

"It was even more uncanny than if we had found it in the wilderness," he wrote. "But those [pyramids] were to some extent exposed to the eyes of the world - but still totally unknown in the western world." Fred Meyer Schroder, 1912

Pyramids in China

There are many pyramids and temple structures in Chichen Itza, Mexico, the most famous is El Castillo or the Temple of Kukulkan, built around the 9th – 12th Century AD. Built to the God Kukulkan, the Yucatec Mayan feathered serpent deity. Each four sides has 91 steps, with a final step serving as a platform for the top, added together this produces 365, the number of days in a solar year. Beautifully designed and built in accordance with astronomical and astrological criteria, orientated in such a way that on the spring equinox the Sun's shadow creates the illusion of a serpent God descending from the sky down the side of the pyramid. There is also a temple pyramid with striking similarities to El Castillo, known as the Sukuh Temple in Indonesia, a Javanese/Hindu temple on the border between central and east Java. Built around 1437 AD on the other side of the world, both structures seem to suggest a common influence even though these two cultures supposedly had no communicative connection. In northern Peru on the planes of Tucume there lie the decaying ruins of around 250 adobe brick pyramids severely ravaged by time. Built by the Sican people between 800-1350 AD, in a location which was once regarded as a major regional centre or even an ancient capital city. Back in Egypt new satellite imaging techniques have made it possible to establish the whereabouts of even more pyramids, yet to be examined, it has been estimated that around 17 further pyramids remain buried under the sands of the desert. a recent attempt to uncover them was thwarted by the political instability which took place in 2011. Time has not been kind to many of these structures, dotted all over the world, it shows clear evidence that our ancestors had an obsession towards building pyramids. Why?

El Castillo, Chichen Itza   Sukuh Temple, Java   Brick pyramid, Túcume

Dogon

The Dogon are an ethnic group of native people living in Mali, West Africa. 500,000 people scattered over hundreds of small villages. They live in social harmony with a strong religious tradition going back thousands of years. Their present location was the result of their community's refusal to convert to Islam a thousand years ago, forcing them to flee and relocate along the base of sandstone cliffs to the Bandiagara Escarpment. The interesting aspect of the Dogon people are their oral traditions, religious teachings past from one generation to the next, going back thousands of years, keeping sacred knowledge secure and preserved by their spiritual leader the Hogon, an older member of the Dogon tribe elected by the community's elders. One of his tasks is to observe the position of the Sun, Moon and stars; he must determine the correct time for his people to plant their crops, failure in this area could have dire consequences for their food supplies.

During the 1930's the French anthropologist Marcel Griaule made a detailed study of the Dogon people along with their oral traditions, he spent years living among the natives, after gaining their trust he was allowed a 33-day intense meeting with a wise elder named Ogotemmêli, during this time Griaule was given access to much of the ancient oral traditions. He reported that the Dogon possessed ancient knowledge of the star system Sirius, and other heavenly bodies which only recently have been confirmed. They believed that Sirius, the brightest star in the sky had two companion stars, po tolo (Sirius B) and emme ya tolo (Sirius C), the orbit cycle of Sirius B around Sirius A takes 50 years. They also say that it is the smallest yet heaviest of all celestial objects, ejecting its essence into creation by its fast spin. According to the French anthropologist the Dogon also knew of Saturn's rings and Jupiter's moons. Griaule and his colleague Dieterlen where baffled by some of this and in their writings, they stated:

"The problem of knowing how, with no instruments at their disposal, men could know the movements and certain characteristics of virtually invisible stars has not been settled, nor even posed" Griaule & Dieterlen[12]

If this is true their prior knowledge of celestial bodies far away from the naked eye can only be explained as, supernatural, a coincidence, an elaborate hoax or a visitation by beings from elsewhere sharing outside knowledge. Amma is the supreme deity of the Dogon, and the Nommo are the "watchers". Amma is described as the intelligent consciousness behind all creation, the awareness within all beings. According to the Dogon belief, Nommo is the collective name for the civilisation that came from the star system Sirius in our ancient past, an amphibious race that set up society here on Earth. The Dogon believe that the radiant frequencies coming from Sirius floods the Earth with rejuvenating and nourishing energy, they perform many ritual ceremonies to maintain the Earth/Sirius connection, preparing themselves mentally, physically and spiritually for the return of the watchers.

Elongated skulls

All over the world skulls have been found with cranial deformations, either an attempt to elongate the skull through artificial techniques or naturally occurring as part of a rear humanoid like species. The artificial cranial deformations come under two general categories.

- 1) The tabular cranial deformation: This is the most popular method used for cranial deformation, using boards on the front, or both front and back of the skull; a new born child's head is bound to restrict natural growth, stimulating new growth towards the top and back of the skull.
- 2) Circumferential method: Constricting bands are wrapped around the baby's head forcing new growth upwards and backwards. The more bands used the greater the exaggeration to the cranial deformation and elongation effect.

Artificial Cranial Deformation

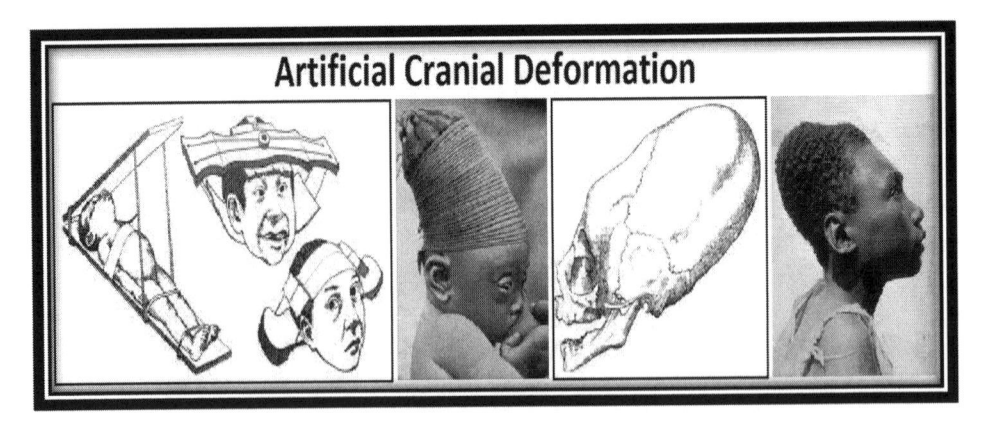

The original purpose behind the practice of cranial deformation seems to have been lost over the course of time. However, many cultures would associate an elongated skull with high intelligence, greater attractiveness, noble origins, status, and even a closer connection to the spiritual realm and the Gods.[13][14] This was a common practice among our ancestors, from as far back as 45,000 years ago to the present day.[15] It found its way onto every continent on the planet, suggesting some prior ancient benchmark, reflecting its way back among later cultural societies in numerous variations. Still prevalent in the 19th century especially in some parts of France. In 1833 a study was conducted by Achille Louis Foville, a French neurologist and psychiatrist, at a private asylum in Seine-Inférieure, Northern France now upper Normandy. He established that 50% of the 431 inmates had some form of cranial deformation, with 11% considered extreme.[16] This was not a minor inconvenience to our ancestors, going through the long process of deforming your baby's head, a painful even dangerous process, took approximately 3 years, for what? what was it all for? was it to look like the Gods, the same Gods who created humanity and who possilbly once lived amongst us? Or was it to look like a race of beings which may have once inhabited the Earth? Possibly highly intelligent, giving the appearance of sophistication with a God like elevated status. Is there any evidence of elongated skulls which don't show signs of artificial cranial deformation, ancient skulls found which appear to have been formed naturally through genetics, the so-called bench mark for this practice?

Paracas

In the late 1920's a Peruvian archaeologist named Julio Tello began excavating and studying an ancient site on the Paracas peninsula, four hours south of Lima. His work uncovered shaft tombs which contained multiple burials, overall Tello unearthed around 300 elongated skulls belonging to the Paracas people. The Paracas culture and society lived on this part of the Peruvian coast up until 2000 years ago, it is suspected that they dwindled in number and migrated up into the highlands. No one knows how long these people have been around and where they initially came from, but evidence during these early excavations concluded they were a culture of fishermen and sea fearers. The Paracas came way before the Inca and before the Nazca, a race of beings with elongated skulls and fiery red hair. Since these early efforts by Tello over 80 years ago, main stream scientists and archaeologists have paid no more attention to the mystery surrounding these bizarre elongated skulls, which could possibly be the remains of a sub-species of humans, which died out many years ago. This lack of interests is a whole mystery in itself. Recently a new breed of independent researchers has been trying to shed more light on the matter. Brien Foerster, an author, researcher and assistant director to the Paracas history museum has written and studied these skulls for years. He believes they could be the descendants of a sophisticated civilisation originating from the Middle East, even Egypt. Many of the skulls show signs of cranial deformation, but a small percentage show even distribution over the cranial elongation, which suggest they could be natural, an original genetic elongated hybrid human. The practice of elongation seems to be most prevalent in the higher classes of Paracan society, the priest or royal elites had the most severe elongations and deformations. It seems the Stranger your head shape the more elevated your position would be in that community; the Elephant Man would have been well looked after. Another anomaly which is often mentioned is the amount of cranial plates found on these skulls; the majority of Homo sapiens have 3 cranial plates when looking at the top of their skulls, but the Paracan elongated skulls have anything from 2 to 5, a skull growth pattern very different from our own, their eye sockets appear larger, the jaws are larger and so is the thickness of bone material forming the skull. Some of the skulls appear to have around 20% more volume than the average human skull. Brien Foerster has managed to acquire permission to have a number of the skulls DNA tested, a difficult process when your samples are over 2000 years old, a full analysis has yet to be conducted, it has taken him many years to get to this stage, numerous hurdles both scientific and political have had to be overcome. A preliminary small-scale test was done with some unusual results. These early tests are by no means conclusive but they suggest a genetic variation different from the common Homo sapiens.[17]

Although the majority of these skulls look as though artificial cranial deformation has been at work, it is still necessary to ask, why are they doing this and who are they trying to look like. It seems as though they are trying to emulate the look of a race who they admired and looked up to, possibly an intelligent race from elsewhere, a race who could have interbred or manipulated the genetics of the indigenous population. Is this one of the reason why the mainstream scientific community avoid the subject? Foerester has suggested these seafaring red headed people came from the Middle East, influencing many indigenous cultures along the way. In the Solomon Islands in the Pacific there is a place called Vanawata, with a culture of people who have traditionally practiced cranial deformation, their oral tradition tells of ancestors coming from Egypt, one of many islands between Egypt and the Paracas peninsula. It is an interesting name for the islands, SOLOMON (three words for the Sun).

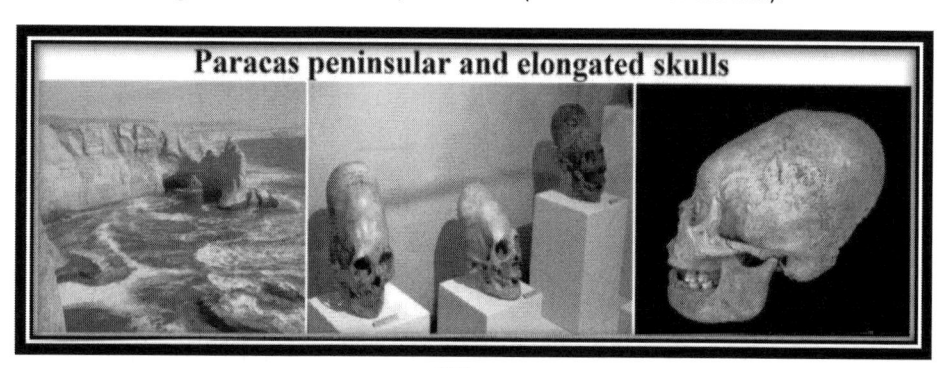

Paracas peninsular and elongated skulls

| Akhenaten Skull | Amarna Princess | Nefertiti |

The skeletons of a baby and an unborn foetus were found in Peru, the unusual thing here was the skulls, both elongated, which could not have been formed from years of artificial cranial deformation, these skulls were natural. Asked in a recent interview Brien Foerster commented about the find.

"These examples are completely natural in shape, and have enormous cranial volume. They are either a different species from us, or, possibly, are a mix of human and alien DNA." - Brien Foerster, 2012, Author and researcher.[18]

The Serapeum

Beneath the sands of Saqqara, North West of the Djoser pyramid, near the ancient city of Memphis is a labyrinth of underground passageways, connected to these passageways are numerous alcoves containing 25 huge granite boxes weighing around 100 tons each. Made from a single piece of hard granite, 4m long, 2m wide and 3.3m high. Granite which came from a quarry 500 miles away. The staggering precision and craftsmanship is breath-taking, leaving any observer in awe, puzzled and perplexed. The surfaces are totally smooth within 2/10000 of an inch, the sides are perfectly parallel and each granite top weighs approximately 30 tons, a design and feat which could not be replicated today with any confidence. The boxes were rediscovered in 1850 by the French archaeologist, Auguste Mariette (1821-81), who had the foresight to use the writings of Strabo, a Greek geographer, from around the time of Christ. This gave Mariette clues enabling him to stumble across the entrance to a labyrinth and all its underground passageways, a place which Napoleon had searched in vain, during his long-extended expedition in Egypt. When Mariette first entered the Serapeum, he reported the boxes to be already empty, looted in a previous Age, all with their lids opened. The official explanation by mainstream Egyptologists suggest the boxes to be sarcophagi, tombs for Apis Bulls, during the Ptolemaic period, where mummified bulls where locked away in these giant granite boxes for all time. The only problem with this explanation is the sheer size of the boxes. Mummified bulls have been recovered in tact elsewhere, found in wooden tombs a fraction of the size. Bulls are usually mummified in the kneeling position and don't take up anywhere near the space we see inside these granite sarcophagi, they would only reach 1.6 m from the ground. The other problem with this hypothesis is that no bulls were ever found in the boxes, not a single one. The word Serapeum comes from the Graeco/Egyptian God Serapis, a politically created religion, designed to unify the Greeks and the Egyptians under the rule of Ptolemy I, during the 3rd century BC, derived from the Egyptian Gods of Osiris and Apis, along with attributes from Greek deities such as Hades and Dionysus. The cult of Serapis continued until pagan religions were suppressed under Theodosius I, in 391AD. Under Ptolemy's deliberate policy to spread the cult of Serapis, a Serapeum was built in Alexandria. The discovery of the Serapeum altered the course of Auguste Mariette's life. He was initially commissioned by the Louvre to find Syrian and Coptic manuscripts for the leaders of various monasteries. Unfortunately for Mariette, at that time, the English were going around snapping up everything before he could get his hands on them. Once his work on the Serapeum was underway Mariette devoted the rest of his life to Egyptology, making detailed notes on the Serapeum, together with all his other findings. Unfortunately, in 1878, while Mariette was in France the Nile experienced the greatest flood of the century, flooding the basement of the Egyptian Museum in Cairo where most of Mariette's notes and manuscripts were stored, his life's work lay underwater for months, much of it was beyond repair. The scale of the catastrophe took its toll on him, prematurely ageing him leading to his death 3 years later. As for the Serapeum no one has come up with a credible explanation, no one knows what they are, who made them, how or why. The only thing we can be sure of is that the Dynastic Egyptians did not possess that level of technology.

"Let me tell you that Mariette's first reports - the detailed discovery of each sarcophagus, each grave, each new underground passage, all through several years - have completely disappeared. This again will not surprise you if you've been following my writings for a while. Everything significant on the Giza plateau tends either to disappear, or if it can't be moved, to be closed to the public" - Antoine Gigal

100 Ton Granite Boxes, Serapeum at Saqqara

Bulls and rams

Throughout the whole of the Egyptian legacy, we see bulls and rams everywhere, statues, deities, myths and writings referring to these sacred animals. Why? What is going on!

When we analyse the whole of the Egyptian period, in relation to the astrological cycle of the Great Year and the binary with Sirius, it all begins to make sense. During the Age of Taurus (the bull) 4300 – 2150 BC, the periods of the Archaic and Old Kingdoms, one of the first Dynastic Pharaohs, prior to Narmer was the Pharaoh Ka, and it is no coincidence that the ancient Egyptian word bull is pronounced "Ka".

The first Pharaoh King was a reflection of the Age of Taurus and the Bull. During this Taurean Age the ancient Egyptians worshiped many deities who they depicted as either a bull or a cow. There was Nut the Goddess of the sky sometimes depicted as a cow, Hathor another Goddess of the sky with attributes such as love, joy and beauty also symbolised as a cow. The cow was a sacred animal throughout those times. During the transition period from Taurus to Aries, we can see the Old Kingdom come to an end, replaced by the 1st intermediate period; this is reflecting the energetic vibrational change emanating from the cosmos. The new Age of Aries is marked by Amenemhat I, and a new epoch of Pharaohs ruling the Middle Kingdom. Amen, Amun and Amon were often depicted as ram deities. This is also around the time Abraham (ram in Aries) enters the scene in the Old Testament. Thutmose I, appears at the beginning of the New Kingdom after the upheavals triggered by the 2nd intermediate period, Thutmose is a constructed name uniting Thoth with Moses, Moses being a personification of the planet Mars, the ruler of the Age of Aries. The proactive physical energy of Mars plays out in the actions of Moses as he liberates and relocates the Jews from Egyptian enslavement during the Exodus.

We also see Ramesses making an appearance during the New Kingdom, in the middle of the Age of Aries. At the Temple of Amun-Ra in Karnak many ram headed sphinx can be seen lining the route, another expression of our Sun in the Age of Aries. Many major deities throughout this 2150-year epoch are depicted as, or associated with, rams. Amun, Khnum, Djedet and Osiris are all synonymous with the ram form.

The Pharaonic Age of Egypt finally came to an end during the transition period from Aries into Pisces, the Age of "I am" was over, the new Age of "I believe" began. Pisces is represented by the two fish and ruled by Jupiter. The Romans took control, adopting a new religion called Christianity, where a Pope, the closest human connection to God was placed on the throne of Peter (Jupiter). With all this evidence pointing to our ancestors living their lives in tune with universal energies, its constellations, cycles of wheels within wheels, the language of the Gods, modern historians, scientists and left-brain academics still dismiss the synchronicity and profoundness of astrology/applied astronomy. Our ancient ancestors had an extremely high level of knowledge concerning astronomical science; their understanding was enormous and exact, so where did this information originate, where and whom did it come from?

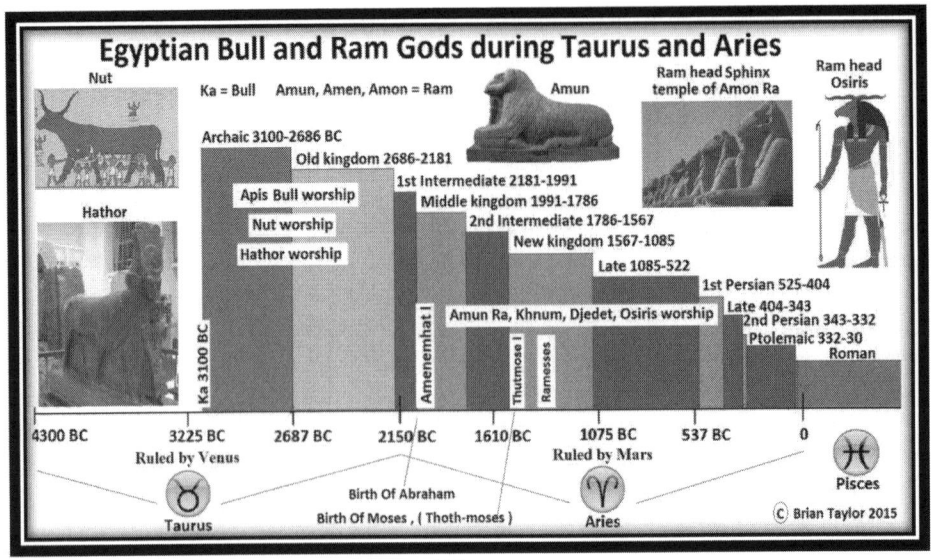

2150 year epoch divided into the 12 signs, 180 years in each sign

- Taurus
- Aries
- Pisces

(Zodiac wheel diagram with labels:)

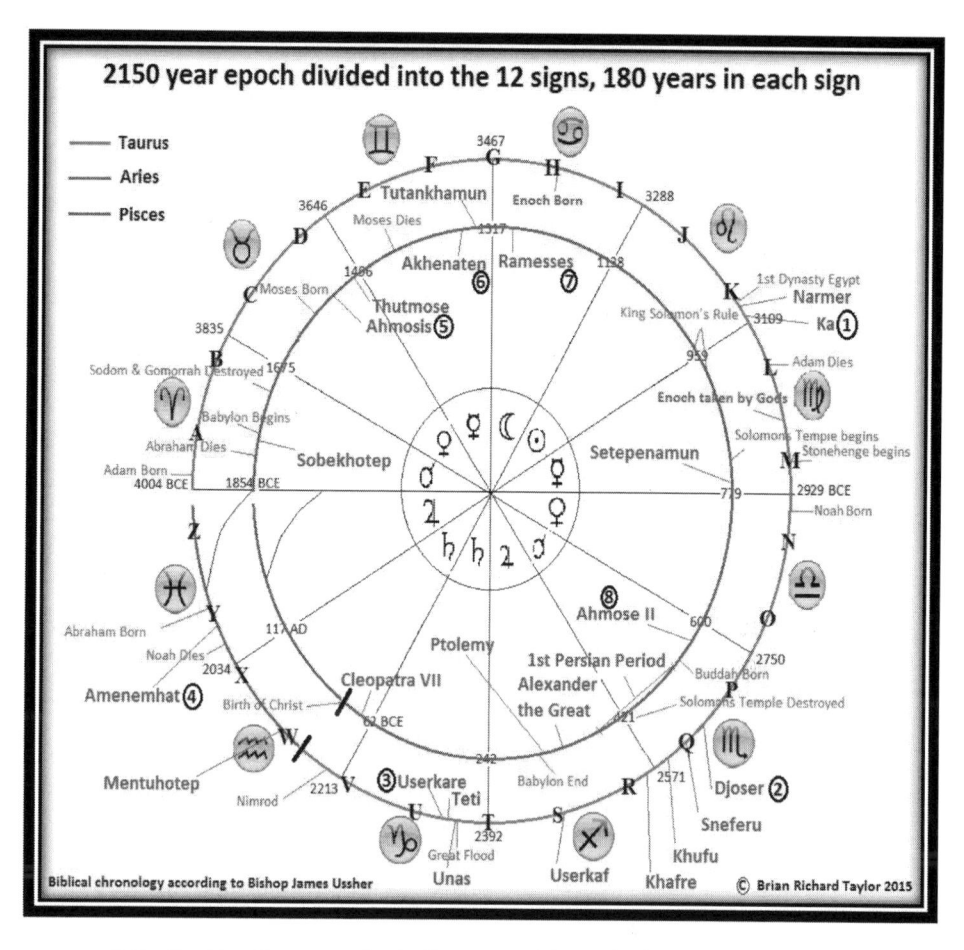

- 3467 F —
- G (Cancer)
- E Tutankhamun
- 3646 — Moses Dies
- Enoch Born — H
- I — 3288
- D (Taurus) — 1486
- Akhenaten ⑥ | Ramesses ⑦ — 1198
- J (Leo)
- Moses Born — 3835
- Thutmose / Ahmosis ⑤
- 1st Dynasty Egypt — Narmer
- King Solomon's Rule — 3109 — Ka ① — K
- C — Sodom & Gomorrah Destroyed 1675
- 959
- Adam Dies
- Babylon Begins
- Enoch taken by Gods — M (Virgo)
- Abraham Dies
- Solomon's Temple begins / Stonehenge begins
- Adam Born 4004 BCE
- Sobekhotep — 1854 BCE
- Setepenamun
- 719 — 2929 BCE — Noah Born
- B (Aries) A
- ♀ ☽ ☉ ☿ ♀
- N
- ♃ ♄ ♄ ♃ ♂
- Z
- ⑧ Ahmose II — 600
- Abraham Born
- Ptolemy
- 1st Persian Period
- O (Libra) — 2750 — Buddah Born
- 11 AD — Y
- Cleopatra VII
- Alexander the Great — 421
- Solomon's Temple Destroyed — P
- Noah Dies 2034 — X
- Amenemhat ④
- Birth of Christ — 62 BCE
- 242
- Q — 2571
- W (Aquarius)
- ③ Userkare / Teti
- Babylon End — R
- Djoser ② — ⑪ (Scorpio)
- Mentuhotep
- Nimrod — 2213 V
- U — T — 2392
- S
- Sneferu
- ♑ (Capricorn)
- Great Flood
- Userkaf X
- Khufu
- Biblical chronology according to Bishop James Ussher
- Unas
- Khafre
- © Brian Richard Taylor 2015

- 1) Ka, the Egyptian name for bull appears right in the heart of the Taurean Age, In Leo, the heart and in the position of the letter K on the zodiac alphabet.
- 2) Djoser, the constellation of Scorpio is in the shape of a J, the opposite house to Scorpio is Taurus, with the letters D and E.
- 3) Userkare, Unas and Teti, at the lowest point in the zodiac wheel, we have the letter T at the very bottom along with U. The motto for Capricorn is "I Use".
- 4) Amenemhat is at the time of Abraham, coming into the sign of Aries, the ram, at the beginning of the epoch of Aries. The planet ruling Pisces is Jupiter, the planet of abundance and expansion, a trigger for the Middle Kingdom.
- 5) Ahmosis and Thutmose, reflecting the time of Moses and the Age of Aries, ruled by Mars.
- 6) Akhenaten dismantles the old Gods in favour of a single God Aten (the Sun disk). This occurs at the top of the chart when the Sun is at its brightest, at the midheaven.
- 7) Ramesses, also appears at the midheaven, in the middle of the Age of Aries the Ram.
- 8) Ahmose II, Opposite Ahmose I, in the house of Scorpio, ruled by Mars.

Looting and the destruction of ancient cultural heritage

It appears to be common practice among warring nations and conflicting empires, to loot, desecrate and dismantle the opposition's ancient cultural heritage, allowing the victors to put forward their version of history unchallenged. Periodically Egypt would succumb to this treatment, during the first intermediate period, following the Old Kingdom, there was a great deal of political chaos, power was divided and temples where pillaged, vandalised and ransacked, allowing new rulers to promote a new version of history. Eventually Egypt became united bringing in the period known as the Middle Kingdom. Akhenaten was guilty of destroying the historical legacy left by his predecessors, to promote his new monotheistic religion of Atenism, the worship of the Sun disk; he removed all evidence of the old polytheistic religions, widely practiced among the Egyptian people. Amen-Ra was removed from temples making way for Aten, all the old mythological history was rewritten, creating a new reality.

Prior to the Roman Catholic Church and Christianity in the Age of Pisces, our ancestors left clues to their understanding and relationship with natural cycles of the heavens, using astrology. It was a wholly science of light, synchronicity and universal wisdom, it was the language of the Gods. Much of this knowledge is thought to have been stored in the Great Library of Alexandria, thousands of ancient writings, manuscripts and scrolls, historical records going back thousands of years. Literature containing esoteric wisdom was not looked at favourably by the new Piscean controllers, who wanted a version of history which supported their power base and future aspirations. The first time the library was threatened was in a fire during the Siege of Alexandria in 48 BC. At that time Julius Caesar was forced to set fire to his own ships in a battle with Ptolemy, but the fire spread and accidentally burnt part of the Great Library. The destruction of the library was limited, occurring in the museum built by Ptolemy. While Caesar was victorious in the final battle Ptolemy drowned attempting to cross the Nile.[19] The library came under attack again during the suppression of a revolt, quashed by Emperor Aurelian in the 3rd century (270 - 275 AD). Aurelian attempted to unify the people within his empire just like Akhenaten tried to do, with a single sun God, which they could worship without betraying their own Gods. Lactantius (early Christian author 250 – 325 AD) suggested that Aurelian would have outlawed all other Gods if he had lived. It was also reported that he had started the process of organising persecutions. He may have taken the opportunity during the invasion to eradicate some ancient history along the way. During this early epoch of Pisces, a new religious order had to be constructed, away from the Age of Aries the ram and Mars, a united belief system associated with the fish of Pisces and the planet Jupiter had to be constructed. In 379 AD Theodosius I became Emperor of Rome, he issued decrees effectively making Orthodox Nicene Christianity the official state church of the Roman Empire. A new state sponsored religion was imposed to unite the people towards this new way of thinking. In 391 AD Paganism was made illegal, laws were made against Polytheism and attacks on old Roman temples were tolerated. In his book *"Byzantium: The early centuries"*, John Julius Norwich places the destruction of the library during the anti – Arian riots, which were fomented after Theodosius's imperial decree of 391 AD.[20] The English historian Edward Gibbon concurred that the library was destroyed along with the Serapeum at Alexandria by the Bishop of Alexandria Theophilus, who ordered its destruction in 391 AD.[21]

Throughout history many armies and warring factions have destroyed historical artifacts or taken them out of context to be displayed in foreign museums. The scattering of ancient artefacts is another aspect of divide and rule. Dividing true historical perspective while painting your own interpretation onto the canvas of history, anyone in the future wishing to analyse a particular historical period at source is handicapped due to lack of contextual evidence. During Napoleons conquest of Egypt, not only did he take a formidable army, he also took 167 savants, intellectuals and scholars who had the task of studying every aspect of Egyptian civilisation and history. During the three-year campaign, they assembled an enormous amount of information, drawings and surveys, finally presenting it in a huge 23 volume publication, called **Description de l'Égypte,** under the orders of Napoleon. The savant's discoveries and documented research initiated interest in Egyptian history and gave rise to the birth of Egyptology. Most of the ancient artefacts collected by the Commission des Sciences et des Arts and the scholars of the Institut d'Egypte were handed over to the British and Egyptian authorities, after the capitulation of Alexandria with the French defeat in 1801. The British acquired most of the important artefacts including the Rosettastone, a key to understanding and deciphering Egyptian hieroglyphs.[22][23]

Roman historiography began after the Punic Wars, documented evidence was necessary to commemorate this important historical event. Quintus Fabius Pictor became one of the first Roman historians, given the task of creating Roman history. His initial writings were not in Latin but Greek, a concerted effort was made to oppose the anti-Roman writings of Timaeus, the Greek author and historian who had been portraying the Romans in a very negative light. Using propaganda with a pro Roman approach, Fabius Pictor's version defended the actions of the Roman State and became the underlying characteristic of future Roman historiography.

During the imperialistic times of European expansion, Portuguese, Spanish, French and British explorers were competing to plunder the world of historical treasures and artifacts. As they promoted their version of sophistication and culture, persuaded by the sword, cannon and musket, they not only enslaved some indigenous people, they also eradicated them like plagues of rats, taking their treasures and sacred artifacts with them. A wealth of ancient knowledge and historical wisdom became scattered, jigsaw pieces to a lost Age of human history. Some forward-thinking explorers made notes and drawings, attempting to undertake some form of serious research into the various cultures they encountered. It is safe to assume that the version of history we are left with today would primarily have originated from the accounts of the butcherers not the butchered, each empire promoting its own cultural values and beliefs through its own unique portrayal of his-story.

Nazi archaeology

Here we see a perfect example of how a belief system within the minds of a unified society can be manufactured to promote social and political ideologies, benefitting the agenda of German National Socialism and the Nazi Party. During this period in the 1930's and 40's a policy to promote Aryan – centric national prehistory began. The Nazi Party wanted to present Germany as the place where superior civilisation started. The Ahnenerbe (Ancestral heritage) organisation was set up under the control of Heinrick Himmler, using Nazi archaeology they set out to prove the pre-eminence of their German ancestors. Himmler was quoted as saying:

"A nation lives happily in the present and the future so long as it is aware of its past and the greatness of its ancestors" H Himmler

Another Nazi organisation steering cultural policy was the AMT Rosenberg, led by Alfred Rosenberg who saw world history as a struggle between Nordic/Atlantic, pure blooded Aryan people who survived the cataclysm, which destroyed Atlantis, and the Semites or Jewish people; in his mind, all races were inferior to the Aryans. He believed that only Germanic people brought culture to the world whereas the Jews propagated evil. The AMT Rosenberg was dedicated to finding archaeological evidence supporting the superiority of the German race. Only artifacts and theories fitting this Nordic version of history would be used along with propaganda to reassure the German people of their true ancestral beginnings. Museums were set up promoting this ideology, together with help from pseudoarchaeology, support for National Socialism and the promotion of German pride. One could argue that the mechanism used by the Nazi's to promote their version of history is similar to the one used to promote Darwin's lineal version of human history, a subtle yet partially credible suggestion which finds its way into the garden of the subconscious via pockets of plausibility.

During the Second World War, the Nazis were accused of looting all kinds of treasures and artefacts. They also had a program in which SS scientists were sent in search of evidence to support Aryan supremacy. Himmler believed that the Aryans were descendants of a superior race of beings who lived in the Golden Age, in the time of Atlantis, a lost civilisation which was destroyed thousands of years ago. He believed survivors moved to higher ground and migrated all over the planet, eventually interbreeding with indigenous populations, diluting and weakening their natural superior Aryan attributes. Determined to prove this theory, Himmler sent his SS scientists on expeditions all over the world, competing for prestige and honour they worked tirelessly for the Reich. They were also on the lookout for the Holy Grail, which they believed to be a cup or bowl used by Christ to consecrate the Last Supper, believing the Grail had special powers Himmler wanted it for himself and the Third Reich.

"We must set race at the centre of life", "Everything we admire on this earth today is the creative product of a few peoples, and originally perhaps one race". Adolf Hitler, Mein Kampf

Iraq

After the first Gulf war in 1991 many ancient artefacts were bought and sold in markets in the south of the country, eventually making their way to the west through a series of open borders. By the time the second Iraq invasion had begun, a network of sophisticated smugglers had developed, who would use the disruption caused by the war to their advantage. During the 2003 invasion, Donald Rumsfeld insisted on only sending the smallest force possible to achieve the objectives set by the US administration. This flawed strategy known as the 'Rumsfeld Doctrine' ultimately caused excessive loss of life and excessive looting. The lack of troops left the gates open for thousands of years of Iraq's artefacts to be taken by various networks, dismantling and erasing a people's history. When Rumsfeld was questioned about the 15,000 objects and artefacts looted from the National Museum in Bagdad, he remarked, "**Stuff happens**". Iraq, Mesopotamia, also known by the ancients as the Fertile Crescent or the cradle of civilisation is where human history goes back at least 10,000 years, it is also home to the Sumerians of nearly 6,000 years ago, and the Babylonians 2,000 years later. To recklessly cause havoc and decimate the history of such an important part of the world, one can't help but cast suspicion on why this was allowed to happen. Not only did organised looters go to town on ancient artefacts but the US military contributed with disregard and even vandalism. Archaeologists have condemned the US military for building their headquarters on top of the ancient site of Babylon, digging trenches 170m long and 2m deep which have caused irreversible damage to our history.[24] To this day thousands of important ancient artefacts relating to the true history of humanity are still missing, making it more difficult to challenge any new perverted forms of history for lack of tangible evidence.

World map

The majority of world maps presented as accurate cartographic depictions of the Earth are in fact distorted; the deception was a concerted effort to present wealthier nations as bigger and more important than they really are. The Mercator projection is a distorted map created way back in 1596, and is the map most people know, which is commonly found on classroom walls. The more accurate Gall-Peters projection, a version of the world presented in 1974 by D. Arno Peters, shows the relative size of each country in realistic proportions. This map is hardly ever seen.

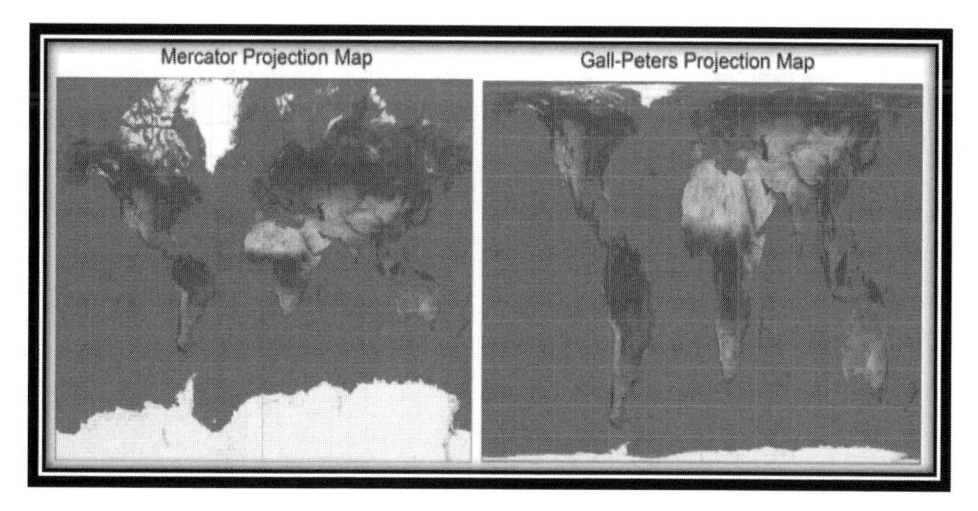

Political correctness and social taboos

Political correctness is just another form of censorship, brought about by the desire to eradicate racism, sexism, hatred and any other forms of behaviour deemed to be offensive to another human being. Unfortunately, this new form of censorship, in a quest to do away with old prejudices, has replaced them with new ones. It declares certain topics, expressions, gestures and thought processes off limits, it has become a participatory self-censoring social engineering mechanism, encouraged by the political classes who seek to steer society towards globalisation. The term political correctness, once a derogatory term used to express the party line during the old Communist Soviet Union, has now become a fashionable phrase and a strait jacket to control the world's population into self-policing one another. The danger with PC is how it effects freedom, as a society you either have free speech or you don't, there is no middle ground, censorship of any kind places freedom of expression into the pages of history, it is a dangerous road to go down, a move towards an open air prison. With certain topics off limits and without the ability to criticise or offend, humanity reduces its options for logical reasoning, debate and investigation. A distorted paradigm of truth, history and human nature is created. Here are a few examples of political correctness at work.

- The term BC (before Christ) has been dropped in favour of BCE (before common era), in an effort not to offend non-Christians.

- The European Parliament proposed to outlaw titles such as 'Miss' and 'Mrs' so as not to cause offence. 'Madame' and 'Mademoiselle', 'Frau' and 'Fraulein' and 'Senora' and 'Senorita' would also be banned.

- Several councils throughout the United States have renamed any term using the word "man" as a prefix or suffix, so as not to cause offence. "Manhole" has been changed to "maintenance or utility hole".

- The old English dessert known as "spotted dick" has been renamed "spotted Richard" by certain UK council bosses, in an effort not to offend some people.

- A school in Seattle, US renamed the "Easter egg" a "spring sphere" in an effort not to offend those who did not celebrate Easter.

- A UK council altered the term "brainstorming" to "thought showers", as local lawmakers thought it may offend epileptics.

- Some US schools now have a holiday tree as opposed to a Christmas tree.

Certain topics are now classed as politically incorrect, unacceptable to be discussed, debated or examined. We are not truly free to discuss many important aspects of modern society and history. To express concern over the official position on a variety of topics is frowned upon in many circles. Any individual with opposing views are now labelled as conspiracy theorists, a one size fits all phrase denouncing anyone who has misgivings towards what their government or officials tell them. It's ironic when most people you ask have deep suspicions about the lies propagated by their governments and media. It is now becoming an offence to offend someone. Although being offended does not cause physical harm, if we continue down this road, it will be an offence for me to show any form of negative disapproval towards my masters. Although I may be offended by their policies, especially those incorporating bombing and killing of innocent people, I will be forbidden from offending them in their psychopathic pursuits.

In many countries throughout Europe it is illegal to deny or grossly play down the events associated with the Holocaust. Anyone having contrary views or feels the need to investigate the official version is advised to suppress these concerns and turn their attention to other matters. Although the truth should not fear investigation, there are many laws put in place which could land you in jail. The death of anyone caught up in any conflict is tragic, but it seems odd that a law ring-fencing this particular event in history is not applied to other wars and other tragic events equally as deplorable.

German laws against Holocaust denial.[25]

130 Incitement to hatred (1985, Revised 1992, 2002, 2005, 2015)

- (3) Whosoever publicly or in a meeting approves of, denies or downplays an act committed under the rule of National Socialism of the kind indicated in section 6(1) of the Code of International Criminal Law, in a manner capable of disturbing the public peace shall be liable to imprisonment not exceeding five years or a fine.
- (4) Whosoever publicly or in a meeting disturbs the public peace in a manner that violates the dignity of the victims by approving of, glorifying, or justifying National Socialist rule of arbitrary force shall be liable to imprisonment not exceeding three years or a fine.

After the fall of Berlin in 1945, the Allies took control of all aspects of German life; they had to rebuild the country from scratch. A strict program of political correctness was initiated, it was known as denazification. The objective was to prepare the German people mentally and emotionally for their new form of governance, to assimilate them into the social norms considered acceptable by their new rulers. All Germans were screened for their political views, and assessed for potential re-education, any views of a pro National Socialist nature were now considered politically incorrect, many of those individuals deemed too far gone for successful re-education were executed.

Climate change

Climate change is fast becoming an emotionally charged issue, where sceptics are viewed as politically incorrect. The establishment of the IPCC's (Intergovernmental Panel on Climate Change) hypothesis on global warming has recently been modified to "manmade climate change", due to the lack of warming over the past 20 years. The predictive models used by the IPCC, which told us that snow would be a thing of the past, and sea levels would rise to swallow up major cities and coastlines, has now been shown to be inaccurate. The truth is that climate has always changed, but this time the establishment wants to blame us for its latest trends. The climate change issue has been hijacked and politicised by the pro-globalists, it is being used as a tool to push forward globalisation policies and alter social behaviour to suit. Powerful lobbyists and financial backers have turned the issue into a belief system, no longer supported by scientific debate, facts or reasoning, it is propelled by a fanatical belief in the overriding assumption that human behaviour is responsible for the majority of new adverse weather patterns. One of the main characters behind the manmade climate change movement is Al Gore, US Vice President 1993 – 2001. Many scientists around the world are not convinced with the hypothesis presented by the manmade climate change lobby and their computer model predictions, although the science and data is still in its infancy, Al Gore and his entourage, insist that the science is settled and the debate is over.

"The debate among the scientists is over. There is no more debate. We face a planetary emergency. There is no more scientific debate among serious people who've looked at the science...Well, I guess in some quarters, there's still a debate over whether the moon landing was staged in a movie lot in Arizona, or whether the earth is flat instead of round."
- Al Gore, The Early Show, CBS, may 31 2006.

"**The science behind climate change is settled, and human activity is responsible for global warming.**" - EPA Administrator Lisa Jackson 2010

"**But the debate is settled. Climate change is a fact.**" - President Obama, 2014 State of the Union address.

"**The science is settled...we're not going to reopen it here.**" - Dr Robert Watson, then Chairman of the Intergovernmental Panel on Climate Change, 1997 during the Kyoto Protocol Treaty negotiations.

The science is not settled and the scientific community are doing what they do best, letting the data and evidence support their conclusions, not fear, emotions or political rhetoric. According to the Global Warming Petition Project, there are 31,487 American scientists; this includes 9,029 with PHD's, who have signed a petition asking the US government to reject the global warming agreement written in Kyoto, in 1997, stating:

"**There is no convincing scientific evidence that human release of carbon dioxide, methane or other greenhouse gasses is causing or will, in the foreseeable future, cause catastrophic heating of the earth's atmosphere and disruption of the earth's climate.**"[26]

The award-winning film "**An Inconvenient Truth** "(2006), is a documentary made where Al Gore calls upon people all over the world to unite in a fight against global warming, because "**Humanity is sitting on a ticking time bomb**". Since its release it has been shown all over the world. In 2007 a British school governor attempted to block the government's plan to screen the film in more than 3,500 secondary schools. A high court judge ruled that the film contained nine key scientific errors. He backed down on banning the film but ruled that it can only be shown with guidance notes to prevent political indoctrination.[27]

Some of the pro global warming/climate change alarmists have become so fanatical about their stance that they have even resorted to manipulating the data to coincide with their doomsday predictions. In 2009 the University of East Anglia's Climate Research Unit, an important source of data for the IPCC, was shown, in leaked emails, to have manipulated scientific data to support the alarmist position on climate change, this became known as "**Climategate**".[28]

Prof Richard Parncutt, a professor of systematic musicology at Karl-Franzers Universitat Graz in Austria, attracted media attention, in 2012, for an internet text which he sent entitled, "**Death penalty for global warming deniers? An objective argument...a conservative conclusion**", where he claimed that global warming deniers could be responsible for the deaths of millions and therefore deserved the death penalty.[29] He later retracted this position. But it shows how science can be perverted and utilised by malevolent forces when politics and emotion are added to the mix. Science is not a belief system nor political, it is built on the accumulation of data and provable facts, anyone insisting that the debate is over has either been compromised or they are not being scientific, debates are never over while new data is being collected and the initial hypothesis is still in its infancy. With thousands of credible scientists opposing the political consensus, alarm bells should be ringing concerning this issue. Without the ability to criticise or offend, we as people are no longer free. Those who seek to censor us or fear the truth have something to hide.

"**Political Correctness doesn't change us, it shuts us up**". - Glenn Beck

"**Political correctness is one of the engines of nannyism. Allowing and even encouraging 'offensive' ideas is vital for the intellectually health of a free society.**" - david Harsanyi

"**There is a term called political correctness, and I consider it to be a euphemism for political cowardice.**" - Milos Zeman

Notes for chapter 8

(1) Arnold C Brackman, A Delicate Arrangement: The Strange Case of Charles Darwin and Alfred Russel Wallace, Published by Times Books, 1980

(2) Graham Hancock, Fingerprints of a global cataclysm 12,800 years ago, Article, 5th Dec 2014, https://grahamhancock.com/ancient-cataclysm-hancock/

(3) David Biello, Did a Comet Hit Earth 12,000 Years Ago?, Scientific American, http://www.scientificamerican.com/article/did-a-comet-hit-earth-12900-years-ago/

(4) D S Allan, J B Delair, Cataclysm!: Compelling Evidence of a Cosmic Catastrophe in 9500 B.C., 1997, Bear & company.

(5) Christopher Dunn, The Giza Power Plant, 1998, Published by Bear & Company

(6) Robert Bauval, Adrian Gilbert, The Orion Mystery, published by three rivers press, 1995

(7) Johan Oldenkamp, The Giza Clock, Presentation, www.pateo.nl, https://www.youtube.com/watch?v=fNpfc3-m0fQ&feature=youtu.be

(8) Zahi Hawass, Interview, Nova Online, http://www.pbs.org/wgbh/nova/pyramid/excavation/hawass.html

(9) Ken Klein, The great pyramid, Lost legend of Enoch, Documentary, 2009, https://www.youtube.com/watch?v=B3r96OWPKXw

(10) Ian Onvlee, The Great Dating Problem, Part 2 - Radiocarbon Dates and Early Egypt, Academia, Page 30, http://www.academia.edu/7715809/The_Great_Dating_Problem_Part_2_-_Radiocarbon_Dates_and_Early_Egypt

(11) The Great sphinx of Giza, Early Egyptologists, https://en.wikipedia.org/wiki/Great_Sphinx_of_Giza#cite_note-11

(12) M.Griaule, G.Dieterlen, 'A Sudanese Sirius System' (trans. of the authors' paper, 'Un Système Soudanais de Sirius',Journal de la Société des Africanistes, 1950

(13) Michael Obladen MD, In God's Image? The Tradition of Infant Head Shaping, Journal of child neurology, Department of Neonatology, Charité University Medicine Berlin, Berlin, Germany, November 2011. http://jcn.sagepub.com/content/27/5/672

(14) Artificial cranial deformation, wikipedia, https://en.wikipedia.org/wiki/Artificial_cranial_deformation

(15) Trinkaus, Erik (April 1982). "Artificial Cranial Deformation in the in Shanidar 1 and 5 Neandertals". http://www.bahaistudies.net/asma/artifical_cranial_deformation.pdf

(16) Achille Louis Foville, Influence des vêtemens sur nos organes: Déformation du crâne résultant de la, Et a la litrairie des sciences medicales, 1834.

https://books.google.co.th/books?id=r4sRAAAAMAAJ&ots=J4mUz6yuU_&dq=Achille+Foville&hl=fr&pg=PP1&redir_esc=y#v=onepage&q&f=false

(17) Brien Foerster, Elongated Skulls of Paracas, Hidden Inca tours, http://hiddenincatours.com/elongated-skulls-of-paracas-a-people-and-their-world/

(18) Brien Foerster, THE PERPLEXING "ALIEN HYBRID" BABY OF THE HIGHLANDS OF PERU, http://hiddenincatours.com/photo-sets/the-perplexing-alien-hybrid-baby-of-the-highlands-of-peru/

(19) Richard Evans, Fields of Death: Retracing Ancient Battlefields, p 182, Pen and sword books LTD, 2013, http://www.amazon.com/Fields-Death-Retracing-Ancient-Battlefields/dp/1848847971

(20) John Julius Norwich, Byzantium: The Early Centuries, 1989, knopf, http://www.goodreads.com/book/show/6103.Byzantium

(21) Edward Gibbon, The History of the Decline and Fall of the Roman Empire, penguin classics, 1989, http://www.amazon.com/History-Decline-Fall-Roman-Empire/dp/0140433937

(22) Erin A. Peters, The Napoleonic Egyptian Scientific Expedition and the Nineteenth-Century Survey Museum, Seton Hall University eRepository @ Seton Hall Theses 2009, http://scholarship.shu.edu/cgi/viewcontent.cgi?article=1037&context=theses

(23) Wikipedia, Capitulation of Alexandria, https://en.wikipedia.org/wiki/Capitulation_of_Alexandria_(1801)

(24) Global policy Forum GPF, destruction of cultural heritage, https://www.globalpolicy.org/humanitarian-issues-in-iraq/consequences-of-the-war-and-occupation-of-iraq/destruction-of-iraqs-cultural-heritage.html

(25) German laws against the holocaust, Wikipedia, https://en.wikipedia.org/wiki/Laws_against_Holocaust_denial

(26) Global warming petition project, http://www.petitionproject.org/

(27) Sally Peck, Al Gore's 'nine Inconvenient Untruths', The Telegraph, 11th Oct 2007, http://www.telegraph.co.uk/news/earth/earthnews/3310137/Al-Gores-nine-Inconvenient-Untruths.html

(28) Christopher Booker, Climate change: this is the worst scientific scandal of our generation, the Telegraph, 28th Nov 2009, http://www.telegraph.co.uk/comment/columnists/christopherbooker/6679082/Climate-change-this-is-the-worst-scientific-scandal-of-our-generation.html

(29) Richard Parncutt, Wikipedia, https://en.wikipedia.org/wiki/Richard_Parncutt

Chapter 9. Perverting spirituality

The human being is not just a two-dimensional biological processing unit of focal consciousness and carnal desires, we are multi-dimensional with infinite potential when connected to higher spiritual realms. For thousands of years systems of control have used division as a mechanism not only to divide universal holistic spirituality away from human consciousness, but also to implant false perverted beliefs designed to disempower the individual and the community. While the majority of the citizens fight and argue amongst themselves, disunited, the controlling powers expand their sphere of influence over their flock, taking full advantage of ancient universal wisdom. A cohesed harmonious society is a powerful antidote to any form of tyrannical, manipulative, governance. Fully aware of this, division is promoted and perpetuated across all aspects of society. In our ancient past, during the Golden Ages of higher expanded awareness, a holistic approach to universal energy united humanity, a combined symphony of frequencies which emanated from the cosmos poured a balanced tapestry of energies over our biological decoding vessels. Over time man's religions singled out particular energetic frequencies, unique characteristics associated with individual planets. Neglecting the balanced approach, monotheistic religions evolved focusing on the frequencies generated by one or two prominent planets. Through this selective approach a whole system of indoctrination and dogma entered the community engulfing each particular religious cult together with its unique methods of worship.

Genesis 1:1 (King James Version)

- **In the beginning God created the heaven and the Earth.**
- **And the Earth was without form, and void; and darkness was upon the face of the deep. And the Spirit of God moved upon the face of the waters.**
- **And God said, Let there be light: and there was light.**

The original translation in Hebrew talk about the "**e·lo·him**" creating the heavens and the Earth. "**El**" is the word for a single God in Hebrew;" **Elohim**" is a plural, suggesting more than one. It should read:

- **In the beginning the Gods created the heaven and the Earth.**

Therefore, there is more than one God; there is a pantheon of Gods, just like in ancient Egypt, Greece and the early Roman Empire. Could the Gods be the planets in our solar system? and the energy resonating from them be the necessary information which we need as building blocks to create and influence a balanced reality. Another explanation for the term Gods could be a reference to an external influence of sophisticated beings which, at one time, possibly participated in our creation and development.

- **And God said; Let us make man in our image, after our likeness: and let them have dominion over the fish of the sea, and over the fowl of the air, and over the cattle, and over all the Earth, and over every creeping thing that creepeth upon the Earth. Genesis 1:26 KJV**

This translation only makes sense when the plural of God is used. **"The Gods said; Let us make man in our image, after our likeness "**. This backs up the holistic planetary approach of all the planets contributing to our likeness. If it was an external influence which manipulated indigenous DNA to produce the likeness described, we can only conclude that this is a feasible and plausible possibility.

- **And the Earth was without form, and void; and darkness was upon the face of the deep. And the Spirit of God moved upon the face of the waters.** Genesis 1:2 KJV

According to the work of Jordan Maxwell, who presents a good argument concerning the original translation. He points out that the ancient writings in Phoenician Canaanite/early Hebrew were misinterpreted, and that we know more about translating ancient manuscripts today than King James did, with his best scholars, all those years ago.[1]

- wə·hā·'ā·reṣ **And the Earth** hā·yə·ṯāh **was** ṯō·hū **without form** wā·ḇō·hū **and void**.[2]

According to Maxwell, and many other theological scholars, it should read:

- wə·hā·'ā·reṣ **And the Earth** hā·yə·ṯāh **became** ṯō·hū **a waste** wā·ḇō·hū **and a desolation**.[3]

If the Earth became a waste and a desolation, this implies it was not in that condition at a previous time, possibly in a prior period the planet was teaming with various forms of life in abundance, certainly in a better condition. After God creates Adam and Eve, the Bible talks about replenishing the Earth's human population. The word "replenish" means to do it all over again, implying the Earth was populated once before.

- **And God blessed them, and God said unto them, be fruitful, and multiply, and replenish the Earth, and subdue it: and have dominion over the fish of the sea, and over the fowl of the air, and over every living thing that moveth upon the Earth.** - Genesis 1:28 KJV

If we apply the cyclical version of history, based on the Great 25,800-year cycle, as opposed to Darwin's lineal version, Genesis 1 begins to make a little more sense. Is it possible that previous human civilisations have dwelled here on the Earth for thousands, even millions of years? A cycle of life which appears to be much older than main stream historians have us believe?

Getting connected

The subconscious is said to make up over 90% of the human brain capacity, it is habitual, emotional and delicately sophisticated. Before man's religions perverted spirituality, I would suggest that humanity had an effective connection to the scope of consciousness offered by nature, a balance awareness between focal, sub and the higher mind(Logos), harmoniously absorbing the energetic frequencies of all the planets and luminaries, without judgment or bias. Maybe our ancestors understood the value of all the universal frequencies, and took great care in handing down and preserving this holistic wisdom for future generations.

All modern religions practice some form of connection to their supreme being. Prayer, meditation, chanting or singing of hymns, a practice which, I suggest, derived from a previous ancient time, when enlightened balanced holistic human beings would join together to energise the collective energy fields around them. Whatever they focused on as a group would influence the electromagnetic plasmatic soup surrounding them, thus tweaking their reality to suit their needs. They did not give away their power by looking outside themselves, to an imaginary saviour in the clouds, created by modern religions, an external God who is expected to iron out all their selfish requirements, they knew their power came from within, from a balanced consciousness, which could be magnified within a united collective.

The whole concept of prayer, meditation, chanting and hymn singing is a repetitive technique stimulating many senses, helping suggestions germinate successfully within the garden of the subconscious. Growing these seeds is a matter of nurturing those suggestions which develop and grow into new beliefs. Any system of control, desiring to dominate the masses, must disguise the human potential within a united collective, offering false or fragmented Gods and masochistic beliefs of hope, which render them powerless, subordinate, and economical slaves to their enlightened masters who keep ancient universal wisdom closely guarded amongst themselves and their limited entourage.

The further we go back in history the more Gods we see being revered. Our ancestors didn't worship one God they worshiped many, a polytheistic pantheon of Gods representing the planets, the cosmos and planetary energies. Only in relative recent history do we see monotheism evolve, possibly to make life easier for the manipulators to steer us from the potential wisdom which can be derived out of the multi-faceted universe.

Seven days of creation

According to Genesis 1, God created the world in 7 days. This whole concept is interesting in a variety of ways, but mainly because the number 7 appears yet again, it can be found all over creation and the natural world. We have 7 days of the week, 7 planets in the ancient zodiac, 7 notes in an octave, 7 colours of the rainbow (bow of RA), 7 chakras in the human body and 7 wonders in the ancient world. If we take the planets as the common denominator, in the order they appear in our weekly cycle, we begin to see a pattern form. The order of creation, according to Genesis 1:2, is in the same order as the planetary days of the week.

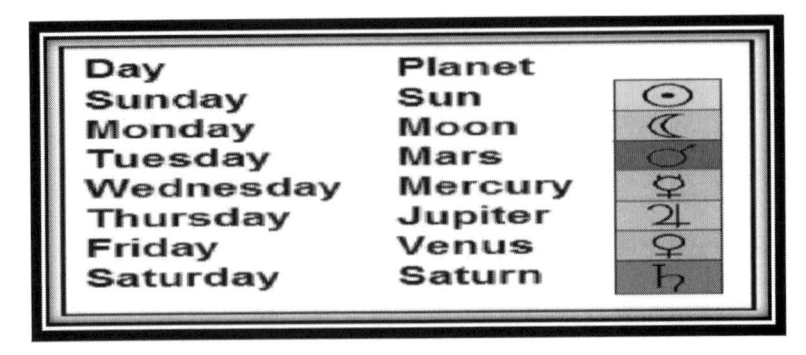

Day	Planet	Symbol
Sunday	Sun	☉
Monday	Moon	☾
Tuesday	Mars	♂
Wednesday	Mercury	☿
Thursday	Jupiter	♃
Friday	Venus	♀
Saturday	Saturn	♄

- Day 1 of creation. **"God said, let there be light"**. The Sun on Sunday.
- Day 2. **"God separated the waters beneath from the waters above"**. The Moon is the planet of internal emotion, typically associated with water.
- Day 3. **"God creates dry land"**. The land surface on Mars is one of the driest places in our solar system.
- Day 4. **"God creates the stars and the heavens"**. Mercury is the planet of communication, connecting Divine consciousness to the cosmos.
- Day 5. **"God creates all creatures that live in the water, all the birds and flying insects, all made with the ability to reproduce"**. Jupiter is the planet of abundance and expansion.
- Day 6. **"God makes Adam and Eve"**. Venus, the planet of love and liking, God made man to his likeness and to his liking. Venus is the ruling planet of Libra, where the Sun gives way to the EVEning.
- Day 7. **"God rested"**. Saturn, Saturday the Jewish Sabbath.

The order in which the planets are represented here is an ancient one, the days of the week in English reflect that order, but this is not unique, it can be found all over the world, in a variety of languages and cultures, people who supposedly evolved independently of each other, express the same seven planets, in the same order. The origins of which must have come from way back in our ancient past, from an ancestral heritage who possessed a comprehensive understanding of the planets and the zodiac, the language of the Gods.

Week days in different languages

Language	Moon Monday	Mars Tuesday	Mercury Wednesday	Jupiter Thursday	Venus Friday	Saturn Saturday	Sun Sunday
Latin	lūnae	martis	mercurī	iovis	veneris	saturnī	solis
Albanian	e Hene	e Marte	e Merkure	e Enjte	e Premte	e Shtune	e Diel
French	Lundi	Mardi	Mercredi	Jeudi	Vendredi	Samedi	Dimanche
German	Montag	Dienstag	Millwock	Donnerstag	Freitag	Samstag	Sonntag
Japanese	月曜日	火曜日	水曜日	木曜日	金曜日	土曜日	日曜日
Thai	วันจันทร์ (wan chan)	วันอังคาร (wan angkān)	วันพุธ (wan phut)	วันพฤหัสบดี (wan paruhat)	วันศุกร์ (wan suk)	วันเสาร์ (wan sao)	วันอาทิตย์ (wan a-tit)
Afrikaans	Maandag	Dinsdag	Woensdag	Donderdag	Vrydag	Saterdag	Sondag
Tagalog	Lunes	Martes	Miyerkules	Huwebes	Biyernes	Sabado	Linggo

Many more examples all over the world   Source : http://www.omniglot.com/language/time/days.htm

Today's major monotheistic religions have a knowledgeable inner core with various levels of outer rings supporting the faithful believers. The inner core acts in a similar way to secret societies, holding the keys to ancient esoteric knowledge, which has been passed down from the old mystery schools of Sumer, Babylon and Egypt, wisdom which derived from the days of polytheism and universal understanding. The main monotheistic religions did not begin this way; they evolved from a pantheon of Gods, which represented the energetic forces of the planets. In the early days of star worship, each culture would practice its own form of star worship, performing different rituals and adopting different names and personifications. As time unfolded, the Gods worshiped by conquering cultures would be seen as superior to the Gods of the vanquished, it was therefore natural to worship the Gods of the victorious.

Today's main religions have singled out specific planets, which are at the centre of their ideology and worship, Judaism with Saturn, Christianity with Jupiter, Muslims with Venus and Buddhism with Mercury. The most obvious reference to this is the day each religion chooses as their preferred holy day, Judaism on Saturday, Christianity on Sunday and Thursday, and Muslims on Friday. In many cultures Monday has been adopted as the first day of the week, as the Moon is the first celestial body from the Earth. If we assign that as our benchmark to our planetary order some interesting correlations begin to unfold.

Judaism and Saturn

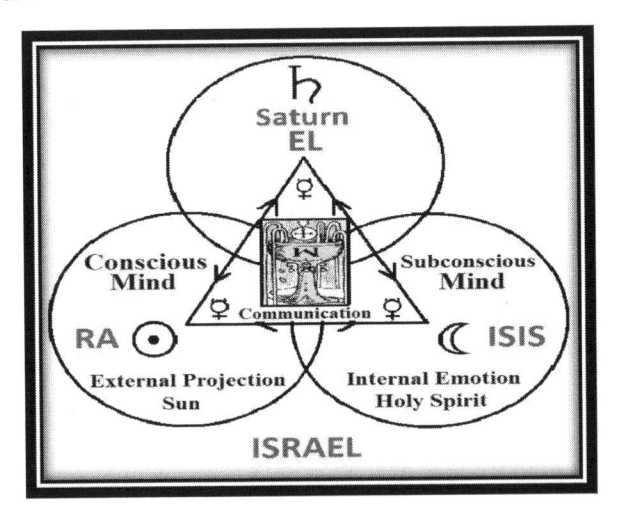

Saturn is commonly depicted as a black cube, also as a 6-pointed star, which in turn makes the number 6 an associate. The most important holy day of the week for the Jewish faith is Saturday, the Sabbath, Saturn's day.

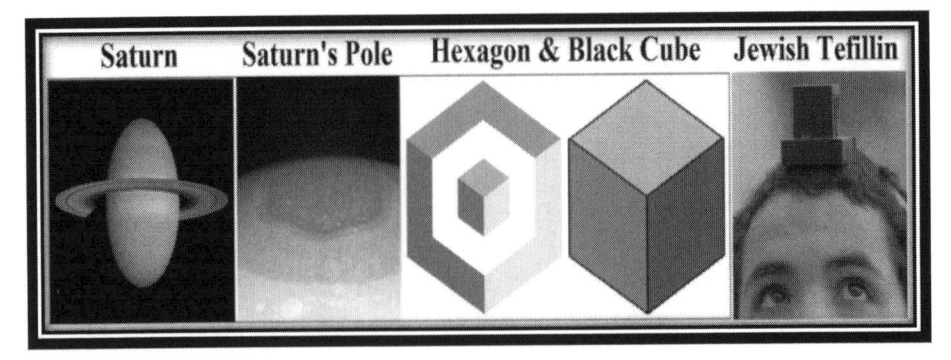

Orthodox history of Judaism

During the Age of Aries and Pharaonic Egypt, the tribes to the north east, between the Nile and the Euphrates were known as Canaanites. A city state system evolved around 1500 BCE in Egypt, Mesopotamia and Canaan. The story of the beginnings of the Israelites start around this time, each city state used the Canaanite people as economical slaves. A man named Moses appears to liberate these slaves from the exploits of the Egyptians, an Exodus of 600,000 men and their families took place, leading them back to the land of Canaan, the Promised Land. They wandered through the desert for 40 years before finally settling in the hills of the West Bank, here they grew from small villages into towns and cities, conquering the old cities of Canaan, they also built a temple in Jerusalem, the First Temple, honouring their single deity, a monotheistic religion with the one God, YHWH. They called themselves Israelites, God's chosen people. Unlike other religions, at that time, who were worshiping many gods, the Israelites taught against polytheism.

The First Holy Temple was sacked by Pharaoh Shoshenq I, around 930 BCE, who carted away most of the treasures. It was stripped again around 700 BCE by the Sennacherib King of Assyria. However, it was finally destroyed by the Babylonians in 586 BCE. At this point the upper classes of the Israelites, the priests, prophets and scribes were marched off to Babylon as captives. Here they organised themselves with their scrolls to write the first five books of the Bible, known as the Torah. Without a city or a temple, they wrote their Bible to keep their faith and traditions alive, they could still worship, pray, perform rituals and keep the Sabbath even while exiled in Babylon. When Babylon fell in 539 BCE the Israelites went back to Jerusalem to build a Second Holy Temple, which was not as grand as the first but allowed them to focus on their religious practices. When Alexander the Great took control of the city in 332 BCE, the Second Temple narrowly escaped being destroyed. It wasn't until 198 BCE when Antiochus the Great came along with the Ptolemaic Army that a rebellion ensued. Antiochus wanted to Hellenise the Jews converting them to Greek polytheism, the rebellion was quashed but later under Antiochus IV an official ban was placed on circumcision and the religious observance of the Sabbath. Furthermore, a statue of Zeus was erected within the Second Holy Temple; and when a Greek official ordered a Jewish priest to perform a Hellenistic sacrifice on a pig, the priest killed the Greek officer and with his five sons fought off their Greek overlords to win their freedom.

The Romans eventually arrived, and took over Jerusalem, their might was too much for most cities to resist. Around 20 BC the Second Temple was renovated and extended by King Herod the Great, a client state king for the Roman Empire. Finally, during the Siege of Jerusalem in 70 AD the Romans flattened the city destroying the temple and much of the Jewish culture. In 132-135 AD during the Bar Kokhba revolt against the Romans, the Jews wanted to rebuild the temple, but when the revolt failed, they were cast out and banished from the city into the surrounding villages and towns. In the 7th century during the expansion of the Muslim Empire a shrine was built on the site of the Jewish temple, the Dome of the Rock. It has stood in the same place for over 1300 years. The Al Aqsa Mosque now stands in the temple courtyard. After WW1, the Zionists were given land in Palestine, their Promised Land. Many Jews settled their before, during and after WW2, with a huge number perishing throughout this turbulent period. After WW2, with overwhelming sympathy for the reported deaths of six million Jews, a recommendation was put forward by the United Nations to form the legitimate "State of Israel". On 14th May 1948 this came into effect. However, it came under criticism, as many felt that the borders of this new state were not clearly defined in the declaration.[4][5][6] In the Six Days War of 1967, the Temple Mount and old city of Jerusalem was captured from Jordan by the Israelis. In 1980 Israel unified East Jerusalem and the Temple Mount with the rest of the city, against opposition from many parties including the United Nations Security Council. The Zionist Jews have a brave ambition to unite all the Jews together within the Promised Land, an area put aside for God's chosen people, from the Nile to the Euphrates. The flag of Israel reflects this ambition. The Star of David, the six-pointed star of Saturn is between two blue lines, which represent the Nile and the Euphrates.

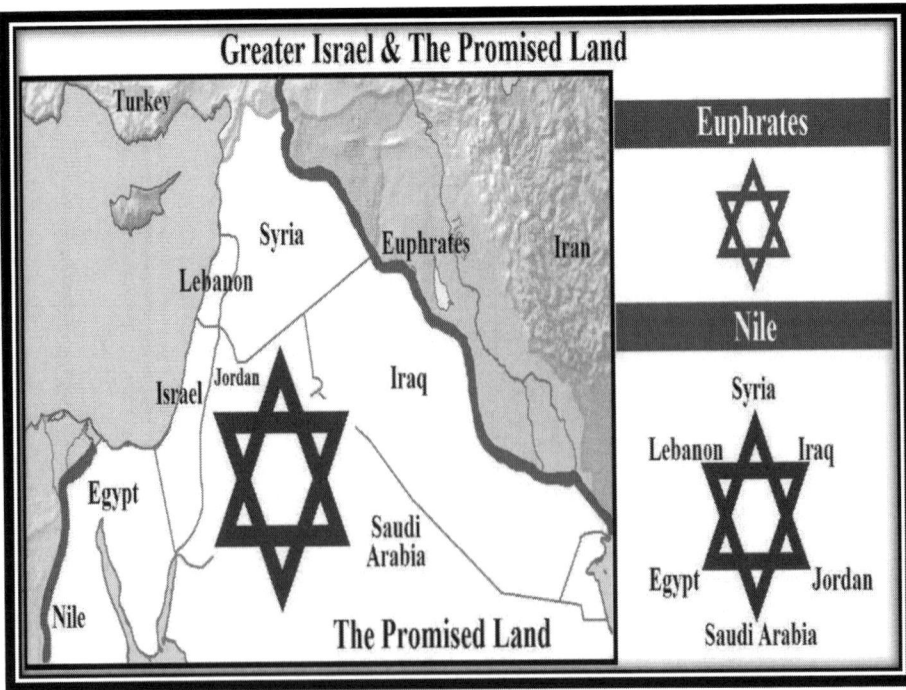

The first five books of the Old Testament, the Judean Torah, are purported to have been written by Moses, Genesis through to Deuteronomy, which is their version of the history of humanity, which according to their timeline began in the Age of Taurus. Could this be the reason for the name Torah? Their legends mention 600,000 men escaping slavery in Egypt under the leadership of a man named Moses, this Exodus happened in the time of Aries ruled by Mars (Marses), a time of hope and liberation, a new beginning with a new set of rules, laws which Moses brought down from Mt Sinai as Ten Commandments from God.

- **"And the glory of the Lord abode upon Mt Sinai, and the clouds covered it for six days"** Exodus X 24:16

They wandered throughout the desert for 40 years before settling in the hills of the Promised Land. The energy of the planet Mars, is a proactive, physical energy, one of movement, motivation and physical doing. They couldn't have chosen a better character to lead them to freedom. Israel has many archaeologists working to find evidence to support the ancient biblical events found in the Torah, events which would legitimise their claim to the Promised Land and a Greater Israel. Unfortunately, the physical evidence uncovered to date does not support the entire biblical hypothesis. The findings lead towards a slow decline in the city state system around the time the Exodus was supposed to have happen. As conditions deteriorated in Egypt, Canaan and Mesopotamia, many of the lower classes, the serfs, slaves and common Canaanites moved out. They took the opportunity to move into the hills to form small communities; these communities grew and united together under common goals and values, creating the early Israelites. Contrary to what the Torah suggests, they were the result of a collapse in the Canaanite city state structure not the cause of it. With a desire to break away from their suppressive lives, under the old polytheistic city states and elitist rule, they had the opportunity to create a fresh, new ideology, cementing it under the worship of one God; the Bible called them "a mixed multitude". A new version of history was put together, painting a romantic view of a peoples struggle and liberation under the guidance and helping hand of God, a chosen people selected for a chosen purpose and promised a chosen piece of land.

During these early years many people were still polytheistic, unwilling to give up the traditions of the past. As each generation emerged, coerced by their leaders, a slow transition took place to create the Jewish faith we see today, a faith which has singled out the energy of Saturn as their primary focus. The combinations of energetic frequencies emanating from Saturn are unique. Submerging oneself in these energies will result in a specific character trait. The energies and characteristics of Saturn are:

- Commands us to get to work and work hard.
- Discipline and responsibility.
- Limitations and restrictions.
- Organising one's time.
- Governs time from birth to death.
- Sense of tradition and conventionality.
- Perseverance and withstanding the test of time.
- Senior status brings authority.
- Structure and order.

It takes 29 years for Saturn to perform one full orbit around the Sun and return back to one's natal chart position; this may be the reason why in Jewish tradition one could not enter into public ministry until the age of 30. Saturn is the 6th planet from the Sun and the 2nd largest after Jupiter, a gaseous giant, 9 times bigger than the Earth, comprising mainly of hydrogen and helium. It has 62 moons, and a visible ring system made from ice particles. Together Jupiter and Saturn account for 92% of the total planetary mass in our solar system. When one looks closely at the lives and habits of practicing Jews, we can identify many of Saturn's energetic characteristics, many being of an admirable quality. Maybe the reason why we see a disproportionate number of Jews in positions of importance and authority is because they align themselves with the characteristics and qualities of this planet, they are the people of Saturn. Being without a homeland for most of their existence the Jews have had a sense of insecurity forcing them to organise themselves well by working hard, being responsible and disciplined while helping to keep their faith and traditions together. This has brought restrictions and limitations to many areas of their everyday lives; their kosher food consumption and preparation requirements can be frustrating and restrictive unless you are habitually accustomed to it. They have a huge sense of tradition and must be applauded for preserving their heritage which has withstood the test of time. They have great respect for their elders and are conventional within the boundaries of time. These are all Saturn's characteristics. A culture aligned with this energetic frequency will inevitably reflect this in their reality. The number six is very important to the Jews, being the number associated with Saturn, it is found in many of their myths, writings and history.

- Sabbath (Saturn's day).
- Saturn is represented as a six-pointed star or a hexagon.
- Six Day War in the 1960s.
- Exodus 600,000 men.
- ISRAEL has 6 letters.
- Noah was 600 years old when the flood of the waters fell onto the Earth.
- Six million Jews died in the Holocaust.
- Siege of Jerusalem (1099), 60,000 people were massacred, 6,000 Jews.
- Exodus V 14:7 "And he took 600 chosen chariots".
- Exodus VI 16:5 "And it shall come to pass on the 6th day, that thy shall prepare that which thy bring in".
- Exodus VII 20:8 "6 days shall thy labour and do all thy work".
- Exodus VIII 21:2 "If thy buy a Hebrew servant, 6 years he shall serve".
- Exodus IX 23:10 "& 6 years thou shalt sow thy land and gather in the increase thereof".
- Exodus X 24:16 "& the glory of the Lord abode upon Mt Sinai, and the cloud covered it 6 days".
- Exodus XI 26:9 "And thou shalt couple fine curtains by themselves and 6 curtains by themselves and shall double over the 6th curtain in the forefront of the tent".
- Exodus XI 25:32 "And there shall be 6 branches going out of the side thereof".
- Exodus XI 26:22 "And for the hinder part of the tabernacle westward thou shall make 6 boards".

- Exodus XII 28:10 The name of the children of ISRAEL "6 of their names on one stone and 6 that remain on the other".
- Exodus XVIII 38:26 "Six hundred thousand, and three thousand and five hundred and fifty".
- Leviticus XIX 24:6 "And thou shall set them in two rows, 6 in a row, upon the pure table before the Lord".
- Leviticus XX 25:3 "6 years thou shall sow thy field, and 6 years thou shall prune thy vineyard and gather in the produce thereof".
- Leviticus XX 25:21 " Then I will command my blessing upon you in the 6th year".

Some people have speculated that the war in the Middle East, essentially comes from the desire of the powerful Zionist factions inside the Israeli government, to expand their boarders to the biblical boundaries of the Promised Land, and that ISIS is a private mercenary army helping to facilitate this outcome. The name ISRAEL is a construct of ISIS, RA and EL..

The Jewish triad consists of Saturn, Sun and Moon worship. The Moon was favoured and worshiped by ancient Hebrews, Arabs and many other cultures in our distant past. The Mesopotamians named their Moon God "Sin or Nanna". This is where the name for Mount Sinai came from, it is Moon worship. The Jews who pray three times a day call their place of worship a **SIN**agog (Synagogue), AGOG means (eagerly, expectantly or merry mood). The interesting thing here is the Christian use of negative terminology to undermine Orthodox Saturn and Moon worship. Saturn has become Satan, Nanna or Sin is the opposite of good and the El of EVE, the evening or night time is considered as evil.

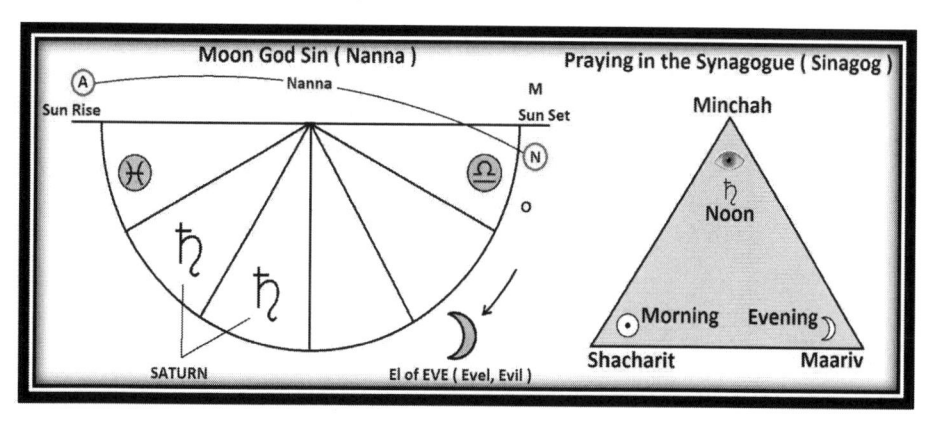

Virtues and vices

There are seven deadly sins and seven virtues, depending upon how an individual wishes to conduct himself. These virtues/vices are derived from the seven planetary energies, the good aspects verses the bad. Saturn's people according to ancient planetary vices, if not careful and aware of their actions, can be prone to avarice (greed).[7] Saturn rules over two signs of the Zodiac, Aquarius and Capricorn. The Motto's for these two signs are "I know" and "I use".

Vices Or Virtues

Planet	Sin	Virtue
Sun	Pride (vanity)	Humility (humbleness)
Moon	Sloth (laziness/idleness)	Diligence (zeal/integrity/Labor)
Mars	Wrath (anger)	Forgiveness (composure)
Mercury	Envy (jealousy)	Kindness (admiration)
Jupiter	Gluttony (over-indulgence)	Temperance (self-restraint)
Venus	Lust (excessive sexual appetites)	Chastity (purity)
Saturn	Greed (avarice)	Charity (giving)

Christianity and Jupiter

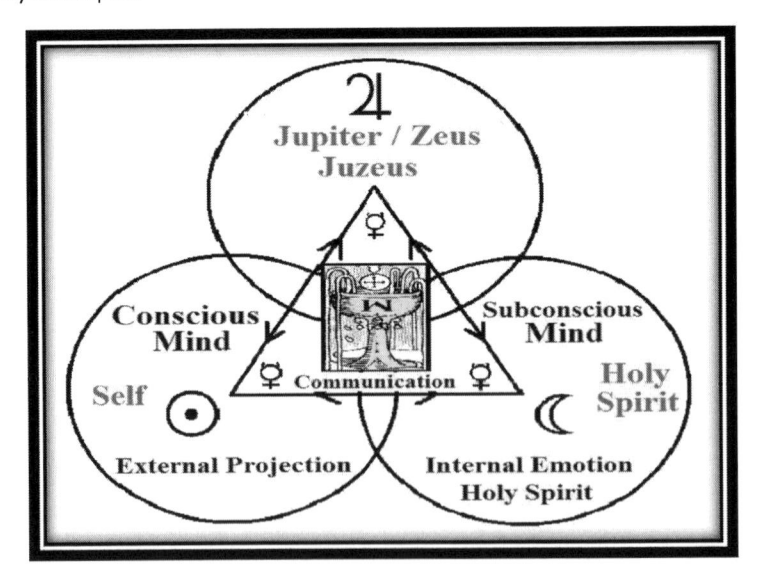

The Christians are people associated with Jupiter, the planet ruling Pisces throughout the 2150 year epoch of the two fish. The Pope sits on the throne of Peter (Jupiter). The religion focuses mainly on the energetic frequencies given off by this planet and the luminaries, aligning their whole belief system with the energetic characteristics of this enormous planetary body. Using the law of attraction, the Christians resonate with Jupiter, bringing forth and emphasising its potential.

Jupiter is the 5th planet from the Sun, the biggest planet in our solar system, 1/10 the diameter of the Sun and 11 times the diameter of the Earth, a gas giant comprising mainly of hydrogen and helium. Jupiter takes approximately 12 earthly years to perform a full orbit of the Sun, this means Jupiter will stay in each zodiac house for approximately 1 year before moving into the next. The planet has a red spot, a giant storm the size of the Earth, which was observed as far back as the 17th century. Jupiter is not alone, it is accompanied by 67 moons, the biggest, Ganymede, has a diameter greater than Mercury. One of its moons is called Europa, which mainly consists of an ice covered liquid ocean.

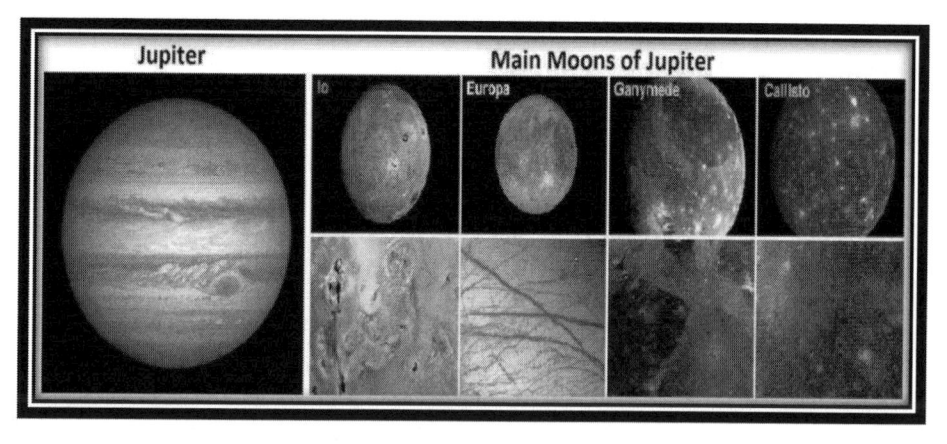

Jupiter's astrological characteristics are a reflection of its size and physical nature. It is the King of the Gods, the planet of plenty, it is tolerant and expansive. Attributes include good luck, bounty, optimism and growth. It comes with morality, gratitude hope and honour. Jupiter can guide you to a sense of purpose and high ideals. Some of its pathways towards fulfilment come through learning, travel, challenges and philosophy. The planet's energy does have a negative side, due to its size, which can lead to blind optimism, excess and overindulgence. Jupiter was the chief deity of the Roman State religion, along with his wife Juno. Jupiter was also known as Jove, Luppiter, Lovis, Diespiter and Zeus in Greek. When humanity entered the Age of Pisces, Jupiter the ruling planet became the new focus of spiritual energy emanating from the cosmos. It would naturally dominate during this epoch of 2150 years. The Romans understood how this all worked, hence why Jupiter became their chief deity offered by the ruling classes as the new state religion. Any form of grass roots spirituality preaching the truth, the light and universal wisdom, would ultimately be targeted as a threat to the establishment, who sought to control all aspects of society. The early Christians were closely associate with Gnostics and Pagans and probably understood ancient universal teachings, holistic wisdom and its heritage. The state eventually took over the running of this New Age Christianity, to control its potential by offering a perverted and diluted version of the truth, organising a new religion taming Jupiterian energies for their own benefit. The Romans threw the early unreformed Christians to the lions, but once the Christian religion was under the control of the ruling classes, this was no longer necessary. Their new weapon was to influence the subconscious and to alter the beliefs in the minds of the masses, steering them on a new path, a path of obedience and control. The vice for Jupiter is gluttony. A recent study for the Journal of Religion and Health, found that

Christians are more likely to have a larger BMI (body mass index) than atheists and other religious groups.

"Evidence of this association was strongest among those affiliated to a Christian religion," Dr Deborah Lycett, a senior lecturer in dietetics at Coventry University.[(8)]

Aligning one's community or nation with the expansive energy of Jupiter will in time manifest these traits in reality, contributing to the Christians expansive domination around the world. Roman Catholicism has become the wealthiest institution on Earth. The Christian faith expanded to nearly every nook and cranny on the planet, leaving no stone unturned. Sunday became the preferred holy day in the Christian week. Seven is their most highly regarded number, it symbolises completeness and perfection, spiritually and physically. The number 7 appears over 700 times in the Bible and is the foundation of God's word. Although Christians are associated with Jupiter, they are also equally aligned with the Sun and the Moon, in a triad, Father, Son and Holy Spirit, choosing the day of the Sun to focus on their faith. Thursday, Jupiter's day is not entirely neglected; Holy Thursday is one of the most important days on the calendar of the Catholic religion. During the Last Supper Juzeus offered himself as the sacrificial lamb, he bids farewell to his followers before prophesising of his betrayal. All around the world bishops and priests celebrate what is known as the institution of the priesthood (Holy Thursday), a mass is held where the bishop washes the feet of 12 priests. The feet are associated with the zodiac house of Pisces, and there are 12 priests one for each house. This is a symbolic reconstruction of the moment when Christ washes the feet of the 12 Apostles. The cross can also represent a 4-pointed star, the day of Jupiter. There is no greater example of Jupiter's expansive gluttony, expressed in the physical realm, than the Christian festival known as Thanksgiving, and it is no coincidence that this festival is celebrated on the fourth Thursday in November. Jupiter rules over two signs of the Zodiac, Pisces and Sagittarius, with motto's of "I believe and I seek".

If we look at the epoch Age of Pisces, ruled by Jupiter, divided into its three decans, we find Mars playing a major role in the first third, a time of marshal, military expansion of the Roman Empire and Roman Jupitarian Catholicism, the emergence of Islam in the second third and finally a global expansion of Christianity in the last third of Jupiter's prominence.

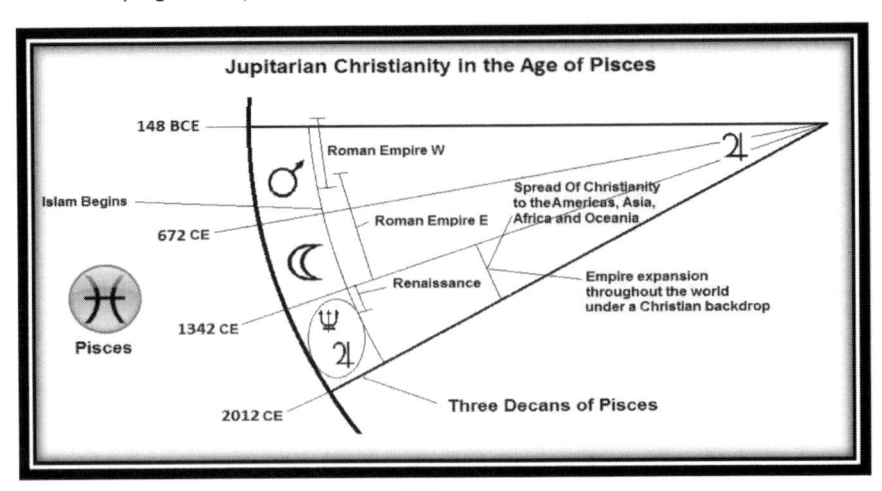

Jupitarian Christianity in the Age of Pisces

Throne of St Peter with zodiac centre

Islam & Venus

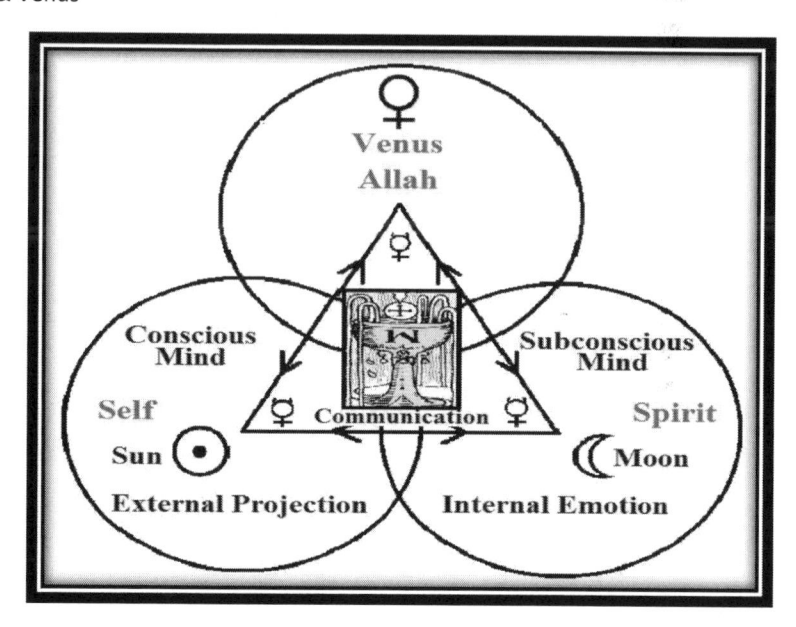

Muslims make up approximately 23% of the world's population; they follow the religion of Islam, based on a book called the Quran, which is considered to be the word of God, revealed by the prophet Muhammad. Muslim is Arabic for "one who submits to God". The planet chosen by this religion is Venus; the planet of love and liking, the number associated with Venus is five along with their holy day on Friday. They pray five times a day and adhere to "the five pillars of Islam". On top of some mosques you will see a crescent moon and a five-pointed star. The top of the mosque roof represents the Sun whereas the crescent Moon and five-pointed star symbolise the Moon and Venus.

Muslims and Venus

If we look at the time Muhammad was born, 570 CE, as a segment of time within the Piscean epoch, we find not only was it in Leo, the lion, on the outer wheel, but he dies and becomes King of Kings to the Muslims in Leo on the inner wheel, a double Leo, in the expansive Age of Jupiter. Such a significant time within the zodiacal timeframe, it was inevitable someone important would appear. From Muhammad's death in 632 CE there were two Caliphates, an expression of the strong will of the double lion wishing to expand in Jupiter. The first Rashidun Caliphate was from 632 – 661 CE, followed by Umayyad Caliphate which ended in 750, coinciding with the move from Leo to Virgo on the outer wheel. This is no coincidence.

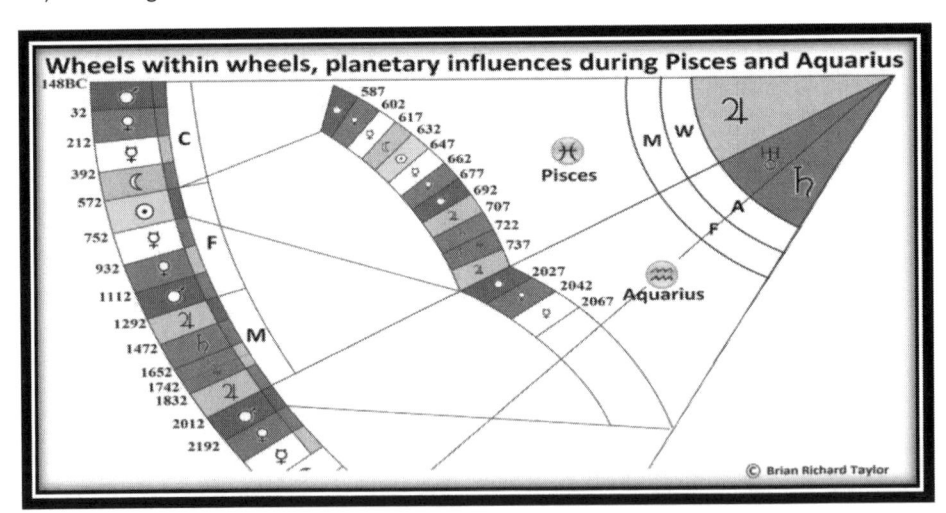

Venus is the second planet from the Sun with an orbit of 224.7 days. It is the brightest natural object in the night sky after the Moon. It is made up of 92% carbon dioxide with an atmospheric pressure 92 times greater than the Earth. It is the hottest planet in our solar system with an average surface temperature of approximately 460 degrees centigrade. The astrological energetic characteristics of Venus are associated with love, liking and the pleasures we take in life, our appreciation of the exquisite nature of things, things which make us happy, the pleasures we derive from our possessions our luxuries and all the good things which surround us. Venus also has a negative aspect or vice; this energy, if misused, can transpire as self-indulgence, self-centred, vain and superficial. The traditional vice for Venus is lust, which is understandable once you comprehend the characteristics of Venus. This could be one of the reasons why some Muslim women are required to wear the Burka, to reduce temptation in the males, keeping them away from lustful vices. Venus rules Taurus

(I have) and Libra (I compliment), one is a fixed earth sign and the other a cardinal air sign, Libra is associated with law and justice, a balance of right and wrong. Sharia law a term which means the "path or way", is a legal framework to regulate those who live within the Islamic system. It deals with all aspects of life. However, there are some harsh penalties. Today's propagated view of Muslims, by western powers, is an attempt to demonise them for economic and political reasons, and the picture they portray is almost an inversion of Venus's planetary energies.

Prior to Muhammad, much of the Arab world were still involved in polytheism or paganism, participating in the Arabian star family worship. The Assyrians considered Athtar/Venus to be the supreme deity who suddenly appeared around 2500 BCE, Assyria and Syria means "the land of Venus". According to Dr Rafat Amari, in his book *"Islam in light of history"* he writes:[9]

Venus stole the title of Allah from the Moon, and both the Moon and the Sun became subjects to Allah, the brightest star.

"If you asked them, who created the heavens and Earth and subjected the Sun and the Moon? They would surely say, Allah. Then how are they deluded? "- Sura 29:61

The Muslim scholar and historian Al Masudi 896 – 956 CE, reveals that Venus was the star of choice worshiped in Mecca, Tathrib and Yemen, which also hosts a Kaaba similar to the one found in Mecca, the Kaaba in Yemen was built specifically for the worship of Venus. Allah became a great and high star which descended every third part of the night to appear to his worshipers. In *"Islam in light of history"* Dr Rafat Amari cites a source from Ali Bin Burnan al-Din al-Halabi, known as the author of Halabieh,

"Allah descends to the heaven of this world when it is the last part of the night. It is clear that, by the word Allah, they meant the morning star which they saw in the third portion of each night."- *Islam in light of history*[9]

In the book of Sahih Bukhari, the book containing the authorised hadith of Prophet Muhammad, we find a subtle but clear indication of the morning star Venus.

" Our Lord, the Blessed, the Superior, comes every night down on the nearest heaven to us when the last third of the night remains, " Volume 2, book 21, number 246, Sahih Bukhari, translated by M. Muhsin Khan.

The worship of Venus suddenly appears around the early time of the Assyrian Empire. Modern theories concerning the birth of Venus are in tune with the work of Immanuel Velikovsky, in his book *"Worlds in collision"*,[10] his hypothesis has been partially corroborated by recent scientific discoveries. It is now believed that around 2500 BCE, Venus entered our solar system, pulled in by Jupiter's immense gravitational force, propelling it towards the position and orbit it occupies today. On its journey Venus took on all the characteristics of a huge comet, with a distinct, bright tail trailing from both sides of its mass, like the horns of a bull. As it moved towards its new position it is thought that it interacted with the Earth on 4 separate occasions, a 52-year cycle of unprecedented upheaval and catastrophe ensued in various parts of the Earth. During this time it has been suspected that the Earth's gravitation turned over, the Sun rose in the west and set in the east, and the North Pole flipped to become the South Pole.⁽¹¹⁾

"**Four times in this period (so they told me) the Sun rose contrary to experience; twice he came up where he now goes down, and twice went down where he now comes up; yet Egypt at these times underwent no change, either in the produce of the river and the land, or in the matter of sickness and death.**" Herodotus Book 2 of his histories, chapter 142.

"I mean the change in the rising and setting of the Sun and the other heavenly bodies, how in those times they used to set in the quarter where they now rise, and used to rise where they now set" Plato, The Statesman, p.49-53.

Due to its time as a comet, Venus has been associated with a beard or "**one with hair**", Venus Barbata,⁽¹²⁾ Venus worshipers would grow their beards to symbolise the comets tail. The Kaaba in Mecca houses a very important stone; it is a meteorite which fell to Earth at the time of Adam, possibly from Venus as it passed by. It was set into the wall of the Kaaba by Muhammad in 605 CE. The stone was believed to have been white, the same colour as Venus when it was first discovered, but went black over time when combined with the bad energy of humans touching it. Some scholars have suggested that the crescent moon on the top of the mosque symbolised the comet Venus, not the Moon, however the overall picture is clear that Venus played a major role in the lives of the people who witnessed its birth and entry into our solar system, a new God was born and thus a new religion.

Venus Comet

Muslims pray five times a day, the first is a pre-dawn prayer meeting known as the Fajr, coincidently the time given for this pray meeting coincides with Venus appearing on the horizon at Mecca in Saudi Arabia.

Venus Appears On The Horizon At Mecca During The Fajr

If we take the average distance of each planet from the Earth, ignoring the Sun, we find the only odd planet in our ancient sequence is Venus, in our weekly list it is situated between Jupiter and Saturn, on Friday. Velikovsky initially assumed that Venus was spawned from an eruption within Jupiter's enormous gaseous mass, but scientists now believe it was pulled in from outside the solar system around 2500 BCE. Is it possible that sometime in our ancient past, Venus had an orbit between Jupiter and Saturn, reflected by the sequence found in our historical days of the week?[13]

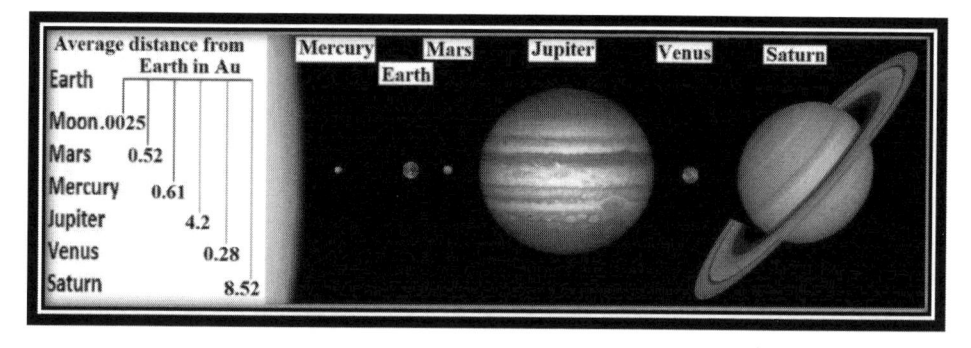

Average distance from Earth in Au	
Earth	
Moon	.0025
Mars	0.52
Mercury	0.61
Jupiter	4.2
Venus	0.28
Saturn	8.52

Buddhism and Mercury

Buddhism emerged from Hinduism. It is a nontheistic religion/philosophy. In Sanskrit the word Budha refers to the planet Mercury,[14] the planet of intellect and communication, this Budha is not to be confused with the Buddha or Gautama Buddha who was a Sage (someone who has attained wisdom). The word Buddha with two d's, in this context means "awakened one or enlightened one". Gautama Buddha was a man born into a wealthy family. His father was elected chief of the Shakya clan, and expected Gautama to follow in his footsteps. When he was 29 years old he left the comforts of the palace to pursue a journey of understanding, discovery and enlightenment. In Buddhism, there is no creator and no supreme God, the only way to salvation is through your own spiritual improvement. The Buddha teaches you to question everything including the Buddha. Through Buddha's teachings (Dharma), he will show the "way or path". It is up to the individual to decide their own route to Nirvana. The Buddhist also believes in reincarnation, the cycle of birth, death and rebirth.

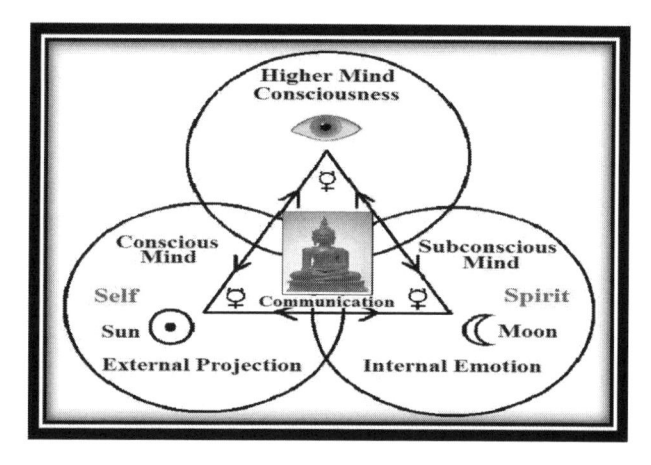

Mercury is the smallest and closest planet to the Sun with an 88-day orbit. The planet has virtually no atmosphere, creating an environment where the surface temperature fluctuates from −173 degrees centigrade during the night to +427 degrees during the day. Its surface is similar in appearance to our Moon having a large number of various sized craters scattered across it.

Looking at Buddhism from an astrological perspective, we find correlations between Mercury, Wednesday and the number three throughout Buddhist traditions and practices. The number three is a common occurrence in Buddhism:

- The three precious Jewels (Buddha (Teacher), Dharma (Teachings), Sangha (Community)).
- Three poisons (Ignorance, Attachment, Aversion).
- The three baskets of the Pali Canon.
- Three aspects of the eight-fold path (Morality, Meditation, Wisdom).
- At the Buddhist temple, when bowing one makes three prostrations with three sticks of incense.
- When making a ceremonial procession around a temple or tomb it is done three times.

The astrological characteristics associated with Mercury, the planet known as the messenger to the Gods, are as follows:

- Communication.
- Intellect.
- Awareness.
- logic & Reasoning.
- Thinking.
- How we express our thoughts.
- To get answers on the physical and psychological level.
- Dexterous and Perceptive.
- Things happen fast with Mercury energy prompting us to move from one thing to the next.
- To express ourselves in all kinds of ways.

Buddhism is a religious philosophy. Through meditation and self-discipline, one can achieve enlightenment. The whole mechanism behind this participatory philosophy fits perfectly well within the characteristics of Mercurian energy. The meditation process facilitates a communicative balance between all levels of consciousness. In peaceful stillness, one can be in the space between thoughts where all possibility exists. Buddha teaches that the unawake mind falls into the trap of the three poisons, and through the Dharma, the teachings of the Buddha, mind training can be achieved, leading one towards a righteous path, eliminating suffering which is caused by the three poisons greed, hatred and delusions.

The timing of Buddha's life also has profound correlations with the astrological zodiac. When we look at his position relative to the biblical history of the world, and his enlightenment

2558 years ago, according to the Thai year, we see he was born in the eighth house, the house of death and rebirth, which is what Buddhism is essentially about. Buddhist monks known as Bhikkhu have 227 rules of conduct which they are supposed to observe. If we take those 227 rules to be degrees of the 360 degree zodiac circle, this position corresponds exactly with the Buddha as he preaches his enlightened teachings.

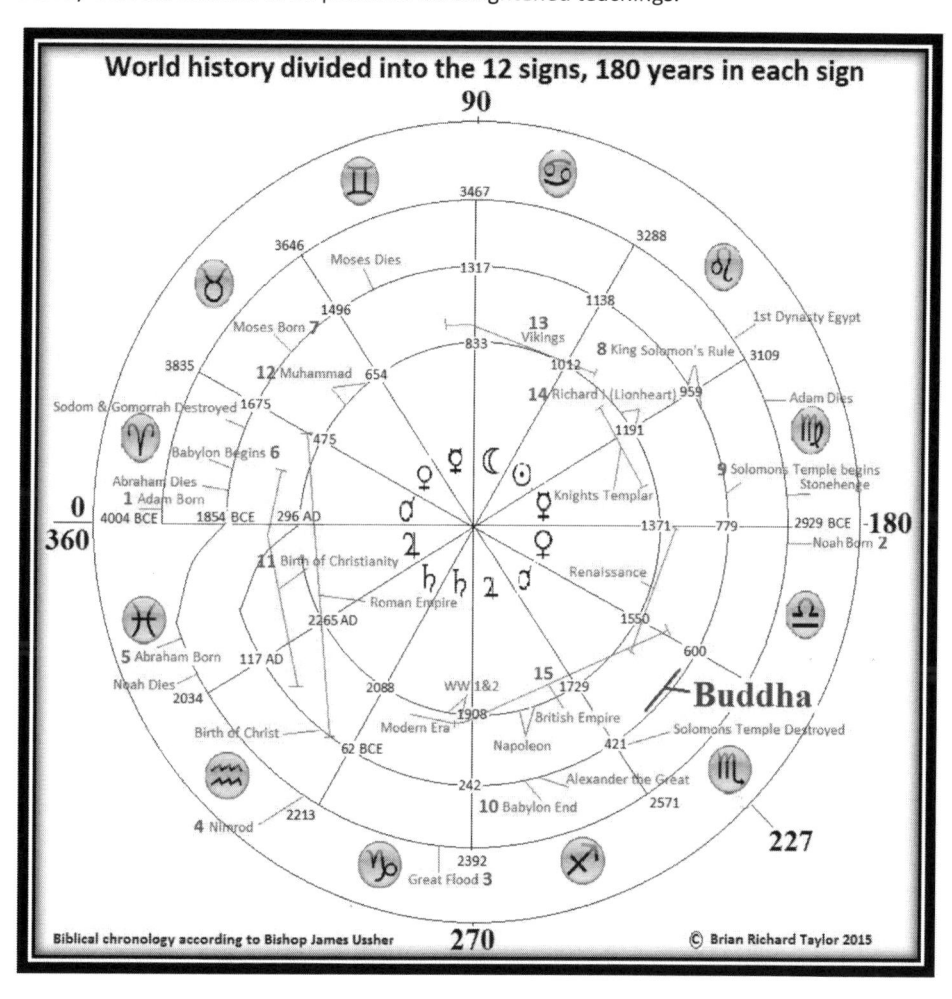

World history divided into the 12 signs, 180 years in each sign

Key points visible on the chart:
- 90 (top), 180 (right), 270 (bottom), 0/360 (left)
- 3467, 3288, 3646, 3835, 3109, 1st Dynasty Egypt
- 1317, 1138, 1496 Moses Born 7, 833, 13 Vikings, 1012, 8 King Solomon's Rule
- Moses Dies, 12 Muhammad 654, 14 Richard (Lionheart) 959, Adam Dies
- Sodom & Gomorrah Destroyed 1675, 475, 1191, 9 Solomons Temple begins Stonehenge
- Babylon Begins 6, Knights Templar, 2929 BCE
- Abraham Dies 1 Adam Born, 4004 BCE, 1854 BCE, 296 AD, 1371, 779, Noah Born 2
- 11 Birth of Christianity, Renaissance
- Roman Empire, 1550
- 2265 AD, 600
- 5 Abraham Born 117 AD, 15, Buddha
- Noah Dies 2034, 2088, WW 1&2, 1729, Solomons Temple Destroyed
- Birth of Christ, 1908 Modern Era, British Empire, 421
- 62 BCE, Napoleon, Alexander the Great
- 4 Nimrod, 2213, 242, 10 Babylon End, 2571
- 2392 Great Flood 3
- 227

Biblical chronology according to Bishop James Ussher © Brian Richard Taylor 2015

Buddhist monks or moonks are instantly recognisable in their orange robes and shaved heads. One explanation for their appearance can be deduced from their role as Moon watchers. Like all monks they are responsible for observing the cycles of the Moon. They shave their heads to symbolise the Moon and the orange robe is thought to represents the colour of the sky during sunset, a time when the Moon slowly becomes the dominant luminary in the sky. Unlike other religions the Buddhists do not focus on an artificially created holy day of the week, instead they base their holy days on the four main phases of the Moon, full moon, new moon and half-moons, harmonising their spiritual connection to nature. Moon days in the Theravadan calendar of Thailand are called "Wan Phra – (Monk Days)", all monks are expected to stay in the temple on these holy days.

Mercury and Buddhism

Mercury rules over two signs of the zodiac, Gemini and Virgo. The energetic mottos for these two signs are "I think" and "I examine", a perfect reflection of the philosophical approach of the Buddhist. Bangkok, the capitol of Thailand is at the heart of this Buddhist nation, the etymology of the name Bangkok is uncertain, although Bang is Thai for "a village situated on a stream", kok could be derived from the old Hebrew word "Kokhav ", which means the planet Mercury.

Hinduism

Hinduism is the main religion in India and many parts of South Asia. Practiced by over a billion people, it is more of a way of life than a religion, a henotheistic (belief in one God while accepting the existence of others) philosophical way of life. The motto for the Hindu is, "plain living and high thinking". It is another Mercury based belief system, the oldest practiced religion in the world, which forms the foundation of modern Buddhism. The main goal of a Hindu is to attain enlightenment, to understand the complete truth of life, to realise that one's soul is identical to the supreme soul, which is present in everything and everyone. There are many paths to enlightenment and it is up to you as to the path you choose. You can be polytheistic, monotheistic, atheistic or humanistic, but Brahma is the supreme creator God who can be seen in many forms.

The Hindu equivalent of the Christian triad is known as the trimurti, Brahma (the creator), Vishnu (the preserver) and Shiva (the destroyer). Just like in Buddhism, meditation is the primary route on the path to enlightenment, the additional art of yoga is use as a tool for discipline, health and balancing the consciousness. The Hindu's do not give their power away to an external man in the clouds, they know that the power of the universe and the creator are both external and internal, they are a part of nature and nature is part of them. They have no religious authority or governing body, no prophets and no holy book like the Torah or Bible. Their roots have a close tie to the understandings and wisdom of the ancient world rather than the rigid monotheistic religions of the modern era. They have a more balanced approach to their conscious connection with universal energy; time has not diluted or altered the fundamental reasoning behind their concept of spirituality.

With Indian astrology or Vedic astrology, history shows us that Indian horoscopic astrology was heavily influenced by Hellenistic practices. The Christian expression "Go to hell" must be referring to polytheistic Hellenistic culture and their social behaviour, anyone turning their back on the rigid dogma offered by Christianity, are naturally assumed to be on the pathway to hell. Jyotisho (Science of light, Vedic astrology) comes in three forms:

- Siddhanta, Indian astronomy.
- Samhita, mundane astrology.
- Hora, predictive astrology.

In 2001 a judgment was passed by the Andhra Pradesh high court, India, favouring astrology, since this, advanced degree courses in Indian astrology are now available in some universities, however the majority of the west's scientific community, a community selling man made global warming and nuclear weapons still consider it to be a pseudoscience.

"Vedic astrology is not only one of the main subjects of our traditional and classical knowledge but this is the discipline, which lets us know the events happening in human life and in the universe on a time scale". - Prashant Bhushan (Indian Lawyer)

Hindu astrologists believe in the connection between the microcosm and the macrocosm, that we are all connected and all part of the whole; it is still an important and major part of the lives of many modern Hindus.

Pantheism

Pantheism is a belief that the universe, from the smallest particle to the whole, is God, It is not a personified deity, it is oneness composed of everything, we are all part of God and all God. This concept of life the universe and all things dates back thousands of years, and is the simplest of all philosophical and spiritual explanations. Although the term pantheism did not exist until the 17th century, many pre-monotheistic religions can be regarded as pantheistic. The ancient Hindu and Egyptian religions all had pantheistic elements about them, suggesting it may be the natural foundation from where human spirituality aligns itself.

Pantheist tendencies appeared among the early Gnostic Christians, it also re-emerged from time to time all over the world in various new forms and pockets. The Roman Catholic Church regards pantheism as heresy, and has put many brilliant scholars and philosophers to death for this very reason, Giordano Bruno being one of them.

Famous Pantheists

Nammalvar (3059 BCE), one of the twelve Alvars
Heraclitus (c. 535 BCE – c. 475 BCE), pre-Socratic Greek philosopher
Giordano Bruno (1548–1600), Italian Dominican friar, philosopher
Ludwig van Beethoven (1770–1827), German composer
Carl Jung (1875–1961), Swiss psychiatrist and psychotherapist
Albert Einstein (1879–1955), German theoretical physicis
D. H. Lawrence (1885–1930), English novelist, poet
Alan Watts (1915–1973), British philosopher, writer
Pete Seeger (1919–2014) American folk singer

Nazism

Although Nazism was not considered as a religion in the traditional sense, it had many features associated with a religious cult, a belief system able to motivate and persuade a nation into contributing and fulfilling the objectives of a political dictatorship. For the purpose of this book, I will regard Nazism as a political religion, and Adolf Hitler as the earthly God figure to the Third Reich, with Uranus as their chosen planet of influence. The characteristics of Uranus run parallel with the characteristics of Nazi Germany during the 1930's and 40's. Enrich Himmler was especially interested in occult matters of an esoteric nature. He purposely designed and built a crypt in the basement of Wewelsbury Castle, near Paderborn Germany. The crypt had an eternal flame centred between twelve pillars, a chamber constructed to symbolise the twelve houses of the zodiac in the Age of Aquarius, with its earthly Nazi rulers reflecting this cosmic energy of Uranus.

Nazi crypt in Wewelsburg castle

The energy emanating from Uranus is associated with:

- Rebellion and revolution.
- Out of the blue events.
- New ways of thinking and of doing.
- New inventions and cutting edge technology.
- Breaking with tradition and the status quo.
- New mold, a new world order.
- Dictatorship.
- Independence and originality.
- Erratic and bazaar behavior.
- Unexpected events sometimes of a violent manner.

As can be seen from the list of characteristics, any form of organised religion or political philosophy aligning itself with these energies, would reflect those characteristics back into their collective reality.

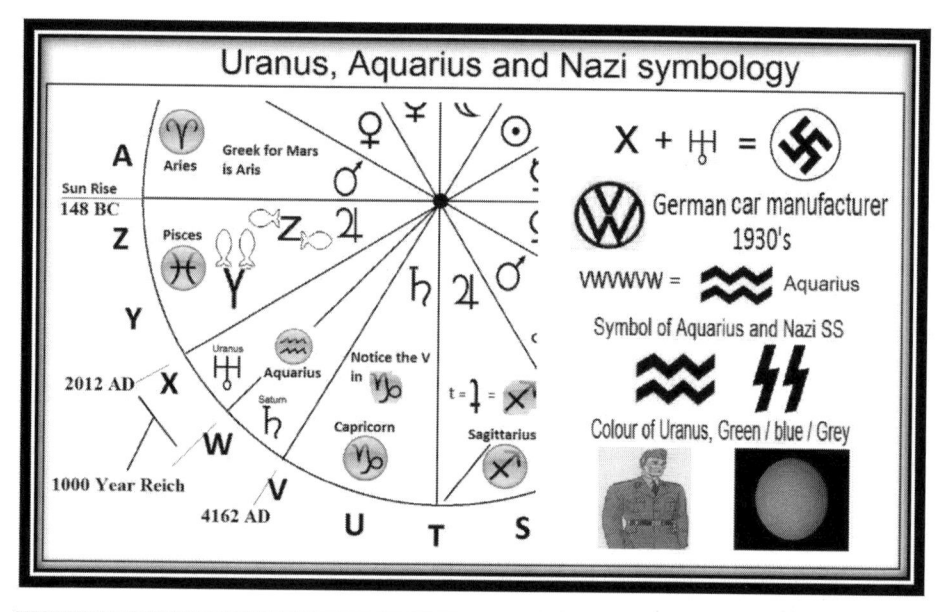

The expansive forces of Jupiter (the Christian west) allied themselves with the restrictive, organised saturnine forces of Bolshevism and Zionism, the two largest planets in our solar system battled it out with Nazism aligned with Uranus. As farfetched as this may seem to most readers, a clue to the deep understanding which the global elites policy makers have of universal energy forces at play, is displayed in some of the names given to Russian military operations, on the eastern front, against the German forces during World War Two, four planet names are used, Mars (the God of war), Jupiter, Saturn and Uranus.[15]

- **Operation Uranus** (1942) - Successful Russian encirclement of German 6th Army in Stalingrad.

- **Operation Saturn** (1942) - Proposed major attack following the Stalingrad encirclement.

- **Operation Jupiter** (1942) - Second phase of failed major offensive against Rzhev salient.

Unfortunately for the Nazis, the Age of Aquarius was not yet upon them, they were still in the Age of Pisces. A premature revolution trying to utilise and enhance Uranus energy for their own political and ideological purposes, being in the final stages of Pisces with Jupiter ruling, any side aligning themselves with Jupiter would have the upper hand. Just like the merging of two water colours, the change over from Pisces to Aquarius is steady and progressive, however many astrologers believe this new Age is finally upon us and the time for revolution is in the air.

"The kingdom of Heaven (**Ouranos** (Greek for Heaven) Uranus) is at hand " - Jesus.

The day chosen for D-day is also significant, a joint venture between Jupiter and Saturn worshipers. June 6th 1944 (6/6/44) was the greatest armada in human history, an alliance between Saturn -6 and Jupiter -4.

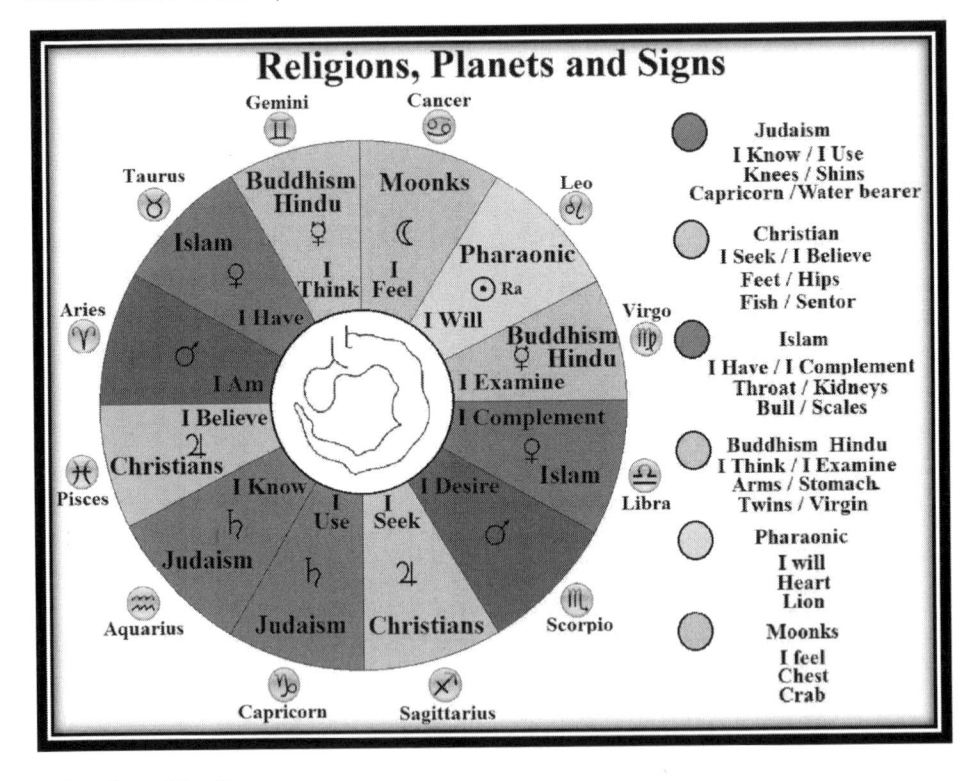

Religions, Planets and Signs

Sign	Religion	I Know / I Use
Judaism		Knees / Shins
		Capricorn / Water bearer
Christian		I Seek / I Believe
		Feet / Hips
		Fish / Sentor
Islam		I Have / I Complement
		Throat / Kidneys
		Bull / Scales
Buddhism Hindu		I Think / I Examine
		Arms / Stomach
		Twins / Virgin
Pharaonic		I will
		Heart
		Lion
Moonks		I feel
		Chest
		Crab

Resignation of the Pope

"I have had to recognize my incapacity to adequately fulfil the ministry entrusted to me" - Pope Benedict XVI resignation statement

The resignation of Pope Benedict XVI is an extraordinary event; it is not something the Catholic Church takes lightly. The last Pope to resign was Pope Gregory XII back in 1415. Some people see this as a clear sign that we are now moving into the Age of Aquarius. The significance of the Pope's timing comes into focus later that day. His resignation of the throne of Peter (Jupiter) was announced at 11:30 am. At 5:59 pm when the planet Jupiter was over head, almost on the mid-heaven, a lightning bolt comes out from the sky striking the very top of the Vatican's roof. But, this event could very well be just a remarkable coincidence.

Pope Resigns

Jupiter above the Vatican 11th Feb, 2013, 5:59pm

Religious and spiritual trinity

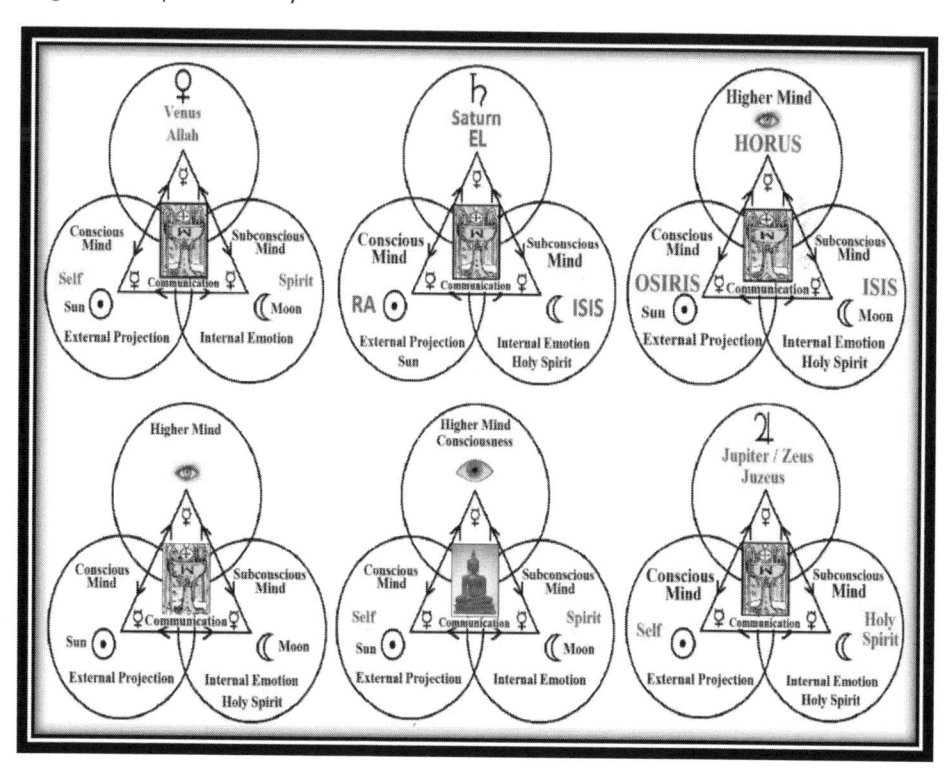

The concept behind the triad, the three aspects of God acting as one, comes from the three areas of consciousness, focal, sub and higher mind consciousness, which correspond to the Sun, the Moon and universal higher mind Logos. This triad can also be represented as the cosmological father and mother giving endless birth and rebirth to their son, A Sun which appears every morning in Aries (The Father) and disappears every evening between Virgo and Libra (The Mother). Most religions have personified this simple process, worshipping the Sun's journey across the sky, from birth to death.

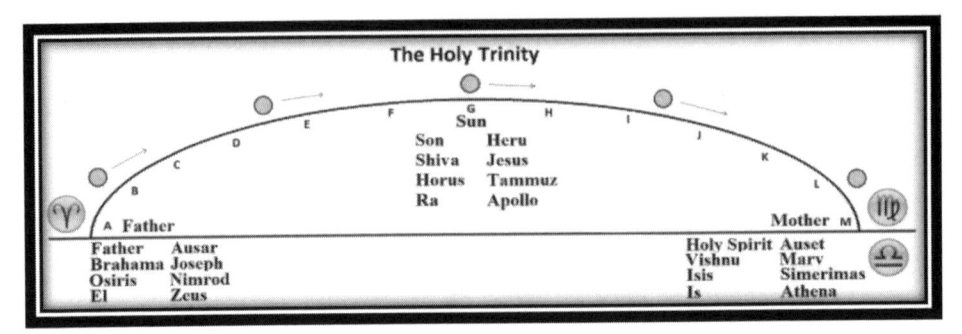

The Holy Trinity

	Sun	
	Son	Heru
	Shiva	Jesus
	Horus	Tammuz
	Ra	Apollo
Father		**Mother**
Father	Ausar	Holy Spirit Auset
Brahama	Joseph	Vishnu Mary
Osiris	Nimrod	Isis Simerimas
El	Zeus	Is Athena

The Sun during the daytime rules the focal consciousness, this is why we are awake and alert during the day. The Moon rules the night, the subconscious, hence why we fall asleep and try to connect with this part of our mind, unfortunately most people have no recollection of their sleep time and their journey into the subconscious. This may improve as our solar system moves closer to its sister star Sirius, reenergising and bringing forth the focal potential of the subconscious.

The Sun rising is considered mescaline; it is the Sun coming out of the feminine waters of the underworld. The Sun appears to come closer, towards us, giving us a bright blue sky. The Sun setting is when the Sun falls back into the waters of the underworld, the subconscious. At this time, the Sun is moving away from us creating a reddish sky. This is the Doppler Effect, hence why blue is synonymous with the male and red/pink synonymous with the female.

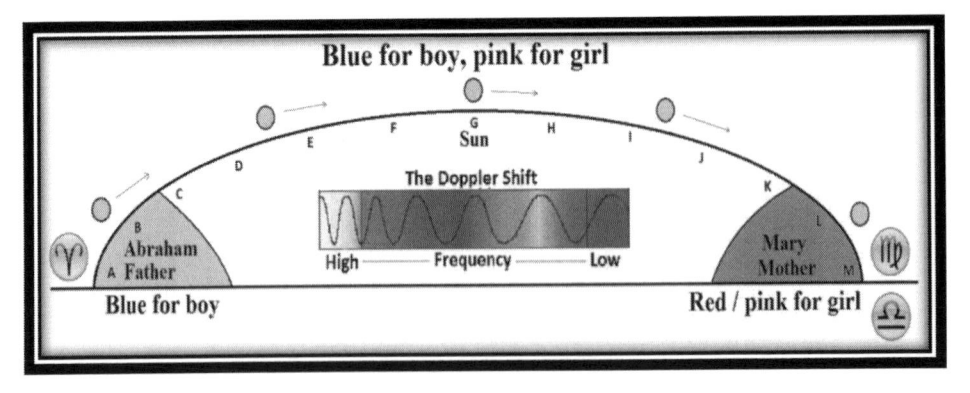

Blue for boy, pink for girl

Sun

The Doppler Shift

High ——— Frequency ——— Low

Abraham A Father — Blue for boy

Mary Mother — Red / pink for girl

The sacred secret

The sacred secret, the Grand Arcanum, the Magnum Opus, the Elixir of Life, enlightenment, self-mastery, whatever you want to call it, knowledge concerning this has been handed down to us through the writings of our ancestors, simple guidelines of how this aspect of the body works and how through self-control and self-discipline one can unlock the keys to enlightenment. Most religions have one major thing in common, the sexual discipline of its male followers, and a doctrine of keeping the seed within.

Self-control over sexual desires In Christianity:

"For it is God's will that you be sanctified: You must abstain from sexual immorality. Each of you must know how to control his own body in a holy and honourable manner, not with passion and lust like the gentiles who do not know God." - Thessalonians 4:3-5

"The fruit of the Spirit is . . . self-control." - Galatians 5:22-23

"And lead us not into temptation, but deliver us from evil" - Matthew 6:9-13

"The flesh is weak" – Mark 14:38

"Flee from sexual immorality. Every other sin a person commits is outside the body, but the sexually immoral person sins against his own body. Or do you not know that your body is a temple of the Holy Spirit within you, whom you have from God? You are not your own, for you were bought with a price. So, glorify God in your body."- Corinthians 6:18-20

"For the one who sows to his own flesh will from the flesh reap corruption, but the one who sows to the Spirit will from the Spirit reap eternal life". - Galatians 6:8

"But each person is tempted when he is lured and enticed by his own desire. Then desire when it has conceived gives birth to sin, and sin when it is fully grown brings forth death". - James 1: 14-15

"Beloved, I urge you as sojourners and exiles to abstain from the passions of the flesh, which wage war against your soul". - Peter 2:11

"And if your right hand causes you to sin, cut it off and throw it away. For it is better that you lose one of your members than that your whole body go into hell." - Matthew 5:30

Self-control in Judaism:

"Semen constitutes the strength of the body, its life, and the light of the eyes. Its emission to excess causes physical decay, debility, and diminished vitality. Thus Solomon, in his wisdom, says: 'Do not give your strength to women' (Proverbs 31:3). Whoever indulges in sexual dissipation becomes prematurely aged; his strength fails; his eyes become dim; a foul odour proceeds from his mouth and armpits; the hair of his head, eyebrows, and eyelashes drop out; the hair of his beard, armpits, and legs grow abnormally; his teeth fall out; and besides these, he becomes subject to numerous other diseases. Medical authorities have stated that for each one who dies of other maladies, a thousand are the victims of sexual excess." - Maimonides (Great medieval Jewish thinker)

"It is forbidden to discharge semen in vain. This is a graver sin than any other in the Torah" - Kitzur Shulchan Aruch

"Whosoever emits semen in vain deserves death, for it is said in Scripture." - R. Johanan

Self-control in Islam

"And those who guard their chastity, except from their wives for then, they are free from blame; But whoever seeks beyond that, then those are transgressors." (23:5-7) Quran

"Masturbation during the daytime of Ramadan breaks the fast, based on the Hadith that a fasting Muslim gives up eating, drinking, and sexual desire for the sake of Allah. Since masturbation is a kind of sexual desire, a fasting Muslim must avoid it. Therefore, masturbation invalidates the fast as does food and as it is one of the sins that if someone does it he or she would be violating the sanctity of this month." - Sheikh Hamed Al-Ali

Self-control in Buddhism and Hinduism

"To refrain from committing sexual misconduct" - The third precept

"Masturbation (sukkavissaṭṭhi) is the act of stimulating one's own sexual organs (sambādha) to the stage of orgasm (adhikavega). In the Kāma Sūtra, male masturbation is called "seizing the lion" (siṃhākāranta). Some people during the Buddha's time believed that masturbation could have a therapeutic effect on the mind and the body (Vin. III, 109), although the Buddha disagreed with this. According to the Vinaya, it is an offence of some seriousness for monks or nuns to masturbate (Vin. III, 111)" Shravasti Dhammika, Guide to Buddhism A to Z

"Celibacy (Brahmacharya) is one of the foundations of Hinduism and masturbation is one of the impediments to purity during the Brahmacharya phase of the life. The word brahmacharya tends to take on a connotation of disciplining the use of and preserving divine energy and is also understood broadly in yoga which can be understood as being applicable as appropriate in different contexts (e.g. faith in marriage, celibacy for spiritual aspirants etc.), in more extreme terms (complete celibacy full stop) or in more specific terms in relation to preserving and sublimating male sexual energy rather than losing it through ejaculation"- Religious views on masturbation[16]

The common theme running through all these religions and philosophical teachings, require self-control from the male, instructing him not to spill his sacred seed unnecessarily. What are they trying to tell us, and what is the main reason behind the barbaric practice of circumcision. In the Jewish tradition, a baby boy is required to be circumcised on the eighth day, after his birth. This is so the child can experience one Sabbath without unwittingly participating in his contract with God. The physical expression of this contractual agreement with God is to have the foreskin of his penis cut off by a senior member of his peers. From an astrological perspective, we see the genitalia, the part of the body associated with Scorpio (I desire) being ceremoniously and intentionally mutilated, imposing saturnine energetic frequencies of control, discipline, responsibility, limitation and restriction. The drawing of blood is the fluid of life, contracting saturnine dominance over the desire for recreational sex, promoting seed retention. Circumcision has become a habitual ritual not only for Jews but other Abrahamic based religions, observed by Muslims and Christians alike.

"Here is my covenant that you are to observe, between me and you and your descendants: Every male among you is to be circumcised. You are all to be circumcised in the flesh of your foreskin, and this is to be the sign of the covenant between me and you. Generation after generation, every male among you is to be circumcised on the eighth day after his birth, including the servant born in your house or the one purchased from a foreigner, who is not of your offspring. "Genesis 17:10-12

Although this ritual was written by Saturn worshipers, it is also practiced by Jupitarians and Venus worshipers, simply because it is thought to promote cleanliness and seed retention.

Chi, Prana, Ruah are all expressions of the creative vitality, the fluid life force breathing energy throughout the body. Most religious practices recommend celibacy amongst the male monks and priesthood; the reason being is that retaining the semen builds up the body's natural life energy, improving physical health, mental health and spiritual awareness. Nearly all paths to enlightenment recommend this practice. Ancients believed the pineal gland (third eye) could be activated with the help of meditation and various esoteric methods including semen retention. An activated pineal gland stimulates the 6th and 7th senses, contributing towards enlightenment and harmony between all levels of consciousness.

Semen is a complexed mixture of chemicals, vast amounts of physical and emotional energy are used in its production, when it is retained, at full capacity; the excess energy is reabsorbed into the body, supporting other vital organs, improving overall health and vitality.

Benefits of semen retention:

Physical

- Increased energy, vitality and drive.
- Optimised immune system.
- Helps with erectile dysfunction.
- Improves alertness.
- Improves physical health and organ function.

Mental

- Improved confidence.
- Better memory.
- Clarity and decisiveness.
- Improved insight and understanding.

Spiritual

- Calmer, a feeling of well being.
- A stronger feeling of spiritual connection.
- Better self-control over mental urges.

Pineal Gland   Eye of Horus   Enlightenment   Ulysses

Nature's cycles, especially Luna cycles have always played an important role, interacting with our biological make up. The human body which is made up of 70% water will be influenced just as much as the tides. Both men and women have a special time of the month (moonth), where their natal Sun/Moon position, cemented within their physical cells, resonates with the frequency of the transiting Moon. Women have a menstrual cycle, from ovulation to menstruation, averaging 28 days, synchronising with the Moon as it orbits the Earth. The term menstruation comes from the Latin mensis, which means (month or moonth). Very little ancient history has been written about the subject, due to most historians of the time being male, but it is believed that in ancient times most women living together in communities menstruated at the same time, around the new Moon.

"What I suggest is that the women of aboriginal Yurok households menstruated in synchrony, utilizing the light of the Moon to regularize their menstrual cycles, and that the menstruating women of (at least aristocratic) households used their shared periods of menstrual seclusion for the practice of spiritual disciplines." - American Ethnologist[17]

Today's modern living pulls women out of sync with nature, artificial lighting and electromagnetic pollution contribute to this distortion and chemical imbalance. Instead of seeing the menstrual cycle as a connection with nature, most women see it as an inconvenience.

The male also has a monthly cycle, a time when sperm production is at its highest. This time is when the Moon moves into the male's natal Sun sign, lasting for 2.5 days. According to Santos Bonacci, a scholar in esoteric wisdom, synchronicity and astrology, a seed is produced by the male which if saved and nurtured, will aid in activating the pineal gland.

"Every twenty-eight and one-half days, when the Moon is in the sign of the zodiac that the sun was in at the birth of the native, there is a seed or Psycho — Physical germ born in the or out of, the Solar Plexus (the Manger) and this seed is taken up by the nerves or branches of the Pneumo gastric nerve, and becomes the "Fruit of the Tree of Life," or the "Tree of good and evil" — viz : good if saved and "cast upon the waters" (circulation) to reach the Pineal Gland; and evil if eaten or consumed in sexual expression on physical plane, or by alcoholic drinks, or gluttony that causes ferment — acid and even alcohol in intestinal tract — thus — "No drunkard can inherit the Kingdom of Heaven" for acids and alcohol cut, or

chemically split, the oil that unites with the mineral salts in the body and thus produces the monthly seed."- Santos Bonacci[18]

The abundance of pornography in modern society is no accident. I would suggest it is encouraged by the controlling factions, as a way to seduce and disempower its citizens away from peak health, heightened awareness and enlightenment. A population of vacant empty vessels are more likely to look outside themselves for guidance, prone to consuming corporate products as a way to plug the holes in their unfulfilled lives, turning a society of wankers into obedient workers for the objectives of a few powerful groups and institutions. The chemical process which takes place in the male body due to sperm retention could be nature's way of ensuring the survival of the species during times of low population. A mechanism designed to heighten awareness with a deeper connection to all levels of consciousness, leading your biological self towards procreation, guiding you to where you need to be in order to find a suitable mating partner. It is therefore recommended by many religions for the individual to be encouraged in the area of self-control and self-discipline, steering himself away from temptation, even tying oneself to a mast like Ulysses, in a desperate attempt to keep the seed within.

There is nothing w-holy about these monotheistic religions, they are only part of the whole. To have a genuine wholly religion, all the planets must be equally represented, as a balancing mechanism for a harmonious reality. The rainbow is not wholly with half the colours missing, the octave will not strike a chord without all its notes. The universe is the energy behind our reality, and we as humans are a reflection of that energy, why handicap ourselves by focusing on only a partial selection of universal frequencies. The further we go back in time to the source of our creation, the more we see a pantheon of energies being worshiped. Did our ancestors know something which we have lost sight of and deviated from today? The ability to understand universal energies and their role in the physical world is not a simple concept; it is the accumulation of knowledge associated with an advanced culture, one with the ability to study the cosmos and its cycles. Is it possible that all those years ago our ancestors were taught by a sophisticated race, a race who's understanding and knowledge allowed them to harness this energy in ways we are unfamiliar with now. They do say in myths and legends that the Gods once walked on the Earth with men. Maybe the descendants of that race are still with us today, using their ancient knowledge to keep themselves in control, while perverting the truth for the rest of us, as a way to divide and rule humanity.

Notes for chapter 9

(1) Jordan Maxwell, Genesis 1:1 correctly translated, Youtube presentation, https://www.youtube.com/watch?v=c9MrElM5WLE

(2) Genesis 1, Interlinear Bible, http://biblehub.com/interlinear/genesis/1.htm

(3) Earth's Age, Beyond Today, United Church of God, March 9th, 2011, http://www.ucg.org/bible-study-tools/booklets/creation-or-evolution-does-it-really-matter-what-you-believe/earths-age

(4) Edwin Black, The Transfer agreement, Tradeselect LTD 2009, https://books.google.co.th/books?id=QjVxPwAACAAJ&dq=transfer+agreement&hl=en&sa=X&ved=0ahUKEwin_uiuuKPJAhUMk5QKHWBbByYQ6AEIGjAA

(5) Harris, J. (1998), The Israeli Declaration of Independence, The Journal of the Society for Textual Reasoning, Vol. 7.

(6) Declaration of Establishment of State of Israel, Israel Ministry of Foreign Affairs. http://www.mfa.gov.il/mfa/foreignpolicy/peace/guide/pages/declaration%20of%20establishment%20of%20state%20of%20israel.aspx

(7) Stereotypes of Jews, Wikipedia, https://en.wikipedia.org/wiki/Stereotypes_of_Jews

(8) Lianna Brinded, Christians are more likely to be fat than atheists, December 2014, International Business Times, http://www.ibtimes.co.uk/christians-are-more-likely-be-fat-atheists-1480732

(9) Dr Rafat Amari, Islam in the light of history, 2004, Religion research institute, http://www.amazon.com/Islam-Light-History-Rafat-Amari/dp/0976502402 & http://www.brotherpete.com/index.php?PHPSESSID=f05b251c1a590b48e0f7d5a2b6d54fab&topic=1240.msg4776#msg4776

(10) Immanual Velikovsky, Worlds in Collision, 1950, http://www.truthseekersministries.org/files/Velikovsky-Worlds-in-Collision.pdf

(11) Kenneth J Dillon, Venus, the Ancient Near East, and Islam, Scientia press, http://www.scientiapress.com/venus-the-ancient-near-east-and-islam

(12) Venus Barbata, Wikipedia, https://en.wikipedia.org/wiki/Venus_Barbata

(13) The Planets, Distances Between planets, http://theplanets.org/distances-between-planets/

(14) Budha, Wikipedia, https://en.wikipedia.org/wiki/Budha

(15) List of military operations on the Eastern Front of World War II, Wikipedia, https://en.m.wikipedia.org/wiki/List_of_military_operations_on_the_Eastern_Front_of_World_War_II

(16) Religious views on masturbation, https://en.m.wikipedia.org/wiki/Christian_views_on_masturbation#Hinduism

(17) Buckley, Thomas (1982). "Menstruation and the power of Yurok women, Conclusion, American Ethnologist, Vol 9, no1, http://anthropology.msu.edu/anp270-us15/files/2015/05/2.2-Buckley-1982.pdf

(18) Santos Bonacci, How To Connect To The Christ Within You, March 2015, http://in5d.com/santos-bonacci-how-to-connect-to-the-christ-within-you/

Chapter 10. Zionism

The majority of people either have no idea of what Zionism is, or they have a distorted view of its true nature and history. A call for a return of Jews to Palestine has a long history. Modern Zionism was created by elements within the British establishment to further the ambitions and aspirations of the British Empire. Their objective was to create a colonial controlled outpost in the Middle East, populated by Jews who would see it as a return to their ancestral homeland. The outpost would be a strategic commercial and military base for further imperialistic expansion using the Jews as a mechanism to drive a wedge between the Arab Muslims and other colonial powers in the area, all seeking to advance their own political or religious ambitions. Palestine is situated between Asia and Europe, whoever controls that area would control trade routes between the two, while securing access to important oil fields. The only problem was how to get the Jews to go along with the idea. Zion is a term used to describe the area around Jerusalem, Zionism is a political philosophy, a call to relocate Jews from all over the world and place them back to where they supposedly came from, the Promised Land, Palestine, mentioned in the Old Testament, between the Nile and the Euphrates. In the middle of the 19th century the British Empire, at the height of its power, was concerned about economic advancements being made by its competitors. The empire had become masters of maritime trade, protecting their trade routes and defending their ports with military muscle. Their competitors on the other hand were industrialising inland, the United States, France, Germany and Russia all posed a potential threat to the British economic dominance, especially if they all united against her. The French had completed the Suez Canal in 1869, enabling goods to flow easily between Europe and Asia. Bismarck had unified Germany in 1871 which encouraged the industrialisation of internal transport links making it easier for other empires and republics to compete with the British. The Empire would do all they could to keep themselves in control, especially by undermining competition in specific areas. Palestine was one of those strategic regions. Its importance became more pronounced after the Suez Canal was opened. Suez is Zeus backwards.

The idea of Jews returning to their homeland is an old one, from the Exodus out of Egypt to the Babylonian conquest of Judea in 641 BCE; Jews have been encouraged to go along with this notion. Even during the annual Passover celebrations, some Jews end their prayers with "next year in Jerusalem ". Daily prayers, another powerful repetitive mechanism used to cement a belief system, include references to, "your people Israel; your return to Jerusalem; and a redeemer shall come to Zion ".

The persecutions of Jews in Spain and Portugal persuaded many to adopt the Christian faith; however, some secretly kept the Judaic traditions alive. The Catholic Church suspicious and intolerant initiated the inquisition and by 1492 had expelled the remaining Jews. In 1516 Venice decided that Jews had to live in secure ghettos, they also had to pay a tax for the privilege, and by 1555 the Pope in Rome followed suit. Jews had already been expelled from England in 1290, only to be allowed back in 1649 under Oliver Cromwell. In 1648 a Sephardic Rabbi named Sabbatai Zevi, claimed he was the long awaited Jewish messiah and would lead his followers back to the Promised Land, unfortunately for Sabbatai most Jews did not see it that way. At the end of the 17th century, Judah he-Hasid Segal ha-Levi, a Jewish preacher, travelled from one Jewish community to another persuading a number of Jews to participate in a new ALIYAH (The immigration of Jews from the diaspora to the Promised Land of Israel). By 1700 he had assembled 1,500 for the long journey, but a third of them died along the way. When they reached the destination, they were broke and found they were not welcome. At that time, there was only around 1,200 Jews living in the city, so the sudden arrival of around 1000 new Ashkenazi Jews created a massive problem. The new comers, viewed with hostility, got into debt trying to build a new synagogue and by 1720 their Arab creditors set fire to the building and took back control. The Turkish authorities blamed all the Jews collectively for the mess and banned the Ashkenazi Jews from the area.[1] The Jewish population within the Holy Land steadily increased after the Christian persecutions of the Reconquista. Following Napoleon's conquest, laws were brought in to emancipate Jews throughout Europe which helped in the decline of their persecution. Britain gave Jews equal rights in 1856 and Germany in 1871. During the competitive Age of Nationalism and expanding empires, Jews ceased to be persecuted for their religious belief, but instead were seen as a different race altogether, anti-Semitism took over from the simple disapproval of Judaic/Saturn worship.

The British established a consulate in Jerusalem in 1838, which at the time was ruled by the Turks and governed from Istanbul, the following year a report was published about the conditions of Jews in the area, a memorandum followed which encouraged European monarchs into supporting the idea of restoring Jews back to Palestine. In August 1840 the Times of London reported that the British government was considering the restoration of a Jewish homeland, and that both Lord Shaftsbury and Lord Palmerston were instrumental in its promotion.[2] Lord Shaftsbury was a proactive advocate for Zionism as early as the 1820's, motivated by an Evangelical revival, which took place between the 20's and 30's. Napoleon in 1799 saw the strategic importance of the area for his own empire, he considered helping the Jews back to Palestine, and prepared a proclamation to this effect. It was only his defeat which put an early end to this proposal.[3] It was important at this time for the British to develop an outpost in the Middle East, due to pressure from colonial competitors, especially the French. There was also the Muslim threat under Muhammad Ali, who by 1832 had united much of Palestine and Syria, he also began to industrialise the region with the intention of turning it into a modern state, Ali also established an Egyptian/French alliance which made it necessary for the British to champion the cause for relocating the Jews back to the Promised Land in order to gain a foothold.

Fathers Of Zionism
Lord Shaftesbury — **Benjamin Disraeli** — **Lionel de Rothschild**

Benjamin Disraeli was a British politician and writer, who came from a wealthy family of Sephardic Jews. He was British Prime Minister twice, once in 1868 and again from 1874 – 1880. A pro Zionist, who with close ties to the House of Rothschild, was able to bring the Zionist dream closer to fruition. Lord Stanley, a Freemason and Conservative Party politician mentions visiting Disraeli in his Diary in January 1851, he talks about " Disraeli's ideas for the restoration of the Jews to Palestine".[4] With a string of pro Zionist and pro Rothschild writings behind him, Disraeli seemed to be the ideal candidate who could turn this idea into a reality.

ISIS cults

Isis cults are the mother of all mystery school cults, Isis being the mother God of ancient Egypt, representing the subconscious, the Moon and the Holy Spirit. Its influence within secret societies is vast. The 19th century was awash with cults and secret societies, initiated from the heart of the British Empire, used to recruit and single out useful members of the community for the purposes of serving each cult and advancing hidden agendas. Disraeli made two important contacts in his early career; the first was with the House of Rothschild and second with Edward Bulwer- Lytton, Colonial Secretary 1858-59 and member of the British parliament. Lytton was an Arch-priest of an Isis cult in Britain, who wrote the novel *"The last days of Pompeii* "(1834), an Isis cult story. His Isis novel was a catalyst which inspired other Isis cults to spring up around the mid to late 19th century, one of these cults was called "ISIS-URANUS TEMPLE OF THE HERMETIC STUDENTS OF THE GOLDEN DAWN ", (1880's). Another such cult was the Theosophy Society, founded by Madame Helena Blavatsky, who published a book titled *"Isis Unveiled"*.[5]

The Thule Society in Germany (German: Thule-Gesellschaft) had close ties with Helena Blavatsky and the Theosophy Society. The Thule Society was originally a study group in Munich seeking the truth about German antiquated history, with the aim of trying to prove the supremacy of the Aryan race and its ties to the lost ancient city of Atlantis. Their pro German or Volkisch (ethno nationalistic) position would later influence the Nazi Party. In 1919, after WW1, Anton Drexler of the Thule society, together with Karl Harrer, established the Deutsche Arbeiterpartei (DAP) or German Workers Party. The following year Adolf Hitler joined and it became known as National Sozialistische Deutsche Arbeiterpartei (NSDAP). Both Rudolf Hess and Alfred Rosenberg were prominent members of the Thule Society.[6]

All this Isis worship was not just meaningless ritual, it had energy behind it. It's another example of how the elite within the establishment are involved in the occult and know how to exploit energies associated with universal wisdom and ancient astrological synchronicity. This early Isis connection is very important and will be expanded upon later.

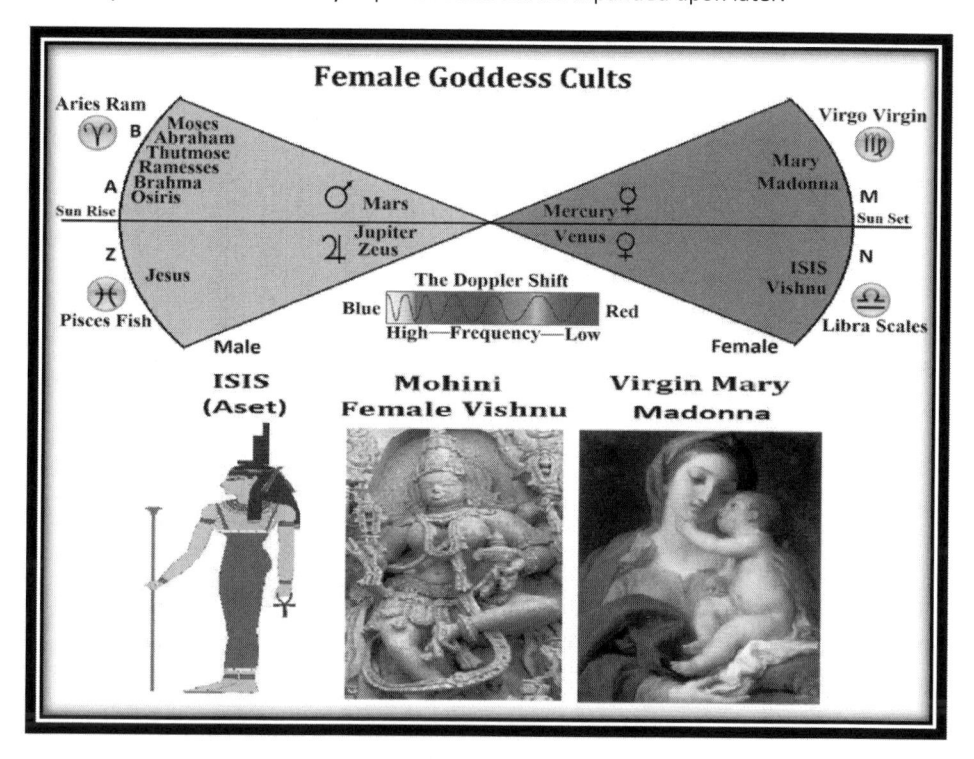

Female Goddess Cults

Diagram showing astrological chart with Aries Ram (Moses, Abraham, Thutmose, Ramesses, Brahma, Osiris), Pisces Fish (Jesus), Virgo Virgin (Mary Madonna), Libra Scales (ISIS, Vishnu), planetary symbols for Mars, Jupiter/Zeus, Mercury, Venus, and The Doppler Shift (Blue High—Frequency—Low Red), with Male/Female axis.

ISIS (Aset) — **Mohini Female Vishnu** — **Virgin Mary Madonna**

In 1862 the Prince of Wales (future King Edward VII), a Freemason, made a visit to Palestine and the Holy Land, not only representing the state but also to do some ground work. After the defeat of the British backed Confederates in the American Civil War, momentum gained for the Zionist project, in 1865 the Foreign Office began preparations for resettlement, a fund called "The Palestine Exploration Fund" was created backed by both Oxford and Cambridge universities along with money from Freemasonry. This exploration fund produced a practical plan to make the country habitable for resettlement. With the construction of the Suez Canal, the potential threat to British pre-eminence was aired by Lord Palmerston (two times British Prime Minister).

"I must tell you frankly that what we are afraid of is losing our commercial and maritime pre-eminence, for this Canal will put other nations on an equal footing with us. At the same time I must own that we are not quite easy on the score of the designs of France. Of course we have every confidence in the loyalty and sincerity of the Emperor, but who can answer for those who will come after him?" Lord Palmerston, Tuchman, Barbara, Bible and Sword, 1956 p 258

In 1862 Moses Hess, a German, French, Jewish philosopher and associate of Karl Marx wrote a book called "*Rome and Jerusalem, the last national question*", in which he calls for the creation of a Jewish socialist state in Palestine. In the latter half of the 19th century various socialist movements sprang up, each one targeting different social and political aspects of society. The Fabians, the Marxists and Hess's Zionist Socialism, were all organised ventures promoted to control the future direction of humanity.

In an effort to control the Canal, Disraeli and the Rothschild's arranged to purchase the Egyptian rulers portion of shares, placing them under the control of the British government. In the late 1870's Jewish philanthropists helped to finance an agricultural resettlement program for Russian Jews who were desperately trying to flee persecution in eastern Europe, the Rothschild's came to their aid sponsoring many new settlements in Palestine. In 1877 Disraeli created a blueprint for a Zionist State, which would be under British rule, ensuring political and economic penetration in the region. In his book *Alroy*, Disraeli reveals his wishes.

"Sire, bear with me. If I speak in heat, I speak in zeal. You ask me what I wish: my answer is, a national existence, which we have not. You ask me what I wish: my answer is, the Land of Promise. You ask me what I wish: my answer is, Jerusalem. You ask me what I wish: my answer is, the Temple, all we have forfeited, all we have yearned after, all for which we have fought, our beauteous country, our holy creed, our simple manners, and our ancient customs." Benjamin Disraeli, Alroy 1828, part 8 chapter 6.

They had the will and the financial backing, all the British needed now was a man who would promote the cause, a man who would successfully convince the Jewish community of the merits for Zionism. The man they approached was Theodore Herzl.

Theodore Herzl was born Benjamin Ze'ev Herzl in 1860, in Pest, East Budapest, Hungary. His parents were German speaking assimilated Jews, his father Jakob Herzl was a successful business man. Theodore's conversion to Zionism was purported to be around the time of the Dreyfus affair in 1894. While he was working as a reporter in Paris he witnessed anti-Semitic protests erupt following the arrest and conviction of a French Jewish Army Captain who was accused of spying for the Germans. This persuaded him to reject Jewish emancipation and assimilation; instead he embraced the notion of moving all Jews out of Europe into Palestine. In 1889 Theodor married Julie Naschauer the daughter of a wealthy Jewish business man, and moved to Vienna. In those days, high society in Vienna would socialise in a network of salons set up by Julie Rothschild, the daughter of the Viennese branch of the banking dynasty, these salons were recruiting grounds for secret societies and Isis cults. Herzl was known to be a regular patron. On March 10th 1896 Herzl was visited by Reverend William Hechler, an Anglican Minister to the British Embassy; Hechler was familiar with Herzl's publications on Zionist issues. This meeting would be the turning point in his career, he wrote in his diary.

"Next we came to the heart of the business. I said to him: (Theodor Herzl to Rev. William Hechler) I must put myself into direct and publicly known relations with a responsible or non-responsible ruler – that is, with a minister of state or a prince. Then the Jews will believe in me and follow me. The most suitable personage would be the German Kaiser." - Theodore Herzl

Hechler arranged Herzl to meet Frederick I in 1896, which led to an audience with Wilhelm II, in 1898. This gave credence to Herzl's movement in the eyes of the Jewish community. Before Hechler's intervention most Jews considered Herzl as a lunatic or a British agent, the majority of Jews considered Zionism to be an assault on Jews and Judaism. This created a split within the Jewish community, those against the homeland and those for it. The problem was that most Orthodox Jews believed that a homeland could only be given to the Jews by a new messiah, as that had not happened and Jesus (Jupiter - Zeus) was not considered as such, a homeland for Jews was out of the question. As Saturn worshipers, their Messiah was not to appear until the new Age of Aquarius, under the traditional zodiacal system where Saturn rules the whole epoch. Under the modern system, Uranus takes precedence for the first 1000 years. This new messiah for the Zionist movement also came in the form of finance from the House of Rothschild, enabling Zionist projects to move forward. Opposition was expressed in the "Pittsburgh Platform", a position adopted by the Central Conference of American Rabbis in 1885.

"We consider ourselves no longer a nation, but a religious community, and therefore expect neither a return to Palestine, nor a sacrificial worship under the sons of Aaron, nor the restoration of any of the laws concerning the Jewish state."[7]

Herzl came to the conclusion that anti-Semitism would be advantageous for the Zionist movement, in the sense that it would make life unbearable for Jews living in Europe, and out of desperation they would eventually move to Palestine. He wrote in his diary:

"**The anti-Semites will be only too happy to give Zionism publicity**." Theodore Herzl

"**The anti-Semites will become our most dependable friends, the anti-Semitic countries our allies**." (The Complete Diaries of Theodor Herzl. Vol. 1, edited by Raphael Patai, translated by Harry Zohn, page 83-84)

"**Herzl regarded Zionism's triumph as inevitable, not only because life in Europe was ever more untenable for Jews, but also because it was in Europe's interests to rid the Jews and relieved of anti-Semitism: The European political establishment would eventually be persuaded to promote Zionism. Herzl recognized that anti-Semitism would be harnessed to his own--Zionist-purposes.**" (Benny Morris, Righteous Victims, p. 21)

During the late 19th century Herzl made regular visits to England. He wrote in his diary.

"Get at one stroke ... ten million secret but loyal subjects active in all walks of life all over the world.... As at a signal, all of them will place themselves at the service of the magnanimous nation that brings long-desired help.... England will get ten million agents for her greatness and influence." Theodore Herzl

Herzl and his colleagues established 'The World Zionist Congress', an organisation which would rally the Jewish people into pushing for resettlement in Palestine. The first congress was held in Basel Switzerland in 1897, attended by 200 participants, they created the political Zionist agenda known as the "Basel Programme".

"Zionism seeks for the Jewish people a publicly recognized legally secured homeland in Palestine." - Statement from the first world Zionist congress.

Herzl wrote in his diary: "Were I to sum up the Basle Congress in a word - which I shall guard against pronouncing publicly - it would be this: At Basle I founded the Jewish State." Theodore Herzl

When Herzl was looking into other possibilities for resettlement, Argentina was one of the options mentioned, when considering this he wrote:

"We shall try to spirit the penniless population across the border by procuring employment for it in the transit countries, while denying it any employment in our country." - Herzl, considering Argentina as a homeland.

He died at the young age of 44 on July 3rd 1904, from cardiac sclerosis. His remains were moved from Vienna to Mount Herzl in Jerusalem in 1949. Before the creation of Israel, with money supplied from wealthy backers, the Zionist's bought up all the land they could. This was known as "land redemption or Jewdifying the land". In 1917, during World War 1, the British conquered Palestine from the Turks, and legalised the Jewish national homeland concept with the Balfour Declaration. The pro-Zionist British dismantled all Palestinian paramilitary groups, leaving them defenceless and leaderless, paving the way for further Zionist settlements. In 1923 the National Socialist German Workers Party (NSDAP), were struggling to get a significant political following, they needed help and financial support. With similar goals towards the Jewish problem, the Zionists and National Socialists decided to help each other. According to the research of Eustace Mullins, the Rothschild backed Zionists offered to support the National Socialists in a joint venture; if they got into power they would round up all the Jews of Europe and try to resettle them in Palestine. This could be the origins of the term NAZI, NA (National Socialist) ZI (Zionist) NAZI. Pro Zionist Jews would be resettled in Palestine under the Haavara Agreement (Transfer Agreement).[8] All the anti-Zionist Jews would be put into labour camps, with the aim of persuading them to convert to Zionism. Mullins speculates that the labour camps were run by Zionist Jews known as "Sonderkommandos" overseen by German soldiers.[9] In 1931 (4,075) Jews immigrated to Palestine, and in 1934 that number had risen to 61,854. During the war the camps inmates were used as slave labour to help with the war effort. The Germans never referred to themselves as Nazi's, it was an allied propaganda creation, used as a derogatory political pun to undermine the cohesive force of National Socialism. It was based on the Austro-Bavarian slang word "Ignatz" which meant simpleton or country bumpkin. One could argue that Adolf Hitler and most of the German High Command were Zionists by definition, because they all wanted to see the Jews relocated out of Europe and into Palestine.

National Socialist and Zionist Coin	Approximate population of Palestine			
	Year	Total	Muslims	Jews	Christians
	1922	752,048	589,177	83,790	71,464
	1931	1,033,314	759,700	174,606	88,907
	1937	1,383,320	875,947	386,084	109,769
	1945	1,845,560	1,076,780	608,230	145,060
	1947	1,955,260	1,135,269	650,000	153,621
	http://www.mideastweb.org/palpop.htm			

Somewhere along the way, and for various reasons, the German's under Hitler went rogue on the geopolitical balance of power. Unable to restrain their expansive aspirations or bring them back to heel, threatened by their strength, the British Empire with the help of its allies, the international financiers and the United States, united in a monumental struggle to tame the beast. From Churchill's perspective, sharing peace with Hitler was not an option; it was all or nothing, a battle to the death. The old power elite would throw all they had at neutralising this upstart; otherwise their own ambitions for globalisation would be finished.

In 1942 there were major epidemics of Typhus plaguing German concentration camps and also soldiers in the field, large amounts of people were dying. At the end of December 1942, in response to this high mortality rate, Himmler wrote a letter to the camps doctors, ordering them to put in place firm counter measures to reduce the number of deaths.

letter from the SS Main Office of Economic Administration to all concentration camps, to Camp Doctors of the Concentration Camps Da., Sh. Bu., Neu., Au., Rav., Flo., Lu., Stu., Gr-Ro., Nied., Natz., Hinz., Mor., Herzog., Mau.

28 December 1942, Medical Activities in the Concentration Camps

"The camp doctors must use all means at their disposal to reduce essentially this death rate in the various camps." and " The SS Reichsfuehrer [Heinrich Himmler] has ordered that the death rate absolutely must be reduced. For this reason the aforementioned has been ordered and a monthly report on this matter is to be submitted to the Chief of the Department D 111, the first report to be submitted on 1 February 1943."- [10]

This led to strict hygiene policies being introduced, to combat lice and other disease-ridden insects, delousing of clothes and new inmates took place, hair was shaved off and belongings removed. Clothes were placed in delousing chambers where Zyclon B crystals were added, these pellets would be heated up to release the poisonous cyanide gas. The residue of this chemical was so powerful it would stain the brickwork of the delousing chambers blue, even after 70 years of weathering.

Delousing with Zyclon B

In the latter stages of the war, the Germans knew they were defeated; the allied bombing campaign was so severe they flattened over 60 German cities. Any city with a population greater than 50,000 was targeted for destruction, in a campaign known as terror bombing, between 1940-45 the number of people killed in German cities is estimated at between 300,000 – 600,000, leaving 7,500,000 homeless. Britain lost 60,000 in similar city bombing campaigns.[11]

Winston Churchill in July 1940

"When I look around to see how we can win the war I see that there is only one sure path. We have no Continental army which can defeat the German military power... Should [Hitler]... Not try invasion [of Britain]... There is one thing that will bring him back and bring him down, and that is an absolutely devastating, exterminating attack by very heavy bombers from this country upon the Nazi homeland. We must be able to overwhelm them by this means, without which I do not see a way through. We cannot accept any aim lower than air mastery. When can it be obtained?" [Extract from Winston S Churchill the Second World War (Volume 2 Their Finest Hour Appendix A), Memo from Prime Minister to Minister of Aircraft Production, 8th July 1940].

Allied Strategic / Terror Bombing of German Cities

The scale of the destruction caused by the Allied bombing disrupted supply lines to the concentration camps. The civilians could not even feed themselves let alone anyone else. The condition of the prisoners by the time Allied forces liberated them was appalling, many had died from starvation and disease, in some cases, barely alive emaciated skeletons would be wandering the camps looking for food, which was made worse by the relentless RAF aerial bombing. Eisenhower and the British wanted film footage to show to the world, footage which would justify their participation and actions towards their German enemies. Sidney Bernstein a British, Jewish pro-Zionist media baron was sent to the camps during the liberation process. He went with his lifelong friend Alfred Hitchcock who was a well renowned film maker of the day. Sidney Bernstein in a television interview, years later, told how he was instructed to make a film which would prove to the world that the claims of atrocities had taken place.

"Our instructions were to film everything which would prove this had actually happened." - Sidney Bernstein [12]

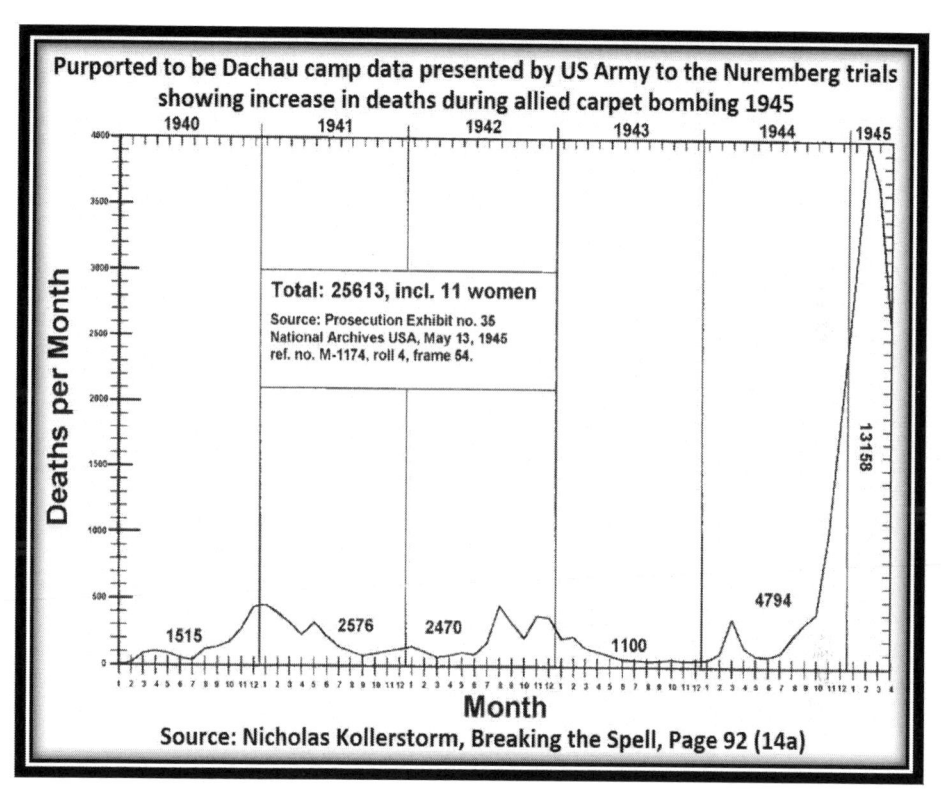

Purported to be Dachau camp data presented by US Army to the Nuremberg trials showing increase in deaths during allied carpet bombing 1945

Total: 25613, incl. 11 women
Source: Prosecution Exhibit no. 35
National Archives USA, May 13, 1945
ref. no. M-1174, roll 4, frame 54.

Deaths per Month

1515, 2576, 2470, 1100, 4794, 13158

Month
Source: Nicholas Kollerstorm, Breaking the Spell, Page 92 (14a)

In July 1945, the documentary they made was shelved by the British Foreign Office, claiming it was too incendiary, and would not favour new relations and the co-operation needed with post war defeated Germans. While films were being made for western public consumption, in the final days of the war, General Eisenhower ordered 19 camps to be built which were big enough to hold the millions of captured German soldiers, under the control of the Western Allies. These camps where known as "**Rheinwiesenlager**"(Rhine Meadow Camps). The prisoners were designated as DEF's (Disarmed Enemy Forces) not POW's, this allowed Eisenhower and their captives to ignore the Geneva Convention of 1929, denying the prisoners of all their basic human rights, right to food and shelter; they were just left out in open fields exposed to the elements. The Allies claimed that out of approximately 2 million

German prisoners, a maximum of 10,000 starved to death, but in James Bacque's book "*Other Losses*"(1989), he estimates the deaths to be in the region of 1 million.⁽¹³⁾

Eisenhower's Rhine Meadows DEF Camps

On April 12th 1945 General Eisenhower visited a German labour camp near the town of Gotha, after his visit he made a statement in which he said:

"I felt that the evidence should be immediately placed before the American and British publics in a fashion that would leave no room for cynical doubt." - General Eisenhower April 1945

In the east, the Soviet Army captured approximately 3 million German's, which were used as forced labour for reconstruction projects. The number of deaths in Soviet POW camps is contradictory, while the Soviet records show 381,000 died, German research suggests the figure is much higher, around 1 million. In 1974 the West German Government set up the Maschke Commission to look into the deaths of German POW's, they concluded that 1.1 million German prisoners died in Soviet prison camps.⁽¹⁴⁾

Armed with the evidence of atrocities carried out on the Jews of Europe during WW2, the Zionist movement could use the sympathy created from Jewish victim status to promote their cause, their desire for an independent state in Palestine was now possible. On 29th November 1947, the UN General Assembly recommended a partition plan for Palestine, to divide the country into two states, one Jewish State and one Arab. Britain was to pull out, ending its Mandate of Palestine on midnight 14th May 1948. David Ben-Gurion the executive head of the Zionist organisation would lead the establishment of the new Jewish State which was to be called "ISRAEL", almost a century after Disraeli had championed the idea among circles within the British elite.

ISRAEL was born ISIS-RA-EL. Just as expected and anticipated by the British, a conflict ensued, the ink had not even dried on Israel's declaration of independence, when an Arab coalition escalated the tension which had been festering since 1917 with the signing of the Balfour Declaration. The anger among the Palestinian Arabs was of no surprise to those watching; the British legitimised the handover of Palestinian land, to a third party, the Zionist Jews. This is no different than the British handing over Indonesia to the Australians, but it wasn't intended to be a smooth ride, it was meant to be a British outpost, occupied by Jews, to drive a wedge and disunite the region, fragmenting the Muslims.

The Arab/Israeli war officially began on 15th May 1948, with an Arab coalition force of around 25,000 soldiers. The IDF initially had 35,000. However, by July this had increased to 65,000, and by the end of the year their numbers had swollen to nearly 100,000 soldiers. The Arabs steadily increased their numbers but couldn't match the pace of the Israelis. The war lasted 10 months and served the Zionists well, not only did it drive a wedge deep into the heart of the Middle East; it was also used as a smokescreen for covert operations which saw the expulsion of some 700,000 Palestinian Arabs from their homes. A similar number of Jews immigrated into Israel due to the conflict and expulsions from surrounding Middle Eastern countries. By the end of the war, Israel not only kept the land granted to it by the UN General Assembly but had managed to capture 60% of the land set aside for the Arabs. The map of Palestine had turned into a map of Israel within a few short years.

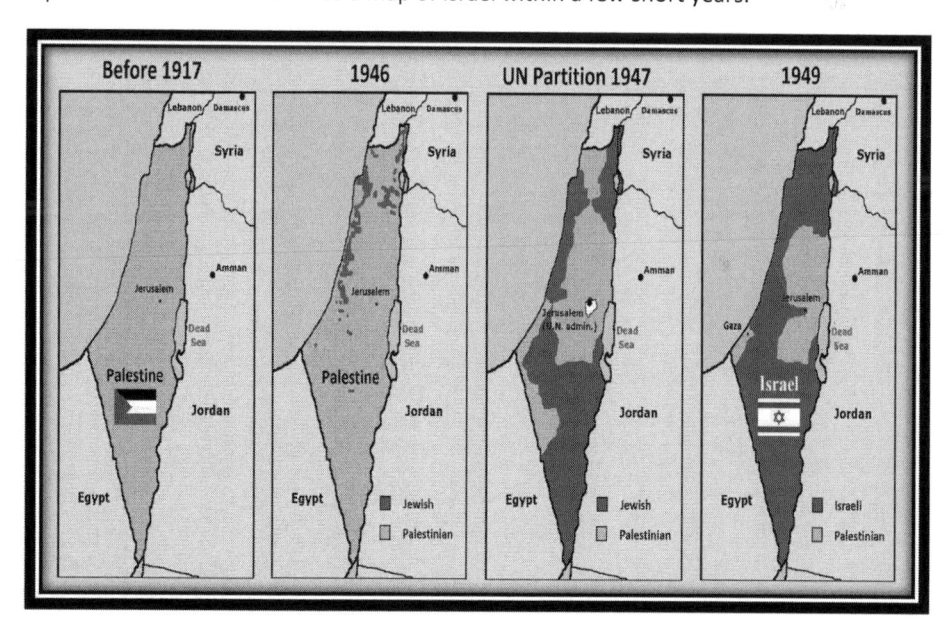

Now Britain had its outpost, to be used as a tool for division, there would never be peace in that area, all in the name of keeping the balance of power tilted in favour of the old colonialists and the British Empire. The Zionist Nation State is used to influence and infiltrate other countries which threaten the new post war globalization project. From its inception many Zionist organisations sprang up throughout the world, lobby groups and sophisticated networks designed to promote Zionist interests, a back door for the British/Rothschild global hegemony.

Zionist Organisations

Adam and Gila Milstein Family Foundation	Gdud HaAvoda	Kvutsat Yovel
Alliance for New Zionist Vision	Gush Emunim	Media Watch International
Alliance Israélite Universelle	Hakhshara	Migdal Oz (seminary)
Ameinu	Hapoel Hatzair	My Israel
American Israel Public Affairs Committee	Hashomer	Na'amat
American Jewish Conference	Hatzohar	The National Institutions House
American Palestine Committee	Histadrut	The National Left
American Zion Commonwealth	Homesh First	Nativ
American Zionist Movement	Hovevei Zion	Nefesh B'Nefesh
AMIT	Im Tirtzu	Odessa Committee
Armée Juive	Institute for Zionist Strategies	Palestine Land Development Company
Artists4Israel	International Academic Friends of Israel	Partners for Progressive Israel
Arzenu	International Fship of Christians and Jews	Partnership2Gether
Tzvi Avisar	Palestine Jewish Colonization Association	Poale Zion
Aytzim	Israel Campus Roundtable	Quebec-Israel Committee
Bar-Giora (organization)	Israel lobby in the United Kingdom	Religious Zionists of America
Bilu	Israel lobby in the United States	Scholars for Peace in the Middle East
Birthright Israel	Israel Project	Swiss Union of Jewish Students
Centre for Israel and Jewish Affairs	JCall	Tarbut
World Zionist Congress	Jerusalem Emergency Committee	The Temple Institute
The David Project	Jewish Agency for Israel	Tzohar (organization)
Ephraim Israel National Convention	Jewish Defense League Chapters	Union des étudiants juifs de France
Ephraim Union	Jewish Internet Defense Force	United Israel Appeal
European Friends of Israel	Jewish Labour Movement	Women for Israel's Tomorrow
European Union of Jewish Students	Jewish National Fund	World Union of Jewish Students
Ezra USA	Jewish Resistance Movement	World Zionist Organization
Facts and Logic About the Middle East	Jewish Territorialist Organization	Yesha Council
Farband	Jung Borochovistim	Zionist Commission
Friends of the Israel Defense Forces	Keren Hayesod	Zionist General Council
		Zionist Organization of America

Source https://en.wikipedia.org/wiki/Category:Zionist_organizations

While the Israeli lobby groups, like AIPAC (American Israel Public Affairs Committee) pressure the United States into annually supporting Israel, not only financially but militarily, the anti-Zionist Jews protest against the whole concept of Zionism and its contradictions towards Judaism. The British/Rothschild Empire has managed to use Zionism as a mechanism to infiltrate the US political system, while making the US pay Israel for the privilege of having their republic manipulated from within. Since its conception in 1948, Israel has become the biggest beneficiary of US foreign aid with a whopping $121 billion, around $3 billion per year. It is the old British way of control, play two sides off against one another, while the empire watches from a safe distance.

Jews against Zionism

Fringe Orthodox Jews known as Neturei Karta consider themselves as true Jews, upholding the undiluted traditions of Judaism. This group opposes Zionism and calls for its dismantlement, along with an end to the state of Israel, believing that real Judaism can only have a homeland when the new Jewish messiah comes. Pro Zionist media outlets have labelled Iranian President Mahmoud Ahmadinejad as anti-Semitic, although he has a good relationship with the Neturei Karta Rabbis and has clarified his position many times. He is not anti-Semitic but opposes Zionism and its policies. Unfortunately, many people in the west see Zionism and Judaism as the same thing, and anyone who criticises the policies or actions of the Zionist regime are considered anti-Semitic, they even go so far as to suggest the Zionist critic is also a Holocaust denier.

Mahmoud Ahmadinejad meets Naturie Karta Rabbis 2007

During the televised meeting with Iranian President Ahmadinejad the Netarei Karta Rabbis clearly state that the Jews and Arabs have lived in peace for hundreds of years, everything changed with the arrival of Zionism, and that many anti-Zionist Rabbi leaders, faithful to old school Torah Judaism died in German concentration camps.[15] Incidentally at the Nuremburg International Military Tribunal, which was initiated as far back as December 1942, the Germans were charged with killing 4 million prisoners at the 3 camps known as Auschwitz (main camp), Birkenau and Mankowitz. This figure was an estimate supplied by the Soviets. They also estimated the number of deaths at Majdanek to be 1.5 million, which the Majdanek Museum later reduced to 78,000, of which 59,000 were Jews. In 1990 the original plaque at Birkenau which commemorated 4 million deaths was removed only to be replaced five years later. The new plaque had been revised down to 1.5 million, and the official number at the Auschwitz Museum is even less at 1.1 million, of which 90% were Jews.[16] An appalling figure. However, the initial total of 6 million is still used to this day, even though the numbers have been officially revised, it has such emotional baggage attached to it that anyone daring to question its validity is frowned upon.

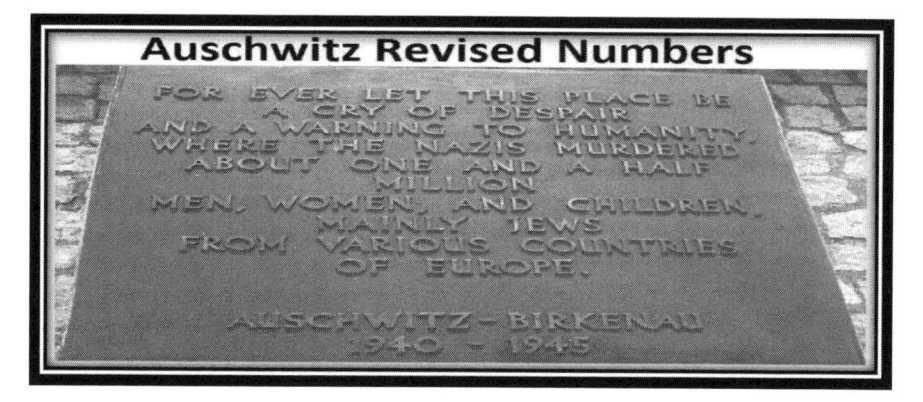

Auschwitz Revised Numbers

FOR EVER LET THIS PLACE BE
A CRY OF DESPAIR
AND A WARNING TO HUMANITY,
WHERE THE NAZIS MURDERED
ABOUT ONE AND A HALF
MILLION
MEN, WOMEN, AND CHILDREN,
MAINLY JEWS
FROM VARIOUS COUNTRIES
OF EUROPE.

AUSCHWITZ - BIRKENAU
1940 - 1945

Judaic Black Hats Of Saturn Worship

When the Soviet Army liberated Auschwitz in 1945 they took away the German records which had been kept on all the inmates, the arrivals, departures, deaths and even religious category. In 1989 President Gorbachev of the USSR released these documents in 46 volumes. These so-called Auschwitz death books cover the period from July 1941 to Dec 1943 and contain the death certificates of just over 68,000 individuals, of which 29,000 were categorised as Jews. The records show a significant increase of deaths in the summer of 1942 due to the Typhus epidemic. Another interesting statistic is the percentage of Jews who died at Auschwitz compared to the number of Catholics. According to the figures, which have been well presented in the book "Breaking the Spell" by Nicholas Kollerstorm 2014, only 42% of the total deaths during this period were Jews, less than the number of Catholics.[17] After the War, Germany was made to pay reparations to Jewish survivors of the Holocaust, which they are still doing to this day. It has become big business with approximately 6 million Jews receiving some form of benefit of this nature. Germany has paid approximately $89 billion to Jewish victims of Nazi persecution since 1952. It is important to point out that few payments have been made to any other group caught up in the Holocaust. The first Israeli Prime Minister David Ben-Gurion in 1951 made a claim against Germany for compensation and reimbursement of resettling 500,000 Holocaust survivors, they asked for 1.5 billion dollars which would be $13,700,000,000 in today's money, They also claimed $6 billion for stolen Jewish property which the Nazi's allegedly pillaged.[18] Every few years one of many Zionist organisations finds another ageing Nazi to wheel out and put on public display in another show trial, keeping the Holocaust and Jewish victim status alive in the minds of each new generation.

"The German government has committed to pay nearly 800 million euros for the care of elderly Holocaust survivors as a result of negotiations in Israel between Berlin and a fund for Jewish victims of Nazi aggression. Nearly 60,000 people will benefit from the aid money." - May 29th 2013, Spiegel online international

"Germany announced last week that it had secured approximately $250 million from the German government to be paid to Holocaust survivors who were children at the time of the war. Beginning on January 1, one-time lump-sum payments of €2,500, or about $3,280, will be paid to the approximately 75,000 remaining Holocaust survivors all over the world in reparations for the psychological pain and suffering that they suffered as children as victims of the Holocaust." By Maya Shwayder, Jerusalem Post, 09/06/2014

From 1948 onwards Israel has steadily expanded its influence and territory in its new homeland, with aid and help from various sources around the world; they have transformed the country into a wealthy nation and a major military presence in the region.

"Palestine belongs to the Arabs in the same sense that England belongs to the English or France to the French. It is wrong and inhuman to impose the Jews on the Arabs... Surely it would be a crime against humanity to reduce the proud Arabs so that Palestine can be restored to the Jews partly or wholly as their national home" — Mahatma Gandhi

"People who call themselves supporters of Israel are actually supporters of its moral degeneration and ultimate destruction." — Noam Chomsky

"If every single Jew born anywhere in the world has the right to become an Israeli citizen, then all the Palestinians who were chucked out of Palestine by the Zionist Government should have the same right, very simple." — Tariq Ali

"When modern political Zionism emerged around the turn of the twentieth century, most Orthodox Jews opposed it." - David Novak

In Simon Schama's book *"Two Rothschild's and the Land of Israel"*, Schama speculates that the Rothschild's, through various commercial enterprises, own approximately 80% of the land within Israel.[19] The British/Rothschild/Zionist outpost known as Israel is essentially another commercial and military base for the empire and the House of Rothschild, the richest and most powerful banking consortium on the planet. It spreads its tentacles throughout the world avoiding criticism by controlling media outlets and shielding itself behind Jewish Holocaust victim status. Zionism is just another tool being used to bring about world unity, a global socialist society under the complete control of the hidden hand, the international banking consortium, the House of Rothschild. Israel today has become the 11th most powerful military force on the planet and one of four countries holding nuclear weapons not recognised by the NPT (Nuclear Non-proliferation Treaty). They maintain a policy of ambiguity, although their nuclear weapons program was exposed back in 1986 by Mordechai Vanunu, an Israeli nuclear technician, who ended up in prison for what they considered as treason.

Worlds Most Powerful Militaries

Country	Rank	Active Personnel	Tanks	Aircraft	Nuclear Warheads	Aircraft Carriers	Submarines	Budget
United States	1	1,430,000	8,325	13,683	7,506	10	72	612,500,000,000
Russia	2	766,000	15,000	3,082	8,484	1	63	76,600,000,000
China	3	2,285,000	9,150	2,788	250	1	69	126,000,000,000
India	4	1,325,000	3,569	1,785	80-100	2	17	46,000,000,000
UK	5	205,330	407	908	225	1	11	53,600,000,000
France	6	228,656	423	1,203	300	1	10	43,000,000,000
Germany	7	183,000	408	710	0	0	4	45,000,000,000
Turkey	8	410,500	3,657	989	0	0	14	18,185,000,000
South Korea	9	640,000	2,346	1,393	0	0	14	33,700,000,000
Japan	10	247,746	767	1,595	0	1	16	49,100,000,000
Israel	11	176,500	3,870	680	80-200	0	14	15,000,000,000

Source : Global Firepower, The centre for arms control and non-proliferation. http://armscontrolcenter.org/ 2014

Due to the nature and purpose of Zionist Israel, there will never be peace in the Middle East; the whole idea is to create division, allowing British/Rothschild multinational enterprises to expand, swallowing up competitors. The psychopathic nature of the beast has no concern for human welfare. The treatment of the Palestinians has become a benchmark for any other group or nation willing to resist or oppose the conglomerates objectives. Since its creation, Israel has been involved in numerous wars, two Palestinian intifadas, and a perpetual stream of conflicts with its Arab neighbours over territory and boarder disputes.

The United States political system has become awash with Zionist and pro Zionist supporters, a politician in the US will find it extremely difficult to advance in their career unless they express pro-Israeli/pro Zionist sentiments. Prior to the creation of Israel, the British would use their own agents to influence American policy, now the batten has been passed to the Zionists. The United States foreign policy has supported the Zionist position in the Middle East since its conception, and will continue to do so. The extent to which this influence has penetrated American politics was exposed during a speech given to the US congress by Israeli PM Benjamin Netanyahu, on March 3rd 2015. During his 40:30 address he was interrupted 39 times by rapturous applause, 23 of which were standing ovations. This level of appreciation is unusual, I suspect even the president wouldn't get this kind of attention, but most politicians don't like to bite the hand that feeds them.

House of Rothschild

Mayer Amschel Rothschild	Amschel Mayer Rothschild Frankfurt	Solomon Mayer Rothschild Vienna	Nathan Mayer Rothschild London	Carl Mayer Rothschild Naples	James Mayer Rothschild Paris

The Rothschild family/dynasty came to dominate European banking during the late 18th and 19th century. By the middle of the 1800's they had become the richest family in the world. It all began in 1743, when Amshal Moses Bauer opened a money changing house in the Jewish ghettos of Frankfurt. He had eight children, the fourth being Mayer Amschel Bauer, who inherited the business in 1755 after the premature death of his father from smallpox. To promote his money lending business Amschel hung a red shield from the front of his premises. His customers and the local community referred to his business as the "**Red Shield Firm**". Eventually Mayer Amschel Bauer change the family name over to Mayer Amschel Rothschild (Red shield). He soon discovered that lending money to royalty and governments was far more lucrative than lending to the general public, plus he had the added security of the loans being secured against future taxation. Mayer had 10 children, 5 of which were boys. When they were old enough he sent them out to create private banks in five of the most prominent European countries, with the intention of dominating the worlds banking system.

Working together as a network of Rothschild banks, they would finance both sides of European political and physical conflicts, collecting vast profits from all the chaos which they helped to support. Nathan in London took advantage of Napoleon's defeat at Waterloo by taking control of England's stock and bond markets. It is also suspected that this is when he secured control over the Bank of England. He managed to get the news of the outcome of the battle ahead of everyone else, using his own private couriers and carrier pigeons. With this knowledge, he began slowly selling stocks and bonds, which set off a panic in most of the markets, investors who watched his actions assumed England had lost the war. Once the prices bottomed out, Nathan instructed his agents to begin buying everything up at giveaway prices. By the time the official news of Wellington's victory arrived in London, prices went through the roof. Nathan was now laughing, most of the important aspects of England's commercial and financial infrastructure now belonged to the Rothschilds.

By the middle of the 19th century they had become the wealthiest family on the planet. In 1850 James Rothschild in France was said to be worth 600 million francs, 150 million more than all the other French banks combined. With this wealth came power, and with most of Europe's monarchs and governments in debt to this family of bankers, they now had the power to influence policy. The lender is always master over the borrower.

Masters at organisation and control, the family now had the opportunity to direct the future course of human history. Combining power with established European royalty and aristocracy, they united to help propel the British/Rothschild Empires to the next phase of global imperialistic domination. They worked together to undermine the American Republic, the German Republic, Russia under the Tsar, China, Africa and anywhere else which had ambitions of independence, the goal was globalisation under their control.

They financed the Rockefellers, the Coon-Logans, the Harrimans, the Vanderbilts, the Carnegies, the Morgans and Cecil Rhodes, all acting under the direction of the lender, the House of Rothschild. By controlling a country's private central bank and owning the majority of stocks in the country's industrial and commercial infrastructure, they would steer the nation in any direction they desired. Occasionally they would come up against a rogue leader, who wanted freedom, liberty and sovereignty. They were soon dealt with and brought back under control. During the First World War JP Morgan was assumed to be the richest man in America, but after his death it was discovered that he was just another agent for the House of Rothschild. Governments, monarchs and business over many parts of the world gradually succumbed to the parasitic influence of Rothschild finance, failing in their duty to shield their subjects from the ravages of debt slavery, instead turning on their people to service the interest on huge loans through various methods of unfair taxation. Much was written about the Rothschilds during the 19th century, but once they took control of the media and its outlets, they could sensor what was being said about them, essentially going underground.

"The few who understand the system, will either be so interested from its profits or so dependent on its favours, that there will be no opposition from that class." "Let me issue and control a nation's money and I care not who writes the laws." – Mayer Amschel Bauer Rothschild, 1744-1812

"History records that the money changers have used every form of abuse, intrigue, deceit, and violent means possible to maintain their control over governments by controlling money and its issuance." – James Madison, 1751-1836

"A power has risen up in the government greater than the people themselves, consisting of many and various powerful interests, combined in one mass, and held together by the cohesive power of the vast surplus in banks." – John C. Calhoun, Vice President (1825-1832) and U.S. Senator, from a speech given on May 27, 1836

"The Government should create, issue, and circulate all the currency and credits needed to satisfy the spending power of the Government and the buying power of consumers. By the adoption of these principles, the taxpayers will be saved immense sums of interest. Money will cease to be master and become the servant of humanity. "- Abraham Lincoln, 1809-1865

"These international bankers and Rockefeller-Standard Oil interests control the majority of the newspapers and the columns in those papers to club into submission or drive out of office officials who refuse to do the bidding of the powerful corrupt cliques which compose the invisible government." – Theodore Roosevelt as reported in the New York Times, March 27th, 1922

"By remaining behind the scenes, they (the Rothschild's) were able to avoid the brunt of public anger which was directed, instead, at the political figures which they largely controlled. This is a technique which has been practiced by financial manipulators ever since, and it is fully utilized by those who operate the Federal Reserve System today." – G. Edward Griffin, (born November 1931), American political commentator, writer and documentary filmmaker.

"The Rothschild's belong to no one nationality, they are cosmopolitan . . . they belonged to no party, they were ready to grow rich at the expense of friend and foe alike." - John Reeves's book The Rothschild's: The Financial Rulers of Nations (1887)

The Rothschilds were not initially in favour of Zionism, but once interwoven with the British Empire and the British elitist establishment, they began to warm towards the concept, helping to promote and finance the project. Queen Victoria was not heavily involved with the Rothschilds but her Son the Prince of Whales (later King Edward VI), a Freemason, became a close friend of Nathaniel Rothschild, from their early days as students at Trinity College Cambridge, till his death in 1910.

In 1878 the Prince was guest at Lord Rosebery's wedding to Hannah Rothschild, a wedding in which Disraeli gave away the bride. Edward would often invite Rothschilds to Sandringham for social gathering and vice-versa. Queen Victoria no doubt under pressure from Edward allowed Nathaniel to become a Baron in 1885, and when Edward became King he promoted Baron Nathaniel Rothschild to the Privy Council the following year. This close relationship cemented the foundations for the new British/Rothschild/Zionist Empire which was to be the foundations of 20th century globalisation, working together to take control of the world's resources and monopolising their positions in global commerce and industry, using their multinational corporations and banks to control and enslave humanity while they decide the direction of the new global political system.

There has always been a close relationship between Jews and Freemasonry, both working together to oppose the old Roman Catholic Empire. Some Masonic Lodges are exclusively Jewish but since the creation of Zionism, I suspect Zionist Jews have replaced the traditional Saturn worshipers. There has been 51 Jewish Grand Masters in the US, and Israel is the host to 60 Masonic Lodges. Together both Zionism and Freemasonry work as an intellectual army influencing geopolitics and the globalisation project.

The ISIS connection

The elite have always had access to the occult, ancient esoteric wisdom and knowledge; they use it to keep themselves at the top and in control of the rest of us. They display this knowledge in their symbols, ceremonies and actions, if you know what to look for you can see it all around. The Isis cult is a major part of this tradition, as we move into the Age of Aquarius the elite are controlling the game, they want to be the creators of the new Gen(ISIS), the Sun setting on the old Age and the birth of the new. Isis is the feminine deity of the ancient world, signifying the spiritual realm and a virgin birth; it is also associated with the colour red which is synonymous with the Sun setting.

The British/Rothschild/Zionist (BROZI) Empire is setting up a socialist globalist world government run by unelected bureaucrats, an old Soviet style socialist dictatorship. Red is used to represent many forms of socialism. The red shield which hung from the original Frankfurt House of Rothschild is an esoteric expression of this symbolism. Most Rothschild financed socialist revolutions, including Marxism, Bolshevism and Maoism, have all used red to reflect their political persuasion and possible Rothschild/Isis influence. However, it is all command and control dictatorships and the centralisation of power.

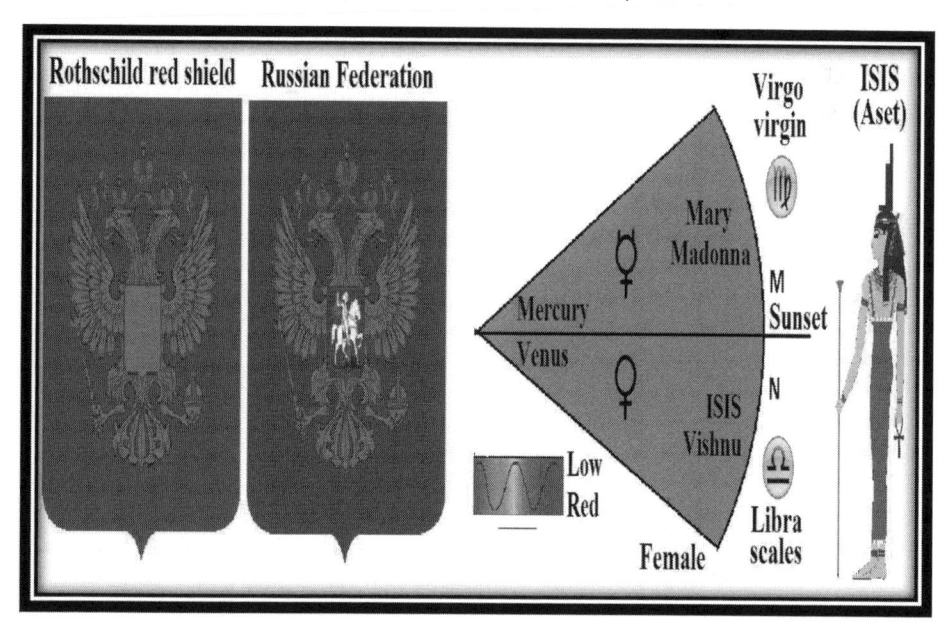

Symbols Of Socialism

Is it the case, that ISIS the Islamic State is a mercenary army financed by BROZI interests to destabilise the Middle East and overthrow various countries which seek strong independence, countries who are not playing ball with the globalisation project? Portrayed in the western media as enemies of democracy and western interests, Isis finds it easy to get hold of all the latest weaponry needed for their campaign of terror, weapons manufactured in the US. Coincidently Israel (ISIS-RA-El) appears to be one of a small group of countries immune to Isis aggression.

"**Logistical support and the secret supply of "arms on a massive scale". Reports were cited that MI6 had cooperated with the CIA on a "rat line" of arms transfers from Libyan stockpiles to the Syrian rebels in 2012 after the fall of the Gaddafi regime.**"The Guardian[20]

The resulting refugee crisis is a designed spinoff of the whole Middle East project, millions of economic migrants posing as Syrian refugees have flooded onto the streets of Europe. This has the added bonus for the globalists in disuniting each sovereign nation, frustrating unity within all communities, undermining cohesion and preventing them from rising up against the projects latest objectives. The last thing the globalists want are strong independent unified nations, working together against them. The Muslim refugees were recently accused of going on a raping rampage through the streets of Cologne Germany. This is a clear case of Lust being played out as a vice associated with worshiping the planet Venus. Without adequate guidance and discipline all the negative aspects of Venus will manifest around its followers.

Virtues And Vices

	Saturn	Jupiter	Mars	Sun	Venus	Mercury	Moon
Saturn	PRUDENCE	SOBRIETY	PERSEVERANCE	FIDELITY	FIDELITY	CONTRITION	OBEDIENCE
Saturn	avarice	obstinacy	presumption	incorrigibility	seduction	insensitivity	stupidity
Jupiter	CLEMENCY	TEMPERANCE	VALOR	TRUTHFULNESS	MODESTY	MAGNANIMITY	ABSTINENCE
Jupiter	despair	gluttony	murder,curse	irreverence	insolence	sadness	roistering
Mars	DILIGENCE	FRUGALITY	FORTITUDE	PIETY	FEAR	CONTRITION	COURAGE
Mars	cruelty	sensuality	anger	rage,injury	fornication	heresy	diffamation
Sun	GRANDEUR	LIBERALITY	GENEROSITY	FAITH	HONESTY	MAGNANIMITY	HOLINESS
Sun	greed	impudence	temerity	conceit	sacrilege	idolatry	haughtiness
Venus	DISCRETION	CHASTITY	CONSTANCY	PIETY	JUSTICE	CONSCIENCE	VIRGINITY
Venus	selfishness	dissolution	arrogance	vanity	lust	curiosity	concupiscence
Mercury	DIPLOMACY	AFFABILITY	DARING	TRUTHFULNESS	POLITENESS	HOPE	HUMILITY
Mercury	larceny	impotence	betrayal	falseness	adultery	envy	lying
Moon	TENDERNESS	FRIENDSHIP	PATIENCE	FIDELITY	CANDIDNESS	CONSCIENCE	CHARITY
Moon	infidelity	inconstancy	impatience	disobedience	weakness	mass frenzy	sloth

This table is based on Fr. Jean d'Aubry's keywords for the virtues and vices associated with the 7 planets.

The London Olympics of 2012 was a blatant expression of a British/Zionist alliance. The official logo designed by Wolff Olins, cost a staggering £500,000. When the individual pieces are rearranged from their 2012 depiction, the word Zion appears. In the Unspoken Bible the original meaning of the word Zion defines the stars of the zodiac.[21]

Logo for London olympics spells ZION

The Zionist IDF (Israeli Defence Force), a military outfit, has been conducting training exercises with American and British police, teaching them army tactics and strategies. The procedures in place in Israel, dealing with terrorism and the Palestinian threat, are being shared with what are supposed to be American and British public servants.[22] One can only speculate as to why this new kind of training is necessary, maybe Gaza and Palestine are examples of what we are to expect in other parts of the world if the globalisation project is resisted.

Notes for chapter 10

(1) Dov Noy, Dan Ben-Amos, Ellen Franke, Folktales of the Jews, Volume 1: Tales from the Sephardic Dispersion, Page 38, The Jewish publication society, Philadelphia. https://books.google.co.th/books?id=vW-9E_fFSOUC&pg=PA39&dq=%22the+hurvah+synagogue%22&lr=&cd=10&redir_esc=y#v=onepage&q=%22the%20hurvah%20synagogue%22&f=false

(2) Gerhard Falk, The Restoration of Israel: Christian Zionism in Religion, Literature and politics. Page 17, http://www.amazon.com/The-Restoration-Israel-Literature-University/dp/0820488623

(3) Napoleon Bonaparte, Letter to the Jewish Nation from the French Commander-in-Chief Buonaparte, (translated from the Original, 1799). http://www.napoleon-series.org/ins/weider/c_jews.html#Appendix 2

(4) Benjamin Disraeli, John Alexander Wilson Gun, Benjamin Disraeli Letters: 1848-1851, volume 5, page 404, University of Toronto press incorporated, 1993. http://www.jstor.org/stable/10.3138/9781442671287

(5) Mark Burdman, How Britain's Biggest Racists Created Zionism, The Campaigner Unbound, http://www.campaigner-unbound.0catch.com/how_britains_biggest_racists_created_zionism.htm

(6) History of the Thule society, http://www.bibliotecapleyades.net/sociopolitica/sociopol_thule05.htm

(7) Pittsburgh Conference in 1885, Reform Judaism. https://www.jewishvirtuallibrary.org/jsource/Judaism/pittsburgh_program.html

(8) Haavara Agreement, Wikipedia, https://en.wikipedia.org/wiki/Haavara_Agreement

(9) Eustace Mullins, THE NAZI ZIONIST PARTY AND THE HOLOCAUST, Speech, Salmon Arm BC, Canada, August 2000. https://www.youtube.com/watch?v=LO5sbwGCR7A

(10) Nuremberg document PS-2171, Annex 2. NC&A "red series," Vol. 4, pp. 833-834. http://www.loc.gov/rr/frd/Military_Law/pdf/NT_Nazi_Vol-IV.pdf

(11) Strategic Bombing during WW2, Wikipedia, https://en.wikipedia.org/wiki/Strategic_bombing_during_World_War_II#cite_note-140

WW2 bombing, Justice for Germans, http://justice4germans.com/wwii-bombing/

(12) Sidney Bernstein, Chief of the film section at the suprime headquarters allied expedition force (SHAEF). http://www.theguardian.com/film/2015/jan/09/holocaust-film-too-shocking-to-show-night-will-fall-alfred-hitchcock

(13) James Bacque, Other losses, (1989), Stoddart publishers, http://www.amazon.com/Other-Losses-Investigation-Prisoners-Americans/dp/0889226652

(14) German prisoners of war in the soviet union, Wikipedia, https://en.wikipedia.org/wiki/German_prisoners_of_war_in_the_Soviet_Union#cite_note-16

(15) President Ahmadinejad Meets Neturei Karta Rabbis - 9/24/2007, Youtube, https://www.youtube.com/watch?v=R-r04SQ97_Q

(16) Auschwitz-Birkenau Memorial and Museum, http://auschwitz.org/en/

(17) Nicholas Kollerstorm, Breaking the spell, 2014, Castle Hill Publishers, http://www.amazon.com/Breaking-Spell-Holocaust-Reality-Handbooks/dp/159148071X

(18) Reparations Agreement between Israel and the Federal Republic of Germany, Wikipedia, https://en.wikipedia.org/wiki/Reparations_Agreement_between_Israel_and_West_Germany

(19) Simon Schama, Two Rothschild's and the Land of Israel (Collins, London, 1978), http://www.abebooks.co.uk/Two-Rothschilds-Land-Israel-Schama-Simon/14948680363/bd

(20) Seumas Milne, Now the truth emerges: how the US fuelled the rise of Isis in Syria and Iraq, 3rd June 2015, http://www.theguardian.com/commentisfree/2015/jun/03/us-isis-syria-iraq

(21) Israel's Zion, The unspoken bible, http://www.usbible.com/Astrology/Israels_zion.htm

(22) Global Research, December 07, 2014, Why are London's Police Travelling to Israel? American and British Police Trained in Israel, http://www.globalresearch.ca/why-are-londons-police-travelling-to-israel-american-and-british-police-trained-in-israel/5418432

Chapter 11. Controlling information

Before the ancient Chinese invented paper, during the Han Dynasty (206 BC - 220 AD), clay tablets were used to record the language of the day, a laborious task which allowed records to withstand the harsh tests of time. When paper was invented as a new medium, at the start of the Piscean Age (I believe), the rulers of the day realised how important it was to control what was being written. Few people could read, and those that could regarded the written word as gospel, the Age of belief was born. Until 1455 when Gutenberg invented the printing press, only selected individuals were chosen to produce or reproduce hand written books, usually within religious circles, keeping important information and knowledge away from the common man. After the invention of the press, there was an explosion in literacy which propelled Europe through the Renaissance, a period of enlightenment between the 14th and 17th century; a change moving civilisation out of the Middle Ages towards the start of the Industrial Revolution. We are now entering the Age of Aquarius (I know), ruled by Uranus, which brings forth new technology in an energetic frequency which has contributed to the creation of the internet and the Information Age, an Age of knowledge and knowing.

"Whoever controls the media controls the mind" Jim Morrison (The Doors)

For centuries, the influential elite have understood the power of controlling the flow of information, what the average person gets to see and hear. Throughout the years, the control system has steered the main stream media in a particular direction, influencing most of the information which passes through our lives. Using multinational corporations, they have managed to swallow up competition and independent outlets. During the early 1980's, the main stream news media in the United States was controlled by approximately 50 large corporations. Today just 6 mega corporations own and control 90% of all we watch, hear, read and think.[1] Corporations like:

NBC Universal, CBS Corporation, News Corporation, Viacom, Walt Disney, Time Warner.

These corporations decide the variety and scope of what enters the mind through the 5 senses, essentially programming the belief systems required to perpetuate and expand their control.

"The conscious and intelligent manipulation of the organized habits and opinions of the masses is an important element in democratic society. Those who manipulate this unseen mechanism of society constitute an invisible government which is the true ruling power of our country. ...We are governed, our minds are moulded, our tastes formed, our ideas suggested, largely by men we have never heard of. This is a logical result of the way in which our democratic society is organized. Vast numbers of human beings must cooperate in this manner if they are to live together as a smoothly functioning society. ...In almost every act of our daily lives, whether in the sphere of politics or business, in our social conduct or our ethical thinking, we are dominated by the relatively small number of persons...who understand the mental processes and social patterns of the masses. It is they who pull the wires which control the public mind." -Edward L Bernays

"Our minds have been poisoned and our accepted beliefs are unnatural and artificial."
— Bryant McGill

"The smart way to keep people passive and obedient is to strictly limit the spectrum of acceptable opinion, but allow very lively debate within that spectrum...."
― Noam Chomsky

"The major media-particularly, the elite media that set the agenda that others generally follow-are corporations "selling" privileged audiences to other businesses. It would hardly come as a surprise if the picture of the world they present were to reflect the perspectives and interests of the sellers, the buyers, and the product. Concentration of ownership of the media is high and increasing. Furthermore, those who occupy managerial positions in the media, or gain status within them as commentators, belong to the same privileged elites, and might be expected to share the perceptions, aspirations, and attitudes of their associates, reflecting their own class interests as well. Journalists entering the system are unlikely to make their way unless they conform to these ideological pressures, generally by internalizing the values; it is not easy to say one thing and believe another, and those who fail to conform will tend to be weeded out by familiar mechanisms." -Noam Chomsky, Necessary Illusions: Thought Control in Democratic Societies

"**Official truths are powerful illusions**" -John Pilger

"**The man who never looks into a newspaper is better informed than he who reads them, inasmuch as he who knows nothing is nearer to truth than he whose mind is filled with falsehoods and errors. He who reads nothing will still learn the great facts, and the details are all false.**" -Thomas Jefferson (3rd US President)

Fortunately, we now have the internet, still open and available for the majority to use. The internet has enabled alternative views to be aired in the public domain. The manipulation of information has become the new front line in a war to control the collective consciousness of humanity. Alternative media with its limited funding, grows daily at the expense of the mainstream, a new generation of inquisitive and disillusioned citizens, sick of being lied to, have set out to uncover the truth on a variety of topics. Awash with information the internet has become a battle ground in a new information war, a battle for minds. Though the curtain is slowly lifting on the wizard and his trickery, the control system is steadfast, it will continue on the course it has set for humanity, using every trick in the book, it will try to pollute the pond of truth by misleading the inquisitive with lies and falsehoods, aided by the best technology available, they conceal their deceit behind new lies.

Mainstream media

Media mind control has developed into a precise science. To every 1 positive news report, there are 17 negative ones. This is no accident. With the consolidation of media power into fewer hands, it has never been easier for the global corporations to influence the output of content, shaping the social norms required for their globalisation project. Working together this network of mega corporations guide human perception down the road of compliance, servitude and guided opinions. Without the consent or approval of the focal mind, the subconscious absorbs everything witnessed by the 5 senses, storing it indefinitely like a powerful computer. With this in mind, we act as we do because of our habitual subconscious beliefs. It is therefore important to take control of what you allow into your brain. Your focal consciousness and will power need to take the reins and steer the subconscious away from negativity and corporate mind manipulation. The mainstream media is the propaganda arm of governments and corporations, setting out to disrupt the human collective's connection to higher mind universal Logos consciousness with propaganda stimulating manufactured consent.

We are bombarded with negative energy, telling us we live in a dark, dangerous, sinister world, where wars are necessary for peace and surveillance is necessary for safety. Telling us the only way to feel good about ourselves and escape our hazardous and frightening existence is to work hard and consume more corporate products. It informs us that the world outside has gone terribly wrong, telling us we need to look outside ourselves, toward the controlling powers for answers to problems which they have helped to create. The individual's exposure to this negative view of the world contributes and upholds the negative and divisive beliefs already established during childhood, and with each negative report they water the seeds of fear and disempowerment. With this perverted mind-set the body transmits manipulated energy back into the collective, reinforcing subordination and hopelessness, falling straight back into the hands of the control system.

Even though the alternative media try to uncover the truth, the shear fact that it is dealing with lies, deceit and propaganda, sets in motion more negativity. For our reality to be positive, happy and peaceful, the mind must focus on those things, shielding the subconscious from the negativity offered to us. Whatever we focus on breathes life into that frequency, which we energise and put back into the collective. To reprogram the subconscious, one must turn away from the manipulation of corporate media, turn instead to the natural rhythms and cycles of life, the wonders which surround us, even simple things have beauty.

TV

Tell lie vision is the greatest mass mind controlling device of the 20th century. This innocent looking device which sits quietly in the corner of most living-rooms has become the resident hypnotist for generations of naive onlookers. It places the viewer into a trance like state allowing the free flow of information and suggestions to enter the subconscious unchallenged and unedited.

"Watching television is like taking black spray paint to your third eye." — Bill Hicks

"I find television very educating. Every time somebody turns on the set, I go into the other room and read a book." — Groucho Marx

"If everyone demanded peace instead of another TV set, then there'd be peace." - John Lennon

"The main purpose of TV, to make you believe in everything you see around you, is real. And then, direct you, by using your own power against you, to make you go to where they want you to go." — VicDo

"Television is simply automated day-dreaming." - Lee Lovinger

In 2013 the average viewer in the United Kingdom watched 4 hours of television a day.[2] If the average life expectancy is 70 years, that equates to 11.6 years watching television. It is no coincidence that the TV stations produce what they call "programmes", that is exactly what they are designed to do, programme subconscious beliefs. It is also no coincidence within the English language that the term "broadcast" is used, as the control system broadly cast their magician like wizardry throughout the whole community. For most television viewers, their sense of world reality is shaped by what is reported on the TV news. From the early days of their childhood they have come to believe that only truth comes from figures of authority, and to most unconscious onlookers, the mainstream media has become that authority. They watch and believe unquestioningly everything the evening news tells them. From their trance like perspective, if it doesn't appear on the evening news it is not something they need to be concerned about. Likewise, if it does appear on the evening news it must be important and true. The tell-lie-vision has come on a long way from the early days of the 1950's. The digital version is far more powerful, almost instantly placing the viewer into an alpha state dissociative trance. A picture paints a thousand words. Using flashing lights, spinning circles, symbolism and the latest in surround sound, the magician locks the focal conscious mind onto the screen, opening up the subconscious to multi layered subliminal suggestions designed to influence and reprogram a desired belief system into the masses. Notice how the evening news, along with spinning circles and flashing lights, opens up with a countdown sequence like the hypnotist who counts down with a calm authoritarian voice. The human eye is naturally drawn to the circle over other shapes, hence why we look into the eyes of people when we meet, we look at their round faces, at their round breasts and buttocks, all round, comfortable and soft in comparison to many other unnatural shapes.

The Great British soap opera has become a major part of many people's lives, hours sat in front of the goggle box, mesmerised by low grade dramas, pointless plots and wailing women. Soap is generally used to wash things; in this case it's the brain. According to a recent survey 34 million Brits average 143 minutes per week watching soaps, that equates to 1 whole year over an average lifetime.[3]

The majority of people have an underlining assumption that the main stream media, especially its news broadcasts and documentaries are under some form of legal obligation to present the truth. In the US, there is no law against the media distorting or falsifying its reports or content. This was exposed in a Florida court case back in 2003, the case of Jane Akre and Steve Wilson; a husband and wife team of reporters hired by FOX to investigate on behalf of WTVT in Tampa Bay, Florida. The couple began work on a four-part series about bovine growth hormone (BGH), and the dangers associated with drinking the milk produced by cows treated with it. The documentary reported how supermarkets continued to assure the public about the safety of the milk even though they were aware of certain adverse effects from the BGH product. Lawyers working for the company who produced the product put pressure on FOX to change the documentary before broadcasting, washing over the dangers in order to maintain their impressive sales of BGH. The two reporters were told to alter the documentary, effectively removing the evidence and associated dangers; they refused to lie and were fired. The reporters sued FOX in 2000 for wrongful dismissal using protection under whistle blower law. They won their initial case and were awarded $425,000 compensation. Fox appealed and in 2003 the Florida Second District Court of appeals unanimously overruled the initial settlement, the two reporters lost their case.

"In a stunningly narrow interpretation of FCC rules, the Florida Appeals court claimed that the FCC policy against falsification of the news does not raise to the level of a "law, rule, or regulation," it was simply a "policy." Therefore, it is up to the station whether or not it wants to report honestly." - Court Ruled That Media Can Legally Lie[4]

News papers

There are four large news agencies, producing and collecting over 90% of foreign news for the world's newspapers, United Press International, Associated Press, Reuters and Agence France Presse. These big media corporations have a common agenda, based in the west, they have a bias towards western ideology and the aspirations of their owners. The third world which represents over 2/3rds of the global population account for only 25% of news reports managed by these four corporations. Interwoven within the control grid of government agencies and larger corporations, the power and influence which these four news agencies have over the way the world sees itself is enormous.

"Regiment the public mind every bit as much as an army regiments their bodies."-Edward Bernays, Propaganda 1928

The evolution of this media monopoly goes back to the 19th century, in 1816 Paul Julius Reuter was born to Jewish parents in the town of Kassel Germany and from his humble beginnings he created the Reuters News Agency. Moving to England in 1845, he used telegraph technology to establish one of the world's first news agencies. In 1847, he returned to Germany to set up a publishing company, Reuters & Stargardt. The following year, after upsetting the German authorities with a publication he moved to Paris, where he translated newspapers and business articles into German. In 1851, he came back to London with his family and became a naturalized British citizen. By 1858 he managed to convince the London Times and several other English papers to subscribe to his news service, soon his news service became indispensable to the British press. His new success and powerful role in media brought him to the attention of the elite and the highest levels of government. His agency in 1865, was the first to bring the news of President Lincoln's assassination, later that year he opened an office in Egypt, laid his own cables across the North Sea, connecting England with France and Germany, Reuters served as news agents for the US, the Far East and even South America. At this time, the company had two main competitors, the Havas Agency in France and the Wolff Agency in Germany, both run by fellow Jews. After a meeting, they agreed to share the monopoly on news. Havas was to have South America while the three shared Europe, leaving the rest of the world to Reuters. This joint cartel lasted for approximately 50 years, until the end of WW1. With his connections in high places Paul Julius Reuter became **Baron Julius de Reuter** by the Duke of Saxe-Coburg-Gotha in 1871. He remained managing director until his retirement in 1878, by this time the company had become a major joint stock company.

Propaganda and WW1

On 8th August 1914, four days after Britain had declared war on Germany, the British government passed the Defence of the Realm Act, which ushered in a variety of social controls and censorship mechanisms.

"**No person shall by word of mouth or in writing spread reports likely to cause disaffection or alarm among any of His Majesty's forces or among the civilian population**" Defence of The Realm Act 1914 (censorship)

Britain had no propaganda agencies at the outset of the war, but soon established one at Wellington House, under a man called Charles Masterman. By 1918 this agency became more organised, joining up with other similar government agencies to create the Ministry of Information. At the start of the conflict the British cut all undersea communication cables to Germany, ensuring it had the monopoly on the transmission of news from Europe to all the press agencies who were feeding the news around the world. With the help of Reuters and the other news agencies, using censorship, propaganda and spin, the British managed to generate support and sympathy across its Empire and the world. Wellington House called on journalists and newspaper editors to write and disseminate articles sympathising with the British while countering statements made by the Central Powers. Even with this backdrop by 1916 Germany had nearly won the war. Britain and France were bogged down in a bitter, stagnant struggle, holding ground but making few gains while they patiently waited for help from the United States.

Woodrow Wilson elected on his promise to keep the United States out of the war was about to show his allegiance and his true colours. His job now was to turn public opinion against Germany using all forms of propaganda available, utilising news agencies and media outlets. At that time, a large portion of the American population were of German descent, they wanted no part in the war, especially against Germany. Wilson had to call in professionals, with an executive order, On April 13th 1917 the **Committee On Public Information** was set up, also known as the Creel Committee[5]. An independent organisation specifically designed to influence American public opinion, through a prolonged propaganda campaign, toward supporting US participation in WW1. With Edward Berneys on board, the father and guru of modern propaganda and advertising methods, the committee recruited 75,000 volunteers, called (Four Minute Men), who would go up and down the country giving four-minute pro war speeches at social groups and gatherings, using every form of media available from newspapers to radio and movies. It was estimated, by the end of the war that the Four Minute Men had made 7.5 million speeches to 314 million people in 5,200 communities. After the ceasefire and armistice, with the final defeat of Germany, the participants who fought for the Central Powers reflected on the war and tried to understand how they went from nearly winning in 1916, to a humiliating defeat.

"It was during the War, however, that we had the best chance of estimating the tremendous results which could be obtained by a propagandist system properly carried out. Here again, unfortunately, everything was left to the other side, the work done on our side being worse than insignificant. It was the total failure of the whole German system of information – a failure which was perfectly obvious to every soldier – that urged me to consider the problem of propaganda in a comprehensive way." - Adolf Hitler Mein Kampf (War Propaganda in WW1, Chapter VI)

In 1951 Sir Rodrick Jones published a book titled "*A life in Reuters*", in the book he talks about the time he was chosen to be the new managing director, shortly after the death of Baron Herbert de Reuter in 1915, the Baron had shot himself due to the crash of the Reuters Bank. After being chosen to be the new head of Reuters, Sir Rodrick Jones was invited to dine with the then head of the House of Rothschild.

"**Shortly after I succeeded Baron Herbert de Reuter in 1915, it so happened that I received an invitation from Mr. Alfred Rothschild, then the head of the British House of Rothschild, to lunch with him in his historic New Court, in the City.**" Sir Rodrick Jones (*A life in Reuters*)[6]

Books

"**No matter how busy you may think you are, you must find time for reading, or surrender yourself to self-chosen ignorance**". - Confucius

"**Whenever you read a good book, somewhere in the world a door opens to allow in more light**" Vera Nazarian

"**If you only read the books that everyone else is reading, you can only think what everyone else is thinking**" Haruki Murakami

"**There are worse crimes than burning books. One of them is not reading them.**" Joseph Brodsky

Books are far more important than most people give credit for. The ability to read has a significant relationship on one's life chances. Reading during childhood has a positive influence on cognitive development. In 2014, 46% of young adults in the UK between the ages of 16-24 do not read for pleasure, it is also the case with 35% of all UK adults. We also find that 60% of the prison population have difficulty with basic literacy skills.[7]

Books have an advantage over other forms of media because they slow down the absorption process, allowing the reader to internalise what they are focusing on. Generally, the writer has taken the time to establish the truth and facts to his best ability. The reader considers each idea, accepting it or coming up with an alternative, based on good reasoning. Books are permanent, they out live the writer by many decades, keeping the ideas alive from one generation to the next, a form of stability within the flux of social change and evolving norms. Any system of control will find it necessary to monitor all books circulating within its boundaries, keeping a tight grip on information that may undermine their legitimacy or question their many motives and objectives, with the power to suppress the circulation of material which could threaten their overall aspirations for the future.

Tyrannical governments over the centuries have resorted to book burning, censorship or seizure of unwanted literature. Throughout history there are many documented cases of book burning. In the 3rd century BC, in ancient China, under the Qin Dynasty, the Emperor ordered the burning of texts and 460 Confucian scholars alive. The Library of Alexandria, one of the largest and most significant libraries of the ancient world, was attacked and burnt on four known separate occasions, from the Romans in 48BC, under Julius Caesar, to a decree from Pope Theophilus in 391AD. In each case they tried and succeeded in destroying valuable information, ancient writings possibly running contrary to their latest beliefs.

Most people are aware of public book burning events which took place in the 1930's, during the rise to power of the German National Socialist Party. Few are aware of a book and literature burning program which took place in Japan after the occupation in 1945-6. Where the United States with GHQ (Government Headquarters) instructed the occupying army to search and confiscate any book or publication which favoured the Japanese over the new occupying forces, also any writings which painted the United States in a bad light. Of course, GHQ called it "confiscation of propaganda material". The occupation forces confiscated what they could get their hands on, over 7,700 different books, articles and pamphlets from all over Japan, literature from book stores, second-hand book sellers, government offices, warehouses, and distribution centres. Some of these books were previously classified as Japanese history. The idea was to take full control of the population's new belief system, to have full mastery over reprogramming their minds. Most of this material was taken away and burnt, never to be seen again.[8] They say the victors write the history books, they don't mention burning other versions of history.

Book Burning

Today the mainstream media has evolved into a well-oiled machine, it is designed to manufacture consent, regiment the minds of social classes, change tastes and attitudes, while ultimately limiting our perception of reality. Different strains of the media target different intellectual levels within society and social hierarchy. Setting the agenda and standards to follow for the intellectual and managerial classes, while filling the rest of the media with distractions designed to keep the wilfully ignorant masses focused on unimportant diatribe, such as scandals, sex, personalities, sporting events, music and fashion. Paying presstitutes to keep the vast majority occupied with unimportant issues, while the elite expand their power of influence and move the rest of society further towards their totalitarian globalisation project. Modern media has essentially become an extension of the education/indoctrination system which began in childhood, keeping the correct subconscious seeds watered at the expense of undesirable ones. With skilful control of the educational system, they manage to keep left brain intellectually aware academics at the top end of the influential job market; a self-policing process keeping the status quo from venturing too far off today's acceptable social norms, rewarding only those people who are suitably socialised to prop up the control system's agenda. Most media editors are successfully employed only because they have a track record of not upsetting the apple cart. They are chosen because they have a belief system running parallel to the overall agenda; through self-censorship they keep their jobs and the large corporations happy. The speed at which news is disseminated around the globe from western news agencies is instant. We now witness a single story or piece of propaganda, designed to be aired simultaneously across the globe, for greatest impact. One news item will enter the minds of millions at the same time, shooting straight into the collective consciousness from sheer volume of witnesses alone. With the aid of spinning circles, flashing lights and authority figures the media sends out information that flies past the focal conscious mind through into the subconscious and becomes our new collective reality without any meaningful challenge, or enough time to rationalise or process information in the traditional manner. Their scientific media machine, a weapon of mass deception, will even make you believe that Saddam Hussain had weapons of mass destruction. Just like the old days of church gatherings, when a large group of people would get together in close proximity to focus on a specific topic, they energised their immediate collective with prayers and hymns, stimulating both the conscious and subconscious in line with the collective's wishes with intent. With enough participants and a strong belief, prayers are sometime answered and a new reality is born.

Internet technology

Like most things in life, there is good and bad to be found. The internet is no exception, it is incredible technology when considering fifty years ago most people didn't even have a fridge. The speed at which technology has advanced is breath taking, especially for any generation who grew up before the 1980's. While having a world of information and convenience at one's fingertips, there is also a world of disinformation. It takes a keen and skilful eye to decipher fact from fiction, with hours of cross referencing and source tracking, to form a sensible conclusion. The internet offers great surveillance potential for the control system, mainly the ability to store, track and record all electronic activity, a digital footprint of thoughts, conversations, feelings and desires. They have the ability to psycho analyse every individual from their digital footprints, along with all their friends, fantasies and perversions.

Most people freely offer information on social media sites like Facebook, which have done a better job of collecting personal information, than some of the most sophisticated intelligence agencies could have dreamed of. Some people may say that if you have nothing to hide, what is the problem. The control system use all the information gathered to tweak policy; ensuring predictable outcomes are running in line with their computer models for globalisation. Once dissent is noticed and moves anticipated, contingencies can be put into place to remove any threat. There is no turning back once the technological control grid is comprehensively in place, it will be full steam ahead with unstoppable obedience and hard labour until the control system's death star is finally complete.

The assumed latest technology available to the general public, which is found in the shops and on-line stores, sometimes superseding products of even 6 months prior, are in fact dated throw outs of the control system's secret and black projects, military projects, toys and tools used by advanced government agencies. They have all the latest high tech gear while we, the general public, get an inferior version of their obsolete throw outs. For example the first electromechanical computer was built and used by the United States Navy in 1938, the torpedo data computer, which used trigonometry to solve the problem of firing a torpedo from a boat into a moving target.[9] The first internet was known as ARPANET and was brought online in 1969 under a contract led by the Advanced Research Projects Agency.[10] With today's leaps in technology, as rapid as they are, one can only speculate as to the kind of technical advancements available behind the scenes to the control system and the elite.

Another aspect to consider is the effect this new technology has on brain function. A person using the internet on a regular basis will biologically modify themselves to become compatible with the new tasks required; the brain will essentially rewire itself, changing its neural pathways to suit these new objectives. The next phase of this globalisation project, to which future generations will be subjected to, is the merger of human biology with artificial technology, known as transhumanism. Once this takes place and accepted by the majority, the control system will have the power to manipulate humanity however and whenever they see fit, creating a subservient hybrid species of obedient workers. Hopefully I won't be around by then to be subjected to it.

Mobile phones

Society is changing. The cell phone is at the forefront of this transition, a technology which on one hand allows people to communicate anywhere in the world instantaneously, but on the other hand distracts them from participating in a traditional cohesive way within their local community. The phone is changing the way we interact. According to OFCOM, 93% of UK adults own/use a mobile phone. The average person spends 90 minutes per day using the devise, this figure increases to a whopping 3 hours 36 minutes among young adults aged between 16-24.[11][12] In addition to these facts, a study by KPCB found that the average person looks at their cell phone 150 times per day.[13] The human brain is being rewired to accommodate this new technological way of living. Prior to this a person would get to know the people within their immediate proximity, they would have a three-dimensional connection with these people when communicating. All senses would be energised by both participants, giving a full spectrum of awareness when sharing time and space together. Eye contact, touch, smell, and an overall feeling stimulated by the individual's electromagnetic aura which is given off as they transmit their conscious energy into their surroundings. The cell phone is only capable of a one-dimensional connection. The focal consciousness attached to the screen becomes distracted from the real things taking place around them, dislocating them from the real world and their natural ability to energise the collective consciousness, essentially neutralising their capacity to contribute in a 3-dimensional way. The cell phone, a corporate device is enabling a new form of socialization to occur, this will no doubt take the form of an opportunity to promote whatever belief system is desirable for the further expansion of corporate interests, advancing a monoculture of technically locked in, isolated, indebted, consumerist, automatons.

Definition of Addiction: - **The state of being enslaved to a habit or practice or to something that is psychologically or physically habit-forming, as narcotics, to such an extent that its cessation causes severe trauma.**

For this technology to work a huge infrastructure has been installed across the whole planet, 5 million phone towers have been erected transmitting electromagnetic frequencies to all but isolated areas, an ocean of microwave frequencies, clouding the natural resonance of the Earth. We live in a super fog of electromagnetic energy, a background millions of times more active than any generation witnessed before the 1980's. God only knows the long term effects of living within this soup, a social experiment where only time will tell the true biological dangers involved. In this time of great change, the transition from Pisces into Aquarius, from a cosmic energy of belief to one of knowing, is it possible that the control system has anticipated this change, a universal frequency destined to energise and take humanity to higher levels of inspirational conscious knowing? This may explain why they have put in place an artificial counter measure, designed to pollute the Earth's natural cycle with a fog of electromagnetic energy under their control.

What's the frequency, Kenneth ?

Inside the brain there is a gland called the pineal gland, this gland is sensitive to light and dark, when the gland senses the dark, usually during sleep, it will begin to produce a chemical called melatonin; this chemical is the body's natural way of repairing itself and fighting off disease. The production of melatonin is our best defence against diseases like cancer. light is also an electromagnetic frequency, which now has to compete with a 24-hour onslaught from modern technology, artificially created magnetic fields, tricking the pineal gland into assuming it is still light, reducing its ability to instigate the production of necessary melatonin. This could be why cancer rates have increased? This barrage of electromagnetic energy is also interfering with our natural auric fields, a two-way flow of energy within the body's biological transmitter/receiver. When we interact with the collective we now have to compete with an ocean of technologically generated fog.

There is another aspect to this electromagnetic fog, an aspect which can only be theorised at this present time. During the transition phase from Pisces to Aquarius, the ruling planet Jupiter gives up its throne over to Saturn and Uranus. The associated spectrum of energy resonating from Saturn is favourable to the control system and its plans for further expansion, whereas the spectrum of frequencies coming from Uranus are not so desirable, the rebellious and revolutionary nature of Uranus seem to contradict any form of control. One must ask is it possible therefore, that the controlling elite are well aware of this and are using technology to neutralise the energy coming from Uranus or neutralising our ability to be influenced by it. This could in some way explain the use of phone masts, vaccinations, GMO's and chemtrails, electromagnetically and biologically interfering with us, while at the same time allowing and encouraging the energy coming from Saturn. With the law of attraction in play, just like a radio tunes in to a particular frequency, we bring that frequency into our perceived reality. The control system now has the technology to align a nation's population with the frequency of Saturn; bringing all Saturn's attributes into focal reality. At the same time, un-tuning the population's focal consciousness or beliefs away from any energetic alignment with Uranus, stopping its rebellious energy from manifesting within our collective reality.

Hollywood

A magician's wand was traditionally made from the wood of a holly tree. With the help of the United States film industry, casting their magician's wand, the control system has managed to reorganise the habits and opinions of the masses. With special effects, factory made scripts and state of the art sound effects; the modern cinema has become a gateway challenging old beliefs while offering up new ones, targeting the subconscious, nurturing favourable seeds while poisoning others. Huge swathes of the population go to the movies, enjoying the thrill and excitement of escaping into the entertainment world within the big screen, oblivious to the influence on their subconscious minds and the belief system they first went in with. Sat in rows like battery chickens, mesmerised by the sounds and images, creating a trance like hypnotic collective consciousness within the cinema walls, stimulating multiple senses within a framework of suggestible believability.

Who Controls Hollywood? According to a recent article written in the Los Angeles Times by the American journalist, Joel Stein, titled "**WHO RUNS HOLLYWOOD**". Mr Stein stated:

"**The Jews are so dominant; I had to scour the trades to come up with six Gentiles in high positions at entertainment companies. When I called them to talk about their incredible advancement, five of them refused to talk to me, apparently out of fear of insulting Jews. The sixth, AMC President Charlie Collier, turned out to be Jewish.**"

He noted:

"**When the studio chiefs took out a full-page ad in the Los Angeles Times a few weeks ago to demand that the Screen Actors Guild settle its contract, the open letter was signed by: News Corp. President Peter Chernin (Jewish), Paramount Pictures Chairman Brad Grey (Jewish), Walt Disney Co. Chief Executive Robert Iger (Jewish), Sony Pictures Chairman Michael Lynton (surprise, Dutch Jew), Warner Bros. Chairman Barry Meyer (Jewish), CBS Corp. Chief Executive Leslie Moonves (so Jewish his great uncle was the first prime minister of Israel), MGM Chairman Harry Sloan (Jewish) and NBC Universal Chief Executive Jeff Zucker (mega-Jewish). If either of the Weinstein brothers had signed, this group would have not only the power to shut down all film production but to form a minyan with enough Fiji water on hand to fill a mikvah.**"

In the article Stein says he called up Abe Foxman, Chairman of the ADL, to ask him:

"**Why don't more Jews just come out and boast at this great accomplishment? Foxman responded by admitting that yes, it's true that most of the top execs "happen to be Jewish." In fact, Foxman told Stein, "All eight major film studios are run by men who happen to be Jewish.**""- (14)

With this in mind, it would be fair to assume that most of what comes out of Hollywood would have a leaning towards the aspirations and common collective beliefs held by all these good people, people holding positions of power within the corporate structure of this massive Media Empire. It is a major achievement by a minority group within the host nation of the United States, having such a large percentage from one particular faith influencing events. Years of worshiping Saturn must have had an influential effect.

Western governments have also had close ties to its nation's movie industry, from the early days of WW 1, through WW 2 and up to the present, playing a role in shaping public opinion towards the goals of its residing government and corporate lobbyists. I would suggest that it is only a matter of time until Hollywood produces a romantic movie glorifying drone attacks on civilians in the Middle East. The vast majority of Hollywood's war film catalogue paints a very biased view of world events and history, coming at it from the victor's perspective, portraying Native American Indians as unsophisticated savages, Germans as inhumane, industrial murdering Jew haters, engaged in world domination. Arab Muslims as potential terrorists and so on. All designed to propagate a chosen belief system and alter our perception towards the next phase of the control systems agenda.

Corporate music industry

The entertainment industry consists largely of, the TV industry, Hollywood movies and the music industry, controlled by those who seek to socially engineer humanity in a certain direction. Music is an energetic frequency which has the ability to create emotions and alter moods. It is not easy to become a member of the mainstream musical establishment, and during the past few decades the artists that manage to climb to the top of the main stream music world are noticeably promoting corporate interests and globalisation, along with Saturn symbolism. The act of symbolism and ceremony are all part of drawing one's frequency in line with what one is representing, through the law of attraction the artist creates the intention to harmonise the collective and influence reality. Music is very much a right brain activity, a free-thinking area of limitless possibility and imagination. The control system is selective as to the type of material they want the average person exposed to. Their selective methods decide who is and who isn't promoted.

It is noticeable if you know what to look for in occult symbolism (occult meaning hidden) amongst the rich and famous within the music industry. Hand signs resembling the number 6 or gestures looking like goat horns are common place. Satan or Baphomet, usually depicted as half human and half goat, similar to Capricorn, the zodiac sign ruled by Saturn. Hand gestures of this type give off intention and resonate with the energetic frequency of Saturn. Wherever intention goes energy then flows. Pentagram symbols, meant to represent goat's horns are also commonly seen throughout this industry.

With all this considered, the average person going about their daily lives are virtually blind to the true nature of the world unfolding around them. The mechanisms in place which control the majority of information they digest keep them financially subservient and subordinate to a small group of powerful interests. Much of main stream reporting is tainted with bias, their version of truth can be as opposite as black is from white, with important relevant facts left out. The shaped opinions of the obedient classes, who on the whole acceptingly absorb these deceptions allied with truths, show no further desire to question official versions of major events, events which have knock on effects, shaping their lives and their children's lives. This acceptance locks society into a corner, unable to ground themselves to a solid foundation of truth as they service their masters with their programmed opinions and beliefs. It has been well understood that a well-informed citizenry capable of critical thinking is part of what is necessary in order to keep their controllers in check. When the controllers hold all the cards they eventually take all the power and all the wealth.

"**Our liberty depends on the freedom of the press, and that cannot be limited without being lost.**" - Thomas Jefferson[15]

"**Whenever the people are well informed, they can be trusted with their own government that whenever things get so far wrong as to attract their notice, they may be relied on to set them to rights.**" - Thomas Jefferson[16]

"Only a free and unrestrained press can effectively expose deception in government." - Hugo L Black[17]

"When one millionaire has ten newspapers and ten million people have no newspapers — that is not freedom of the press." - Anastas Mikoyan[18]

Notes for chapter 11

(1) Ben H. Bagdikian, The Media Monopoly, Sixth Edition, (Beacon Press, 2000), pp. xx-xxi

(2) BBC NEWS, 18 March 2013, Entertainment & Arts, http://www.bbc.co.uk/news/entertainment-arts-21828961

(3) Press association, Huffington Post entertainment, 7/12/2011, http://www.huffingtonpost.co.uk/2011/12/07/average-briton-spends-one-year-watching-soap_n_1133490.html

(4) Liane Casten, Court Ruled That Media Can Legally Lie, CMW REPORT, Spring 2003, http://www.projectcensored.org/11-the-media-can-legally-lie/

(5) The Committee On Public Information, 1917 , http://en.wikipedia.org/wiki/Committee_on_Public_Information

(6) Sir Rodrick Jones, A life in Reuters, Hodder and Stoughton, London (Jan. 1, 1951)

(7) The reading agency, Reading facts, http://readingagency.org.uk/news/reading-facts003

(8) Nishio Kanji, Breaking the Seal on the GHQ Burned Books, Society for the Dissemination of Historical Fact, http://www.sdh-fact.com/book-article/217

(9) Terry Lindell, The torpedo data computer, http://maritime.org/tech/tdc.htm

(10) Mary Bellis, The first internet, about.com inventors, http://inventors.about.com/library/weekly/aa091598.htm

(11) number of adults using mobile phones in uk, Facts and Figures, http://media.ofcom.org.uk/facts/, Adults between 16-24 usage, http://stakeholders.ofcom.org.uk/market-data-research/market-data/communications-market-reports/cmr14/uk/

(12) Mobileinsurance.com, 7th Mar 2013, By The Mobile Insurance Team, 90 min per day on cell phone, http://www.mobileinsurance.co.uk/blog/average-britons-spends-almost-34-entire-days-on-mobile-phone-per-year/

(13) Kleiner Perkins Caufield & Byers (KPCB) partners, 28th May 2014, checking phones per day, http://www.kpcb.com/internet-trends

(14) Joel Stein, Who runs Hollywood, Los Angeles Times, 19 dec 2008, http://articles.latimes.com/2008/dec/19/opinion/oe-stein19

(15) Thomas Jefferson, Writing to Dr James Currie, The Library of congress, Jan 28, 1786, http://memory.loc.gov/ammem/collections/jefferson_papers/mtjquote.html

(16) Thomas Jefferson, Writing to Richard Price, The Library of congress, Jan 8th 1789, http://memory.loc.gov/ammem/collections/jefferson_papers/mtjquote.html

(17) Hugo L. Black, (New York Times Company v. United States, 1971) , Wikiquote, http://en.wikiquote.org/wiki/Freedom_of_the_press

(18) Anastas Mikoyan, quoted in "Traveling With Mikoyan Quote By Quote" - Time Magazine, 26 jan 1959, http://en.wikiquote.org/wiki/Freedom_of_the_press

Chapter 12. The attack on education

When all aspects of consciousness are working together in harmony, with a balanced left/right mind connection to the spirit, our capacity to become the greatest version of ourselves is enhanced. The control system is in a constant battle, in an attempt to disrupt this fragile balance, beginning early with the modern educational system. It has become no more than layers of indoctrination, using subtle yet sophisticated processes, in an effort, to turn its subjects into left brain intellectual awareness, and useful servants for the controlling system's advancing agenda, as George Carlin eloquently put it.

"There's a reason that education sucks. And it's the same reason that it will never ever, ever be fixed. It's never going to get any better. Don't look for it. Be happy with what you got, because the owners of this country don't want that. I'm talking about the real owners now, the real owners, the big wealthy business interests that control things and make all the important decisions. Forget the politicians. The politicians are put there to give you the idea that you have freedom of choice. You don't. You have no choice. You have owners. They own you. They own everything. They own all the important land. They own and control the corporations. They've long since bought and paid for the Senate, the Congress, the state houses, and city halls. They got the judges in their back pocket. And they own all the big media companies so they control just about all of the news and information you get to hear. They got you by the balls. They spend billions of dollars every year lobbying, lobbying to get what they want. Well, we know what they want. They want more for themselves and less for everybody else. But I'll tell you what they don't want. They don't want a population of citizens capable of critical thinking. They don't want well-informed, well-educated people capable of critical thinking. They're not interested in that. That doesn't help them. That's against their interest. That's right. They don't want people who are smart enough to sit around the kitchen table and figure out how badly they're getting fucked by a system that threw them overboard 30 fucking years ago. They don't want that. You know what they want? They want obedient workers, obedient workers. people who are just smart enough to run the machines and do the paperwork and just dumb enough to passively accept all these increasingly shittier jobs with the lower pay, the longer hours, the reduced benefits." George Carlin, quote from Dumb Americans.

The educational system requires children to be pulled from the influence and safety of their family unit as early as possible. The young child starts life with an inquisitive mind, exploring its home and surroundings, actively involved within a healthy left/right brain balance. The control system needs to prepare that child for a life time of useful work. To ensure a modicum of compliance and success, a saturnine left-brain indoctrination process begins in earnest. We have already established in a previous chapter that the child has become the property of the state, it is now expected to fulfil its lifetime duty in representing the legal fiction which was set up by the government when the parents unwittingly signed the birth certificate. The state must now perform its role in moulding that human resource or unit of productivity on which vast sums of future government borrowing will depend.

"Each child belongs to the state" William H Seawell, professor of education, University of Virginia 1981

Once the child becomes part of the schooling process a new energetic collective frequency will start to influence the child and its development. The programming of its subconscious with a belief system running in line with new social expectations and projections for the next generation begins. Training at school aims to educate out of us the right brain function, children begin schooling chaotically creative, thinking in a very right-minded manner, yet the longer they stay within the schooling environment the tamer their imaginations become.

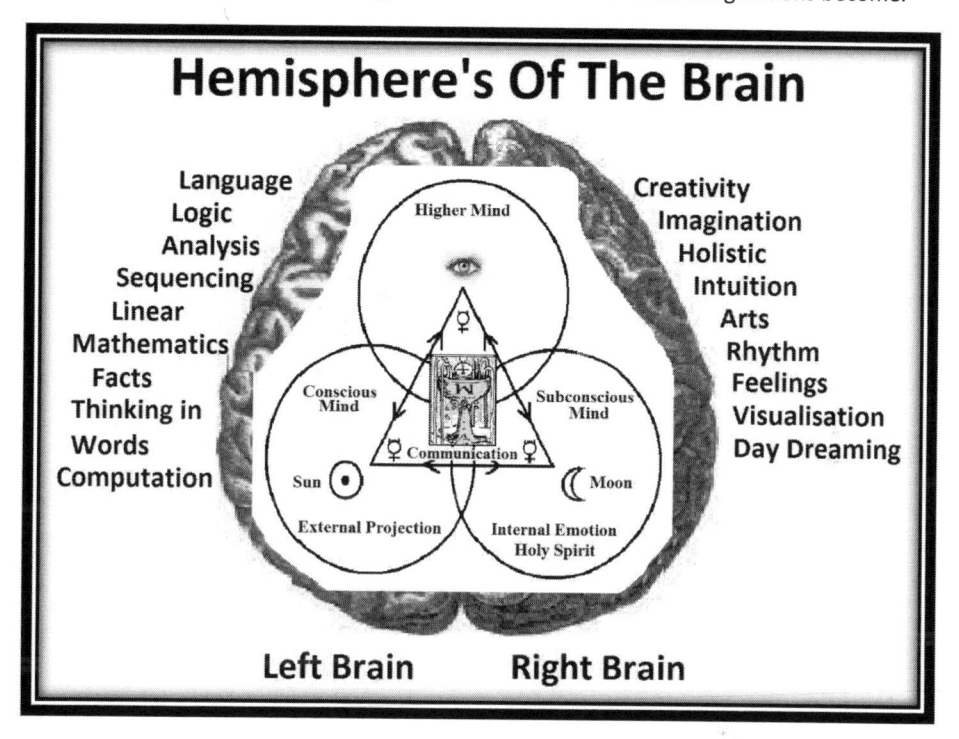

Hemisphere's Of The Brain

Left Brain
- Language
- Logic
- Analysis
- Sequencing
- Linear
- Mathematics
- Facts
- Thinking in Words
- Computation

Right Brain
- Creativity
- Imagination
- Holistic
- Intuition
- Arts
- Rhythm
- Feelings
- Visualisation
- Day Dreaming

Higher Mind
Conscious Mind — Communication — Subconscious Mind
Sun ☉ — Moon ☾
External Projection / Internal Emotion / Holy Spirit

With all these attributes interwoven and related to focal consciousness, it seems reasonable to assume that the conscious mind is clearly linked to the functional integrity of the left side of the brain. It is therefore also reasonable to assume that the attributes relating to internal emotion and the subconscious can be linked to the functional attributes of the right side. Between these two hemispheres, connecting both sides of the brain, is a super highway of neural fibres called the Corpus Collosum. This Mercurian attachment is the biological communicative route balancing the conscious and subconscious minds. A balanced connection between all these aspects of awareness essentially represent the Holy Grail of consciousness.

Objectives within the modern educational system include obedience and subordination within a competitive sense of limitation. They want the child to believe that truth comes from authority and intelligence is the ability to remember and repeat. Non-compliance is punished while accurate memory and repetition is rewarded. Overall, they want each person to conform intellectually and socially within the parameters set by the state, essentially producing a generation of left brain automatons. Any form of uniqueness or individuality outside the remit dictated from above is quashed at a very early stage. Children who have problems suppressing their right brain activity are labelled as difficult, day dreamers or even boys and girls with one of many newly invented illnesses like ADD (Attention Deficit Disorder), which unsurprisingly comes with an array of manufactured medications.

"We spend the first year of a child's life teaching it to walk and talk and the rest of its life to shut up and sit down. There is something wrong there." Neil Degrasse Tyson

If you suggested a couple of hundred years ago that a family should turn over their children to strangers, who they know nothing about, and for those strangers to work on the minds of their children, out of sight for approximately 12 years. You would have been quickly chased out of the village, labelled as insane. But that is just what we are doing. We assume the system has our best interests at heart. With government initiatives like "No child left behind", and the Catholic Church's initiative of "No child's behind left", it is clear that the system desires full control over those developing young minds. With children so closely connected to higher realms of spiritual consciousness, a potential, if not restrained early, could generate loose ripples within the community's collective, undermining control away from the hands of the manipulators.

"The whole educational and professional training system is a very elaborate filter which just weeds out people who are too independent and who think for themselves and who don't know how to be submissive and so on, because they are dysfunctional to the institutions." Noam Chomsky

"I have never let my schooling interfere with my education" Mark Twain

"Play is the highest form of research" Albert Einstein

"Children must be taught how to think not what to think" Margaret Mead

"Educating the mind without educating the heart is no education at all" Aristotle

"Spoon feeding in the long run teachers us nothing but the shape of the spoon" E Forster

"School is the advertising agency which makes you believe that you need the society as it is" Ivan Illich

"It is nearly impossible to become an educated person in a country so distrustful of the independent mind" James Baldwin

"There is nothing more unequal than the equal treatment of unequal people" Thomas Jefferson

"The only thing that interferes with my learning is my education" Albert Einstein

"It is a thousand times better to have common sense without education than to have education without common sense" Robert Green Ingersoll

"Education is a system of imposed ignorance" Noam Chomsky

"He alone who owns the youth, gains the future" Adolf Hitler

The modern school

If the modern schooling system is seen as a tool used by the state to prepare the future collective for its role in the projected ambitions of that control system, then we see it in a totally different light. Some schools in western countries are becoming more like prisons than learning facilities, with students photographed, x-rayed, scanned, snooped and sniffed at before they enter the class room. This is not just a free society's reaction to outside threats; it is a subtle way to program and condition the student's subconscious minds into accepting it as a norm, a benchmark of what modern freedom and democracy represents in the name of safety. Preparing the students to participate and uphold the new transformations in the society which the control system is working towards. As it progresses, slowly unfolding its array of checks and tracking mechanisms, the older members of society deflated with frustration, find it difficult adjusting to any new lack of privacy, their old benchmark of liberty with few restrictions become just another ageing memory. As the control system gains more and more ground, its grip grows tighter as its tentacles spread into all aspects of our lives, requiring any new submissive collective to fulfil their roles unquestioningly, posing no threat as they accept their new version of normality. It will even go so far as to pervert science and distort history to create the mind-set required for the next 20-year cycle.

Schools or Prisons

"Education is a weapon whose effect depends on who holds it in his hand and at whom it is aimed" Joseph Stalin

Home schooling

The assumed proper method of education is a collective assumption that the state knows better. When your child enters the schooling system, submerged in the energetic frequency of the class room, it is essentially brought up by the collective influence of the other children, the lowest common denominator of the culture. If the same child spent its developing years amongst a group of scientists, a totally different kind of adult would emerge. It is well documented that the majority of home schooled pupils out perform their rivals in the mainstream. There are many reasons for this. At present only 3% of all school aged children in the United States are home schooled, a number which steadily increases year on year. There are many benefits for both the family and the pupil when considering the options on educating their children at home as opposed to mainstream public education.

- 1) You can teach them quicker, in greater depth over more subjects.
- 2) Feed them better, keeping the child away from processed foods.
- 3) Give them self-confidence and self esteem.
- 4) Keep them away from abusive teachers and pupils.
- 5) Home schooling is cheaper.
- 6) You can live almost anywhere.
- 7) Many schools will not take un vaccinated children.
- 8) Keeps the family unit closely together during the child's developing years.
- 9) You can have days off at convenient times which suit the whole family.
- 10) The child will have more time to pursue extra interests.

A study took place back in 1997 which demonstrated on average that pupils who were home schooled performed 30-37% better than their public school counterparts, in all subjects.[1] The most important thing you can give to a child is self-confidence and the skills to find things out for themselves. Take either of those two things away and the child literally struggles through life handicapped. It is puzzling how heavily funded professional institutions, with professional teachers can't seem to match the academic standards of the home schooled children who, on the whole, receive their guidance by parents with little or no previous teaching experience. It is another example where government intervention interferes and stifles the natural progress and ability of human development. But of course they don't want a population of well informed, critical thinkers, they want obedient workers.

"**We want one class of person to have a liberal education and we want another class of persons, a very much larger class of necessity in every society, to forgo the privilege of a liberal education and fit themselves to perform specific difficult manual tasks.**" Woodrow Wilson US President

Repetition

The whole process of modern institutional education is to fill the left brain with facts that can be recalled on demand. The exam system rewards people who are particularly good at this, allowing them to continue up the academic ladder, enabling them to become the next generation of teachers and professors who will teach the future generation to become teachers and professors, a perpetuating system safeguarding the established methods of learning, a system in which subjects are divided into compartments, isolating perspective, and reducing the concept of the universal interconnecting greater whole. Unfortunately, genius does not come from repetition or filling the mind with facts. Genius is the ability to see things with higher levels of consciousness. Of course, depth of understanding is necessary along with facts in any given subject. But higher levels of consciousness can see things from multiple perspectives holistically.

"**The intellect has little to do on the road to discovery. There comes a leap in consciousness call it intuition or what you will, the solution comes to you and you don't know how or why.**" Albert Einstein

This is one reason why a left-brain education can only achieve a modicum of greatness. An education based on the expansion of all levels, within a balanced consciousness, could be a better way to promote greater leaps in human evolution and progress.

Debt

The borrower is always slave to the lender. It is another method used to control people's behaviour and limit their scope of independence. The modern western educational system has slipped backwards by design, placing enormous debt burdens upon a new generation of students, with costs increasing year upon year, resulting in a loss of opportunity for the common man to participate. Regardless, there are still large numbers of upper and middle-class families sending their children to these institutions, hoping to give their offspring a better chance of placing a foot on the ladder of prosperity and fulfilling family expectations. The steady implementation of this student debt policy, far removed from the golden days of free education for all, is no accident, it is part of an overall strategy to control human resources. It is vital for the continued expansion and survival of the new globalisation project, through corporate control, that eager new members will devote their lives and energies to continuing this cause. The greater its expansion, the greater its control, and the more mechanisms of control will be introduced guaranteeing its influence. A graduate without debt is free to choose a destiny according to his or her heart/mind moral compass, seeking a journey through life which suits their character, natural abilities and aspirations. This may run counterproductive to the requirements of an expanding system of control which surrounds them. Once the burden of debt is attached, the students have very little choice but to participate, as cogs, somewhere within the corporate machine. Choosing which open air prison they want to dedicate the majority of their energy and sacrifice their most productive years. According to a 2014 report by the Institute of fiscal studies, UK students are now graduating with an average debt of £44,000, With the majority expected to make repayments well into their 50s,[2] a sure way to trap a generation into debt slavery, obedience and servitude. Accepted by most as the norm, the generation who put in place free education for all can only stand back and wonder what happened. There always seems to be enough money for war, enough for political campaigns, enough for governments to bailout bankers, but the nurturing of the minds of our young has become more of a privilege than a necessity, only available to the people of means. Knowledge is not wisdom and corporate education is not the only road to Rome. With home schooling and internet access, one can educate independently of government organisations, many suggesting it as the superior option, certainly preferred by a growing number of parents.

You cannot force wisdom and knowledge onto someone who does not want or have the inner desire to understand its true value. You also cannot stop an individual who has a thirst for knowledge, wisdom and truth from exploring their curiosity, even with limited funds, some of the greatest thinkers throughout history, were self-educated, guided by intuition and a balanced consciousness. A recent study performed by the Federal Reserve Bank of New York, concluded that only 27% of college graduates have jobs closely related to the subject that they majored in.[3] With all this in mind, careful consideration is necessary when guiding your child towards their first steps of independence.

International curriculum

To establish globalisation without too many unexpected disruptions, an international curriculum is being implemented across the globe, a curriculum with common objectives.

Corporations and policy makers are together setting the direction of this new form of indoctrination, a system designed to train the new global man to fit well into a new form of planned economy and collectivism. Organisations and initiatives like Common Core in the United States; "Education for All" through a UNESCO initiative; and Common Purpose in the United Kingdom, have all been set up to implement the changes necessary. They have been working for many years away from public scrutiny, designed to propel and implement future sustainable development (Agenda 21). These new forms of education initiatives are training processes, created to discourage independent thought and curiosity, dehumanising the learning process with an abundance of standardised testing, collectively acting as a harness suffocating traditional education. Its prime objectives are to alter the student's attitudes, values and beliefs, subtly programming the subconscious with a new state focused perspective. The political, economic and industrial elites want limited learning for lifelong labour. Partly funded by the Bill and Malinda Gates Foundation, Common Core is now operational throughout the US, brainwashing students with assignments designed to install a new belief system.

Common Core assignment question on man made climate change

After reading the text the student is expected to answer several questions about what they have read.

"By the early 21st Century, people knew that the massive use of fossil fuels was heating up the planet. But people didn't stop their destructive lifestyles. They just kept using up earths recourses. The ice sheets melted and the earths crust shifted. In 2130, the oceans began to rise over farmland and cities, in 300 years most of the eastern Unites States was covered with water."

Common Core exercise encouraging flu shots

- News reports predicted that this winter's flu __EPIDEMIC__ would be very bad.
- Our state's health department tried to _____ people to the importance of getting their flu shots as early as possible. Unfortunately the disease spread so quickly that many people did not have a chance to protect themselves.
- The symptoms of this year's strain of flu left even strong people _____ and unable to take care of themselves.

> **Common Core; Suggesting your rights are privileges given to you by your government not inalienable rights given to you by GOD**
>
> Name   Date
>
> ## Being a Good Citizen
>
> What is a citizen? If you were born in the United States, you are a citizen. That means you are a member of our country. Sometimes people who are not born here want to become citizens. They do this by asking the government to make them a citizen. This is called naturalization.
>
> When you are a citizen you have rights. <u>Rights are special privileges the government gives you.</u> In our country, you have free speech. You are also given the right to choose a religion. In America, the press is free to tell you what is happening in the world. The Bill of Rights lists the freedoms given to citizens. These rights are very important. Many people in the world do not have freedoms like we do.
>
> <u>Because the government gives us rights,</u> we have the duty to be good citizens. But, what does it mean to be a good citizen? How can you be part of giving back for the freedom you have? Being a good citizen means you show your love to your country. You can do this by being courteous to the symbols of America. Singing our National Anthem and respecting our flag are ways to show how much the United States means to you.

"We are what we think. All that we are arises with our thoughts. With our thoughts we make the world." Gautama Buddha

Programming

Young children are sensitive to all aspects of energy; their minds for the first 6 years of life are in what is referred to as a hypnogogic state, similar to the state a hypnotist induces when he is implanting suggestions. They are so sensitive that they can pick up on just the anxiety in the air given off by their parents. During these formative years the bulk of a child's belief system is programmed into their subconscious. All future patterns of behaviour emerge from the experiences during this important development phase. If we see the subconscious as a garden and the focal consciousness as seeds being offered in the form of suggestions, each child starts life with an empty garden collecting seeds from his environment and experiences which begin to germinate. There are seeds of love, anger, envy and compassion, seeds for every type of thought and emotion. Once they are planted, our focal thoughts decide their fate, either helping them grow or allowing them to perish. If you dwell on hate and anger, those weeds will be fed by your focal energy, spreading throughout your subconscious garden. Eventually the weeds of hate and anger will take over every aspect of that garden, influencing all areas of life. It is up to the individual how much focal energy is given to each seed which will mature into a personal garden, and a belief system. The controllers set out to influence these important years, by requiring children to start school at an earlier age, subtly planting necessary beliefs required for all participants of the new global society.

There is a law in the universe, a powerful law, known as the law of attraction, we naturally develop into cosmic magnets, with our thoughts and feelings we send out a spectrum of vibrations, once aligned, those matching vibrations flowing all around us will become more noticeable and appear in abundance. We essentially get more of the same coming back. Hence why, if we go looking for trouble, trouble will find us. To access higher mind wisdom and influence one's reality, there needs to be a good communicative balance within all layers of consciousness. The thoughts and intentions of the focal mind must be in line with a positive belief system embedded within the subconscious, the frequencies must be the same and then in line with the energy flowing from the macrocosm. If the focal mind has been sabotaged by a bombardment of negative thoughts, the individual will become detached from beneficially influencing his own reality. A consciously aware individual can take control of his thoughts, making necessary changes to the programming within the subconscious. Attention must be shifted towards peace in the space between thoughts, emptying the mind of trip wires, negativity and excess baggage, opening it up for all possibility to manifest within. These are the magical moments of inspiration and intuition. For many people it is necessary to weed unwanted growths of inharmonious programming, in some severe cases the whole field must be ploughed over allowing space for a new belief system which is allied with desirable focal intentions. A new positive subconscious mindset would then be able to grow without doubt or resistance benefiting from the universal laws of attraction, giving the individual more control over creating their own reality. Once in tune he must first ask, then believe, and finally he will receive. Negative thoughts and negative energy go against our natural equilibrium; they create doubt and resistance against desired intentions, perverting what you eventually attract. The circumstances of our lives are always a vibrational match to our own energy. If you are judgemental towards others, who have what you desire, you will keep yourself in a state of resistance, as you cannot belong to a club in which you despise the current members. Just imagine the potential of humanity if each individual was programmed with a positive, balanced belief system, enabling an abundance of intuition, inspiration and wisdom connected to higher levels of conscious awareness. From that, a whole new frequency would resonate throughout human society, influencing each other towards unity and advancements for the greater good.

"The greatest discovery of my generation is that human beings can alter their lives by altering their attitudes of mind." -William James

"Watch your thoughts; they become words. Watch your words; they become actions. Watch your actions; they become habit. Watch your habits; they become character. Watch your character; it becomes your destiny." -Lao Tzu

"Nurture your mind with great thoughts, for you will never go any higher than you think." -Benjamin Disraeli

"A man is but the product of his thoughts what he thinks, he becomes." -Gandhi

"When you change the way you look at things, the things you look at change." -Dr. Wayne Dyer

"We are shaped by our thoughts; we become what we think. When the mind is pure, joy follows like a show that never leaves." -Buddha

It is essential for the control system's survival, that its subjects are imprisoned within left brain academic intellectual awareness. The whole idea of a society full of independent universally enlightened citizens is not acceptable, especially if the global elite wish to keep themselves at the helm. To control the world's educational system with a global curriculum is one more step towards their desired end. The evolution of which, has many safeguards built within it. Most children succumb to left brain programmed awareness; some colourful individuals who have difficulty shaking off their natural right brain connections are sometimes cruelly labelled and told they have learning difficulties. From that moment on their fragile subconscious will carry a programmed belief that they are not normal, disabling them with a learning difficulty, activating a restrictive barrier of disbelief in their own ability, rendering the child consciously handicapped. If you put a label on someone they invariably start to believe it, they become that label, essentially casting a spell over them.

Why English

Each language is part of the unique identity of a particular group of people. Language is a left-brain expression, vocalising the thoughts and feelings passing through our focal and subconscious. Each language operates a unique frequency, vibrating within a culture. Just like a song the overall language can invoke all kinds of feelings and emotions, resonating through to the subconscious. Certain languages have a natural bias towards cohesion and happiness, others towards authority and obedience, like the planets in our solar system, each one vibrates its own unique qualities. With globalisation unfolding, it would seem sensible for the control system to choose a language that helps them achieve their goals and fits neatly with the projected society which they are trying to create. English has a track record for invoking obedience and discipline within a culture, hence the British Empire. The structure of the language is the building block for left brain development and subconscious programming. English vibrates a song of compliance, obedience and seriousness. It would not be in the interest of the control system to choose a language like Thai for the global project, instead of obedience and compliance you would get a world full of happy people, with smiling faces, singing and laughing all day. That would not be good for a serious global totalitarian takeover. With English being adopted as the global language, cultures merging into duel speaking societies are in danger of losing their original identity and unique perspective on life, a way of life which evolved from that authentic way of communicating. Spelling within the English language, does exactly what it says, it casts a spell, a suggestion into the subconscious, subliminally tweaking the mind. English has its roots in Latin, a language associated with the energetic allegiance to Saturn. In the works of Virgil, he comments that Latin is spoken by Saturn's people.

"Latinus calls his people the nation of Saturn, either because he reigned in Latium over the same people; or because they governed themselves by the principles of justice and equality, and walked in the steps of that God".[4]

Many Languages are expressions of the "now"; they do not have a developed concept of past, present and future. For this reason, their societies will predominantly live in the moment, care free and oblivious to future planning. The globalisation project requires a language which thinks in past, present and future terms, hence why English is preferred. Anyone living in the now will struggle to understand usury and other economical concepts.

Changing your belief system

A belief system grown out of influence and environmental factors can be difficult to change; they develop from parents, groups, authority figures and emotional impacting events. During their formative years, most people nurture a belief system similar to that of their parents, their ethnic group, religion and culture. The subconscious is like a garden full of influential seeds either dismissed or watered by focal attention and stimuli. The focal conscious mind may have a desire to change a habit which has been nurtured for 20 years, smoking for instance, each time a person lights up a cigarette they are reassuring the subconscious that they like to smoke. They even have special smoking times, like after dinner, while drinking and after love making, they really go to town convincing the subconscious how much they love to smoke. So, when they consciously decide to stop one day, they have a massive conflict of interest. The focal conscious mind wants to be a none smoker but the more powerful subconscious believes he loves to smoke. Having precedence over the focal consciousness, and being the part of the mind, which controls habitual behaviour, a conflict ensues and the person finds he is unable to stop. The only way to reverse a habit of a lifetime and change the belief system is to convince the subconscious that it desires to be a non-smoker, bringing it in line with the conscious minds new requirements. Making the decision at a conscious level is not enough, the subconscious right brain is predominantly emotional in nature, changing its programming needs to be done through various emotional stimuli, through the 5 senses.

We learn in 3 main ways, seeing, hearing and feeling, by using all our senses bringing them in line with the new resonant frequency of the focal consciousness, we can convince the subconscious to change its mind too. Imagery and symbolism stimulates the subconscious as does hearing repetitive reinforcing affirmations like repeating that you are no longer a smoker. Mild electric shock treatment has been used for many years to stimulate the feeling and touch senses, known as (Adverse counter conditioning), it goes straight into the subconscious. This along with other tools in the spectrum of stimuli, self-hypnosis can go a long way towards success when trying to reprogram a new belief system, digging out the old seeds from the subconscious garden and nurturing positive new ones.

A study was carried out in 1985, at a clinic in Seattle, where 327 clients wanted to give up smoking. 52% of all clients achieved their goal of total abstinence from cigarettes after graduating from the electric shock treatment.[5] The secret of success with self-hypnosis is positive attitude and a belief in one's inner ability to alter their attitude, mind and reality. First ask, then believe and you will receive. All levels of consciousness must be in harmony for things to manifest in the way you want.

Saturn connection

The law of attraction suggests that like energies attract more of the same. There is a common denominator in all this, the qualities of the left brain, the unique qualities of the English language, the evolution of the control system, the structure of the corporations and the mentality of the global elite; they all possess Saturnine energetic qualities, we essentially live in a world focussing on Saturn. The energy's associated with this planet include, control, responsibility, limitation, authority, hard work, restriction, discipline and time. To take full advantage of the law of attraction, calling on its power could explain many social anomalies. Satan worship Is Saturn worship, ceremonies and rituals designed to focus the conscious mind on resonating physically with the energy of Saturn, drawing on its power by tuning in to its characteristic frequencies. Is it any wonder allegations of Satan worshipping rituals run rampant amongst the rich and famous?

Graduation

Saturnine square black cap and gown

Graduation is proof that your mind has been squared off into left brain academic intellectual awareness, proof that you now resonate the saturnine qualities of seriousness and hard work. A sufficient standard of programming has now been installed into the mind of the graduate, a belief system full of compartmentalisation and division, designed to keep humanity fragmented and endlessly competing with one another while the control system expands around them, competing divisions like class, income, status, education, religion, race and sexuality. Unfortunately for the graduates, with an average student debt of around £44,000, the hidden agenda would be the last thing on their minds.

"Everything is energy and that's all there is to it. Match the frequency of the reality you want and you cannot help but get that reality. It can be no other way. This is not philosophy. This is physics." -Darryl Anka

Notes for chapter 12

(1) HSLDA, Research supplement, Academic Statistics on Home-schooling, https://www.hslda.org/docs/nche/000010/200410250.asp

(2) Claire Crawford, Wenchao Jin, Report R93, Institute for fiscal studies, April 2014 http://www.ifs.org.uk/comms/r93.pdf

(3) Jaison R Abel, Richard Deitz, Agglomeration and Job Matching among College Graduates, Dec 2014, http://www.newyorkfed.org/research/staff_reports/sr587.pdf

(4) Virgil, Opera, or the works of Virgil, Page 403, https://archive.org/details/publiivirgiliim03virggoog

(5) J W Smith, NCBI, 1988, Long term outcome of clients treated in a commercial stop smoking program, http://www.ncbi.nlm.nih.gov/pubmed/3361624

Chapter 13

Astrological natal charts of famous people

A natal chart is a zodiac wheel depicting the position of the planets at the exact moment of birth. It is very important to have the correct time and place when calculating a natal chart, otherwise the universal energies locked into your specific character at that time and place would be inaccurate. Every person is different, their unique biological expression of universal energies can be decoded and translated from a basic understanding of astrology and the ability to read a birth chart.

"Astrology is assured of recognition from psychology, without further restrictions, because astrology represents the summation of all the psychological knowledge of antiquity." CG Jung

"A child is born on that day and at that hour when the celestial rays are in mathematical harmony with his individual karma. His horoscope is a challenging portrait, revealing his unalterable past and its probable future results. But the natal chart can be rightly interpreted only by men of intuitive wisdom: these are few". Sri Yukteswar

"Astrology has no more useful function than this, to discover the inmost nature of a man and to bring it out into his consciousness, that he may fulfil it according to the law of light." Aleister Crowley (The complete Astrological Writings)

"Virtually every major move and decision the Reagan's made during my time as White House Chief of Staff was cleared in advance with a woman in San Francisco [Quiqley] who drew up horoscopes to make certain that the planets were in a favourable alignment for the enterprise" - Donald Regan[1]

The elites have used the ancient wisdom of astrology, the language of the Gods, for thousands of years, they prefer to keep it to themselves, they want the average person to be ignorant and handicapped, when it comes to esoteric occult wisdom you're not invited. The serfs are to be kept in the dark, to remain asleep, concentrating instead on their designated role, which is to serve the aspirations of the elite classes. Astrology is generally mocked and ridiculed by the vast majority, who know very little about it. Judged to be a pseudoscience, while exclusively understood and utilised by a small group of well-informed individuals.

They say the highest form of ignorance is when you reject something you know very little about, this is true with astrology. Chapter 2 gave a brief outline of what the natal chart represents and what we can expect to uncover from it. In this chapter, we shall look at a few examples of natal charts of famous people throughout history, people relevant to this topic and this book. The first chart is of Napoleon Bonaparte, born on August 15th 1769 on the Island of Corsica.

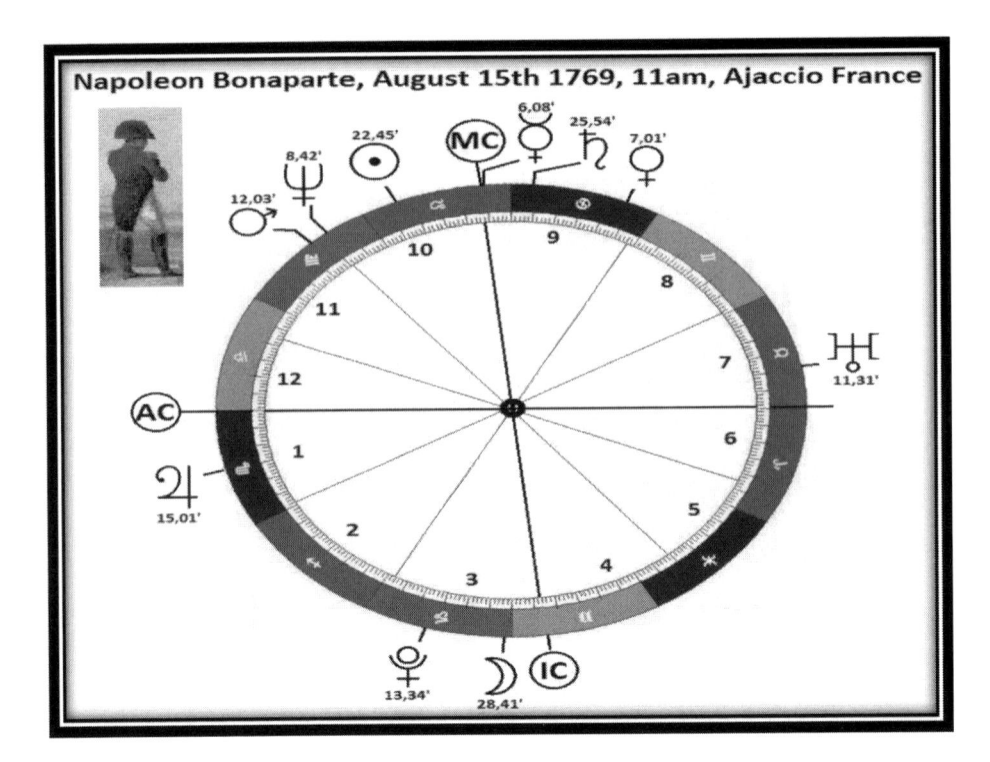

Most of Napoleon's major planets are in the southern hemisphere, this is at the top of his chart, denoting a person who is concerned with outside events, he prefers to be in the public realm as opposed to being at home, a career orientated individual.

Sun sign: This represents the external projection, focal consciousness the will and creative life force of the individual. Napoleon's Sun is in Leo, fixed, fire; individuals with a Leo Sun tend to have the characteristic traits of a Lion. It is a sign of strong will power; these are people who feel important, even conceited, with a noble inner core and determination to influence the world with big dreams, ambitions and plans for the future. Like the lion they can appear lazy and relaxed but when they spring into action it is done with intense determination, tenaciously holding onto situations and people for long periods, before giving up.

Moon sign: The Moon represents the Inner emotions, the subconscious. It's our deepest personal needs, habits, reactions and instincts. The Sun acts while the Moon reacts. Napoleon has his Moon in Capricorn; these people are generally calm, cool and collected, able to keep their emotions under control with a cool head in adverse conditions. This will quickly give them a reputation for being a pillar of strength. In order to feel secure, they plan well in advance, and have a need for recognition and respect from others.

Ascendant: This is what is coming into view from the universe, on the eastern horizon at the moment of birth. It represents the type of person we are trying to be. It shows our natural reactions to new people and situations. Napoleon's Ascendant is just entering the energy of Scorpio, signifying a person with a great deal of presence, a person who is not to be messed with, commanding respect and in some cases fear. They are people who get noticed, either loved or hated, with a strong desire to control their environment, naturally gifted at organisation and strategy.

Midheaven (MC Medium Coeli), this is the middle of the sky at the moment of birth. It represents career and social standing, our reputation and life's path. Napoleon's MC is also in Leo, giving him more than a lion's share of will power and tenacious determination, enabling him to attain the lofty goals in life, courageous, noble and professionally ambitious people, with great potential for leadership. They can see the big picture as well as the fine detail. They can be stubborn but are well equipped for taking control in a crisis. They possess a natural sense of timing but have the potential for over developed egos.

Planets in the twelve houses

Jupiter in the 1st house, Jupiter is the planet of abundance and expansiveness, the first house is the house of self. Napoleon has an abundance of self-belief and self-expansion. In the sign of Scorpio, it gives him a desire to expand the self and the focal consciousness.

Moon in the 3rd house, the house of communication, The Moon is the planet of emotional need and satisfaction. This person will be an emotional communicator, airing his views from within the subconscious. In Capricorn (I use), he will feel the need to use his emotional communication skills with others.

Saturn, Venus and Mercury in the 9th house, Saturn is the planet of structure, hard work, responsibility and organisation. Venus is the planet of love and liking, while Mercury is the planet of communication. The 9th house is the house of Philosophy, higher learning and travel. A person with these planets in the 9th house will work hard and structure their aspirations towards their particular philosophy, they like to travel and talk about travelling. They will love and like higher mind thinking and philosophical concepts. Gaining pleasure organising themselves in this area of life. In time Saturn's influence will manifest restrictions and frustration in this area too. The backdrop sign to this house is Cancer, this will give Napoleon a deep subconscious understanding of his philosophical approach, together with Mercury, stimulating his ability to communicate his knowledge and philosophy.

Sun in the 10th house, the Sun represents the will, the focal consciousness. The 10th house is the house of career, profession and social standing. This person has the will to succeed in his profession with a great capacity to lead others while finding it uncomfortable taking orders from someone else. They are people who function well in the public eye, competitive and authoritative. Also, being in the sign of Leo, this throws more will power into the mix.

Mars in the 11th house, Mars represents proactive energy and the 11th house is the house of friends, groups and organisations. This person will be proactive within groups and organisations, using co-operation and coordination to achieve their ambitions.

Napoleon's natal chart has three dominant signs and three dominant houses, which stand out more than the rest. These are signs and houses with the most elements in them. His dominant signs, in order, are Leo (I will), Capricorn (I use) and Scorpio (I desire). His dominant houses are 10 (career), 3 (communication) and 9 (philosophy/travel).

Consequently, the description of the planetary energies influencing this individual accurately reflect Napoleon's personal characteristics.

Main aspects: I shall concentrate on the two major conjunct aspects in Napoleon's birth chart. A conjunction is when two planets or points in the chart are together, within 10 degrees of one another. This combines the individual frequencies of the planets to create a unique combination of energies. Napoleon's Midheaven (MC) is conjunct with Mercury (communication), the mixture of these two puts emphasis on Napoleon's communication skills in the area of career, giving him a sharp clear mind, which he will use to get ahead in achieving his goals. The other aspect is a conjunction between Neptune (dreams/illusions) and Mars (proactive), this combination propels the individual in the direction of his dreams, finding the motivation and the tools to carry out somewhat illusory ambitions.

Napoleon's astrological body

Each sign represents different areas of the body, the feet in Pisces to the head in Aries.

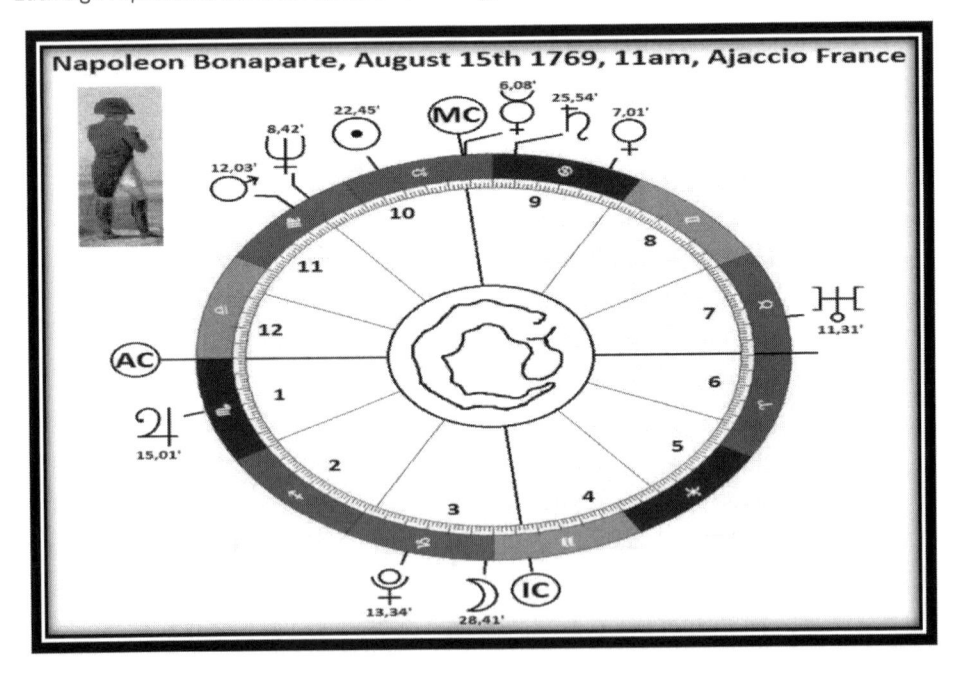

Napoleon has Uranus in the throat. This is a planet of surprises, out of the blue events, revolutionary and independent energy. This would manifest itself in a variety of unpredictable ways. According to French historian Henri Guillemin, It was common for Napoleon to shock people with unexpected comments, especially insults to the ladies.

"He was a man who didn't prevent himself from making barbaric noises, no matter where he was, reception or council of state".[2]

In Cancer Napoleon has the planets Venus and Saturn. This sign represents the chest and the stomach. Venus the energy of love and liking will evoke an appreciation for breasts and the chest. Breasts were very much in vogue after the revolution, the old whalebone and lace look was out while breasts were in. Not only did Napoleon proudly portray himself with his chest out like a robin, he most probably had a liking for women's breasts too.

"How happy I would be if I could assist you at your undressing, the little firm white breast, the adorable face, the hair tied up in a scarf a la Creole." - Napoleon writing to Josephine

Saturn on the other hand is the planet of restriction and frustration, possibly causing problems for him during his life. It's interesting to note that when reading his autopsy, carried out on May 6th 1821, his Doctors where of the opinion that he died from stomach cancer.

"Signed off by no fewer than seven doctors in attendance, that indicate Napoleon expired ultimately from stomach cancer. For the record, Napoleon's grandfather, father, his brother Lucien, and three of his sisters also died from stomach cancer." - Napoleon's autopsy[3]

His heart is heavily influenced by Mercury and the Sun. The Sun is the focal consciousness, the external will. Having this in Leo, the sign of the will, multiplies the person's will power; coupled with Mercury, the planet of communication, suggests that this individual shall impose his will with a strong heart/mind connection, making his will felt by all.

Napoleon has Mars energy in the intestines and gut. Mars is the planet of proactive, physical energy. People with a proactive gut are more likely to have large appetites, physically stimulating the intestines. His autopsy once again confirms this. His weight had increased over the years, from 67kg in 1800, to 90kg by 1820.

"Upon opening the abdomen, the omentum was found remarkably fat". [4]

Jupiter is found in Napoleon's sex organs, this denotes a person with an abundance of sexual energy and an expansive sexual appetite. The facts corroborate this. He was renowned for having a long string of affairs, it has even been suggested that he dabbled with homosexuality. The French historian Henri Guillemin goes into detail about Napoleon's affairs and also his incestual relations with his three sisters. Another French historian Frederic Masson (1847-1923) writes:

"Of course Bonaparte had mistresses, just like every other married man"-*"I couldn't even keep track of the number of affairs Napoleon was involved in"*. Frederic Masson

"They say Victor Hugo was a Satyr? He was an altar boy compared to Napoleon." "Of course there were actresses, Miss George, Miss Bourgoin and there were his employee's wives or should I say the wives of his ministers, high society women and not so high, brought in by his suppliers, Talleyrand, Duroc, Murat and Junot." Henri Guillemin

Josephine spread a rumour about Napoleon having sex with his three sisters; this is understandably when you consider his sisters didn't get along with Josephine. But Madame De Remusat did get along with the sisters, and she mentions it in her memoirs.

"The three sisters offered themselves to him, and finally Caroline has admitted it publically. She was very proud to say that she had sex with her brother." Henri Guillemin

"When he was at the academy, he became very close with Laugier De Bellecour, Laugier had a nick name, they called him "The Nymph". Gourgaud, who accompanies him at Saint Helena, was a homosexual. "Henri Guillemin

Finally we see the Moon in the area around Napoleons knees, in Capricorn. The Moon represents sensitivity, an area of his body which would either start out sensitive or become sensitive.

"During the battle for Toulon Napoleon was wounded several times. The first was on his forehead, and it bled profusely. On the night of December 16th his horse was shot out from under him and he was wounded in the chest, but it was minor. On December 17th, in the final assault on Fort Mulgrave, Napoleon suffered a bayonet thrust on the inner side of his left thigh just above his knee. It was so severe that for a time amputation of his leg was considered." - Friedman Peter[5]

Influential years

One cycle of the zodiac wheel can also represent an average life cycle of 72 years, each sign being 6 years of life. Starting at the Ascendant we go around in a clockwise direction, any planet in a particular year should have greater influence during that time period.

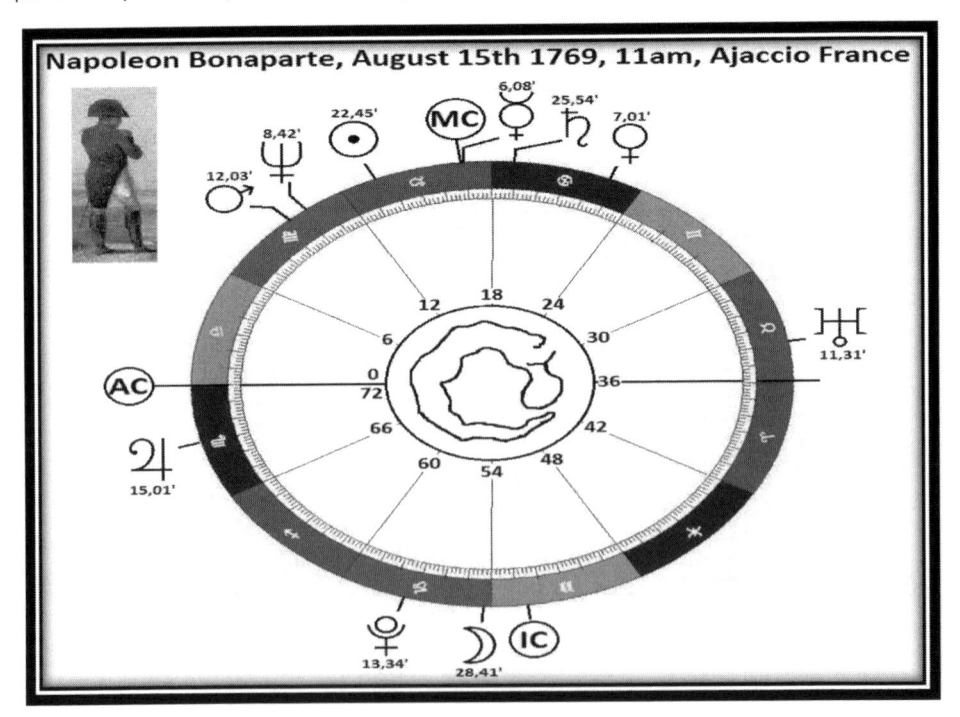

Mars appears in Napoleon's chart around the 9th year. The planet of proactivity and physical energy, situated within the mutable earth sign of Virgo. In 1778 Napoleon moved to France and secured a scholarship at the Royal Military College, he enrolled at the age of 9. Mars in Virgo (I examine) in the 9th year influences a physical mutable change in Napoleon's Earthly proximity.

In his 16th year the MC and Mercury play a major role in influencing events. The Midheaven (MC) represents career, our life's path. Mercury is the planet of communication. At the age of 16, on October 28, 1785, Napoleon graduates as Second Lieutenant in the artillery from Ecole Militaire and shortly after begins his life as a soldier.

Saturn appears in Napoleon's chart in his 19th year. Although this is the planet of restriction, frustration and limitation, Saturn also brings structure and meaning to our environment. The planet of responsibility, definition and self-control, it is also associated with authority. In a backdrop of the emotional water sign of Cancer (I feel). On July 14th 1789 Paris erupted into riots, the start of a ten year period of unrest, the revolution had begun.

The planet Venus appears around the age of 23, a planet of love and liking. During this time Napoleon witnesses the dethroning of King, Louis XVI along with the storming of the Tuileries Palace, he also moves back to Corsica with his family.

Uranus in Taurus (I have) influences Napoleons 33rd year, the planet of out of the blue events. The positive aspects of this planet's energetic frequencies are associated with enlightenment and progressiveness, whereas the negative expression is associated with revolution, rebellion and irresponsibility. On August 4, 1802, a new constitution is adopted, making Napoleon First Consul for life, effectively the King of France, in all but title.

Napoleon's descendent is between his 35th and 36th year. The descendent represents everyone outside of you; it represents what and whom you are attracted to. This is the year on December 2, 1804; Napoleon crowns himself Emperor in Notre-Dame Cathedral, Paris. The other interesting point to consider is the sign the descendent is placed. It is situated on the cusp between Aries (I am) and Taurus (I have). You couldn't pick a more suitable astrological chart position to be crowned Emperor.

From 36 to 42 Napoleon lives in his natal Aries years, from 1805 - 1811, the years of (I am), his ego must have been huge during that period. Following Aries, he moves into the Piscean years, from 1811 - 1817, the motto for Pisces is (I believe). Still with a strong belief in himself and his ability, he over reaches his capacity and is finally defeated on June 18th 1815, at the Battle of Waterloo. He is exiled to the Island of Saint Helena on October 16th 1815, where he spends the rest of his life.

Napoleon died in 1821 at the age of 51, he dies in the 4th zodiac house in Aquarius, the 4th house represents home environment. The Imum Coeli (IC), the opposite of the Midheaven (MC) is situated very close to his moment of death. The IC symbolises the need for security, home and family. It also describes the circumstances that we encounter during the final phase of our lives.

It is clear to anyone with an ounce of awareness and an open mind that the natal chart of Napoleon is an accurate reflection of his personality and characteristics, the chart would not be suitable for any other person. From this we can see how the symphonies of energies surrounding us determine and influence what and who we are. We are not born into this world but out of its energetic kaleidoscope of possibilities, generated from the position and interaction of huge heavenly bodies gracefully moving through space.

Adolf Hitler

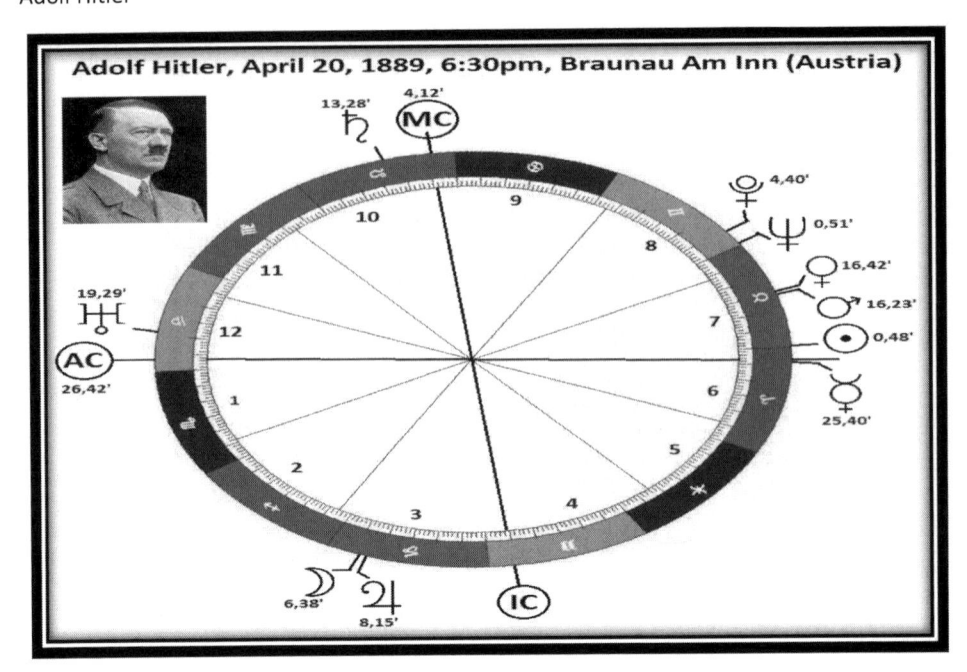

Adolf Hitler, April 20, 1889, 6:30pm, Braunau Am Inn (Austria)

The main bulk of Hitler's planets are positioned in the western and southern hemispheres of the chart. Planets in the southern hemisphere, the top half of the chart represent a person who likes to be out in the public realm, a person who takes action, career orientated as opposed to being an introverted homely creature. Many planets in the western hemisphere, denotes a person who is the opposite of self-sufficient, a person who relies heavily on others to fulfil their life's purpose and objectives.

Hitler's Sun sign, his external projection of focal consciousness, is 0.48 degrees Taurus, this puts his Sun position on the cusp of Aries (I am) and Taurus (I have). These people are natural leaders, a powerful force to be reckoned with. They can be authoritative and bold. They need to watch out because they have a tendency for being too forceful, steam-rolling over other people's opinions and desires. He has the mutable decan energy from Aries (I am) combined with the cardinal decan of Taurus (I have), creating the energy of someone who will find a way to get what they want. Hitler's Sun position is in the same place on the zodiac as the crowning moment of Napoleon when he became Emperor.

Hitler's Moon sign, his inner emotions and subconscious can be found in Capricorn. The same as Napoleon, these people feel the need to be productive and useful. They keep their emotions under control, appearing calm, cool and collected. They are good planners and have a subconscious need for recognition and respect, seen by many as pillars of strength in the community.

Hitler's Ascendant (the type of person he projects to others), his natural reaction to new people and situations, is situated in Libra (I compliment), a balanced sign which sees both sides of things. These people come across as nice, pleasant and fair, attracting others to them without effort. They give the impression that they can solve problems and smooth things out. Most Libra Ascendants pay a great deal of attention to their appearance, their clothes, their hair and even their style of walk; they are diplomatic and persuasive people.

His Midheaven (MC), which represents the career, social standing, reputation and life's path, is situated in Leo (I will). Once again, the same as Napoleon, having huge will power and tenacity to achieve the higher goals they set themselves, courageous, ambitious and noble, they are people with a sense of destiny for greatness. They are highly organised who understand the bigger picture as well as the fine details. These people can also become stubborn, fixed in their minds about a direction they wish to go in.

Planets in the twelve houses

Jupiter and the Moon are in Hitler's 3rd house, the house of communication. Jupiter the planet of abundance and expansion will give him enormous natural ability to communicate to others. The Moon represents the subconscious, the inner emotions, also in Capricorn (I use); he will use communication effectively to express his emotions.

Mercury is in Hitler's 6th house, the house of health and service to others. Mercury the planet of communication will influence Hitler to communicate about these aspects of life, being of service to others, his health or as he saw it, the health of the nation, this is in a backdrop sign of Aries (I am), this would play out as "I am going to communicate my service to others and the health of the nation".

The 7th house is the house of others and partnerships, Hitler has 3 planets here, the Sun (will), Mars (proactive/action) and Venus (love and liking). He has strong will power and proactive energy when getting involved in partnerships of any kind, political partners or sexual partners. Venus energy will make him happy and like the idea of being involved in partnerships.

In Hitler's 8th house we see Neptune and Pluto, the house of rebirth, transformation and sex. Neptune has the energy of illusion and dreams, Pluto is the planet of transformation, endings, renewal and rebirth, its negative aspect is general destruction. These people pay attention to their dreams and like to analyse them. They lean towards sexual fantasies and role play. They feel that their needs at this level are out of reach. They may not see their partners clearly due to their need for extraordinary or fantastical experiences. It's interesting to note here that in Walter C. Langer's 1943 report for the American Office of Strategic Services (OSS), he describes Hitler as having repressed homosexual tendencies and suggested that he was an impotent coprophile.

Saturn is in the 10th house, the planet of seriousness, responsibility, limitation, restriction, structure and meaning. The 10th house is the house of career and social status. People with Saturn in the tenth house take their careers and social standing more seriously than others. They have an innate desire to lead. They can shoulder immense responsibility with ease. Saturn will also bring frustration to this area, in time.

Finally, in Hitler's 12th house we see Uranus, The planet of out of the blue, surprising events, rebellion and originality. The 12th house represents the house of self-undoing and karma. It is where we sabotage ourselves, and become the creators of our own downfall, it also represents secret enemies. So, Hitler's downfall will essentially come from secret enemies, out of the blue events and surprises.

Dominant signs and dominant houses

Hitler's dominant signs are Taurus (I have), Libra (I compliment) and Leo (I will), a person who will stubbornly defend their territory just like the bull of Taurus protecting its field. He will complement the people who surround him with his balancing Libran diplomatic skills; he shall possess strong will power from the energy of Leo, the backbone to fulfilling his ambitions. His dominant houses are 7 (partnerships), 6 (service to others) and 3 (communication). He needs to be in some form of partnership with others to achieve his life's goals, to feel that he is of service to others, and have good communicative skills to achieve his objectives.

Main aspects

Hitler is unusual with six conjunctions, the three strongest ones are Mars (proactive) and Venus (love/liking) in Taurus (I have), this is a person who is proactive in doing what makes him happy, but can come across as selfish, it is his way or the highway. The Sun (will) is conjunct with Mercury (communication) in Aries (I am), suggesting this person has great capacity to communicate his will, but can come across as domineering and forceful. The Moon (internal emotion) is conjunct with Jupiter (abundance) in the 3rd house of communication and in Capricorn (I use). This person will have an abundance of emotion and passion when communicating, he will use it to its full potential.

Hitler's astrological body

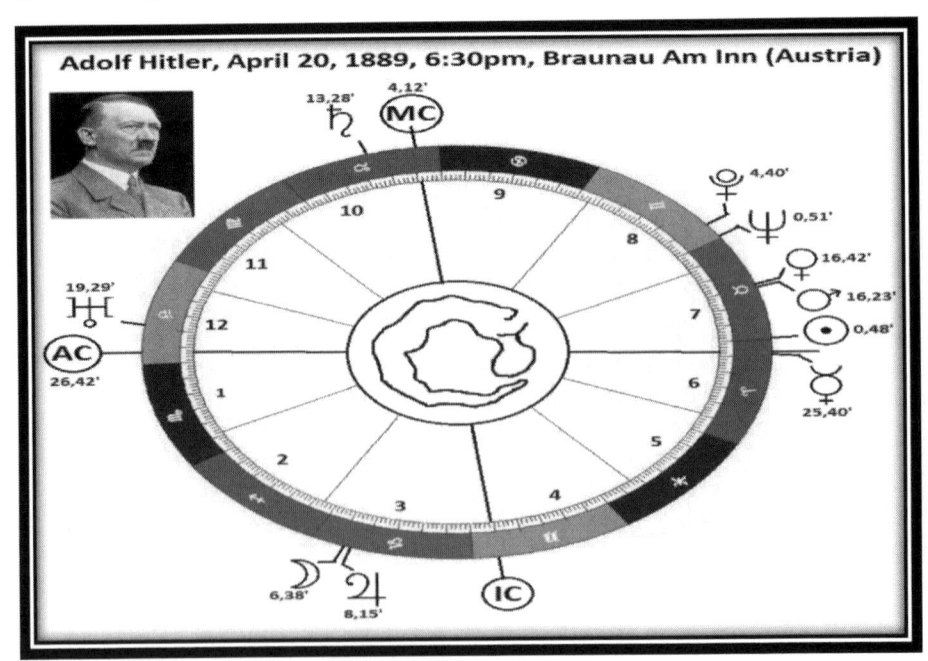

Mercury (communication) is in Hitler's head; his main medium of communication is through his head. It's no surprise that he is one of the most recognised people in history.

The Sun (will), Mars (proactive/physical) and Venus (love/liking), are all present in Hitler's throat. This is a person who will use his voice proactively (Mars), to express his will (Sun) which he loves and likes (Venus).

Hitler has both Pluto and Neptune in his arms, planets of illusion, dreams and transformation. Is this the real influence behind the Nazi salute?

Saturn is in Leo, the area of the zodiac associated with the Heart, Chest, Spine, Spinal Column and Upper back, the planet of frustration and restriction can cause problems for Hitler in these areas at some point in his life.

In an interview in 1985 one of Hitler's doctors, Gunther Schenck recalling Hitler's last few days in the bunker. "**His spine was hunched, his shoulder blades protruded from his bent back, and he collapsed his shoulders like a turtle... I was looking into the eyes of death.**"

Schenck also said that Hitler had three major illnesses, "**Colitis, which probably represented the irritable bowel syndrome and included constipation and diarrhoea, as well as two maladies that were not diagnosed until 1944: arteriosclerotic heart disease and Parkinson`s disease.**"[6]

Uranus is situated in Libra, the area of the body associated with the kidneys; Uranus is the planet of surprises and out of the blue events.

Schenck said. "**Hitler`s initial complaints were the colitis that had bothered him for years, a mild kidney condition and a problem with a leg injury suffered during World War I.**"[7]

Finally, we see the Moon and Jupiter in the first portion of Capricorn, the area associated with the knees and above the knees. Jupiter is the planet of expansion and abundance, maybe the influence behind Corporal Hitler becoming a dispatch runner for the German Army during WW1. The Moon is the planet of emotion and sensitivity. On October 7th 1916 near Bapauma, France, Hitler was wounded by a shell blast, above the knee, in the left thigh, eventually healing but making the area far more sensitive.

Influential years

In 1903 Saturn appears in Hitler's birth chart, the planet of restriction, frustration and seriousness. This is the year his father dies. It is interesting to note that this year falls in the backdrop of Leo; a sign ruled by the Sun, the Sun happens to also represent the father figure in a person's life.

The Midheavern (MC) which represents the career or life's path is in Hitler's 16th year. In 1905 Hitler lived in Vienna on an orphan's pension, a bohemian lifestyle with some occasional support from his mother. He was twice rejected from the Academy of Fine Arts in Vienna (1907 - 1908). The MC is 9 degrees away from Saturn; this is within range of what is known as a conjunction, when two planets or aspects in the heavens are close enough to mix energies, forming a union. Here Saturn will influence Hitler's career with its restrictive and frustrating energy which maybe the underlining reason for his disappointments. In the sign of Leo, he has the will to succeed but Saturn restricts the outcome.

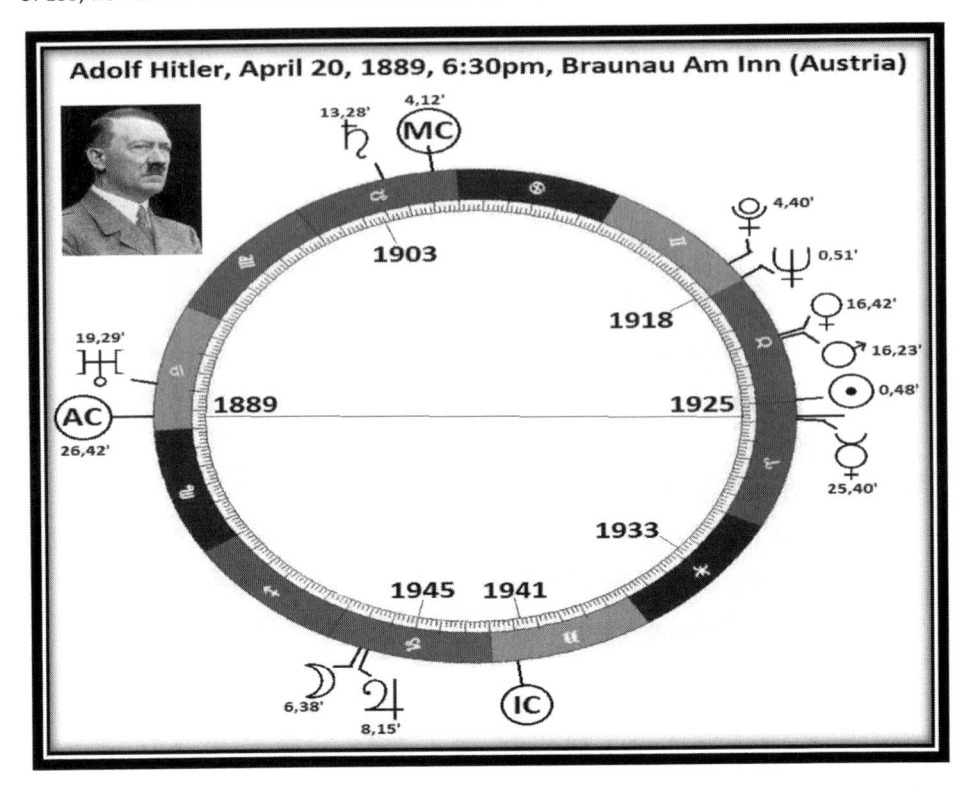

Adolf Hitler, April 20, 1889, 6:30pm, Braunau Am Inn (Austria)

World War 1 breaks out in 1914 which begins in Gemini on Hitler's chart. The sign of duality, split mind and split thinking, life or death, war or peace, win or lose. This is also associated with the arms and hands. Gemini is also the sign of thinking. During the war Hitler would have had a great deal of time to ponder, to think and reflect on his circumstances and that of the German people. Two planets influence the final stage of Hitler's war from 1917 to 1918, the planets of Pluto (Transformation, endings and new beginnings) and Neptune (Illusions/dreams), these mark the last phase, the turnaround from possible victory to defeat, the illusion of winning, and a new beginning with the end of fighting on November 11th 1918.

During Hitler's Taurus (I have) years, the planets Venus (love and Liking) and Mars (proactive/physical) join in a conjunction between 1920-21, This is the time the Nazi party is formed, this also happens to be in the zodiac house of partnerships. Hitler throws his Mars energy into the party and likes what he is doing. Taurus is a sign associated with the throat, the vocal side of an individual. Hitler develops into a great speaker. He recalls in his book "*Mein Kampf*" the first occasion he addressed a meeting at a beer cellar.

"I spoke for thirty minutes, and what before I had simply felt within me, without in any way knowing it, was now proved by reality: I could speak! After thirty minutes, the people in the small room were electrified and the enthusiasm was first expressed by the fact that

my appeal to the self-sacrifice of those present led to the donation of three hundred marks." Adolf Hitler (*Mein Kampf*)

After a failed coup in 1923, Hitler goes on trial the following year. He decides to defend himself in court. The Sun (The self) is prominent at this point in Hitler's chart. It is all about Hitler, the making or breaking of the self. On the cusp of Aries (I am) and Taurus (I have), the throat and the head are the major body parts at this time. Leading and propelling Hitler's vocal skills and his will in this court room drama.

"Overnight, Hitler became a nationally and internationally known figure due to massive press coverage. The judges in this sensational trial were chosen by a Nazi sympathizer in the Bavarian government. They allowed Hitler to use the courtroom as a propaganda platform from which he could speak at any length on his own behalf, interrupt others at any time and even cross examine witnesses."

"Rather than deny the charges, Hitler admitted wanting to overthrow the government and outlined his reasons, portraying himself as a German patriot and the democratic government itself, its founders and leaders, as the real criminals."

"I alone bear the responsibility. But I am not a criminal because of that. If today I stand here as a revolutionary, it is as a revolutionary against the revolution. There is no such thing as high treason against the traitors of 1918."[8]

On April 4th 1924, Hitler was sentenced to 5 years in prison for treason.

In 1925 Mercury comes into the picture. The planet of communication, in Aries (I am). At this time Hitler wrights his famous book about his struggle (*Mein Kampf*).

Hitler becomes Chancellor and leader of Germany in 1933, in the sign of Pisces (I believe). At this point he firmly believes in what he is doing, for the greater good of Germany and its people. This is also at the start of his 4th house, the house representing the home and home environment, where our foundations are laid. It also represents family history, cultural and social norms, our ancestry, roots and heritage. All these aspects will be cultivated during this time along with Hitler's plan for a Greater Germania. The sign behind the fourth house goes from Pisces (I believe) to Aquarius (I know) a definitive shift from apprehensive belief in oneself, to an all-knowing arrogance. An interesting side note, the symbol for Aquarius has modest similarities to the symbol for the Nazi SS.

Symbol for Aquarius and Nazi SS

The Imum Coeli is situated around 1941, this is opposite to the Midheaven (MC). It is the point which describes the circumstances that we encounter during the final phase of our lives. On June 22nd 1941, Operation Barbarossa begins with the German invasion of the Soviet Union. This turns out to be a major contribution to Hitler's downfall, as with Napoleon, Russia turns out to be too much for the Germans. The other factor which sealed Hitler's fate came on December 11th 1941, a few days after Pearl Harbour, Hitler and Mussolini declared war on the United States.

From 1942 to the end of WW2 Hitler spends his final years in Capricorn (I use), which is in his 3rd house of communication. Capricorn is a cardinal earth sign, it is proactive in an earthly physical sense. At this time Hitler is using the whole nation, communicating his orders to defend the earth which they stand on to the last man.

Although there is a consensus amongst astrologers, that the precise time of death is almost impossible to determine from chart analysis, it is not impossible to predict the method of death. The 8th house is the house of birth, death and rebirth; it represents how we shake off the old to make way for the new, and how we end relationships or jobs etc. A planet within the 8th house generally has greater influence than the ruling planet of the sign it falls in. If you are a person who frequently experience sudden breakdowns in your relationships you can also expect this type of scenario to play out in your exit from this physical realm. The 7/8th house cusp carries more weight in this matter than the 8th/9th house cusp.

Death in the 8th house

Sign (Ruler)	Description
Aries (Mars)	Sudden, possibly violent, head or brain configured
Taurus (Venus)	Slow, generally peaceful, maybe due to overindulgence, throat
Gemini (Mercury)	Possible multiple causes, mental deterioration, lungs and breathing
Cancer (Moon)	At home, overeating may be a factor, stomach
Leo (Sun)	Probable cardiac problems, some drama
Virgo (Hygeia)	Often a quiet demise in modest circumstances, not dramatic, digestive system
Libra (Venus)	Not difficult, maybe related to kidney function
Scorpio (Ploto)	Possibly confined or violent, alcohol
Sagittarius (Jupiter)	Abroad or away from home, possibly overindulgence
Capricorn (Saturn)	Slow degenerative demise probably in old age
Aquarius (Uranus)	Sudden, possibly unusal demise, rare disease, blood problems
Pisces (Neptune)	Confused; cause of death obscure or uncertain, alcohol, poison, drugs, mistake, suicide

Transformation
Rebirth Death
Sex
9 8
7

Napoleon Bonaparte

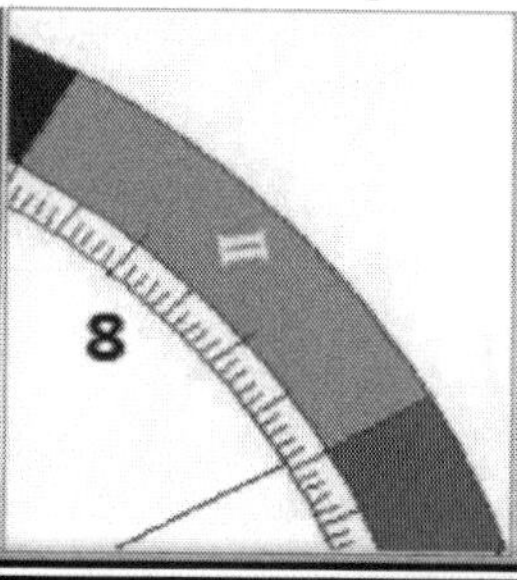

Napoleon 8th house begins on the cusp of Taurus and Gemini.

Taurus (Venus): slow, generally peaceful, maybe due to overindulgence, throat.

Gemini (Mercury): Possible multiple causes, mental deterioration possible,

lungs and breathing.

Napoleon died peacefully at home from stomach cancer.

Adolf Hitler

Hitler has Neptune and Pluto at the front of his 8th house.

Pisces (Neptune): Confused; cause of death obscure or uncertain, alcohol, poison, drugs, mistake, suicide.

Scorpio (Pluto): Possibly confined or violent, alcohol.

Hitler was reported to have died from suicide in 1945, a combination of poison and gun shot to the head.

John F Kennedy

John F Kennedy has Mars, Mercury and Jupiter right at the forefront of his 8th house.

Aries (Mars): sudden, possibly violent, head or brain configured.

Gemini (Mercury): Possible multiple causes, mental deterioration possible, lungs and breathing.

Sagittarius (Jupiter): Abroad or away from home, possibly overindulgence.

John F Kennedy was assassinated while on a visit to Dallas in 1963. The fatal shot was to the head.

John Lennon

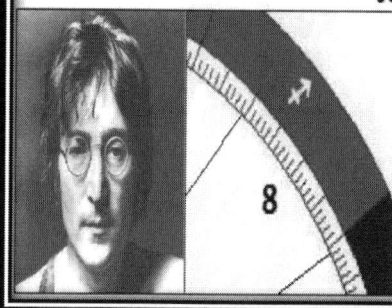

John Lennon's 8th house begins on the cusp of Scorpio and Sagittarius.

Scorpio (Pluto): Possibly confined or violent, alcohol.

Sagittarius (Jupiter): Abroad or away from home, possibly overindulgence.

John Lennon was shot in the entrance area to his New York apartment in 1980.

Princess Diana

Princess Diana has Uranus, Mars and Pluto in her 8th house.
Aquarius (Uranus): Sudden, possibly unusual demise, rare diseases, blood problems.
Aries (Mars): sudden, possibly violent, head or brain configured.
Scorpio (Pluto): Possibly confined or violent, alcohol.

Princess Diana died in a car crash in Paris 1997.

Elvis Presley

Elvis Presley has Pluto in Cancer within his 8th house.
Scorpio (Pluto): Possibly confined or violent, alcohol.
Cancer (Moon): At home, overeating may be a factor, stomach.
Elvis Presley had a heart attack, brought on by overeating and an unhealthy life style, he died on the toilet at home, he weighed approximately 260 lb's when he went.

When an individual's natal chart is analysed and broken down, it paints a picture of who you are dealing with. Unaware of how the universe works, most people assume we are only products of our upbringing. This is true to some extent, but knowledge and understanding of this energy allows us, in advance, to see deeply what and who we are. It is a useful tool and our own personal biological and emotional user guide.

Giordano Bruno

The Italian philosopher and scientist Giordano Bruno, born in 1548, believed that the only way human civilisation was to survive, thrive and liberate itself, was to cast off the perverted shackles of bigotry, ignorance and superstition which surround all man's religions. He called for the return to ancient universal wisdom and the science of light and philosophy, the backbone of Egyptian, Greek and Roman civilisation. For this he was tracked down by the Roman Catholic Church and burnt alive, tying his tongue during the execution, to prevent him from communicating with the crowd as they watched his agonising death. He died on 17th Feb 1600.[9]

Giordano Bruno 1548 - 1600

Notes for chapter 13

(1) Donald Regan. For the Record: From Wall Street to Washington, (San Diego: Harcourt Trade Publishers, 1988)

(2) Henri Guillemin, French (1903-1992), Napoleon sex life and personality reviled, TV presentation, https://www.youtube.com/watch?v=mcjoErIQRXM

(3) Friedman Peter, Napoleons Death, 2011, Napoleon.org, http://www.napoleon.org/en/reading_room/articles/files/479165.asp

(4) Ibid

(5) Ibid

(6) Dennis L. Breo, (copyright) 1985, American Medical Association. Hitlers Medical file, Chicago Tribune, http://articles.chicagotribune.com/1985-10-14/features/8503090891_1_dr-theodor-morell-dr-ernst-gunther-schenck-drug-firms

(7) Ibid

(8) Jabril Faraj, Adolf Hitler goes on trial for treason, The history place, World History Project, http://worldhistoryproject.org/1924/2/26/adolf-hitler-goes-on-trial-for-treason

(9) Frank Gaglioti, A man of insight and courage, 16 February 2000, Published by the International Committee of the Fourth International (ICFI). https://www.wsws.org/en/articles/2000/02/brun-f16.html

Chapter 14. Astro-geopolitics

Most nations have adopted a political system based on their religious heritage, formulating laws and social guidelines reflecting these beliefs. The lives of its citizens, who are mainly unaware of the planetary forces influencing their cultural development, continue to fuel their political machines without any thought or consideration as to the nature of its construct. Western politics evolved from a Christian/Jupiter, Judaic/Saturn foundation, the expansive and abundant characteristics of Jupiter, a gas giant, helped to propel the Christian religion and consequently its political ideologies throughout the known world, eventually becoming the largest of all the religious and political systems. Allied with Saturn's characteristics of organisation and control , this form of political ideology has been a major contributor towards the modern globalisation project.

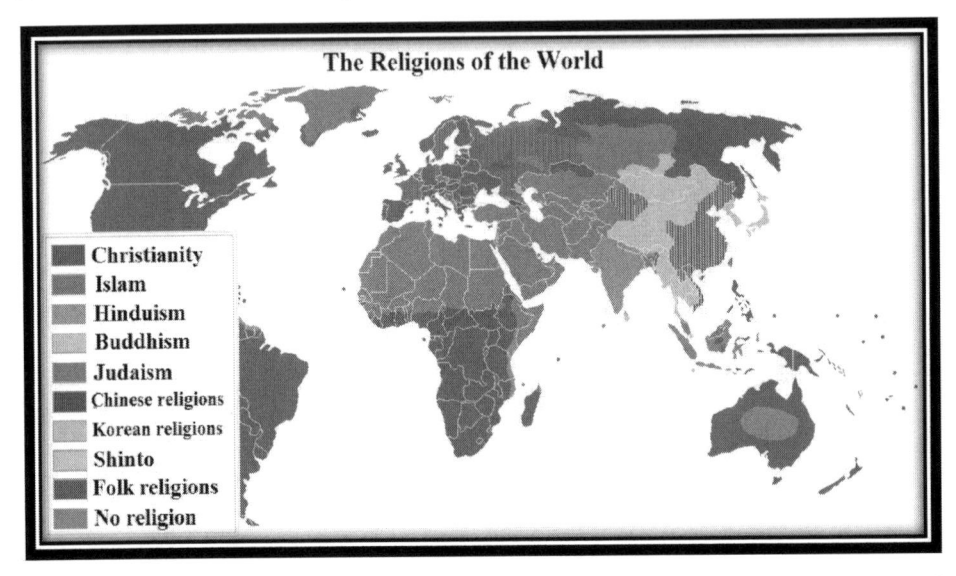

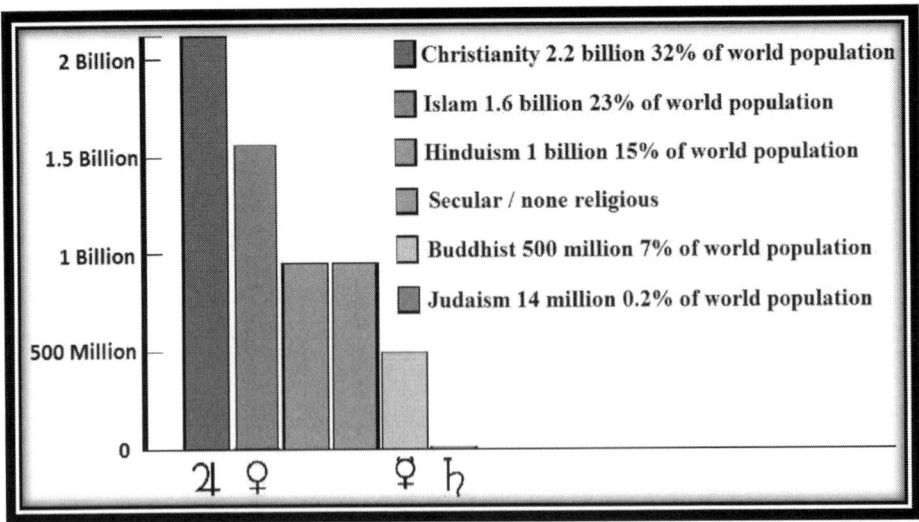

The Religions of the World

- Christianity
- Islam
- Hinduism
- Buddhism
- Judaism
- Chinese religions
- Korean religions
- Shinto
- Folk religions
- No religion

- Christianity 2.2 billion 32% of world population
- Islam 1.6 billion 23% of world population
- Hinduism 1 billion 15% of world population
- Secular / none religious
- Buddhist 500 million 7% of world population
- Judaism 14 million 0.2% of world population

The largest and oldest denomination of Christianity is the Roman Catholic Church. As the Roman Empire expanded, churches sprang up in most major cities under the empires rule. The mother of all these churches was situated in Jerusalem, but after the Romans destroyed the city in 70AD, the church in Rome became the next best thing. In 313 AD Emperor Constantine published the "*Edict of Milan*",[1] this gave legal status to Christianity and paved the way for it to become the state religion. This new alliance between religion and politics gave the Roman Catholic's the authority to persecute all its enemies in an effort to maintain and expand its sphere of influence, led by their supreme authority figure, known as the Pope. From his headquarters in Vatican City new and inventive ways were designed to advance this Jupitarian religion, claiming it to be the only true Christian denomination. The word Catholic is derived from the Greek word "καθολικός" (Katholikos) meaning "universal", ironic when you consider its subtle deviation from universal holistic wisdom to monotheistic Jupiter worship.

Jupiter is the ruler of two zodiac houses, Pisces and Sagittarius, signs associated with **belief and seeking,** both mutable signs, one fire and one water. These signs are expressions of intuition, belief and imagination, together with an active and optimistic approach to adventure and world exploration. With all these traits aligned with the expansive nature of Jupiter, it was no surprise to find any religious/political system associating itself with this energy growing exponentially throughout the world during this time. In 1610 Galileo named the 6th closest moon of Jupiter and 6th largest moon in the solar system Europa. The Jewish attachment to Saturn has brought about many of those characteristics in the evolution and development of Judaism, the limiting and restrictive nature of Saturn has placed the Jews in the minority with only 0.2% of the world's population compared with 32% for the Jupitarian/Christians. Jewish discipline, structure and hard work enabled them to survive even though environmental factors in many cities throughout Europe restricted their ability to conduct business on a level playing field. In many cases they found themselves having to perform usury as a necessity to survive. The Jewish people with no homeland used money as a form of security, a prop to bring some form of stability to their otherwise insecure lives. Lending money developed and grew from simple goldsmiths to large international banking corporations we see today. The Judaic/Saturnites realised they had mastered control of themselves but not the people around them, what they needed was allies, they also realised that the lender is always master over the borrower. Over time the opportunity presented itself for usury to encircle European governments and monarchs in debt, transferring more power into the hands of the lenders. The Saturnites would lend to all sides and persuasions, even both sides of one conflict. The expansive nature of the Jupitarians made them a favoured choice when choosing a strong alliance, both sides needed each other to survive and grow. The Jupitarians could expand their empire with money supplied by the Saturnites, while the Saturnites would be allowed to prosper unmolested in the majority of Jupitarian controlled colonies, implementing usury wherever they went. The Judaic/Christian alliance was a natural development out of the biblical alliance of the Old and New Testaments, the two largest planets in the solar system working together to dominate the world, a partnership which is now at the forefront of the globalisation project.

Venus worshiping Islam accounts for 1.6 billion people, 23% of the world's population, on the whole a peaceful and traditional way of life, complementing the environment. Many

Muslim countries have a strong theocratic dimension to their countries political structure, keeping the Islamic faith at the forefront of Muslim life. They understand the expansive nature of Christianity and the controlling influence Judaism/Saturn worship can have over their lives. They choose to limit their involvement in the adventures of the Judaic/Christian alliance, choosing instead to express themselves through the energetic characteristics of Venus. Both Taurus and Libra are ruled by Venus, and like the bull in the field, the Muslims are happy to be left alone to live their lives how they see fit. The bull is not expansive, he has no desire to take over the field next to him, he will compliment his surroundings, but if you try and take over his field you may be in for a nasty surprise. Muslims are still forbidden to involve themselves in usury; the Quran is quite specific on this matter.

"Allah does not bless usury, and he causes charitable deeds to prosper, and Allah does not love any ungrateful sinner." (Quran, Al-Baqarah, 2: 276)

The Christians were against usury in the early years and throughout the medieval period, only later, during the Commercial Revolution was it allowed, when it was practicable for the Christians and the Jews to work together, bolstering their own ambitions. The Muslims have not deviated from the teachings in the Quran; the majority still see usury as a mechanism of enslavement. This has become an obstacle for the Jupatarian/Saturnine globalisation project, seeking to shackle all humanity under debt slavery, to a few powerful men at the top. Since the 9/11 attacks in New York, Muslims around the world are steadily and progressively being vilified by western propaganda, western controlling elites are adamant that nothing will hold back globalisation, not even Allah. They are gambling on subduing the Islamic world into submission, resistance is not an option. Iraq, Afghanistan, Libya, Syria, Yemen, Lebanon, Egypt, Gaza, the list goes on. Iran is the Jewel in their Islamic crown. The war hawks in the United States would like nothing more than to eradicate Islam from the Earth; the Muslim approach to usury is the main resistance holding back global domination of debt slavery. The tiny planet of Venus, representing the energy of love and liking, is up against the two biggest gas giants in our solar system.

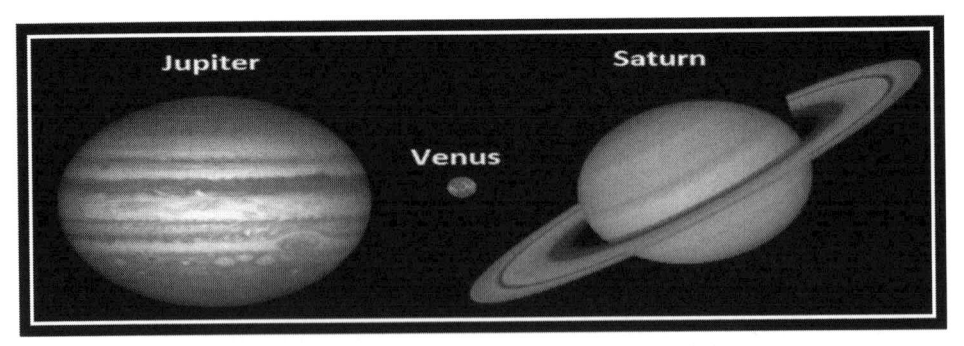

Western propaganda inverts, 180 degrees, the whole concept and energies associated with Islam, determined to sow the seeds of hate in the minds of its followers and the children under its influence. The characteristics of love, liking, having and complimenting are now portrayed by western propagandists as hate, dislike, needing and disharmony, the same demonising tactics used on Germany during WW1 and WW2, and the same vilifying tactics use to paint the Soviet Union in a bad light during the cold war. The controlling elites have mastered the art of getting their enemies entangled in conflicts and wars, all for political reasons, and for the purpose of opening up new opportunities for international financiers and corporations. Many people in the west are now fearful of Muslims, absorbing the perverted propaganda which makes them look outside themselves, towards their own governments for protection, the same institutions propagating the fear. Most people involved in various forms of religion are civilised, moral and spiritual, a small percentage take it to the extreme, this is true in most walks of life, the fanatic is common place in all aspects of society. From 9/11 onwards there seems to be a conscious effort by certain elements within the Judaic/Christian world to associate the Islamic faith, as a whole, with a minority of extreme Muslim fundamentalists. It is a technique which works predominantly on the simple minded. Unfortunately, over the past few decades, this now represents a large number of people throughout the western hemisphere. People are people, no matter where they are born or what group they associate themselves with. Muslims are no more extreme than Christians or Jews, extremists can be found in all religions, it is not necessarily the religion which makes them extreme it is their underlining character. If the same person took up golf or knitting, I would suspect they would approach both these activities with equal amounts of extreme vigour. The truth is that Christians can be just as psychopathic, with a long track record for being more evil than the devil they turn from. If we look at the statistics we find that Christians are 7 times more violent than Muslims. It is the Muslims who should be frightened of the Christians not the other way around. Extremism of any kind can be utilised by malevolent organisations and secret societies into pushing forward their own extreme aspirations and objectives, these people can be brainwashed into killing while naively believing the cause to be genuine and righteous.

"Seven times more people have died in Christian wars: 113.8 million compared to the 16.4 million who died in Muslim wars. There are more Christians, but only about 50% more, nothing like seven times more."[2]

According to the Centre for Research on Globalisation, American's alone have killed up to 30 million people all over the world, with an estimated 90% of them being civilians. They have initiated 201 armed conflicts out of the 240 which have occurred from 1945 to 2001.[3]

"Why of course the people don't want war. Why should some poor slob on a farm want to risk his life in a war when the best he can get out of it is to come back to his farm in one piece? Naturally the common people don't want war neither in Russia, nor in England, nor for that matter in Germany. That is understood. But, after all, it is the leaders of the country who determine the policy and it is always a simple matter to drag the people along, whether it is a democracy, or a fascist dictatorship, or a parliament, or a communist dictatorship. Voice or no voice, the people can always be brought to the bidding of the leaders. That is easy. All you have to do is tell them they are being attacked, and denounce the peacemakers for lack of patriotism and exposing the country to danger. It works the same in any country." Hermann Goering

Wheels within wheels

This moment, the now, is the present moving through space, mixing with energetic forces and frequencies on its journey into the future. The cyclical order of the zodiac, a perpetual loop changing throughout the Great Year, is an important expression of nature's characteristics and cycles. The Age or epoch one is in will be influenced greatly by its ruling planet, i.e. Jupiter in Pisces. Within that epoch another 12 zodiacal divisions can be created spanning the Age, and each subsequent portion can also be divided by another 12 divisions, and so on. Wheels within wheels, from the Great Year all the way down to a clock face with its 60 second cosmic cycle. An experienced chart reader can appreciate the universal forces at play behind geopolitical events. Universal energy influences the biological focal consciousness and the subconscious. The geopolitical world is a projected reality emanating from the collective consciousness of active and energised human participants.

"We are what we think. All that we are arises with our thoughts. With our thoughts we make the world." Gautama Buddha

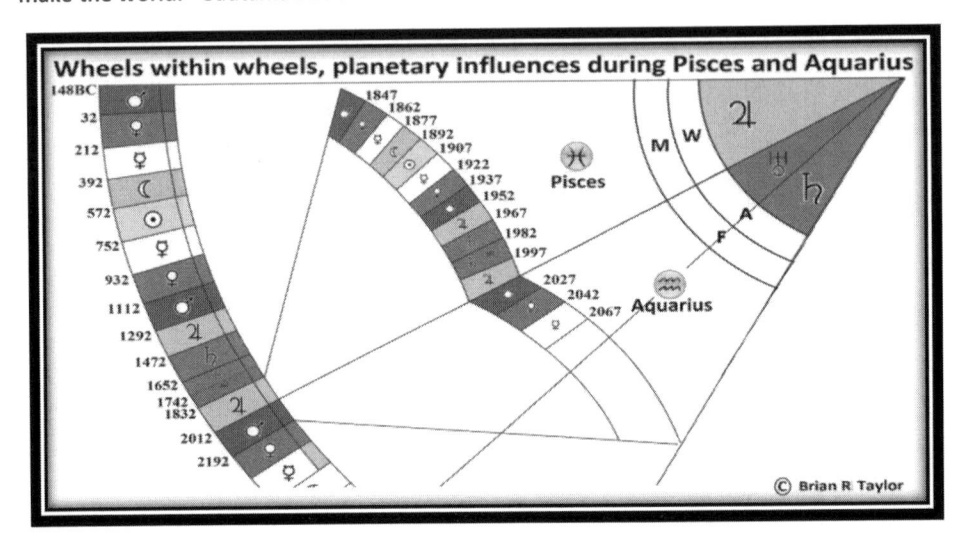

Wheels within wheels, planetary influences during Pisces and Aquarius

To understand the chart above, we need to break down the main planetary influences during any given time period. During the 2150 years of Pisces, Jupiter was the master of the house. That whole-time period was overshadowed with Jupiterian energy, together with the outer wheel are inner wheels of less significance, but significant enough to be noticeable, giving the observer an insight as to what to expect during any given time period. We are now in the crossover between Pisces and Aquarius, we have a new benchmark, 2012, thanks to the Mayan calendar and the Popes resignation of his Jupiterian throne. If we take a trip back in time we can see the significance of the inner and outer wheels/zodiacs as they turn during the Age of Pisces.

148 BC- 32 AD: Mars the God of war, the start of a new zodiac cycle in Aries, cardinal fire, a proactive frequency of movement and physical energy. During this time, we see the Roman Empire expand its physical influence throughout the Mediterranean. The Roman republic had established its supremacy in the region. By 133 BC Rome had conquered Spain and found itself in a cycle of perpetual war in one place or another. The population of the capital had now grown to over 100,000 people, considered large in those days. Macedonia, Greece and Carthage were annexed; only one kingdom remained a challenge to Roman supremacy,

Pontus and the Hellenistic Mithradates to the east. In 88 BC, the Mithradates attacked and overran the Asian provinces controlled by Rome, 60,000 Roman citizens were executed. By 86 BC Greece fell into the hands of the Mithradates putting great strain on the young Roman Empire. Although Rome was under pressure from civil strife, they managed to organise a counter attack, defeating the Mithradates to restore their eastern frontiers, by 66 BC the threat from the east was dissolved and the coast from Pontus to Syria was annexed to Rome. Under the leadership of Julius Caesar (49 BC – 44 BC) Rome managed to conquer Gaul, they even succeeded in conducting multiple raids on Britain. During this period rival generals were competing for power, the republic began to fragment, with its final end after the civil wars of 49-30 BC and absolute power in the hands of Octavian, the first Emperor of Rome. In 27 BC he was given the title Augustus which means "great or venerable". By 32 AD around the time Jesus Christ was purported to have been crucified, the era of Mars (martial) was coming to a close; its influence would not be extinguished but would move away from the foreground. Rome had firmly established itself as a great, all powerful empire, stretching all over the Mediterranean; even Britain was close to being absorbed.

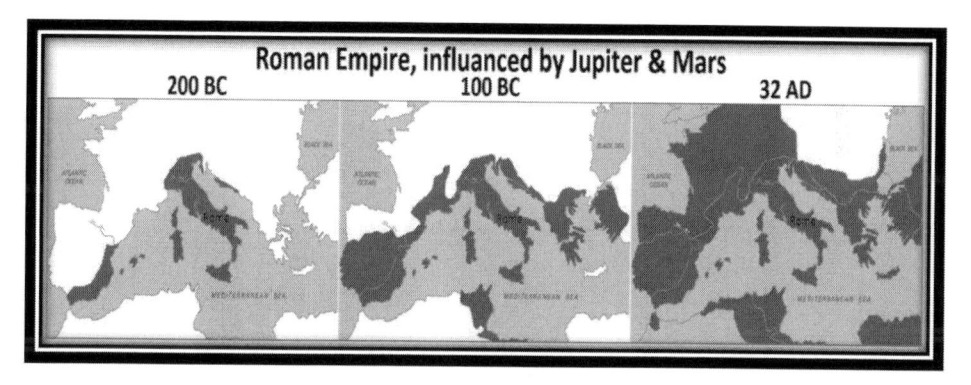

32 AD – 212 AD: 180 years of Venus (love and liking) in Taurus influencing global events. For the sake of this exercise I am only going to focus on Europe and the west, this is mainly for practical reasons; otherwise this book would be too long and take a lifetime to write. During this period, one would expect Venus's influence to be somewhat similar to the stable bull in his field, a time of consolidation, holding onto territory gained during the martial phase of imperialistic expansion. During the Julio - Claudian period 27 BC – 68 AD modest expansion continued, swallowing up most of Britain. After Flavian's dynasty was over in 96 AD, a century of stability ensued. The English historian Edward Gibbon wrote:

"If a man were called upon to fix that period in the history of the world during which the condition of the human race was most happy and prosperous, he would, without hesitation, name that which elapsed from the deaths of Domitian (96AD) to the accession of Commodus (180 – 192AD)." Edward Gibbon[4]

Venus, the planet of love and liking, reflected back into human reality during this happy period of human history. The population of Rome also reflected this by reaching an estimated half a million people, the most populated city in the world in its day. Throughout this period the succession of Emperors were happy to maintain existing European territorial limits, with the exception of the Dacians and the Parthians.

Roman Empire, influenced by Jupiter & Venus

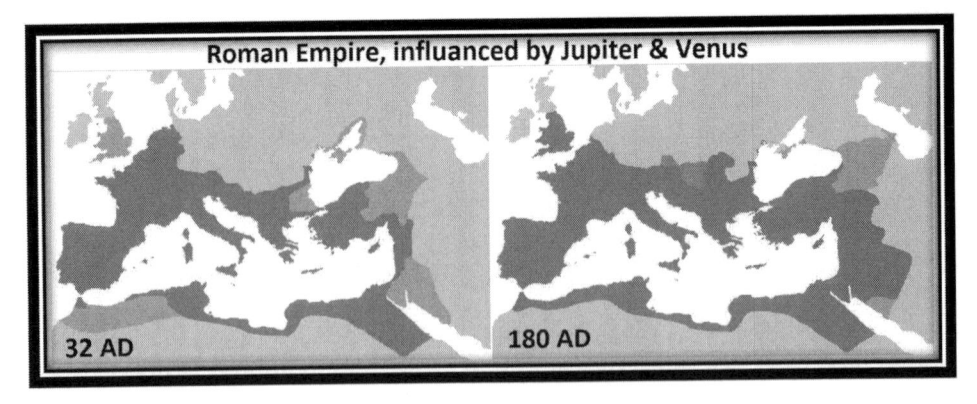

32 AD — 180 AD

212 AD – 392 AD: Mercury comes into the picture with the two minds of Gemini (I think), a period in which the Roman Empire had too many minds, all wanting a piece of the action, eventually leading to its split in 330 AD a notorious characteristic of Gemini's influence. From 235 – 285 Rome had 15 different Emperors making it weak and disunited, allowing its enemies to grow threatening Rome from all sides. Pressure came from Persia and Gaul. Diocletian managed to stabilise the empire from 284 to 305, but it eventually fell into a state of turbulence and civil war. From the ashes emerged a strong victor, Constantine the Great (324 – 337), Not only did he restore the empire but he is remembered for two important decisions.

- He converted to Christianity, which subsequently became the dominant religion throughout the empire.
- A new capital was founded on the site of Byzantium in 330 AD; this eventually became known as Constantinople.

An empire restored, but with two capitals, east and west, just like the two twins in the sign of Gemini.

Rome's two capitals in Gemini

Rome • Byzantium (Constantinople)

392 AD – 572 AD: The sign of Cancer, ruled by the Moon. This is a period of Jupitarian expansion within the Moon and the subconscious, the beliefs and belief systems associated with internal emotions. Although Constantine had made Christianity the state religion, it was

not formalised until 391 AD when Emperor Theodosius outlawed all forms of heresy and closed all Pagan temples. As the Roman Empire in the west began to decline, Christian intellectuals within the empire sought to create a government within the church and a body of belief which all Christians could accept, essentially the church would now take over from the old Roman military rule. This was also the time when monks (moonks) appeared on the scene. Early Christians serious about worship came together to form communities, they were able to support each other in what became known as monasteries. St Benedict (480 – 543) of Italy was one of the first and most famous early organisers of the monastic movement, expanding his particular brand of monasteries throughout Europe. These organised communities, pockets of self-sufficient civilisations, attracted some of the most literate and learned people around at the time. As the world outside drifted into decline following on from the empires collapse, everyday life inside the monasteries was relatively good.[5]

Monks Moons & Monasteries

572 AD – 752 AD: Leo, ruled by the Sun, the will. This period is dominated by the arrival of the Prophet Muhammad (570 – 632), a new King in the sign of Leo, the last prophet of the Gods, who would lead all Muslims to follow the teachings of Islam. Not only does he appear in the Sun sign on the outer wheel, his death coincides with the Sun on the inner wheel, a double Sun signifying someone extremely significant. There were two major caliphates during this period which took place after the death of Muhammad. The Rashidun and the Umayyad caliphates both resulted in the expansion of the Muslim Empire while holding back the imperialistic ambitions of the Catholic Church.

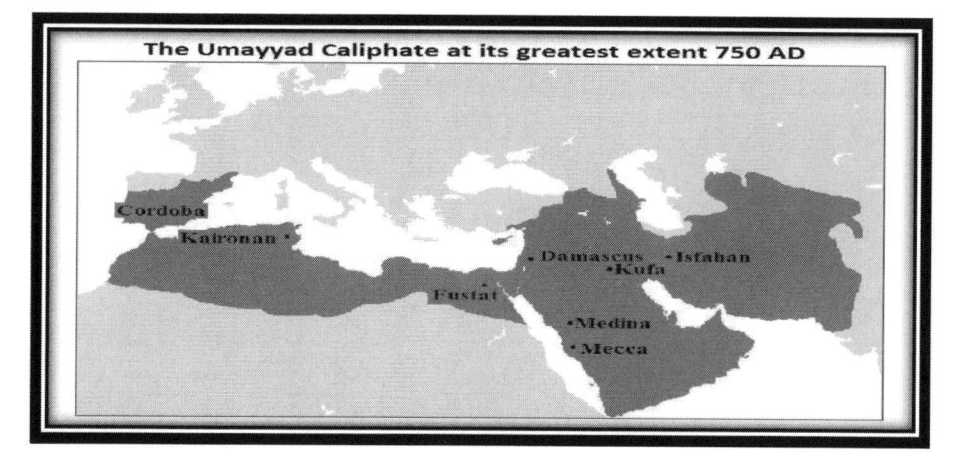

The Umayyad Caliphate at its greatest extent 750 AD

752 AD – 932 AD: Mercury in Virgo, The Vikings, a race of seafarers and explorers of Germanic Nordic, Scandinavian origin. The source of the name Vikings is uncertain; some scholars believe it refers to Vik dwellers, an area from which they came. I will refer to them as Kings of Virgo (**Vir**go - **Kings**). They explored the coasts of the North Atlantic, Europe, North Africa, Russia, Constantinople and the Middle East, raiding, trading and settling, influencing existing settlements and creating new colonies. They expanded their territories from the late 8th century right up to the Norman conquest of England, influencing and being influenced by various cultures along the way. Regarded as a non-literate culture, they did have a simple alphabet and left many descriptions of themselves on various runestones. The interesting correlation between this time period and the Vikings can be found in the Gods which they worshipped, they had two main Gods, Odin and Thor. Odin is Woden or Mercury and Thor is Jupiter, the same two planets heavily influencing this 180-year time period. The motto for the sign of Virgo is "I examine" which is precisely what the Vikings did along most of Europe's coast line.

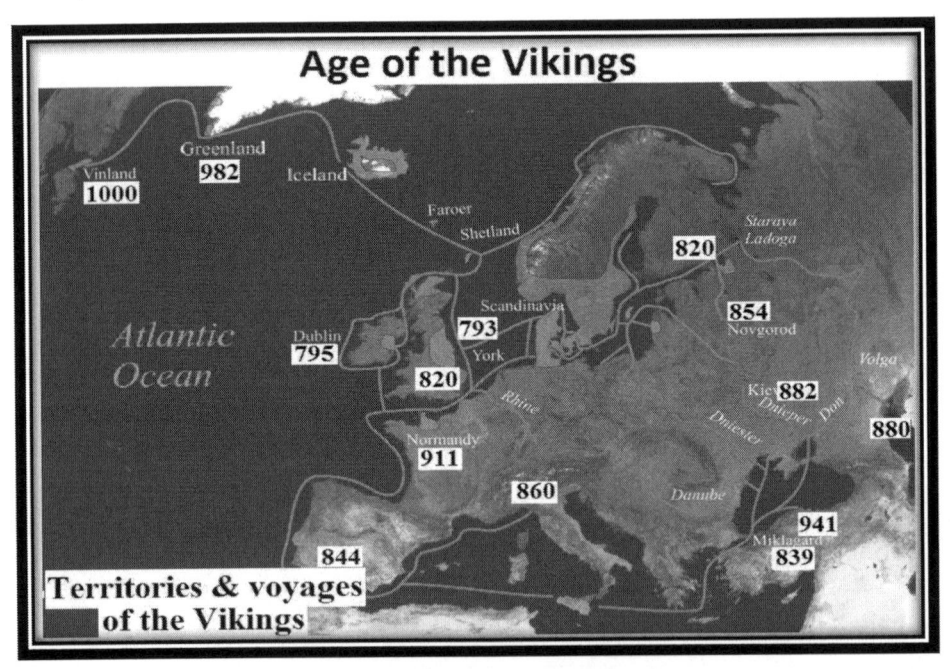

Age of the Vikings

Territories & voyages of the Vikings

The Vikings (Virgo Kings)

ODEN = MERCURY

THOR = JUPITER

932 AD – 1112 AD: Venus in Libra, the sign of balance and complementation. Libra is the sign of the setting Sun as we now enter the Dark Ages. This was a period in Europe that saw the emergence and expansion of the Normans, descendants of Norsemen Vikings, who gave their name and settled in the region of Northern France. This newly evolving Norman culture was a blend of Old Norse language, Norse religious tradition mixed with local Catholic women who spoke a Gallo-Romance language. This new Norman identity began to emerge in the first half of the 10th century; it spread throughout Europe, England and what was to become the Crusader States of the Near East. The Normans were credited not only for their military achievements but for various judicial and political arrangements which they introduced throughout their conquered territories. After the famous Norman conquest of England in 1066, they expanded their influence with the help of Normans from Italy, France and England who later served as avid fighters during the crusader years. The result of Norman expansion helped to create a new balance of power throughout Europe and the Middle East. I would suggest that it is no mere coincidence that the letters 'N' and 'O' are associated with the sign of Libra in our Zodiacal alphabet.

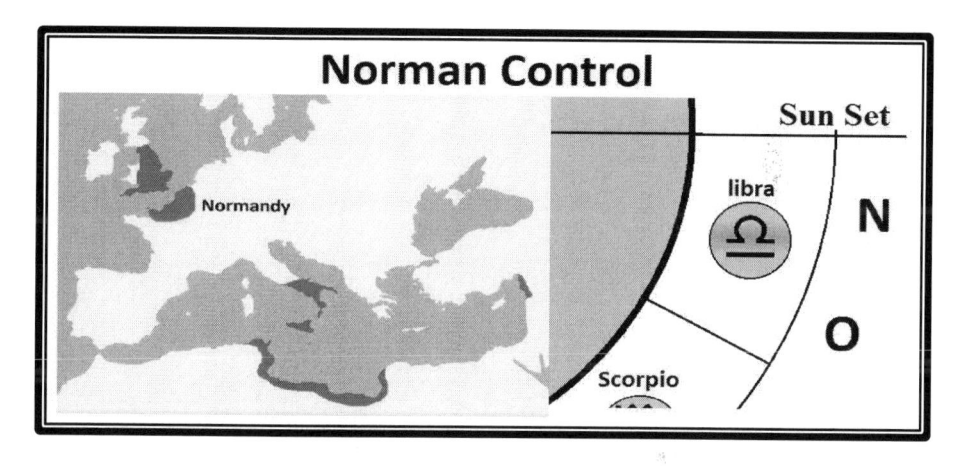

Norman Control

1112 AD – 1292 AD: Scorpio ruled by Mars, the God of war and physical movement. This is universal energy driving the Crusades, which were military campaigns sanctioned by the Roman Catholic Church, they began in 1096 when the Emperor of Constantinople sent a message to the Pope asking for military assistance to fend off threats from the Muslim Turks. The Pope responded by rallying support from Catholic soldiers, mercenaries and Christian extremists, all joining together in a Crusade against this rising Muslim threat. Their initial objective was to free up the Holy Land which at the time was controlled by Muslims, and also to unite Christians in both the east and the west, creating a more powerful Roman Catholic Empire. A complex 180-year struggle ensued; Mars the God of war was unleashed yet again. After battling the Turks, the Crusaders finally reached Jerusalem on 7th June 1099, both Jews and Muslims fought together to repel the attacking Christians, the attackers eventually entered the city on 15 July massacring the remaining Jews and Muslims. As a result of this first campaign, four new Crusader States were formed, Edessa, Antioch, Tripoli and Jerusalem. Many Crusades followed this first one but on a smaller scale, some more successful than others. The Crusades were essentially expansive military conquests of the Catholic Church, using religion to flex its imperialistic muscle.

After 180 years of battling for control the Crusading nations and participants fell into disunity, the decline of the papacy's moral authority along with the rise of nationalism saw an end to the era of the Crusades. Jerusalem finally fell back into the hands of the Muslims after the Siege of Acre in 1291, forcing many Christians to flee or succumb to a gruesome end.

The Crusades

1292 AD – 1472 AD: Jupiter in Sagittarius, (I seek), the Inquisitions. The expansive ambitions of the Catholic Church came under pressure from various religions and alternative beliefs. Paranoid elements within the church, suspicious of the motives behind recent converts initiated the Inquisitions, a quest to seek out and destroy the enemy within. Centaur Chiron, the half man half horse archer of Sagittarius sprang into life looking for its next target, the Catholic Church went on a man hunt. Anyone found guilty of heresy, a provocative belief or theory which opposed the establishments adopted beliefs, would pay the ultimate price.

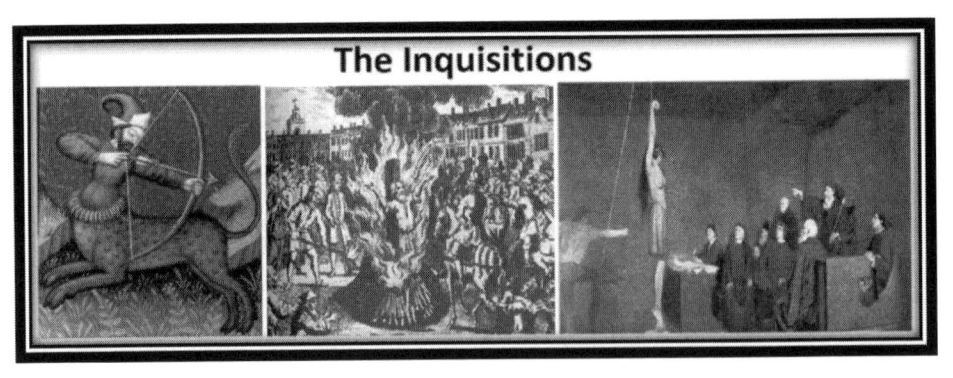

The Inquisitions

1472 – 1742: Saturn in Capricorn and Aquarius, (I use, I know), the important characteristics of Saturn begin to influence human society during this period.

- Commands us to get to work and work hard.
- Discipline and responsibility.
- Limitations and restrictions.
- Governs time, organise one's time.
- Structure and order.

The Commercial Revolution was under way, which expanded trade routes and empires. The most disciplined and structured organisations would dominate, spreading their influence to all corners of the globe. Time became important during this period; Chronos' influence brought forward the mechanical clock. Due to the invention of the escapement, oscillating timekeeping devices and spring driven clocks began to appear in the 15th century, they flourished over the next 100 years. The whole concept of the clock changed society, governing the day to day lives of the majority of working people, a major tool in commanding them to get to work and to work hard. For commerce to thrive with ease a fluid mechanism of exchange was necessary, the Judaic Saturnine community were at the spearhead of this business. Their roots as goldsmiths, money lenders and facilitators of usury paved the way for them as pioneers of the new banking industry. The first modern private central banks appeared, like the Bank of England (1694), an institution created to enable government and industry to borrow large sums with ease. This was the new micro Age of Jupitarian/Saturnian expansion, joining forces to initiate a Judaic/Christian Empire, the first major steps towards modern globalisation.

Expansion of Saturn with Jupiter

1742 AD - 1832 AD : Uranus in Aquarius, revolution, rebellion, out of the blue events and new technology, all aspects of the planet Uranus, the daddy of Saturn. The characteristics of Uranus are:

- Rebellion and revolution.
- Out of the blue.
- New ways of thinking and new technology.
- Breaking with tradition.
- Independence and originality.
- Unexpected events, sometimes violent.
- Erratic and bazaar behavior.

The Great Awakening of the 1730's – 40s, was an Evangelical movement which swept through Protestant Europe and the American Colonies, a movement that made Christianity personal and challenged the status quo and the established authority within the church. It was a precursor to the influential energies of Uranus and the mood of the people.[6]

The Industrial Revolution begins in the middle of the 18th century, with the introduction of new manufacturing processes, new machines, chemicals, technology and new processing techniques, helping to make production more efficient, which led to the rise of factories and the factory system. This revolution was felt in nearly all areas of daily life, leading to a long period of sustained growth in population and living standards.

In November 1755, Pasquale Paoli declared Corsica an independent sovereign state, a Corsican republic, not only the birth place of Napoleon but a taste of things to come. Both the American Revolution (1776) and the French Revolution (1789) erupted, a time of great change and challenges for both the citizens and the establishment. The desire for independence was strong; the influence from Uranus to break away from tradition and develop new ways of thinking was certainly playing out in the real world. By 1832 the situation had stabled out, the establishment had weathered the storm.

Uranus and Revolution

1832 – 2012: Although the second inner wheel is less influential than the outer zodiac and the ruling planet of the epoch, the influences are enough to be more than just coincidence. As the energetic frequencies of one planet move to make way for a new God, subtle changes take place within the human consciousness, sparking transformations to their projected reality. Here we will focus on the changes made by the inner wheel to the Jupiterian/Piscean Age. With the benchmark of expansion overriding energetic influence during this epoch of the outer wheel, a double Jupiter backdrop, we still see subtle variations on the inner wheel adding to the combined energies during this time period.

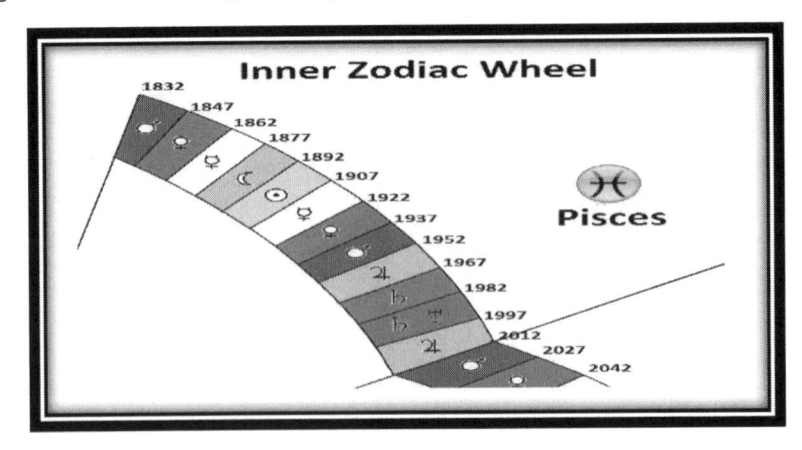

Inner Zodiac Wheel

1832 – 1847: Mars in Aries. By 1832 the Industrial Revolution was well under way, creating enormous growth in many aspects of society, growth which came at a price. The transition from the traditional harmonious rhythms of a placid rural life came at a cost to basic human happiness. This period was known as "The Troubles", a period of economic and social distress.[7] Peoples everyday lives underwent enormous physical change due to new industrial and technological innovations, a time synonymous with unemployment, poverty and riots. Riots were springing up everywhere, England, Wales, America and Europe. Farmers, agricultural workers and factory workers, fearfully perceiving new technology as a threat to their livelihoods, machines where smashed, buildings burnt and violence erupted. There were the reform riots 30's, The Paris riots; Belgian riots, national uprising in Poland, Prussian riots 33-34, Swing riots 30's - 40's, Nativist riots Philadelphia 1844, etc. The period also witnessed anti-immigration and anti-black riots throughout America.[8]

1847 – 1862: Venus in Taurus. This was a period of greater stability, like the bull in his field, a time of prosperity, optimism and stable achievements. Although the troubles of the 30's and 40's were not entirely over, most people were looking forward to the future and moving on, great achievements had been made in science and technology, many Victorians looked towards science as the answer to everything. To celebrate these achievements, the Great Exhibition of 1851, in the magnificent Crystal Palace, London, was organised, an excuse to show off the empires cutting edge achievements to the world. Reflecting back on this period, many saw it as one of the best in the Victorian Age.

"Of all decades in our history, a wise man would choose the eighteen-fifties to be young in".[9] - G. M. Young, Victorian England: Portrait of an Age

1862 – 1877: Mercury in Gemini, the period of communication. Here we see the Jupitarian expansion ally with the communicative aspects of Mercury. The growth of railway networks was at its peak. The first transcontinental railroad was completed in 1869; also in the same year, the Suez Canal in Egypt was opened (Suez is Zeus spelt backwards). In 1866 the first transatlantic telegraph cable was laid between America and Europe. All these practical achievements brought the world closer together, communication had never been easier.

1877 – 1892: Moon in Cancer, the female aspect of the focal and subconscious. Queen Victoria becomes Empress of India in 1877, the jewel in the crown of the British Empire. She essentially takes the role as mother or Goddess of India, an aspect of Moon energy.

1892 – 1907: Sun in Leo. These were the golden years of the City of London,[10] the financial heart of the world. London was all powerful and dominant; the British gold standard reigned supreme all over the world. The empire was at its apex, it seemed unstoppable going from strength to strength. The financial aspect of the empire, with all its aspirations, was instrumental in its future role as the main power throughout the world; those who controlled the finance controlled the beast.

1907- 1922: Mercury in Virgo. This is the tipping point at which the Sun begins to set on the old order, making its way into the underworld. A balancing act approaches, a balance of two opposites, night and day, good or bad, life or death. In this case it is Germany verses the British Empire, WW1, the greatest clash of mechanised warfare in the belly of Europe, a time to re-examine the whole structure and nature of European power, birth pains of the Virgin giving birth to a new order.

1922 – 1937: Venus in Libra. The inter-war years, another period of calm, stability, and reflection. After the treaty of Versailles this new balance of power takes effect, positioning Germany for the next round.

1937 – 1952: Mars in Scorpio. The God of war, betrayed by the stab in the back, the sting of the scorpion, round two, WW2 ignites, pulling the empire and Germany into an all-out war of annihilation, everything was at stake here, the whole globalisation project was under attack, challenged by the greatest military machine ever compiled in the history of the world, with a different view of globalisation. Unfortunately for the National Socialist's Jupiter was always going to be on the side of the victors, it rules the next time period (52-67), with triple Jupiter there was only ever going to be one outcome, those who allied themselves with Jupiterian energy, the Allies.

1952 – 1967: Jupiter in Sagittarius, a triple Jupiter. With a new Queen and a war behind it, the new Jupitarian/Saturnine Empire had a post war boom, the whole of the western world enjoyed this well-deserved time of expansive prosperity. The British Prime Minister, Harold Macmillan, made a famous speech in July 1957:

"Most of our people have never had it so good" - Harold Macmillan

1967 – 1989: Saturn in Capricorn and Aquarius. Here we see the restrictive nature of Saturn moving into play. Although the world was still expanding under the overriding energy of Jupiter, Saturn plays a small role throughout this time period. The 1970's saw a stagflationary recession throughout most of the western world, putting an end to the post war boom. High unemployment coincided with high inflation. In 1967 the Saturnian Six Day War took place, helping Israel to take control of the Promised Land. The world came off the gold standard, leaving national currencies to the mercy of private central banks that were now free to inflate them into oblivion.

1989 – 1997: Uranus in Aquarius. Revolutions, rebellions, new technology and out of the blue events are all characteristics of this planet. We see the Berlin wall come down with German reunification, the collapse of the Soviet Union, the first Gulf War, British Prime Minister (Margaret Thatcher) forcibly removed from office. We saw the Asian financial crash of 97 and the Internet Revolution, all aspects of Uranus energy.

1997 – 2012: Jupiter in Pisces, the final piece of the Piscean Age, the end of a 2150-year era, with another triple Jupiter. Here we see an all-out push for globalisation, the next phase in an attempt to control all of humanity under one all-powerful geopolitical system. Since the 9/11 attacks, this expansive period saw an escalation of military force with the US and the United Nations involved in many parts of the world. The rush for global control had moved up a gear.

Planetary Influences From 1832 - 2012

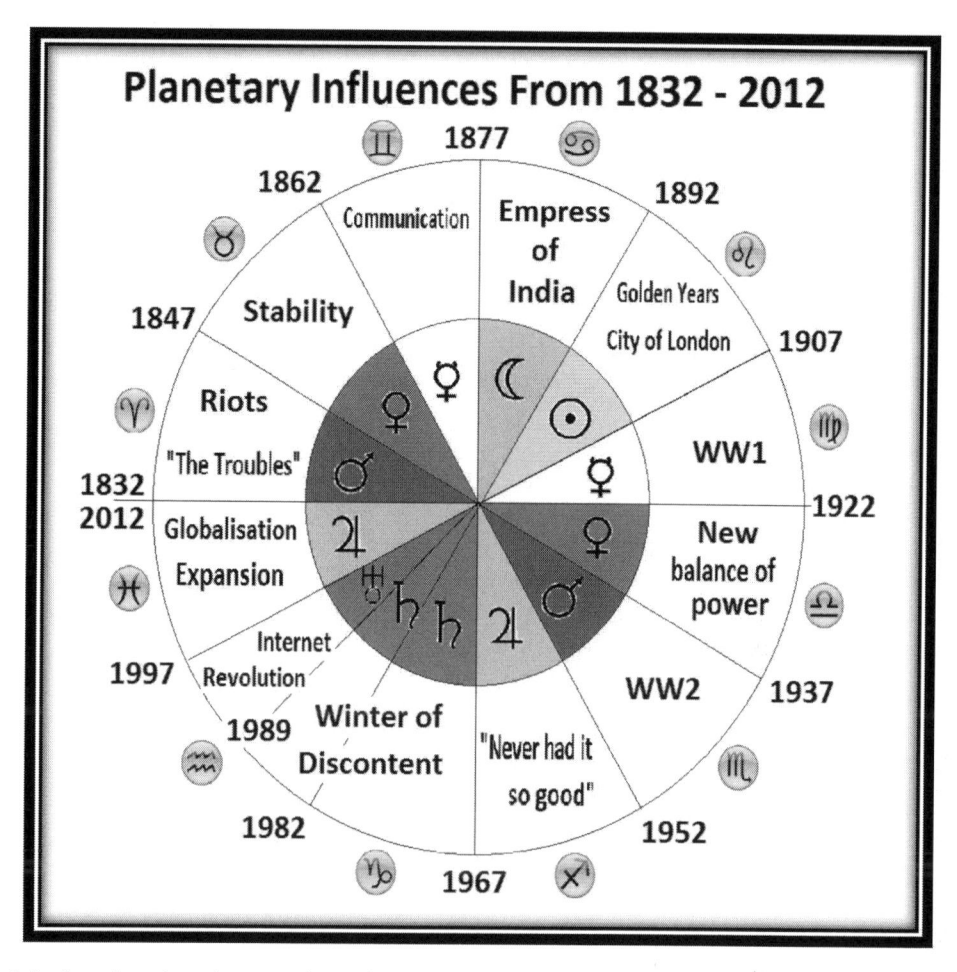

[Circular chart showing planetary influences across zodiac signs from 1832 to 2012, with dates and events labeled around the wheel:]

- 1832 / 2012 (Pisces ♓) – Globalisation, Expansion
- 1847 (Aries ♈) – Riots, "The Troubles"
- 1862 (Taurus ♉) – Stability
- 1877 (Gemini ♊) – Communication
- 1892 (Cancer ♋) – Empress of India
- 1907 (Leo ♌) – Golden Years, City of London
- 1922 (Virgo ♍) – WW1
- 1937 (Libra ♎) – New balance of power
- 1952 (Scorpio ♏) – WW2
- 1967 (Sagittarius ♐) – "Never had it so good"
- 1982 (Capricorn ♑) – Winter of Discontent
- 1989 (Aquarius ♒) – Internet Revolution
- 1997 – Internet Revolution

It is clear that there is a correlation between the planets and geosocial events, playing out in the real world. There are two explanations for this.

- 1) Our ancestors and controlling elites were aware and involved in this science. It is possible they initiated events to suit the astrological time they were in, as though this was a template, a time-line map given to them by the Gods, which they adhered to.
- 2) The energies and frequencies emanating from the planets and combination of planets do influence our consciousness, and thus our projected reality.

I would suggest that the first explanation could have been a possibility in the ancient world, but not so much in the modern era, although the elites do possess this knowledge. It's clear to see that planetary correlations are more than coincidental; something real and tangible is taking place. The other possibility is a combination of the two, where the elites aware of these natural energy cycles use them to their advantage, they develop geopolitical policies which run parallel and in tune with the natural energy cycles of the planets and the universe. Why swim against the tide if you can swim with it.

The future

"I have seen the future and it is very much like the present, only longer." - Kehlog Albran, the Profit

"Prediction is very difficult, especially if it's about the future." - Nils Bohr, Nobel laureate in Physics

The new Age of Aquarius has two planets ruling throughout this sign, Uranus dominating the first 1000 years followed by Saturn for the last. Unlike the Jupiterian Age of expansion, the main energy influencing this epoch is one of revolution, rebellion and individuality. For the first 180 years, Mars in Aries dominates the outer wheel, and also the inner wheel until 2027. These universal energies are driving the human collective towards a great deal of physical change. The possibility of war throughout this period is greater than ever before, with new kinds of wars, using new forms of technology. Double Mars signifies physical movement and martial like activity, massive migrations of people relocating is more likely to occur in this energetic backdrop. Many surprising out of the blue events are possible, sending shockwaves through society, bringing social and political change. With Jupiter out of the picture, the expansion of the human population will subside, under Saturn's influence Earth's population will be restricted, controlled and organised. The 500,000,000-figure suggested by the Georgia Guide-stones could become a realistic possibility.

The globalists have their work cut out, under this combination of energies; their push for global governance under a one all-powerful system should be met by resistance from many aspects. The rebellious, free thinking, independent nature of Uranus will no doubt frustrate the progress towards a totalitarian super state. Not only is resistance likely, physical force will be imposed by the state to maintain obedience, as a minority they must reign in all forms of dissent to keep their fragile system of control together. Pocket rebellions and organised revolutions are likely to occur during this double Mars (martial) phase, eventually levelling off under the influence of Venus between 2027 and 2042. The main body of universal influence will still come from the ruler of the Age, and the dominant planet on the outer wheel, Uranus and Mars, instigating dramatic, sometimes violent changes to our lives and the institutions we try to hold together. New technology will always be a major part of the Uranus cycle, offering both liberation and control. While most people regard technology as a tool of progress and sophistication, the control system will always use it to their advantage, as a mechanism of surveillance and order.

The elite have always known what was coming; they know the science of applied astronomy and what was on the horizon, the grid of control which has been slowly erected, like a strait jacket around humanity, could be their attempt at preparing for this energetic changeover. At this time the greatest threat to humanities economic and cultural systems, do not come from manmade climate change, AIDS, Muslim terrorists, asteroids or super volcanoes. The greatest threat to our fragile way of life is ourselves, it is the unleashing of a natural process, a cycle of awakening to the new Age of "knowing", the Age of Aquarius, mixed with the revolutionary energy of Uranus and Mars, the God of war. Consequently, anyone reading this can now appreciate what we are up against, a journey into a future of uncertainty, surpassing anything witnessed throughout the expansive Age of Pisces.

"You will hear of wars and rumours of wars, but see to it that you are not alarmed. Such things must happen, but the end is still to come." - Matthew 24:6 (NIV)

The good news is that there is no end, well not until the universe implodes and all the lights go out permanently, which is not going to happen any time soon. The cycle of life and death is perpetual; the Ages come and go, round and round, wheels within wheels. Life is just a ride, sometimes rough sometimes smooth, but it continues in one form or another. You are an expression of infinite universal consciousness, having a biological experience, you should not be afraid or worried, as one great man put it,"**the only thing to fear is fear itself**".

By bringing all humanity under a one size fits all globalised system; the elite can ensure the collective consciousness of humanity is tamed from the unwanted effects of Uranus. Our personal connection to the higher mind, together with a balanced consciousness will be under attack by the elite, intended to limit the ingress of natural frequencies which oppose their control. Humanity will be kept busy and distracted, in an attempt to place them in a constant state of stress and fear, stifling natural rhythms and their ability to connect. Restrictions on movement are more likely as we progress into the future; movement is an important part of positioning the biological body to where higher levels of consciousness require it to be. Without freedom of movement one's life purpose can be greatly restricted. Using all mechanisms available, tools such as diet, vaccination, education, propaganda, drugs, alcohol, pornography and consumerism, the control system will use various combinations to socially engineer the new citizen in order to keep them under control as we move into this New Age.

"Diet, injections, and injunctions will combine, from a very early age, to produce the sort of character and the sort of beliefs that the authorities consider desirable, and any serious criticism of the powers that be will become psychologically impossible. Even if all are miserable, all will believe themselves happy, because the government will tell them that they are so." - Bertrand Russell, The Impact of Science on Society, 1951.

It is already happening

Much of this is already taking place. Since 9/11 the world has seen an endless run of wars, with no foreseeable end, their war on terrorism is limitless. The control systems definition of a terrorist can easily grow to incorporate anyone who questions their authority, legitimacy or their version of the truth. Terrorism can be used as a smokescreen to quickly bring in the new globalised world which they have been working towards for some time.

The cosmic energy which has been promoting the Jupiterian/Saturn alliance is fading as Jupiter is steadily being replaced by Uranus. The Roman Catholic Church is losing its God and therefore its legitimacy. Looking at the zodiac it appears there is a natural cycle following on from a Jupiterian expansion period, a cycle towards Mars, wars and proactive upheaval. This could be what we are seeing now with the American Empire, such wealth, gluttony and greed in the hands of a small group of elitists, who during the expansion period, prior to 2012, made enormous gains. Some of these people have suffocated under the weight of their own desire for more, falling out of touch with their spiritual connection to source and humanity. Like all vice ridden emperors and kings; they eventually destroy their own empires.

If we look further forward along the timeline of Aquarius, after 1000 years Uranus will move out of the limelight, leaving Saturn to dominate the remaining 1000 years. This is around the time I suspect George Lucas's Star Wars was portrayed. The Saturnian control system during this period will be so technologically advanced they will be more than capable of creating an artificial moon. George Lucas's famous Death Star has a uncanny resemblance to Mimas, one of Saturn's 62 moons. Maybe George Lucas was trying to tell us something.

Saturn's Moon Mimas   **The Death Star**

The next time Uranus appears in the outer zodiac wheel of the Aquarian Age is between the years 3892-3982, a 90-year period when rebellious energy would be at its peak, this is when the republic would have a better chance at liberating themselves from the Empires Death Star. Darth Vader is a play on words, Vader is Dutch for father and Darth represents dark. Consequently, Dark Father could be George Lucas's future version of (old father time, Cronos) another expression of Saturn.

Notes for chapter 14

(1) Edict Of Milan, Wikipedia, https://en.wikipedia.org/wiki/Edict_of_Milan

(2) Eric Rudolph, Are Christians more violent than Muslims, Abagond, https://abagond.wordpress.com/2013/04/24/are-christians-more-violent-than-muslims/

(3) Joachim Hagopian, It's Time to Stop "Supporting Our Troops": Thirty Million People Killed by U.S. Since the End of World War II, Dec 13, 2015, Global Research, http://www.globalresearch.ca/its-time-to-stop-supporting-our-troops-thirty-million-people-killed-by-u-s-since-end-of-world-war-ii/5495538

(4) Edward Gibbon, The History of the Decline and Fall of the Roman Empire, (1776-88), Penguin Classics. http://www.amazon.com/History-Decline-Fall-Roman-Empire/dp/0140433937

(5) Steven Kreis, Christianity as a cultural revolution, 2001, the history guide, http://www.historyguide.org/ancient/lecture15b.html

(6) First great awakening, wikipedia, https://en.wikipedia.org/wiki/First_Great_Awakening

(7) The Victorian era, "Time of Troubles", http://victorian-poetry.bloomyebooks.com/p/the-age.html

(8) Riots, 30's – 40's , http://www.historyhome.co.uk/peel/ruralife/swing.htm , http://www.teachushistory.org/second-great-awakening-age-reform/articles/historical-background-antislavery-womens-rights-1830-1845 , http://philadelphiaencyclopedia.org/archive/riots-1830s-and-1840s/,

(9) G M Young, Victorian England, Portrait of an age, first published 1936, 1964, oxford UP. http://www.goodreads.com/book/show/1320386.Victorian_England

(10) David kynaston, The City Of London Volume 2: Golden Years 1890-1914, Publishers: Random house 2015, https://books.google.co.id/books?id=625zBgAAQBAJ&printsec=frontcover&dq=city+of+london+the+golden+years&hl=en&sa=X&ved=0ahUKEwj-lNvD9OnJAhVW-GMKHYwCA1cQ6AEIIzAA#v=onepage&q=city%20of%20london%20the%20golden%20years&f=false

Chapter 15. Non-human entities

The world we experience is only a perception based on our ability to decode the energetic fields and frequencies surrounding us. Our five senses limit our ability to decode what actually exists in the space we occupy. Just because our biological radio is tuned to radio 4, does not mean radios 1 and 3 do not exist, therefore the existence of other forms of energetic consciousness undetectable by our bodies limited sensory perception cannot be discounted. People who have heightened senses have the ability to connect into other frequencies and dimensions, allowing them to interact with various forms of non-human entities. Our history is riddled with myths and legends, stories of encounters with strange beings, such as angels, demons, ghosts and spirits. But what exactly are we dealing with?

The different varieties of non-human entities could be as numerous as the leaves in a forest, it is impossible to put a figure on. The four main types I will concentrate on here are:

- Spiritual.
- Interdimensional.
- Extra-terrestrial/Terrestrial.
- Hybrids/Trans human.

Spiritual entities

"We are not human beings having a spiritual experience. We are spiritual beings having a human experience." - Pierre Teilhard de Chardin

As we have already discussed in previous chapters, there is a higher mind or Logos consciousness which most of us are tethered to, a spiritual realm of infinite variations and expressions of Divine consciousness. How we interact or make the most of that connection is up to the individual. Some of our ancestors believed that the planetary bodies within our solar system also had a focal and subconscious aspects to them, radiating from their centres outwards, positive and negative energy commonly depicted as angels, archangels and demons. A planet's aspect or angle towards another body is an arch; the archangel is nothing more than the angle between two bodies. In an electric universe, the angle between bodies is most important, it is the main driving mechanism of varying influence. Each planet and luminary has a personified character for specific energies, corresponding to their individual angels, demons and archangels.

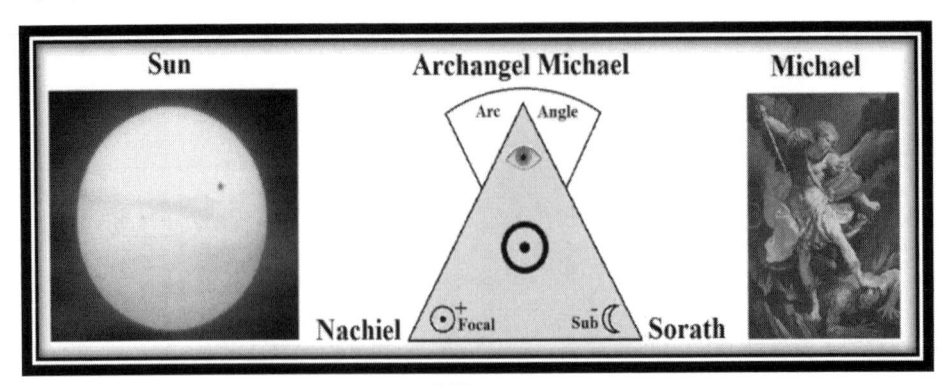

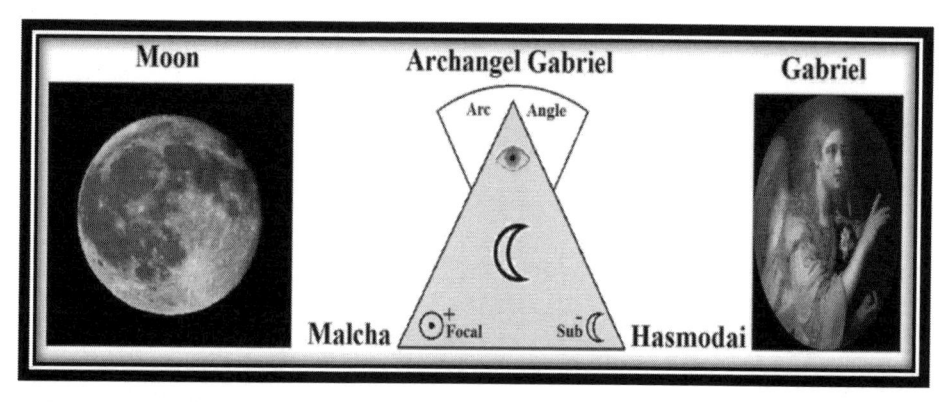

Moon	Archangel Gabriel	Gabriel
	Arc / Angle — ☾ — Malcha (⊙⁺ Focal) / (Sub⁻ ☾) Hasmodai	

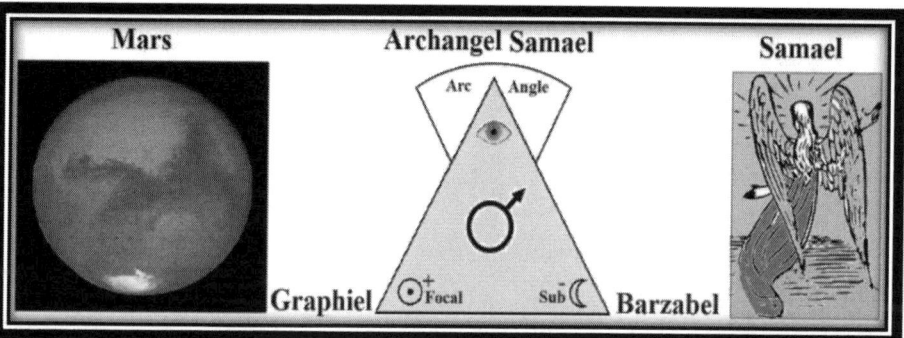

Mars	Archangel Samael	Samael
	Arc / Angle — ♂ — Graphiel (⊙⁺ Focal) / (Sub⁻ ☾) Barzabel	

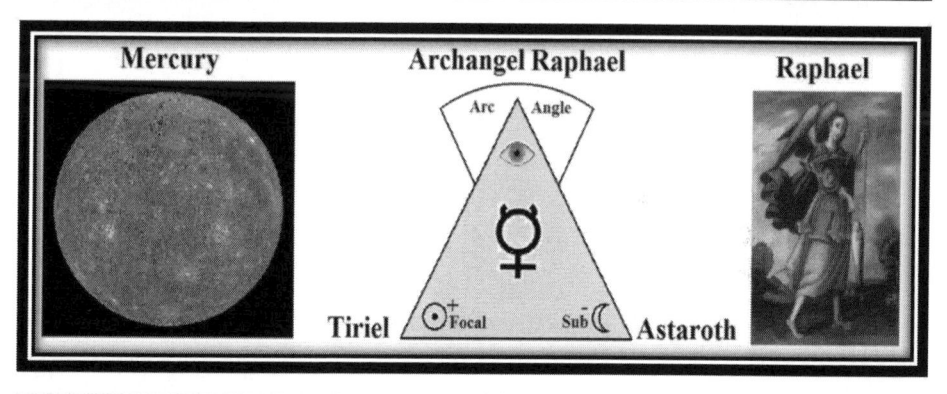

Mercury	Archangel Raphael	Raphael
	Arc / Angle — ☿ — Tiriel (⊙⁺ Focal) / (Sub⁻ ☾) Astaroth	

Jupiter	Archangel Sachiel	Jophiel
	Arc / Angle — ♃ — Jophiel (⊙⁺ Focal) / (Sub⁻ ☾) Hishmael	

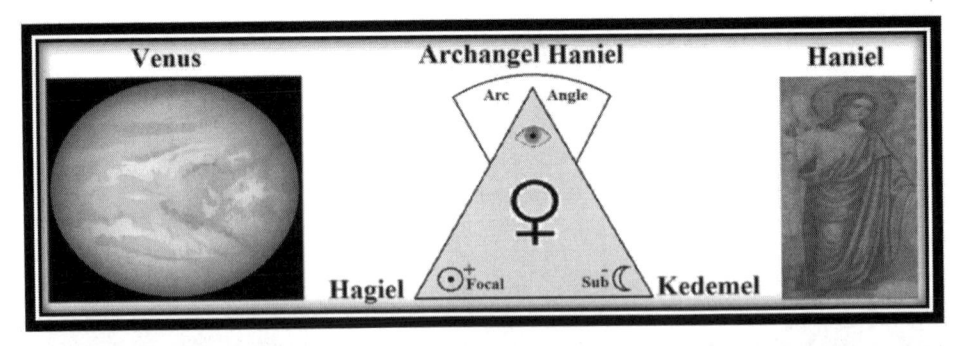

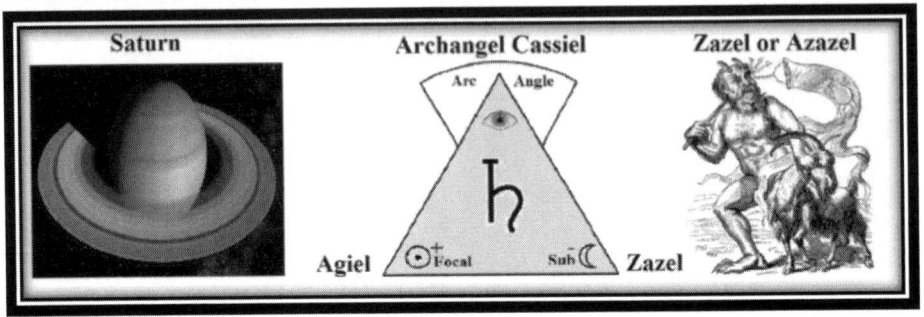

In the Age of Aries, during the time of the Pharaohs, the angle of the Sun in the sky was referred to as Horus, divided into hourly portions, this became a way to monitor time and is where we get the word "hour" from. The importance of the Sun's angle in the sky has an electromagnetic influence on our biological decoding mechanism, hence why our focal awareness appears stronger during the day than it is at night. Throughout the Age of Pisces, under the Christian influence, this angle of Horus became known as Archangel Michael, the arc and angle of the Sun in the sky. On the Aleph.se web site under the heading Egyptian Gods, they point out the similarities between Horus and Archangel Michael.

"It is interesting to notice the strong similarities to the Archangel Michael in the religions of the Book, and the fact that Michael is said to be the protector of the Nile delta."[1]

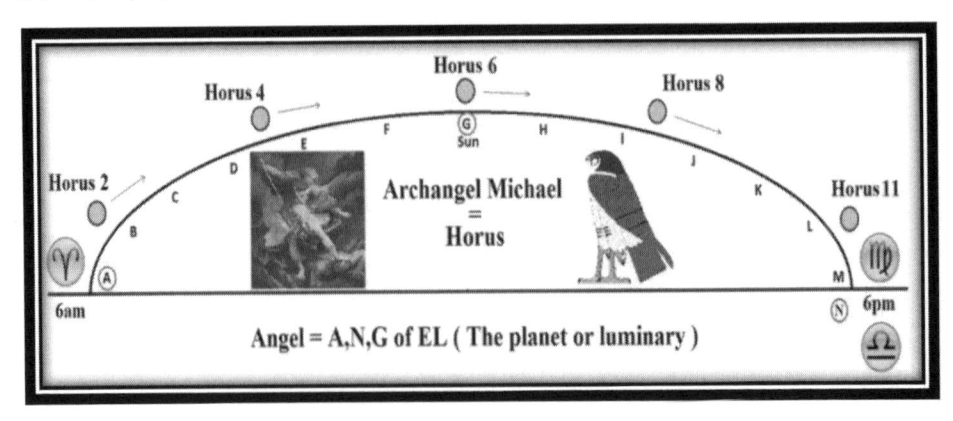

It is also no coincidence that each of the archangel's names end with "EL", this is simply a reference to the planet or luminary to which the angel/angle refers to.

The war in heaven

"And there was war in heaven: Michael and his angels fought against the dragon; and the dragon fought and his angels, and prevailed not; neither was their place found any more in heaven. And the great dragon was cast out, that old serpent, called the Devil, and Satan, which deceiveth the whole world: he was cast out into the earth, and his angels were cast out with him." - Revelations 12: 7-9 (KJV)

"How art thou fallen from heaven, O Lucifer, son of the morning! [how] art thou cut down to the ground, which didst weaken the nations! For thou hast said in thine heart, I will ascend into heaven, I will exalt my throne above the stars of God: I will sit also upon the mount of the congregation, in the sides of the north: I will ascend above the heights of the clouds; I will be like the most High." - Isaiah 14: 12-14 (KJV)

The war in heaven is not about angelic beings with feathered wings fighting off demonically possessed red eyed rebels from the dark recesses of God's kingdom, it is more likely to be referring to the time when Venus fell out of its old orbit into its present position, Lucifer comes from the Latin "lux ferre" meaning" light bringer ". In Isaiah 14:12, Venus is referred to as "the Sun of the morning", the morning star which precedes the Sun rising at 6am. The scripture talks about Lucifer (Venus) falling from heaven, it then mentions how Venus begins its journey of ascension into heaven. In revelations, there is a war between Archangel Michael and these fallen angels, which are cast out into the Earth. It all begins to make sense when you look at it from an astrological point of view. Venus moved from its original orbit thousands of years ago, its angles relative to the other planets fell out of position, on a course towards the Earth, as mentioned in Immanuel Velikovsky's 1950 book *Worlds in collision,* Venus made its way earthwards as a huge comet, given the appearance of a fiery dragon with a long visible tail. As it passed by the Earth on four separate occasions it caused the Earth to rotate in the opposite direction, the poles shifted and chaos ensued. This would explain the battle between the angle of Venus in the sky and the angle of the Sun (Archangel Michael). Finally, when Venus settled into its new orbit, closer to the Sun and it's ascension into heaven, Michael, the Sun, had essentially defeated Lucifer by finally rising in the east. During this process, many meteors would have broken away from the dragon comet and entered the Earth's atmosphere, giving the appearance of angels falling to Earth. I suspect it is one of these meteors which found its way to Mecca and is now housed in the famous Kaaba, in the very heart of Venus worshiping Islam.

We can now appreciate that the concept of angels and demons do not exist in the manner commonly defined by man's religions, personified expressions of planetary angles designed to manipulate emotions in the hearts and minds of men, making it easier for outside sources to control humanity. Instead of frightening depictions of demons, Satan, Lucifer and hell, there are magnificent planets, luminaries, stars and a universe full of various forms and expressions of consciousness which stretches far beyond the human imagination in a limitless cycle of birth, death and rebirth. With Venus in its new orbit and all the other planets stable, this latest version of electromagnetic planetary equilibrium, creates new angular interference patterns that emanate towards the Earth, a new symphony of frequencies influencing human epi-genetics, in a new era of biological conscious expression. This could be the mechanism behind the Adam and Eve story, a different line up of planetary Gods casting a new combination of conscious vibrations, which became the breath of life entering the nostrils of Adam, a flesh and blood man as a reflection of the universe, "as above so below". It is no surprise to see a correlation between human consciousness and universal consciousness. The ratio between the focal conscious and subconscious can be observed throughout the universal. The Subconscious tethered to the spirit realm is the internal emotional aspect of the mind commonly represented by water, the Moon, the feminine and the night. A recent study of the universe found that it is made up of 70% dark and 30% light energy.[2] We also know that water makes up approximately 70% of the Earth's surface, leaving 30% for the land.[3] It is therefore no surprise to find that the human body is also made up of 70% water.[4] The star Sirius, which it has been suggested, represents the subconscious aspect of our solar system's binary, is 2.3 times the mass of our Sun, which equates to a ration of 70/30.[5] From this you would expect the human mind to have the same ratio for the sub and focal consciousness. However, the established view on this matter estimates the capacity of the subconscious to be a whopping 95%. The task of measuring the subconscious is not easy, it is based mostly on speculation rather than hard scientific evidence, so the figure of 95% is pure guesswork. Pure logic in this matter would expect the 70-30 ratio to continue, "as above so below".

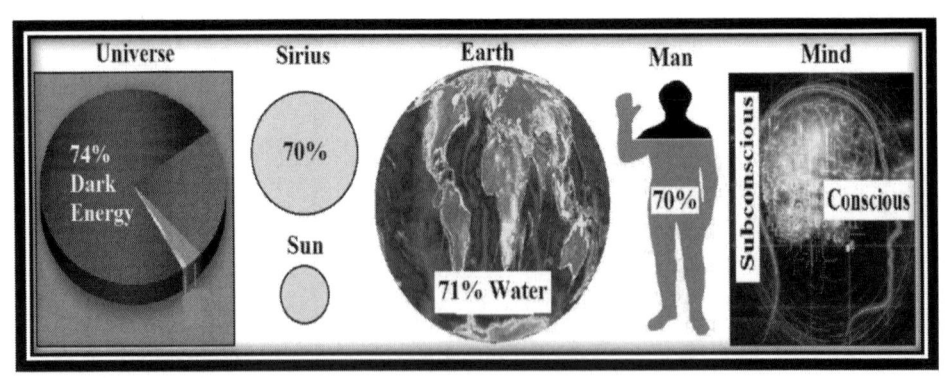

Universe	Sirius	Earth	Man	Mind
74% Dark Energy	70% / Sun	71% Water	70%	Subconscious / Conscious

Spirit and soul

The soul is the immortal essence of the biological living being, the connection between focal consciousness and the higher mind Logos. The spirit on the other hand is regarded as feminine, the internal emotional connection to Logos, an aspect and point of awareness which continues after the physical body expires. The Adam or Atman is an expression of the soul whereas Eve represents the feminine spirit.

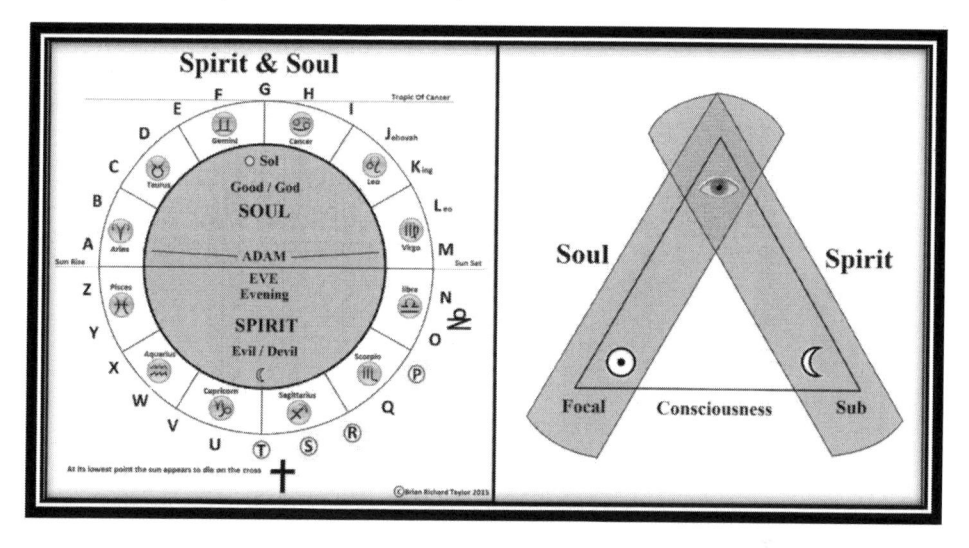

To eat or feed from the tree of knowledge is to understand and experience both good and evil. It is to enter the physical realm and experience the Earth as a biological living being, as a person born in (SIN), in the physical realm of the sine wave formed by the zodiac cycle. It is to live and experience physical cycles of day/night, summer/winter and time within space. Existing within mortal sin in which your physical body, after approximately 70 years, will surely die. Eve the spirit ate from the tree and gave to Adam, the soul, who also ate, together as soul and spirit, they entered this world, their eyes were opened and they found themselves naked in the flesh.

"And so it is written, the first man Adam was made a living soul; the last Adam was made a quickening spirit." - 1 Corinthians 15:45 (KJV)

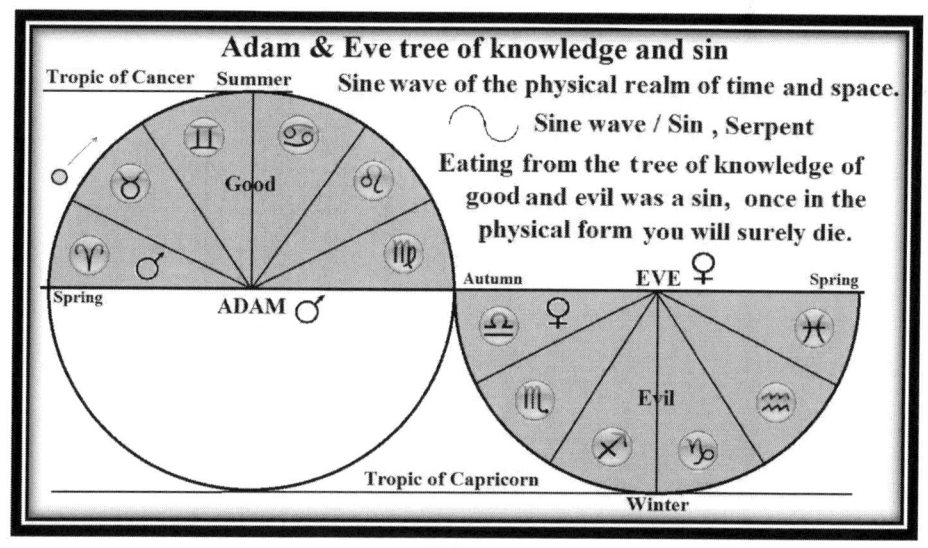

"The Lord God formed man of the dust of the ground, and breathed into his nostrils the breath of life; and man became a living soul." - Genesis 2:7

To enter this earthly plane in a physical form and to experience its limitations within time and space, is to move along the zodiacal sine wave of seasons and Sun cycles.

"The soul that sinneth, it shall die." - Ezekiel 18:20 (KJV)

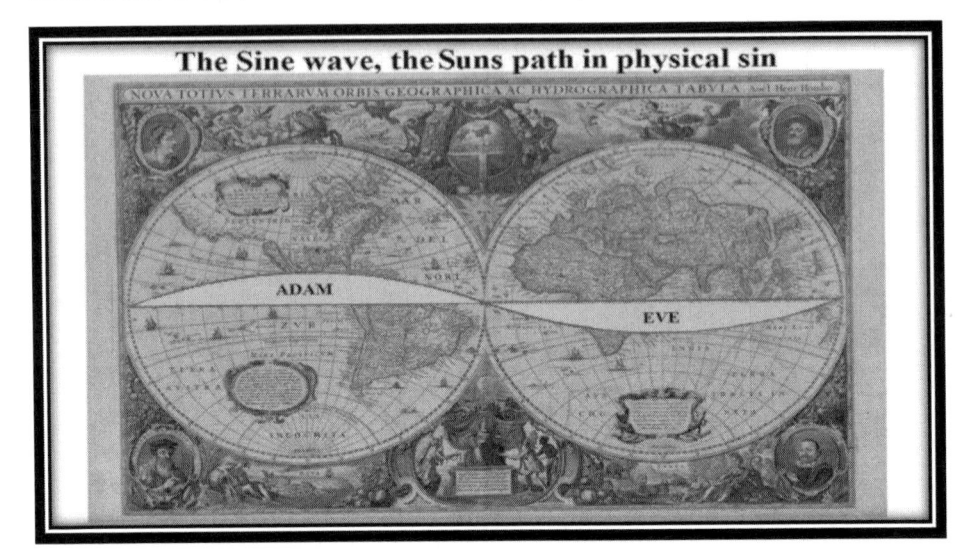

The Sine wave, the Suns path in physical sin

Adam the soul represents the male who is generally considered more physical and practical when it comes to earthly things, whereas Eve the spirit, who represents the female, is understood to be more emotional and in tune with her feelings. Although everyone possesses a soul and a spirit, the male is traditionally more soulful and the female more spiritual. This male/female union complement one another, together creating a full circle of spirit and soul.

The average human life of approximately 72 years is one full sine wave cycle, from this the physical biological body dies but the spirit continues, just as it did before the physical experience began. Most religions explain the soul and spirit in some form or another, with a common theme connecting our physical experience to the eternal higher mind Logos consciousness. In Hinduism, the Atman (individual self) is their version of the Adam.

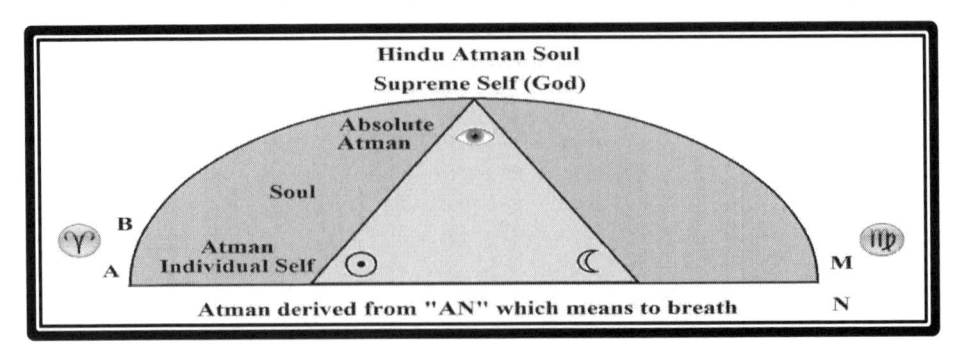

Hindu Atman Soul
Supreme Self (God)

Atman derived from "AN" which means to breath

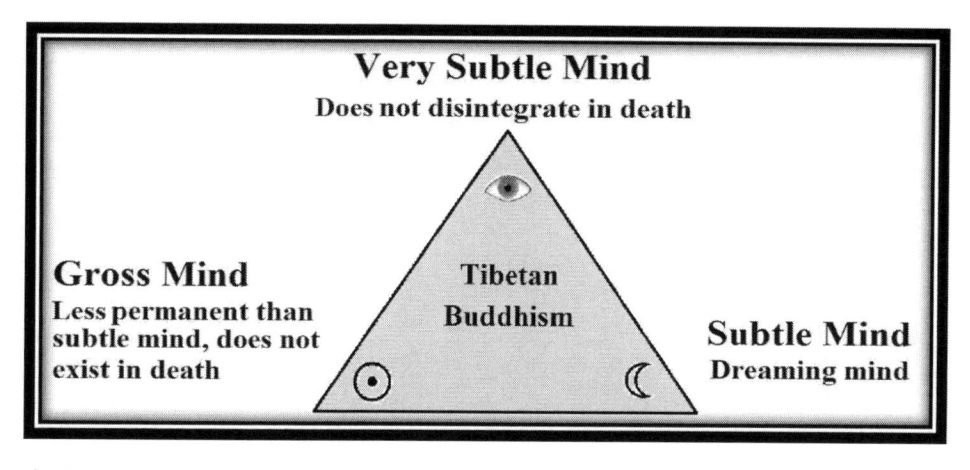

Very Subtle Mind
Does not disintegrate in death

Gross Mind
Less permanent than subtle mind, does not exist in death

Tibetan Buddhism

Subtle Mind
Dreaming mind

Plato divides the soul or psyche into 3 separate parts, each part is related to specific areas of the body. Plato's definition runs in line with the Adam/Daytime concept of the soul. It is also worth mentioning that the word used to describe the part of the body which primarily comes into contact with the physical Earth is also known as the sole. The Hebrew Bible mentions the first King of a united Israel back in the 11th century BCE, his name was King Saul.

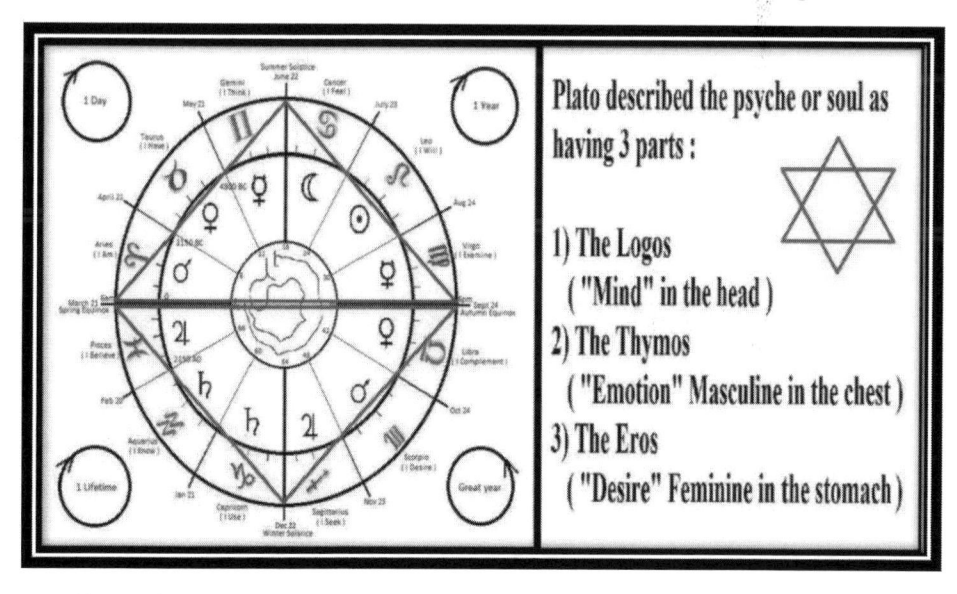

Plato described the psyche or soul as having 3 parts:

1) The Logos
   ("Mind" in the head)
2) The Thymos
   ("Emotion" Masculine in the chest)
3) The Eros
   ("Desire" Feminine in the stomach)

Tutankhamun's mask

Tutankhamun was originally named Tutankhaten by his father Akhenaten, who abandoned the traditional Egyptian polytheistic planet worship in favour of monotheistic Aten Sun disk worship. After only ten years at the age of 19 the young Pharaoh Tutankhamun died ending his rule in 1323 BC. Although he was only around for a short time, he eventually became one of the most famous of all the Egyptian Pharaohs. His solid gold death mask weighing in at 22.6lbs is a mystery to most viewers, but its secrets can easily be revealed when looking at it from an astrological perspective.

Tutankhamun's death mask

The gold mask and coffinette depicts the Pharaoh holding a shepherd's crook in his left hand and a flail in his right. The crook symbolises the left side or left brain in mescaline Aries while the flail represents the right side in feminine Virgo.

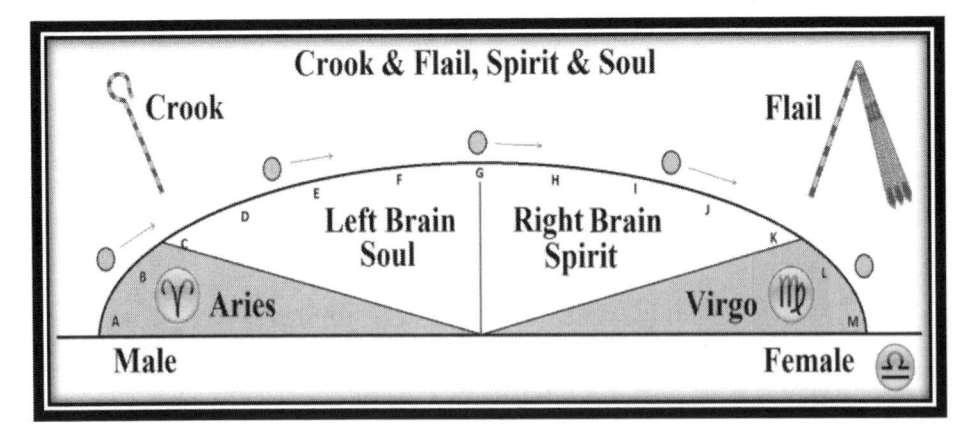

Crook & Flail, Spirit & Soul

Crook — Left Brain / Soul — Aries — Male
Flail — Right Brain / Spirit — Virgo — Female

The Pharaoh's headdress (known as a nemes) is made up of blue and gold stripes; above the neck you see one Egyptian calendar month divided into three decans (ancient Egyptian weeks consisted of 10 days each). Below the neck a second month is depicted, a masculine month above and a feminine month below. This also symbolised upper and lower Egypt. The 12 houses or signs of the zodiac alternate from masculine to feminine, beginning with masculine Aries. The bottom month has 30 gold strips (day) and 28 blue strips (night), this is most likely a representation of the solar and lunar cycles or the feminine monthly cycle. The top month only has 27 blue stripes possibly referring to the sidereal Luna cycle of 27.3 days as opposed to the synodic Luna cycle of 29.5 days. Around the neck are 12 bands of various colours, could this be the 12 houses of the zodiac in various elements?

The top of the head dress is probably the most mysterious with a vulture and cobra proudly protruding from the forehead. Running in line with my thesis I suggest the vulture represents the focal conscious mind, the soul, the male, the daytime and Upper Egypt, whereas the Cobra (the serpent) represents the subconscious, the spirit, the night, the feminine and Lower Egypt.

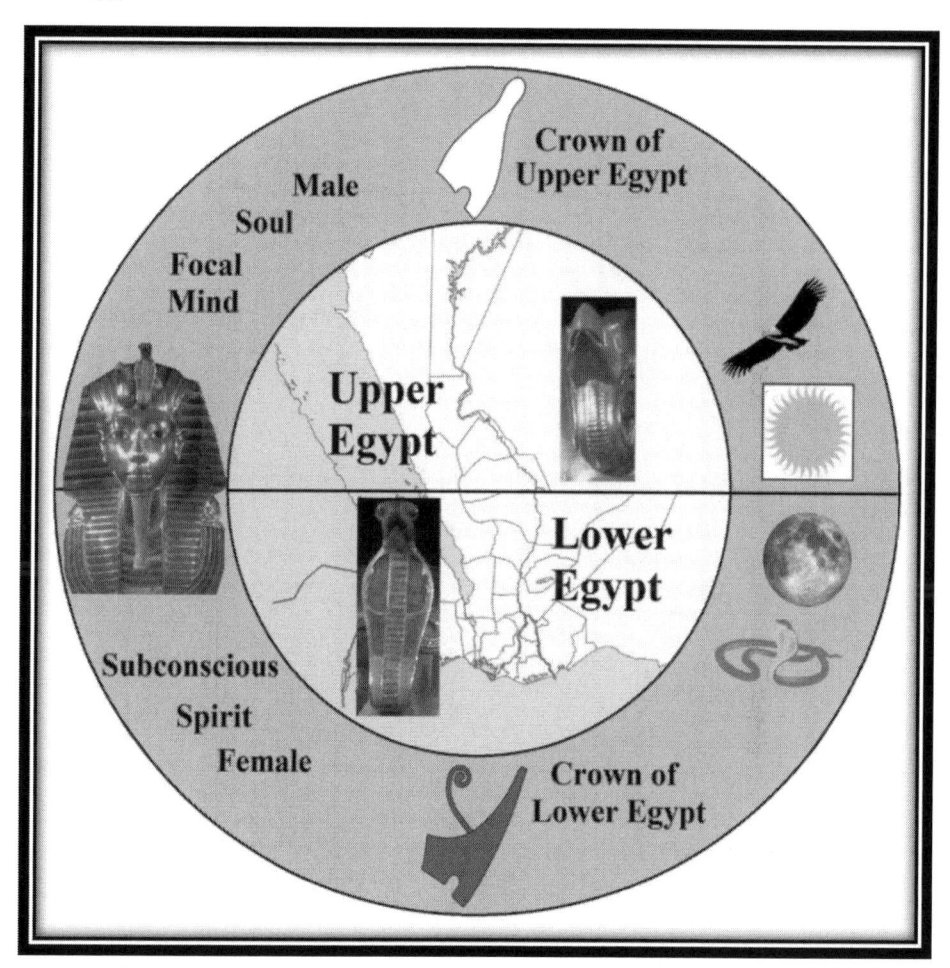

The vulture is a bird which hunts during the day, it is used in many cultures to symbolise the Sun. The cobra on the other hand is a snake like the serpent who spoke to Eve in the Garden of Eden; it is predominantly a nocturnal hunter which represents the night. The cobra on Tutankhamun's nemes is larger than the vulture; this is because the subconscious is superior to the focal mind in capacity and scope. Tutankhamun's beard is also offering a hint of Sun symbolism, considering the Pharaoh is a human representation of the Sun God Ra, his face symbolises the Sun when it is close to the horizon, the Sun's reflection on the water resembles the pattern and length of Tut's beard.

Sun on the water, Tut's beard

All around us are spirits of one kind or another, with various motives, just like the variety of people in our physical world. Using the law of attraction, we attract spirits to us in much the same way as we do people. Seeds are planted in the garden of our subconscious via thoughts and suggestions coming from our focal mind. Whatever we focus our attention on, or occupy our minds with, stimulate those kinds of seeds which grow within our subconscious/spiritual garden. The Adam/soul exercises the will to nurture whatever seeds are desired while the Eve/spirit connects with the fruit grown from the seeds planted by Adam and the focal consciousness. The garden and its fruit acts as a beacon attracting other spirits resonating at a similar frequency.

"Therefore, by their fruits ye shall know them."- Matthew 7:20 (KJ21)

These spirits or non-human entities will help to amplify the assortment of energies and frequencies growing in your spiritual garden. Just like thousands of rain drops on a tin roof this amplified energy filters its way out and into our physical reality, creating new experiences for the individual who was focusing on specific things. If you focus on good things, good things will come to you, it is the same with bad things. The fighter preoccupied with conflict and death, has a garden to match his thoughts, this attracts the appropriate spirits which help him manifest his reality. The fighter will live by the sword and die by it.

When one dies or separates from the physical body they begin a journey into the spirit world. The only thing which has changed, from their perspective, is that their point of attention within their consciousness has shifted into spirit form, many will have guides to help them on their journey, but some stay Earth bound for various reasons, hanging around for a while unaware they have died, others stay bound due to unhealthy attachments to families, homes, businesses and other earthly familiarities. A portion stay due to perverted spiritual beliefs or an expectation of being destined for hell. Those who cannot accept that they are dead sometimes appear as ghosts or apparitions seeking attention. On the whole, most spirits ascend into the spirit world smoothly.

It is believed, in many cultures, that most people will have at least one guardian spirit protecting them from harm throughout most, if not all, of their lives. A guardian spirit is generally considered to be someone who you have a connection with, either in this life or a past one; it could be a deceased family member, an ancestor or a friend. In their spirit form, they look out for you, preserving your safety and interests.

The human connection to the spirit realm is not easily apparent at this point in history. Our proximity to the Sirius star system may have some bearing on this. Sirius is a luminary, another expressive representation of our subconscious, its distance from the Sun could explain why our physical consciousness does not easily interact with our subconscious and spiritual side, which may possibly improve as the Sun and Sirius move closer together. During the day time when the Sun's energy stimulates our focal consciousness, our spiritual awareness is not at its peak due to earthly physical distractions. When the Sun goes down our focal awareness subsides. From midnight to around 4am, when the Sun is on the other side of the Earth, our spiritual awareness improves, this is known as the "witching hour". Anyone wishing to connect with spirits, ghosts or other entities in this realm are advised to do it during this time period. Spiritual activity doesn't increase during these hours, it is just that our ability to sense spiritual connections appears to increase because the Sun is out of the way. Another requirement for successfully connecting with the spirit realm is to be relaxed and at peace, allowing the mind to wander wherever it wishes to go. When in fear or anxiety one tends to be grounded to lower energy vibrations within this physical plane creating an obstacle towards spiritual interaction.

The spirit world is abundant with every type of spirit for all eventualities, whatever you wish to do in the physical realm can be catered for and helped into reality by like-minded spirits. You set the seed, nurture the idea, and the spirits will help you turn them into reality. This is why you often see individuals who break away from their old lives, sometimes moving to new places, find the universe and synchronicity working in their favour. People, places and information appear to come to them at the moment when they most need it. It is as though their connection to a higher source of consciousness is working in their favour, something most people will put down to just coincidence. When you meet someone, who has similar spirits interacting with them, you will automatically feel a connection, that is because you already know them on a subconscious/spiritual level.

With unlimited potential within the spiritual realm, the person has a duty to his fellow humans when it comes to nurturing virtuous seeds as opposed to feeding a spiritual garden full of weeds and vices. The control system's influence over what we see and hear ultimately impacts the collective subconscious, and by massaging public perception they align the collective with the required energy spheres throughout the spirit realm. Consequently, by drawing in necessary spiritual influences which amplify our collective thoughts they can easily promote their agenda. This is one of the dangers associated with globalisation and the new Technological Age. The control system now can influence the whole planet with any belief, whether true or false, simultaneously, whereas before, when we had millions of individual bulk heads acting independently, with enough time to process ideas and suggestions, we could alleviate big disasters preventing the ship going down too quickly. Without the bulkheads, the human collective subconscious can be steered to a tipping point, using propaganda and relentless media exposure, an atmosphere of war can be artificially stimulated. Furthermore, as the war drums begin to beat pro war spirits will infest the minds of the unquestioning masses, amplifying their desire for revenge and blood, and once they pass the point of no return, a disastrous sequence of events will be set in motion as Pandora's box is opened and the hounds of hell are released.

Children's spirits, are untainted and pure, they are generally happy in their simple gardens, closely connected to their spiritual roots. They have not yet become corrupted by perverted beliefs which confuse and attract malevolent spirits, watched closely by their guardian spirit who keep them at a safe distance, away from unwanted influences.

The term spirit has been adopted to describe strong distilled alcoholic beverages, ironic for a substance which poisons and wrecks the body, giving a false sense of spiritual highs. While the drink upsets the chemical balance of his body it will eventually turn into depression, disrupting a balanced consciousness. The drunks spirits may find themselves sharing their garden with pro alcohol spirits, which help draw other alcoholics to him from all walks of life.

Interdimensional entities

It is generally accepted that we live within the constraints of three spatial dimensions and one of time, but is this accurate? Time is restricted to a single dimension when looking at it from a rigid lineal perspective. One could speculate that time has three dimensions past, present and future. If we look at this closely we see a correlation between space, time and consciousness. Space has three dimensions X, Y and Z. Time has three and so does consciousness with Focal, Sub and higher mind Logos. Instead of looking for a fourth dimension within the realms of spatial awareness, one may discover more through an understanding of our relationship to the spiritual and conscious realms. The interaction between these three realms is as real as time is with space, combining to create our earthly experience. One could argue that we already live in a nine-dimensional reality.

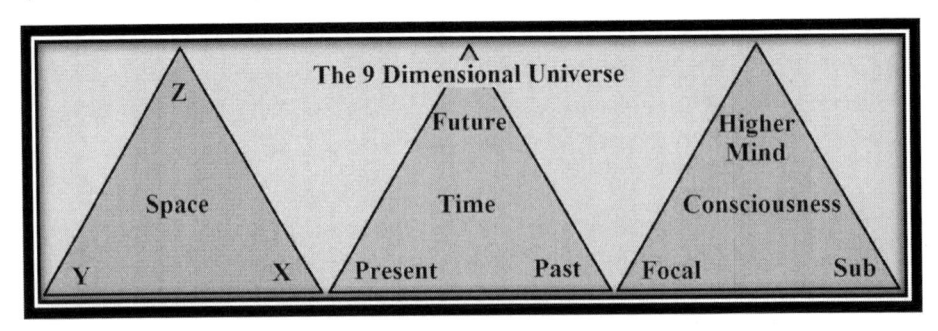

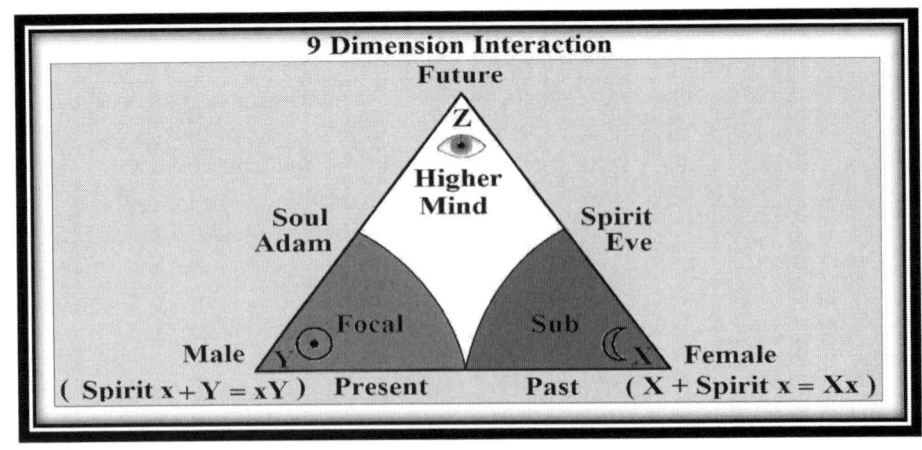

The 9 Dimensional Universe

Space: Z, Y, X

Time: Future, Present, Past

Consciousness: Higher Mind, Focal, Sub

9 Dimension Interaction

Future — Z — Higher Mind

Soul Adam — Spirit Eve

Focal — Sub

Male Y — Female X

(Spirit x + Y = xY)   Present   Past   (X + Spirit x = Xx)

From a practical point of view, we can see how these dimensional interactions play out in our simple earthly experience. For example, the subconscious is the part of our mind which stores everything we ever did in our past, while our focal consciousness is primarily concerned with the present and what we do in the now. The X and Y chromosomes assigned to both male and female can be expressed as a spacial X or Y coordinate with a added spiritual dimension (x) added. In the male we see both X and Y chromosomes whereas in the female we fine a double X. The future is only known by the higher mind Logos consciousness, but through the soul or the spirit one can draw any variation of the future he or she desires.

One can appreciate that with multiple dimensions it is possible to interact in all manner of combinations, just as we have the ability to move through space in our limited physical bodies, spirits also move freely in their spheres of familiarity. In our minds, we can recollect the past and imagine the future, stimulating our perspective of life and influencing our present. Sightings of UFO's, ghosts and other kinds of apparitions could just be various expressions of universal consciousness moving between dimensions.

As we interact with the spirit world during sleep, other dimensional entities could be doing the same in our world in much the same way. UFO's and apparitions have a tendency to appear from nowhere and disappear just as quickly. It is far more plausible than the traditional view of extra-terrestrial visitors travelling billions of miles from outer space, to unpack their buckets and spades for a two-week holiday here on the Earth.

Extra terrestrials

Beings from outer space have fascinated people for centuries; the idea of an interstellar race visiting the Earth, even interacting with us on various levels is legendary. There are many documented reports of sightings and encounters with all kinds of strange creatures, but distinguishing the extra-terrestrial from an interdimensional could be difficult and confusing. Due to the vastness of space, and the time it would take to get here, the probability of extra-terrestrial life visiting the Earth seems unlikely, which makes the interdimensional explanation far more favourable. The existence of extra-terrestrial life, given the infinite size of the universe, is more or less a certainty, the question is can they get here?

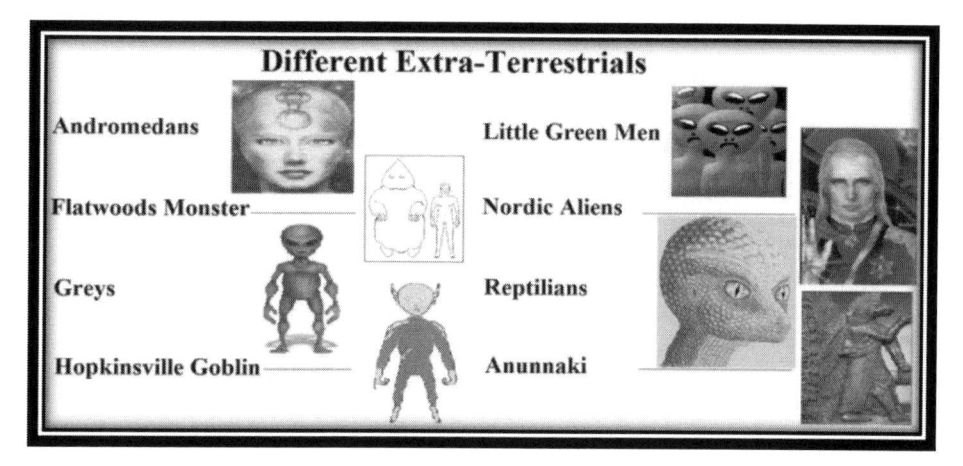

Different Extra-Terrestrials

- Andromedans
- Flatwoods Monster
- Greys
- Hopkinsville Goblin
- Little Green Men
- Nordic Aliens
- Reptilians
- Anunnaki

Some people including prominent scientists have serious doubts as to the validity of the American manned space missions to the Moon, believing that the whole Apollo program was not what we think it was. Their reasons for doubting the official version of events are numerous, but one criticism is that humans cannot withstand the accumulative effects of the radiation out in space,[6] and to provide adequate protection would make any rocket so heavy it would never get off the ground. If this is the case, other biological entities wishing to visit the Earth would encounter similar difficulties. Any advanced alien civilisation with a desire to interact with earthlings would find another less time-consuming way of getting here, star-gates have been suggested as one possibility. To simplify the complexity of this subject I will put extra-terrestrials, with star-gate technology, along with the interdimensionals, whether they use machines to move through time and space or they have natural interdimensional abilities, from our perspective, the result is still the same.

Who is in control?

Many people are convinced that non-human entities have been influencing man's affairs since the beginning of time, it is even speculated by some that we are the result of scientific experiments by outside entities manipulating our genetics. Zecharia Sitchin a Soviet born American wrote many books about an alternative to the origins of the human race. One of only a hand full of people able to decipher ancient Sumerian clay tablets, he pieced together a different version of history. Sitchin believed that a highly advanced race of human like beings came to Earth from the planet Nibiru, approximately 450,000 years ago. Sitchin speculates that the planet is part of our solar system with an elliptical orbit, far beyond Neptune.[7] According to Sitchin the Sumerians called these visitors the Anunnaki (the offspring of Anu (sky God)), who are also suspected as being the Nephilim mentioned in Genesis.

"The Nephilim were on the Earth in those days--and also afterward--when the sons of God went to the daughters of humans and had children by them. They were the heroes of old, men of renown." - Genesis 6:4 (NIV)

The King James translation refers to the Nephilim as giants.

"There were giants in the earth in those days; and also after that, when the sons of God came in unto the daughters of men, and they bare children to them, the same became mighty men which were of old, men of renown." - Genesis 6:4 (KJV)

This could explain the existence of megalithic structures which are found all over the world. Not an easy feet for us to construct and move around, but a piece of cake for giants with advanced technology. The Sumerian writings talk of how the Anunnaki came to this planet looking for rare minerals, and in order to mine the minerals, they created a slave race of humanoids known as Homo sapiens, they mixed their Anunnaki genes with the native Homo erectus, creating the basis of what we are today. It is also though that they created a superior race with a greater percentage of the Anunnaki gene, these became the rulers who were given the "**divine right of Kings**", a superior Anunnaki/Human hybrid blood line.

Zecharia Sitchin | **Anunnaki** | **Nephilim**

"We saw the Nephilim there (the descendants of Anak come from the Nephilim). We seemed like grasshoppers in our own eyes, and we looked the same to them." - Numbers 13:33 (NIV)

"And there was yet a battle in Gath, where was a man of great stature, that had on every hand six fingers, and on every foot six toes, four and twenty in number; and he also was born to the giant." - 2 Samuel 21:20 (KJV)

"For only Og king of Bashan remained of the remnant of giants; behold his bedstead was a bedstead of iron; is it not in Rabbath of the children of Ammon? Nine cubits was the length thereof, and four cubits the breadth of it, after the cubit of a man." - Deuteronomy 3:11 (KJV)

A bed of 9 X 4 cubits would be equivalent to 13.5 X 6 feet. When you compare this to a standard king-sized bed of 6.6 X 6.3 feet, you can appreciate the scale. One can only imagine how big the Nephilim/Anunnaki were, but it makes sense from the perspective of the Nephilim ruling elite, to create a slave race half their size or less. When one looks at the picture held by Zecharia Sitchin, you can clearly see the size of the ruler, even in a sitting position he appears at the same level as the other men who stand before him.

"These four were born to the giant in Gath, and fell by the hand of David and by the hand of his servants." - 2 Samuel 21:22 (KJ21)

David & Goliath

The ruling classes throughout history have sought to keep their blood lineages pure and undiluted by breeding incestuously amongst themselves. If their DNA is indeed special with a greater percentage of superior genetics, descending from the Gods of the ancient world, then one would understand and expect them to keep this tradition. If these God like creatures did come to the Earth and interbreed with the ape man, creating us and our ruling elite bloodlines, we could expect the elite to have a greater spiritual connection to these extradimensional beings. There could be an argument made to suggest that although we are confined to this 4-dimensional space time reality, the descendants of the Gods, those with superior DNA, have a natural interaction with other dimensional realms, especially those resonating with their genetic frequencies. I would also suggest that if the Anunnaki/Nephilim came here, then why not various other beings and entities, also mixing with life on Earth, producing all kinds of hybrid offshoots, this would explain why there are different races in different parts of the world. Although man was made in the image of the Gods, we seem to have limited potential when it comes to accessing other dimensional realities, could this be due to our recent monotheistic mentality, limiting our modern spiritual/universal connections, a method imposed upon us by our rulers to keep us under control? When we look at the ancient Star of David Kabbala symbol with its 7 planetary/spiritual building blocks, we can only speculate as to why modern religions isolate themselves away from polytheism and the 7 planets. This could also be the key to expanding human consciousness in a multi-dimensional way.

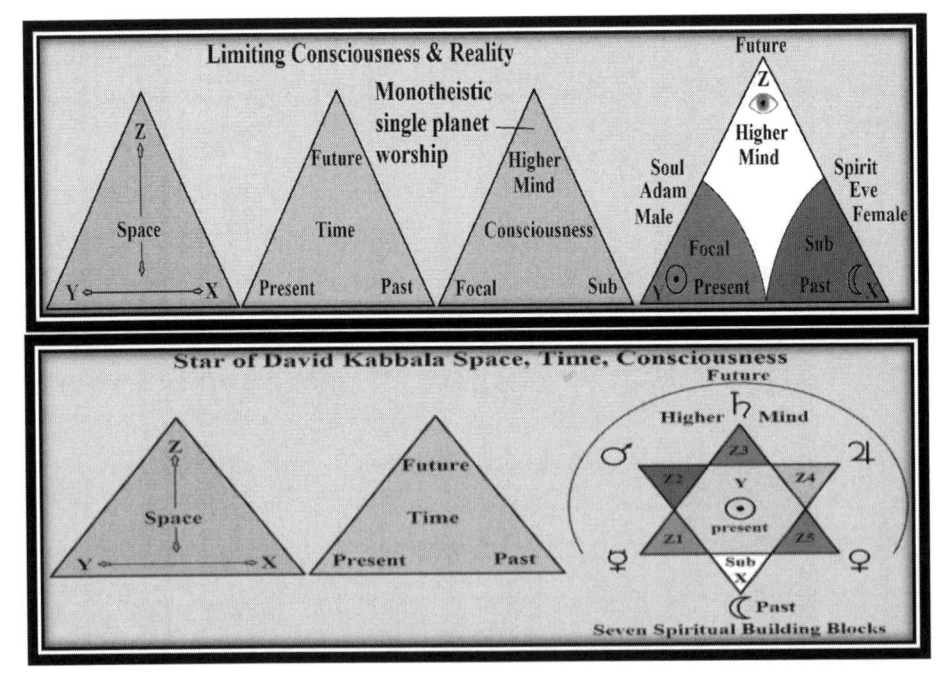

When we expand our awareness towards higher levels of spiritual consciousness, opening ourselves up to a greater array of planetary frequencies, we energise our spirit/soul connection to the Logos, allowing our five senses, in a paranormal way, access to a greater number of frequencies and therefore expanded realities. At present humanity is locked in a vicious cycle of division stimulated by various kinds of monotheistic planet worship, feeding each religion with a narrow frequency band of reality, suppressing their ability to influence their own futures. If humanity united under an umbrella of polytheistic holistic universal energy, which expanded their consciousness, we may find that our physical reality is far more harmonious and balanced.

"No problem can be solved from the same level of consciousness that created it." - Albert Einstein

The various races we see on the planet today could be the result of thousands of years of successful interbreeding between Homo-erectus, interdimensionals and hybrids. Over time those races which no longer served the evolving interests of non-human entities have, through various methods, been eliminated. Only recently has main stream science concluded that all the races on the planet are from the same source. This is true in the sense that they all have a lineage to Homo-erectus, but there are obvious differences both physically and consciously. If non-human entities are responsible for the way we are, it wouldn't be the first-time science swung in favour of a political position to disguise the truth. It seems that any ancient race with an active spiritual and soulful connection to their higher mind, and the rhythms of nature, have either been eradicated or reduced to a pitiful existence, superseded by modern races eager to support suppressive systems of control. This was true in both North and South America, the Aborigines of Australia and the elongated skulls of the Paracas, Africa too has seen its fair share of racial evolutionary change. To get one race to annihilate another is not easy, intrinsically most people do not want war, they are not interested in organising themselves into fighting machines to kill each other. Only when psychopathic rulers pervert beliefs and nurture hatred, is it then possible to persuade people to participate in these types of non-human activities of killing each other enmasse. It is as though a non-human influence initiates and accelerates this type of behaviour, and once the ball is rolling the energy created engulfs and poisons the minds of those involved until the flames of hatred eventually subside. When the fever is over those who are left are bewildered as to how it all began. Non-human entities favour the psychopath, technology and the corporation structure because they are easily manipulated towards fulfilling anti human objectives.

Each race on Earth is slightly different, both in look and behaviour. This could be explained by the interbreeding of various entities and/or proximity of that race's first biological manifestation in the flesh, the position on the Earth of each race's Adam in comparison to the position of the planets and universal energy which influenced the DNA and epi genetic configuration, when the Gods first breathed life into their nostrils. A mixture of proximity and non-human biological interaction seems to be the most plausible explanation and could be the reason for our racial differences.

Is it possible that interdimensionals have been here for a long time, and are the hidden hand behind our various governments, a continuity of change pushing humanity towards the next phase of non-human control and manipulation? The push for globalisation could be the result of non-human interference, it seems that although the majority of humanity want independence and sovereignty, the policy makers are forcing globalisation upon the whole planet. When we analyse history, it has always been a battle for one's freedoms, each generation fighting against the suppression of liberty and their ability for self-determination. The power structures have always sought for greater control into fewer hands, pulling humanity into a net of manageable slavery, servicing the elite's interests.

In May 2013 former, Canadian Defence Minister and 23-year parliamentarian Paul Hellyer testified at the "Citizen Hearing on Disclosure Conference" in Washington DC. In his testimony to a packed audience he stated:

"At least four species of alien have been visiting Earth for thousands of years." "There are live ET's on Earth at this present time, and at least two of them are working with the United States government." "There are different species with different agendas." "Tall whites are living on United States air force property and working in cooperation with the US air force and sharing technology." "We live in a cosmos teaming with life of various sorts" "Is being kept secret by the same vested interests who control our destiny, who are these vested interests and what are they up to. The cabal comprise of members of three sisters, the CFR, the Bilderbergs and the Trilateral Commission. The international banking cartel, oil cartel, members of various intelligence organisations and select members of the military, together have become a shadow government of not only the US but of much of the western world. The aim of the game is a world government, comprising members of the cabal who are elected by no one and accountable to no one, and according to Mr Rockefeller the plan is well advanced."- Paul Hellyer, former Canadian defence minister.[8]

On the night of February 20th 1954, while on vacation to Palm Springs, President Eisenhower went missing, after he reappeared rumours emerged speculating that he had been taken to Edwards Airforce Base to meet with ET's/The Anunnaki. Eisenhower's cover story of an emergency dentist visit did not wash with many people, leaving room for all sorts of theories as to what he had been up to. Retired Command Sergeant Major Robert O Dean stated that Eisenhower did in fact visit the air base along with a group of representatives, who made contact with entities from another world.

"Among the group that greeted the Annunaki in 1954 at Rurak, which is now Edwards Air Force Base. There was an Arch Bishop from Los Angeles by the name of Mike McIntyre, he had been invited to be present when they landed to meet them, because Icke (Eisenhower) thought somebody ought to be representing the church here, you know; and they brought McIntyre over from LA, to Rurak. They were there for two days, and these guys scared the shit out of everybody with their technology, and they talked openly. The two hovered over the runway for two days, never landed, no legs or nothing they just hovered over the damn runway. It's all on film, but the other guys come out, landed right in front of the hanger got out and went over shook hands or whatever I don't know what the hell they did. McIntyre was present because Icke had invited him. After it was all over with after the second day and these guys get back in their ship and off they go; our intelligence people got a hold of McIntyre and says Arch Bishop you got to understand something, you can't talk about anything you've seen, this is beyond top secret, you can't say a word about what we have just experienced here." - Robert O Dean, Retired Command Sergeant Major[9]

It seems logical to assume that any external race would connect with humanity through influential channels, avoiding the majority of mankind. One could also make the assumption that any large organisation with the potential to influence and advance any non-human agenda would be targeted for infiltration. Powerful institutions, corporations and influential psychopaths present themselves as favourable targets. It has been suspected for many years that some secret societies, with their secret rituals, are tapping into other dimensions, seeking guidance from external entities. While other entities interact with our reality, they prefer we stay consciously naïve unable to interfere with theirs.

Even with the version of history we are presented with, many stories and accounts have been documented regarding unexplained phenomena and non-human entities. During the Renaissance, various artists depicted strange objects in the skies on what would generally be considered as classical artwork.

The Baptism of Christ 1710, Aert de Gelder

Crucifixion of Christ, Visoki Dečani Monastery

Carlo Crivelli, Annunciation with St. Emidius (1486)

Is it possible that the whole of human civilisation has developed under the guidance of these non-human entities, and we are essentially a slave race created from start to finish, with traces of obvious interbreeding intentionally filtered out from modern society or kept hidden, out of sight and away from scrutiny, allowing the Darwinian theory of lineal evolution to go unchallenged? During his lifetime Leonardo da Vinci accomplished many things, not only was he a great artist and inventor, he was also a stickler for accurately recording detail, among some of his drawings and sketches there are a selection of grotesque heads. If they are a true reflection of what he was witnessing, one may wonder as to what other varieties of beings coexisted with humanity even in our not so distant past.

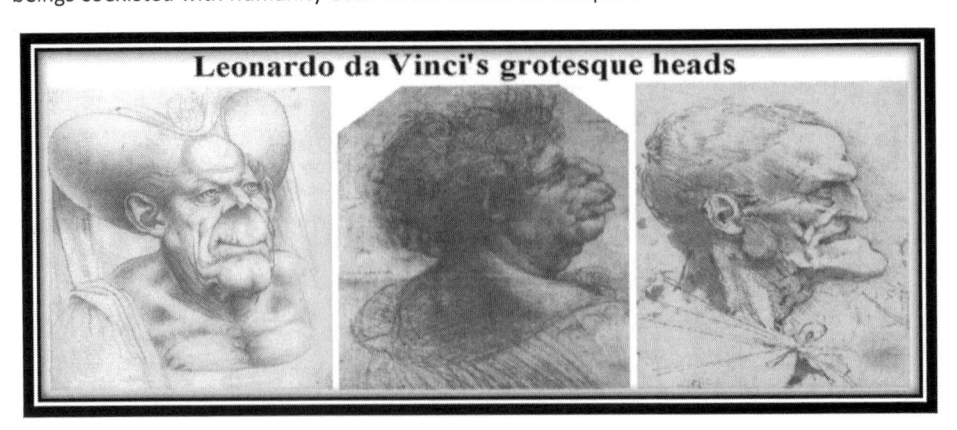

Leonardo da Vinci's grotesque heads

The Pharaoh/Masonic connection

After the decline of the pharaonic Egyptian dynasties, the bloodline powers behind those dynasties moved with the times, expanding their influence out of Egypt and into Europe, starting with Rome, transforming it, under Julius Caesar, from a republic into a new Egyptian style imperialistic dictatorship. The descendants of powerful wealthy families intermarried keeping their wealth protected. From there the Roman Catholic Church evolved giving credence to the Knights Templar's who battled with the Muslims for control of old strategic cities in the Middle East, spreading their own Christian grip over trade and commerce. When the Templar's lost their headquarters at the Siege of Acre on May 18, 1291 bringing an end to the crusades,[10] many suspect they moved their wealth and power over to Switzerland, which coincidentally was established on 1st August 1291 along with a flag resembling the cross of the Templars. It is also speculated that elements of the ancient wealth and power of the Pharaonic bloodlines went to Switzerland with the Templars, taking their gold with them. Swizz banks have always been at the centre of world banking, financing both sides of wars, while remaining neutral, a safe haven for the mega wealthy and elite bloodlines.

The Freemasonic movement evolved from the Knights Templar concept, using their pharaonic knowledge, traditions and Isis cults. Is it possible that the real power behind international finance, multinational corporations and globalisation still rest in the hands of the descendants of the power which once ruled Egypt? When one looks around western cities we find pharaonic/Masonic Isis cult Egyptian symbolism everywhere, obelisks are found all over the world, with St Peters square hosting one of the biggest. It is also no coincidence to find Swizz guards protecting the Vatican, an old partnership between the Templars and the Catholic Church's corporate headquarters. The Washington monument is also a huge obelisk, paying homage to pharaonic/Masonic Isis cults. The Statue of Liberty or Goddess Libertas is the Roman equivalent of the Egyptian Goddess Isis, presented as a gift from the French Grand Orient Temple Masons to the Freemasons of America.[11] It is also important to note that the name AMERICA is very close to the Egyptian Sun God Amen Ra, (AMEn RicA). The power behind this cult has not gone away, it is real, and I suspect they are the financial backers and policy makers behind this latest version of ISIS in the Middle East.

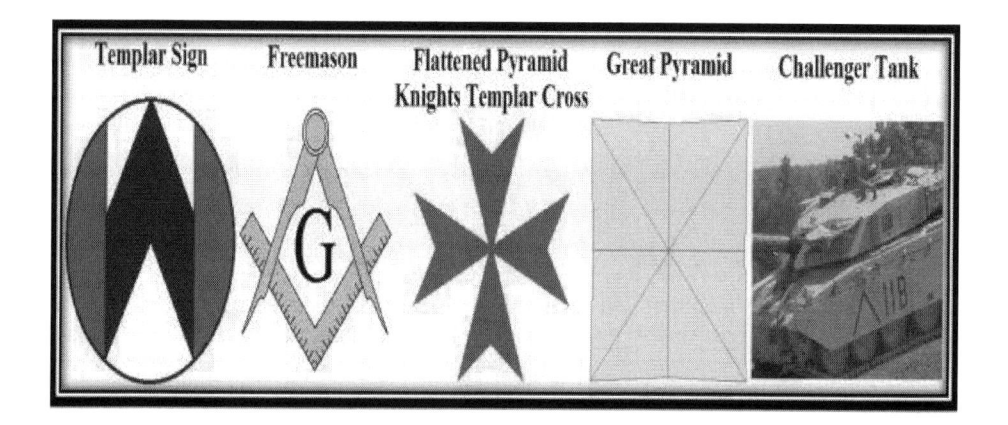

Pharaonic / Masonic, Knights Templar Cross

The Orthodox Hebrews have a long history of being persecuted and used by pharaonic power, hence the Exodus and the creation of organised Judaism, this persecution never went away and continued under the pharaonic/Masonic/Zionist movement, which just happen to have had their first conference in Basel, Switzerland. Maybe the ancient Pharaoh's were a race of interdimensional hybrids, with the intention of reorganising the human gene pool, targeting specific races for extinction during the past 5000 years? Who knows what they have in store for the rest of us? It would explain why Prince Philip would like to come back as a super virus, killing the majority of humanity.

Satanic rituals

What most people consider as satanic rituals, could be just other form of interdimensional interaction. From ancient times to today, all over the world, rituals, ceremonies and gatherings, tap into powerful external influences. The true nature and purpose of some rituals are closely kept within inner circles; trusted participants guard the keys to these other dimensions, believing they will share in earthly wealth and prosperity as long as they uphold their oaths and promises. Child/virgin sacrifice is a common theme, synonymous with occult rituals. The sacrifice of the pure spirit/soul of the child is an expression of dedication and worship to the entities outside our reality. It is a gift of loyalty, destroying a pure hearted biological reflection of the physical balanced universe at that given moment, offering one's service and control over to a non-physical entity. When the child is sacrificed during a terrifying traumatic ritual, its body naturally produces high levels of adrenalin, along with many other chemicals. Drinking this blood is said to possess hallucinogenic qualities, allowing easier connection to other dimensions during ceremonies. The cremation of care at bohemian grove is based on this type of ceremonial worship, who knows what goes on in secret.

Many people feel that there is an anti-human agenda playing out across the world, a future course unfavourable to the aspirations of humanity, confusing many observant people, who can't quite figure out what, where or why things are unfolding the way they are. Just as we humans have tried to colonise and influence other countries, it is not unreasonable to assume interdimensional entities are colonising other dimensional realities. Through various compartmentalised organisations, corrupt governments, secret societies and industrialised militarisation these entities seduce humanity towards interdependency, forcing them in a direction they will find hard to escape. Once the technological grid is in place, humanity will be trapped, no longer masters of their environment, but subordinate to an electronic globalised enslavement grid, possibly controlled from other dimensions. They may even seek to alter our physical environment, drawing it closer towards a compromise between both dimensional realities, allowing them to coexist. Climate change and geoengineering could be one of many ways of making this possible. Maybe this has been a reoccurring situation throughout history, where humanity is only free when restrictive technological is destroyed either by internal civil conflicts or by cosmic cataclysms, this maybe one of the reasons for the scattered relics of our ancient megalithic past.

Intrusive thoughts and mind parasites

Many people suffer from intrusive thoughts, unwelcome disharmonising involuntary thoughts, entering the focal mind from within. These thoughts come from the subconscious, the spirit realm, sometimes habitually reoccurring, paralysing and anxiety provoking. Our focal consciousness is stimulated by our five senses and the people and things which surround us; likewise, the subconscious is similarly stimulated by suggestions and stimuli taking place by our connection to the spirit realm. Most people have a spirit/soul connection to higher mind consciousness, self-policing their thoughts and actions for the greater good of the collective. Even though many people experience intrusive thoughts, most disregard them, brushing them aside. The garden of the subconscious which we nurture during our lives attracts spirits of similar frequencies. The psychopath on the other hand is a vacant vessel with little or no spirit/soul connection to the Logos. Their subconscious will be an ideal playground for non-human entities to infest, making uncensored suggestions which feed into their focal projected ego's. The psychopath operates without conscience, service to self, with little empathy or regard for others; they do not have a connection to the higher mind therefore they have no stake in the collective outcome, only what they can gain for themselves in this one physical experience. Their subconscious can be targeted by entities with various non-human agendas. This makes the psychopath an ideal candidate for compromised corporate and political leadership.

Intrusive thoughts can come from malevolent influences, designed to deviate, disunite and disempower mankind, another divide and rule tactic making it easier to enslave humanity. Just as the serpent in the garden was able to seduce Eve with its suggestions, we as individuals must be aware and in control of our thoughts, some not our own, coming from within. Life can be made easier if we focus on the now, as opposed to dwelling on the past or fearful of the future, it is a simple but helpful guide for having command over one's thoughts, also meditating and focusing on the good while dismissing the negative.

"Let your eyes look directly ahead and let your gaze be fixed straight in front of you." - Proverbs 4:25

"For from within, out of the heart of men, proceed evil thoughts, adulteries, fornications, murders" - Mark 7:21

"Finally, brothers and sisters, whatever is true, whatever is noble, whatever is right, whatever is pure, whatever is lovely, whatever is admirable - if anything is excellent or praiseworthy - think about such things." - Philippians 4:8

```
                    The Psychopath
         Adam                ⊙              Eve
         ♂         Soul  Higher Mind  Spirit  ♀
                      No Spirit / Soul
                        Connection
Focal Consciousness                        Subconscious Open to
Open To Suggestions    ⊙ Focal    Sub ☾    Suggestion From Non
From Surroundings                          Human Entities
      Projecting Ego         Body
                    The Psychopath
```

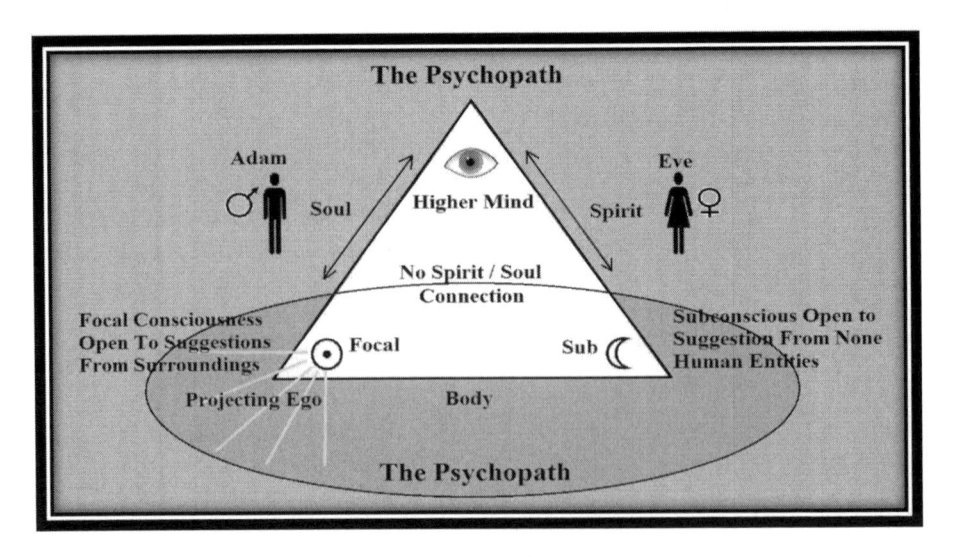

Cloning and synthetic humanoids

In this modern world of division and competition, there is a possibility that advanced technology exists in the area of cloning and synthetic humanoids, manufactured in an attempt to influence humanity towards non-human goals. The advantage of this form of technology to any group of elite controllers is self-evident, and it has been speculated by some that it is real and has been around for decades. As with many secret governmental programs and black operations, sensitive technology of this nature would never be made public, and as with all technology, what enters the main stream is years behind what government and military are working on behind the scenes. It has been over 20 years since Dolly the sheep was cloned back in the 1990's. I would suspect with the best scientists, unlimited budgets and no ethical rules holding them back, scientists somewhere working in military projects have already mastered this technology. The clone or synthetic humanoid may look like us and act like us but will essentially be a factory-made psychopath, devoid of a spirit/soul connection, a perfect vessel for the non-human entities to utilise. With the emergence of transhumanist technology, our traditional biological bodies will no longer be sovereign, especially if we are forced, through legislation, to be microchipped with devices capable of tampering with our body's natural resonant frequency. If clones are being mass produced, acting as an army of representatives, this would explain why society is moving in the direction it is, and if this really is the case, as some suspect, we truly are heading into a very dark future, with non-human entities at the helm. It would also make more sense when viewing our inhumane past, if we consider opposing entities, equally as psychopathic, initiating conflicts using their subordinate human races as cannon fodder, and any previous race or organisation seeking independence from this form of control would find themselves being dealt with severely.

Underground bases

According to Philip Schneider, a US ex-government geologist and structural engineer, who became involved in building underground military bases during the late 70's, there are many different races of alien beings living deep underground, and have been with us for thousands of years.[12] Schneider also stated that the US has 131 active deep underground military bases, and there are 1477 all over the world. Many people are aware that billions of dollars annually are siphoned off from tax payers money into black budget secret military government operations, and because the US holds the world's reserve currency, they have a bottomless pit to tap into. On September 10th 2001, the day before 9/11, the then Secretary of Defence, Donald Rumsfeld, admitted to losing $2.3 trillion of Pentagon money, with absolutely no idea as to its whereabouts.[13]

In August 1979 Schneider was working on a new deep underground military base down in New Mexico, when the drilling machine they were using repeatedly broke. He suspected something was not quite right when dozens of green and black barrette soldiers showed up. Consequently, when his team was sent down to inspect the drilling machine all hell broke loose.

"I was involved in building an addition to the deep underground military base at Dulce, which is probably the deepest base. It goes down seven levels and over 2.5 miles deep. At that particular time, we had drilled four distinct holes in the desert, and we were going to link them together and blow out large sections at a time. My job was to go down the holes and check the rock samples, and recommend the explosive to deal with the particular rock. As I was headed down there, we found ourselves amidst a large cavern that was full of outer-space aliens, otherwise known as large Greys. I shot two of them. At that time, there were 30 people down there. About 40 more came down after this started, and all of them got killed. We had surprised a whole underground base of existing aliens. Later, we found out that they had been living on our planet for a long time, perhaps a million years. This could explain a lot of what is behind the theory of ancient astronauts. Anyway, I got shot in the chest with one of their weapons, which was a box on their body that blew a hole in me and gave me a nasty dose of cobalt radiation. I have had cancer because of that." - Philip Schneider 1995

Schneider was only one of a handful of people with level one security clearance, and possibly the only one speaking out publicly about what he knew. He says there were nine underground bases in and around area 51, employing 18,000 people in shifts, developing and testing technology shared by non-human entities. The act of speaking out put Schneider in a compromising position, he was essentially breaking his official oath and ultimately the law. This could be one of the reasons for his mysterious premature death in January 1996, only a few months after going public.

The huge sums and resources involved in building these DUMB's (Deep Underground Military Bases) derive from fear and insecurity. Money which could be used to eradicate human suffering and poverty is being spent on this underground world. One has to ask why is it of benefit to humanity or is it primarily for non-human entities to exist and interact unmolested, deep under the Earth, shielded from the electromagnetic influences of cosmic planetary bodies (The Gods), which stimulate the rest of human activity? It is possible that these Godless players have already mapped out the future of the Earth and all its inhabitants, hiding themselves from the effects of their non-human agenda, artificial humanoids living in an artificial environment promoting an artificial future of transhumanism. It is as though there is a breakaway civilisation, one with all the money, technology and connections to this other world of interdimensional non-human activity, and the rest of us, surface dwellers, existing in an open-air prison on the unwanted scraps the elite leave behind, a prison designed to keep us busy and distracted. Maybe when this breakaway civilisation has reached its goal, and built its death star, they will have no more use for us surface dwellers? Not only do we hear reports of underground bases but also undersea ones too. William Cooper, ex US Naval Intelligence Officer, while serving on a submarine out in the Pacific, witnessed a UFO come out of the sea and fly off.

"When I left the Air Force I went into the Navy, and this is where everything began to happen for me. I had originally intended to just go from service to service and do something that very few people have ever done before. I was a very adventurous, very crazy young man, and I thought that that would be a pretty exciting life. I volunteered for submarines, and while on the submarine USS Tyroot, SS-416, on a transit between the Portland/Seattle area and Pearl Harbor, which was our home port; the Pearl Harbor sub base, as the port lookout I saw a craft, saucer shaped, the size of a Midway class carrier, aircraft carrier, for those of you who don't know how big that is; it's huge, come up out of the water approximately two and a half nautical miles off the port bow, which is about 45 degrees to the left of the pointy end of the submarine. It tumbled slowly on its own axis, and went up into the clouds. It appeared to be moving slowly to me at a distance of two and a half nautical miles, but in reality, it was moving pretty fast because it came up out of the water, did a few tumbles, and it was gone!" - William Cooper[14]

In 2002, Gary McKinnon, a Scottish systems administrator and computer hacker was arrested for hacking into 97 US Army, Navy, Air Force, Department of Defence and Nasa computers, looking for evidence of suppressed advanced technology. He was charged with penetrating the biggest military computer hack of all time. During this 13 month period of system penetration it has been speculated that he discovered secret documentary evidence of all kinds of off world technology including, anti-gravity, free energy and reverse engineered alien space craft. His activities caused such an embarrassment to the US authorities that they sought to extradite him to the US for trial and throw him in jail for 60 years, setting an example to other hackers. In 2012 the British Home Secretary Theresa May announced that the extradition order had been blocked and that McKinnon would be safe in the UK for the time being.[15]

Star-gates and portals

The disruptions in the Middle East are multifaceted, not as simple as the main stream media have us believe. This area is at the heart of the ancient world, Sumer, Babylon, Egypt and Mesopotamia; all have secrets buried of the past, remnants of ancient history and hidden technology. As we hurtle through space entering a new phase of cosmic energetic influence, is it possible that ancient portals and star-gates have reactivated, opening up conduits to other dimensions? some people believe so, and that one aspect of the wars unfolding in that area are to determine which factions have ultimate control over this technology. During the morning hours of December 9th, 2009, as many Norwegians were preparing for a state visit from the US President, Barack Obama, a mysterious blue and white light appeared from the east, over the mountains of northern Norway. Initially the light started out as a blue beam but transformed into a twisting spiral of white light, turning into a giant spiral hundreds of miles in diameter, rotating for several minutes before being swallowed up by a black hole which appeared from the centre moving outwards. Those who witnessed it said it was not a natural phenomenon but a mysterious anomaly unusual for those parts.[16]

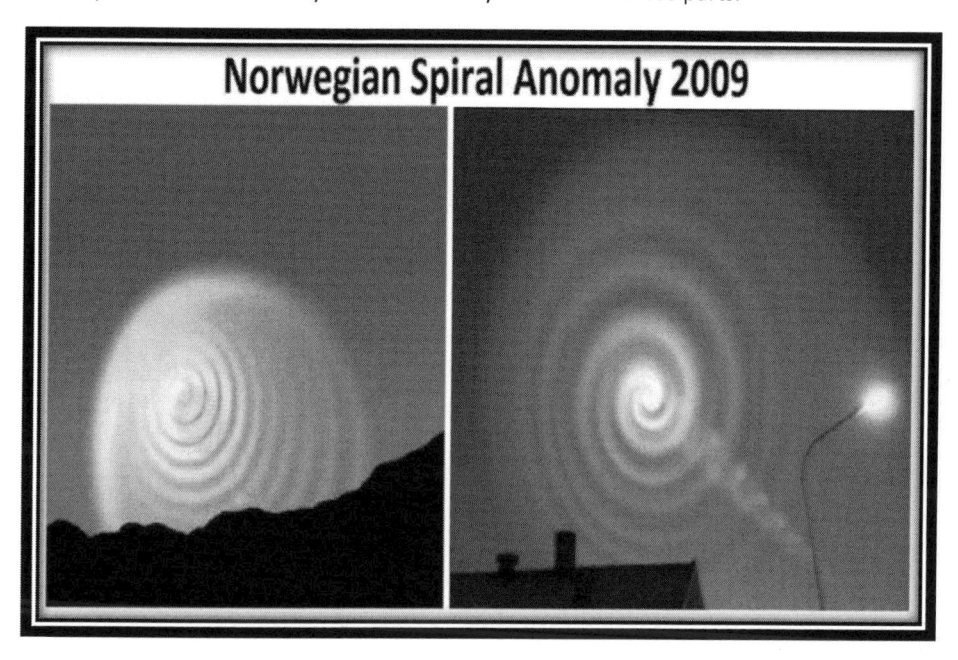

Norwegian Spiral Anomaly 2009

With the geopolitical situation unfolding in the world, one can't help but wonder whether this forced integration and refugee policy is an effort to make it easier for non-human entities and synthetics to assimilate, going unnoticed in this new multicultural globalised society. Anonymity in a crowd is what they seek, allowing them to advance their control over the native surface dwellers, as they pave the way for the next phase of human evolution and globalisation. With their superior technology, they will decide who and what survives in this brave new unfolding world. Is it the case that sometime in our past, our ancestors, surface dwellers, ultimately became aware of these manipulating factions, and united in an attempt to free themselves from the shackles placed upon them by this secret hidden hand, and unfortunately were annihilated in a fierce retaliatory war, sending humanity back to the Stone Age? It is only speculation but a plausible one with all things considered. It appears that the main priority of these non-human entities, is to keep hidden and away from public scrutiny. Our civilisation which continues under the illusion they are alone would never suspect or see outside their basic paradigm, they will continue to believe they are in control of their own destiny, until it is too late.

Notes for chapter 15

(1) The Egyptian Gods, Horus, http://www.aleph.se/Nada/Mage/Egypt/Gods.html

(2) NASA, Dark Energy, Dark Matter, http://science.nasa.gov/astrophysics/focus-areas/what-is-dark-energy/

(3) Matt Williams, What percentage of Earth is water, Universe today, 2014, http://www.universetoday.com/65588/what-percent-of-earth-is-water/

(4) NASA, Following the water, http://www.nasa.gov/vision/earth/everydaylife/jamestown-water-fs.html

(5) University Bulletin: A Weekly Bulletin for the Staff of the University of California, Volume 4, page 28, Office of Official Publications, University of California, 1955, https://books.google.co.th/books?id=ovA2AQAAMAAJ&pg=PA28&lpg=PA28&dq=sirius+has+2.3+times+the+mass+of+the+sun&source=bl&ots=vBD5dSZgrv&sig=6sY-dXkVOUvw0c09dNVLMAB8md0&hl=en&sa=X&ved=0ahUKEwjBnrDtxu_KAhVSHY4KHQ6qBKMQ6AEIIzAC#v=onepage&q=sirius%20has%202.3%20times%20the%20mass%20of%20the%20sun&f=false

(6) Karl Tata, Space Radiation Threat to Astronauts Explained, May 2013, http://www.space.com/21353-space-radiation-mars-mission-threat.html

(7) Zecharia Sitchin, http://www.sitchin.com/

(8) Paul Hellyer, Ex Canadian defence minister, testimony, Citizen hearing on disclosure, May 2013, YouTube, https://www.youtube.com/watch?v=JDuqZbjxB_E

(9) Robert O Dean, Interview, 2013, YouTube, https://www.youtube.com/watch?v=G8GGSq5mxbU

(10) Siege Of Acre, Wikipedia, https://en.wikipedia.org/wiki/Siege_of_Acre_(1291)

(11) Statue of liberty, Freemasonry watch, http://freemasonrywatch.org/statue_of_liberty.html

(12) Philip Schneider, Preparedness expo 95, Presentation. 1995 https://www.youtube.com/watch?v=xedmfAgx8eg

(13) ALEEN SIRGANY, CBS January 29, 2002, The war on waste, CBS evening News. http://www.cbsnews.com/news/the-war-on-waste/

(14) William Cooper, The UFO Conspiracy, speech 1990, http://www.sacred-texts.com/ufo/cooper1.htm

(15) Gary McKinnon, BBC interview, 2012, YouTube. https://www.youtube.com/watch?v=XacevWeOkHg

(16) Norwegian spiral anomaly, 2009, YouTube science channel, https://www.youtube.com/watch?v=FgWgsstTx-8

Chapter 16

Globalisation

Globalisation comes with both positive and negative aspects. It is the inevitable next step in the evolution of human social development, the progression from villages to towns and towns to cities; we are now witnessing the nation states merge with their neighbours to create continental unions, which will eventually lead to the one all-encompassing globalised system. The process of unification has not been easy, it has been slowly creeping up on us for centuries. The vast majority of people do not like change, which is understandable, if that change leads them into unknown waters and given the choice they will resist. There are too many people all with different opinions, if the globalisation project takes on board all these views, modifying its strategies to accommodate, it would take too long and never see the completion of its ultimate aim. It is therefore necessary to boldly force through its agenda, whatever the consequence and collateral damage. At present, they appear to have a window of opportunity which they are aggressively utilising, all systems are go for the final sprint to the finishing line, the amount of crockery smashed along the way seems unimportant to them now, and once they get to the finishing line they will rebuild and recalibrate society to fit in with the new system they wish to implement. It is easier to build a new system if the old one is out the way first, a controlled demolition of the old world may be necessary.

Once the Marxist socialists of the east merge with the Fabians of the west, we will essentially be in a global socialist system, Ironic when you consider that National Socialism was the big bad wolf of the 20th century, and global socialism is the next step up from that. I suspect this form of governance would give people choices in all the areas which don't threaten the continuity of power, which they will be permitted to serve, providing they are of use and behave in line with the required political correctness.

The advantages of globalisation:

- Countries can specialise in those areas which they are naturally good at.
- Larger markets are created.
- More competition with cheaper prices.
- More choice of goods from all over the world.
- Removal of borders and less regulation on movement.
- Standardisation of units, measures and procedures.
- Reduced costs to military and border defence.
- Reduced overall cost to bureaucracy.
- Promotes peace between nations.
- Relieve poverty and redistribute wealth.

The advantages of globalisation, once in place and running efficiently, can outweigh the pain and sacrifice humanity has to go through to get there. It is a great opportunity to reset society, casting off redundant traditions to create a brave new world. In the right hands and under wise management globalisation offers immense benefits for the future of humanity.

An optimistic view of globalisation

Globalisation can be portrayed as a positive achievement, an optimistic vision for the future, a world with a civilised border-less community, freedom for all to enjoy and prosper. Globalisation has made life easier in some ways and can continue to do so. Technology allows individuals to work almost anywhere in the world, coordinating their affairs from portable hand-held devices. With borders relaxed, free movement allows us to enjoy the world like never before, we can mix with people from all cultures, in all walks of life. It has opened up markets to poor communities enabling them to improve their basic standards, helping them interact with more people, removing feelings of isolation. English, the global language, now allows people to understand one another, reducing tension and misunderstanding. There is no need to be frightened of other countries, cultures or their people, we are all part of the human race, wanting to live in peace and harmony, to pull together in a shared common cause under a common system for the greater good of all and future generations.

"Together we can help transform the global economy into a global community." -- Robert Alan Silverstein

"We must ensure that the global market is embedded in broadly shared values and practices that reflect global social needs, and that all the world's people share the benefits of globalization."-- Kofi Annan

"We are committed with our lives to building a different model and a different future for humanity, the Earth, and other species. We have envisaged a moral alternative to economic globalization and we will not rest until we see it realized." -- Maude Barlow

"Changing the structure and rules of the global economy will require a mass movement based on messages of compassion, justice, and equality, as well as collaborative and democratic processes ... If we stay positive, inclusive, and democratic, we have a truly historic opportunity to build a global movement for social justice." -- Medea Benjamin

The disadvantages of globalisation

- The loss of sovereignty and independence.
- The slow erosion of unique cultural ways of living.
- Interdependency.
- If you don't like the system you live under you have no alternative.
- A single system if corrupted will be very difficult to pull back, it can easily become totalitarian.

- Alternative forms of living, the pursuit of your individual version of happiness may be restricted.
- A monoculture will eventually evolve from years of globalization.
- Disease spreads more easily.
- Multinational corporations have the potential to make every city the same.

The main disadvantage with the globalisation project, which will eventually be controlled by one global government, is the possibility of that government being compromised by corrupt interests. No matter how good the measures are to prevent this, history shows us it will eventually be compromised. The other major objection is that a single system may not be suitable for everyone, in which case they are stuck with no alternative to escape to.

The control of humanity has always been the big issue. The ones holding the batons of power are not going to suddenly relinquish their position, if they did, anarchy would ensue leading to absolute chaos, out of which would come instability and gang mentality. Somebody has to be in control, so why not them? We cannot all be captains of the ship or as rich as they are, it is just a cruel fact of life. Every generation has had its masters and its servants. It is up to the majority who are servants to reign in the exploitative powers of their masters, so don't be frightened to say no once in a while.

"I would define globalization as the freedom for my group of companies to invest where it wants when it wants, to produce what it wants, to buy and sell where it wants, and support the fewest restrictions possible coming from labour laws and social conventions." -- (Percy Barnevik, President of the ABB Industrial Group)

"Globalization, as defined by rich people like us, is a very nice thing... you are talking about the Internet, you are talking about cell phones, you are talking about computers. This doesn't affect two-thirds of the people of the world." -- Jimmy Carter

"There's two globalizations. There's the globalization of the elites, of the corporations, represented by the World Bank, the IMF, the World Trade Organization. That's the global state. It's a secret global government information. There's another globalization that's grass roots globalization. The Fair-Trade Networks, the Sister Cities, Sister Schools, Citizen Diplomacy, the work we do at Global Exchange, linking people up at the grass roots. That represents majority forces. The elite globalization represents minority forces. The elite globalization is about making money. It's money values. The people's globalization, the democratic mass globalization is about life values. So you got two paradigms, the money cycle and the life cycle and they're in contestation." -- Kevin Danaher

"Recognizing that the current form of globalization is nothing more than a generalized downward levelling in which global corporations are extracting more and more of the wealth, power, and productive energies from communities and the environment is the right approach... And knowing that in every specific battle, what we are fighting for is merely the substitution of the human agenda for the corporate agenda is what can guide and sustain us." -- Robin Hahnel

A pessimistic view of a future under globalisation

The new globalisation project is a modern-day extension of the old colonial power system, with the same players and their descendants in control. They are using the multinational corporation as a substitute for military conquest and dictatorial rule. After the Second World War the IMF and World Bank were set up to help facilitate the reconstruction of European economies. Many underdeveloped countries, which had been exploited for centuries by the old colonial system, were encouraged to borrow huge sums, opening up their borders to free trade, persuading them to participate in the international economic community. Conditions were placed on these loans allowing a steady infestation of multinationals and global financiers together with common purpose policies. New factories and sweat shops were built to produce cheap goods for western markets, creating economic labour camps and human resource processing zones. These underdeveloped countries were encouraged away from self-sufficiency and independence. Pressure would be applied using trade agreements, debt and sanctions to any government veering off international policies, occasionally if they failed to fall in line regime change would be sanctioned.

The future of everyday life under globalisation, once it reaches its completion phase, will be an extension of the same progressive policies of power consolidation which we have witnessed throughout the centuries. The controllers of these globalist institutions will hold all the cards; they will use humanity as a commodity for their own private use. People will only be allowed to exist to serve these institutions, any form of criticism or descent will not be tolerated. At present the vast majority of people show no interest in political matters, preoccupied with fashion and consumerist tat, they leave that job to their compromised representatives, who get fat and rich legislating freedoms away. Previous generations were unable to prevent the erosion of their national sovereignty, setting a precedent of apathy which will open us up for the final totalitarian takeover. The controllers have never been interested in individual welfare, seen as a tool, as foot soldiers to be used to facilitate the expansion of their power. Once they have total control throughout the world, under a system all encompassing, they can set about remoulding global society in their image, reduce the population of the Earth to what they consider as sustainable. People will have no rights, just privileges, granted to them by the system, for service to that system. We are and always have been building our own prison, a death star for the empire, a brave new world.

Brave New World

When we look at who the main players are in the push for globalisation, a better picture emerges. There is a triad of power behind this venture, the roots of which have been with us for a very long time.

- The Crown Corporation, London.

- The Roman Catholic Church, Vatican.
- Rothschild Zionism, Israel.

Very little goes on in the world today without some form of interference or control by one or all of these players. The major multinational corporations and Crown Corporation are interdependent and interlinked, their shareholders and subsidiaries essentially act as a monolithic entity, expanding their markets under the umbrella of globalisation. Zionism is at the forefront of the modern monetary system; the world essentially borrows from their banks on interest. The Vatican still a powerful organisation cooperates with the Crown and world Zionism, to push forward its own influence. From the old colonial system came the new commercial colonisation, with help from international finance, a new method of control was utilised. After the Second World War, the dream of a New World Order, under this corporate/financial system was becoming a real possibility. All efforts were focused to bring this about. The United States Corporation, a subsidiary of the Crown Corporation, has been used as military muscle for this ambitious project, countries or rulers opposing free trade (globalisation) for multinational corporation and finance have been targeted, overthrown, or overrun.[1]

- Philippines 1948-54 **CIA directs war against Huk Rebellion.**
- Puerto Rica 1950 **Independence rebellion crushed in Ponce.**
- Korea 1951-53 **U.S./South Korea fights China/North Korea to stalemate.**
- Iran 1953 **CIA overthrows democracy, installs Shah.**
- Guatemala 1954 **CIA directs invasion after gov't nationalized U.S. company lands.**
- Egypt 1956 **Suez crisis.**
- Lebanon 1958 **Army & Marine occupation against rebels.**
- Vietnam 1960-75 **Vietnamese war for independent communism.**
- Cuba 1961 **CIA-directed exile invasion fails.**
- Iraq 1963 **CIA organizes coup that killed president, brings Ba'ath Party to power.**
- Indonesia 1965 **CIA and UK assisted army coup.**
- Chile 1973 **CIA-backed coup ousts elected president Allende.**
- Angola 1976-92 **CIA assists South African-backed rebels.**
- Nicaragua 1981-90 **CIA directs exile (Contra) invasions.**
- Granada 1983-84 **U.S Invasion four years after revolution.**
- Panama 1989 **Nationalist government ousted.**
- Iraq 1990 & 2003 **First and Second Gulf wars.**
- Afghanistan 1998 **Attack on former CIA training camps used by Islamist groups.**
- Pakistan 2005 **CIA missile and air strikes on alleged Al Qaeda and Taliban.**
- Somalia 2006 **Special Forces advise invasion that topples Islamist government.**
- Yemen 2009 **Cruise missile attack on Al Qaeda.**
- Libya 2011 **NATO air strikes and missile attacks against Qaddafi government.**
- Syria 2011 **War against President Bashar al-Assad's government.**

All these countries have one thing in common, their wish to be independent from the dictates of the international economic community, or globalisation in its present state. Their desire to be self-sufficient was not acceptable in the eyes of the globalists, who insisted everyone play their expected part in bringing their ambitions into fruition. Even democratically elected nationalistic governments like Allende in Chile and Sukarno in Indonesia, were targeted for military coups, and overthrown by western backed military generals. After seizing power, they would deregulate and re-privatise the country's infrastructure, opening the doors once again for progressive assimilation towards globalisation. This action would also send a clear message to other countries who wanted to go it alone, a shot across the bow, **bringing them back** on course, self-sufficient independence is not an option. Vietnam was an interesting case because Ho Chi Minh broke away from mainstream communism, suspecting it had been compromised by international finance and western interests. His desire to have a truly independent Vietnamese revolution, uniting both north and south under their own system was frowned upon by the globalists, who saw the spread of independent communism, a version which they had no control over, as a threat to their future plans.

While the globalists where constricting choice on an international and national level, they were also targeting humanity on an individual level. While offering more choice to the average citizen, in areas which could not undermine the spread of globalisation, they restricted choice on anything which did. All mainstream political parties, media and education became pro-globalist, in an effort to set a new benchmark for normality. Anyone opposing or exposing its dangers were viewed as extreme or at least outside the acceptable view of normal consensus. Individual freedoms, which were once proud expressions of common law, have steadily been eroded and constricted by the imposition of more corporate legislation, freedoms once taken for granted move further into the distance as the buckles on our corporate strait jackets are tightened.

Most of the Christian/Judaic world has accepted globalisation as their natural destiny, oblivious to whose hand is on the tiller, they see it as a progression towards a brighter future. They know the ship left port a long time ago, and most people wish to stay asleep throughout the journey, they only want to be woken up when they get to the destination. It is a Disney ride to some, who are happy to appear neutral while enthusiastically working in the tank factory to pay their mortgage. For many people, they have little interest in outside matters, the whole world can annihilate itself, as long as their favourite game show is still aired together with an ample supply of beefburgers, beers and ball games.

The Islamic world in the Middle East has resisted globalisation more than any other region on Earth. Why is this? Can the answer be found in astrology? If we look at the nature of Venus worship, reflected by the two signs ruled by Venus, Taurus and Libra, (I have & I compliment). A people who have all they need to live the life they want, which complements the surroundings in which they reside, are not going to want to change. Like the bull of Taurus in his field, he is happy with what he has. He doesn't want McDonalds or Walmart setting up shop in the corner of his plot, He certainly does not need Nike shoes or Adidas sweat shirts to run around looking like a premier league super star. The bull is happy to be left alone, which is what any sensible person would do, but oh no, the globalists want to poke and prod the bull, annoy it and make it do things it does not wish to do. This is a problem for the globalists. They need to persuade the Islamic Middle East, the stubborn bull, to play ball otherwise their plan for global dominance, under one system, will stall. All the trouble we see unfolding in the Middle East is just that. Multiple plans and players designed to force globalisation and the assimilation of the Islamic world with the Christian/Judaic world of finance and commerce. Just as the forced integration policies of the 90's and 2000's, promoted multiculturalism all over Europe and many parts of the world, these wars and disruptions in the Middle East are forcing Muslim refugees onto predominantly Christian countries in an effort to assimilate for globalisation. The more, all round, chaos they cause the better it is for the globalists, who will have an easier job implementing their new global system if the old one has been demolished, just like in Libya, Berlin and Syria.

Globalisation of the Islamic World

ISIS the Islamic State a militant group of Salafi Jihadist fighters. The name given to this group is interesting for the time period we are in, the beginning of the new Age of Aquarius, the Genesis of that Age. Genesis means "Gen (Greek for, Born or produced by), esis (ISIS), the mother God, the Virgin (Virgo), married to Osiris, giving birth to the new Sun in this new Age of Aquarius.

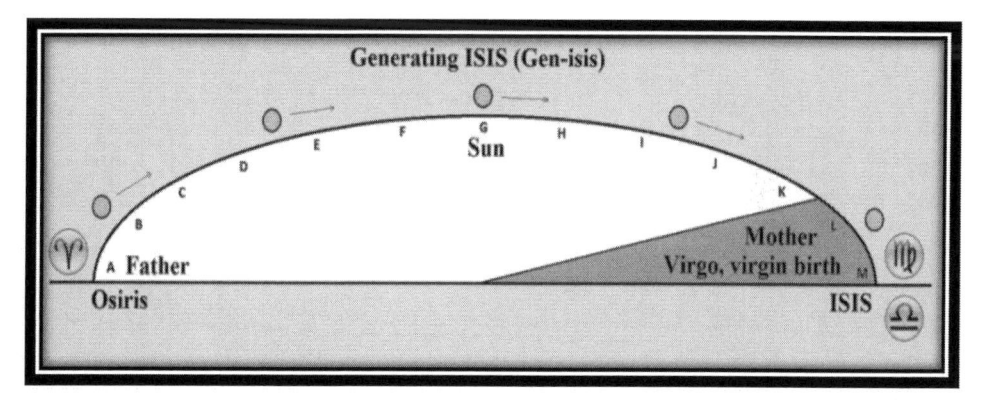

Generating ISIS (Gen-isis)

Father — Osiris

Mother — Virgo, virgin birth — ISIS

The desire to control the whole world is an old one, placing humanity under a single ruling system has been on the go for a very long time. The more sophisticated we become with better communication and technology, the easier it is to control us. Large conflicts such as WW1 and WW2 are not isolated struggles, wars to end wars; they were major eruptions of organised rebellion against the same continuous program. The war for global governance never ended, it just altered its tactics and its targets. Neither is neutrality an option, they will find some way of sucking you into some form of compromising entanglement. The founding fathers of America were specific about staying neutral, they knew, from history, how the

European political game worked. Thomas Jefferson in his first inaugural address spoke about foreign entanglements.

"Equal and exact justice to all men, of whatever state or persuasion, religious or political; peace, commerce, and honest friendship with all nations, entangling alliances with none" - Thomas Jefferson, First inaugural address, March 4th 1801.

After WW2, most formidable organised resistance had been smashed. However, small pockets still existed in various places. Intelligent agencies and secret services were called upon to manage these threats. One such operation was called operation "Gladio", a series of covert military assignments conducted by what was known as a "stay behind army". In his book, "*NATO's secret armies: operation Gladio and terrorism in Western Europe*", the Swiss historian, Daniele Ganser points to a collaboration between the CIA, British Secret Services and European Secret Services, working together under NATO. After WW2 networks of clandestine armies were set up to undermine the spread of communism. According to Ganser, this secret army linked up with right wing terrorist groups to undermine, manipulate and harass left wing political parties. He also claims that over the subsequent decades, Gladio agents were involved in numerous terrorist attacks on their own European citizens.[2] With all this in mind and the immense control the establishment has over the mainstream media, it is not out of the question for them to stage more fake attacks which they can blame on their latest enemies, justifying new invasions and new legislation, bringing the minds of its citizens on board with their latest plans, who are expected to continue working and paying for it.

Many geopolitical commentators have suggested World War Three is already under way, apart from an official declaration, especially when you consider the amount of countries participating in this latest version of political arm twisting. All the dynamite is being laid, when the big event takes place, igniting it, the shock wave will be enough to bring about the changes necessary to advance the whole planet towards totalitarian global governance. The real game is control, you are the enemy and the political classes are your masters. At this moment, the old American Republic still has cobwebs of resistance in its ageing constitution; the second amendment is one of them.

"A well-regulated militia being necessary to the security of a free state, the right of the people to keep and bear arms shall not be infringed." - 2nd Amendment, Constitution for the United States of America.

All presidents after 1871 were acting for the interests of the UNITED STATES Corporation, as opposed to the American Republic; one by one they have eroded the inalienable rights of the American citizens, shackling them to a mountain of corporate legislation. The right to bear arms was specifically designed to rein in tyrannical governments and foreign takeovers from within, giving the people a final line of defence against the abuse of power. The constitution limited the power of government, who were there to serve the people, not the other way around. The globalisation project cannot allow citizens to have firearms, power of this nature can only be allowed in the hands of the masters or those who have proven themselves loyal. An ongoing attempt has been underway in the U.S to reverse the second amendment, to take all guns out of circulation. Shootings, especially mass shootings, are used to promote gun bans. Some mass shootings in recent years have been suspected as being government sponsored psyops, secret exercises designed to alter public opinion against gun ownership. One such case was the Sandy Hook Elementary School shooting in Newtown Connecticut, 2012, where Adam Lanza, acting alone, was reported to have shot and killed twenty-seven people including twenty school children. The whole of America was appalled at this horrifying act. According to Wolfgang Halbig, a school safety expert and ex state trooper, important questions have not been answered concerning the official version of events. Casting doubt in many people's minds as to what really happened, suspecting it could be a giant hoax.[3] This investigation is still ongoing.

The endgame of globalisation may look good for humanity from an optimistic/naive perspective, but one cannot help feeling a little uneasy, when much of its expansion is done covertly, the sinister aspect to it all should ring alarm bells. When your government lies to bring about change, you suspect something is wrong. When it kills innocent people as a result of those lies, you know something is wrong. When your government legislates, forbidding criticism of their extreme actions, you know something is very wrong, but now you can't do anything about it, and when your government comes for you, it's all over.

Soldiers obeying orders   **Citizens obeying gun laws**

With Jupiter's optimism and expansive influence slowly moving out the picture, a new era of saturnian contraction along with Uranus's revolutionary rebelliousness is emerging, maybe the reason behind the mad rush to bring about globalisation is because Jupiter's energy is fading, the window of opportunity will eventually close.

Before WW1 you didn't need a passport for international travel, border restrictions were few. Only after the passing of the British Nationality and Status Aliens Act 1914 was it required.[4] Before you could travel almost anywhere you wanted, do business anywhere and live anywhere, the global currency had already been in place for thousands of years, it was known as gold and silver. To protect yourself you carried a firearm, and because others were armed you also had to behave in a manner which was not confrontational, showing respect for other cultures and their people. In essence, the world and freedoms we once had are being exchanged for the new world of globalisation, one in which you need permission and valid documents from elitist corporations to do almost anything. You need to use a fiat currency which loses its value with debt attached. You can travel anywhere you wish if you have purchased the right visa from the right corporate authority, you can also do business anywhere you wish as long as you have enough corporate money and the right corporate permits. To protect yourself you must be completely disarmed, but pay tax in order to supply local government policy enforcement agencies enough money to keep you relatively safe from those who have no corporate currency and can't afford permits which would allow them to do legitimate work.

Airport security has recently become an area of aggravation and frustration for many travellers, with new levels of paranoia and compliance. Since the 9/11 attacks and the incident with the underwear bomber, security has taken on a whole new meaning. Most airports employ private firms to fulfil this role, with Israeli security companies leading the way, some of which were responsible for the airport security during the 9/11 attacks and the underwear bomber.[5] After such major compromises you would expect a rethink over the running of airport security, unless it was all part of a grand plan. When you consider the forces at play involved in the globalisation project, it is no longer a surprise. There is little doubt that the threat from terrorism is real, but to what extent does it truly threaten the lives of most individuals? The whole concept of terrorism can easily be utilised by the global entities for political purposes. The more fear they can generate the greater their mechanism of persuasion countering that fear, all in the name of keeping us safe from the Islamic bogie man. In a time of heightened security and purported terrorist threats, one would think the most logical course of action, would be for the U.S government to encourage all its citizens to arm themselves, protecting their families and communities from this growing threat, but the opposite is the case, the power structure want to see all its citizens disarmed. This places doubt over the validity of these claims, with suspicion mounting towards other agendas.

All this fear along with new restrictions is helping to boost corporate sales. Water once used as an agent to put out fire, is now seen as a substance capable of bringing down an international airline. It is now forbidden to take water past security, since then sales of bottled water inside airport terminals, at inflated prices, has risen. The ban of any liquid greater than 100ml is another money spinner for the corporations and manufacturers, who can now sell tiny amounts of the same product at high prices. Airport security has become big business, with all kinds of scanning machines and devices, all to prevent terrorism and make us feel safe from strangers wearing exploding underpants. More security and screening techniques condition the people into accepting corporate authority, domesticating society into acquiescing as subordinates to their corporate masters, the level of security witnessed today will not be reduced, it will only increase to the next level, This type of corporate control is synonymous with Saturnian energy, It is no surprise to see Zionist Israel leading this field.

If we all lived in a town with no crime we would not need to pay for a police force, we would not need to buy insurance cover or lock anything away, corporate sales of burglar alarms and security devices would cease. Any corporation in this line of business would do well to sponsor criminal activity, which would stimulate demand, creating massive profits for themselves and their shareholders, expanding their sphere of influence over the community and the legislative process.

"One has to realize that the powerful industrial groups concerned in the manufacture of arms are doing their best in all countries to prevent the peaceful settlement of international disputes, and that rulers can achieve this great end only if they are sure of the vigorous support of the majority of their peoples." -- Albert Einstein

Globalist policies are being implemented all over the world simultaneously, any participant dragging their feet will have pressure with consequences placed upon them. While the west stagnates allowing the underdeveloped countries to catch up, the change which some of these countries are going through is huge. A generation brought up with rice fields and wooden carts are now being thrust into the Information Age, a change some cannot cope with. The pace is fast, accepted as positive progress, it races full steam ahead, as more and more nations are brought to heel, the level of security around our leaders increases. I remember as a child, anyone could walk along Downing Street to view No.10, but now the security is more like the estate of a Columbian drug cartel, not an office representing freedom and democracy. The President of the U.S drives around in a car which is so heavily reinforced, it would be the only thing left in a nuclear exchange. It certainly makes one wonder whether this kind of security is a consequence of their policies, are they treading on too many toes? even Hitler didn't need to drive around in a fortified tank.

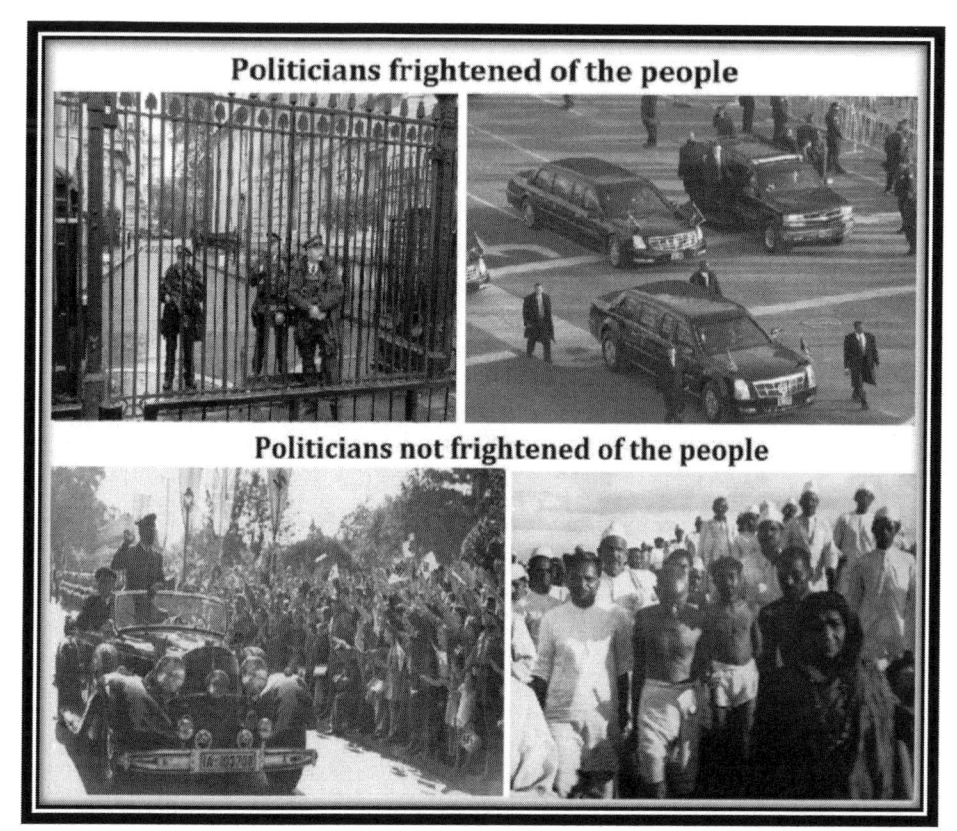

As the process of globalisation unfolds, humanity has a great opportunity to become proactive in its development. If we all sit back and do nothing, the tyrants will continue with more of the same. It is up to all of us to become proactive, physically and emotionally steering this new Age in a direction which will benefit the many as opposed to the few. Throw off the shackles of deceit, the dogma and ideologies which serve the self. Seek the truth and stop supporting false idols with false hope that train you to look outside yourselves for the answers, we have the answers, they are simple, they are written in our hearts. Each one of us can make a difference, be the change you want to see in the world and make this globalisation project fit for your children and their children.

Notes for chapter 16

(1) Dr Zoltan Grossman, A century of U.S Military intervention,
http://academic.evergreen.edu/g/grossmaz/interventions.html

(2) Daniele Ganser, NATO's secret armies : operation Gladio and terrorism in western Europe, Frank Cass Publishers, 2004.
http://www.goodreads.com/book/show/765633.NATO_s_Secret_Armies

(3) Wolfgang Halbig, Wolfgang Halbig Files Lawsuit, "Sandy Hook Was Not Operating" in 2012, School Safety Expert Says, March 7th 2015,
http://memoryholeblog.com/2015/03/07/wolfgang-halbig-files-lawsuit-sandy-hook-was-not-operating-in-2012-school-safety-expert-says/

(4) British Nationality and Status Aliens Act 1914,
http://www.legislation.gov.uk/ukpga/Geo5/4-5/17/enacted

(5) Mike Rivero, All 9/11 Airports Serviced by One Israeli Owned Company, What really happened, http://whatreallyhappened.com/WRHARTICLES/ICTS.html

Conclusion

As we move through the transition from Pisces into Aquarius, great changes are taking place. It is a natural and inevitable cycle for humanity and the universe. Cosmic frequencies will stimulate our consciousness, perception and reality, moving steadily into a new epoch of "knowing". Many people at this moment feel the world around them is changing, but are confused as to what is really behind the changes. Frustrated by the systems they have been living under and supporting throughout their lives, systems which are straining under the pressure of deceit and corruption. Humanity is awakening from a naïve daze of Piscean belief which it has been living under for thousands of years. People all over the world are beginning to see things in a different light, undermining what they previously believed to be real. Many have become suspicious of the control system and sense a greater force behind global events and Earth changes, they don't know what it is but they feel it.

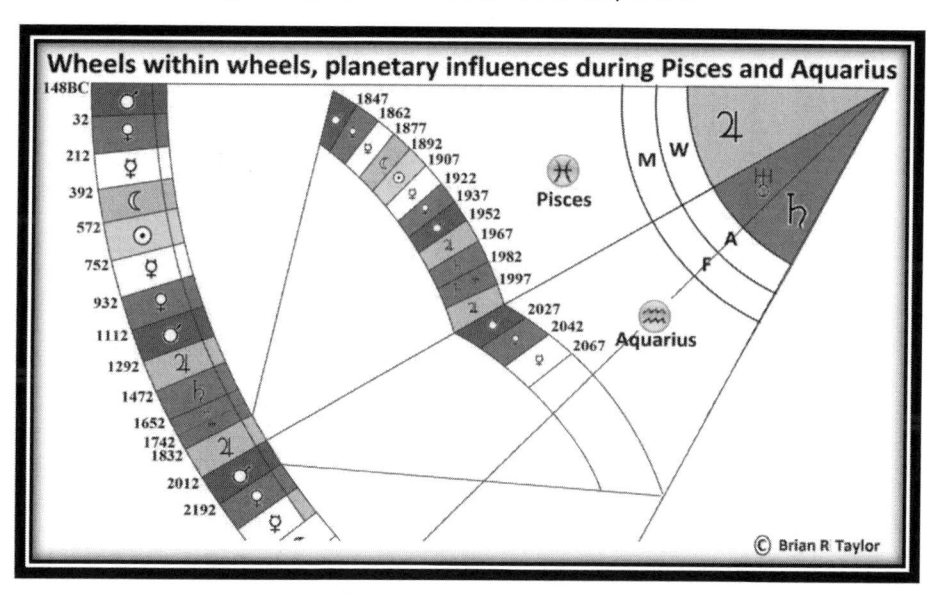

Wheels within wheels, planetary influences during Pisces and Aquarius

© Brian R Taylor

From 2012-2027 there is tremendous cardinal energy coming from Mars, the planet of proactivity, the ancient God of war, the cardinal start or Genesis (generating ISIS) of this new Age, an Age where we see ISIS being created to ferment war and the proactive movement of millions of people. The sequence of universal energy according to the zodiac is the true language of the Gods, whether it plays out internally or externally is based on individual perceptions, the fact is that it will play out anywhere from our consciousness to the far corners of the universe. Uranus, the daddy of Saturn will resonate 1000 years of unpredictability, revolutions, independence and new technology. We are also coming around to another 84-year revolutionary cycle of Uranus. Mix this together with a Saturnian back drop from traditional astrology, we should see restrictions and contractions in many areas inherited from the Jupetarian Age, even to the point of global population reduction. Although Mars' energy is strong during this period, it does not mean we are all going to kill each other, we still have will power and choice; we can choose our battles and our reality by resisting and restraining certain influences.

The control system will become more sophisticated with new forms of technology, battling against a society seeking independence and freedom. It certainly will not be mundane. The journey for anyone living through this time will be interesting and full of surprises. By the end of the third decade, around 2027, the global situation should settle back down, although it won't cease. It is similar to the beginning of the Piscean Age where the Romans were expanding their influence for the first 180 years; we are in a similar cycle, but this time under the ruler-ship of the unpredictable revolutionary planet of Uranus.

Many people are now aware that most traditional government organisations within the fabric of society are mechanisms of control, not for the benefit of individual freedoms, but for the advancement of their globalisation project. Having a basic understanding of applied astronomy/astrology, the language of the Gods, helps one decipher the forces at work behind our physical reality. It is the difference between knowing the road ahead as opposed to driving on an unfamiliar dirt track in the dark. Any organisation or system of control seeking the upper hand will, without doubt, require all the information they can to cover all contingencies, this includes a comprehensive understanding of the language of the Gods. The main objective of all governments and systems of control is to keep hold of power, while offering candy with one hand; they quietly disarm you with the other. Without appreciating this, one can become a little confused as to the motives behind these organisations. To understand their modus operandi better, I will refer once more to Michael Ellner's quote:

"Everything is backwards, everything is upside down. Doctors destroy health, lawyers destroy justice, psychiatrists destroy minds, scientists destroy truth, major media destroys information, religions destroy spirituality and governments destroy freedom." — Michael Ellner.

It is necessary for any system of control to organise its information institutions, not for the benefit of its people, but to continue in its quest for unchallenged dominance. The possibility of non-human influence interfering in our world from top down becomes more credible the further one looks into this subject. Maybe the Gods have always been at the helm with their representatives here on this Earth. Education within the modern university system is not designed to expand the mind of the individual, instead of the holistic universal approach to wisdom they compartmentalise knowledge by limiting the potential of the human mind, offering only 1 degree of understanding as opposed to 360 degrees found with the holistic zodiacal approach. With his mortar board and mind squared off, up to his neck in debt, the graduate slots neatly into this brave new society as a fresh enthusiastic obedient worker.

Science in modern times has also been targeted and politicised, the method of funding is all important. If you want specific results you just need to fund the team working on one side of a theory, while denying funds to any studies which contradict your required outcome. Manmade climate change and HIV/AIDS both fall into this category. In a court of law and in a perfect world both the prosecution and the defence have an equal share of time and funds necessary to uncover the truth, unfortunately this does not always apply to modern science.

It is all put in place in an effort to distract and disempower the human collective, those at the top know what our real potential is and the influence, if united, we have over our reality. They keep us busy with day to day petty squabbling and fear, worries over terrorism, climate change, economic collapse and disease, while they continue to fashion the world how they like. What they don't want you to know is:

"You are God. You are the "I AM that I AM". You are consciousness. You are the creator. This is the mystery, this is the great secret known by the seers, prophets, and mystics throughout the ages. This is the truth that you can never know intellectually. "- Neville Goddard, The power of awareness.[1]

With our thoughts, we truly do make the world and as stewards over our focal consciousness, we have a duty to one another and the collective, to be selective and to filter what stimulates our five senses and thoughts. We are therefore guardians over the subconscious and our connection to the spirit world. If we only focus on good, as a collective, we shall only know and experience good. If we focus on death and destruction we will only know the seeds of hatred which we plant. The control system will intentionally influence our five senses, stimulating our subconscious and our ability to manifest their reality as opposed to our own, giving all our power over to them. Stop listening to them, by observing them we are giving them energy, breathing life into their nostrils and their creations. The universe will give us what we need, not necessarily what we think we need or what the control system convinces us to want. Your destiny is the course of least resistance, guided by your higher mind and connection to the Logos, your true needs and wants will be taken care of.

"You're I AM-ness, your Consciousness, is the way in which you change your world. Whatever you attach to I AM you become. As you affirm with feeling, I am illumined, inspired, loving, harmonious, peaceful, happy and strong, you will resurrect these qualities that lie dormant within you, and wonders will happen in your life. When men and women help you in the realization of your dreams, they are playing their part and are messengers testifying to your beliefs and convictions. You wrote the play, and other men and women execute the parts conforming to your concept of yourself." - David Allen, The power of I am.[2]

Knowing one's own unique position within time and space, through the knowledge and understanding of one's own astrological birth chart is akin to having your own personal biological instruction manual. Without understanding one's own strengths and weaknesses, life can become unnecessarily difficult. Knowing oneself in this way, allows us to flow with natural rhythms and universal energetic cycles. When in tune, your life purpose becomes self-evident and the path made easy. Understanding consciousness is the key to expanding it, the modern crapitalist world of corporate consumerism requires armies of shallow reactionary automatons, surviving to stimulate and service mammon, discouraged from looking deeply into the meaning of life, or taking that sophisticated journey towards enlightenment.

The same financial, oligarchic and corporate interests behind the British Empire have not gone away, in this latest form of imperialism, known as globalisation, their secret societies and global organisations still hold the baton of power. One must not confuse the new British Empire with the British people; they too are caught up in its web of deception and control. Elements within this web have clearly handicapped humanity through various rival monotheistic planet worshipping cults, enabling the establishment to create division in both our physical and spiritual realms. They carefully play one faction off against the other while steering us all in the direction they require.

The People Don't Know Their True Power

Unfortunately, the majority of people guard their set of beliefs vigorously, believing that their view of the world is the most accurate. If their belief system is challenged, even with provable facts, many will still stand by their position. There is a parable in the bible reflecting this, Jesus and Barabbas, the essence of the story suggests if you offer the crowd the choice between Jesus (the truth & the light) or Barabbas (the deceiving lying criminal), the crowd will always choose Barabbas. It is harder to convince someone they have been conned than it is to con them initially.

We may never know who is really in control. Just as the majority of workers within a corporation do not know the shareholders or get to meet the CEO, most of humanity is not even aware of other realities or dimensions outside the five senses, sharing our experience with various other interdimensional entities and spirits. Once we surpass our ignorance we may one day become masters of our own destiny. I suspect wars are not initiated by humans alone, although it may seem so when viewed from our limited perspectives. It could be the result of non-human interference pushing humanity to a point of self-destruction, in an attempt to promote new levels of non-human control. Whether humanity will ever unite again in a common cause for life, liberty and happiness is yet to be seen, what can be seen is the fast erosions of our options to unite against globalisation and whoever or whatever is in control. This is why any form of independent national unity is seen as a threat to globalisation and world stability.

Most people live busy lives, this is not always by choice, leaving no time to think clearly about philosophical questions, what is going off around them and the purpose of their short lives. They are preoccupied with non-issues concerning corporate procedures and commerce, which neutralises their capacity to tune into natural universal cycles. Modern living appears to be unwisely pulling us further away from cosmic cycles, detaching us from nature's umbilical cord. Although we are changing on a conscious level, it has always been like this, the only constant in this universe is change. It seems to me that the secret to prosperity, happiness and fulfilment in this life, is to be at peace and in harmony with the universe and the rhythms and cycles of nature.

Desiderata

Go placidly amid the noise and the haste, and remember what peace there may be in silence. As far as possible, without surrender, be on good terms with all persons.

Speak your truth quietly and clearly; and listen to others, even to the dull and the ignorant; they too have their story.

Avoid loud and aggressive persons; they are vexatious to the spirit. If you compare yourself with others, you may become vain or bitter, for always there will be greater and lesser persons than yourself.

Enjoy your achievements as well as your plans. Keep interested in your own career, however humble; it is a real possession in the changing fortunes of time.

Exercise caution in your business affairs, for the world is full of trickery. But let this not blind you to what virtue there is; many persons strive for high ideals, and everywhere life is full of heroism.

Be yourself. Especially, do not feign affection. Neither be cynical about love; for in the face of all aridity and disenchantment, it is as perennial as the grass.

Take kindly the counsel of the years, gracefully surrendering the things of youth.

Nurture strength of spirit to shield you in sudden misfortune. But do not distress yourself with dark imaginings. Many fears are born of fatigue and loneliness.

Beyond a wholesome discipline, be gentle with yourself. You are a child of the universe no less than the trees and the stars; you have a right to be here.

And whether or not it is clear to you, no doubt the universe is unfolding as it should. Therefore, be at peace with God, whatever you conceive Him to be.

And whatever your labours and aspirations, in the noisy confusion of life, keep peace in your soul. With all its sham, drudgery and broken dreams, it is still a beautiful world. Be cheerful. Strive to be happy. - Max Ehrmann, "Desiderata"[3]

Notes for the conclusion

(1) Neville Goddard, The Power of Awareness, Chapter 27, http://www.thepowerofawareness.org/chapter-twenty-seven

(2) David Allan, The Power of I Am, 2010, page 9, http://api.ning.com/files/NNXWrUWlpudTq9f*8XxK*2p3I9Fan7dFrKK52Dgy9gR6M4QUQridGPJBTa61erDuIL77npicGEyA*L24VqmKfwsMXrypEGPG/DavidAllenThePowerofIAM.pdf

(3) Max Ehrmann, Desiderata, Poem, 1927, https://en.wikipedia.org/wiki/Desiderata

Author's Bio

Brian Taylor was born in a small town in the suburbs of Nottingham, England during the late 1960s. After graduating with BSc (Hons) in construction management from Leeds Polytechnic in 1992, he spent most of his time working as an engineer. After many years fascinated by the bigger questions of life, he chose to take time away from western society, to pursue a journey of discovery. With an open mind and an optimistic belief in himself, he decided to see where destiny would take him.

During his many years travelling mostly throughout Southeast Asia, he discovered the answers to many of the questions which he had been carrying for years. At this time he wrote two books, the first one entitled *'Language of the Gods'*, was a comprehensive breakdown of how the controlling elite divide and rule humanity from a physical perspective, with an astrological overtone. His second book *'Metaphysics of the Gods'* looked into how universal energies are the building blocks for our perception of reality, within a feed-back loop of human consciousness. At this stage in his journey, he began to understand the mechanisms in play relating to how we influence our reality. A profound moment, and the most important and valuable lesson an individual can learn in a limited lifetime. From this core knowledge he revisited history to see if it made more sense. This was when he wrote *'Metaphysics of WW2'*.

As the years progressed Mr Taylor noticed an increase in obesity in western tourists visiting Southeast Asia. American and British tourists in particular, appeared to have developed some unhealthy eating habits in comparison to the Asians, who, on the whole, ate a relatively healthy and modest diet. This prompted Mr Taylor to investigate the subject from a metaphysical perspective, not only to benefit others, but also himself. This resulted in the book *'The Metaphysical Diet'*. To add to the series of books on metaphysics and suspecting that humanity was being steered in a direction which was not entirely righteous Mr Taylor next decided to investigate Kabbalah in relation to astrotheology and the globalisation project. This resulted in his book *'The Left Hand Path'*.

Finally, after more years of travelling and still evermore fascinated and puzzled by life's deeper questions, Mr Taylor focused on research regarding our connection to the spirit realm. This resulted in the book *'When The Spirit Takes Over'*.

B R Taylor's Natal Chart

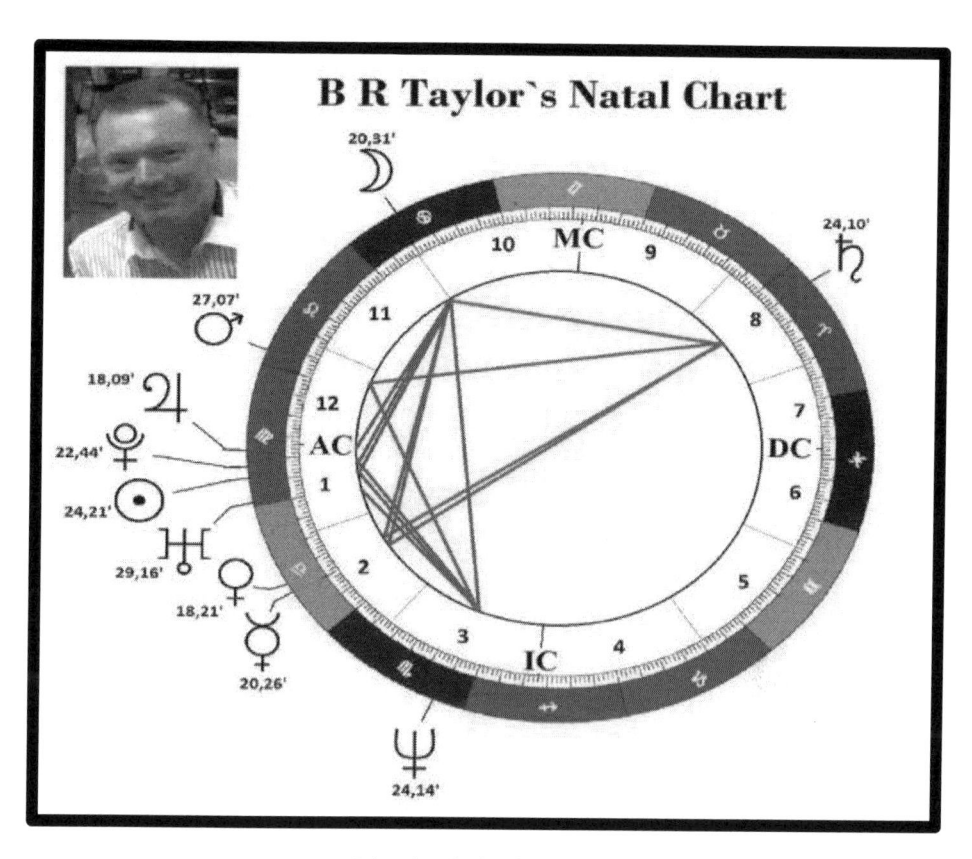

Other books by this author

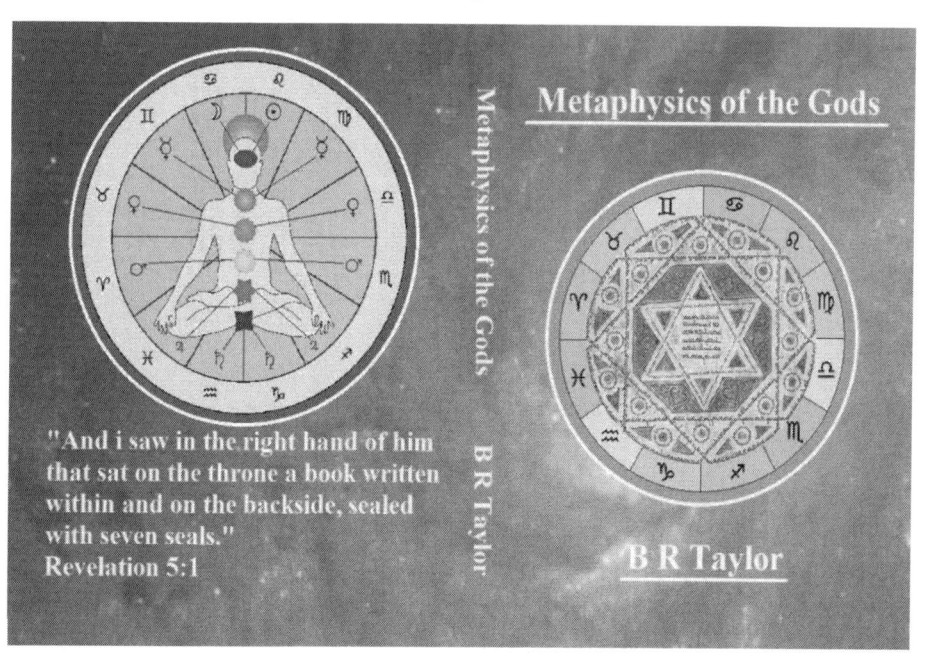

Metaphysics of the Gods

"And i saw in the right hand of him that sat on the throne a book written within and on the backside, sealed with seven seals."
Revelation 5:1

Metaphysics of the Gods

B R Taylor

Metaphysics of WW2

B R Taylor

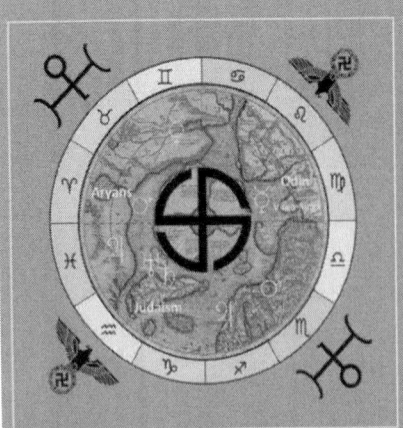

If you think you understand WW2, think again! Until you have looked into the metaphysical (beyond the physical) aspect of the subject, together with the astrological timing in which it took place, you really are only scratching the surface. Many war historians and scholars concern themselves with the people, places and events surrounding WW2, but neglect the bigger picture. This is the only book of its kind to give you the big picture.

The Metaphysical Diet

B R Taylor

Only recently has the three meal a day mentality become accepted as the norm. We are a generation overeating. Our habitual nature has been hijacked and steered in a sinister and unhealthy direction, in order to underpin and support a corporate system reliant on excessive consumption. Most diets fail because they focus on momentary solutions to deep rooted problems. This is the only book of its kind to explain the astrological and metaphysical mechanisms at play behind obesity, and how, without spending a fortune, one can learn to sow new seeds of health, wealth and happiness within the powerful mind of the subconscious.

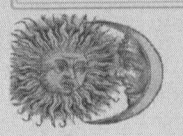

The Left Hand Path

The word sinister comes from the Latin for left. It is the new direction for humanity. This book examines Kabbalistic, astrological and occult forces behind the new globalisation project, exposing its sinister left hand agenda as we move further into the new Aquarian Age.

B R Taylor

When The Spirit Takes Over

This book explores the spiritual aspect of consciousness, and what we can expect when the physical body expires and our conscious perspective transcends into an alternative reality. The book also explores our relationship with other realms, entities and dimensions, together with the possibility of reincarnation being a plausible concept.

B R Taylor

Websites by this author

www.BRTaylorMetaphysics.com

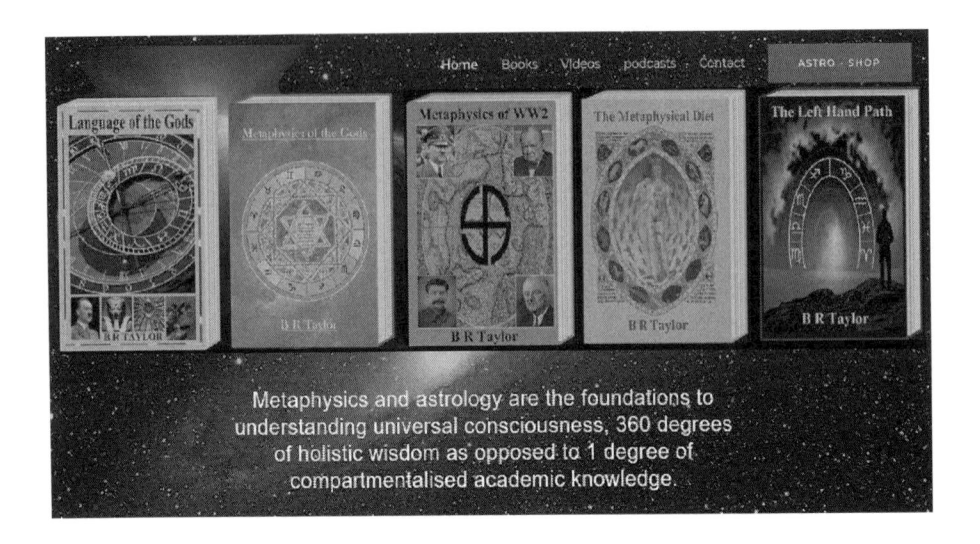

B R Taylor's Youtube channel

https://www.youtube.com/channel/UC6lc7_8H0JGdrDhpQWuvfBQ

https://twitter.com/BRTaylor14

Printed in Great Britain
by Amazon